The Adams Papers

SARA MARTIN, EDITOR IN CHIEF

SERIES II

Adams Family Correspondence

Adams Family Correspondence

HOBSON WOODWARD, SARA MARTIN,
MIRIAM LIEBMAN, GWEN FRIES, AMANDA M. NORTON,
NEAL E. MILLIKAN, SARA GEORGINI, R. M. BARLOW
EDITORS

Volume 16 • November 1804 – July 1809

THE BELKNAP PRESS
OF HARVARD UNIVERSITY PRESS
CAMBRIDGE, MASSACHUSETTS
AND LONDON, ENGLAND

2025

Copyright © 2025 by the Massachusetts Historical Society • All rights reserved

Printed in the United States of America

Funds for editing *The Adams Papers* were originally furnished by Time, Inc., on behalf of *Life*, to the Massachusetts Historical Society, under whose supervision the editorial work is being done. Further funds were provided by a grant from the Ford Foundation to the National Archives Trust Fund Board in support of this and four other major documentary publications. In common with these and many other enterprises like them, *The Adams Papers* has continued to benefit from the guidance and cooperation of the National Historical Publications and Records Commission, chaired by the Archivist of the United States, which from 1975 to the present has provided this enterprise with major financial support. Important additional funds were supplied from 1980 to 1993 by The Andrew W. Mellon Foundation, The J. Howard Pew Freedom Trust, and The Charles E. Culpeper Foundation through the Founding Fathers Papers, Inc. Since 1993, *The Adams Papers* has received major support from the National Endowment for the Humanities, and matching support from The Packard Humanities Institute, through the Founding Fathers Papers, Inc., and from The Charles Francis Adams Charitable Trust, The Florence J. Gould Foundation, The Lyn and Norman Lear Fund, and anonymous donors. Any views, findings, conclusions, or recommendations expressed in this publication do not necessarily reflect those of the National Endowment for the Humanities.

∞ This volume meets all ANSI/NISO Z39.48-1992 standards for permanence.

Library of Congress Cataloging in Publication Data (Revised for vols. 5–16)

Adams family correspondence.
   (The Adams papers: Series II, Adams family correspondence)
   Vols. 3–4 edited by L. H. Butterfield and Marc Friedlaender.
   Vols. 5–6 edited by Richard Alan Ryerson et al.
   Vols. 7–11 edited by Margaret A. Hogan et al.
   Vols. 12–13 edited by Sara Martin et al.
   Vols. 14–16 edited by Hobson Woodward et al.
   Includes bibliographical references and index.
   Contents: v. 1. December 1761 – May 1776–v. 2. June 1776 – March 1778–[etc.]–v. 16. November 1804 – July 1809.
    I. Butterfield, L. H. (Lyman Henry), 1909–1982. II. Friedlaender, Marc, 1905–1992. III. Ryerson, Richard Alan, 1942– . IV. Hogan, Margaret A. V. Martin, Sara. VI. Woodward, Hobson. VII. Series: Adams papers: Series II, Adams family correspondence.
E322.1.A27   929'.2   63-14964

ISBN 0-674-00400-0 (v. 1–2)
ISBN 0-674-00405-1 (v. 3–4)
ISBN 0-674-00406-X (v. 5–6)
ISBN 0-674-01574-6 (v. 7)
ISBN-13 978-0-674-02278-2 (v. 8)
ISBN-10 0-674-02278-5 (v. 8)
ISBN-13 978-0-674-03275-0 (v. 9)
ISBN-10 0-674-03275-5 (v. 9)
ISBN 978-0-674-05784-5 (v. 10)
ISBN 978-0-674-07244-2 (v. 11)
ISBN 978-0-674-50466-0 (v. 12)
ISBN 978-0-674-97718-1 (v. 13)
ISBN 978-0-674-24090-2 (v. 14)
ISBN 978-0-674-24773-4 (v. 15)
ISBN 978-0-674-24774-1 (v. 16)

This edition of *The Adams Papers*

is sponsored by the MASSACHUSETTS HISTORICAL SOCIETY

to which the ADAMS MANUSCRIPT TRUST

by a deed of gift dated 4 April 1956

gave ultimate custody of the personal and public papers

written, accumulated, and preserved over a span of three centuries

by the Adams family of Massachusetts

The Adams Papers

ADMINISTRATIVE COMMITTEE

Benjamin C. Adams
Katherine Babson
Joyce E. Chaplin
Rodney Mims Cook Jr.
Annette Gordon-Reed
Sally E. Hadden
R. J. Lyman
Kenneth P. Minkema
John Adams Morgan Jr.
Louisa Thomas
Lisa Wilson
Hiller B. Zobel

EDITORIAL ADVISORY COMMITTEE

Joseph J. Ellis
Edith B. Gelles
Linda K. Kerber
Gordon S. Wood

The acorn and oakleaf device on the preceding page is redrawn from a seal cut for John Quincy Adams after 1830. The motto is from Cæcilius Statius as quoted by Cicero in the First Tusculan Disputation: *Serit arbores quæ alteri seculo prosint* ("He plants trees for the benefit of later generations").

Contents

Descriptive List of Illustrations — ix

Introduction — xv
    1. Tranquility at Peacefield *xvi*   2. Soldier of Fortune *xx*
    3. Principles, Politics, and Party *xxiii*   4. Notes on Editorial Method *xxvii*   5. Related Digital Resources *xxvii*

Acknowledgments — xxxi

Guide to Editorial Apparatus — xxxiii
    1. Textual Devices *xxxiii*   2. Adams Family Code Names *xxxiii*
    3. Descriptive Symbols *xxxiv*   4. Location Symbols *xxxv*
    5. Other Abbreviations and Conventional Terms *xxxvi*
    6. Short Titles of Works Frequently Cited *xxxvi*

Family Correspondence, November 1804 – July 1809 — 1

Appendix: List of Omitted Documents — 441

Chronology — 451

Index — 459

Descriptive List of Illustrations

1. "THE PRAIRIE DOG SICKENED AT THE STING OF THE HORNET," BY JAMES AKIN, 1806   83

   After the United States and France agreed to the Louisiana Purchase in 1803, Spain and the United States were unable to agree on the boundary between the newly acquired territory and the Spanish-held Floridas. President Thomas Jefferson reported to Congress in his 3 December 1805 annual message that negotiations between the two nations failed to settle the issue. Seeing an opportunity to duplicate the Louisiana success, the president on 6 December secretly asked Congress to appropriate $2 million to settle U.S. claims to West Florida and purchase East Florida.

   In closed-door debate in the House of Representatives some members argued that the payment would ultimately enrich Napoleon Bonaparte since France had forced an alliance with Spain against Great Britain. Nevertheless Congress approved the appropriation and the president signed the bill into law on 13 February 1806. Senator John Quincy Adams hoped the action would halt "all the vapouring against Spain" (JQA, *Diary*, 17 Jan.). Despite Jefferson's success in Congress, public opposition led the president to forgo the plan. The territory remained Spanish and the boundary dispute lingered until 1819 when John Quincy negotiated the Adams-Onís Treaty, in which Spain ceded both East and West Florida to the United States.

   American engraver James Akin (1773–1846) drew this cartoon in 1806. The cartoon is the earliest known to be signed by Akin and was likely printed in Newburyport, Massachusetts, where he worked at the time. It depicts Jefferson as a prairie dog, a likely reference to an animal captured by Meriwether Lewis and William Clark on their expedition through the new American territory. Akin's Jefferson is stung by the hornet Napoleon and vomits a $2 million payment. A French diplomat clutching maps of East and West Florida declares it "a gull for the People" (David Carson, "That Ground Called Quiddism: John Randolph's War with the Jefferson Administration," *Journal of American Studies* 20:71–92 [April 1986]; *Annals of Congress*, 9th Cong., 1st sess., p. 11–16, 18–20, 266–267, 1131–1132; David Narrett, "Geopolitics and Intrigue: James Wilkinson, the Spanish Borderlands, and Mexican Independence," *WMQ* 69:118 [Jan. 2012]; Gilbert Din, "A Troubled Seven Years: Spanish Reactions to American

Claims and Aggression in 'West Florida,' 1803–1810," *Louisiana History* 59:409–452 [Fall 2018]; U.S. Senate, *Exec. Jour.*, 9th Cong., 1st sess., p. 36–38, 40–42; JQA, *Diary*, 6 Feb. 1806; Plumer, *Memorandum of Proceedings*, p. 379–380, 425; Maureen O'Brien Quimby, "The Political Art of James Akin," *Winterthur Portfolio* 7:60, 66–68 [1972]; Philadelphia *United States Gazette*, 20 Aug. 1805, 19 May 1806).
Courtesy of the Library of Congress.

2. DETAIL FROM "CARACCAS AND GUIANA," BY JOHN MOFFAT, 1817   89

When U.S. relations with both Great Britain and Spain worsened in 1805, Venezuelan expatriate Francisco de Miranda seized the opportunity to pursue his longstanding goal of liberating Venezuela from Spanish rule. Miranda came to the United States to solicit support, arriving in New York in November and meeting the next month with Thomas Jefferson and James Madison in Washington, D.C. He received no official support and returned to New York, where he purchased the ship *Leander* and outfitted it for a military expedition.

Miranda sailed from New York City on 2 February 1806 with a crew that included William Steuben Smith, son of Abigail Adams 2d and William Stephens Smith. Two schooners joined the expedition in the West Indies, and the convoy sailed to Venezuela where it was attacked by coastal forces on 27 April. The smaller vessels were captured; fifty-seven sailors were tried on 12 July, and ten were executed. The *Leander* returned to the West Indies, where Miranda won limited British assistance for a second incursion. On 20 June a four-vessel convoy sailed from Barbados, landing briefly in Coro, Venezuela, on 3 August, where local forces repelled the landing party. Returning to the West Indies, the remaining recruits split the proceeds when the *Leander* was sold in the fall of 1807. Miranda returned to England and the younger Smith to the United States. Some of the captured seamen who survived imprisonment in Venezuela were released with British assistance between 1807 and 1810.

A detail from engraver John Moffat's map depicts the area targeted by the expedition, including Coro, where Miranda and his men went ashore. Moffat engraved the map for John Thomson's *New General Atlas*, Edinburgh, 1817, plate 70 (vols. 6:267, 9:410; Introduction, Part 2, below; JQA to WSS, 16 April 1806, and note 2, below; Gordon S. Brown, *Latin American Rebels and the United States, 1806–1822*, Jefferson, N.C., 2015, p. 27–31; William Spence Robertson, *Francisco de Miranda and the Revolutionizing of Spanish America*, Washington, D.C., 1909, p. 363, 369, 377–378, 379, 381, 385, 386, 392).
Collection of the Massachusetts Historical Society.

3. FAMILY RECORD, BY ANN HARROD ADAMS, 1806–1825   189

"I could descant for a page or two in praise of my Daughter's genteel shapes—her jetty-locks & *darkling* eyes—the perfect symmetry of her *nose—just like her father*," a doting Thomas Boylston Adams wrote to his cousin William Smith Shaw on 3 August 1806 (below). Thomas Boylston and Ann Harrod Adams, who married on 16 May 1805, welcomed their first child, Abigail Smith Adams, on 29 July 1806. The

Descriptive List of Illustrations

eighth Adams grandchild was baptized in Quincy by Rev. Peter Whitney Jr. on 31 August. Eighteen months later on 9 February 1808, the couple welcomed a second child, Elizabeth Coombs Adams, who was baptized by Rev. Joshua Bates of the First Church of Dedham on 13 March. "I pray that this newcomer together with her elder sister, may prove a comfort to your succeeding years," John Quincy Adams wrote to his brother on 12 March (below).

In the pictured "little journal" of a family record, Ann documented the milestones of each of her children's lives, noting important events and health concerns. Written in narrative form, she detailed when Abigail and Elizabeth started walking, talking, and cutting teeth, recorded their vaccinations, and described how they fared with whooping cough, scarlet fever, and chicken pox (AA to AHA, 24 March 1805, and note 7; TBA to William Meredith, 30 July 1806, both below; Sprague, *Braintree Families*; JQA, *Diary*, 31 Aug.; TBA to JQA, 19 Feb. 1808, below; Louis A. Cook, ed., *History of Norfolk County, Massachusetts, 1622–1918*, 2 vols., N.Y., 1918, 1:440; TBA to JQA, 15 March, Adams Papers).

From the original in the Adams Family Papers. Collection of the Massachusetts Historical Society.

4, 5. SHEHEKE AND YELLOW CORN, BY CHARLES BALTHAZAR JULIEN FÉVRET DE SAINT-MÉMIN, 1807   220, 221

Chief Sheheke (ca. 1766–1812), his wife Yellow Corn, and their son White Painted House arrived in Washington, D.C., on 28 December 1806 with other members of the Mandan Nation to meet with President Thomas Jefferson. They accompanied Meriwether Lewis, whom they had helped survive a North Dakota winter during his exploration with William Clark of the territories acquired in the Louisiana Purchase. French-Canadian trader René Jusseaume traveled with the delegation as their interpreter.

Senator John Quincy Adams saw the delegation at Jefferson's annual New Year's Day levee where they were served "a great plenty of ice creams, apple pies, cakes, & a variety of wines." In his Diary Adams reported, "I paid the customary visit to the President. His Rooms were very much crowded— The most distinguished visitors were a number of Indians—Osages—and a Mandan chief with two women, and three children" (JQA, *Diary*, 1 Jan. 1807). The visitors also attended a performance of acrobats that evening. Representative William Plumer of New Hampshire recorded in his diary that after the main event "the whole was closed with a grand Indian dance," though Sheheke and Yellow Corn "took no part in the exercise" (Plumer, *Memorandum of Proceedings*, p. 553–554).

Lewis commissioned artist Charles Balthazar Julien Févret de Saint-Mémin to create these 1807 charcoal-and-chalk portraits before Sheheke and Yellow Corn were escorted home by a retinue of soldiers and trappers (vol. 13:xiv; Elizabeth A. Fenn, *Encounters at the Heart of the World: A History of the Mandan People*, N.Y., 2014, p. 255, 323; William E. Foley and Charles David Rice, "The Return of the Mandan Chief," *Montana: The Magazine of Western History*, 29:5

[Summer 1979]; James J. Holmberg, ed., *Dear Brother: Letters of William Clark to Jonathan Clark*, New Haven, 2002, p. 118; Jefferson to the Mandan Nation, 30 Dec. 1806, DLC:Jefferson Papers).
Courtesy of the New-York Historical Society.

6. THE *CHESAPEAKE* AND THE *LEOPARD*, BY IRWIN JOHN DAVID BEVAN, CA. 1875–1940   277

Tense Anglo-American relations ratcheted up on 22 June 1807 when the U.S. frigate *Chesapeake* was stopped by the British warship *Leopard* near the mouth of Chesapeake Bay. Earlier in the year, several sailors deserted the British Navy in the area, so the *Leopard*'s commander, Salusbury Pryce Humphreys, demanded that Captain James Barron of the *Chesapeake* allow a search party to board. When Barron refused, the *Leopard* fired, killing three sailors and injuring eighteen. The British then boarded and impressed four seamen from the U.S. vessel.

John Quincy Adams shared in the widespread public anger over the event. He helped draft a Boston resolution condemning the affair in which "our Citizens have been wounded and murdered, and the Flag of our Nation insulted and violated" (Boston *Democrat*, 11 July). The incident proved a spur to the passage of the Embargo Act of 1807, which John Quincy supported. The Massachusetts senator's backing of Thomas Jefferson's response to the crisis drew criticism from Federalists and contributed to his departure from the Senate. In his Diary, John Quincy wrote, "I should *have my head taken off*, for apostasy, by the federalists— I have indeed expected to displease them, but could not help it— My Sense of duty shall never yield to the pleasure of a party" (JQA, *Diary*, 11 July).

British watercolorist Irwin John David Bevan (1852–1940) was a naval historian who later illustrated historic naval battles, including this view of the *Leopard* and *Chesapeake* engagement (AA to AA2, 19 June 1808, and note 3, below; Monroe, *Papers*, 5:629; John Marshall, *Royal Naval Biography*, 4 vols., London, 1823–1835, 2:891, 892–893; Wood, *Empire of Liberty*, p. 647; TBA to JQA, 27 Dec. 1807, and note 3, below).
Courtesy of the Mariners' Museum and Park.

7. ELIZA SUSAN MORTON QUINCY, BY CHARLES BALTHAZAR JULIEN FÉVRET DE SAINT-MÉMIN, 1797   405

"When You see Mrs Quincy present my Love to her and tell her her little sophia is very well grows finely and is very lively and sprightly," Abigail Adams wrote to her daughter-in-law Louisa Catherine Adams on 19 January 1806 (below). Eliza Susan Morton Quincy, like Louisa, was in Washington, D.C., while her youngest child, Maria Sophia, remained in Quincy. Eliza's and Louisa's lives had much the same rhythm at the time. Eliza's husband, Josiah Quincy III, served in the House of Representatives from 1805 until 1813, overlapping with John Quincy Adams' tenure in the Senate from 1803 to 1808.

As wives of public servants whose responsibilities called them to

Descriptive List of Illustrations

the nation's capital, and as the mothers of young children with whom traveling was difficult, Eliza and Louisa faced tough choices. At times, they accompanied their husbands to Washington, D.C., entrusting the care of their children to friends and family in Massachusetts. The infant Sophia Quincy and four-year-old George Washington Adams were included in the "family of little ones" watched by Mary Smith Cranch, while John Adams 2d stayed at Peacefield with Abigail and John Adams (AA to JQA, 9 Feb. 1806, below). During other periods Eliza and Louisa remained in Boston, while their husbands traveled to the capital. For both, correspondence formed a lifeline during these periods of separation, bringing news and serving as a conduit of information for a broader family and social circle. Abigail wrote to Louisa that Eliza's letters home always included updates on family members, and she thanked Eliza directly for keeping her informed. For both, correspondence helped ease the pains of separation. "I am greatly obliged to you for your notice of my dear little babe," Eliza replied to Abigail on 6 April, and she returned the favor by reporting on John Quincy's "better health, and spirits" (below).

Charles Balthazar Julien Févret de Saint-Mémin completed this engraving of Eliza and a companion portrait of her husband in 1797 (vol. 12:168; AA to LCA, 19 Jan. 1806; AA to Eliza Quincy, 24 March; Eliza Quincy to AA, 6 April, and note 2, all below; *Biog. Dir. Cong.*; LCA to JQA, 26 Feb. 1809, below).

Courtesy of the National Portrait Gallery, Smithsonian Institution.

Introduction

During the nearly five years from November 1804 to July 1809 covered in volume 16 of *Adams Family Correspondence*, Abigail and John Adams hosted all ten of their grandchildren in the halls and meadows of Peacefield. While the founding couple nurtured and molded the lives of a new generation, their adult children engaged in fresh pursuits in a widening world. John Quincy Adams faced tests in the Senate, Abigail Adams 2d (Nabby) guided her husband and children through foreign and frontier endeavors, and Thomas Boylston Adams stepped tentatively into politics. Nabby is especially prominent, laying the groundwork for her son William Steuben Smith to depart on an overseas venture, serving as a political sounding board for her mother, seeing her son John Adams Smith graduate from college, and moving to a frontier settlement with her husband and children. These stories and many more unfold in the 236 letters published in the volume.

The developing nation was tested in the western Atlantic, as the arc of Adams family correspondence swept toward the end of the first decade of the nineteenth century. There was significant discussion of international intrigue in South America; family members wrote about Francisco de Miranda's bid to challenge Spanish control of Venezuela, which was of personal interest because Nabby's son William joined the enterprise. Anglo-American affairs were also of paramount importance to the Adams family and the nation during this time. Great Britain continued to fuel tensions by impressing sailors from American vessels, harassing a nation whose navy was not yet strong enough to answer with military might. When Massachusetts senator John Quincy Adams voted for President Thomas Jefferson's plan to punish Britain with a trade embargo, Abigail decried the policy's severe impact on local families and challenged her son to explain his stance. John Quincy mounted equally vigorous defenses in the press and in letters to his family, but his explanations were for naught. The Massachusetts General Court replaced him in the Senate, addressing dissatisfaction with his policy positions dating back to his entrance into Congress.[1]

Abigail turned sixty the month the volume opens and John celebrated his seventieth birthday soon afterward. They reveled in having family near. John Quincy and Louisa Catherine were in Massachusetts during most Senate recesses. Nabby escaped tumultuous times in New York to spend almost a year under the parental roof. Youngest son Thomas Boylston resided at Peacefield and married Ann Harrod, and the couple had two children. As usual John and Abigail supervised all, while watching, and offering adroit commentary on, the politics of the time.

1. TRANQUILITY AT PEACEFIELD

"Hush child; don't you see I am writing?" Abigail Adams wrote of a young one tugging at her sleeve. This time it was five-year-old John Adams 2d, who sought help finding a coin lost in the grass. "I sit writing in my chamber with all the Chit Chat of two Girls, and little John who is on a Visit to me," Abigail wrote to Abigail Adams 2d at a time when Peacefield echoed with the voices of the founding couple's grandchildren and nieces and nephews.[2] While Abigail depicted herself as a harried caregiver in some of the 68 letters she authored here, it was clear that she relished her time with grandchildren. She is most often a doting parent and grandparent in correspondence that continues to provide an intimate look at the management of a complex American household. The matriarch of Peacefield directed the activities of domestic servants of her choosing, handled household finances and her own investments, oversaw the procurement of goods from Boston markets, clothed and fed the family, advised the ailing on medical care, tracked the travels of relations and guests, and cared for grandchildren who ranged in age from newborn to young adult. Historians of economics, technology, food and clothing, medicine, education, child rearing, and the interplay of race, gender, and class in early America will all find material of value.

While caring for grandchildren close at hand, Abigail did not neglect her adult children, even when they were far away. She advised John Quincy Adams to stave off hunger in the Senate chamber by carrying

[1] Vol. 15:312, 331; AA to AA2, 19 June 1808, and note 3, below.
[2] AA to AA2, 13 May 1809, and note 19, below.

Introduction

crackers in his pocket and counseled late son Charles Adams' widow, Sarah Smith Adams, through a courtship.[3] Of special interest is Abigail's 1808 and 1809 correspondence with Nabby and granddaughter Caroline Amelia Smith while they were living in a remote homestead in central New York. Abigail offered motherly advice, endorsing Nabby's plan to make maple sugar as a way to reduce dependence on foreign imports, and instructing Caroline that assisting her parents in their rustic household would reward her with serenity "beyond the possession of gold and Rubies."[4] Abigail took time to correspond with friends as well, carrying on spirited exchanges with Eliza Susan Morton Quincy, Hannah Phillips Cushing, and Hannah Carter Smith.

John Adams was a less visible but nevertheless ubiquitous resident of Peacefield. The former president invested in curating his legacy. Volume 16 features fifteen letters by John, missives that showcase his efforts to shape the collective memory of his life and work. A November 1804 request by John Quincy that his father resume his autobiography elicited reluctance from the senior Adams: "I can recollect no part of my political Life, without pain." Nevertheless, on the very day he wrote those words, John took up his pen to resume the dormant project.[5] There was reason for the retired chief executive to be concerned about his public image. Mercy Otis Warren's depiction of his statecraft in her 1805 *History of the Rise, Progress and Termination of the American Revolution* led to a rancorous epistolary debate between John Adams and the author, a rift that will play out fully in the *Papers of John Adams* but is on display in this volume as the Adamses struggled to maintain a friendship with the Warrens.[6] More congenial to John's project was a laudatory March 1809 letter from the editors of the *Boston Patriot* to the "father of New-England," which drew a meditative response from Peacefield that was published in the newspaper. The exchange was a precursor to a long-running series in which John published letters from his archives and offered explanatory and sometimes exculpatory comment.[7] As he looked back on his experiences as a diplomat and executive, reminiscences crept into his letters with his grandchildren, who for the first time appear as correspondents in the series.[8]

---

[3] AA to LCA, 8 Dec. 1804; to AA2, 31 July 1808, and note 4, below.
[4] AA to AA2, 8 May 1808; to Caroline Amelia Smith, 17 Nov., both below.
[5] JA to JQA, 30 Nov. 1804, and note 3, below.
[6] AA to AA2, 8 Dec. 1808, and note 6, below.
[7] AA to AA2, 10 April 1809, and note 3, below.
[8] JA to John Adams Smith, 27 March 1806, and notes 1 and 2; 14 Dec. 1808, and note 3, both below.

Thomas Boylston Adams, while residing at Peacefield, tried his hand at the family business. In November 1804 he made a bid for election to the United States House of Representatives. After losing that contest, he resolved to remain closer to home and won Quincy's seat in the Massachusetts General Court in May 1805.[9] The youngest Adams son enjoyed proximity to power, touting to a friend in Philadelphia his "access to members of our Legislature" and promising to investigate legislative obstacles to a business proposal: "I will converse with some Gentlemen whom I believe to be competent judges of the subject of your letter and without betraying your secret, avail myself of their intelligence."[10] During Thomas Boylston's year in the State House, John Quincy counseled him on how to succeed as a legislator.[11] He served only one term, however, losing his seat when a sea change in Massachusetts politics saw Democratic-Republicans assume control of government for the first time. His lack of advancement did not escape his parents' notice. His mother in a letter to her sister Elizabeth Smith Shaw Peabody caught herself extolling John Quincy's talents before adding that her purpose was not to "depreciate the good and amiable qualities of my other Son," who "being so much younger, and not having been placed in such conspicuous stations, cannot be supposed to have the knowledge and experience of his Brother."[12] Legal work and property management rather than politics became the focus of Thomas Boylston's professional pursuits, and his sixteen letters printed here reflect his growing confidence as a lawyer.

The greatest change for Thomas Boylston at age 32 came in May 1805 when he and Ann (Nancy) Harrod concluded a long courtship and married, soon adding two children to the family, in 1806 Abigail Smith Adams and in 1808 Elizabeth Coombs Adams.[13] While Nancy is quiet in this volume, the correspondence of Abigail and others makes it clear that as a New Englander she integrated easily into her new husband's Yankee family. When Nancy accompanied Thomas Boylston to Boston during his year in the state legislature, Abigail drew her into the management of Peacefield by asking her to purchase chocolate, currants, and cloth.[14] The two quickly became confidants. A short let-

[9] William Smith Shaw to JQA, 5 Nov. 1804, and note 4; JQA to TBA, 2 Jan. 1806, and note 4, both below.
[10] TBA to Thomas Cadwalader, 19 Feb. 1806, below.
[11] JQA to TBA, 5 Feb. 1806, below.
[12] AA to Elizabeth Smith Shaw Peabody, 18 July 1809, below.
[13] AA to AHA, 24 March 1805, and note 7, below; Descriptive List of Illustrations, No. 3, above; TBA to JQA, 19 Feb. 1808, and note 4, below.
[14] AA to AHA, 28 April 1806, below.

Introduction

ter from Abigail in 1807 is striking in its intimacy and warmth: "Commit this hasty scratch of My pen to the flames my dear Nancy. it is written more to shew you how much I bear you in mind, and how tenderly I love you than to afford you any entertainment."[15] That was unlike notes Abigail wrote to the spouses of her other children, none of whom were born or raised in New England. Abigail was also enamored of Nancy's infants, writing of Elizabeth, "The little one is a very beautifull Baby, quiet as a Lamb, fine dark Eyes, and black Hair."[16]

In contrast to her sister-in-law, Louisa Catherine Adams met with both joy and tribulation during these years. Louisa oversaw a growing family, caring for her children, George Washington Adams and John Adams 2d, and worrying when others cared for them in her absence. She and John Quincy faced extended periods of separation as she sometimes stayed behind in Washington, D.C., with her mother and sisters and other times remained in Boston while her husband traveled to the federal capital. One separation was particularly difficult. Having stayed in Washington, D.C., while her husband and children went to Quincy, on 22 June 1806 Louisa suffered the birth of a stillborn child. She was resolute in the aftermath, writing to John Quincy that she feared her labor "would have terminated an existence which though of little use I flatter myself is of some consequence to you." After recovering her health, she took the first opportunity to reunite with her husband and sons, whom she characterized as "all I hold dear in this world."[17]

Fourteen months later, Louisa gave birth to a healthy son, Charles Francis Adams. Abigail rejoiced in this grandchild too, calling the baby "My Boy Charles" and teasing that he would have to be well behaved if he expected to "claim an equal share of the Love and affection of his Grandmother with his Brothers."[18] Louisa wrote 37 of the letters printed below, gaining strength and stature as an emerging voice in the Adams clan. Often politics and family life intersected, as when she wrote to her husband that John Adams "cannot account for the Vote of a *certain friend* of mine. it never caused me the slightest anxiety," Louisa reported, "as I know your opinions to be generally form'd upon mature reflection and deliberation and almost always correct. he has tax'd me once or twice upon two of your former votes as if he suspected my having been concern'd in the subject, which makes me smile."

---

[15] AA to AHA, [*post* 6 *July 1807*], below.
[16] AA to AA2, 8 May 1808, below.
[17] LCA to JQA, 24 June 1806, and note 1, below.
[18] AA to LCA, 4 April 1808, below.

Louisa gently communicated the conversations with her father-in-law, adding her opinion as she did. "Is it fair mon Ami, for a man, thus to condemn, without knowing upon what grounds you have acted? I think not."[19] Louisa offered comment on rumored duels, Anglo-French relations, political intrigue in capital society, and the treatment of enslaved people.[20] Her correspondence also provides insight into family life, telling of managing household finances, socializing at Boston dinners, dancing in Quincy, and helping to turn aside the unwanted attentions of a Boston lawyer toward her sister Catherine Maria Frances Johnson.[21]

John Quincy and Louisa might have settled permanently in Massachusetts if events had gone in another direction. When the eldest Adams son was installed as the Harvard College Boylston Professor of Rhetoric and Oratory on 12 June 1806, he stood at a crossroads. The senator and former diplomat would soon turn forty years old and faced a choice between a secure life teaching the elite youth of New England and the exhausting, sometimes maddening, but always invigorating life of public service modeled by his father. The 69 letters that John Quincy authored in the volume reveal that for a while he did both, continuing his legislative work while embracing his academic role with his usual exactitude. He wrote and delivered 36 lectures on the power and importance of oratory, and during three years of teaching he needed a classroom substitute only three times. But his academic career was a short one. John Quincy ended it in July 1809 when he accepted a commission as United States minister to Russia.[22] A faithful heir, John Quincy turned away from a career in education to continue in public service, a path from which he would never again waver.

2. SOLDIER OF FORTUNE

"Let us cultivate a little candour in judging of others," Abigail Adams 2d wrote to her mother on 3 December 1804; "I have never found that those who were most disposed to condemn the follies of others, were the most perfect themselves." Nabby's parents had long disapproved of the activities of her husband, William Stephens Smith, ob-

---

[19] LCA to JQA, 15 Feb. 1807, below.
[20] LCA to AA, 11 Feb. 1805; 6 Dec.; to JQA, 29 June [1806]; 6 July, all below.
[21] LCA to JQA, 21 Feb. [1809], Adams Papers; 21 Jan. 1807; 20 Feb., and note 5; JQA to LCA, 5 March 1809, and note 5; 9 March, all below.
[22] JQA to LCA, 15 June 1806, and note 1, below.

Introduction

jecting when his land speculation resulted in unsettled finances and extended absences from his wife and children. Nabby handled the criticism with equanimity, remaining loyal to her husband but taking action to advance the well-being of her children. "I shall do what appears to me to be my duty," she wrote, "and hope in every situation to find support and consolation."[23] The Adamses' displeasure was particularly acute when the Smiths sent their eldest son, William Steuben Smith, on a covert military raid to Venezuela. Members of the extended Adams family learned of the venture only after the young adventurer had departed.[24]

As with many Adams stories, the foreign adventure of William Steuben Smith was both public and private, as the young man joined Francisco de Miranda's ill-fated attempt to liberate Venezuela from Spanish rule. Miranda met William Stephens Smith when both served in the American Revolution. They renewed their friendship while Smith served as John Adams' secretary in London in 1785. The Venezuelan expatriate returned to the United States in late 1805 to organize his expedition. When he sailed from New York City on 2 February 1806, Nabby's eighteen-year-old son was at his side. Nabby wrote two letters to Miranda before his departure, which are among five by her printed below. As she consigned the care of her child to Miranda, the apprehensive mother requested "guidance and protection" for her "young and inexperienced" boy, but she believed he was in good hands: "I can say that I do not know any person to whom I could with so much confidence entrust him— permit me to wish you a pleasant passage, and success, in the object of the enterprise." That confidence gave way to angst as the Smiths and Adamses followed news of Miranda's activities over the next year. An American press report in the summer claimed that the younger Smith was captured by Venezuelan coastal forces. That proved false, but the family was unsure how he fared in a second clash at Coro, Venezuela, until he finally wrote that he was safe.[25]

Like most in the family, John Quincy disapproved of his nephew's activities, writing to Louisa, "This quixotic adventure at the outset of life, is just calculated to make him fit for nothing upon this Earth."[26]

[23] AA2 to AA, 3 Dec. 1804, below.
[24] AA2 to Francisco de Miranda, 13 Jan. 1806, and note 1; 29 Jan., both below; New York *Commercial Advertiser*, 3 June; New York *Public Advertiser*, 29 April 1807.
[25] Descriptive List of Illustrations, No. 2, above; JA, *Papers*, 17:301; AA2 to Francisco de Miranda, 13 Jan. 1806, and note 1; 29 Jan.; JQA to WSS, 16 April, and note 2; to LCA, 9 July, note 6, all below.
[26] JQA to LCA, 28 Nov. 1806, below.

For Abigail, her grandson's participation "could never have met with his Grandfathers or My assent or consent, if it had been known to us before he had saild," although she admitted to some amusement at the Jefferson administration's entanglement in Miranda's scheme.[27] John declared that the United States' unintentional involvement in a private military venture demonstrated a need for a stronger naval presence. "The Attention of all Europe has been turned by all these means so much to this quarter of the World," John wrote, "that We shall e'er long be obliged to turn our Thoughts to some means of preservation and defence."[28]

Nabby remained defiant during the months of uncertainty. "I did not expect when he went away that his excursion would have excited Such a Spirit as it has amongst us," she wrote to Hannah Carter Smith, "or that he would have been made of so much consequence as to excite such various conjectures and Surmises. many of them time and events will contradict I presume."[29] Nabby was vindicated when William Steuben returned, surprising John Quincy on 12 September 1807 as William passed through Boston on his way to Quincy. Having departed college without a degree, he lived at Peacefield while considering careers in commerce and the military. Finding no success, he solicited and received an appointment as John Quincy's secretary and prepared to depart for Russia in 1809.[30]

"Mirandas Wild enterprize" did not leave the senior members of the Smith family unscathed.[31] William Stephens Smith lost his federal post as surveyor for the port of New York and was indicted in U.S. Circuit Court for his involvement in organizing the expedition. The exact nature of his role remains murky. Critics charged that he helped to recruit sailors, obtained arms and supplies, and engineered the official clearance of the vessel from New York Harbor.[32] While her husband fought the charges, Nabby took her son John Adams Smith and daughter Caroline Amelia Smith to spend most of 1807 in Quincy with her parents. Abigail reveled in their time together, but the idyll abruptly terminated when William Stephens Smith arrived in Quincy, acquitted but unemployed, in January 1808 to escort his wife and children to a cabin in the Chenango Valley of central New York.

[27] AA to Mercy Otis Warren, 9 March 1807; to JQA, 16 Jan., both below.
[28] JA to JQA, 7 Jan. 1807, below.
[29] AA2 to Hannah Carter Smith, 12 March 1806, below.
[30] JQA, *Diary*, 12 Sept. 1807; AA to AA2, 18 March 1808; JQA to William Steuben Smith, 5 July 1809, and note 1, both below.
[31] AA to JQA, 16 Jan. 1807, below.
[32] WSS to JQA, 23 March 1806, and note 1; JQA to WSS, 16 April, and note 2, both below.

Introduction

"When you was really gone," Abigail lamented after Nabby and Caroline's departure, "I felt the full force of Your absence and sat down without a wish to move from my chair the whole day or to see any one."[33] To fill the void, Abigail embarked on regular epistolary exchanges with both. Most of Nabby's and Caroline's return letters are lost, leaving Abigail's side of the correspondence to reveal the dynamics of their relationships, especially how Abigail engaged her granddaughter. "You must write me how you spend your time, what are your daily occupations and amusements, what acquaintance you make with the quail, the partridge, and the pheasant," Abigail asked of Caroline.[34] Her letters to the teenager are rife with guidance for a girl who had had to trade friends and the comforts of home for a wilderness dwelling. Avoid boastfulness and maintain a serene countenance, Abigail advised, for "pride you know was not Made for Man, nor Woman neither." The tenor of the times also demanded attention to the politics of the day, Abigail admonished her granddaughter: "You say you hate politics; but when your native country is so seriously threatened, you cannot be a descendant from the spirit of '76, to be totally indifferent to what is passing."[35]

3. PRINCIPLES, POLITICS, AND PARTY

Anglo-American relations had been largely stable since the mid-1790s, but external pressures began to build a decade later as war in Europe renewed and intensified. The self-crowned emperor Napoleon continued his quest to expand the French empire to the edges of Europe. Great Britain, looking to maintain its naval dominance and global commercial avenues, had little respect for neutral nations profiting from European war. The United States was swept into the fray. Britain's need for warship crews caused it to step up impressment from American ships, a practice seen as a gross violation of United States sovereignty. Changes to British navigation laws restricted access to ports for United States merchants, carrying economic consequences. The resulting erosion of Anglo-American relations created tensions among the American populace that had sharp repercussions for John Quincy Adams. The Massachusetts senator, who represented a Federalist stronghold, sided with Democratic-Republicans on how

---

[33] AA to AA2, 14 Jan. 1808, below.
[34] AA to Caroline Amelia Smith, 24 Jan. 1808, below.
[35] AA to Caroline Amelia Smith, 17 Nov. 1808, and notes 1 and 7, below.

the United States should respond to an increasingly hostile Britain. It was not the first time he had drifted from his Federalist Party roots, having supported the Louisiana Purchase in his first congressional session.[36] During the four subsequent sessions covered in this volume, John Quincy consistently prized independent thought over the party interest. Those choices led to vociferous criticism from New England Federalists.[37] More distressing on a personal level was his need to explain himself to his mother and father. The process brought forth an uncharacteristic ambivalence as John Quincy struggled to chart his way. "It grieves me to see him sacrificing the best years of his life in so painful and unprofitable a way," Louisa Catherine Adams confided to Abigail Adams. "It would however cause me infinite pain to see him give it up."[38]

Successive military engagements increased Anglo-American tensions. On 25 April 1806, the British warship *Leander*, intent on impressment, fired on the American merchant sloop *Richard* in New York waters, killing a mariner. Then near the mouth of Chesapeake Bay on 22 June 1807 the British warship *Leopard* fired on the United States frigate *Chesapeake*, killing three sailors and injuring eighteen. The clashes did more than kill and maim Americans; they wounded the nation's pride in its budding military. John Quincy was in Boston when news of the attack on the *Chesapeake* arrived. He joined local citizens in drafting a statement that called the action "a most wanton and cruel outrage."[39] Federalists and Democratic-Republicans were equally angry, but the parties differed on how the United States should respond. Thomas Jefferson had few options to counter British aggression. The United States Navy was not a serious threat to its British counterpart and any move to arm merchant vessels or privateers would likely lead to war. The president chose economic sanctions in the form of three escalating embargo laws passed by Congress between April 1806 and March 1809. John Quincy supported the first two measures, actions that proved ineffective and drew the ire of Federalists as merchants saw their cargoes pile up and their fortunes shrink.[40] The Federalists walked a fine line, however, as they opposed the militant ac-

---

[36] Vol. 15:312, 331; AA to AA2, 19 June 1808, and note 3, below.
[37] TBA to JQA, 27 Dec. 1807, and note 3; JQA to TBA of 6 Feb. 1808, and note 4; TBA to JQA, 24 March, and note 3, all below.
[38] LCA to AA, 27 Nov. 1804, below.
[39] JQA to LCA, 1 May 1806, and note 5, below; Descriptive List of Illustrations, No. 6, above; Boston *Democrat*, 11 July 1807.
[40] JQA to TBA, 20 Jan. 1806, and note 2; TBA to JQA, 27 Dec. 1807, and note 3; JQA to LCA, 8 Feb. 1809, and note 5, all below.

Introduction

tions advocated by the most vociferous Democratic-Republicans for fear they would lead to a catastrophic war. They effectively demanded that Jefferson, and by extension John Quincy and his congressional colleagues, draw an alternative retaliatory option from a barren arsenal. When no option was offered, Massachusetts legislators ousted John Quincy from his Senate seat effective at the end of his term. The repudiated senator chose not to wait and resigned on 8 June 1808.[41]

John Quincy's disillusionment with Federalists' principles and his high-profile departure from the party agenda mirrored larger shifts in early American political culture. By the early 1800s New England Federalists fought to uphold the Jay Treaty and to shed the stain of the Alien and Sedition Acts. Democratic-Republicans, nurturing their bases in southern and western states, rallied around the Louisiana Purchase and pushed for greater trade with France. Overall, John Quincy followed the family commitment to federalism. He believed that a tripartite constitutional government was best, and he feared that the brawl of party spirit could upset that balance. Yet on questions of economy and expansion, the founding Federalist's son now magnetized to Democratic-Republican views. A cordial, albeit arm's-length, relationship with Jefferson did not help to soothe his parents' worries. A trio of pinchpoints drove the Adamses to question John Quincy's shifting allegiance. The first was the pain that they and their friends felt from the economic vise of the embargo. A second was the family's general distrust of Democratic-Republican principles. Even John Quincy persisted in recommending to his brother that artisans and tradespeople should be chosen by their politics, advising, "Never deal with democrats if you can avoid it; and where a choice is offered you for your custom, depend upon it, the federal tradesman will use you best."[42] A third source of tension was the perception that the son's actions would reflect on his father. An anonymous letter in the New York *Herald* in January 1808 warned John Quincy to "think of the reputation of your Worthy father & pause before it be too Late."[43] The Adams patriarch adopted a more philosophical attitude toward his son's activities, perhaps because he too felt that the Federalist Party was losing its way. "It is your Grandfather who has been Steady to his System, and the Pretended Federalists, who have fled from it," John Adams wrote to a grandson.[44]

---

[41] AA to AA2, 19 June 1808, and note 3, below.
[42] JQA to TBA, 21 Nov. 1805, below.
[43] JQA to TBA, 6 Feb. 1808, and note 3, below.
[44] JA to John Adams Smith, 14 Dec. 1808, below.

John Quincy's politics produced a particularly extraordinary set of family letters over five days in February as the senator's mother, father, and brother wrote from their respective desks at Peacefield to query his turn from the Federalists. Abigail wrote that reports of John Quincy's connections to the Democratic-Republicans "staggerd my beleif" and prompted her to ask for an explanation: "I take it for granted that You will neither in public or private Life do any thing which you are unwilling to own, or to affix Your Name." A protective Abigail never wavered from viewing her husband's presidency as "the Halcion Days of America" and extolling his sacrifices: "I trust future Generations will feel the benifit of the sacrifices we have made; and do justice to the Memory of those, who have sufferd much, and endured much for their benefit."[45]

John advised his son to follow his conscience, and if that meant supporting Democratic-Republican James Madison for president, "I apprehend it will not redound to your Popularity or mine." Thomas Boylston Adams adopted a sharper tone, declaring that "a man is known by the company he keeps" and warning his brother that "for any of our family to aid the measures of the present Administration, however congenial those measures may be with the true interests of the Nation, will be looked upon as damnable heresy, by those who call themselves federalists."[46] John Quincy responded to Abigail and Thomas Boylston, letters he knew would be read by his father. His votes were motivated by principle, he argued, not by party allegiance, and when issues dictated that he side with Democratic-Republicans, he did so regardless of the political consequences. "My situation has been difficult—my conduct, governed by my best judgment, under a deep conviction of the perilous State of the Nation, and of my own duties in the Station where I have been placed," son wrote to mother. "I could wish to please my Country— I could wish to please my Parents— But my duty, I *must* do— It is a Law far above that of my mere wishes."[47]

One of John Quincy's more provocative actions was to caucus with Democratic-Republicans as they nominated James Madison as the party's presidential candidate in early 1808. When Madison won, Abigail recognized that the new administration would have to deal with the Anglo-American storm clouds that were growing ever darker. "Whether Commerce is ever again to shake of her shackles, as re-

---

[45] AA to JQA, 15 Feb. 1808; to AA2, 29 Aug.; to SSA, 20 Jan., all below.
[46] JA to JQA, 19 Feb. 1808; TBA to JQA, 19 Feb., both below.
[47] JQA to AA, 24 Feb. 1808; to TBA, 12 March, both below.

Introduction

spects America, is doubtfull, not I fear untill she can do it, by the power of her own Navy, and the Thunder of her own Cannon."[48] John Quincy joined the new president's team to shelter the nation from political tempests, accepting a commission as United States minister to Russia.[49] On the last day of July 1809 as her son prepared to embark across the Atlantic to resume diplomatic service, this time in St. Petersburg, Abigail penned a poignant goodbye. In it she quoted a poem that promised to safeguard her eldest son and his young family within a shield of love, declaring it, "Your Mothers Legacy May a blessing accompany it."[50]

4. NOTES ON EDITORIAL METHOD

For a complete statement of Adams Papers editorial policy as revised in 2007, see *Adams Family Correspondence*, 8:xxxv–xliii. Readers may also wish to consult the descriptions of the editorial standards established at the beginning of the project in *Diary and Autobiography of John Adams*, 1:lii–lxii, and *Adams Family Correspondence*, 1:xli–xlviii. These statements document the original conception of the Adams Papers project, though significant parts of them have now been superseded.

The only major addition to the 2007 policy regards the selection for publication in the *Adams Family Correspondence* series of some correspondence between John Adams and John Quincy Adams. In general, we will include those letters only when they focus substantially on family matters. If their contents revolve largely or entirely around diplomatic and political affairs, they will be reserved for consideration and likely inclusion in the *Papers of John Adams* or the *Papers of John Quincy Adams*. John Quincy's letters to other family members—especially Abigail, to whom he often wrote at the same time as he did to his father—will continue to be published routinely in the *Adams Family Correspondence* books.

5. RELATED DIGITAL RESOURCES

The Massachusetts Historical Society is committed to making Adams family materials available to scholars and the public online. Four

---

[48] AA to AA2, 3 Nov. 1808, below.
[49] William Steuben Smith to JQA, 1 July 1809, and note 1, below.
[50] AA to JQA, [31 July 1809], below.

Adams Family Correspondence

digital resources of particular interest to those who use the *Adams Family Correspondence* volumes are the Adams Papers Digital Edition; the John Quincy Adams Digital Diary; the Online Adams Catalog; and The Adams Family Papers: An Electronic Archive. All are available through the Historical Society's website at www.masshist.org.

The Adams Papers Digital Edition, a project originally cosponsored by the National Endowment for the Humanities, Harvard University Press, and the Massachusetts Historical Society, offers searchable text for 52 of the Adams Papers volumes published through 2020. There is a single consolidated index for volumes published through 2006, while the indexes for more recent volumes appear separately. This digital edition is designed as a complement to the letterpress edition by providing greater access to a wealth of Adams material.

The John Quincy Adams Digital Diary presents verified and searchable transcriptions, alongside manuscript page images, from the 51-volume Diary that John Quincy Adams composed over nearly seventy years. This project was supported by the Amelia Peabody Charitable Fund, Harvard University Press, and private donors, and builds on work completed by the Society as part of The Diaries of John Quincy Adams Digital Collection.

The Online Adams Catalog represents a fully searchable electronic database of all known Adams documents, dating primarily from the 1760s to 1889, at the Massachusetts Historical Society and other public and private repositories. The digital conversion—based on the original Adams Papers control file begun in the 1950s and steadily updated since that time—was supported by the National Historical Publications and Records Commission and the Massachusetts Historical Society, and was initiated with Packard Humanities Institute funds in 2009. The catalog allows public online access to a database of nearly 110,000 records, with some 30,000 cross-reference links to online, printed, and microfilm editions of the items, or to websites of the holding repositories. Each record contains information on a document's author, recipient, and date and on the location of the original, if known. The Adams Family Papers: An Electronic Archive contains images and text files of all of the correspondence between John and Abigail Adams owned by the Massachusetts Historical Society as well as John Adams' Diaries and Autobiography. The text is fully searchable and can also be browsed by date.

The letters printed here may be supplemented with the letters of John Adams and John Quincy Adams published, respectively, in *The Works of John Adams*, edited by Charles Francis Adams, 9:589–624,

Introduction

and *Writings of John Quincy Adams*, edited by Worthington Chauncey Ford, 3:62–333. Also of interest will be the *Diary and Autobiographical Writings of Louisa Catherine Adams*, edited by Judith S. Graham, Beth Luey, and others, 1:217–284. Future volumes of the *Papers of John Adams* will provide considerably more coverage of John's public activities during these years.

Intertwined personal and public accounts of local, national, and international events reveal a maturing and expanding Adams family. As a growing nation pushed further onto western frontiers and became entangled in South American politics, an uneasy economic standoff with Great Britain threatened to draw the United States into war. The evolving political terrain prompted John Quincy Adams to turn from the Federalist associations of his parents and chart a new course. Through it all, the Adams letters offer portraits of each member of the family—Abigail and John ensconced at Peacefield, John Quincy and Louisa Catherine Adams shuttling between Boston and the federal capital, Abigail Adams 2d ushering her children into adulthood, and Thomas Boylston Adams adding a new branch to the family tree. The Adamses are one of the nation's best documented families, and their letters continue to enlighten and enliven our understanding of the past.

Hobson Woodward
January 2025

Acknowledgments

The dedicated work of past and present staff of the Adams Papers editorial project made possible the creation of volume 16 of the *Adams Family Correspondence*. Editorial assistant Sarah Hume, administrative assistant Molly Mullin, and intern Lucy Wickstrom made valuable contributions. We are grateful to our copyeditor, Ann-Marie Imbornoni, who continues to add finesse and polish to our text.

Many colleagues at institutions throughout the country provided important assistance in the creation of this volume. We are indebted to Brianne Barrett at the American Antiquarian Society; Carolle R. Morini at the Boston Athenæum; Lisa Williams at the Mariners' Museum and Park; Eleanor Gillers at the New-York Historical Society Museum & Library; Laura Morrill and Diane Shewchuk at the Albany Institute of History & Art; Kathryn Gehred at Virginia Humanities; Krystal Appiah and Adam Stevenson at the Albert and Shirley Small Special Collections Library at the University of Virginia; Jennifer E. Stertzer and the other editors at the Papers of George Washington; Mary K. Wigge and Tyson Reeder at the Papers of James Madison; and Lisa A. Francavilla at the Papers of Thomas Jefferson: Retirement Series. The reference staff and librarians at Harvard University's Houghton, Lamont, and Widener libraries also provided essential resources.

Our continued thanks goes to Kenneth and Kevin Krugh of Technologies 'N Typography in Merrimac, Massachusetts, who typeset our files with great care. At Harvard University Press, we appreciate the support of Christine Thorsteinsson, Managing Editor; Emily Silk, Editor; Tim Jones, Director of Design and Production; Abigail Mumford, Associate Director of Production; Jillian Quigley, Editorial Assistant; and Eric Mulder, Production Designer.

The Adams Papers continues to enjoy the unwavering encouragement of the Massachusetts Historical Society. We thank especially former president Catherine Allgor; Brenda M. Lawson, Senior Vice President for Collections & Content Development and Interim President; Jack Sheehan, Vice President and Chief Financial Officer; Peter Drummey, Chief Historian & Stephen T. Riley Librarian; Carol Knauff, Vice President for Programs & External Affairs; William Beck, Lead Web Developer and Software Engineer; Anne E. Bentley, Curator of Art & Artifacts, Emerita; Chris Coveney, Chief Technology & Media Officer; Tammy Hamond, Controller; Elaine Heavey, Director of the Library; Nancy Heywood, Lead Archivist for Digital & Web Initiatives; Ondine E. Le Blanc, Worthington C. Ford Editor of Publications; Victoria McKay, Director of Development; Kanisorn Wong-srichanalai, Director of Research; Conrad E. Wright, Sibley Editor; Laura Wulf, Photographic & Digital Imaging Specialist; Mary E. Yacovone, Curator of Rare Books & Visual Materials; and all of the members of the Library–Reader Services department. As always, the project appreciates the steadfast support of the Society's Adams Papers Committee.

Guide to Editorial Apparatus

The first three sections (1–3) of this guide list, respectively, the arbitrary devices used for clarifying the text, the code names for prominent members of the Adams family, and the symbols that are employed throughout *The Adams Papers*, in all its series and parts, for various kinds of manuscript sources. The final three sections (4–6) list, respectively, the symbols for institutions holding original materials, the various abbreviations and conventional terms, and the short titles of books and other works that occur in volume 16 of the *Adams Family Correspondence*.

1. TEXTUAL DEVICES

The following devices will be used throughout *The Adams Papers* to clarify the presentation of the text.

[. . .]	One word missing or illegible.
[. . . .]	Two words missing or illegible.
[. . . .][1]	More than two words missing or illegible; subjoined footnote estimates amount of missing matter.
[ ]	Number or part of a number missing or illegible. Amount of blank space inside brackets approximates the number of missing or illegible digits.
[roman]	Conjectural reading for missing or illegible matter. A question mark is inserted before the closing bracket if the conjectural reading is seriously doubtful.
~~roman~~	Canceled matter.
[*italic*]	Editorial insertion.
{roman}	Text editorially decoded or deciphered.

2. ADAMS FAMILY CODE NAMES

First Generation

JA	John Adams (1735–1826)
AA	Abigail Adams (1744–1818), *m*. JA 1764

Second Generation

AA2	Abigail Adams (1765–1813), daughter of JA and AA, *m*. WSS 1786
WSS	William Stephens Smith (1755–1816), brother of SSA
JQA	John Quincy Adams (1767–1848), son of JA and AA
LCA	Louisa Catherine Johnson (1775–1852), *m*. JQA 1797

Adams Family Correspondence

CA	Charles Adams (1770–1800), son of JA and AA
SSA	Sarah Smith (1769–1828), sister of WSS, *m.* CA 1795
TBA	Thomas Boylston Adams (1772–1832), son of JA and AA
AHA	Ann Harrod (1774–1845), *m.* TBA 1805

Third Generation

GWA	George Washington Adams (1801–1829), son of JQA and LCA
JA2	John Adams (1803–1834), son of JQA and LCA
MCHA	Mary Catherine Hellen (1806–1870), *m.* JA2 1828
CFA	Charles Francis Adams (1807–1886), son of JQA and LCA
ABA	Abigail Brown Brooks (1808–1889), *m.* CFA 1829
ECA	Elizabeth Coombs Adams (1808–1903), daughter of TBA and AHA

Fourth Generation

LCA2	Louisa Catherine Adams (1831–1870), daughter of CFA and ABA, *m.* Charles Kuhn 1854
JQA2	John Quincy Adams (1833–1894), son of CFA and ABA
CFA2	Charles Francis Adams (1835–1915), son of CFA and ABA
HA	Henry Adams (1838–1918), son of CFA and ABA
MHA	Marian Hooper (1842–1885), *m.* HA 1872
MA	Mary Adams (1845–1928), daughter of CFA and ABA, *m.* Henry Parker Quincy 1877
BA	Brooks Adams (1848–1927), son of CFA and ABA

Fifth Generation

CFA3	Charles Francis Adams (1866–1954), son of JQA2
HA2	Henry Adams (1875–1951), son of CFA2
JA3	John Adams (1875–1964), son of CFA2

3. DESCRIPTIVE SYMBOLS

The following symbols are employed throughout *The Adams Papers* to describe or identify the various kinds of manuscript originals.

D	Diary (Used only to designate a diary written by a member of the Adams family and always in combination with the short form of the writer's name and a serial number, as follows: D/JA/23, i.e., the twenty-third fascicle or volume of John Adams' manuscript Diary.)
Dft	draft
Dupl	duplicate
FC	file copy (A copy of a letter retained by a correspondent other than an Adams, no matter the form of the retained copy; a copy of a letter retained by an Adams other than a Letterbook or letterpress copy.)
FC-Pr	a letterpress copy retained by an Adams as the file copy
IRC	intended recipient's copy (Generally the original version but received after a duplicate, triplicate, or other copy of a letter.)
Lb	Letterbook (Used only to designate an Adams Letterbook and always in combination with the short form of the writer's name

	and a serial number, as follows: Lb/JQA/29, i.e., the twenty-ninth volume of John Quincy Adams' Letterbooks.)
LbC	Letterbook copy (Used only to designate an Adams Letterbook copy. Letterbook copies are normally unsigned, but any such copy is assumed to be in the hand of the person responsible for the text unless it is otherwise described.)
M	Miscellany (Used only to designate materials in the section of the Adams Papers known as the "Miscellanies" and always in combination with the short form of the writer's name and a serial number, as follows: M/CFA/31, i.e., the thirty-first volume of the Charles Francis Adams Miscellanies—a ledger volume mainly containing transcripts made by CFA in 1833 of selections from the family papers.)
MS, MSS	manuscript, manuscripts
RC	recipient's copy (A recipient's copy is assumed to be in the hand of the signer unless it is otherwise described.)
Tr	transcript (A copy, handwritten or typewritten, made substantially later than the original or later than other copies—such as duplicates, file copies, or Letterbook copies—that were made contemporaneously.)
Tripl	triplicate

4. LOCATION SYMBOLS

CSmH	Huntington Library
Ct	Connecticut State Library
DLC	Library of Congress
DNA	National Archives and Records Administration
DNDAR	Daughters of the American Revolution, Washington, D.C.
ICN	Newberry Library
InU	Indiana University
MB	Boston Public Library
MBAt	Boston Athenæum
MBBA	Boston Bar Association
MBBS	Bostonian Society
MCR-S	Harvard University, Radcliffe Institute for Advanced Study, Schlesinger Library
MH-Ar	Harvard University Archives
MHi	Massachusetts Historical Society
MQA	Adams National Historical Park
MWA	American Antiquarian Society
NjMoHP	Morristown National Historical Park
NAlI	Albany Institute of History and Art
NHi	New-York Historical Society
NIC	Cornell University
OClWHi	Western Reserve Historical Society
PHi	Historical Society of Pennsylvania
ViLoGH	Gunston Hall Library and Archives
ViU	University of Virginia

5. OTHER ABBREVIATIONS AND CONVENTIONAL TERMS

Adams Papers
> Manuscripts and other materials, 1639–1889, in the Adams Manuscript Trust collection given to the Massachusetts Historical Society in 1956 and enlarged by a few additions of family papers since then. Citations in the present edition are simply by date of the original document if the original is in the main chronological series of the Papers and therefore readily found in the microfilm edition of the Adams Papers (APM, see below).

The Adams Papers
> The present edition in letterpress, published by The Belknap Press of Harvard University Press. References to earlier volumes of any given unit take this form: vol. 2:146. Since there is no overall volume numbering for the edition, references from one series, or unit of a series, to another are by writer, title, volume, and page, for example, JA, *D&A*, 4:205.

Adams Papers, Adams Office Manuscripts
> The portion of the Adams manuscripts given to the Massachusetts Historical Society by Thomas Boylston Adams in 1973.

APM
> Formerly, Adams Papers, Microfilms. The corpus of the Adams Papers, 1639–1889, as published on microfilm by the Massachusetts Historical Society, 1954–1959, in 608 reels. Cited in the present work, when necessary, by reel number. Available in research libraries throughout the United States and in a few libraries in Canada, Europe, and New Zealand.

Anna Thornton Diary
> Anna Maria Brodeau Thornton, Diary, DLC:Anna Maria Brodeau Thornton Papers.

Catalog of the Stone Library
> Catalog of the Books Housed in the Stone Library, Adams National Historic Park, Quincy, Massachusetts, unpublished typescript of Stone Library card catalog, MQA, 1994.

A New Nation Votes
> Philip J. Lampi and others, comps., A New Nation Votes: American Election Returns, 1787–1825, American Antiquarian Society and Tufts University: elections.lib.tufts.edu.

Oxford Art Online
> Oxford Art Online, a compendium of online art resources including Grove Art Online (formerly the Grove *Dictionary of Art*), the *Benezit Dictionary of Artists*, and others: www.oxfordartonline.com.

6. SHORT TITLES OF WORKS FREQUENTLY CITED

AA2, *Jour. and Corr.*
> *Journal and Correspondence of Miss Adams, Daughter of John Adams, . . . Edited by Her Daughter* [Caroline Amelia (Smith) de Windt], New York and London, 1841–[1849]; 3 vols.

Guide to Editorial Apparatus

Note: Vol. [1], unnumbered, has title and date: *Journal and Correspondence of Miss Adams,* 1841; vol. 2 has title, volume number, and date: *Correspondence of Miss Adams . . . Vol. II,* 1842; vol. [3] has title, volume number, and date: *Correspondence of Miss Adams . . . Vol. II,* 1842, i.e., same as vol. 2, but preface is signed "April 3d, 1849," and the volume contains as "Part II" a complete reprinting, from same type and with same pagination, of vol. 2, above, originally issued in 1842.

Adams, *Geneal. History of Henry Adams*
Andrew N. Adams, comp. and ed., *A Genealogical History of Henry Adams, of Braintree, Mass., and His Descendants,* Rutland, Vt., 1898; 2 vols.

AFC
Adams Family Correspondence, ed. L. H. Butterfield, Marc Friedlaender, Richard Alan Ryerson, Margaret A. Hogan, Sara Martin, Hobson Woodward, and others, Cambridge, 1963– .

AHR
American Historical Review.

Allgor, *Perfect Union*
Catherine Allgor, *A Perfect Union: Dolley Madison and the Creation of the American Nation,* New York, 2006.

Amer. Antiq. Soc., *Procs.*
American Antiquarian Society, *Proceedings.*

Amer. Hist. Assoc., *Ann. Rpt. for* [year]
American Historical Association, *Annual Report,* 1889– .

Amer. *State Papers*
American State Papers: Documents, Legislative and Executive, of the Congress of the United States, Washington, D.C., 1832–1861; 38 vols.

ANB
John A. Garraty, Mark C. Carnes, and Paul Betz, eds., *American National Biography,* New York, 1999–2002; 24 vols. plus supplement; rev. edn., www.anb.org.

Annals of Congress
The Debates and Proceedings in the Congress of the United States [1789–1824], Washington, D.C., 1834–1856; 42 vols.

Bemis, *JQA*
Samuel Flagg Bemis, *John Quincy Adams,* New York, 1949–1956; 2 vols. Vol. 1: *John Quincy Adams and the Foundations of American Foreign Policy;* Vol. 2: *John Quincy Adams and the Union.*

Biog. Dir. Cong.
Biographical Directory of the United States Congress, 1774–2005, Washington, D.C., 2005; rev. edn., bioguide.congress.gov.

Boston Directory, [year]
Boston Directory [title varies], issued annually with varying imprints.

Boston, [vol. no.] *Report*
City of Boston, Record Commissioners, *Reports,* Boston, 1876–1909; 39 vols.

Bostonian Socy., *Pubns.*
Bostonian Society, *Publications.*

Bryan, *Hist. of the National Capital*
Wilhelmus Bogart Bryan, *A History of the National Capital from Its Foundation through the Period of the Adoption of the Organic Act,* New York, 1914–1916; 2 vols.

Cambridge Modern Hist.
  The Cambridge Modern History, Cambridge, Eng., 1902–1911; repr. New York, 1969; 13 vols.

Catalogue of JA's Library
  Catalogue of the John Adams Library in the Public Library of the City of Boston, Boston, 1917.

CFA, *Diary*
  Diary of Charles Francis Adams, ed. Aïda DiPace Donald, David Donald, Marc Friedlaender, L. H. Butterfield, and others, Cambridge, 1964– .

Chase, *History of Haverhill*
  George Wingate Chase, *The History of Haverhill, Massachusetts, from Its First Settlement, in 1640, to the Year 1860*, Haverhill, 1861.

Clay, *Papers*
  The Papers of Henry Clay, ed. James F. Hopkins, Mary W. M. Hargreaves, and others, Lexington, Ky., 1959–1992; 10 vols. plus supplement.

Col. Soc. Mass., *Pubns.*
  Colonial Society of Massachusetts, *Publications*.

Columbia Hist. Soc., *Records*
  Records of the Columbia Historical Society, Washington, D.C.

Cranch, *Reports of Cases in the Supreme Court*
  William Cranch, *Reports of Cases Argued and Adjudged in the Supreme Court of the United States* [title varies], 9 vols., Washington, D.C., 1804–1815.

DAB
  Allen Johnson, Dumas Malone, and others, eds., *Dictionary of American Biography*, New York, 1928–1936; repr. New York, 1955–1980; 10 vols. plus index and supplements.

Dexter, *Yale Graduates*
  Franklin Bowditch Dexter, *Biographical Sketches of the Graduates of Yale College with Annals of College History*, New York and New Haven, 1885–1912; 6 vols.

Dicy. Canadian Biog.
  Dictionary of Canadian Biography, Toronto, Canada, rev. edn., 1966– , biographi.ca.

DNB
  Leslie Stephen and Sidney Lee, eds., *The Dictionary of National Biography*, New York and London, 1885–1901; repr. Oxford, 1959–1960; 21 vols. plus supplements; rev. edn., www.oxforddnb.com.

Dolley Madison Digital Edition
  Papers of Dolley Madison Digital Edition, ed. Holly C. Shulman, rotunda.upress.virginia.edu/dmde.

Edmund Quincy, *Josiah Quincy*
  Edmund Quincy, *Life of Josiah Quincy of Massachusetts*, Boston, 1867.

Essex Inst., *Hist. Colls.*
  Essex Institute Historical Collections [title varies], 1859–1993.

Evans
  Charles Evans and others, *American Bibliography: A Chronological Dictionary of All Books, Pamphlets and Periodical Publications Printed in the United States of America* [1639–1800], Chicago and Worcester, Mass., 1903–1959; 14 vols.; rev. edn., www.readex.com.

Guide to Editorial Apparatus

Felt, *Memorials of William Smith Shaw*
    Joseph B. Felt, *Memorials of William Smith Shaw*, Boston, 1852.

First Fed. Cong.
    Documentary History of the First Federal Congress of the United States of America, March 4, 1789 – March 3, 1791, ed. Linda Grant De Pauw, Charlene Bangs Bickford, Helen E. Veit, William C. diGiacomantonio, and Kenneth R. Bowling, Baltimore, 1972–2017; 22 vols.

Franklin, *Papers*
    The Papers of Benjamin Franklin, ed. Leonard W. Labaree, William B. Willcox, Claude A. Lopez, Barbara B. Oberg, Ellen R. Cohn, and others, New Haven, 1959– .

Greenleaf, *Greenleaf Family*
    James Edward Greenleaf, comp., *Genealogy of the Greenleaf Family*, Boston, 1896.

Harvard Quinquennial Cat.
    Harvard University, *Quinquennial Catalogue of the Officers and Graduates, 1636–1930*, Cambridge, 1930.

History of Hingham
    History of the Town of Hingham, Massachusetts, Hingham, 1893; 3 vols. in 4.

History of Weymouth
    History of Weymouth, Massachusetts, Boston, 1923; 4 vols.

Hoefer, *Nouv. biog. générale*
    Jean Chrétien Ferdinand Hoefer, ed., *Nouvelle biographie générale depuis les temps les plus reculés jusqu'à nos jours*, Paris, 1852–1866; 46 vols.

Isenberg, *Fallen Founder*
    Nancy Isenberg, *Fallen Founder: The Life of Aaron Burr*, New York, 2007.

Jackson, *Papers*
    The Papers of Andrew Jackson, ed. Sam B. Smith, Harriet Chappell Owsley, Harold D. Moser, Daniel Feller, Michael E. Woods, and others, Knoxville, Tenn., 1980– .

JA, *D&A*
    Diary and Autobiography of John Adams, ed. L. H. Butterfield and others, Cambridge, 1961; 4 vols.

JA, *Earliest Diary*
    The Earliest Diary of John Adams, ed. L. H. Butterfield and others, Cambridge, 1966.

JA, *Legal Papers*
    Legal Papers of John Adams, ed. L. Kinvin Wroth and Hiller B. Zobel, Cambridge, 1965; 3 vols.

JA, *Papers*
    Papers of John Adams, ed. Robert J. Taylor, Gregg L. Lint, Sara Georgini, and others, Cambridge, 1977– .

Jay, *Selected Papers*
    The Selected Papers of John Jay, ed. Elizabeth M. Nuxoll and others, Charlottesville, Va., 2010– .

Jefferson, *Papers*
    The Papers of Thomas Jefferson, ed. Julian P. Boyd, Charles T. Cullen, John Catanzariti, Barbara B. Oberg, James P. McClure, and others, Princeton, N.J., 1950– .

Jefferson, *Papers, Retirement Series*
: *The Papers of Thomas Jefferson: Retirement Series*, ed. J. Jefferson Looney and others, Princeton, N.J., 2004– .

Jefferson's Memorandum Books
: *Jefferson's Memorandum Books: Accounts, with Legal Records and Miscellany, 1767–1826*, ed. James A. Bear Jr. and Lucia C. Stanton (*The Papers of Thomas Jefferson*, Second Series), Princeton, N.J., 1997; 2 vols.

JER
: *Journal of the Early Republic*.

JQA, *Diary*
: *Diary of John Quincy Adams*, ed. David Grayson Allen, Robert J. Taylor, and others, Cambridge, 1981; 2 vols.; rev. edn., *John Quincy Adams Digital Diary*, ed. Neal E. Millikan and others, www.primarysourcecoop.org/jqa/.

JQA, *Lectures on Rhetoric*
: *Lectures on Rhetoric and Oratory, Delivered to the Classes of Senior and Junior Sophisters in Harvard University*, 2 vols., Cambridge, 1810.

JQA, *Writings*
: *Writings of John Quincy Adams*, ed. Worthington Chauncey Ford, New York, 1913–1917; 7 vols.

Kaplan, *Men of Letters*
: Catherine O'Donnell Kaplan, *Men of Letters in the Early Republic: Cultivating Forums of Citizenship*, Chapel Hill, N.C., 2008.

Kapsch, *Building Washington*
: Robert J. Kapsch, *Building Washington: Engineering and Construction of the New Federal City, 1790–1840*, Baltimore, 2018.

LCA, *D&A*
: *Diary and Autobiographical Writings of Louisa Catherine Adams*, ed. Judith S. Graham and others, Cambridge, 2013; 2 vols.

Madison, *Papers, Presidential Series*
: *The Papers of James Madison: Presidential Series*, ed. Robert Alan Rutland, J. C. A. Stagg, Angela Kreider, and others, Charlottesville, Va., 1984– ; 8 vols.

Madison, *Papers, Retirement Series*
: *The Papers of James Madison: Retirement Series*, ed. David B. Mattern and others, Charlottesville, Va., 2009– .

Madison, *Papers, Secretary of State Series*
: *The Papers of James Madison: Secretary of State Series*, ed. Robert J. Brugger, Mary A. Hackett, David B. Mattern, and others, Charlottesville, Va., 1986– .

Marshall, *Papers*
: *The Papers of John Marshall*, ed. Herbert A. Johnson, Charles F. Hobson, and others, Chapel Hill, N.C., 1974–2006; 12 vols.

Mass., *Acts and Laws*
: *Acts and Laws of the Commonwealth of Massachusetts* [1780–1805], Boston, 1890–1898; 13 vols.; *Laws of the Commonwealth of Massachusetts* [1805–1838], Boston, 1806–1839; 11 vols.; *Resolves . . . of the Commonwealth of Massachusetts* [1806–1838], Boston, 1806–1838; 9 vols.

MHS, *Colls., Procs.*
: Massachusetts Historical Society, *Collections* and *Proceedings*.

Guide to Editorial Apparatus

Miller, *Treaties*
: *Treaties and Other International Acts of the United States*, ed. Hunter Miller, Washington, D.C., 1931–1947; 8 vols.

Monroe, *Papers*
: *The Papers of James Monroe*, ed. Daniel Preston, Robert Karachuk, and others, Westport, Conn., 2003– .

Monthly Anthology
: *Monthly Anthology and Boston Review*.

Morris, *Diaries*
: *The Diaries of Gouverneur Morris*, ed. Melanie Randolph Miller and Hendrina Krol, Charlottesville, Va., 2011–2018; 2 vols.

Morris, *Papers*
: *The Papers of Robert Morris, 1781–1784*, ed. E. James Ferguson, John Catanzariti, Elizabeth M. Nuxoll, Mary A. Gallagher, and others, Pittsburgh, 1973–1999; 9 vols.

Namier and Brooke, *House of Commons*
: Sir Lewis Namier and John Brooke, eds., *The House of Commons, 1754–1790*, London, 1964; 3 vols.

NEHGR
: *New England Historical and Genealogical Register*.

NEQ
: *New England Quarterly*.

OED
: *The Oxford English Dictionary*, 2d edn., Oxford, 1989; 20 vols.; rev. edn., www.oed.com.

Oliver, *Portraits of JA and AA*
: Andrew Oliver, *Portraits of John and Abigail Adams*, Cambridge, 1967.

Oxford Classical Dicy.
: Simon Hornblower and Antony Spawforth, eds., *The Oxford Classical Dictionary*, 3d edn., New York, 1996.

Paige, *Hist. of Cambridge, Mass.*
: Lucius R. Paige and Mary I. Gozzaldi, *History of Cambridge, Massachusetts, 1630–1877, with a Genealogical Register*, 2 vols., Boston and Cambridge, 1877–1930.

Papenfuse, *Pursuit of Profit*
: Edward C. Papenfuse, *In Pursuit of Profit: The Annapolis Merchants in the Era of the American Revolution, 1763–1805*, Baltimore, 1975.

Pattee, *Old Braintree*
: William S. Pattee, *A History of Old Braintree and Quincy, with a Sketch of Randolph and Holbrook*, Quincy, 1878.

Philadelphia Directory, [year]
: *Philadelphia Directory* [title varies], issued annually with varying imprints.

Pierce, *Foster Genealogy*
: Frederick Clifton Pierce, *Foster Genealogy*, 1 vol. in 2, Chicago, 1899.

Plumer, *Memorandum of Proceedings*
: *William Plumer's Memorandum of Proceedings in the United States Senate, 1803–1807*, ed. Everett Somerville Brown, New York, 1923.

Princess Louise, *Forty-five Years*
  Princess Louise of Prussia (Princess Anton Radziwill), *Forty-five Years of My Life, 1770–1815*, transl. A. R. Allinson, London, 1912.

Princetonians
  James McLachlan, Richard A. Harrison, Ruth L. Woodward, Wesley Frank Craven, and J. Jefferson Looney, *Princetonians: A Biographical Dictionary*, Princeton, N.J., 1976–1991; 5 vols.

Repertorium
  Ludwig Bittner and others, eds., *Repertorium der diplomatischen Vertreter aller Länder seit dem Westfälischen Frieden (1648)*, Oldenburg, 1936–1965; 3 vols.

Roof, *Smith and Lady*
  Katharine Metcalf Roof, *Colonel William Smith and Lady: The Romance of Washington's Aide and Young Abigail Adams*, Boston, 1929.

Schom, *Napoleon Bonaparte*
  Alan Schom, *Napoleon Bonaparte*, New York, 1997.

Shaw-Shoemaker
  Ralph R. Shaw and Richard H. Shoemaker, *American Bibliography: A Preliminary Checklist for 1801–1819*, New York, 1958–1966; 22 vols.; supplemental edn., *Early American Imprints*, www.readex.com.

Sibley's Harvard Graduates
  John Langdon Sibley, Clifford K. Shipton, Conrad Edick Wright, Edward W. Hanson, and others, *Biographical Sketches of Graduates of Harvard University, in Cambridge, Massachusetts*, Cambridge and Boston, 1873– .

Sprague, *Annals Amer. Pulpit*
  William B. Sprague, *Annals of the American Pulpit; or, Commemorative Notices of Distinguished American Clergymen of Various Denominations*, New York, 1857–1869; 9 vols.

Sprague, *Braintree Families*
  Waldo Chamberlain Sprague, comp., *Genealogies of the Families of Braintree, Mass., 1640–1850*, Boston, 1983; repr. CD-ROM, Boston, 2001.

Treat, *Treat Family*
  John Harvey Treat, *The Treat Family: A Genealogy of Trott, Tratt, and Treat*, Salem, Mass., 1893.

U.S. House, *Jour.*
  Journal of the House of Representatives of the United States, Washington, D.C., 1789– .

U.S. Senate, *Exec. Jour.*
  Journal of the Executive Proceedings of the Senate of the United States of America, Washington, D.C., 1789– .

U.S. Senate, *Jour.*
  Journal of the Senate of the United States of America, Washington, D.C., 1789– .

U.S. *Statutes at Large*
  The Public Statutes at Large of the United States of America, 1789– , Boston and Washington, D.C., 1845– .

Washington, *Papers, Presidential Series*
  The Papers of George Washington: Presidential Series, ed. W. W. Abbot, Dorothy Twohig, Jack D. Warren, Mark A. Mastromarino, Robert F. Haggard, Christine S.

Patrick, John C. Pinheiro, David R. Hoth, Jennifer Stertzer, and others, Charlottesville, Va., 1987- .

Washington, *Papers, Retirement Series*
  The Papers of George Washington: Retirement Series, ed. W. W. Abbot, Edward G. Lengel, and others, Charlottesville, Va., 1997–1999; 4 vols.

Whitmore, *Families of Payne and Gore*
  W. H. Whitmore, comp., *The Genealogy of the Families of Payne and Gore*, Boston, 1875.

Winsor, *Memorial History of Boston*
  Justin Winsor, ed., *The Memorial History of Boston, Including Suffolk County, 1630–1880*, Boston, 1880–1881; 4 vols.

WMQ
  William and Mary Quarterly.

Wood, *Empire of Liberty*
  Gordon S. Wood, *Empire of Liberty: A History of the Early Republic, 1789–1815*, New York, 2009.

VOLUME 16

Family Correspondence

November 1804 – July 1809

Adams Family Correspondence

John Quincy Adams to John Adams

Dear Sir. Washington 3. Nov^r: 1804.

I wrote you a few lines from New-York, enclosing a copy of Commodore Morris's Defence, for M^r: Shaw— The day after which I left that City and came on multum jactetus mare et terris—to Philadelphia in the Land-Stage, and thence to Baltimore by the way of Newcastle and Frenchtown; chiefly by water—A mode of conveyance to me much more agreeable than that of a Stage Coach over the chaotic roads on this side of Philadelphia— I arrived here last Monday—the 29$^{th.}$—the very day upon which I had fixed for my arrival, before I left Quincy—[1] I should have preceded my reckoning by one day, but for a very long passage of 36 hours from French-town to Baltimore, a distance which seldom calls for more than an eight or ten hours sail— A smooth Sea, and a fair Sky, made however some compensation for the want of wind, and made the length of the voyage only tedious— I found my wife and children well—And all the family with whom we reside, also in good health—[2] But from the State of New-York to that of Virginia inclusive, they have had in all the interior Country a Season uncommonly sickly— I pass'd a couple of hours at Philadelphia with D^r: Rush whose accounts were truly melancholy—[3] The mortality has not been in any proportion to the universality of disease, but from the concurrent testimony of every body I have seen, possessing the means of information, the harvests have ve[ry] considerably suffered, by the want of people to get them in.

As I arrived soon after the middle of the day at Philadelphia, I stop'd there, only one Night—when at the earnest invitation of my brother's friends M^r: and M^{rs}: Rutter, I took the bed in their house, which he formerly occupied— They appear very much to regret his loss, and speak of him with the most cordial affection.— I called at Dennie's lodgings, and also at the Office where the Port-Folio is published, but did not find him at either—⁴ I likewise left a letter from my brother for M^r: Ewing, at that Gentleman's Office, but did not see him.⁵

Since my arrival here, I have called upon the President, who had some conversation with me respecting the conduct of the British frigates on our Coast, during the course of the last Summer, and respecting, the trade of arms and Ammunition principally carried on from New-York to S^t: Domingo— He said nothing relative to the controversies with Spain, or to the murmurs of Louisiana.

As to the British frigates, there is no official information of that disapprobation by the British Government, upon the conduct of their Officers, which has been announced in the newspapers— Nor does it appear that the Captain of the Cambrian and Leander, or either of them have been recalled— But they have not given any recent cause of complaint; and by the letters from M^r: Monroe, the Ministry give him perfect satisfaction upon every representation made by him on the subject— The conduct of their Ships and Officers in the European Seas, is also generally such as is satisfactory to him— The disposition of the present Ministry, is also very amicable—⁶

The trade from New-York to S^t: Domingo, is a subject of grievous complaint to the French Minister, who peremptorily demands that our Government should interfere to suppress it— The Blacks give such excessive prices for arms and ammunition, that several merchants in New-York have fitted out, and are still fitting out vessels to send them these Articles in some instances they have armed the ships, in force sufficient to force their way through, in case of attack by the french privateers—⁷ M^r: Jefferson thinks, that on the return of any of these armed vessels, if they should have fought with a french privateer and killed one of her men, *our* Judges ought to hang every man on board the American Vessel, for Murder— He draws his inference from the Common Law Principle, that homicide committed in support of an unlawful Act is Murder— But common Law Rules should not be applied to the objects which essentially belong to the Laws of Nations— I questioned the accuracy of his argument, but asked him why the Government had not interfered, to *prevent* the arming of these vessels at New-York— He said the Law would not bear them out in such interference, though he admitted it had been done, at an early period of the late War— This he first said was by virtue of a temporary Law; but afterwards recollecting himself, said it had been done, without a Law, and submitted to— But that had it been contested the authority of the

November 1804

Government could not have been supported for the measure— Hence I conclude we shall have a Law for such an authority at the approaching Session

I have seen General Wilkinson, who has taken a house here to reside during the Session— I imagine he waits for an Answer from you to his letter— His *power* to prescribe roundheads to his Officers, is denied at the War-Office, and therefore the Court-Martial on Major Butler hangs heavily upon him—[8] Colonel Burrows is also here, and as I hear has fully and honourably settled his Accounts— But his health is very low.[9]

I am, Dear Sir, ever affectionately and dutifully your's.

RC (Adams Papers); endorsed: "J. Q. Adams / Nov. 3. Ans^d 16. 1804." Some loss of text due to wear at the edge.

[1] JQA departed Quincy on 16 Oct. to attend the 2d session of the 8th Congress in Washington, D.C. He visited AA2 and WSS in New York City from 21 to 23 Oct., resuming his journey on the 24th and arriving in the federal city on the 29th. From New York, JQA wrote to JA on 23 Oct., not found, enclosing a copy of Richard Valentine Morris, *A Defence of the Conduct of Commodore Morris during His Command in the Mediterranean*, N.Y., 1804 (vol. 15:280; JQA, *Diary*).

[2] LCA and JQA resided with Ann Johnson Hellen and Walter Hellen when in Washington, D.C., at the Hellens' residence on K Street (LCA, *D&A*, 1:188).

[3] Newspapers in Philadelphia and New York described a sickness prevalent in Pennsylvania's rural interior as a seasonal "bilious" fever or one accompanied by ague. There were also 56 deaths reported in Philadelphia during the week prior to JQA's 25 Oct. visit with Benjamin Rush, including 11 from various fevers (Philadelphia *United States Gazette*, 18, 24 Oct.; Hudson, N.Y., *Bee*, 23 Oct.; JQA, *Diary*).

[4] Joseph Dennie Jr. may have resided at this time at 113 Walnut Street, the home of Samuel and Sarah Jones Rutter, where TBA previously resided. Later in the year a Philadelphia directory listed Dennie at 25 North Second Street, the location where Hugh Maxwell printed *Port Folio* (vol. 15:87; *Philadelphia Directory*, 1804, p. 66, 157, Shaw-Shoemaker, No. 7044; *Philadelphia Directory*, 1805, p. [116], Shaw-Shoemaker, No. 9139; Harold Milton Ellis, "Joseph Dennie and His Circle," *Bulletin of the University of Texas*, no. 40:178 [15 July 1915]).

[5] No correspondence has been found between TBA and Samuel Ewing, an attorney recorded at 30 Walnut Street in Philadelphia (vol. 15:364; *Philadelphia Directory*, 1804, p. 79, Shaw-Shoemaker, No. 7044).

[6] JQA met with Thomas Jefferson on 31 Oct., and one of the topics discussed was "the impressments by the British frigates upon our Coast." During the summer of 1804 the British Navy harassed merchant vessels entering and exiting New York Harbor, halting and boarding ships ostensibly to search for British sailors but also to impress U.S. seamen. Two of the British vessels involved were the *Cambrian*, Capt. William Bradley, and the *Leander*, Capt. Alexander Skene, both of which had previously patrolled the harbor to deter French vessels from sailing. The New York press decried the "outrages practised" by the British Navy and reported from mid-August on captures and impressments. In late August Secretary of State James Madison informed Jefferson that in his communications with Anthony Merry, the British minister denied any wrongdoing and left the "continuance of the evil at the pleasure of the British Commanders." From London in early September James Monroe reported his discussions on the subject with the British ministry and informed Madison that Bradley had been relieved of his command (vol. 15:399; JQA, *Diary*; Marie Jeanne Rossignol, *The Nationalist Ferment: The Origins of U.S. Foreign Policy, 1789–1812*, Columbus, Ohio, 2004, p. 173; Stephen Budiansky, *Peril-*

ous Fight: America's Intrepid War with Britain on the High Seas, 1812–1815, N.Y., 2012, p. 38–39; Jefferson, Papers, 44:265, 267, 300–301; New York American Citizen, 20, 22 Aug.; Monroe, Papers, 5:252, 254, 255).

[7] The idea of an independent Haitian military sparked concern in the United States. As reports surfaced in spring 1804 that U.S. merchant vessels traveling to the West Indies were arming to protect against French privateers, French chargé d'affaires to the United States Louis André Pichon argued that the real purpose was for munitions trade with Haiti, in violation of U.S. neutrality. In May Pichon wrote to Madison, "It is clear that American citizens, under the eye of their government, are conducting a private and piratical war against a nation with which the U.S. is at peace." Though the Jefferson administration discussed the issue, it took no action until the fall. The president requested congressional action in his 8 Nov. address, for which see JQA to TBA, 12 Nov., and note 1, below, and the House of Representatives took it up on 12 November. Jefferson signed the resulting bill into law on 3 March 1805. It required armed merchant vessels traveling to the West Indies and anywhere on the coast between Cayenne and Louisiana to be bonded for twice the value of the vessel, arms, and equipment carried; required an inventory of munitions aboard to be accounted for on return to the United States; prohibited bonded vessels to other ports from traveling to the West Indies; and penalized violators with forfeiture (Ashli White, Encountering Revolution: Haiti and the Making of the Early Republic, Baltimore, 2010, p. 125–126; Jefferson, Papers, 44:x, 591–592; Madison, Papers, Secretary of State Series, 7:xxiv–xxv, 185–189; U.S. Statutes at Large, 2:342–343).

[8] Gen. James Wilkinson wrote two letters to JA on 12 Sept. 1804 (both Adams Papers), seeking information on the regulation of U.S. Army uniforms during JA's administration and discussing the court-martial of Col. Thomas Butler. Butler (1754–1805) commanded the army's 2d Regiment of Infantry. After Butler refused to cut his hair, in violation of an 1801 "order for regulating the Uniform of the Head," and defied an order to take command of Fort Adams in Mississippi Territory in 1802, Wilkinson ordered Butler's court-martial in May 1803. Found guilty of the first act, Butler continued to violate the uniform regulation. He was again court-martialed in July 1805 and punished with the loss of his command and pay for one year, although he died before the sentence was enforced. Wilkinson characterized his actions to JA as an attempt to demonstrate his authority regarding uniforms and to combat insubordination that resulted from having his orders questioned. JA replied to Wilkinson on 16 Nov. 1804 (LbC, APM Reel 118) that he could not recollect having so empowered the general and questioning whether "a General or a secretary of war, or a President, or all of them together have such authority without an act of the Legislature" (Jefferson, Papers, 41:155–157, 42:597).

[9] Col. William Ward Burrows (1758–1805) was the first commandant of the U.S. Marine Corps, appointed in 1798 under JA's nomination. He resigned his position on 6 March 1804, owing to ill health (ANB).

William Smith Shaw to John Quincy Adams

Dear Sir   Boston 5 Nov. 1804

I hope by this time, you have safely arrived at Washington and found Mrs. Adams family and friends in good health— I send by the same mail with this three of Parks of papers containing four numbers with the signature of Publius Valerius and will send the others as they appear.[1] You will see in these papers that Dr Eustace's brother has made an assault on Park in consequence of a publication which appeared in his paper of tuesday the 30 Oct. signed with his name— I also inclose with this, the statement of Charles P. Sumner the gentleman who accompanied Eustace—[2]

November 1804

I have seen the letters in Silesia as published in London— It is a small octavo, printed on good paper with a handsome type and sells for three dollars—there is but one copy in town & that was sent out to Eben Larkin. They are prefaced with a shot advertisement merely stating that they were written by the eldest son of the late president of the United States at that time an American minister at Berlin to his brother in Philadelphia—that they were not originally intended for public view but that young Mr. Adams at the request of some gentleman of distinguished taste to whom they were shewn permitted them to be printed in the port folio—that from that work they are now for the first time collected and are offered to the British public as a faithful picture of the interesting province of Silesia by the hand of a gentleman a scholar and a statesman[3]

7th. Nov—

I send you Russels paper of this morning in which you will see some account of the late election— Quincy is chosen by a majority of 90— Mitchell has lost his election and we are told that the democratic list of Electors has generally prevailed in that District— The federalists are very much disheartened in this town and have strong apprehensions that they have lost the electoral ticket and that there will be eight or ten democratic representatives sent to Congress— Stedmans reelection I understand from rumor is doubtful— Sever as was expected will be rechosen by a large majority[4]

Your mother has been confined to her chamber with her old complaints almost ever since you left Quincy but is now very much better. Dr & Mrs Welsh came from there last evening and they think her very fast on the recovery

With respectful attachment I am / your very grateful humle. Sert

W S Shaw[5]

RC (Adams Papers); addressed: "[. . . .] Esqr / [. . .] in Congress / Washington"; endorsed: "W. S. Shaw. 5. 7. Novr: 1804. / 16. Novr: recd:"; notation: "Free." Some loss of text due to a torn manuscript.

[1] Shaw sent JQA the Boston *Repertory*, 26, 30 Oct., 2 Nov., which contained four of five parts of a series by JQA as Publius Valerius that condemned the "Virginian faction" in Massachusetts politics. In the series, JQA called on the citizens of Massachusetts to elect individuals to Congress "who will support your own Interests." Let the people of Virginia elect their own representatives, he wrote, and "let it be your care on your part to elect men, who shall have no bias on their minds, the tendency of which will be to prostrate your legitimate rights at the feet of Virginian policy." The final installment appeared in the 6 Nov. issue. The *Repertory* was edited by Dr. John Park (1775–1852), Dartmouth 1791, a former naval surgeon who had begun his newspaper in Newburyport in 1803 before transferring it to Boston in Feb.

1804 (Edward H. Hall, "Reminiscences of Dr. John Park," Amer. Antiq. Soc., *Procs.*, 7:69, 70, 78, 81, 93 [1890]).

² In his Boston *Repertory*, 30 Oct., Park penned a piece decrying the decline of federalism in Massachusetts and the growing influence of Democratic-Republicans. Dr. William Eustis was one of the politicians who drew Park's ire. Park accused Eustis of having witnessed "the scene of usurpation which has prostrated our rights" and "like cowards—nay I may say like traitors, abandoned the interests of their constituents." In response to this affront, Eustis' younger brother Jacob (1759–1834), accompanied by Boston lawyer Charles Pinckney Sumner (1776–1839), confronted Park to demand evidence and an apology. When the newspaper editor refused to apologize, a physical altercation ensued. The *Repertory*, 2 Nov., defended its position on William Eustis, claiming its comments were restricted to his "publick conduct." The article summarized the incident and lambasted Jacob Eustis for resorting to violence but did not name Sumner, being "convinced he did not come as an abettor of violence." Sumner also issued a statement about the events in the Boston *Democrat*, 3 Nov., which, although not found, Shaw enclosed with this letter (Henry Lawrence Eustis, "Genealogy of the Eustis Family," *NEHGR*, 32:208, 211 [April 1878]; CFA, *Diary*, 2:248; William Sumner Appleton, *Record of the Descendants of William Sumner of Dorchester, Mass., 1636*, Boston, 1879, p. 176).

³ For the publication of JQA's *Letters on Silesia, Written during a Tour Through that Country in the Years 1800, 1801*, London, 1804, see vol. 15:438. Ebenezer Larkin (1767–1813) was a bookseller at 47 Cornhill in Boston (Janice Gayle Schimmelman, *Books on Art in Early America: Books on Art, Aesthetics and Instruction Available in American Libraries and Bookstores through 1815*, New Castle, Del., 2007, p. 232; *Boston Directory*, 1805, p. 79, Shaw-Shoemaker, No. 8057).

⁴ Shaw sent the Boston *Columbian Centinel*, 7 Nov., which reported partial results from the 5 Nov. election for Massachusetts' presidential electors and members of the U.S. House of Representatives. The Democratic-Republican ticket prevailed for the state's nineteen presidential electors, prompting the *Columbian Centinel* to comment, "It has been emphatically a struggle whether *Massachusetts* would voluntarily consent to be considered a colony or dependence on *Virginia*, or a free, sovereign and independent State." The congressional races that drew comment from Shaw included that of Josiah Quincy III, who narrowly defeated the incumbent, William Eustis, to represent the Suffolk District; Nahum Mitchell (1769–1853), a Federalist, who lost to Rev. Joseph Barker for the Plymouth seat; and William Stedman, who retained his seat for Worcester. Ebenezer Seaver defeated TBA by a margin of nearly 1,000 votes to claim the Norfolk District seat (vol. 15:448; Walpole, N.H., *Political Observatory*, 17 Nov.; A New Nation Votes; *Biog. Dir. Cong.*).

⁵ JQA wrote letters to Shaw of 9 and 26 Nov. and 17 Dec., which record a robust flow of publications sent by JQA to his cousin and pertain to business that Shaw was transacting on JQA's behalf (all MWA:Adams Family Letters).

John Adams to John Quincy Adams

My dear Sir   Quincy Nov. 6. 1804

I thank you for my Letter from N.Y and the Pamplet inclosed. Commodore Morris's Defence contains Information which appears to be wanted by our President and all his Ministers, by his senators and Representatives, by his officers and Men of his Navy, and by the commercial Citizens of our Country.¹

To besure to protect the Commerce and Seamen in the Atlantic and Mediterranean and blockade Tripoly, all with a large ship or two is rather too hard Work for a Commodore: but enough of this.

Yesterday You met and so did We. our Town gave 85 Votes to the

Fed and 21 to the Anti. Braintree gave a Majority of four to the honest Candidate.² We have heard no further. Quincy gave 90 Votes to the Fed. Ticket and 27 to the opposite, making 117 Votes many more than ever were given in this town. The Choice of Rep came on in the afternoon. A number who voted in the Morning for Electors went to dinner and returned too late to vote for Rep. So that the Numbers were Smaller on both sides.

I wish to know whether the Vice President takes his seat.³

Your Mamma is ill, but We hope better than She has been— My Love to your Wife and Children and regards to all the Family.

I miss you, beyond expression. Thomas is very good, but he is So taken up with Business of many and various kinds, that I can not have him allways of Evenings as I had you. Alass I fear I cannot have you again So Steadily another Summer.— Pray write me as often as you can at least as you used to do, by inclosing any Papers of importance.

With the tenderest affection and highest Esteem / I am &c

J. Adams

RC (Adams Papers); internal address: "J. Q. Adams Esq."

¹ See JQA to JA, 3 Nov., and note 1, above.
² A reference to TBA, who garnered a majority of the Quincy vote in his unsuccessful bid for the Norfolk District congressional seat and earned four more votes than Ebenezer Seaver in Braintree (Boston *Columbian Centinel*, 7 Nov.; A New Nation Votes).
³ Despite indictments for murder in New York and New Jersey following his duel with Alexander Hamilton, Aaron Burr continued to serve as vice president and took his seat as president of the Senate on 5 November. For JQA's comments, see his Diary entry for the day and his letter to TBA of 1 April 1805, and note 3, below (vol. 15:408; U.S. Senate, *Jour.*, 8th Cong., 2d sess., p. 411; JQA, *Diary*).

John Adams to John Quincy Adams

My dear Son   Quincy Nov. 9. 1804

The Republicans have exerted their Energies, and propagated their lying Pamphlets So Secretly, and with Such effect as to make Federalists almost doubt their Empire in Massachusetts. They do not yet despair however: but their majority will not be So great as they expected. The Defection of the County of Essex is greater than was foreseen. The Causes of this are many. more than I know perhaps. The Name of Mr Gerry carries more Weight with it than the federalists will allow or are aware of, and Mr Sullivan is more known than any upon the List of federal Electors.¹ He has connected his family too, with So many families who are wealthy numerous active and influencial on the federal Side, that a great deal of Management for him is visible enough to me. Another Thing I believe the Measures of the

General Court, were not popular with numbers: The General Ticket was not relished, and Some other Steps had a Tendency to hazard the Union, as they imagined.[2] It opened new prospects to them. They did not See, where they were likely to end. Mr Sullivan is reported to have made incredible Efforts on the last Circuits, and with more Success than was thought in his power. He has been Scolding and quarrelling with Judges and Lawyers the whole time, and the Language he has held to Grand Jurors and Witnesses and Party's may be easily conjectured. He is and will be as memorable an Example of Ambition as Hamilton or Burr. If he has carried the Election he has merited as much of that Party, I cannot call it his party, as Mr Burr did four years ago, and they had better take him for V. P. than my old Friend Clinton.

Your Brother you know was overpersuaded by the Feds against his Inclination and Judgment as well as mine, to permit his name to be used, and the Result has been only to Shew, to what a degree certain Sorts of People in Norfolk are under the dominion of the Halles, and Poisardes of the town of Boston.[3] Quincy however did him great honor and Braintree more than was expected.— On my own Account, and on his, there is reason to rejoice. The Exchange of Quincy for Eustis is a greater Thing than the Republicans imagine.— He will not be afraid to confess among his Constituents when he comes home, the real Thoughts of his head and feelings of his heart, upon public affairs as Eustis has been, or advised and constrained to be, by his friends.

Thomas is gone to Haverhill: Your Mother has been very ill and in a different State from any of her Symptoms before. But she is better We hope and Dr Warren gives Us chearing hopes of her recovery. Sickness in the Family, Absence of my sons who are all the Companions I have, with various perplexities, are Tryals: but I keep Up a good heart as usual. My Love to your Family including all. My dear Boys I long to See. How does that charming little fellow George do.? Tell him, I will write him a Letter as soon as he can read it

I pity you, in your Situation: But Patience and Perseverance will carry you with honor through all Difficulties. Virtuous and Studious from your Youth, beyond any other Instance I know I have great Confidence in your Success in the service of your Country, however dark your prospects may be at present. Such Talents and Such Learning as you possess, with a Character so perfectly fair and a good humour So universally acknowledged, it is impossible, you can fail, except in Conjunctures when I should think it an honor to go with you to the Guilotine. You and I have clasped each other together in our Arms, and braced our feet against the Bed boards and Bedsteads to prevent

November 1804

Us from ~~being~~ having our Brains dashed out against the Planks and Timbers of the ship, thunders roaring over our heads and Lightenings flashing down Men upon the Deck, the Winds raging in a Hurricane, The Masts cracking, the ship shivering trembling under Us in Agonies, every joint and plank crashing, as if ~~every~~ the Butts must start in a moment.[4] In Twenty political storms of as much danger to the ship as this, have I weathered through, while the ~~dastardly poltron~~ Petit Maitre, who now tyrannizes at our expense dared not trust his damask Person on the Sea, And here I am alive and hearty Yet.— I am determined to write you, and will write as I please. If the Peepers violate publick Faith, and get Stung by a Wasp in the folds of the Paper, let them have the Smart for their reward

I am &c   J. Adams.

RC (Adams Papers); internal address: "J. Q. Adams / S. U. S."; endorsed: "My Father— 9. Nov^r: 1804. / 19. Novr rec^d: / 20. d^o: Ans^d:."

[1] Votes for Democratic-Republican candidates increased significantly in Essex County between the 1802 and 1804 congressional elections. Although Federalists retained the seat for the Essex North District, the party saw its margin of victory shrink by 25 percent. In the Essex South District, Democratic-Republican incumbent Jacob Crowninshield retained his seat with a 20 percent increase in his margin of victory. Elbridge Gerry and James Sullivan were the state's at-large presidential electors for the Democratic-Republican ticket (*Salem Register*, 5 Nov.; Pittsfield, Mass., *Sun*, 3 Nov.; A New Nation Votes).

[2] The actions by the Mass. General Court with ramifications for the presidential election of 1804 included its refusal to ratify the 12th Amendment; its resolve to petition the state's federal senators for a constitutional amendment to change apportionment to a system based solely on free residency rather than the three-fifths clause; and the decision to move to a general party ticket in determining presidential electors for the 1804 election, for all of which see vol. 15:318, 390–391, 395, 397. Public sentiment against changing how electors were selected was embodied in the pamphlet *The First Book of the Dying State of Federalism, to Which Is Added the Federal Obituary*, 1804, Shaw-Shoemaker, No. 6301.

[3] *Les dames de la halle* and *poissardes* were Parisian market women and fishwives who protested food shortages and rioted during the French Revolution (Paul R. Hanson, *Historical Dictionary of the French Revolution*, 2d edn., Lanham, Md., 2015, p. 93).

[4] JA in his autobiography included a similar account of the storm he and JQA endured aboard the Continental frigate *Boston* in Feb. 1778 (JA, *D&A*, 4:12).

Abigail Adams to John Quincy Adams

My Dear son   Quincy Nov$^{br.}$ 11th 1804

I am desirious of writing You a few lines just to assure you that I am able to hold a pen, and that I hope my Health is not in a more declining State than when You left me, altho I have not been able to leave my chamber since; except to ride a little way a few times; I think I have gained a little strength the last week tho I have not got the better of the most debilitating of my complaints— a loss of strength, and such a relaxation of the Solids without any feverish symptoms is new to me: tho I have often sufferd much before by a feverish habit; my appetite is rather better than it was.

we want to hear from You, and from mrs Adams and family. I shall not attempt to scetch any politics your Father writes to you— I will however say something to you respecting the Letters lately publishd from the late Lord Chatham to his Nephew. I am sure they must have commanded Your attention. a part of his 5th Letter so intirely meets my own sentiments upon a subject you will be at no loss to find, if you will be so good as to give it an attentive perusal— at the Same time I do not think you so far advanced in life as not to profit by the advise—in short I believe it to be Your duty, to Yourself, your Family and country, to consider his sentiments upon the subject infalliable— and to strive to follow his advise.[1] I will not Say mine— if I had not thought it of essentiall concequence I should not with a feeble & trembling hand, said thus much—

with a kind remembrance to all the family I am / Your truly affectionate / Mother A Adams

RC (Adams Papers).

[1] In the fifth letter of his *Letters Written by the Late Earl of Chatham to His Nephew Thomas Pitt*, London, 1804, William Pitt the elder advised his nephew on acceptable behavior, praising gentility and especially politeness (p. 29–39).

John Quincy Adams to Thomas Boylston Adams

12. Nov^r: 1804.

I have sent you under another cover, a copy of the President's Message, with the documents, and the Journals of both Houses—[1] We have hitherto done nothing, and this week being destined to horse-racing, will of course be passed in doing more nothing.[2] This morning came a Message, with nominations for appointments, consisting only of those which have been made during the recess— The only one deserving remark is that of M^r: Monroe, as Envoy Extraordinary to Spain, in the room of M^r: Pinckney, he *intending to return*.[3]

M^r: William Pinckney, the former Commissioner, associated with Messrs: Gore and Trumbull, has arrived—And the report in circulation is that he is to be appointed Attorney General, instead of M^r: Lincoln, who is to resign— For this however I do not vouch—as M^r: Wright behind me is this moment assuring his neighbour M^r: White, that there is nothing in it, and that M^r: Lincoln will not resign.[4]

November 1804

16. Nov^{r:} 1804.

The attendance upon the races has been so faithful and punctual that both Houses of Congress have scarcely been able to meet enough to adjourn, untill this day— And now on meeting we have found nothing better to do than to adjourn over untill next Monday— Next week I suppose we shall begin upon some business.

I received last Evening a letter from my father, and am grieved to hear of our dear Mother's illness—[5] The accounts of your Elections give great satisfaction to the Virginians.— My wife and children are well, as were M^{r:} Cranch's family, when I last saw him two days ago.

RC (Adams Papers).

[1] The 2d session of the 8th Congress convened on 5 Nov. with a quorum in place in the House of Representatives; the Senate achieved a quorum two days later. Thomas Jefferson submitted his annual message to both houses on 8 Nov., reporting the ongoing depredations against neutral shipping and the need for regulation of U.S. merchant vessels. The president noted Spanish recognition of the U.S. right to the territory acquired in the Louisiana Purchase, although he acknowledged that boundary questions remained to be settled and the territorial governance of Louisiana required further congressional action. Jefferson also offered significant comment on relations with Native Americans, continuing to articulate his vision for improved commercial relations as the best means to secure peace. William Duane published the address as *Message from the President of the United States to Both Houses of Congress. 8th November, 1804*, Washington, D.C., 1804 (vol. 15:410; *Annals of Congress*, 8th Cong., 2d sess., p. 10, 11, 677–678, 682; Jefferson, *Papers*, 44:680–685).

[2] The Washington Jockey Club held horse races between 13 and 15 Nov. (vol. 15:452).

[3] In a message dated 9 Nov., Jefferson submitted a list of 31 interim appointments made during the congressional recess, including James Monroe as minister extraordinary and plenipotentiary to Spain. The Senate confirmed Monroe's appointment on 20 Nov., as a replacement for Charles Pinckney, who had served as the U.S. minister to Spain since 1801. Pinckney was recalled in Oct. 1804, after requesting to return to the United States. His recall, however, did not arrive before he and Monroe entered treaty negotiations with Spain. Pinckney ultimately continued in his role through the end of the negotiations in May 1805 after which Monroe immediately returned to London, where he continued to serve as the U.S. minister at the Court of St. James's. Pinckney remained in Spain through Oct. 1805 (Jefferson, *Papers*, 44:522, 702–703; U.S. Senate, *Exec. Jour.*, 8th Cong., 2d sess., p. 473; Madison, *Papers, Secretary of State Series*, 7:52–53; Monroe, *Papers*, 5:xxiv, 394).

[4] Rumors that former Anglo-American claims commissioner William Pinkney would succeed Levi Lincoln as attorney general had circulated since July 1804. Lincoln resigned his post in a letter to Jefferson of 26 Dec., and although James Madison suggested Pinkney as one of Lincoln's possible successors, James Breckinridge assumed the office in Aug. 1805. JQA's Senate colleagues were Robert Wright (1752–1826), who represented Maryland from March 1801 until his resignation in Nov. 1806, and Samuel White (1770–1809), who served for Delaware from 1801 until his death (vol. 15:405, 406; Jefferson, *Papers*, 45:244–246, 275; *Biog. Dir. Cong.*).

[5] JA to JQA, 6 Nov. 1804, above.

John Quincy Adams to Thomas Boylston Adams

26. Nov.r 1804.

Yours of the 14.th: came to hand Saturday Evening—24.th: [1] I suppose you were not inconsolable at the loss of your election, and that your expectations had not been raised very high of a different issue— As to the electoral Ticket, I am certainly not one of those who can say I told you so— Nor am I one of those who can say I am not sorry for it— But I do not think crimination against any body can be of any avail in the case— The Junto folks I have no doubt did all they could; but they are not *popular*, in their opinions or their measures— The other Class of federalists are not *popular* neither— Nothing can be more conclusive than the issue of the two last elections in Massachusetts, to prove the increasing popularity, of the General Government, and increasing *unpopularity* of *all* its opponents— The next Spring elections as you anticipate will complete the Revolution, and bring in Democrats to rule Massachusetts like the rest— But what then?— Why then in a given number of years the democrats will in their turn be run down, and yield their places to men better or worse than themselves— *Change*, is the only unchangeable characteristic of our Governments, and we must make ourselves content under it.

I was very glad to receive the letter you speak of, and of the freedom with which it spoke out—[2] But as my most ardent wish is that the writer may in future enjoy *tranquility of mind*, I wish it were possible he could see the course of things with more indifference— Try to engage his mind in something other than public affairs— For these will henceforth never affect him, but unpleasantly, and the less he feels on this subject, the more he will enjoy—[3] I am happy to hear our dear mother is so much better, and pray for her perfect restoration.

Your's.

RC (Adams Papers); internal address: "T. B. Adams Esq.r."; docketed: "Nov.r 1804 J. Q. A."

[1] Not found.

[2] JQA referred to JA's letter of 16 Nov., in which JA likened politics to a "Diabolical Miasmata, which engender political Delirium, and Spread Contagion endemically or epidemically, from one Man and one State to another." The Democratic-Republicans' "vile Corruption" had finally overwhelmed Massachusetts, he wrote, influencing recent elections in light of the fact that Thomas Jefferson would again "infallibly be chosen." JA further commented on the president's foreign policy, faulting his views of maritime law as it pertained to U.S. trade with Haiti (Adams Papers).

[3] Responding to JQA's comments here, JA wrote on 6 Dec., "While Life and Breath and being last, I shall love my Country: and neither the Interests of Posterity nor the Happiness of the present Generation, can ever be indifferent to me." He then reflected on his lifetime of public service, lamenting the partisan press and rise of political factions (Adams Papers).

November 1804

Louisa Catherine Adams to Abigail Adams

Washington Nov[br:] 27[th.] 1804

I have delayed writing dear Madam longer than I intended, in the hope of giving you a more favorable account of M[r.] Adams's health, which has been extremely indifferent ever since his arrival. I was much surprized and grieved to see him look so ill when he returnd I thank God he is now better though I am apprehensive while he continues in public life there is little chance of his enjoying perfect health owing to the extreme anxiety of his mind, in the present unprosperous and unpleasant situation of affairs. Nothing surely can be more irksome than such a situation as he now fills, devoted as he is to his Country, and feeling how impossible it is to render her any essential service, but obliged to witness the evils which it is utterly out of his power to prevent, and which hourly spread from one end of the Union to the other It grieves me to see him sacrificing the best years of his life in so painful and unprofitable a way it would however cause me infinite pain to see him give it up his talents are so superior and he is so perfectly calculated for the station in which he is placed his manners are so perfectly pleasing and conciliating and his understanding is so refined even his enemies envy and admire him you dear Madam who feel this as sensibly as myself will be able to reconcile these seeming contradictions and excuse my sometimes regreting he ever quitted Boston and a profession to which he was an honor—

M[r.] A. recieved a letter from his father which gave us ~~the most~~ more pleasing accounts of your health than we have had for sometime[1] I offer my prayers to heaven for your perfect restoration and hope shortly to hear from yourself of your compleat recovery—

Accept my thanks for the things you were so good to send to me and the Children who are very well[2] Georege grows a fine stout Boy and goes to School every day[3] The family desire to be respectfully remember'd to the President Your Son and Louisa Smith as does / Dear Madam Your / Affectionate daughter   L

RC (Adams Papers); addressed: "M[rs:] A. Adams / Quincy Near / Boston"; docketed by JA: "M[rs] J.Q.A to A A / 1804."

[1] JA to JQA, 16 Nov., for which see JQA to TBA, 26 Nov., and note 2, above.
[2] The items AA sent were likely the "cloaths cheese &c" and "current jelly" she mentioned in her 8 Dec. reply to LCA, below.
[3] Since 1 Nov. GWA had attended a school run by "a M[rs:] Lee" (JQA, *Diary*).

John Adams to John Quincy Adams

My dear Son   Quincy Nov. 30. 1804

In your Letter of the 19th, which I have received with its Inclosures, you mention a Letter of the Sixth received from me but take no notice of another, whose date as I take no Copies I cant remember. I have written you, two before this.[1]

Your Mother is much better, and now lives with Us but is So zealous about the affairs of the Family that I am almost as anxious for her, as when She was confined.

The Stiffness of temper you mention, never appeared to me, more than was honest and justifiable, excepting as Dr Swift excepted. "If the World had a dozen Arbuthnots, I would burn my travels: but even he has his fault: an ugly Slouch in his gate."[2] thats all.—

you request me to commit to Writing, the principal Incidents of my Life.— Alass! Alass! Alass! What can I Say? I can recollect no part of my political Life, without pain. Every Scene of it presents So much Jealousy Envy, treachery, Perfidy Malice without cause or provocation and revenge without Injury or offence, which forever Surrounded me, that I cannot look back upon it without a kind of Scepticism in my own memory and a doubt whether I should be believed even by my own Children.[3] You may depend on this, ["]I am a Man more Sinn'd against than Sinning."—[4]

The Memoirs of Sully have ever been to me a melancholly Book.[5] They are, as they are given to us, by posthumous Compilers from a mountain of Rubbish, the description of an honest Man running the Gauntlet through all the ranks of Society. I dare to compare myself to him in this particular, and to affirm that I have Seen and felt more of its pains than he did: with this infinite difference, that he Served a Master, whose Understanding and Justice protected and rewarded him and I have Served one who neither knew my services nor cared for me, after they were Secured.— If I Should write the Truth and the whole Truth and nothing but the Truth, like a faithful Witness, I should be believed by very few, and must reveal to posterity the Weaknesses of many great Men, whose Intentions were generally upright, and whose Characters ought to be esteemed and even revered by Posterity. My Work would be called an Hymn to Vanity. It would be one continued rapture of Vanity from one End to the other.— Do not Suspect from this that I am a Pharisee, thanking God that I am not like other Men.[6] No I am the Publican praying God to be mercifull to me a Sinner. I have fallen far short of my Duty in my own Judgment as well as in the sight of God. But among Men, where is the Man, whom I have injured? I know him not.

Yesterday was our Thanksgiving.[7] Thomas is gone to Haverhill. Brother Cranch and his Family dined with Us. Mr Whitney gave Us a Solemn a vehement discourse upon the times. The late monstrous conduct of the People has Spread a gloom, but far from intimidating our Pastor it appears to have arroused him.

This the thirtieth of November, to recollect a Jingle of Edmund Jennings, We should do well to remember. The Preliminaries of Peace in 1782 were signed on this day, and many valuable millions of Land obtained without fifteen millions of Dollars, or a breach of the Constitution.[8]

I promise myself much pleasure next Summer, in the society of my Children. I hope Politicks will not be so dark As to destroy all Comfort. New England appears to me, like a Knight on Horseback in full Armour placed on the Pinnacle of a Monument or Steeple in the posture of full Gallop. With Love to all I am / affectionately

J. Adams[9]

RC (Adams Papers); internal address: "J. Q. Adams Esq."; endorsed: "My Father. 30. Nov^r: 1804. / 10. Dec^r: 1804. rec^d: / 12. d^o: Ans^d:."

[1] JA was referring to his letters to JQA of 6 and 9 Nov., both above. In his letter to JA of 19 Nov., JQA commented on AA's health and TBA's career and reported his delight in having spent the summer with his parents (Adams Papers).

[2] In his 19 Nov. letter, for which see note 1, above, JQA wrote that he hoped his "stiffness of temper" did not convey a lack of affection and respect for his parents (Adams Papers). In responding to his son's self-reflection, JA fused two references from Jonathan Swift's correspondence: the first from a letter to Alexander Pope of 29 Sept. 1725 and the second from a letter to Dr. John Arbuthnot of 25 July 1714 (vol. 13:275; *Works of Alexander Pope*, 10 vols., London, 1871, 7:54).

[3] JQA's 19 Nov. 1804 letter also renewed a request that JA "commit to writing, an account of the principal incidents of your own life," adding that such a memoir would gratify his children and benefit his country. JA acquiesced. On 30 Nov., he resumed the writing of his autobiography, a pursuit he had begun in 1802 but laid aside after finishing short sections on his ancestry, parents, and boyhood. He completed part one, "John Adams," in June 1805 and did not resume again until Dec. 1806, for which see JA to JQA, 7 Jan. 1807, and note 5, below (vol. 15:xxiii; JA, *D&A*, 3:253, 261; 4:1, 270).

[4] Shakespeare, *King Lear*, Act III, scene ii, lines 59–60.

[5] *Memoirs of Maximilian de Bethune, Duke of Sully, Prime Minister to Henry the Great*, 4th edn., 6 vols., London, 1763, a copy of which is in JA's library at MB, along with an eight-volume French edition published in London in 1767 (*Catalogue of JA's Library*).

[6] Luke, 18:11.

[7] Gov. Caleb Strong issued a proclamation on 18 Oct. 1804, declaring a day of thanksgiving in Massachusetts for 29 Nov. (Boston *Repertory*, 23 Oct.).

[8] For Edmund Jenings, see JA, *D&A*, 2:355–356, and for the Anglo-American preliminary peace treaty, see JA, *Papers*, 14:103–109.

[9] JA wrote again to JQA on [28 *Nov.*] and 2 Dec., expounding on maritime law, Massachusetts politics, and the French government and its influence in the United States. He also commented on legislation to regulate the collection of customs revenue then under consideration in Congress (both Adams Papers).

Abigail Adams Smith to Abigail Adams

My Dear Mother: New-York, Dec. 3d, 1804.

Your two letters of November I have received, and am rejoiced to find that you recover strength.[1] I have suffered a great deal of anxiety of mind upon account of your indisposition. At times I feel as if I could fly almost to see you, and be with you. When I lose you, this world will appear to me a desert.

I do not complain, but my mind has suffered much; perhaps I am too prone to anticipate evil: I shall do what appears to me to be my duty, and hope in every situation to find support and consolation, that temporal things can neither give or take away.

We have all some failings; none of us are perfect; and let us cultivate a little candour in judging of others. I have never found that those who were most disposed to condemn the follies of others, were the most perfect themselves.

I cannot flatter the vanity of any one, even to gain their good opinion. I hate the little tittle tattle that lays the foundation of dissensions and differences. Half the people in the world have nothing to say, if they did not meddle with the affairs of others, and animadvert upon them. I can say with Hamlet—

> "How weary, stale, flat, and unprofitable,
> Appear to me all the uses of this world:
> 'Tis an unweeded garden, things rank
> And stale in nature possess it merely."[2]

Yours, affectionately, A. Smith.

MS not found. Printed from AA2, *Jour. and Corr.*, 2:184–185.

[1] Not found.
[2] Shakespeare, *Hamlet*, Act I, scene ii, lines 133–137.

Abigail Adams to John Quincy Adams

My dear son Quincy December 7th 1804

You have been so good in writing to your Father and Brother that I ought not to complain that You have not particularly addrest a Letter to me, tho I wanted to know how George was grown, and whether he rememberd you and what he had to say to you. John I think you told me was quite different in his temper and disposition, more sturdy and harder to manage. these are Subjects much more interesting to me than the politicks of the present day. as we have no rewards to expect, for *Services renderd*, we have not any dissapointments to endure— I have often heard that prosperity & Success is More dangerous than adversity.

I wrote you a few lines one day when I was very weak and feeble, and intended to inclose you Stuart receit for My portrait. whether I did, or not I am not able to say, but as I have not Since been able to find it, I hope I did. the Letter was written about a fortnight after you went away, and was sent, I think with the first which your Father wrote you after you went from here—[1] I have Since been fearfull that you did not receive it as you have not made any mention of it, or the receit. Brisler has had the pork salted down as you desired. I have taken the Legs shoulders &c to Bacon for you and had the lard tried up, and put into a pot for use

Mrs Brisler has put up two more pots of Butter for you and saved you a hundred wt of cheese. the remainder he has put by for sale. Your cider is made and put into Your cellar. the other articles I advised them to keep in their own, through fear of Rats or other Thiefes. Brisler wanted me to write and ask you if You would have the Grainary painted. he says that he can get it done for about 12 dollors, and he thinks it would be a great saveing—

Mrs shaw has shut up her House and removed to Boston. it is not like she will ever return to live in it again It will be to sell, or Let in the spring. I do not imagine it will sell for half what it cost; the turning the road from it has sunk its value—[2] should it be to be let reasonably I have thought whether You would not like to hire it, and let your own— I only mention it for your consideration—

Your uncle Cranch is much afflicted with his Legs indeed the humour spreads over him and I am fearfull will end his days very soon. he has been confind to his Room & bed for several days with a voilent cold and oppression upon his Lungs. The Death of Bishop Parker was Sudden and unexpected it was paralitic[3]

I am better much than when you left me— I do not however go out but to ride, have not been to meeting since you went away— Your Brother has been several days confined, looks pale & feels Rheumatism Your Father has a lame knee, weak and swelld, it has not yet confined him. he is gone to day to dine with the club[4] we all rejoice to see your hand writing. rewards and honors crowd thick upon the Democrats, whilst honest Men are striped of their plumes to decorate—

so it goes up up up—and then it must go down down down again—
Yours most affec'ly.   A A—

RC (Adams Papers); addressed: "J Q Adams / Washington"; endorsed: "My Mother. 7. Dec^{r:} 1804. / 17. Dec^{r:} rec^{d:} / 19. d^{o:} Ans^{d:}."

[1] AA's letter to JQA was dated 11 Nov. and likely accompanied JA's letter of 9 Nov., both above. She did not include the receipt from Gilbert Stuart; see her letter to JQA, 30 Dec., and note 4, below.

[2] Judith Proctor Shaw (ca. 1763–1806) was the widow of Boston merchant William Shaw, whose real estate included an eighty-acre property along the Plymouth Road (later Adams Street) in Quincy and portions of smaller acreages in Milton and Braintree. To meet the probate requirements to settle the estate, part of which was held in trust for the Shaws' son Francis, Judith Shaw had to petition the Mass. General Court for authorization to sell the land. The legislature approved her petition on 13 March 1805, and the property was advertised for sale from 1 April (Sprague, *Braintree Families*; *Boston Commercial Gazette*, 24 March 1806; Mass., *Acts and Laws*, 1804–1805, p. 378–379; Boston *Independent Chronicle*, 1 April 1805).

[3] Episcopal bishop Samuel Parker (b. 1744), pastor of Boston's Trinity Church, died on 6 Dec. 1804 (*Sibley's Harvard Graduates*, 16:76, 77, 83; Boston *Repertory*, 7 Dec.).

[4] For JA's participation in the weekly fish club, see vol. 15:342, 343.

Abigail Adams to Louisa Catherine Adams

My Dear Mrs Adams   Quincy December 8th 1804

I received Yesterday Your Letter of Nov^{br} 27th. and was rejoiced to learn that you and the Children were well. I was just contemplating writing a Letter to my son to chide him for not writing to inform me, how George was grown, and improved, what he said when he saw his Pappa again, and how Master John came on, whether he is as grave as his Brother George was how Master Georges socks fitted him, and whether Mamma let him wear them. sundry of these domestic matters interesting only to those who are Mammas, and Grandmamas— also whether Capt Brackets vessel had arrived safe with the cloaths cheese &c and a small Box containing some current jelly.[1] I am glad to learn from You that George goes to school. Mrs Judge cushing when she arrives has two pr more socks which I could not get finishd soon enough to send by mr Adams—

I regreet to hear that my dear sons health is not good. he lost his flesh so the last winter that he did not recover it through the summer. I do not think that he took sufficient excercise. his pen and Books engrossed almost his whole time— I wish You would not let him go to congress without a craker in his pocket the space between Breakfast and dinner is so long, that his stomack gets filld with flatulencies, and his food when he takes it neither Dijests or nourishes him. this and too great an anxiety of mind wears upon his constitution, and impairs

December 1804

his health. the first may be remedied by taking a dry bisquit and a Glass of wine—the latter I fear is constitutional and habitual— he must Strive however to get the better of that, which he can neither prevent, by his anxiety or remove by his assiduity. all who know him, know him for a Man of strickt honour and integrity, candid and liberal towards those who differ from him in opinion, where their views are honest. I can readily assent to your well drawn portrait, but there is one thing in which we must also unite, that of prevailing upon him to pay more attention to his personal appearance upon this subject I have labourd to convince him of its necessity even as it conduces to his usefullness in Society—and as the writer in the port folio calling himself a British Spy, observes with respect to mr Parsons, "that whilst the sublimity of his Genius intitles him to admiration, the cut of his coat, the strangeness of his wig, or the coulour of his neckcloth; are the subjects of reprehension."[2] It is in vain to talk of being above these little decorums— if we Live in the world and mean to serve ourselves and it, we must conform to its customs, its habits and in some measure to its fashions.

My health I thank God is much mended. I have regained my appetite, and in some measure my strength. my flesh, it will be long before I recruit if ever. it went of like the snow under a hot Sun. My decline was so rapid—that I had very little expectation of living more than a few months— the day before my son left Quincy, my spirits were So deprest with the Idea that I should never see him again, I sufferd an anguish which I kept to myself, and strove to appear cheerfull, that I might not embitter his journey with painfull reflections— the next day after he left me I was confined to my Chamber; & for six weeks growing daily weaker, & more feeble. since then, the complaint I labour under has gradually subsided, and I have gained Strength, and Spirits— I hope My Health may be confirmd, and that I may yet be permitted to welcome you both with your little ones at Quincy the next Spring. How is your good Mother and your Sisters? tender them my regards. let me hear frequently from you & Yours. Louissa request me to present her regards, and thanks for your kind remembrance of her— Thomas must answer for himself. he has not been well the last fortnight.

affectionatly Yours, Abigail Adams

RC (Adams Papers); addressed: "Mrs Louissa Adams. / Washington"; endorsed by JQA: "AA. to L. C. A. 8. Dec^r: 1804."; notation by CFA: "To the Same—"

[1] Capt. James Brackett sailed vessels from Boston to Charleston, S.C., including the brig *Katy*, which was reported arriving in Alexandria, Va., on 26 Nov., although helmed by a Captain Covell (vol. 12:328; Boston *Columbian Centinel*, 21 Dec. 1803; Philadelphia

American Daily Advertiser, 27 Feb. 1804; *New York Commercial Advertiser*, 5 April; Alexandria *Daily Advertiser*, 26 Nov.).

² AA quoted from "The British Spy in Boston. Letter II," which appeared in *Port Folio*, 4:45 (10 Nov.). The article heaped lavish praise on the professional abilities of JQA's legal mentor, Theophilus Parsons, but condemned his "unpolished" manner of dress.

Abigail Adams to John Quincy Adams

my Dear son   Quincy December 18th 1804

I last week received Your Letter of December 3d in replie to mine of Novbr 11th. not having made any mention of it before I thought it had miscarried.¹ I am very sorry to learn by it, that you have been unwell. You must not let the mind wear so much upon the Body. Your disposition to a Sedentary Life prevents You from taking that regular excercise which the Body requires to keep it in a healthy State. I used frequently to remind You of it during Your stay here. You Eat too little; and studied too much. You observe in a Letter to Your Father, that you had an apparent Stiffness of temper.² now that I smiled at. if you had said that You had contracted a reserve and a coldness of address upon entering company which was not natural to you, I would have assented to it, and rejoiced that You had made the discovery as a means towards a Remedy I have accounted for it from several causes. one Your having resided abroad during Such critical periods as you witnessd both in Holland and England, You were obliged in Your public capacity to be constantly upon your gaurd, that nothing improper escaped you either in words or looks— the constant state of anxiety for your Family Served to fix a weight of care upon Your Brow incompatible with that ease and freedom for which You was once noted. Your constant application to your pen & Your Books has had as great an influence as either of the other causes; for frequently after having been a short time absent from them, your pleasentness & ease would revive, the Brow contracted with care would unbend, and the whole countanance be lightned up into social good humour. could not the student be left in the study, and a smile illumine the face when an old acquaintance appeard, a smile which is So cheering that I think I could not feel Myself, happy not thus to meet my Friends, or be received by them— possessing all the most valuable requisites of virtue knowledge honour and integrity I am anxious that you should ~~possess~~ have what Lord Chatham calls, Benevolence in Trifles—³ I know it to be in the Heart; to the outward Man only It is wanting— I have been the more free in my remarks and observations because; tho others may make the Same, they will not so readily account for the causes which produce the affects, or view them perhaps with so much candour.

I thank You my dear Son for the solicitude you express for my Life and Health. without the latter in a tollerable degree, the former would soon be a burden to myself and others— whilst I can be usefull, I hope they may be continued to me. I have recoverd my strength beyond what I thought 5 weeks ago I ever should again my spirits have also returnd. my flesh is not of so much concequence Your Father I think is as well as he was through the summer except that he has a weakness & swelling in one of his knees which prevents him from walking so much as he likes. I believe it to be Rheumatick— for your cough if it is not much better try the cough drops which cured Mrs Cranch after the Physicians had in vain exerted their skill— I beg You would not go such a length of time as you did last year without some refreshment— I know your stomack fills with wind, and then Your food will not nourish you—

You must take the advise You gave Your Father, and feel less for the state of public measures.—[4] they are tending to concequences which few if any of the actors see through. I feel much for Judge Chase.[5] I believe him to be an honest and upright judge. so Do most of his percecutors—and upon their heads may the ignominy rest thou shall not bear false witness.

Your uncle cranch is confined to his chamber, never I fear to leave it. he suffers inexpressible agony from the itching of his Legs.

Thomas will write you himself.

My Love to Mrs Adams. Do not let George forget Quincy, and his Grandparents—

Your most affectionate / Mother   A Adams—

Present my Regards to mr Tracy & Bayard. assure them that I entertain a high esteem for them

RC (Adams Papers); endorsed: "My Mother 18. Dec^{r:} 1804. / 27. Dec^{r:} rec^{d:}."

[1] In his letter to AA of 3 Dec. JQA noted his relief at his mother's recovery of health. He reported suffering from a cold and commented on upcoming congressional activities, including the impeachment trial of U.S. Supreme Court justice Samuel Chase. He also responded to AA's recommendation that he read particular "letters from lord Chatham to his nephew," for which see her 11 Nov. letter, and note 1, above.

[2] See JA to JQA, 30 Nov., and note 2, above.

[3] *Letters Written by the Late Earl of Chatham to His Nephew Thomas Pitt*, London, 1804, p. 36.

[4] See JQA to TBA, 26 Nov., above.

[5] For Chase's impeachment, see LCA to AA, 11 Feb. 1805, and note 2, below.

John Quincy Adams to Abigail Adams

My dear Mother. Washington 19. Dec[r:] 1804.

I do not exactly recollect the date of my last Letter to you; but if it went safely you must have received it very shortly after the date of your favour of the 7[th:] which I received the evening before last.[1] Indeed I am a little surprized that you had not received it before— By that you will find that in the frequency of my letters to my father and brother, I have not been forgetful of my dear mother.— Stuart's receipt for the portrait was not enclosed in your former letter; but I hope you will find and forward it— Stuart is now here, and perhaps if I had the right to call on him for the picture he might be induced to finish it, under the apprehension, that it would be liable to injure his reputation by its being exhibited in the owner's possession, in its unfinished state— At any rate, it is so excellent a likeness, that being the only one extant of you, I am very anxious to have it in our own power; to whomsoever of us it may rightfully belong.

My children, with gratitude to Heaven, I have to say, have enjoyed fine health ever since my return here; but the youngest had suffered so severely by his teething in the summer, and the illness which this had brought on him, that he had pined away to an object really pitiable— He appeared to me to be smaller when I came here, than he was when I left him seven months before.— His weakness was proportionable to this decline— But he has been growing plump and ruddy, every day since my return; and at length is able to run alone— This he has however done only these two or three days. His temper has been affected as might be expected by the state of his health— He is much more easily affected, and more fractious than his brother— I hope however that as he recovers his health and strength, his disposition will again sweeten, and grow tractable.

George has regularly been to school, for the last six weeks, and learns to read, though not very fast— His health is excellent, and has been uninterrupted the whole Summer through— His growth is not very rapid and he is small for his age— His Spirits are as high as his health, but I find him easily managed. I study his character and disposition with close observation— The most remarkable feature I discover, and it gives me some concern, is a volatile Spirit, which it is impossible to fix upon any thing. It would indeed be absurd at that age, to expect steadiness, or assiduous application to single objects, and I am willing to flatter myself that a habit of attention may be acquired, where it

December 1804

has not been bestowed by Nature— I am afraid there is too much truth in an observation of Lady Mary Wortley Montague's, that the most extravagant and groundless of all Castles in the Air, are those we build on the hopes of our children's virtues or happiness in the world—[2] After all the pains we can take, Nature and Fortune ninety-nine times in a hundred contrive to disconcert all our purposes— Yet we should never be weary of well-doing.

I am very glad to hear that M^r and Mrs Briesler, have been laying in provisions, to be prepared for us on our return; which I hope will be by the last of March— We shall have occasion for such vegetables as can be preserved untill that Season, and I hope they will have some for us, as well as the pork and Bacon— If Mrs Shaw's house should be to let on very reasonable terms, and an opportunity of letting mine should offer, it would suit our convenience much better than it will be suited to find ourselves confined in the narrow bounds of my native mansion— But for this additional convenience, I cannot afford to be at much expence.— There is one want which will be of the utmost pressure, and which I must beg you to look out for providing us in, at a seasonable time—I mean of Servants— A Man, or boy, to do the ordinary business of a family, and a woman able to do our Cookery, will be indispensable; with these we can begin our house-keeping, as we shall have one Maid with us.

I am much grieved to hear so unpromising accounts of my Uncle Cranch's health; and still hope he may recover from complaints which have so often afflicted him— Of my father, brother and yourself, I wish your next letters may give more pleasing information.

Mr Pickering invited me a few days since to dine with him, in company with the deputies from Louisiana, who came with the remonstrance; and I accepted his invitation— There are three of those Gentlemen—Messrs Sauvé, Derbigny, and Detréhan; the two former frenchmen born; but long resident in the Country from which they come— The third, a native of Louisiana— He speaks only French; his Colleagues are familiar with our language—[3] They are men of modest and pleasing manners, with the vivacity and sprightliness natural to their Nation; well acquainted with the world, and as far as I could judge, well-informed— They express their entire reliance upon the Justice and Honour of Congress; but they do not appear to be well satisfied with their reception here. In fact hitherto very little attention has been paid to them or their representations; nor is it probable that much will this winter be done to remove their complaints— The Governor is apparently one of their heaviest grievances, and he has just been re-appointed, under the Government Act, which commenced its operation the 1st: of October— The [pro]hibition of the Slave-trade is another very obnoxious point with them— But this I hear will be infle[. . . .] They also claim under the 3d: Article of the Treaty, and *the President's promises*, ha! ha! ha! [. . . .] GOVERNMENT— But this is thought food too strong for their baby Stomachs—So they are likely to go home as they came, with hardly a good word to soften their disappointment.

The french Minister, General Tureau, has the field of diplomacy wholly to himself this Winter— What his Negotiations are I know not; but he has a great fondness and taste for Music.— He is in extreme anxiety for the fate of his wife, and two daughters, who with his two Secretaries of Legation sailed from Nantes in an American Vessel, full three months since, for New-York, and have not yet arrived.[4]

This City is dull this Winter, beyond example— There are no balls nor Assemblies— No foreign Ministers to make great entertainments, and scarcely such a thing as private parties of Company, where the Ladies and Gentlemen can see one anothers faces— This is no sacrifice to me; and perhaps no disadvantage to the public— The warring interests of the District of Columbia are again in full employment, and will take up half our time the remainder of the Session.

Ever affectionately yours.   J. Q. Adams.

RC (Adams Papers); addressed: "Mrs: A. Adams. / Quincy."; endorsed: "J Q Adams Decbr / 19 1804." Some loss of text due to placement and removal of the seal.

[1] JQA's previous letter to AA was dated 3 Dec., for which see AA's reply of 18 Dec., and note 1, above. Her letter of 7 Dec. is also above.

[2] On 27 Oct. JQA noted in his Diary that he was reading a recent edition of the works of Lady Mary Pierrepont Wortley Montagu, which he had purchased in New York as a gift for LCA. The edition was likely *The Works of the Right Honourable Lady Mary Wortley Montagu*, 5 vols., London, 1803, and his reference here was to Montagu's comment about spinning daydreams about her grandchildren, made in a 20 Sept. 1754 letter to her daughter Mary Wortley Montagu Stuart, Countess Bute (4:274): "You will laugh at the castles I build in relation to my grand-children; and will scarcely think it possible those I have never seen should so much employ my thoughts" (JQA, *Diary*; *DNB*, entry on John Stuart, 3d Earl of Bute; *OED*).

[3] JQA dined with Timothy Pickering on 15 Dec. 1804 in the company of Pierre Sauvé (b. 1759), Pierre Augustin Bourguignon Derbigny (1769–1829), and Jean Noël Destréhan (1754–1823), who had carried a petition from Louisiana residents to Congress seeking redress for the 26 March law establishing the territorial government, for which see vol. 15:341, 353. The remonstrance was largely penned by Edward Livingston. It argued for "above all, the privileges of a free representative government" and bristled against the idea that Louisianians were too ignorant for self-government, a characterization that had been propagated by territorial governor William Charles Cole Claiborne and repeated in Congress during the debate of the government bill. The petition was introduced in the House of Representatives on 3 Dec. and referred to committee. Despite the fact that the committee recommended extending the right of self-government, the act to establish the government for Orleans Territory did not include such a provision. Instead, the law, which Thomas Jefferson signed on 2 March 1805, authorized a state government when the free

population reached 60,000, with a 25-person elected assembly and a governor and legislative council appointed by the president (JQA, *Diary*; New Haven *Connecticut Herald*, 6 Nov. 1804; Stanley Clisby Arthur, George Campbell Huchet de Kernion, Charles Patton Dimitry, *Old Families of Louisiana*, New Orleans, 1931, p. 81; Jefferson, *Papers*, 45:468; *Biog. Dir. Cong.*; Julien Vernet, "Too Ignorant to Elect Suitable Men," *Louisiana History*, 60:160–161, 164–165 [Spring 2019]; *Memorial Presented by the Inhabitants of Louisiana to the Congress of the United States*, Washington, D.C., 1804, p. 4, Shaw-Shoemaker, No. 7541).

[4] Louis Marie Turreau de Garambouville (1756–1816) served in the Continental Army in the American Revolution before serving in the French revolutionary army. He was minister plenipotentiary to the United States from 1804 to 1811. He arrived in the United States on 18 Nov. 1804 and was received by Jefferson on 23 November. His wife, Marie Angélique Lequesne Ronsin Turreau (b. 1767), two of their children, and members of the legation traveled separately from Nantes. Issues with their ship necessitated a change of vessel in Faial Island, and they arrived at Charleston, S.C., aboard the Portuguese brig *Union*, Capt. Antonio Francisco de Medeiros, on 28 March 1805 (Madison, *Papers, Secretary of State Series*, 6:157, 8:383; New York *Daily Advertiser*, 26 Nov. 1804; Washington, D.C., *National Intelligencer*, 26 Nov.; *Philadelphia Gazette*, 1 Dec.; *New-York Gazette*, 14 Jan. 1805; Charleston *Carolina Gazette*, 29 March).

Thomas Boylston Adams to John Quincy Adams

Dear Brother   Quincy 23d: December 1804

I did not think to receive a reply to my letter of the 2d: instant, before I had the Mail charged with another and on the way to Washington Yet so it is, and I am now to acknowledge your favor of the 13th: which came to hand yesterday with enclosures—[1] The Journals of the H. R. I have received to No 14 inclusive & but three sheets of the journal of Senate. Bills, Messages & Reports, in abundance.

As you have kindly administered consolation to me, at divers times when circumstances wore the appearance of being adverse, and I derived relief and encouragement from your counsel, I trust you will not be regardless of similar suggestions from me, under ~~your~~ the present mortifications & embarrassments, which you say are incident to your publick capacity. You enjoin it upon me, in one of your late letters not to abandon or become listless to the publick cause in consequence of the gloomy & unpromising aspect of affairs in this quarter.[2] This is wholesome advice and I hope to practise it, but the advice I have for you, though exactly opposite may be equally salutary to you. I think it is manifest from the strain of your letters, that you lay the publick cause too seriously to heart and give too much dominion to the crosses and vexations, which are strown along your path, by the wayward nature of the times. It would abundantly relieve your mind if you could adopt the language of the Clownish Costard & say, "Welcome the sour cup of prosperity— Affliction may one day smile again &—till then, sit thee down, sorrow!"[3] Your solicitude, though stimulated by the best of motives cannot abate one ~~jot~~ drop the overwhelming torrent of

Democratic frenzy, and although you may often be left without a coadjutor in the exercise of your publick duties, there is that, in honest intentions, which will console you, even in solitude. I know nothing of the conduct of the federalists this session, but there are those here, who think them censurable for their silence with respect to the impending impeachment. The yeas & nays do not give us the reasons which govern the votes, and there is so much interest excited by this extraordinary & unprecedented attack upon the Judicial character, that many think a formal protest of the minority, ought to be entered of Record.

The system of appointments and nominations to office as detailed by you, is farcical enough. The controul given to the Senate as the Constitutional Council of the Executive authority, in the business of appointments, has been fairly tested under the two last administrations, and I think it is apparent, that, of all their powers, it is the most obnoxious or the most nugatory. If a majority harmonize with the President, as is now the case, the power of controul, is never exercised & therefore useless, as a mere pageant of office; if the majority be hostile, adverse or excessively tenacious of exercising the right of rejecting candidates selected by the President, such as in his opinion may be most fit for the office to be filled, then the power becomes injurious to the publick service and outrageously clashes with the executive prerogative. It never can do any good and may do much harm.

Poor M:̲ Perez Morton! He is doubtless severely disappointed by the preference of M:̲ Bodoin as a foreign Minister and we do not know of any expected vacancy, which he will like; but he must have something either at home or abroad, speedily, or his patience will flag—[4] He can't afford to wait much longer for his sop. How would the Collector's Office at Boston suit him? Or a Judge-ship in New Orleans?

I am glad to hear that General Turreau wears gold lace and a buttonhole bauble, if it were only for the sake of mortifying the red-breeches philosopher. Plain—simple—Republican Thomas Jefferson, must persuade the Ambassador of his Imperial highness to throw away his legion of honours, before he can bring him to a costume fit for the meridian of Washington— Let him try—the difference may all be reconciled by *an If*.

I have read in the Port Folio, the Review of M:̲ Cranch's Reports, and am well pleased with it. So are we all. There is some wholesome castigation administered where it was much wanted.[5] I am heart-sick when I think of the shameful degradation of official character, throughout every stage of violence committed against the judiciary. There is no sin in the Catalogue of their offences so damnable in my estimation. You have whipped the greater and the smaller culprits, but the old Beelzebub deserves a lash of scorpions. When you see Cousin Cranch give my love to him, and shew him the verses herewith enclosed— They will be prized by him for the sake of the author, who is no other than his venerable father, who wrote them while sorely afflicted with a rheum or humour, which has visited his legs for some time past, and confined him to his chamber The lines, upon which the humours of the old gentleman vented, were posted upon trees & sign posts, in this town, a short time since and are ascribed to Willson M— the *woolen draper*—when you read them, you will think they bear strong marks of *fustian*, or some such stuff of an inferior quality.[6]

We had a Town-meeting, about a fortnight ago, at which it was voted to enlarge our Meeting-house in the Spring, and a Committee was chosen to receive proposals, should any be made, to carry the plan into effect.[7] I suppose it is desired by the Committee, that those who want pews should make it known, so that the numbers to be accommodated may be calculated. Would you have your name put down for one? I think the enlargement of the building will be undertaken by several of the town-gentlemen and I will join them if I can see my way clear— The sale of pews will more than requite the expence of alteration.

M^r: Richard D Tucker of Boston, desired me some time ago to enquire of you the character of a black fellow, who lived some-time in your family; he understood you discharged him for dishonesty, but wishes to be made certain by your testimony as to the fact. I do not remember the name, but presume you will.[8]

Present me kindly to your wife & all friends at Washington. I thank you for your warm wishes on my behalf— Alas! Had they been realized, it could never have happened more seasonably, for the weather has been intensely cold for the last three-weeks—a warmer spell has commenced, but I calculate upon sundry alterations in the weather before your anticipation becomes my condition. My friend at the Hague, Macqueen, had a favorite exclamation when things went cross with him—viz—"Dam'—all hard bargains!"[9] So say I.

Affectionately Your's   T. B. Adams.

RC (Adams Papers); addressed: "John Q Adams Esqr: / Senator of the United States / Washington City"; internal address: "J. Q. Adams Esqr:"; endorsed: "T. B. Adams. 23. Dec^r: 1804. / 2. Jan^y: 1805. rec^d: / Ans^d:."

¹ No letter from TBA to JQA of 2 Dec. has been found. For JQA's 13 Dec. reply, see note 4, below.

² JQA offered TBA this advice in his letter of 19 Nov., after learning of TBA's failed congressional bid: "Remember that listlessness will never have any effect at-all: make yourself known as much as possible, and do not despise the cause of the public so much as to leave it in the lurch— Do not suffer your temper to be soured, with the want of present success— There is more merit in bearing up against depression, and keeping a placid and chearful heart in ill-fortune; than in commanding all the votes in the world" (Adams Papers).

³ Shakespeare, *Love's Labour's Lost*, Act I, scene i, lines 315–317.

⁴ In a letter to TBA of 13 Dec., JQA reported on his colleagues' reactions to the Massachusetts elections and commented on recent federal appointments from Massachusetts, including James Bowdoin Jr. as U.S. minister to Spain. JQA noted that Bowdoin was not the popular choice even among "his friends here of his own party" and that after JQA spoke in favor of the nomination a fellow senator questioned Bowdoin's "*capacity*" and believed the appointment should have gone to Perez Morton. "Now I sincerely believe that even in point of abilities Mr. Bowdoin is fully equal to Morton," JQA wrote to his brother. "And as to character and reputation, all comparison between them would be ridiculous" (Adams Papers).

⁵ The first volume of William Cranch's *Reports of Cases in the Supreme Court*, for which see vol. 15:438–439, was reviewed in *Port Folio* 4:49 (8 Dec.), which praised the work as "clear, methodical, and correct; neither obscured by brevity, nor perplexed with diffuseness." In commenting on some of the court cases, the review criticized the court's decision in Marbury *v.* Madison and condemned the case of Hodgson *v.* Dexter, for both of which see vol. 15:153, 154.

⁶ The enclosed lines written by Richard Cranch have not been found. Wilson Marsh Jr. (1750–1828) was a Quincy draper (vol. 11:284; Sprague, *Braintree Families*).

⁷ The meetinghouse of the First Church of Quincy was enlarged by fifteen feet in 1805, bringing the dimensions of the structure to 61 feet by 56 feet. This structure remained in place until the current church was built in 1828 (Pattee, *Old Braintree*, p. 234–235).

⁸ Richard Dalton Tucker (1771–1842) was a partner in the Boston mercantile firm Davenport & Tucker, which operated from 23 and 24 Long Wharf. The African American man was likely the same servant JQA referenced in 1802, who has not been further identified (vol. 15:180; George Chandler, *The Chandler Family. The Descendants of William and Annis Chandler*, Worcester, Mass., 1883, p. 506; *Boston Directory*, 1805, p. 41, 154, Shaw-Shoemaker, No. 8057).

⁹ Both JQA and TBA socialized with an English shopkeeper named McQueen at The Hague (M/TBA/2, 19 Feb. 1795, 22, 24 June, 15 Sept., 4 April 1796, APM Reel 282; JQA, *Diary*, 27 July 1796, 14 Oct., 11 Sept. 1814).

Abigail Adams to John Quincy Adams

My dear son   Quincy december 30th 1804

Your affectionate Letter of december 19th reachd me a few days since, and found me and the rest of the family in good Health, and Spirits, blessing for which we ought to be truly thankfull. as all the Gifts of Providence are enhanced and enjoyed with tenfold pleasure when attended by them, we can never so justly appreciate the blessing we enjoy, as when we are deprived of them

I was glad to hear so good an account of Master George. You must not look for an old head upon Young shoulders.— a Grave sedate Boy, will make a very mopish dull old Man to my Grandmother I often refer for wise and just observations upon Humane nature, and as a consolation for my own volatile giddy disposition, she used to quote the old

December 1804

adage, wild colts make the best Horses. I used to be more afflicted by Georges grave deportment before he was two years old, than you can be now by his volitility and am really rejoiced to hear that he is a wild Boy— George has that within him which will show itself in time to his honour & Your pleasure, or I have no skill in Physiognomy. as to the other little Gentleman whom You, and Mrs Adams describe as very fractious time may cure that tendency to irritability, but it requires much care and attention to rear Such a child or his temper may be Spoiled for Life.

I shall attend to your request respecting help. I have a woman in my Eye to whom I will speak as soon as I can see her she has lived with me; and last year lived with mrs T Greenleaf[1] I think She would answer for You. she is an old Maid concequently has her oddities, but she is used to house keeping, and is prudent. as to a Man; You know how difficult it is to procure help of that sort for the country, and Boys are much trouble and little service— I can tell mr shaw to make inquiries respecting the House & place of Mrs shaws of Robert Shaw in Boston.[2] I presume Yours would let for 80 or 90 Dollers with the Garden & peice of Ground which mr Whitny occupied I think I have a Tennant in my Eye who would give you that for it.[3]

I have found Stuarts receipt and now inclose it to you. I have thoughts of writing him a few lines when You call upon him for the portrait. I wish he could be prevaild upon to Execute the one of your Father, which was designd for the State House in Boston—[4] Genius is always eccentrick I think. superiour talents give no Security for propriety of conduct; there is no knowing how to take hold of this Man, nor by what Means to prevail upon him to fullfill his engagements.

I have a request to make you. it is to immorttalize my Juno— you know many of her virtues, her affectionate attachment, her good humour, her watchfullness, and her sportive graces together with her personal Beauties— then she is as chaste as Diana— Homer has immortalized the dog of Ulyssus—Johnson had his favorite   and Cowper his spanil Beau, all celebrated in verse and why not my favorite Juno?[5]

we have had an uncommon cold & Snowe December, the weather very fluctuating—not more than one fair day at a time—a day or two sleighing, then a rain succeeded by cold and Ice. yet it very healthy. I have been much benifitted by the cold weather. I am anxious for your Health My dear son. the Straitness upon your Breast, and your cough are undoubtedly a Rheumatic affection, but not the less to be attended to on that account. for many Years I was sadly afflicted in that way, not a winter past that I did not experience more or less of it. many times I could not lie down in My Bed without two or three pillars— I pray you to take some advise and not to neglect yourself untill you and Your friends have cause to regreet it— I shall send mrs Adams a recipe for a mixture which I have found very benificial, have both taken and given with good effect.

Your uncle cranch remains much as he was your Father is very well; Thomas cannot be otherways whilst his darling is with me, tho he has kinks of the Rheumatism entaild upon all of you— Your Father has read two Romances this winter, tempted by the Eves—and I think he enjoyed them as highly as a Girl in her teens

company comeing in obliges me to close my Letter, but not untill I have subscribed Your / affectionate Mother   Abigail Adams—

RC (Adams Papers); endorsed: "My Mother 30. Dec[r:] 1804. / 10. Jan[y:] 1805. Rec[d:]."

[1] The servant who was employed by the Adamses and Mary Deming Price Greenleaf has not been identified. Greenleaf (ca. 1767–1855) was the wife of Thomas Greenleaf (vol. 12:540; Greenleaf, *Greenleaf Family*, p. 210).

[2] Boston merchant Robert Gould Shaw (1776–1853) acted as Judith Proctor Shaw's attorney in the sale of her husband William's estate, for which see AA to JQA, 7 Dec., and note 2, above. The younger Shaw, who later became wealthy as a merchant trading in China, had apprenticed with his uncle and took control of his businesses upon William's retirement (Lorien Foote, *Seeking the One Great Remedy: Francis George Shaw and Nineteenth-Century Reform*, Athens, Ohio, p. 3, 16, 17–18, 27; Boston *Independent Chronicle*, 1 April).

[3] Rev. Peter Whitney Jr. moved out of the John Quincy Adams Birthplace in April 1804, and the property remained vacant until JQA and LCA returned to occupy it during the summer in April 1805 (vol. 15:343; Laurel A. Racine, *Historic Furnishings Report: The Birthplaces of Presidents John Adams and John Quincy Adams*, Quincy, 2001, p. 196, 198).

[4] AA enclosed the 20 May 1800 receipt from artist Gilbert Stuart for the portrait of her that Stuart did not complete until 1815. The artist completed at the same time the portrait of JA that the Mass. General Court had commissioned to hang in the house of representatives shortly after JA became president (vol. 14:xiii–xiv, 248; Oliver, *Portraits of JA and AA*, p. 132, 135).

[5] Argos was Odysseus' dog in Homer's *Odyssey*. Samuel Johnson wrote, "I had rather see the portrait of a dog that I know, than all the allegorical paintings they can show me in the world," and William Cowper penned several poems to a spaniel named Beau: "The Dog and the Water-Lily," "On a Spaniel, Called Beau, Killing a Young Bird," and "Beau's Reply" (Homer, *The Odyssey*, transl. Robert Fagles, N.Y., 1997, line 329; James Boswell, *The Life of Samuel Johnson*, rev. edn., 5 vols., London, 1831, p. 218; *Poems by William Cowper*, 3 vols., Baltimore, 1810, 3:13–14, 80–82).

John Quincy Adams to John Adams

My dear Sir.   Washington 5. Jan[y:] 1805.

I have now two letters from you, and one from my mother, which ought to be answered more particularly, than my time will admit—[1] The business of the Session has been delayed, untill such an accumulation has taken place, as will very much hurry the close of our Time— And although I might perhaps without injury to the public, suffer the business to be done without taking much trouble about it myself, as whatever trouble I do take will certainly be to little purpose, yet I feel a sense of duty impelling me to devote all the leisure I have to searches of information, to understand more fully the subjects upon which I am called to act— Hence my time at present is very much abridged, for correspondence with my friends.

Judge Chase's memorial, requesting Time, untill the first day of the next Session, to prepare his answer, and for trial, I suppose you will see, in the public papers— The day fixed upon for his trial is the 4th: of next month.²

Mr: Giles continues to be our *Director*; and in general meets with little opposition, to what he thinks beneficial to the public service— He has lost much of the vehemence in his manner which struck me when I first heard him speak in public; in the year 1791.— And he treats his opponents with a very pointed civility— I wish his principles had moderated in proportion to his manners.³

The Vice-President, is treated by his former Friends with a degree of distinction and respect to which he had before this Session, long been a Stranger— His case is held out as being eminently entitled to compassion— He seems to be under a deeper personal obligation to one member of the Senate, than from his situation, he ought to be, and the effect of this obligation is too perceptible on his conduct as President.⁴

I am, Dear Sir, ever faithfully yours'.⁵

RC (Adams Papers).

¹ JQA referred to AA's letter of 18 Dec. 1804, above, and JA's letters of 14 and 22 Dec. (both Adams Papers). In the letter of the 14th, JA commented on the Jefferson administration and the forthcoming Massachusetts elections, noting, "Of one Thing I am well convinced that if ever a Party was damned to judicial Blindness, it is the Federalists." In his letter of 22 Dec., JA praised the recent appointment of James Bowdoin Jr. as U.S. minister to Spain and condemned partisanship and the struggle between legislative and executive powers. He also informed his son: "I know not what you may find, among my Papers after my death. If I Should breath the Air, for Some time longer on this congregated Ball, I may commit a few minutes to Writing: but I have been the most careless of Men in preserving Memorials or notices of any kind."

² Samuel Chase on 2 Jan. 1805 asked the Senate for additional time to prepare his defense against articles of impeachment. The following day, the Senate denied his request, ordering his trial to begin on 4 February. The Washington, D.C., *National Intelligencer*, 4, 5 Jan., reported the news, and it was reprinted by the Boston press from 12 Jan. (Adam A. Perlin, "The Impeachment of Samuel Chase: Redefining Judicial Independence," *Rutgers Law Review*, 62:751 [Spring 2010]; Boston *Democrat*, 12 Jan.; *New-England Palladium*, 15 Jan.).

³ JQA first heard William Branch Giles speak in the House of Representatives in Feb. 1791. Giles (1762–1830), who served Virginia in the House from 1790 to 1798 and then again from 1801 to 1803, was appointed to the Senate on 11 Aug. 1804 to fill a vacancy caused by the resignation of his state's junior senator, Abraham B. Venable. Giles took his seat on 5 November. On 29 Nov. he moved for a committee to draft Senate rules for impeachment, about which JQA wrote, "He seems to wish for

debate; but cannot get it.— Debate on this subject with him or his party would be ridiculous." Five days after this motion, on 4 Dec., Giles resigned his Senate seat in favor of his election the same day to the seat vacated by Wilson C. Nicholas' resignation, thus making Giles Virginia's senior senator (*Biog. Dir. Cong.*; JQA, *Diary*, 7 Feb. 1791, 29 Nov. 1804, 10 Dec.).

[4] In late November and early December, an address circulated in the Senate soliciting New Jersey governor Joseph Bloomfield to shield Aaron Burr from prosecution under his indictment in the state for the murder of Alexander Hamilton. According to JQA, Giles both "drew up and procured the subscriptions of the party in the Senate" for the address (JQA, *Diary*, 26 Nov., 7 Dec.; Isenberg, *Fallen Founder*, p. 276).

[5] JQA previously wrote letters to JA on 11 and 24 December. On the 11th he noted the increased use of recess appointments and described the norms and practices for debating confirmations, specifically commenting on recent nominations of Massachusetts men for federal posts, including Benjamin Austin Jr. as commissioner of loans. JQA also repeated his request that JA pen his memoirs. In the letter of 24 Dec., JQA characterized the new French minister, Louis Marie Turreau de Garambouville. He also commented on congressional inactivity, suggesting that federal lawmakers would not take up the constitutional amendment on apportionment proposed by Massachusetts, for which see vol. 15:397. JQA wrote again to his father on 24 Jan. 1805, reflecting on public service and drawing comparisons between his sensitivities to his current role and the challenges JA faced during the American Revolution (all Adams Papers).

Hannah Quincy Lincoln Storer to Abigail Adams

Dear Madam   Jan[ry] 12 1805—

Yours and the President Company On the thirtieth to dine, will add much to the pleasure of that day, in which Brattle street Society will be again blessed with a *Minister* Approved of without a dissenting *Voice*. As You once were members there I thought it would be pleasing to You—if So, I hope your State of health will be Such as to admit of Your gratifying us.[1]

The *Solemn* Ceremony commences at Eleven [o]Clock, or before if possible— Your Sons Company is requested, and the Ladies in the family.—

M[r] Storer pleads his want of Sight as his excuse for not sending in his own hand writing his invitation to President Adams and Son.—

You'll join Me dear Madam in wishing that both Minister and People, may be made instrumental of much Spiritual satisfaction to each other. in this beleif I rest, assuring you of the Compli[ts.] of the Season from each present with those of / Your attached friend

H. Storer

RC (Adams Papers); internal address: "Madam Adams—"

[1] On 30 Jan. Joseph Stevens Buckminster was ordained as minister of Boston's Brattle Street Church, which the Adamses had attended in the early 1770s. Buckminster (1784–1812), of Portsmouth, N.H., Harvard 1800, was the son of Sarah Stevens and Rev. Joseph Buckminster, who gave the sermon during his son's ordination. The new minister served the Boston congregation until his death (vol. 10:264; Boston *Repertory*, 5 Feb. 1805; *ANB*).

January 1805

John Adams to John Quincy Adams

My dear Sir Quincy Jan. 20. 1805

I received in Season, your kind Letter of the 5th: and have been So very busy that I have not found time to acknowledge it, till now. When I write to you it is with no Expectation of any Answer, unless it be in a bare Acknowledgment to Some of Us, i.e. to me, your Mother or your Brother of the receipt of my Letter.[1] I know that the public Business must as it ought to engage all your time and thoughts. The Transactions in Congress at the present Period will be of great Importance to this Country, especially the Mediterranean War The Government of Louisiana, and the Impeachment of the Judge: and whatever part you may take in them, although at present it may appear inefficacious, may be hereafter of more consequence to your Country, than you may now imagine.

I have been uncommonly engaged and interrested in Reading Shakespeare, and particularly his Historical Drama's which I have read through once with Attention, and have almost compleated the Second time. During that Period of the English History, that Ballance of the Constitution, from which its Liberty results, and in which it excellence consists was not formed. The commons had not an independent Share in Legislation, and were not well represented, the Powers of the House of Lords were not well defined, the Prerogatives of the Crown were not exactly limited, the Judges held their Commissions durante Beneplacito the Habeas Corpus Act was not known and Magna Charta was a mere Piece of Parchment which every tryumphant Faction neglected or violated, at its pleasure even much more than our national and State Constitutions are disregarded at this day. These Plays of the great Poet if they are read by any one, with a view to the Struggles between the Red Rose and the White Rose, that is to the Treachery Perfidy Treason Murder Cruelty Sedition and Rebellions of rival and unballanced factions, if he can keep his Gravity and his Attention from being diverted by the Gaiety and Drollery of Falstalf, Pistol Nym, Peto, Fluellin and the rest of those Rakes, & Bullies he will find one of the most instructive Examples for the perusal of this Country. Hitherto We have gone no further than a few Duels, in actual Violence. In Slander We have gone as far as any nation and for any thing I know as far as human nature in its depravity can go. The Parties in England availd themselves of Religion, the Catholic and the Puritan, as Pretexts, and sought the Aid and Alliances of Scotland and France, alternately, very much as ours do.— Our Presidents and Governors have not yet Wealth enough to give Dowers with their Daughters to Bonapartes Brothers or Nephews, nor are they rich enough to demand Royal or Imperial Girls for their sons. But Suppose a Hamilton or a Burr, at the head of victorious Armies and President at the same time, and with Sons and Daughters to dispose of, and what then? Why then it will be Said

> O America! what might'est thou do, that honor would thee do,
> Were all thy Children kind and natural!
> But see thy fault! France or England hath in thee found out
> A nest of hollow Bosoms, which he fills.[2]

With regard to Judge Chace's Tryal, were I in your Situation I would read every Impeachment, that is to be found in the State Tryals. So much I may say to you, without Suspecting myself of the least desire to influence your Judgment.

With regard to Mr Giles you may if you please give my Compliments to him and ask him in my name whether our Nation is now as Democratical as he wishes, or not. This jocular Question I suppose I may ask him without offence to him which is far from my Intention.

The Union of the red Rose and the white Rose, that is of the Livingstons and Clintons seems to have compleatly tryumphed over the Vice President for the present in New York.[3] I feel much interested on the public Account in the Question what is to be his Course after the fourth of March. I am told that his Party in this State, who were very violent against him at first are changing their Language, I Suppose in consequence of Letters from Washington, and they now say that he ought to be pardoned even if upon Tryal he should be found guilty.

RC (Adams Papers); addressed by TBA: "John Q Adams Esq^{r:} / Senator of the US / Washington City"; endorsed: "My Father 20. Jan^{y:} 1805. / 9. Feb^{y:} rec^{d:}." Tr (Adams Papers).

[1] JQA had yet to acknowledge JA's two previous letters, dated 24 Dec. 1804 and 8 Jan. 1805. In the first, JA reflected on the "History of Jealousies," political rivalries he had witnessed over the years, before commenting on the balance of powers in France and the French Revolution. In the second letter JA both encouraged and commiserated with his son about the "humiliations in public Life." He also decried the nation's sectionalism: "According to my Observations and Opinion the Southern Men have been actuated by an absolute hatred of New England and have been joined in it most cordially by the Germans Irish and Dutch in all the middle States. Nothing but their fears ever restrained them from discarding Us from their Union. Those Fears, as their population increases So much faster

January 1805

than Ours diminish every day: and were they not restrained by their Negroes they would reject Us from their Union, within a Year" (both Adams Papers).

[2] A slightly modified quotation from Shakespeare, *King Henry V*, Act II, Prologue, lines 16, 18–21.

[3] Factions within New York's Democratic-Republican Party supporting DeWitt Clinton or Aaron Burr continued to battle through the 1804 gubernatorial election, which saw a coalition of Clinton and Brockholst Livingston supporters unite behind Morgan Lewis' successful candidacy against Burr (vol. 15:218, 357; Isenberg, *Fallen Founder*, p. 252).

Abigail Adams to Hannah Carter Smith

My dear Friend   Quincy Jan^{ry} 26 1805

My mind is so anxiously engaged for You my Dear Friend, and your Family that I cannot think of any thing else; tho I am unacquainted with any details respecting the misfortune which has assaild you, I cannot but think that your family ought not to suffer for debts which were not your own; and that you have a right to secure to yourself and children as much property as would have been yours, if mr smith had dyed insolvent the Law perhaps may be against me, but I hope you will consider this subject, and secure such moveables as you can consistant with justice & honor. You have Friends who can advise you upon this subject. you know where you may deposit whatever you may wish to send away. mr smith and Family are so well beloved, that I hope and trust he will find benevolence & kindness, from all to whom he is responsible— I pray that you may be supported under this Severe & unexpected trial, and that Mr Smith will not suffer it to sink and depress his spirits so as to impair his Health & injure his future usefullness— excuse me if I have said more than I ought, and be assured that it is from the interest I feel for You and your Family that I am thus urgent with you. My kindest regards to mr smith, and be assured no change of circumstances can alter the Love and regard of

                                                   Abigail Adams[1]

RC (MHi:Smith-Carter Family Papers); endorsed: "A Adams / Quincy 26 Jany 1805."

[1] For William Smith's financial failure, see AA to LCA, 27 Jan., and note 5, below. AA previously wrote to Hannah Smith on 22 Jan. (MHi:Smith-Carter Family Papers) to offer assistance in caring for any of the Smith children and receiving any goods they wished to send, for which she enclosed cards to be attached to trunks. William Smith's sister Elizabeth Smith replied on the family's behalf on 23 Jan., thanking AA for her concern and offer of help (Adams Papers).

Abigail Adams to Louisa Catherine Adams

My dear Mrs Adams   Quincy Jan'ry 27th 1805

inclosed You have a Letter to mr Rutledge which you may if you like send to Your Brother if you think it will be of any service to him.[1]

we yesterday received a few lines from mr Adams of the 14th from which I learnt You were all in tolerable Health.[2] I want to know if his cough has left him, and whether he has any thing of the Rheumatism in his Limbs— I would have him pay particular attention to his cough, and if he is not quite relieved put a Blister between his shoulders. coughs are dangerous if of long continuence. Louissa has a severe attack of the Rheumatism in her neck one shoulder and arm. she has not been able to dress or undress or lay down in her bed without being Bolsterd up with pillows for these ten days. a cough also attends her— the pain at times has been extreem—and she has not yet got much relief— I cannot be sufficiently thankfull that I am so well as to be able to go out, & to attend to my family. the colder the weather, the better I have been, and we have had the hardest winter since the year 1780— a Snowstorm this day which promises to be deep—and I wish the Snow would last untill April; but we have had but one thing steady which is unsteadiness; no sooner have we had a fine snow & cold enough to make it fine travelling, before a rain has dissolved our prospect—a true Emblem of humane Life— to day we put forth like a flower of the feild. to morrow are cut down, & cast away into oblivion— So teach us to number our days—thou Maker of our Frame, that we may apply our Hearts unto Wisdom—[3] Mr Adams I know will lament the Death of mr Davis, he who lost his wife about a year since, and was Treasurer— he died of a Lung fever, universally regreeted—[4]

Mr Adams and You will also be distrest to learn that our good Friend mr smith has met with a Sad Catastrophe by indorsing Bills to a large amount for Mr Goreham who faild for a Sum twice as much as he is worth; and has involved mr smith and his family in the greatest Distress—[5] I do not know of any Calamity which has So affected me for a long time— it excites universal sympathy & compassion throughout all the Town. no family were more beloved—or did more good with their property—

Mr Adams mentiond to me in one of his Letters that You would want a woman when you return here. Prudy Newcombe who formerly lived with you; and has been with a mrs Vesecy ever since would serve you again— Mrs Dexter told me yesterday that her Mother was desiri-

January 1805

ous She should live with you when you come, and if You would like to have her, You will let me know that I May engage her.⁶

If mr Adams should see mr Cranch, let him know that his Father is better than he was the beginning of winter and his Mother who was here Yesterday as well as usual as were both his Sisters—

I hope my little Boys are well. tell them of their Grand Parents at Quincy where I hope to see them before many Months—

My Love to your Mother and Sisters / From / Your affectionate

Abigail Adams

RC (Adams Papers); notation by CFA: "To the Same—"

¹ In a letter of 19 Dec. 1804 (Adams Papers), LCA requested from AA a letter of introduction for her brother, Thomas Baker Johnson, to former South Carolina congressman and Charleston lawyer John Rutledge Jr., because, LCA reported, Johnson had "got a situation" at the College of Charleston. AA's enclosed letter of introduction to Rutledge has not been found, although a Dft dated [*ca.* 27 Jan. 1805], filmed at [1802?], is in the Adams Papers. In the 19 Dec. 1804 letter, LCA reported purchasing a horse for JQA's health, which he was not using, and asked for AA's help, believing that through their joint effort JQA might "oblige us by taking more care of himself" (*Biog. Dir. Cong.*).

² Not found.

³ Psalms, 90:12.

⁴ Thomas Davis (b. ca. 1756), who was appointed Massachusetts treasurer in June 1792, died on 21 Jan. 1805. His wife, Elizabeth Hanckley Davis, died on 26 April 1803 (Boston *Columbian Centinel*, 27 April, 23 Jan. 1805; Newburyport *Essex Journal*, 27 June 1792; Newburyport *Impartial Herald*, 23 Sept. 1797).

⁵ Joint financial dealings of William Smith and Boston merchant Stephen Gorham (1747–1826) included co-ownership of a merchant vessel and the underwriting of marine insurance on several others that were captured in the 1790s. Smith held several debts on Gorham's behalf, including one promissory note for $6,000 that came due on 12 Feb. 1805. Smith's resulting insolvency led to a 27 Feb. indenture, where he assigned the bulk of his property for pro rata payment to his numerous creditors. Interest in three vessels and their related cargos, valued at $33,000, and Smith's Court Street residence and seven other pieces of real estate satisfied only a fraction of his total debt (*First Fed. Cong.*, 22:1908; Dudley Atkins Tyng and others, *Reports of Cases Argued and Determined in the Supreme Judicial Court of . . . Massachusetts*, 17 vols., Boston, 1864–1866, 5:42–52, 10:366–368; *French Spoliations: A Condensed Report of the Findings of the Court of Claims*, Washington, D.C., 1912, p. 15, 59–60, 91, 99).

⁶ JQA requested AA's assistance in finding household help in his letter of 19 Dec. 1804, above. Prudence Newcomb (1791–1860) was the daughter of Jerusha Adams Newcomb (1767–1848), and the sister of Elizabeth Newcomb (1787–1832), who had also previously worked in JQA and LCA's household. Jerusha was an Adams cousin and also the aunt to two boys who later served in the household, for whom see JQA to AA, 9 Aug. 1806, and note 3, below (vol. 15:183; Adams, *Geneal. History of Henry Adams*, 1:412, 432; Sprague, *Braintree Families*).

John Adams to John Quincy Adams

Dear sir   Quincy Jan. 27. 1805

Your favour of the fourteenth, with its ample Enclosures of Documents, has arrived in good order.—¹ I deliver all the Journals of Senate and House, all the printed Bills and other printed Papers you Send me, to your Brother, who I presume preserves them all in order for your Use and his own.

The Season here has been unexampled. We have had an Abundance of Snow but it has been melted almost as fast as it has fallen So that We have never had more than Eight or ten Incles at a time on the Ground. From November to this day We have had an Alternation of Snows and Rains. A Snow has fallen, very level, of a certain depth, Say Eight or ten Inches and given Us cold Weather and fine Slaying for two or three days: then a rain has come and melted it, then another Snow and then another rain. At this moment it Snows, and all the Trees encumbered with a load of that Spotless commodity, like Dutch Ladies arrayed in white Robes the Emblems of Innocence and Purity. With all this We have had more of extream cold Weather than has been known for many Years. Thaws have not been So compleat, but that Snow and Ice enough has remained for Slays and Sleds, So that neither Business nor Pleasure has been much interrupted.

Mr Bayard, will be your Friend, and a powerfull Accession to your little flock. My Compliments to him.

A Writer in the Paladium lately has taken my name in vain and given great offence.[2] Motions have been made about it in the House, which will give it great Celebrity. Sydenham and Rush pretend that in a City infected with an Epidemic fever, all other diseases are converted into the prevailing Contagion.[3] Upon Some Such Principle I Suppose, that punishment of Libels, will operate in favour of the present Administration, for the Same reason that they injured the former. Who the Libeller is I have not the Smallest Conjecture or Suspicion, nor have I heard of any intimation of him from either party. I wish that both Parties would let my name alone. It is no pleasure to me, to have my name employed like the Air as vehiculum Soni dissonantis. In this case to be Sure it is not unskillfully or rather not unartfully employed to ~~put~~ make impressions upon Some minds and put Language into Some mouths. In france Such a machine would have been framed into a Vaudeville, in England into a Ballad. But I think Poetry is not naturally predominant in American Minds. There have been very few proofs of Imagination as yet exhibited. It is amusing however to See the galled horse, wince.

A Cock roosted, in the night upon the Backs of a Stable of Horses and there he crowed Scratched, peck'd and eased his nature, in great Pride and Security, till at last he provoked one of the Spirited Coursers to shake himself so suddenly and violently that he dashed Canticleer down on the floor among the Horses feet. These in their Turn Stamped

January 1805

and kicked and Snorted in such manner, that the Cock, affrighted, ran about among the feet and Legs till despairing of his Life he Squatted and cryed out "Pray Gentlemen dont let Us tread upon one another?" This Fable of Daniel De Foe will apply very well to McFarland and Allen, and their Semblables. They who could read Freneau, Lloyd, Peter Markoe, Andrew Brown, Bache, Callender Duane, Greenleaf Cheetham, Wood and Austin with delight, for a dozen Years together, one would think would be ashamed to rage so furiously at a few Lines. Surely not more impudent insolent or false than whole Volumes of their own Libellers.[4]

My Amusement, Since I left Shakespears historical plays, has been reading in Henry's history of Great Britain, the Chapters in the Several Volumes upon Civil and Military History.[5] His Arrangement is very convenient for me.— The everlasting Efforts of ambition and Avarice to obtain their Objects: The never failing Pretexts of Religion and Liberty to disguise them. The unblushing Application to foreign Powers France, Germany, the Pope, Holland Scotland, Ireland Wales and the Mob, to assist their Party and increase their Strength, excite my Indignation, while the poor ignorant misguided deceived cheated and oppressed People, excite my Compassion and afflict my humanity. Alass! when will it be otherwise.?

His Worship and I have employed our late Evenings in reading The Tryal of Dr Sacheverells Impeachment. The D^r told our Louisa's Great Grandfather, Salmon that the Tryal published, was nothing like the real Tryal and that a true one was written and would be published in Holland. I should like to see his Account of it: but I never heard that it was printed. The D^r it Seems lost nothing by his Impeachment or punishment. What was his fate after the accession of the Hanover Family I know not. The Tryal of Sacheveral brought in the Tory Ministry in place of the Duke of Marlborough and Ld Godolphin.[6] The Tryals of Lion, Callender, Brown &c brought in Jefferson.[7] The Peace of Utrecht and the Tragedy of Cato demolished Harly and Bolingbroke.[8] The Peace with France and the Deviltry of Hamilton, and Company destroyed the Federal Faction and with them, the Friends of honest impartial Government who were not of that Faction. Such are the Sudden Changers when Nations are nearly equally divided and all have their prejudices fomented, their imaginations exalted and their Passions inflamed.— How are passions to be allayed, and the People to be united.? I know not. I believe they will have their Course. We know not what that Course is and have reason to dread its bloody and cruel Catastrophy, as well as its Consequences unfavourable to

Liberty. The People are right in many of their Opinions and in none more than this, that when a Military Spirit gets up gives a tone to Society and commands the Fashion all is undone in our Government. The Garrulity of Age.[9]

RC (Adams Papers); endorsed: "My Father— 27. Jan^{y:} 1805. / 9. Feb^{y:} rec^{d:}." Tr (Adams Papers).

[1] Not found.

[2] The *New-England Palladium*, 18 Jan., reported a claim that Democratic-Republicans "have raised a bugbear" about Federalists' support for monarchy. The paper refuted the "absurdity" of such a notion by listing a series of actions by Thomas Jefferson but substituting JA's name. "If Mr. Adams had hired a base calumniator, one Callender for instance, to invent the most scandalous lies ... he *would have been no monarchist, but a good republican*" was one among more than ten examples offered dating back to Jefferson's governship of Virginia.

[3] Thomas Sydenham (ca. 1624–1689) was an English physician who espoused the practice of clinical observation. He researched and wrote on epidemic diseases, and his best known work on the subject is *Observationes medicae*, London, 1676 (*DNB*).

[4] JA quoted from Daniel Defoe's 1702 essay "The Shortest Way with Dissenters" in his criticism of Phineas Allen (1776–1860), editor of the Pittsfield, Mass., *Sun*, and the unidentified McFarland. Among the list of printers and newspapermen who drew JA's censure was Philadelphia playwright Peter Markoe (JA, *Papers*, 18:295, 21:107; Ebenezer Clapp, comp., *Record of the Clapp Family in America*, Boston, 1876, p. 34).

[5] Robert Henry, *The History of Great Britain, Written on a New Plan*, 2d edn., 6 vols., Dublin, 1789–1794, for which see vol. 10:321–322.

[6] JA was also reading *A Compleat Collection of State-tryals, and Proceedings upon Impeachments for High Treason*, originally published in 4 vols., London, 1719. The work included the impeachment of Anglican minister Henry Sacheverell, who delivered on 5 Nov. 1709 an incendiary sermon attacking nonconformists as "false brethren." Although impeached and found guilty by the House of Lords, Sacheverell received a light sentence at the direction of Queen Anne. Popular response to the sentencing led to riots and ultimately the downfall of the ministry, which included the lord high treasurer Sidney Godolphin, 1st Earl of Godolphin. John Churchill, 1st Earl of Marlborough, was a captain-general of English forces and instrumental in the War of Spanish Succession. When Queen Anne died in 1714, she was succeeded by George I, England's first Hanoverian king.

The *Collection of State-tryals* was edited by English historian and travel writer Thomas Salmon (ca. 1679–1767), suggesting a familial link with Louisa Catharine Smith, whose maternal grandfather was William Salmon of Harvard, Mass., son of Thomas Salmon of London. Two versions of the published trials are in JA's library at MB: an abridged edition, *A New Abridgement and Critical Review of the State Trials and Impeachments for High-Treason*, London, 1738, edited by Thomas Salmon; and a ten-volume compilation comprising the six-volume 3d edn., London, 1742, and four supplemental volumes from the 2d edn., London, 1746, both of which were edited by Sollom Emlyn (*DNB*; *Vital Records of Harvard, Massachusetts, to the Year 1850*, Boston, 1917, p. 300; *Catalogue of JA's Library*).

[7] For the prosecutions of Matthew Lyon and James Thomson Callender under the Sedition Act, see vols. 13:334 and 14:228, respectively, and for the charge of libel against Andrew Brown Jr., see vol. 15:127.

[8] Robert Harley, 1st Earl of Oxford, and Henry St. John, 1st Viscount Bolingbroke, led the Tory ministry in Britain from 1710 to 1714, at the end of Queen Anne's reign and supplanting the Godolphin-Marlborough power base before falling out of favor. Oxford was imprisoned in 1715 for his association with the Treaty of Utrecht of 1713, while Bolingbroke championed Joseph Addison's *Cato. A Tragedy*, an act that contributed to his dismissal and the dissolution of the ministry (*DNB*).

[9] JA next wrote to JQA on 7 Feb. 1805, encouraging his son in his public service and affirming his long-held belief in a tripartite balance of powers in government (Adams Papers).

January–February 1805

John Quincy Adams to William Smith Shaw

Dear Sir. Washington City 3. Feb^y: 1805.

I have received your letter enclosing M^r: Bradford's Sermons which I have read with much pleasure; and informing me of the cruel misfortune which has befallen M^r: Smith, for whom, and his excellent lady and family, I feel very much distress'd—[1] If there was any one merchant in Boston on whose safety and stability I should have confided more than any other, he was the man; and to find him thus overwhelmed by the torrent of another's failure was the more afflictive, for being so totally unexpected.

I now enclose you two orders to receive the rent when due from M^r: Dexter, and from Delisle—[2] I hope they will both be punctual this time; as on my return home I shall be much in want of the money; and I hope to see you before or by the last of March.

I suppose you will see by the newspaper Reports of the debates in Congress, that the Georgia-Land-Claims have given rise to debates something more than animated in the House of Representatives—[3] Though it is doubtful to me whether the newspapers themselves will give all that has occurr'd— Not a Law of any material importance has yet been enacted this Session; which has now only one month longer to live.

M^rs: Adams and the children, with the rest of the family here are well, excepting M^r: Hellen, whose Constitution is scarcely able to stand so severe a winter, as we have had for nearly two months; and which continues at the moment I write, as bitter as at any day hitherto.

I remain ever truly yours. John Quincy Adams.

RC (MWA:Adams Family Letters); addressed: "M^r: William S. Shaw. / Boston. / Massachusetts."; internal address: "M^r: W. S. Shaw—"; endorsed: "John Q Adams / An 25 Feb"; notation by JQA: "*Free* / John Quincy Adams. / S. U.S."

[1] Neither Shaw's letter nor the enclosure has been found, although the latter was likely Alden Bradford, *A Sermon Delivered at Plymouth, December 21st, 1804; The Anniversary of the Landing of Our Fathers in December, 1620*, Boston, 1805, Shaw-Shoemaker, No. 8072. Bradford, for whom see CFA, *Diary*, 2:411, had served as the minister for the Congregational Church in Wiscasset, Maine, from 1793 to 1801. He left and served as a clerk for the Mass. Supreme Judicial Court in Lincoln County, Maine, until 1811 (*DAB*).

[2] The enclosed orders have not been found but were for Andrew Dexter Jr. and Caton Delisle, the tenants of JQA's Court Street and Half-Court Square properties, respectively (vol. 15:386, 431).

[3] On 29 Jan. 1805 Virginia representative John Randolph launched a two-day tirade on the floor of the House opposing the proposed settlement of Yazoo land claims. The issue originated with a 1795 Georgia law that transferred millions of acres of western lands to four land companies and provoked massive specu-

lation, much of which was based on fraudulent surveys. The legislature rescinded the law in 1796. It nullified existing contracts and reclaimed the land, although speculation continued and resulted in numerous legal challenges. In Jan. 1802 Thomas Jefferson established a federal commission to negotiate with Georgia representatives; by April the parties reached an agreement where the United States paid Georgia $1.25 million to cede its western lands and to set aside up to 5 million acres to settle claims. Congress passed a bill for settling claims in March 1803 but effectively deferred consideration of claims until the next session. When the issue came before the House in Feb. 1804, Randolph spearheaded opposition and again successfully deferred consideration. His objection to the federal settlement of Yazoo claims was his belief that it violated state sovereignty. When the House again took up the issue in Jan. 1805, the Virginian attacked the corruption that led to the Yazoo controversy, directing his ire not just at the Federalists who allowed it to happen but also at moderate Democratic-Republicans who now condoned it by supporting the settlement of claims. The *Boston Commercial Gazette*, 11 Feb., called Randolph's harangue "shameless impudence" and "matchless effrontery." His lambasting of his colleagues, however, was successful, and the issue was again tabled. Randolph continued to stymie congressional efforts to settle the claims, and it was not until 1810 that the U.S. Supreme Court decided the issue in Fletcher v. Peck, for which see JQA to LCA, 5 March 1809, and note 1, below (vol. 11:149; Charles F. Hobson, *The Great Yazoo Lands Sale: The Case of Fletcher v. Peck*, Lawrence, Kans., 2016, p. 2, 3, 77, 78, 80–81, 92, 93, 94–95, 97–98).

Louisa Catherine Adams to Abigail Adams

My Dear Madam   Washington Feb$^{ry.}$ 11$^{th.}$ 1805

I recieved your two kind letters a few days since and was much affected by the account of poor Louisa's illness and the dreadful misfortune which has befallen M$^{r.}$ Smith and family our much esteem'd friends[1] too well am I enabled by sad experience to participate in their affliction on my first entrance into what is called the world I learnt this painful lesson and though I was shielded from the blow which crushed my family I yet felt it keenly and the moment in which it happen'd perhaps render'd my situation more exquisitely painful than theirs the repeated villainies of those who my father thought his best friends and in whom he placed an unlimited confidence broke his spirit and finally terminated an existence which had for sometime become burthensome surely no blame can or ought to attach to a man for having indulged too favorable an opinion of his fellow creatures and if it is a weakness it is of a nature so amiable none but the worst of men would dare to condemn it this subject awakens every feeling of my heart and makes me shudder at the depravity of human nature which under the spurious semblance of virtue can commit the deepest crimes and reduce whole families to misery and frequently to disgrace and death. when nex you see M$^{rs:}$ Smith have the goodness to make my affectionate respects and tell her how sincerely I participate her sorrow—

February 1805

Washington, *spite of the impeachment* is very dull[2] Miss Wheeler is here and as usual very much admired it is said M[r:] White is addressing her[3] We have had some very warm work in the house and M[r.] R. and M[r.] D–c—— are to decide it *a la mode* that is to in a duel M[r.] R. is engaged in two or three *others* one it is said with Beau D.—[4]

Miss Kitty Johnson who married M[r] Brent is a distant relation of ours and not my Sister as you imagined[5] was there any likelihood of a wedding taking place in our family shortly you should certainly be informed of it.

Poor M[rs:] Barry has been nearly burnt to death by an accident but is now much better and D[r.] Eustis who attends has hopes of her entire recovery.—[6]

I will thank you dear Madam to tell Prudy that I will take her again when I return and if we should get M[rs.] Shaws house to make William do up the garden a little that is to sew some different sorts of Peas some mustard and cresse some pepergrass Lettuce and set out some cabbage plants I should be glad to have done before we return as we may probably not get home untill the middle of April.

M[r.] Adams has entirely lost his cough and is much better in health and spirits the children are both well as are all the family except Eliza and M[r.] Hellen who suffer with a breast complaint but not dangerous—

The family unite with me in best respects to the President and Thomas and Louisa tell Thomas his friend M[r] Ewen is here and has informed that I am to have the pleasure of finding a new relation at my return I did not expect to hear such a piece of news from a stranger—[7]

Adieu dear Madam I have just heard that M[rs.] Cranch is confined but do not know which it is a girl or a Boy[8] believe me your affectionate daughter   L C Adams.

RC (Adams Papers); addressed: "M[rs:] Adams"; endorsed: "Mrs L Adams / Feb'y 11 1805."

[1] See AA to LCA, 27 Jan., and note 1, above.

[2] The House of Representatives passed eight articles of impeachment against U.S. Supreme Court justice Samuel Chase on 4 Dec. 1804, alleging the associate justice misused the law for partisan purpose, committed legal errors, and espoused political rhetoric from the bench to incite fear. Chase's trial in the Senate began on 4 Feb. 1805 and lasted until 1 March. His defense, led by Robert Goodloe Harper and Luther Martin, rooted Chase's actions within judicial precedence and norms and raised larger questions about judicial independence, judicial review, and the scope of the House's power to impeach. On 1 March the Senate, with all 34 senators in attendance, acquitted Chase of all charges (vol. 15:346; Adams A. Perlin, "The Impeachment of Samuel Chase: Redefining Judicial Independence," *Rutgers Law Review*, 62:748, 749, 752, 753–754, 767, 773, 777, 780 [Spring 2010]; *Annals of Congress*, 8th Cong., 2d sess., p. 747–762).

[3] Susan Wheeler (1776–1839), the daughter of Norfolk, Va., merchant Luke Wheeler, spent the winter in Washington, D.C. Though

courted by Delaware senator Samuel White, whom LCA described as "a polished and elegant man; a favourite of the Ladies," Wheeler married Como. Stephen Decatur in 1806 (Jefferson, *Papers*, 45:732; Washington, D.C., *Daily National Intelligencer*, 28 Dec. 1839; *Biog. Dir. Cong.*; LCA, *D&A*, 1:215, 2:492).

⁴ The House member at odds with John Randolph was probably William Dickson (1770–1816) of Tennessee. Dickson was a land speculator and favored the proposed Yazoo land claims settlement in the face of Randolph's opposition, for which see JQA to William Smith Shaw, 3 Feb. 1805, and note 3, above. Randolph's conflicts with John "Beau" Dawson of Virginia may have stemmed from the same debate when he suggested Dawson "go home and take a little *Essence of Roses* as a tonick to brace his nerves" (*Biog. Dir. Cong.*; Daniel S. Dupre, *Transforming the Cotton Frontier: Madison County, Alabama 1800–1840*, Baton Rouge, La., 1997, p. 27, 29; Philadelphia *Aurora General Advertiser*, 12 March; New York *Commercial Advertiser*, 12 March).

⁵ On 6 Jan. LCA's cousin Catherine Walker Johnson married William Brent (vol. 15:445).

⁶ Likely Joanna Gould Barry (d. 1811), the wife of Washington, D.C., merchant Capt. James Barry (Jefferson, *Papers*, 35:349; Baltimore *Federal Republican*, 21 Oct. 1811).

⁷ Probably Samuel Ewing, with whom TBA had recently corresponded (JQA to JA, 3 Nov. 1804, and note 5, above). For TBA's marriage to AHA, see AA to AHA, 24 March 1805, and note 7, below.

⁸ Anna (Nancy) Greenleaf Cranch gave birth to a daughter named Elizabeth Eliot (d. 1860) on 3 Feb. (Greenleaf, *Greenleaf Family*, p. 222).

Abigail Adams to Ann Harrod

my dear Nancy   Quincy Feb'ry 19th 1805

I received last Evening Your Letter by the hand of mr Adams, and the little matters accompanying it. you execcuted my commission quite to my satisfaction.¹ accept my thanks in return. I have regreeted that you have had such wet Streets in Town, after having experienced So much confinement at Quincy. To know that we can go, and come at our pleasure, is a privilege, even when we do not use it, and a privilege whose worth we estimate like many others by its loss.

Louissa who thanks You for your kind Letter, & friendly sympathy, has been more afflicted by pain since You left us than before. for three days last week she could not use her needle.² You can judge how ill she was from that circumstance. Yesterday she used the warm Bath, and had a better night in concequence of it.

we needed not your absence to convince us what a deprivation it would be to our social circle by the fire side. I continue to read Burns, to feel for, pity and admire him, poor fellow. he felt Povertys cold wind, and crushing rain beat keen and heavy on him. he justly observes, "in the comparative view of wretches the Criterion is not what they are doomed to suffer, but how they are formed to bear" with Burns vivid Immagination, his delicate sensibility, his strong and ungovernable passions, his high sense of honour and pride of independence, he was ill calculated to bear the "insolence of office, or the proud Mans contumely"³

February 1805

I am sometimes led to question whether the fine and delicate sensibilities of the soul are a real blessing. they so often are wounded by the insensible, by the unfeeling beings which surround them, of which much the larger portion of Mankind are composed, that like the Rose of Cowper they are shaken by the rude Blast, or witherd by cold neglect, instead of having the tear of Sorrow wiped away by the sympathizing hand of congenial tenderness— yet who that possesses them would be willing to exchange them for a cold hearted apathy, and a stoical indifference a fine tuned instrument is soonest put out of order, Yet what lover of Musick would wish to possess in Preference, an ordinary, instrument?

> "Dearly bought, the hidden treasure
> Finer feelings can bestow;
> Chords that vibrate sweetest pleasure
> Thrill the deepest notes of woe"[4]

I hope my dear Nancy that You will have a favorable time to Return to your Family and Friends—to whom present my kind Regards, as well as to my dear Sister when You see her. I conclude this Letter with my wishes, however unavailing, that the time may not be far distant, which will give me a legal right to call You mine. in the mean time be assured that I both Love, and esteem You and subscribe your affectionate / Friend Abigail Adams

PS
Miss Juno wags her kind remembrance to you. she feels the loss of one kind benefactor, looks up and solisites for favour from those who remain, and seldom seeks in vain

RC (Adams Papers); addressed: "Miss Ann Harrod / Boston"; endorsed: "Mrs A Adams"; notation by ECA: " 'Burns.' "

[1] Not found. This is the first extant correspondence between AA and her future daughter-in-law AHA.

[2] There is no extant correspondence between AHA and Louisa Catharine Smith.

[3] AA was then reading *The Works of Robert Burns . . . in Four Volumes*, Liverpool, 1800, and quoted first from Burns' letter "No. CXXXVIII" (2:423) and second from Shakespeare, *Hamlet*, Act III, scene i, lines 79, 81.

[4] In this paragraph AA referenced William Cowper, "The Rose," and quoted Burns, "On Sensibility," lines 13–16.

Abigail Adams to Louisa Catherine Adams

My dear Mrs Adams   Quincy Feb'ry 24th 1805

I received two days since Your Letter of Febry th 11. it contain information the most agreable, that mr Adams was in better Health and spirits is cheering news to me. I feared through want of attention to himself that his cough would fix upon his Lungs, and produce very allarming concequences— the Time is fast approaching when Congress must rise, whether they have done good, or whether they have done evil. I hope it will not rise with the indeliable disgrace of condemning a just and upright Judge, who if he has err'd has fully proved that, his errors were those of the judgment, not of the Heart. I fear there are too many Members who have no other criterion to Judge of right & wrong than the vote of their Party. I should not fear for the Judge if he had competant Judges to try him, but if I appreciate the talents of those who sit in Judgment upon him arright. with a few exceptions, they have not had Legal nor Parlementary information if they had heads capable of receiving it, sufficient to qualify them to decide upon the merits of the cause at issue before them. how they may be enlightned by the able counsel of the Judges, I know not My most fervent petition is that, Justice may flow down as a River, and Righteousness as a mighty stream;[1] and that for the honour and happiness of our common Country, "no foes may ravish her, and no false friend, betray Her, while professing to Defend."[2]

The season has been uncommoly severe through the whole winter, untill ten days past. the snow is disolving gradually but will keep us bad Roads for a long time. I fear You will have bad travelling for your return. You must take it leisurely and from Nyork may not find it bad by water at the season You propose. Mrs shaw was at Quincy a fortnight ago. I then askd her what she proposed to do with her House. she said sell it, if she could. she afterward applied to the Judge for leave. the Judge could not give her permission upon account of the will, so that she must petition the Legislature, which is now in session. if she should not sell, she would Let it, but at what rent I am unable to say. in a few days I suppose the result will be known— I have desired mrs dexter to Let Prudys Mother know that You shall depend upon her— I will see her as soon as the snow banks will permit me to ride there—

Louissa thanks You for Your kind sympathy. she is very little better suffers pain continually, and is fearfull that the contraction of the

February–March 1805

Musels in her neck and shoulder will be made durable— I hope not, but I never saw a more obstinate Rheumatism—

Thomas sighs that his Friend Ewens report cannot be true, whatever his wishes are, and I believe them very sincere Prudence whispers him, they must be delayed. he is ready to sing the Scotch song

> "O why should fate Sic pleasures have;
> Lifes dearest bands untwining?
> or why Sae sweet a flower as Love,
> depend on fortune's shining?"

"a hungry care, is an unco care["] says Burns

> "Syne as ye brew, My Maiden fair;
> Keep mind that ye Maun drink the yill"[3]

Present me affectionately to all Your family. we were very glad to hear Mrs Cranch was safe with a fine daughter but my sister did not know that there was one in prospect till she heard that it had arrived. she was accordingly saved Much anxiety—

when ever You come on, You will give us pleasure to come and take Your residence with us, untill You can make Your arrangements else where. with my Love to my Son and My Grandsons, I am most affectionatly / Yours   A Adams

RC (Adams Papers); addressed by TBA: "Mrs: L. C. Adams / Washington City"; endorsed by JQA: "A. A— to L. C. A. 24. Feby: 1805."; notation by CFA: "To the same—"

[1] Amos, 5:24.
[2] William Cowper, "Table Talk," lines 332–333.
[3] Here, AA quoted Robert Burns. The first four lines were a repeated refrain in the song "O Poortith Cauld and Restless Love," while the next three lines were from the poem "The Country Lassie," lines 28, 31–32.

Abigail Adams to John Quincy Adams

my Dear son   Quincy March 11th 1805

As Congress are now up for this Season, You will be thinking of returning as Soon as the Roads will permit, and that will be soon, unless we should have a renewal of winter. the two last weeks of Fe'bry and March as far as it is gone, has been very fine Weather, uncommonly So. the grass springs, and the trees bud, too soon for a climate so liable to Sudden changes; I fear You will not get Mrs shaws House. it will be advertized immediatly & Sold. there is some prospect that Robert Shaw may be the purchaser. if he Should, he will let it—but their object is to sell in preference.

You will congratulate me that I have prevaild upon Your Father, to let the lower Farm to Michel to the halves, & that for 5 Years: I am sure we shall do much better in that way, than the one we have been in.

You will see by the papers that Rivalship & party spirit, have adopted club Law—instead of the Sword and pistol. I am sorry for Mr s—— Children, particularly William who is really an estimable Man— nothing but the regard for them and the respectable, and powerfull connections they have formed by marriage have restraind the tongues & pen's of those who have had it in their power to display the Character of mr s—— in its true light. this buisness was commenced a fortnight ago by mr Blake upon the exchange between him and mr sullivan—after which Blake went into the insureance office, and there publically made declarations Similar to those this day publishd in the Centinal—[1]

the public are anxiously waiting the result of the important trial which has for several weeks occupied the senate. O may our Country be saved from the ignominy and disgrace which will attach to it, should the judge be sentenced as Guilty— can it be possible? I have foreborne to say a word untill the subject was decided. the next week will put us out of our suspence—

Your Brother is just come in from dedham court—where he has been all the week—[2]

I inclose a Bill which if you can as well as not, pay for me as you come through Philadelphia it would oblige me, and I will repay You upon your arrival here.[3] the reason of my requesting it is, that a Boston Bill is as great a Rarity, or a Bill of the United Stats; as a silver dollor; or an Apple Blossom in March. whilst the Bills of all the Country Banks are as plenty as Rose Bugs in June; and as pernicious, as it must be amidst such a variety impossible to ~~prevent~~ detect counterfeites.[4]

Since I began this Letter I have been informd that William Baxter has offerd his House to let.[5] he asks two Hundred dollors a year for the House Garden Barn &c. it is large & has a fine Hall above stairs which would do for a Library— the house is finishd in a plain Stile and has not any Yard before it. upon many accounts it is to be preferd to mrs shaws the situation is in the center of the Town. Marketting may be had at the door, and it is in the best Neighbourhood. he made the offer of it to Your Brother, and wished him to go and see it— I think he asks too much. if he would make an abatement and put up a fence before the door it will suit you better than your own, and it will be nearer to your Farm than mrs shaws if you could have had that.

March 1805

If You should have opportunity to write and give any directions respecting it, I will endeavour to see them executed.

My Love to Mrs Adams and the Children from / your affectionate / Mother
Abigail Adams

RC (Adams Papers); addressed by TBA: "John Q Adams Esq^{r:} / Washington City"; endorsed: "My Mother 11. March 1805."

¹ Electioneering in Massachusetts ramped up in advance of the April gubernatorial contest, where Federalist incumbent Caleb Strong again defeated Democratic-Republican challenger James Sullivan. Several local newspapers recounted an exchange between Sullivan and Boston lawyer Joseph Blake Sr. after Blake questioned Sullivan's fitness for office by raising Sullivan's previous association with a democratic society in Boston and subsequent denial of his involvement. Blake also accused the Massachusetts attorney general of appropriating a $3,000 legal settlement and not accounting for the funds with the state treasury. The charge was both reprinted and refuted in the Boston *Independent Chronicle*, 11 March, while the Boston *Columbian Centinel*, 9 and 13 March, also reported on the exchange. AA's sympathies lay with Sullivan's son William (1774–1839), Harvard 1792, a Boston attorney and Federalist who eschewed his father's politics (Boston *Independent Chronicle*, 28 Feb., 7 March; Boston *Columbian Centinel*, 6 March; A New Nation Votes; Thomas C. Amory, *Memoir of Hon. William Sullivan, Prepared for Early Diary of Massachusetts Historical Proceedings*, Cambridge, 1879, p. 3, 5]).

² The Mass. Supreme Judicial Court session for Norfolk County was set to begin at Dedham on the first Tuesday in March, or 5 March (Mass., *Acts and Laws*, 1802–1803, p. 602–603; Boston *Columbian Centinel*, 24 Nov. 1804).

³ Enclosure not found.

⁴ The Mass. General Court in 1799 passed a law prohibiting unincorporated entities from issuing currency, and banning Massachusetts bank notes under $5. Notes as low as 25 cents from out-of-state banks were therefore in wide use, though subject to counterfeiting. The legislature addressed the issues in 1805 by authorizing notes as low as $1 and in 1809 by requiring Massachusetts banks to print notes with special plates to curb counterfeiting (L. Carroll Root, "New England Bank Currency," *Sound Currency*, 2:255, 256 [1 June 1895]).

⁵ William Baxter Sr. (1768–1829) resided on School Street, across from Franklin Street (Sprague, *Braintree Families*; Pattee, *Old Braintree*, p. 301, 306).

Abigail Adams to Ann Quincy Packard

Quincy.— March 11. 1805.

With the only and beloved daughter of my late venerable and respected friend, I shed the tear of sympathy, and with a full heart participate in the sorrowful event, which has deprived her of one of the most tender and affectionate of parents.— One of the best of Mothers,—one of the kindest of friends,—one of the pleasantest companions,—and one of the most exemplary of women.—¹

To me she was "a friend of more than fifty years ripening."— my earliest,—my constant, and my oldest Friend.—

Dear departed spirit,—wilt thou still be my friend in those regions of immortal bliss to which I trust thou art translated,—and whither I hope e'er long to follow thee.—

With D'Johnson I can say that hope dictates what revelation does not confute, that the union of souls may still remain, and that we who are struggling with[2] sorrow and infirmity, may have our part in the attention and kindness of those who have finished their course, and are now receiving their reward

> "Hope wipes the tear from Sorrow's eye
> And Faith points upward to the sky."[3]

It is more than fifty years since my acquaintance commenced with her, who in that period became your Mother.— I was then a child, and carried by my Grandmother,[4]—to visit with her your grandmother,[5]— whom she taught me from my earliest years to venerate, as well as to love, and respect your mother,—and this long before any connexion in the family united us in closer bonds.—[6] The early impressions I received were indelibly stamped by time, and impressed by my own judgment, as I advanced in life,[7]—and became more capable of appreciateing the many virtues of your late excellent parent, in the various relations she sustained of daughter, wife, & mother; in each of which she had few equals,—and I have never known her superior.— You have reason for gratitude and thankfulness that she was spared to such an advanced age,—and as few of its infirmities as the lot of humanity permits.— Always possessing a cheerfulness and a vivacity which whilst it enlivened it delighted, for it was chastened with dignity & decorum.

["]Peace and esteem is all that age can hope"[8] These she enjoyed through life, and having fixed her hopes and expectations upon a solid foundation. She is gone to reap the fruit of a well spent life.

"Heaven gives us friends to bless the present scene Resumes them to prepare us for the next."— Let us my friend improve this dispensation to that useful purpose, and whilst we reflect upon the many endearing qualities, and bright virtues which adorned the life and conversation of your dear, departed parent;—strive to emulate her example, and transplant them into our own lives;—then we shall honour her memory, and transmit it with lustre to Posterity.—[9] This is the present wish & ardent desire, of your sympathising friend

Abigail Adams.[10]

Tr (MHi:Quincy Family Papers); notation: "Letter from M^rs: Adams / to M^rs: Packard." Dft (Adams Papers).

[1] Packard was the daughter of Col. Josiah Quincy and Ann Marsh Quincy, whose death was reported in mid-February. Packard lived in Marlborough, Mass., where her husband, Rev. Asa Packard, served as a minister (vol. 8:448; Boston *Repertory*, 19 Feb.; Boston *Columbian Centinel*, 20 Feb.).

[2] In the Dft, AA added here: "sin," completing her quotation of Samuel Johnson, *The Idler*, No. 41.

³ Anne Steele, "To the Same on the Death of Her Child," lines 23–24. In the Dft AA added the paragraph: "Scarcly had the Grave closed over the remains of my esteemed Friend Madam sargent Relict of the late judge e'er it was again opend to receive the remain of one still dearer to me." She was referring to the recent death of Mary Pickering Leavitt Sargeant, widow of Nathaniel Peaslee Sargeant (vol. 12:186; Steele, *Poems on Subjects Chiefly Devotional*, 3 vols., Bristol, Eng., 1780, 2:34; Boston *Repertory*, 5 Feb.).

⁴ A mark at this point refers to a note at the bottom of the page: "Mrs: John Quincy.—"

⁵ A mark at this point refers to a note at the bottom of the page: "Mrs: Marsh, wife of Rev J. Marsh of Braintree.—"

⁶ In the Dft, AA instead wrote, "Bonds of consanqunity." Packard's maternal grandmother was Ann Fiske Marsh, the wife of former Braintree minister Rev. Joseph Marsh, and her paternal grandmother was Dorothy Flynt Quincy (1678–1737); both women likely knew AA's maternal grandmother, Elizabeth Norton Quincy (vol. 9:10; Nina Sankovitch, *American Rebels: How the Hancock, Adams, and Quincy Families Fanned the Flames of Revolution*, N.Y., 2020, xiii–xiv).

⁷ In the Dft, AA wrote instead of the preceding, "confirmed impressed by my own observation and approbation as I advanced in Life and the difference of Age Diminishd between Us."

⁸ Here and below, AA quoted Edward Young, *The Complaint; or, Night Thoughts*, Night V, line 657; Night IX, lines 388–389.

⁹ In the Dft, AA instead closed the letter: "That you may derive support and consolation from a firm belief in that Being Who disposes all events and Governs in infinate wisdom & mercy and whom we are assured does not willingly afflict but would wipe all tears from all Eyes—is the sincere / and fervent desire of / Your sympathizing / Friend."

¹⁰ Packard replied on 18 March, thanking AA for her condolences (Adams Papers).

Louisa Catherine Adams to Abigail Adams

Dear Madam   Washington City March 17 1805

We have been under the necessity of delaying our journey a few days on account of the marriage of Harriet which took place on thursday evening at eight o-clock[1] since which I have been so much engaged with company and preparations for my departure It has not been in my power to write you untill this morning—

We propose leaving this place on Tuesday morning and shall probably reach Quincy in about a fortnight Caroline will not return with me being engaged to pass the Summer with Mrs. Harper at Baltimore[2] I shall therefore take Eliza on with who has been in a very delicate state of health and to whom it is thought the journey and change of air will prove very servicable I thank you for your invitation and with pleasure accept it[3] George has an unpleasant breaking out round his mouth and I do not think he is quite well otherwise. John is just recovering from his innoculation for the Kine Pox his arm is still very sore—[4]

We were sorry to learn by your last letter that Louisa still continued so unwell[5] I hope with you that the spring and mild weather will entirely restore her pray remember me to her affectionately—

Adieu my dear Madam pray make our best respects acceptable to all our friends and believe me your very affectionate

L. C. Adams

RC (Adams Papers); addressed: "M^rs: A Adams / Quincy near / Boston"; endorsed by Louisa Catharine Smith: "Mrs L C Adams / March 17th: 1805."

¹ On 14 March Harriet Johnson married George Boyd, whom LCA described as "a very fascinating handsome man" (LCA, *D&A*, 1:213).
² Catherine Carroll Harper (1778–1861) was the daughter of Mary Darnall and Charles Carroll of Carrollton and had married Robert Goodloe Harper in 1801 (*ANB*; Catherine O'Donnell, *Elizabeth Seton: American Saint*, Ithaca, N.Y., 2018, p. xi).
³ LCA, JQA, GWA, and JA2, accompanied by LCA's sister Eliza Jennet Dorcas Johnson, traveled by stage, sailing vessel, and hired carriage from Washington, D.C., to Quincy between 19 March 1805 and 5 April. Their trip was delayed more than a week in Philadelphia owing to the children's illness from whooping cough and chicken pox. They also made a brief stop in New York City to visit AA2 from 31 March to 2 April (JQA, *Diary*; LCA, *D&A*, 1:224).
⁴ JA2 received his vaccination against smallpox on 1 March (JQA, *Diary*).
⁵ AA to LCA, 24 Feb., above.

Abigail Adams to Ann Harrod

my dear Nancy   Quincy March 24th 1805

I have had an inflamation for several days past in my Eyes, which has prevented either my reading or writing, and must plead my excuse with you, for not Sooner thanking You for the pleasure afforded me by Your excellent Letter, and of communicating to you Mrs smiths request in her last Letter, of being particularly remembered to you, and of saying to you that she hoped e'er long to become acquainted with You.¹

I see by the paper that You have had a repeated call to Sympathize with the Family, which so lately follow'd the Head of it to the Silent Mansions of the Tomb. the wise Man assures us, that it is be[tter to go to the house of] mourning; than the House of feasting,² for by it [. . . .].³ altho personally a stranger to mr Kemball his connection with the family of my much esteemed Friend Madam Sargent, the loss he sustained by the Death of her to whom he was to have been united.—⁴ his consequent declineing Health, and many other circumstances, which were frequently our Subject of conversation the last winter, interested me much in his Character, and Melancholy fate.

> "A lecture, silent, but of sovereign power!
> And what its worth? ask Death beds, they can tell.["]⁵

I hope agreable to your conjecture that he has done all in his power for Mary, whom according to your account, has been, Nurse, sister, and Friend.⁶ may she receive a higher remuniration than any pecuniary reward in his power to bestow, the consciousness of having bound up the broken heart, and poured balm into the afflicted mind, tho she

March 1805

could not avert the fatal shaft, which was commissoned to unite him, in happier Realms to his departed Friend—

and now my dear Nancy, having paid the debt of sorrow to departed worth it cannot be improper to consider the living, and as this is a mixed state of Joy and Greif, the transition will not be an unnatural one. if I call Your attention to the subject of the last letter, which *you* received *from* my son, and which he put into my hand for perusal, previous to his Sending it—the propositions which he there made received my approbation. I have only to add that if you can wave all difficulties I shall do all in my power to render Your situation agreable to you and hope that You will feel, that You have only exchanged one Parents House, for an others.[7]

That we may prove mutual comforts and blessings to each other, is the sincere and ardent wish of / Your affectionate

[Abigail Adams]

Louissa desires to be kindly rememberd to You, as I also do to your parents & sisters. tell Your Friend Mary that I sympathize with her in her repeated afflictions—[8]

PS. I have been favored with the disposal of this letter, and now forward it with great pleasure. I took the liberty to underscore the words above, *you* & *from*, lest you might expect I had taken a liberty with your last letter—and if you should it would only *be true*; for, after writing my answer to it, I committed it with a benediction to the flames; Mother asked to see it; "it is burnt["] said I, "for fear of accidents," and if you have a mind to burn mine by way of retaliation, I shall be much obliged to you. My Mother has said so much about poor Kimball, that I will only add, that I sincerely lament his untimely end.

Adieu

RC (Adams Papers); addressed by TBA: "Miss Ann Harrod / Haverhill"; endorsed: "M^rs A Adams." Some loss of text where the signature was removed.

[1] Not found.
[2] Ecclesiastes, 7:2.
[3] Four words missing.
[4] Haverhill, Mass., attorney Jabez Kimball (b. 1772), Harvard 1797, died on 19 March. Kimball's betrothed was likely Arria Sargent (b. 1779), the daughter of Epes and Dorcas Babson Sargent, who died on 1 February. The Kimball and Sargent families were further connected through AA's friend Mary Pickering Leavitt Sargeant, whose husband, Nathaniel Peaslee Sargeant, was the grandson of Judith Kimball Peaslee (vol. 12:186; *Haverhill Museum*, 19, 26 March; *New-England Palladium*, 5 Feb.; Emma Worcester Sargent, *Epes Sargent of Gloucester and His Descendants*, Boston, 1923, p. 12; E. A. Kimball, *The Peaslees and Others of Haverhill and Vicinity*, Haverhill, 1899, p. 28).
[5] Edward Young, *The Complaint; or, Night Thoughts*, Night II, lines 647 and 51.
[6] Kimball's caregiver was likely Mary Harrod (1772–1871), AHA's older sister (vol. 7:273; Treat, *Treat Family*, p. 270).

7 No correspondence between AHA and TBA is extant for this period. AA wrote again to AHA on 15 May, reiterating her support for the couple's forthcoming marriage and praising AHA's character. "From the knowledge I have of your disposition, your education and habits," AA wrote, "I have the fullest assurance that you will discharge them in such a manner as to approve yourself to your own mind, and diffuse pleasure and happiness to all." AA also noted her regret at being unable to "sanction your union" in person. AHA and TBA married in Haverhill on 16 May in a ceremony conducted by Rev. Isaac Tomkins (AA to AHA, 15 May, printed in Charles Hamilton Autographs, Catalog No. 42, 1970, item 2; Boston *Columbian Centinel*, 18 May).

8 TBA added the second postscript.

John Quincy Adams to Thomas Boylston Adams

My dear Brother.   New-York 1. April 1805.

It is so long since I gave my father notice of the time when we intended to take our departure from Washington, and of course expected to greet you at Quincy, that I am apprehensive you will begin to feel some anxiety on our Account— I have therefore determined to write you this line, though I hope to tread so close upon the heels of my Epistle, as to be with you by the time, it has performed the task of announcing our approach— If I should get the start of it, and arrive first, I shall only have to change parts, and prepare you for its reception.

Shortly before leaving the *Metropolis*, I wrote to my father two long Letters, which he has doubtless ere this received—[1] In the first of them I told him we meant to depart the 18th:— I believe, in the last I mentioned we might be detained a day or two later— In reality we commenced our Journey on the 19th:—and coming from Baltimore by the Chesapeak and Delaware water Stages through Frenchtown and Newcastle, landed at Philadelphia, the 21st: in the afternoon— We lodg'd at Mrs: Roberts's, where we found several agreeable fellow boarders, and among them your old friend Geo: W. Smith—[2] My eldest Son had been unwell before we left Washington; he became still more so at Philadelphia, and his illness detained us there five or six days longer than we had intended— We finally took the Stage there last Friday (29th:) and reached Paulus Hoek the next day soon after noon— But in the midst of a North-East Storm, we thought best to pass the Night there, and yesterday Morning came over to this City.

Thus much may suffice you for our itinerary Journal— Perhaps you are more curious for an account of incidents than a detail of roads— First then—At Baltimore we found Judge Cushing and his Lady travelling the same course with ourselves; but in their own Carriage— They also arrived at Philadelphia while we were there, and left it before us;

but whether they have yet arrived in New-York I have not heard— We still expect to get home before them.

Secondly, from Baltimore to Philadelphia, we had the company of M^r: Burr the late Vice-President, and of Commodore Preble, the Mediterranean hero—the latter is a man very agreeable to my taste, by the unassuming simplicity of his manners; but whether the original seducer of mankind, has embodied himself in the person of the little *ex-vice*, I am not competent to pronounce— This I will say; that I defy Man, Woman or Child, so to withstand the powers of his fascination, as to part from him after such a transitory association, without feelings of good-will towards him— The last act of his political life I had witness'd, in the delivery of an Address to the Senate in praise of dignity, order, and *Morality*—[3] M^r: Burr the Moralist, was now become the most amiable, attentive and complacent of travelling companions— I had kept him at arms length the whole Session of Congress— I had felt it a cruel degradation to the Body itself, to have for a President at such a time, and on such an occasion, a Man under a legal accusation of Murder, and I could not forgive him for taking the Seat— But now, when he was a private Citizen again, and in circumstances of obvious difficulty, struggling with misfortune and maintaining a deportment superior to it—I had not strength of mind enough to retain in their full inflexibility the resentments even of Virtue— I felt a degree of compassion for the Man, which was almost ready to turn to Respect— He was more than barely civil to me and my family— I could not help feeling for him in return more kindness, than I was willing to acknowledge to myself—infinitely more than I suffered myself to shew him; and perhaps more than is justly consistent with that character which on a cool and distant estimate I cannot help believing to be his.

At Philadelphia we were visited by a great number of friends and acquaintance of your's and of your mother's, besides our own— From many of them we received proofs of that hospitality which has so long been known to you— But in the kindness of your Associates there was an ardour and vivacity, which attested the cordial sincerity of their unanimous declarations of affectionate regard for you, and of their continual mourning for your loss— Dennie was with me every hour and minute that I could be with him, and entertained me with a banquet of recent literature, which after the famine of a Congressional Session was more grateful to me, than all the delicacies of sensuality that human invention has devised from the days of Apicius, to those of the great men Julien and Othello Pollard.⁴ Ewing scarcely left us, for a Moment, but when the indispensable calls of business took him off— D^r: Rush and his family, M^r: Hopkinson and Meredith we frequently saw, and still with new friendly obligations— We were also at M^r: Breck's—M^r: T. Francis's—M^r: James Greenleaf's, and the last day I past there, I dined with another of your friends whom I had not known before; M[^{r}: McCall.] I was twice at your friend Rutter's and M^{rs}: Rutter called to see M^{rs}: Adams— Your apar[tment] is occupied by a D^r: Chapman, a young man lately from Edinburgh, originally a Virginian, and who is trying his medical Fortune in Philadelphia—⁵ M^r: Rutter in consequence of a severe cold, has lost his voice, to such a degree that he can speak only in a whisper— He has been several weeks in this condition, and told me it was not a new thing to him— M^{rs}: Rutter is very anxious for an Answer from you, to her last Letter.⁶

Here, our acquaintance is not so extensive, nor are our friends here of the same class; if I may so express myself— Col^l: Smith and the family are well, and his brother Justus is here with him— I have call'd on M^r: Fitch, M^r: King, and M^r: M'Cormick; and this Evening have taken tea with D^r: Mitchill, who is I believe not personally known to you, but with whom as a man of Science and Letters⁷ I have formed a sort of amicable intercourse, touching as little as possible upon politics.

M^r: Fitch is about to sail for New-Orleans; being as he says tired of walking the Streets of New-York; and intending to purchase there a sugar-plantation; for which he is doubtless well qualified, and which he may fairly hope to render profitable— As accustomed to the climate of Jamaica, he is not afraid of that of Louisiana.⁸ D^r: Mitchill shewed me a letter from M^r: Livingston at Paris, enclosing several patches of seal-skins given him by Sir Joseph Banks; with the furs in a different state of preparation—⁹ M^r: L— announces his intention to bring home with him many useful agricultural inventions and improvements.

I have engaged a passage on board a Providence Packet, which is to sail with the first fair wind— The time fixed for departure was 1/2 past 3 of this afternoon (2. April) But we have an easterly air bordering on a calm neither of which will allow us to go— If we sail tomorrow, we may hope to see you as early as next Sunday or Monday— In the mean time with remembrances of duty and affection to all the fire-side, I am as ever, faithfully yours.

RC (Adams Papers); addressed: "Thomas B. Adams Esqr / Quincy.—"; internal address: "T. B. Adams Esqr."; endorsed: "J. Q. Adams Esqr / 1 April 1805 / 11. Rec^d:." Some loss of text where the seal was removed.

April 1805

[1] JQA's "long" letters to JA were of 8 and 14 March and offered detailed comment on the impeachment of Samuel Chase. In the 8 March letter, JQA noted his reticence to write on the subject until the trial closed. The business was ended as it pertained to Chase, he wrote, but he worried that "the Spirit which impelled to the prosecution" was "far from being subdued or abashed." He then offered substantial analysis of the partisan attack on the judiciary that began with the impeachment of John Pickering two years earlier. JQA continued his discussion of the "crisis which appears to be hastening upon us" in his letter of 14 March, believing that actions taken by the House of Representatives after the Chase impeachment, including the immediate introduction of a constitutional amendment permitting the removal of federal judges on joint petition of Congress, constituted an attempt to undermine the authority of both the judiciary and the Senate. In both letters, JQA also reported their plans to return to Quincy, and in the letter of the 14th he noted that JA2 had been vaccinated for smallpox (both Adams Papers).

[2] Probably dry goods merchant George W. Smith, who had a shop at 158 North Second Street in Philadelphia (1810 U.S. Census, Penn., Philadelphia Co., Philadelphia Upper Delaware Ward, p. 440; *Philadelphia Directory*, 1805, p. [204], Shaw-Shoemaker, No. 9139).

[3] Aaron Burr took leave of the Senate on 2 March in a speech delivered, according to JQA, "with great dignity and firmness of manner." Burr praised the character of the senators and the impartiality with which they conducted business, believing, "It is here if any where, that our Country must ultimately find the anchor of her safety" (JQA, *Diary*; Isenberg, *Fallen Founder*, p. 282).

[4] JQA drew a parallel between the literary and culinary worlds, from first century Roman gastronome M. Gavius Apicius to two modern, acclaimed Boston chefs. "Julien" was Jean Baptiste Gilbert Payplat (1753–1805), a steward from 1786 for the French consul at Boston Philippe André Joseph de Létombe, who left his position and opened a dining establishment in the city in 1793. Julien's rival was Othello Pollard (b. 1765?), an African American chef who operated establishments in Boston and Cambridge between 1796 and 1806 (*Oxford Classical Dicy.*; David S. Shields, *The Culinarians: Lives and Careers from the First Age of American Fine Dining*, Chicago, 2017, p. 25, 28, 29, 30; JA, *Papers*, 14:159).

[5] In addition to Samuel Ewing, Benjamin Rush, Joseph Hopkinson, and William Meredith, JQA's socializing in Philadelphia included visits with the families of Samuel Breck Jr. and Thomas Willing Francis. On 28 March 1805 he and LCA likely dined at the home of merchant Archibald McCall (1767–1843). The resident in TBA's former lodgings was Dr. Nathaniel Chapman (1780–1853), a former student of Rush's who served as physician of the First Troop Philadelphia City Cavalry (vols. 11:212, 13:550; JQA, *Diary*; John W. Jordan, ed., *Colonial and Revolutionary Families of Pennsylvania*, 3 vols., 1911, reprint edn., Baltimore, 2004, 1:408; *ANB*).

[6] Not found.

[7] While in New York City, JQA called on Eliphalet Fitch and Rufus King, merchant Daniel McCormick, and Samuel Latham Mitchill, for whom see note 9, below (vol. 7:442).

[8] Fitch, a distant cousin of JA's, was a sugar merchant and the former receiver general of Jamaica. By November Fitch was in New Orleans, advertising his services as a notary public and later as a justice of the peace. He died in New Orleans in 1810 (JA, *Papers*, 20:348; *Louisiana State Gazette*, 3 Dec. 1805; New York *Public Advertiser*, 7 March 1807; New York *Evening Post*, 4 Sept. 1810).

[9] On 1 April 1805 JQA passed the evening with Mitchill (1764–1831), University of Edinburgh 1786, a politician then serving in the Senate who had been a professor of chemistry, botany, and natural history at Columbia College between 1792 and 1801. In his Diary JQA further described the samples that had been sent to Mitchill from Robert R. Livingston as "several pieces of seal-skins with the long fur, the short fur, and work'd into Cloth." Livingston had visited London in May 1804, where he likely met with Sir Joseph Banks, the noted botanist and president of the Royal Society (vol. 7:212; JQA, *Diary*; *Biog. Dir. Cong.*; Jefferson, *Papers*, 44:217).

Thomas Boylston Adams to William Smith Shaw

Dear Shaw— Quincy 24th: April 1805

I want the form of a petition to be presented to the Court of Sessions, praying for a Committee to be appointed to assess damages, in case of property damaged by the proprietors of the Middlesex Canal—[1] If you can not find a form, this side of Cambridge, you must go there and obtain one from the Clerks Office of the Sessions, where I presume you will find some on file—

Our Petition must be presented in June & I want to know whether it is necessary to describe by boundaries the farm damaged & the nature of the Estate held by the proprietors also the quantity of land taken away, & generally what damages must be laid in the petition—

Do not fail to procure this information soon, as I am resolved to enter with Spirit upon the recovery of damages—

Your's   T B Adams

RC (MHi:Misc. Bound Coll.).

[1] For the dispute regarding the extension of the Middlesex Canal through AA and Elizabeth Smith Shaw Peabody's Medford farm, see vol. 15:453–454. TBA wrote to Shaw about the matter again on 5 Sept., asking that Shaw present a petition at the Middlesex County Court of Sessions, slated to open in Concord on 9 Sept. (MHi:Misc. Bound Coll.).

John Quincy Adams to Walter Hellen

Dear Sir. Quincy 2. May 1805.

Your favour of the 22d: ulto: came to hand a few days since— If it suits your convenience to keep the horse at the original cost it will be perfectly agreeable to me; my wish to have him sold was only upon the supposition that he was of no use to you.[1]

I received at the same time with your last letter one from Mr: Cranch, in which he declines undertaking the Administration of Mr: Johnson's Estate; owing to the difficulty of finding security *to the large Amount* required—[2] It seems to me somewhat extraordinary that security should be required in so large a sum, as to render it almost impossible for any body to administer.

My trunks and boxes from Alexandria, arrived here almost as soon as ourselves— Notwithstanding this arrival and several others the price of flour untill within a very few days has kept at Boston up at least as high as you have seen it marked in the Boston Gazette.[3]

We have been settled now for about a week in our own house, and are all well, excepting the children— George has the whooping cough, which he must have caught at Philadelphia— His brother we suppose has also taken it from him; but as yet has it so lightly that we cannot be certain of the fact.

M^rs: Hellen and your children we hope are well— I beg to be remembered affectionately to them, and the girls, and remain, Dear Sir, truly your's.

LbC (Adams Papers); internal address: "M^r: Walter Hellen."; APM Reel 135.

[1] The letter from Hellen to JQA has not been found but was presumably in reply to JQA's of 11 April (LbC, APM Reel 135), in which JQA enclosed funds to settle his account with Hellen, including the cost of caring for the horse LCA purchased late in 1804. JQA also indicated his willingness to have the horse sold, if possible (LCA to AA, 19 Dec., Adams Papers).

[2] No correspondence has been found between William Cranch and JQA regarding the settlement of Joshua Johnson's estate, for which see vol. 15:200. JQA noted having a "long conversation" with Cranch about it on 8 March 1805 and received Cranch's letter on the subject on 30 April (JQA, *Diary*).

[3] The cost of flour remained relatively steady in Boston throughout April, with the *Boston Commercial Gazette*, 1, 8, 15, 22, 29 April, recording current prices for superfine ranging from $12.50 to $13 per barrel but dropping to $12 to $12.25 by 6 May.

Abigail Adams Smith to Thomas Boylston Adams

My Dear Brother   New York june 10th 1805

a week or two past we had your Marriage announced in our news papers and I have been congratulated upon it by many of your friends, and I confess have been waiting ever since for a communication from yourself, to offer my congratulations to you, upon an event that I most cordially wish and expect will be productive of your happiness[1]

permit me to present myself to my new sister through your mediation which I presume must be most acceptable to her from the amiable character I have universally heard her represented I am predisposed to Love and admire and respect her. I hope before many months are elapsed to have the pleasure of a personal interview with you all

your friend Robert Hare made us a visit the other day and inquired very particularly after you— it is said that he is soon to marry Miss Kean[2] what think you of it?

remember me to all friends and beleive me affectionately your / sister   A Smith

RC (InU:Lafayette MSS Coll.).

[1] The New York *Spectator*, 25 May, announced AHA and TBA's marriage.
[2] The rumors about Philadelphia chemist Robert Hare Jr.'s pending nuptials to "Miss Kean" proved unfounded. Hare married Harriett Clark in 1811 (*ANB*).

William Stephens Smith to Abigail Adams

Dear Madam New York August 10th. 1805

Agreable to your wish, expressed Some months past, M^{rs:} Smith, accompanied by Miss Caroline and Our son William, pay you a visit.[1] I lament that it is not in my power to accompany them, but agreable to the old tune, I cannot leave my post, as Besides the paper War is recommencing, and as We are Threatned with a broad side, I must recive it, & proceed to action, against the Clintonian faction.— M^{rs:} S. takes with her the first papers, relative to the commencement of the War— the attack in the first instance is directed against the enemies advanced fire ships, Cheetham & Coleman. Our Battery is in high mettle this morning you will notice the progress of the action and laugh to see what a dust the flies make—[2] With particular respect to The President & congratulations to Thomas & his Bride, I am with great / regard, Madam—Your most / Obed^{t:} Humble Servt

W: S: Smith

RC (Adams Papers).

[1] AA2, Caroline Amelia Smith, and William Steuben Smith visited Quincy from 13 Aug. to 11 November. Of the correspondence between members of the Smith family during that time, only two letters from WSS to AA2 remain extant. The first, dated 3 Sept., sought news of the Harvard College commencement and commented on New York politics. The second, written on 4 Sept., discussed JA's legacy and condemned attacks against his father-in-law's character: "No longer a living reproach to the mean and frivolous who compose the mass of every generation, he imperceptibly becomes their veneration and delight; and those talents, which once called forth the shafts of envy, and the censure of malevolence, are then encircled with a wreath of bays" (JQA, *Diary*; WSS to AA2, 3 Sept., NHi:William Stephens Smith Coll.; AA2, *Jour. and Corr.*, 2:185–187).

[2] WSS was referring to an ongoing New York City newspaper war. William Coleman (1766–1829), a lawyer who edited the *Evening Post* from its 1801 founding until his death, ignited the most recent brawl on 5 Aug. 1805 by printing a statement claiming he was "authorised to say" that the rival *Morning Chronicle* was under new ownership. *American Citizen* editor James Cheetham joined in on 6 Aug., claiming that an unnamed incoming editor of the *Morning Chronicle* was known to be "a grovelling villifier of the President of the United States." Later the same day, *Morning Chronicle* editor Peter Irving called the claim "a direct falsehood" and labeled Coleman an "officious *wise acre.*" The *Morning Chronicle*, which had earlier printed pseudonymous letters authored by WSS, followed up on 12 Aug. with a renewed attack on both rival editors that belittled Domitor, a pseudonymous defender of Cheetham, by referring to him as Dormouse (vol. 15:272–273; Martha J. Lamb and Constance Cary Harrison, *History of the City of New York*, 3 vols., N.Y., 1877–1896, 3:478; Stephen F. Knott, *Alexander Hamilton and the Persistence of Myth*, Lawrence, Kans., 2002, p. 21, 22).

August–November 1805

Hannah Phillips Cushing to Abigail Adams

Scituate September 10th. 1805.

I was much disappointed My Dear Madam in not having it in my power to see you again before we went to Newport & also in not calling on M^{rs} J Adams & Miss Johnston to have renewed my invitation to them that they would give us the pleasure of a visit this summer. I regret that I did not see them the day we were at Quincey; Delays are dangerous. Court held at Boston till Fri^y eve^g prier to its opening on Mon^y at Newport so That the time was too short without our encroaching on the Sabbath, which is always an unpleasant circumstance.[1] We were in hopes ere this to have seen Miss Smith here. Our family is a pleasant one in which I think she would pass her time agreeably; & nothing should be wanting in my power to render it so. Our Sisters, Miss Cushing, & Mrs Bowers are passing the summer here. Neither of them you have seen. Mrs Jackson is spending a few weeks with us.[2] We cannot be thankful enough that her health & spirits are entirely restored. She often speaks of & wishes much to see you & do my dear Friend gratify us all in favoring us with your company. Our family has been large but five will leave us this week.

I hope you have been blessed with health since we parted & that the remainder of your days may glide away without pain or sickness. Be so good as to write a line respecting it &c. Mr Cushing has his usual health & spirits. He wishes with me to be remembered with due regards to all the family.

H Cushing

RC (Adams Papers); internal address: "Mrs Adams."

[1] The U.S. Circuit Court was in session at Boston from 1 to 14 June. The Newport, R.I., session would have opened on 17 June (Boston *Independent Chronicle*, 20 June).

[2] The Cushings' visitors were William Cushing's sister Abigail Cushing (1748–1824) and Hannah Cushing's sisters Margaret Phillips Bowers (1759–1831) and Esther Phillips Parsons Jackson (vol. 15:427; James S. Cushing, *The Genealogy of the Cushing Family*, Montreal, 1905, p. 49; James Carnahan Wetmore, *Wetmore Family of America, and Its Collateral Branches*, Albany, N.Y., 1861, p. 500).

John Quincy Adams to Abigail Adams

My dear Mother. New-York 17. November 1805.

We embarked at Providence on Tuesday morning, as I wrote you we purposed to do; and after a tolerably pleasant passage of three days and Nights arrived here the day before yesterday about noon; much to the satisfaction of my Sister and her children; who have thus reached the end of their Journey.

But we for our part have accomplished not more than one half of ours; and we have taken Seats in the Stage for Philadelphia, which goes to-morrow morning; I hope we shall get there on Tuesday.—[1] My wife and Eliza Johnson, are still severely afflicted with their coughs; and I cannot flatter myself that they will obtain relief from them untill we have finished our Journey.

The weather has hitherto very much favoured us— We have found it very moderate untill this day; when a North-west wind blows with its natural vehemence and keenness— The Season is not so far advanced here as we left it behind us— On our approach to this City, we saw many remnants of verdure upon the fields; and we find the leaves now just falling from the trees.

M^r: Otis proceeded upon his Journey yesterday Morning; and is I presume before this time in Philadelphia—

I have just returned from Church, where I have heard a Sermon from Dr Smith, the President of Princeton College.[2]

I have been very much amused by looking over the volumes of prints and the coloured drawings presented by the Emperor Napoleon to the Academy of Arts, of this City— They are in this house, and consist of very beautiful engravings from Antique Statues, Architecture, and Sculpture—Views in Egypt, Syria, France and Italy, painted on pasteboard by french Artists, and executed with great taste and elegance; and models from Antique Statues, the spoils of Italy, deposited in the National Museum at Paris—[3] They are all well selected to give an idea of the greatness and magnificence of the new Emperor, and they all have a very immediate relation to himself or his family.

There is much conversation here, on the prospect of a War with Spain; of which however I have no conception— M^r: Skipwith has arrived somewhere in Virginia from France, and says our differences with the Spanish Government were unsettled, and likely to remain so; and in Florida there have been some menacing appearances; but all this is no reason for War—[4] General Miranda, is in this City, and I have met him both at M^r: King's house and at the Col$^{l's:}$— He has lately arrived from England; but with what views I have not learnt—[5] It is said he has lands in the Territory of Louisiana; and perhaps within the disputed boundaries.— General Moreau is said also to be in this City, but I have not seen him.[6]

Our anxiety to hear from you, and particularly respecting the health of our children increases, as the days slip away in succession— We

November 1805

depend upon having a letter from you by the time we shall reach Philadelphia; though it should only be two days later than our own departure— In the meantime, with my duty and affection to your family round, I remain, ever faithfully your Son

John Quincy Adams.

RC (Adams Papers); addressed: "M^(rs:) Abigail Adams. / Quincy."; endorsed: "J Q Adams / 17 Nov^(br) 1805."

[1] JQA, LCA, and Eliza Jennet Dorcas Johnson, accompanied by AA2, William Steuben Smith, Caroline Amelia Smith, and "Rose," presumably a servant, departed Quincy for Providence, R.I., in a hired carriage on 11 Nov. and traveled by ship to New York City, where they arrived on 15 November. After resuming their journey on the 18th, JQA, LCA, and Johnson remained in Philadelphia from 19 to 26 Nov. and finally arrived in Washington, D.C., on 29 November. JQA's letter to AA from Providence was dated 12 Nov. (Adams Papers) and noted that they were in relatively good health and were traveling with Samuel Allyne Otis Sr. (JQA, *Diary*).

[2] JQA attended New York's First Presbyterian Church on Wall Street, where the sermon on Genesis 22:2 was delivered by Samuel Stanhope Smith, whom JQA described as "a very good writer, and a very handsome Speaker." Smith (1751–1819) served as president of Princeton College from 1795 to 1812 and was an early writer on race in America (JQA, *Diary*, 17 Nov. 1805; LCA, *D&A*, 1:237; *ANB*).

[3] The New York Academy of Art was founded in 1803 by brothers Edward and Robert R. Livingston, the latter of whom offered an honorary membership to Napoleon and in return secured the donation of books, engravings, and the loan of paintings for the academy. One donation was the first 24 volumes of *Opere di Giovanni Battista Piranesi, Francesco Piranesi, e d'altri*, 27 vols., Paris, 1800–1807, which were then stored at WSS and AA2's home (Rachel N. Klein, *Art Wars: The Politics of Taste in Nineteenth-Century New York*, Philadelphia, 2020, p. 18, 19, 20; JQA, *Diary*, 16 Nov. 1805; *The Charter and By-Laws of the American Academy of the Arts*, N.Y., 1815, p. 31).

[4] Fulwar Skipwith, a U.S. commercial agent at Paris from 1801 to 1808, returned to the United States in Nov. 1805 with news that the Spanish-American negotiators reached a stalemate. Thomas Jefferson included the news, with additional information about events along the disputed Louisiana boundary that were increasing tensions between the two nations, as part of his annual message to Congress on 3 Dec., for which see JQA to AA, 3 Dec., and note 4, below (Washington, *Papers, Presidential Series*, 11:438; Richmond, Va., *Enquirer*, 12 Nov.).

[5] JQA met Venezuelan revolutionary Francisco de Miranda while socializing in New York on 15 Nov. and in Washington, D.C., on 7 and 15 Dec. (JQA, *Diary*). For Miranda's expedition to wrest Venezuela from Spain, see Descriptive List of Illustrations, No. 2, above.

[6] French general Jean Victor Moreau (1763–1813) fell out of favor with Napoleon and was arrested in Feb. 1804 for allegedly participating in a royalist conspiracy. Originally sentenced to two years' imprisonment, Moreau was exiled to Spain. He sailed from Cádiz for the United States and arrived in Philadelphia on 25 Aug. 1805, remaining in the United States for eight years and settling in Morrisville, Penn. The New York press did not begin reporting rumors of Moreau's pending visit to the city until 20 November. He attended a 25 Nov. militia review and dinner to mark the anniversary of the British evacuation of New York in 1783 (Hoefer, *Nouv. biog. générale*; Philadelphia *United States Gazette*, 26 Aug. 1805; *New-York Gazette*, 20 Nov.; New York *Daily Advertiser*, 26 Nov.).

Abigail Adams to John Quincy Adams

my Dear son   Quincy Nov'br 21 1805

Your trusty driver took Such care of Your Letter that he kept it close in his pocket for a whole week after he returnd, untill ragged and dirty it reachd us last Evening 10 days after it was written.[1] it was however very welcome, being the first intelligence which had reachd us of you, from the time You left us.—

I requested your Brother to write to you to Philadelphia, as I was unable too having been attackd by my old Rheumatick complaints the week you left us, and ever Since confined to my Chamber. I have had a distressing cough which has not been usual. I believe I took a sudden cold. I am now so much better as to hope to get below in a few days—

John is very well and very content, always good except when he has a high coulour. his teeth worry him, and make him fractious. his cough is better. he askd once for his Mother, when she would come from Boston? and the day you went away, when he went down to Tea, he lookd round, and seemd dissapointed Said he thought his Pappa was there. Since then he has been told that his Pappa and Mamma were gone to washington, and he is quite content. he like other Children of his age requires the constant attention of some one, to keep him out of harms way, as they say.

George went to his Aunts the day You left him. that humour worrys him; tho he Breaths much easier than he did. he coughs like the hooping cough. his Aunt knows how to take care of him and he is very content and happy. he came with her to see me a day or two past. John & he were much pleased to see each other, tho the right of property could not be settled between them, with out a third person— John is playing about in my chamber shutting the Shutters—and opening them by turns, as an amusement—

I was at Cambridge the Wednesday of the last week, and some of your Friends exprest an anxiety least you should purchase at Cambridgeport a House. they think it a very unwholesome situation, and that you would endanger your Health, and that of your family by living there. mrs Guile told me the corporation had purchased the house Dr Wigglesworth formerly lived in, and had been repareing it, and that it would be to let in the spring, and she did not doubt that You might have it, if you chose You may know the house. I think she said there were 4 Rooms on a floor.[2] I will make further inquiry if You should think best—

November 1805

This I hope will reach You at Washington, comfortably lodged from whence I should rejoice to learn that your health was mended, and that Mrs Adams's cold and Elizas cough had left them upon their journey. I shall deliver the powd[ers] and the directions respecting George to Mrs Cranch.[3] she says he is as go[od] a child as she wishes. tell mr Quincy that his little Girl was very well to day, and grows finely.[4] with abundance of Love regards &c from all Friends present, are joind those of your affectionate / Mother   Abigail Adams.

RC (Adams Papers); addressed by TBA: "John Q Adams Esqr / Senator of the U.S.A / City of Washington"; endorsed: "My Mother 21. Nov^r: 1805. / 3. Dec^r: rec^d: / D^o: Ans^d:"; notation by JA: "Quincy, Novr 25th 1805. Free." Some loss of text where the seal was removed.

[1] That is, JQA to AA, 12 Nov., for which see his 17 Nov. letter, and note 1, above.

[2] Rev. Edward Wigglesworth (1732–1794) was the Hollis Professor of Divinity at Harvard College from 1765 to 1791, residing in a college-owned house on Braintree Street. AA later made clear that the house possibly available for lease was another dwelling, for which see her letter to JQA of 17 Dec. 1805, and note 3, below. In this letter she referenced Elizabeth Quincy Guild (1757–1825), a maternal cousin of hers and the widow of Boston bookseller Benjamin Guild Sr. (vol. 3:322; Paige, *Hist. of Cambridge, Mass.*, 2:813; Collection Overview, MH-Ar:Records of Early Harvard Buildings, 1710–1969; Cecil Hampden Cutts Howard, comp., *Genealogy of the Cutts Family in America*, Albany, N.Y., 1892, p. 63). For JQA's appointment as Harvard's Boylston Professor of Rhetoric and Oratory, the reason he was considering property in Cambridge, see his letter to LCA, 15 June 1806, and note 1, below.

[3] LCA wrote to AA on 12 Nov. 1805, asking her to relay instructions to Mary Smith Cranch about giving castor oil and "black powders" to GWA (Adams Papers).

[4] That is, Abigail Phillips Quincy, the youngest child of Eliza Susan Morton and Josiah Quincy III (vol. 15:523).

John Quincy Adams to Thomas Boylston Adams

My dear Brother.   Philadelphia 21. November 1805.

I wrote to my mother from Providence & New-York, giving her an Account of our progress thus far;[1] but the moment one sets one's foot into Philadelphia, the Squire becomes such a standing topic of enquiry, from all quarters, that it never fails to remind me of the duty of remembrance to him.

We left New-York in the *Diligence* Stage on Monday Morning, and arrived here the next day just at dinner-time, very much fatigued; but after two Nights rest we all find ourselves recruited; and the ladies are much better of their coughs, than at any time since we left Quincy.— By the way, if you or any of your friends should have occasion to travel in the Stage between New-York and Philadelphia, I would strongly recommend to you the *Mail-Pilot*, and *Diligence* lines, which run in opposition to the *Mail* and *Industry* lines;[2] for you must know that the latter have got into Democratic hands; the consequence of which is that their drivers are a set of drunken black-guards, whose insolence is insufferable, and whose intoxication continually endangers the lives of the passengers— Another effect of the new arrangements is, that the *Mail* and *Industry*, have changed all the Inns, at which they stop on the road; and now go to detestable dens, with sign-posts having "Republican Hotel," inscribed upon them, where you can neither get a comfortable bed, nor an eatable meal, and where you can be sure of nothing, but being well fleeced— I do not indeed suppose that this system will continue long; for its natural consequence has already produced such a preference for the Pilot and Diligence, that they are always crowded with Passengers, while the opposite lines are almost deserted— The two lines always start at the same hour; the Stage in which we came was full, from Paulus Hoek— The Industry Stage that started with us had only two passengers— We met on both days the Stages, running to New-York, of the two lines, and always with the same evidence of preference given to the Pilot and Diligence— You will make your reflections upon these facts— Mine have been simply these—In the ordinary transactions of business in life, never deal with democrats if you can avoid it; and where a choice is offered you for your custom, depend upon it, the federal tradesman will use you best.

I called and delivered your letter to M[r:] Ewing,[3] who has your ci-devant Office & chamber, at M[r:] Rutter's— I dined with them yesterday; in company with M[r:] Hopkinson— M[rs:] Rutter is confined to her chamber with a pleurisy,—from which she is however on the recovery— She was disappointed, at my not having a letter from you for her— I apologized for you as well as I could. I have called twice upon Dennie; but have not yet seen him.

The State of Politics here is not so turbulent as when I was here last Spring; but now that the federalists have been set at ease on the danger to the Constitution for which they were so much alarmed, they have leisure to remark that the success of the late Election, was not their success, and they are as much dissatisfied, as they would have been at the loss of the field— They have been indeed too much elated by the issue of the late contest, and have discovered a disposition to dictate in the Elections, without consulting their new Allies the Quids— One of the Senators for this County, recently elected, has resigned, in consequence of which a new one is to be chosen in his stead— A few leading federalists have met together, without admitting any of the *thirds*, and put in nomination a M[r:] Hallowell— But he does not suit the third party, and they are resentful at having been excluded

November 1805

from the federal Meeting; so they are to start a candidate of their own, M^r: Joseph Reed; and the chance is that neither will succeed— The Governor too since his election is secured, has not shewn a disposition so accommodating to the federalists as they expected, and the composition of their Supreme Judicial Court, is a subject, upon which they are very uneasy, and on which their hopes of speedy amelioration, are greatly dashed, by his course of proceeding, & supposed intentions.[4]

24. November 1805.

We have been in daily and anxious expectation of hearing from my dear Mother; but hitherto we have been disappointed— I hope the occasion of this has not been illness either of her, or of our children— To-morrow morning we purpose to proceed upon our Journey, and have already spent much more time here than we had contemplated— We must now content ourselves with the hope of hearing from your quarter when we reach Washington.

I have settled Allibone's Account, and delivered him your letter containing the order for three barrels of flour, which he promises shall be sent by the first opportunity.[5] I have also had the 3^d: volume of the Supplement to the Encyclopaedia, (which is in two parts) packed up at Dobson's, and directed to your father, to the care of M^r: [. . . .] Boston— Dobson says he will send it round by the first vessel, and M^r: Shaw w[. . .] you mention this to him be on the look out, for them when they arrive— D^r: Rush, with whom we dined yesterday, will also send to Dobson's to go by the same opportunity a copy of the New Edition of his Works, which is on the Eve of publication in four Volumes.[6]

I find upon Enquiry that I cannot transfer the Schuylkill Bridge Stock standing in your and your father's names, without powers of attorney for that purpose.[7] I shall therefore sell none of them now, and you will have leisure to send me the powers, in the course of the Winter, that I may sell the Stock on my return.

I have only time to add that I am as at all times, truly yours; with kindest remembrance to your wife.   John Quincy Adams

RC (Adams Papers); addressed: "Thomas B. Adams Esqr: / Quincy."; endorsed: "J Q Adams Esqr / 21st: November 1805 / 24th: D^o / 3^d: Dec^r: Rec^d:." Some loss of text where the seal was removed.

[1] See JQA to AA, 17 Nov., and note 1, above.
[2] By the fall of 1805 these four competing stage lines from New York City to Philadelphia, Baltimore, and Washington, D.C., had been in service for more than a year. All departed from Greenwich, with the Diligence and Mail Pilot offering ferry service to Paulus Hook, N.J. The Diligence departed at 8 A.M., carried

eight passengers, and cost $5 per through fare, while the Mail Pilot departed at noon and cost $8 per passenger for each of its six spots. The Industry left at 8 A.M., six days per week at a cost of $5, while the United States' Mail Stage started at 12:30 P.M. and cost $8 per rider (*New York Commercial Advertiser*, 29 Sept. 1804, 26 Oct. 1805; New York *Evening Post*, 13 Oct. 1804; New York *American Citizen*, 7 Oct. 1805).

³ Not found.

⁴ Pennsylvania politics had long been roiling, with Democratic-Republicans splintering into progressive and conservative factions. Progressives focused on judicial reform, proposing arbitration as a viable alternative to adjudication in the courts and seeking to unseat Federalist judges on the state supreme court, for which see vol. 15:336. By the start of 1805 urban and rural progressives uneasily coalesced behind a plan to convene a state constitutional convention and unseat Gov. Thomas McKean. The conservative Quids combatted this reform coalition by defending the existing constitution, separation of powers, and independent judiciary. They also attacked the progressive newspapers the Philadelphia *Aurora General Advertiser* and the Northumberland, Penn., *Republican Argus*. The Quids defended McKean and urged popular political participation to combat the opposition's reform efforts. In November, McKean was reelected by a slim margin. In the state legislative elections, John Gamble was chosen to represent Philadelphia County in the senate but resigned his seat. JQA accurately predicted that neither Joseph Reed Jr. (1772–1846), who later served as city recorder, nor John Hallowell would succeed in the 28 Nov. special election. Instead, Hallowell, whom supporters characterized as having "unsullied political integrity," narrowly lost to John Dorsey (Andrew Shankman, *Crucible of American Democracy: The Struggle to Fuse Egalitarianism & Capitalism in Jeffersonian Pennsylvania*, Lawrence, Kans., 2004, p. 127–131, 134–135, 136, 140–142, 151–152, 159; Philadelphia *Aurora General Advertiser*, 18 Nov.; CFA, *Diary*, 2:135; Philadelphia *United States Gazette*, 23 Nov.; A New Nation Votes).

⁵ No correspondence between the Adamses and Philadelphia merchant Thomas Allibone has been found. JQA visited Allibone on 21 Nov. to transact business on JA's behalf (vol. 15:118; JQA, *Diary*).

⁶ *Supplement to the Encyclopædia; or, A Dictionary of Arts, Sciences, and Miscellaneous Literature*, 3 vols., Phila., 1800–1803, and Benjamin Rush, *Essays, Literary, Moral and Philosophical*, 2d edn., Phila., 1806 (vols. 13:319, 15:241).

⁷ The previous day JQA visited Dorsey, treasurer of the company established in 1798 to build a bridge across the Schuylkill River from the "West End of the High Street" in Philadelphia. JQA took an interest in the project, visiting the construction site in Oct. 1803 and the recently opened bridge in March 1805. Shares in the Schuylkill Permanent Bridge Company cost $10 each, and JQA, JA, and TBA each acquired twenty shares. JQA purchased the shares from his father and brother at par in 1818 and held all sixty until 1844 (JQA, *Diary*, 17 Oct. 1803, 25 March 1805, 23 Nov., 28 Sept. 1818, 12 Oct., 1 Dec. 1844; *Philadelphia Gazette*, 13 May 1805; Subscription for Shares in the Bridge Corporation, [Phila., 1798,] Evans, No. 50940; M/JQA/12, p. 166, 167, APM Reel 209).

Abigail Adams to John Quincy Adams and Louisa Catherine Adams

my Dear Son and daughter   Quincy Nov^{br} 29 1805

The reason that You did not receive a Letter from me when you arrived at Philadelphia, was oweing to my being so sick that I could not write. I got Your Brother to write, but not so soon as I should, if I had been able. as soon as I could hold my pen I wrote you a few lines, Since which I have received Your Letter from Newyork;[1] I have rejoiced in the fine weather which has followed you ever since You left us. with the exception of a rainy day or two; we have had it un-

November 1805

commonly mild and pleasant, much more so than for a fortnight before you sit out I presume you have by this time arrived in Washington where I hope You have found Your Friends in health. Your children are both in better Health than when You left them. George Breaths quite easy & is hearty & lively goes to school every day to Mrs Turner, who keeps in a Room in Gays House, where she takes Major Barrets two of Capt Brackets & those at Your uncles—[2] John is very well & has lost his cough intirely; he is rather too early a riser even for me, but the nights are now so long that it is not to be expected that children will sleep till it is fully light. He goes to bed about Six—seldom cries, goes by himself into bed, and asks neither for light or any one to stay by him— he is a very pleasent child, and easily managed, with a steady hand. we take care of him ourselves. both Louissa and his Aunt Adams are very fond of him, and he of them— in fine weather I let him walk out I told him I was writing to you and askd him what I should say— shall I say John is good. No shall I say John is Naughty. No. he stood a moment and his little Eyes glistned— say John has got a Beauty new Hat—

Yesterday being Thanksgiving Brother and sister cranch dinned with me, and George with a Group of Mr Nortens Children.[3] mr shaw was up, and brought up mr Quincys Children to Mr Torrys at the Bridge. tell mr Quincy they were very well, as was miss sophia who made me a visit yesterday and grows finely.[4] son having a fellow feeling for Your Friend, you must not forget to tell all this to him, however trivial it May appear to those who are not parents—

Now all family Matters are arranged, I shall turn my mind to those which are National; and begin to look out for the *Message*. Miranda is one of Tallyrands agents I have not a doubt and as such every movement should be carefully watchd.— we shall hear more of that Man. he is capable of troubling the waters, and fishing in them too.

Your Brother & sister are gone to Haverhill

Present me kindly to all Friends and let me hear from You as often as you can

Your affectionate Mother   Abigail Adams—

RC (Adams Papers); addressed by JA: "The Hon[ble] / John Quincy Adams / Senator of the U. States / Washington"; endorsed: "My Mother. 29. Nov[r:] 1805. / 9. Dec[r:] rec[d:]."

[1] TBA's letter to JQA has not been found. The other letters were JQA to AA, 17 Nov., and AA to JQA, 21 Nov., both above.

[2] Probably Lydia Gay Turner (1758–1808), wife of John Turner of Quincy and sister of Henry Turner Gay (1766–1844), who resided on School Street. The students were likely Nathaniel Augustus Barrett (b. 1800) and Samuel Barrett (b. 1801), sons of Maj. John Barrett (d. 1810) and his late wife, Elizabeth, and

Mary Brackett (b. 1796) and Thomas Odiorne Brackett (b. 1799), the eldest children of Capt. James and Elizabeth Odiorne Brackett (Sprague, *Braintree Families*).

[3] Gov. Caleb Strong issued a proclamation on 17 Oct., declaring 28 Nov. a day of thanksgiving in Massachusetts (*New-England Palladium*, 22 Oct.).

[4] Possibly Abner Torrey (ca. 1767–1809). Maria Sophia Quincy (1805–1886) was the fourth child of Eliza Susan Morton and Josiah Quincy III (Sprague, *Braintree Families*; CFA, *Diary*, 1:312; *Boston Evening Journal*, 1 Jan. 1887).

John Quincy Adams to Abigail Adams

Washington 3. December 1805.

This morning I had the satisfaction of receiving your kind letter of the 21st: ulto: which partly relieved me from the anxiety occasioned by the letter of a previous date from my brother, mentioning your illness and confinement—[1] The weather has of late been so remarkably fine and mild in this quarter that I hope its benign influence has been extended to your regions, and has restored you entirely to health— I rejoyce to hear that my boys are so well, and that George behaves himself to the satisfaction of my Aunt.

I wrote to my brother from Philadelphia; and expected to have left that City, the day after I closed my letter to him—[2] But we were about five minutes too late for the Newcastle Packet of that morning, though it carried off all our baggage, and we followed it the next day— We found our trunks safely stored at Newcastle, and continued our route by the way of French-town and Baltimore— We arrived safely here on Friday the 29th: having had the pleasure of Mr: Tracy's company from Philadelphia— We were two Nights out on the Water, and the Packets were so crowded with passengers, that we had hardly 1/3 of a bed to each person— But our friend Tracy has such an inexhaustible fund of pleasantry and good-humour, that I never felt less of tediousness on a journey, in my life, and when we arrived I almost regretted that we had reached the spot of our destination— His health I am sorry to say is far from being so good as his Spirits, though better than when I left him here last Spring.

Both Houses of Congress formed a Quorum yesterday, being the first day of the Session— The Vice-President not being here, Mr: Smith of Maryland was chosen President of the Senate pro Tempore, and Mr: Macon after three trials was chosen Speaker of the House of Representatives— A feeble attempt was made by what they call the Eastern Interest to set up General Varnum as Speaker, but he had only 27 votes— More than one hundred members were present.— There were some scattering votes also for Mr: Smith of Connecticut, Mr: Gregg of Pennsylvania, and M^r: Dawson of Virginia; all which prevented the Speaker from obtaining a positive majority at the two first trials.[3]

The President's Message has just been received, and read— It will probably reach you in the newspaper's as soon as this letter, which dispenses me from giving you many of its particulars— It speaks of our differences with *Great-Britain, and with Spain*, in a tone of Spirit, which has not been usual in the late Communications from the National Executive—Recommends measures for the protection of our Sea-ports—Modifications of the *Militia-Laws*, and more gun-boats— It hints slightly at the materials for 74 gun ships, which are on hand, but without positively recommending their employment. The State of the Treasury is flourishing in the highest degree.[4]

I shall be much obliged to you for any information you can obtain of a comfortable house at or near Cambridge for the next Summer— I shall probably abandon all thoughts of taking M^r: Davenport's house; but I should much prefer a situation near Boston to the place where M^r: Wigglesworth lived—[5]

With my love and duty to my father, and all the family, I remain, my dear Mother, faithfully your's   John Quincy Adams.[6]

RC (Adams Papers); addressed: "M^rs: A. Adams. / Quincy."; internal address: "M^rs: A. Adams."; endorsed: "Mr J Q Adams. / Dec^br 3^d 1805."

[1] TBA's letter to JQA has not been found.
[2] JQA to TBA, 21 Nov., above.
[3] The 9th Congress convened on 2 December. George Clinton as the new vice president did not take his seat as president of the Senate until 16 Dec., and Maryland's Samuel Smith served as president pro tempore in the interim. While Nathaniel Macon (1757–1837) of North Carolina emerged the victor as Speaker of the House, representatives receiving votes included Joseph Bradley Varnum of Massachusetts, John Dawson, Andrew Gregg, and John Cotton Smith (1765–1845), Yale 1783, who represented Connecticut in the House from Nov. 1800 until Aug. 1806 (*Annals of Congress*, 9th Cong., 1st sess., p. 9, 20, 254; *Biog. Dir. Cong.*).
[4] Thomas Jefferson submitted his annual address to Congress on 3 Dec. 1805 and it was read in both chambers the same day. The address was printed in the Washington, D.C., *National Intelligencer*, 3 Dec., and reprinted in the Boston press from 11 Dec.; see, for example, the *Columbian Centinel*, 11 Dec., and the *Repertory*, 13 December. JQA summarized the major points, including increasing military preparedness and countering foreign depredations against shipping and commerce. He also pointed to more uplifting news about the liberation of American prisoners from Tripoli, "friendly discussions" with Tunis, and that diplomacy with several Native American nations yielded treaties and land sales beneficial to the United States. Jefferson also reported on relations with Spain, for which see JQA to TBA, 2 Jan. 1806, and note 2, below (*Annals of Congress*, 9th Cong., 1st sess., p. 11–16, 256–257).
[5] Rufus Davenport was a Boston merchant who operated from No. 23 Long Wharf from the mid-1790s. After 1803 he became a partner in the development of Cambridgeport, speculating in lands and canal development with the hope of creating a port. In Oct. 1805, JQA visited Cambridgeport with Davenport to view properties he had available. Although JQA was interested in one "beyond West-Boston-Bridge," he ultimately could not "reconcile" himself to it (Boston *Columbian Centinel*, 17 Dec. 1796; Boston *Repertory*, 12 Nov. 1805; Paige, *Hist. of Cambridge, Mass.*, 1:176, 179,

180; JQA, *Diary*, 29 Oct. 1805, 7 Nov., 12 May 1806).

⁶ JQA next wrote to AA on 16 Dec. 1805, reporting a lack of "bustle and animation" in Congress despite the president's message. He also voiced his belief that debates about "non-importations and prohibitory duties" would not come to fruition (Adams Papers).

Louisa Catherine Adams to Abigail Adams

Dear Madam   Washington Dec 6th. 1805

After a pleasant although extremely fatiguing journey we have safely arrived at Mrs. Hellens were we found all the family in good health and spirits Mr. Adams's health is much improved and he has gain'd flesh on the journey but I much fear that the exercise he takes will prove too much and again reduce him to his former state of debility—

My spirits and health have both been very indifferent since my arrival and I hourly feel the loss of my Children more sensibly, convinced as I am of the safety and happiness they enjoy still now that I am again perfectly domesticated I feel the want of their Society and the Solitude

I regret was extremely sorry to hear of your indisposition I flatter'd myself you would escape this year from any farther attacks I hope you will entirely lose the Cough before the winter sets in and suffer no farther inconvenience from it—

Mrs: Randolph the Presidents daughter is here[1] I am going to pay my respects this morning I have not yet seen Mrs: Quincey she arrived before us some time the Question of ettiquette still occasions a great deal of trouble here and the heads of department are very much puzzled how to act as it regards Mrs: Merry—who still keeps up her state[2]

Elizas Cough is still very bad Mama and the family unite in best wishes for your health and that of all your family Kiss my darling Children for me over and over gain and remind them constantly of their mother whose every wish on this earth centres in them should you have any apprehension of Georges having worms give him five drops of spirit of Terpentine upon a lump of Sugar every other morning[3] and believe me dear your obliged and affectionate   L C A.

RC (Adams Papers); addressed: "Mrs: A Adams / Quincey near / Boston"; endorsed: "Mrs L Adams / Decbr 6 1805."

[1] That is, Martha Jefferson Randolph, for whom see LCA, *D&A*, 1:216.

[2] For Elizabeth Death Leathes Merry, the wife of British minister to the United States Anthony Merry, and the furor over breaches of diplomatic etiquette on their arrival in Washington, D.C., in 1803, see vol. 15:308, 317, 318.

[3] Physicians like Benjamin Rush recommended oil of turpentine for resolving intestinal worms (Rush, *Medical Inquiries and Observations*, 2d rev. edn., 4 vols., Phila., 1805, 1:226, 231, Shaw-Shoemaker, No. 9290).

December 1805

Abigail Adams to John Quincy Adams

my dear son   Quincy December 17th 1805

I began a Letter to you on the 10 of this month left it unfinishd, and so it is like to remain, an old Letter being of no more value than an old almanack—for to know how things are, when absent from the Scene, is better than to learn how they were a week before. at that period I had not heard of your safe arrival at washington. Since I have received two Letters, one dated the 21st Novbr and the other the 3d of December—[1] we have rejoiced in the fine weather which we presume attended you through Your journey. with the exception of two or three rainy days, we have had it uncommonly mild, and soft, not a single day, like the harshness of the weather the last fortnight you past here— the last week we had two cold North west winday days—but this day is as clear and fine as possible; our People are now employd in sight of my window plowing, breaking up as the Farmers call it—

you have Seen in the papers the choice of mr Ames as President of Harvered colledge—[2] it was a surprize to every one, as he had never been mentiond; it is not thought, that he will accept. he will make a good President if he could be persuaded to take the Chair. I have not heard of any House except the one I mentiond. it is the House mr sewal lived in, three stories high, and a very good House, it is said to be—[3]

Bates put up his pews about 2 oclock in the day, and before dark, the whole number were sold of. Mr Tufts bought the best pew I think in the whole, Number 4, the first Broad Ile pew which Bates made & next to Burrels. it sold for 200 25 dollors they all went off, up the Ile for more than 200— I think the amount of the whole sale exceeded 5000 dollors— the Two Mr Greenleafs mr Apthorp mr Millar & mr A Baxter were purchasers. Major Vinal capt White and dr Lovell of weymouth— in short, I believe ten more would have sold.[4]

We have at length what under the federal administration would have been calld a War message purchased with 15 Million of dollors— and a Minister Sent to provoke it, by the most base and disgracefull conduct— if that has been justly reported—a penny wise administration—the overflowing treasury will soon find ways and Means of disbursment— tell mr Tracy I rejoice in his fine spirits, and wish most sincerely for a confirmation of his Health. I hope he will live to see a reestablishment of federal principles and measures, but I fear there is Some incurable defect at the very core.

By accounts received tis Said by way of Holland: the Austrians are totally defeated.[5] I can Say with Cowper—

> My Ear is pain'd
> My soul is sick with eve'ry day's report
> of wrong and outrage with which Earth is fill'd
> There is no flesh in Mans obdurate heart,
> It does not feel for Man—[6]

Bonaparte is a comet, a blaizing one. Mankind gaze and are astonished at his power—which every Victory increases— You will read in the Centinal of december 14th a Peice first published in the Repertory, asscribed to the pen of Mr Ames—called "the combined powers and France"—[7] you will read it with interest— you will have a much more busy time in congress than was contemplated. You must keep yourself from becomeing too anxious I wish you could get Lodgings nearer the capitol— as You have not the encumberance of children with you, I should suppose you would not find it difficult— I am glad to find from Mrs Quincys Letters that she is so perfectly satisfied with her situation, and accommodations let them know that their little Girl grows finely: what not a word about my own Children? Why I must reserve that subject, for a Letter to their Mamma. I told John I was writing to you. he desired a pencil and peice of paper, and has been sometime employd in writing a Letter to you[8] he says, but he does not Love to see me write. he cannot talk so much; and play round me when thus engaged—

Your Father designs to write to you Soon. I am your truly affectionate / Mother

A Adams

RC (Adams Papers); addressed: "John Quincy Adams Esqr / Washington"; endorsed: "My Mother 17. Dec^r: 1805. / 26. Dec^r: rec^d:."

[1] JQA's letters to AA were dated 17 Nov. and 3 Dec.; he also wrote to TBA on 21 Nov., all above.

[2] The Boston press on 13 Dec. reported Fisher Ames' election as president of Harvard College; see, for example, the Boston *Repertory* and *New-England Palladium*. The news circulated broadly and was reported in Washington, D.C., by Christmas. Ames was to replace Rev. Joseph Willard, who had died in Sept. 1804. He declined the post in March 1806, and the Harvard Corporation elected instead Samuel Webber, which prompted the resignation of the interim president, Eliphalet Pearson (vol. 15:443; Philadelphia *United States Gazette*, 20 Dec. 1805; New York *American Citizen*, 21 Dec.; Washington, D.C., *National Intelligencer*, 25 Dec.; Boston *Repertory*, 7 March 1806; *New-England Palladium*, 14 March). For Webber's installation, see JQA to LCA, 10 May, and note 2, below.

[3] AA mentioned the former residence of Rev. Edward Wigglesworth in her letter to JQA of 21 Nov. 1805, and note 2, above. The house for lease was a nearby dwelling built in 1766 on land purchased from Wigglesworth by Stephen Sewall. Sewall (1734–1804), Harvard 1761, was the Hancock Professor of Hebrew and Oriental Languages at Harvard College from 1764 to 1785 and married Wigglesworth's daughter Rebecca in 1763. The three-story home was located on the site currently occu-

pied by Harvard's Boylston Hall (*Sibley's Harvard Graduates*, 15:107, 109, 112, 113; Paige, *Hist. of Cambridge, Mass.*, 1:691).

⁴ For the expansion of the meetinghouse of the First Church of Quincy, see TBA to JQA, 23 Dec. 1804, and note 7, above. The purchasers of the pews constructed by Weymouth housewright John Bates included Cotton Tufts Jr., Peter Burrell, Daniel Greenleaf, Thomas Greenleaf, George Henry Ward Apthorp, Maj. Ebenezer Miller, Anthony Wibird Baxter, Maj. William Vinal (d. 1818), Weymouth physician James Lovell (1768–1820), and possibly Capt. Elihu White (d. 1836) of East Braintree (vols. 10:357, 12:263, 13:175; Sprague, *Braintree Families*; *Dedham Gazette*, 6 March 1818; *History of Weymouth*, 3:402–403).

⁵ In July 1805 Austria joined Great Britain and Russia in the Third Coalition and by the end of September had amassed 60,000 troops along the Bavarian border, concentrated at Ulm. Between 8 and 15 Oct. French troops defeated an advance division before encircling Ulm and prompting the Austrian offer to surrender on 17 October. The Boston *Repertory*, 17 Dec., published reports from the Netherlands of the French victory at Ulm and the destruction of the Austrian Army (*Cambridge Modern Hist.*, 9:249, 253, 254, 896).

⁶ William Cowper, "The Time-Piece," *The Task*, Book II, lines 5–9.

⁷ The article from the Boston *Columbian Centinel*, 14 Dec., referenced by AA appeared first in the Boston *Repertory*, 10 December. The piece was written before the Austrian defeat was known and argued that the European forces coalescing against France would not be enough to defeat Napoleon's despotism and the complicity of the "base and desperately wicked" within French client states. Britain remained an "invincible" bastion against French imperialism, the newspaper claimed, but the "Coalition, as it affects *England* . . . will deceive her hopes and aggravate her embarrassments." The article also declared that the effects on American commerce would be dire.

⁸ Not found.

Abigail Adams to Louisa Catherine Adams

My Dear Mrs Adams   Quincy, December 17 1805

I received your Letter of December 6th on the 14th and was very glad to hear of Your safe arrival at Washington; the journey at this Season when the days are so short must always be fatigueing. it must have been less so to you than it would have been with the children, tho I doubt not You must miss them very much. they are very well. John is as thick as he is long, has out grown his cloaths. we cannot button his coats, and we are obligd to take out the sleaves of his shirts to lengthen the arm holes— I say to him often, John do not eat so hearty— Grandmam—I stuff like a pig. well John I am writing to Your Mamma what shall I say. please to Say duty to Mamma, and John's a good Boy. who Says so? Grandmamma— he comes again Grandmamma—I did not Say duty to Aunt Eliza. well must I put that in? yes— he is really a very good Boy, and a very pleasent temperd Child, never wants any Severity used towards him: George has more frequent ill turns and does not incline to be so fleshy. I do not think that humour which troubled him so much last year is radically cured altho it does not now shew itself, outwardly. he is very good, pretty Volatile, full of Life and play— I can Easily believe that You must feel a void, not easily supplied tho Your sisters little ones must in Some measure

Supply their place. I am sorry Eliza should take back with her, as dissagreable a companion as she brought with her— to reason and expostulate against the strong arm of fashion, are but weak and feeble weapon's; She is as powerfull in her dominions as Bonaparte is in his. She levels all distinctions. Decency Submits to her Sway, and Modesty looses all her Blushes. even a fig leaf is thought too cumbersome and untransparent for the Vestals of the present day. they have quite an abhorrence to all free Masonary and have no . . . .[1] all, allmost all, may be seen, from the crown of the Head, to the Sole of the foot, but as in early Life they have not been innured to this mode, and fashion, the most delicate and fragile constitutions, fall early and premature Sacrifices.

I wish mr Adams would take lodgings nearer the capitol, tho in the fine weather the excercise may be good for his Health, it cannot be so through the Season— wet & bad weather he must be exposed and will take colds.

My Health is in a great measure restored. I kept close whilst my cough lasted, and in about three weeks it left me. Present my Regards to Your Mother, and the rest of the family. how is Caroline? remember me to her. I thought She appeard to be attached to Boston, and not to dislike Quincy and I felt the more attached to her in concequence of it. next to our Relatives, we feel these local propensities and predelictions

Mrs Adams and Louissa request to be rememberd— tell Eliza not to lose her Spirits— I shall think if she does, that she pines after Quincy—

Yours affectionatly   A Adams

RC (Adams Papers); addressed: "Mrs Louissa Adams / Washington"; endorsed by JQA: "A. Adams to L. C. Adams 17. Dec^r: 1805."; notation by CFA: "To the same—"

[1] Ellipsis in MS.

John Adams to John Quincy Adams

Dear Sir   Quincy December 23 1805

I ought, before now, to have acknowledged the Receipt of your favours and even now I can do no more than acknowledge them, for what Subject have I for a Letter?[1] Shall I send you diagrams of my Grounds, which the fine Weather of November and December has enabled me to plough, for Corn, Potatoes, Barley Clover and Timothy? But what a Miniature picture of a Lilliputian Plantation, would

December 1805

Six Acres and four Acres and three Acres and two Acres appear in Comparison of President Washingtons which as Mr Lear informed me employed five and thirty Ploughs in continual motion all the Year round. But General Washington was a wise man from his Youth, took good care of himself and married a rich Wife; whereas I was a Simpleton from the beginning, took little care of the main chance and married a Girl as poor as myself. My Plough and my Molecule of Compost have been my important Business.

Now for my Pleasures. I have read the Six first Volumes of Gibbon, the three Vol. of Middletons Life of Cicero, and now I am Seriously Studying Tacitus, by comparing him Word for Word with Murphys Translation; and am Surprized to See, how many more Words he is obliged to Use, than his Author. He gives a faithfull Idea of the Sense: but the Grace, the Brevity and the Pomp of the original are wanting, and I fear must never be expected in English.

I have last read the Dialogue De oratoribus Sive De causis corruptæ Eloquentiæ, which you no doubt have read and will Study to perfection.[2] It is a beauty and well deserves your most critical attention. I have a conceit that a more litteral translation than Murphy's would be more like Tacitus. I have half a Mind to try my hand in the attempt. If it should be found to be only an Old Mans Vanity, what Signifys that?

I have given you an Account of my Business and Pleasures: and now for my Amusements which are all Domestic as you know and chiefly in Sports with my Grand Children. John and I are very intimate and he is as hearty and gay as you can wish. George unites with Us delightfully when he makes Us a Visit, is tollerably well but not such an Hercules as John, He behaves remarkably well, and is in high Credit with his Uncle and Aunt Cranch.

Although the World is in Commotion and great Events are struggling for Birth, in which our Country will be more interested than You and I could wish, it would be ridiculous for me to write, any thing about them. So far from being able to reconnoitre the whole Country, I see no part of it. Our Negotiations with Spain and England, for five Years are a profound Secret. If a Want of Skill in the Cabinet, or in the Negotiators have brought Us into Embarrassments and in a danger of War I think the Saddle should be put upon the right Horse: but it will not be. If We get into a War, in my opinion our Country at home, and especially our Elections will become the Sport of foreign Nations as much as ever our commerce has been. Urbem venalem mature perituram Si modo emptorem invenerit.[3] A Country whose Government can be made and unmade by Such Men as Calender,

Paine Duane Andrew Brown, Peter Markoe, &c &c may be bought and sold like Cattle at Smithfield. My Compliments, wherever they are due.
J. Adams.[4]

Better is a fortune in a wife; than with a wife.[5] both united are very pleasent; I believe the wife was the best calculated for the Husband that could have been obtaind, and the Husband for the wife—

RC (Adams Papers); addressed by TBA: "John Q Adams Esq[r:] / Senator of the U.S. / City of Washington"; internal address: "J. Q. Adams Esq."; endorsed: "My Father. 23. Dec[r:] 1805. / 4. Jan[y:] 1806. rec[d:]"; notation by JA: "Quincy Dec[r.] 26[th.] 1805. Free."

[1] JQA last wrote to JA on 6 Dec., commenting that the "style and tone" of Thomas Jefferson's 3 Dec. message to Congress "have not been fashionable of late." He also enclosed a copy of a bill regarding naval appropriations and reported meeting their "old friend" Capt. Pierre Landais (Adams Papers).

[2] JA's library at MB holds two six-volume London editions of Edward Gibbon's *The History of the Decline and Fall of the Roman Empire*, a complete 1777–1788 edition and a 1783 edition that lacks volume 1; the first two of the three volumes of Conyers Middleton's *The History of the Life of Marcus Tullius Cicero*, London, 1755, with JA's marginal notes; and Tacitus, *Works*, transl. Arthur Murphy, 4 vols., Dublin, 1794. Comments by JA in his 29 Jan. 1806 letter to JQA, below, suggest that he was consulting the more recent Tacitus, *Works*, transl. Murphy, rev. edn., 8 vols., London, 1805, which includes "A Dialogue concerning Oratory, or the Causes of Corrupt Eloquence" (8:7–315) and for which see note 2 to that letter (*Catalogue of JA's Library*; JQA, *Lectures on Rhetoric*, 1:145–147). JQA discussed the dialogue in his 15 Aug. Lecture VI delivered during his Harvard College professorship, for which see JQA to LCA, 15 June, and note 1, below.

[3] "A city for sale and doomed to speedy destruction if it finds a purchaser" (Sallust, *The War with Jurgurtha*, transl. J. C. Rolfe, N.Y., 1921, ch. 35).

[4] AA added the following paragraph on the otherwise blank third page.

[5] John Shebbeare, *The Marriage Act*, 2 vols., London, 1754, 2:46.

John Quincy Adams to William Smith Shaw

Dear Sir. Washington 27. Dec[r:] 1805.

I have to thank you for the receipt of your letter of the 14[th:] inst[t:] and for the last number of the Anthology, which came at the same time—[1] I am much pleased with the Spirit of this publication which appears to improve as it advances, and which I hope you will not suffer to flag— I am much flattered by the partiality of the opinion entertained by the Gentlemen that a regular contribution from me would be useful to the success of the work, though I am sensible how far they overrate my resources in their estimate— The State of my health, and the real pressure of occupation which I have upon me, forbids my undertaking to furnish a constant portion of composition for every month, but I hope to prove my good-will to the association and the establishment, by some occasional assistance from time to time— I am even now reading with particular attention the Life of Washington, with a view to the promise I have made respecting it, and although its accomplishment may be delayed untill the work itself shall be out complete, I shall probably make up in point of quantity for the lapse of time—² I shall always be glad to furnish you with any pamphlets or papers which may useful to you; approving much the additional eight pages you propose to give in future, and the objects to which they will be devoted— But I question whether you will have space enough to give the Congressional debates on interesting subjects, unless it be in a very concise abridgment of them.

I shall endeavour to procure answers to the Questions given you by M^r: Thacher, and forward them to you as soon as possible.³

Gen$^{l:}$ Thayer's receipt was enclosed in your letter; but you mention having received $220 from Delille— The sum he should have paid you was $225. I mention this, because I gave an order on you for 50 dollars in favour of M^r: French,⁴ and your funds will fall short, if you have from Delille only $220.

We have hitherto not entered upon any business of material importance; and at this time we are languishing through what is called the Christmas Holidays. Perhaps with the new year we shall commence our serious labours.

You know we have a Tunisian Embassy here;⁵ and there are also deputations from eight or ten Indian tribes on visits to the seat of Government—⁶ The Africans and Americans sometimes meet, and are objects of mutual curiosity to each other.

One of the Committees of the House of Representatives on the Presidents Message has reported to build 50 gun-boats and 6. Seventy-four gun ships. The gun-boats I presume will pass; but I fear the 74's will sink on the passage.⁷

M^r: Quincy and his family here are well— So are M^r: Cranch and his— So are ours— M^r: Quincy thinks he should hear more frequently from you.

Our weather continues remarkably fine and moderate— I keep a thermometrical register at 8. A. M. 3. P.M. and 9. P.M.— I want one kept at the same hours in Boston to compare them together— I have written to my brother about it.⁸

 Your's sincerely   John Quincy Adams.

RC (MWA:Adams Family Letters); internal address: "M^r: Shaw."; endorsed: "Washington 27 Dec / John Q Adams / Ans 17 Jan"; docketed: "1805 / Decr 27."

¹ In his letter to JQA of 14 Dec. (Adams Papers), Shaw summarized his financial transactions on JQA's behalf and sought assistance with an enclosed set of queries, for which see

note 3, below. Shaw also reported that he was sending by the same mail the *Monthly Anthology* and requested a regular contribution from JQA to add "reputation" and ensure the "complete success" of the endeavor. Founded in 1803 by Boston schoolteacher Phineas Adams, the literary journal *Monthly Anthology, and Boston Review* in mid-1804 came under the direction of a group of Boston intellectuals who promoted it as "favourable to the interest of science in general, and of belles lettres studies in particular." Shaw, Arthur Maynard Walter, and Joseph Stevens Buckminster, the minister of Boston's Brattle Street Church, became the prime movers for the journal, although the Anthology Society organized for the purpose in Oct. 1805. The journal survived the transformation of the Anthology Society into the Boston Athenaeum in 1807, but its list of subscribers never topped 500 and the journal folded in 1811 (Kaplan, *Men of Letters*, p. 184, 185, 186, 189; *The Monthly Anthology; or, Massachusetts Magazine*, Boston, 1804, Shaw-Shoemaker, No. 54522; *ANB*).

² JQA had read the first two volumes of John Marshall, *The Life of George Washington*, 5 vols., Phila., 1804–[1807]. By 7 Jan. 1806 he was through the fourth volume, and though he spoke with Marshall about the pending fifth, a review of the work does not appear to have been completed before it was published in 1807 (vol. 15:232; JQA, *Diary*, 6 Nov. 1805, 21, 31 Dec., 7 Jan. 1806, 26 Feb.).

³ Shaw enclosed in his letter of 14 Dec. 1805 (Adams Papers) a list of queries from Peter Oxenbridge Thacher, not found, seeking JQA's "goodness to enquire of some gentleman from Kentucky in Congress respecting them." Thacher (1776–1843), Harvard 1796, was a Boston lawyer. JQA spoke to Kentucky lawyer and senator Buckner Thruston and enclosed a response in a letter to Shaw of 27 Jan. 1806 (MWA:Adams Family Letters), where he characterized Thruston as "a gentleman of the profession, in whose information on this subject, I think the fullest reliance may be placed." JQA also promised to send documents on public affairs as well as his "thermometrical register" (*Genealogy and Biographical Sketches, of the Descendants of Thomas and Anthony Thacher*, Vineland, N.J., 1872, p. 21, 22; *Biog. Dir. Cong.*).

⁴ Likely Moses French Jr., a former Adams tenant (vol. 13:394).

⁵ Tunisian minister Sidi Soliman Mellimelli visited the United States between Nov. 1805 and Sept. 1806. The purpose of Mellimelli's mission was to diffuse tensions between the two nations. In part, Tunis sought indemnification for vessels captured by the United States in April 1805, while Thomas Jefferson sought a peace that was not dependent on U.S. tribute. The Tunisian diplomat and his retinue captured popular interest, and the visit provided consistent fodder for the American press. Negotiations, however, stalled over the issue of tribute, and the president reported their failure to Congress in April 1806 (Jason Zeledon, "'As Proud as Lucifer': A Tunisian Diplomat in Thomas Jefferson's America," *Diplomatic History*, 41:155, 158–159, 175 [Jan. 2017]; Madison, *Papers, Secretary of State Series*, 11:270–272).

⁶ Representatives of several Native American nations were also then in Washington, D.C., to negotiate or finalize treaties with the United States, most of which resulted in Native American land cessions in exchange for payments of cash or goods, promises of military protection, or pledges to settle grievances. Three treaties between the United States and the Cherokee Nation were then in process: the first negotiated 25 Oct. 1805, consented to by the Senate 19 Dec., and proclaimed by the United States 24 April 1806; the second negotiated 27 Oct. 1805, consented to 23 Dec., and proclaimed 10 June 1806; and the third negotiated 7 Jan. 1806, consented to 12 April, and proclaimed 23 May 1807. A treaty with the Creek Nation was negotiated 14 Nov. 1805, consented to 23 Dec., and proclaimed 2 June 1806. Two additional agreements with confederations of Native Americans were also under consideration: one with the Delaware, Potawatomi, Miami, Eel River, and Wea Nations, negotiated 21 Aug. 1805, received Senate consent on 24 Dec. and was proclaimed 24 April 1806; and another with the Wyandot, Ottawa, Anishinaabe, Munsee, Delaware, Shawnee, and Potawatomi Nations, negotiated 4 July 1805, was consented to on 17 Jan. 1806 and proclaimed 24 April. While JQA mentioned the presence of members of the Osage, Sac, and Fox Nations in his letter to TBA of 2 Jan., below, there were no pending agreements with the Osage Nation, and the most recent pact with the Sac and Fox Nations had been proclaimed 21 Feb. 1805 (U.S. Senate, *Exec. Jour.*, 9th Cong., 1st sess., p. 7, 9–10, 11, 15–16, 32; Vine Deloria Jr. and Raymond J. DeMallie, eds., *Documents of American Indian Diplomacy: Treaties, Agreements, and Conventions*,

1775–1979, 2 vols, Norman, Okla., 1999, 1:185, 202, 253; Charles J. Kappler and others, comp., *Indian Affairs: Laws and Treaties*, 7 vols., Washington, D.C., 1903–1971, 2:74, 77, 80, 82, 84, 85, 90).

[7] The House of Representatives on 4 Dec. formed a committee to consider the construction of new naval vessels. The committee issued a report on 23 Dec. proposing appropriations of $250,000 for the construction of fifty gunboats and $660,000 for six battleships. As JQA predicted, Congress approved the former but not the latter. On 16 April 1806 the House passed a bill to fund the gunboats, which the Senate passed with minor amendments on the 18th. The House concurred and the president signed it into law on 21 April (U.S. House, *Jour.*, 9th Cong., 1st sess., p. 188, 209, 393–394, 406, 420; U.S. Senate, *Jour.*, 9th Cong., 1st sess., p. 90, 91; U.S. House, *Report of the Committee Appointed on the Fourth Instant, on So Much of the Message of the President of the United States, as Relates . . . to the Building of Seventy-Four Gun Ships*, Washington, D.C., 1805, p. 4, Shaw-Shoemaker, No. 9612; *U.S. Statutes at Large*, 2:402).

[8] In a letter to TBA of 18 Dec. 1805, JQA commented on both the current furor over U.S. relations with Great Britain and Spain and Joseph Dennie Jr.'s recent legal triumph. He also noted his plan to take thrice daily notations of the temperature in Washington, D.C., and asked his brother to do the same at Quincy twice per day. He thought the comparison would "make a very good closing page for the monthly Anthology" and suggested that if TBA found the project "too much of a philosophical *petty kick-show*," he transfer his request to Shaw (Adams Papers).

John Quincy Adams to Thomas Boylston Adams

Washington 2. January 1806.

We have so little business on hand that it was not thought necessary to commence the year with a Session for transacting it; and this morning we have adjourned for the purpose of letting the Tunisian Minister come and pay us a visit; I cannot employ the leisure of the moment better than in answering your letter of the 15th: and 16th: of last Month.[1]

Your opinion of the Message will probably not be altered by the proceedings of Congress upon it— I never believed that any thing really vigorous would be done at this Session, and every indication since its commencement has confirmed me in the opinion. Although you will see a report of a Committee recommending the building of six seventy-four gun ships and fifty gun-boats, yet you will not expect to see it adopted by the House of Representatives— The Committee on the Spanish aggressions are also about to report— The Committee consists of seven members, Mr: John Randolph being chairman— One Member has been sometime absent, and the others have been divided equally, between two Reports; one made by the chairman, and promising vigorous measures to defend the disputed territory—the other drawn by Mr: Bidwell, and proposing a *second* purchase—with an appropriation from five to ten Millions to buy the *Florida's*.[2]

Yesterday being New Year's day, with all the beau-monde, including Tunisians, Cherokees, Sacs, Foxes and Osages we went to pay the homage of our high consideration to the Presidents— Many of the Indians were in full costume, that is to say three quarters naked— The company was more numerous than I have ever known on a like occasion; having the additional stimulus of curiosity to see the barbarians of both Continents, as well as our own.[3]

I have enclosed a number of documents under cover to your father, for M$^{r:}$ Shaw—And have written his name upon them, that they may be known to be for him.— I suppose you will be in Boston during the greatest part of the two months to come, and shall accordingly address my letters to you there— I hope your legislative functions will not so engross your time, as to prevent your communicating frequently with me.[4]

The Tunisian Ambassador has been to pay his visit— As we could not with propriety receive him into the body of the house, while the house was sitting, we adjourned; but the Vice-President kept the chair and the members their Seats— He took the Secretary's chair, and his two guards had chairs placed for them which they took.— Before he came into the Senate, he had been into the House of Representatives, but they did not adjourn to let him in.[5] A member was speaking when he went in— On coming here he asked our President who the man was, that he heard speaking in the other Room; on being told he was a member of the house, he enquired whether all those men he saw there had a right to speak—being answered in the affirmative, he said that it must take one, two, or three years to finish any business— It was just so he said, in *Italy*, where he knew that sometimes it took *twenty* years to decide a cause. One of our Members undertook to explain to him the difference between our Legislative Assemblies, and a *Judicial* Court; but he said it was all the same— In his Country they never took more than half an hour to finish any business; and he appeared fully convinced of the infinite superiority of *their* mode of transacting affairs.

I will thank you to ask M$^{r:}$ Shaw to be on the lookout for a house for me in Cambridge, and if he hears of any which he thinks will suit me, to enquire and inform me at what Rent it may be had— He mentioned to me before I came away that M$^{r:}$ William Winthrop's house would probably be to let the next Season, and promised to enquire about it—[6] But I have not heard further from him on the subject— I should be willing to engage a house from the first of May, though in the manner we *progress*, (as the Virginians say) I shall probably not get home before June.

1. "THE PRAIRIE DOG SICKENED AT THE STING OF THE HORNET," BY JAMES AKIN, 1806
See page ix

If you see Captain Richard Beale, I wish you to tell him that the Committee of Claims in the House of Representatives have reported against the prayer of his petition, as I always expected they would, and the House will undoubtedly accept their Report— The Chairman of the Committee of Claims to whom I urged with all my power the equity of M{r:} Beale's request, answered me that his resort must be to Captain Nicholson, against whom he had no doubt but he must recover—[7] Without being very sangwine in that expectation, I am at least confident, that it is the only chance he has of recovering at-all.

We are now all well; as are M{r:} Cranch & his family and guests— I am very anxious to hear as good news from Quincy; being a little uneasy on account of George, from what you and my mother in her last Letter say of him—[8] My wife has been unwell, but appears now to be quite recovered.

Your's in all sincerity and affection.

RC (Adams Papers); internal address: "T. B. Adams Esqr—"; endorsed: "J Q Adams Esqr / 2{d:} January 1806 / 15{th:} Rec{d:} / 19{th:} Answ{d:}."

[1] Not found.

[2] Thomas Jefferson on 6 Dec. 1805 sent a confidential message to Congress further detailing the deteriorating situation with Spain. In a closed-door session on the same day, the House of Representatives referred the new message to a committee led by John Randolph and composed of Barnabus Bidwell of Massachusetts, Robert Brown of Pennsylvania, Gurdon Saltonstall Mumford of New York, Joseph Hopper Nicholson of Maryland, John Cotton Smith of Connecticut, and David Rogerson Williams of South Carolina. Mumford was probably the absent committee member mentioned by JQA, who accurately summarized the competing recommendations that emerged from the committee on 3 Jan. 1806. A resolution offered by Randolph called for raising troops to protect the disputed border between the Orleans Territory and the Floridas. A second resolution offered by Bidwell proposed an unspecified appropriation for the settlement of U.S. claims to West Florida and the purchase of East Florida from Spain. House members defeated Randolph's resolution on 11 January. The second resolution, amended to a $2 million appropriation, passed on 16 Jan., for which see Descriptive List of Illustrations, No. 1, above. In March Randolph successfully appealed to the House to make the report and the journal of its secret sessions on the Floridas public, for which see Eliza Susan Morton Quincy to AA, 6 April, and note 4, below (*Annals of Congress*, 9th Cong., 1st sess., p. 1117–1118, 1120–1121, 1131–1132; *Biog. Dir. Cong.*; David A. Carson, "That Ground Called Quiddism: John Randolph's War with the Jefferson Administration," *Journal of American Studies*, 20:85 [April 1986]). For congressional consideration of naval preparedness, see JQA to William Smith Shaw, 27 Dec. 1805, and note 7, above.

[3] JQA, LCA, and Catherine Nuth Johnson attended Jefferson's annual levee at the President's House, which the *Washington Federalist*, 4 Jan. 1806, called "the most brilliant Levee ever known here," noting that companies of light horse and infantry paraded outside. Senator William Plumer of New Hampshire reported that the president greeted guests and "there was a full band of Music which played well & with fine effect. The side boards were numerous & amply furnished with a rich variety of wines, punch, cakes—ice cream." Plumer noted that JQA was one of only three Federalists present, a fact the Boston *Repertory*, 24 Jan., attributed to Federalists not being invited. Among the levee guests were Tunisian minister Sidi Soliman Mellimelli and forty of the Native American delegates who were visiting Washington, D.C. (JQA, *Diary*; Plumer, *Memorandum of Proceedings*, p. 363, 364).

[4] On 8 May 1805 TBA had been elected as Quincy's representative to the Mass. General

Court, serving from 29 May to 14 March 1806. In May 1806 he was a Federalist nominee for one of two Norfolk County seats in the state senate, but those seats went to Democratic-Republicans John Ellis and John Howe. In the same election Capt. Benjamin Beale Jr. was elected to TBA's former seat in the house of representatives (*New-England Palladium*, 10 May 1805; Charles J. Babbitt, *State Library of Massachusetts Hand-List of Legislative Sessions and Session Laws*, Boston, 1912, p. 213; Boston *Repertory*, 21 March 1806; Boston *Columbian Centinel*, 14 May; Boston *Democrat*, 7 May).

⁵ Vice President George Clinton informed the Senate on the morning of 2 Jan. that Mellimelli asked to visit at noon that day. During subsequent debate, JQA argued that no diplomat had yet been afforded such an audience and cautioned against setting a precedent. Other members questioned whether a Tunisian minister should be afforded privileges not even extended to a full ambassador. The solution was to adjourn the Senate and informally host Mellimelli. The diplomat first observed debate in the House of Representatives before visiting the Senate chamber for twenty minutes, with Buckner Thruston conversing with him in Italian and translating for his fellow senators (JQA, *Diary*; Plumer, *Memorandum of Proceedings*, p. 364–365; *Biog. Dir. Cong.*).

⁶ William Winthrop (1753–1825), Harvard 1770, entered the mercantile trade before the American Revolution and later served as a justice of the peace and register of deeds for Middlesex County. He was a benefactor of Harvard who also collected biographies of its alumni and from 1791 resided in an old mansion on Arrow Street (*Sibley's Harvard Graduates*, 17:460, 461, 462; *Boston Commercial Gazette*, 10 Feb. 1825).

⁷ On 4 Dec. 1805 JQA visited the House of Representatives to enlist Josiah Quincy III's aid in presenting a petition from Richard Copeland Beale. Beale, who had served aboard the U.S. frigate *Constitution*, Capt. Samuel Nicholson, sought compensation for expenses incurred during his naval service. Previous requests had already been denied by the naval and treasury departments. The House referred the petition to committee on the same day, and on 13 Dec. the resulting report was read and tabled (vol. 13:64, 102; JQA, *Diary*; U.S. House, *Jour.*, 9th Cong., 1st sess., p. 188, 197).

⁸ See AA to LCA, 17 Dec., above.

Abigail Adams to John Quincy Adams

my Dear son Quincy Jan'ry 9th 1806

This is the first Snow which we have had of any concequence; and this promises to be deep. it began last night and has continued increasing all day. it is now mid day, and the Storm is cold and severe, the wind North. I cannot tell you how the Glass Stands, for when I went in the absence of your Brother & Sister; to take an observation as I promised, the window was frozen down so tight, that I could not open it.—

you gave yourself unnecessary anxiety about George. he is very well, and has never but two days been detaind from school since you went away, and then by a cold, and a trifling complaint in his Bowels. the stopage in his Head is intirely gone. he has a good appetite, grows fast, and is fleshy enough for a running Boy. Master John my Charge, puffs like a very corpulent Man when he has walkd fast. his face is round as an apple Rosy as a carnation, his Eyes Brilliant and sparkling as diamonds his Lips a virmillion. a painter might take Hebe from the exuberence of his Health, and Adonis from the Beauty of his face these are his infant traits; time will harden his features; and the Sun burnish his complexion. he ought not to grow up as handsome as he is now, but what I value more than his Beauty, is his disposition which is very pleasent, and engageing. he is Volatile like all sprightly Children. I cannot fix him to his Letters, but he will learn them soon enough. he talks much more about his Pappa and Mamma than he did when they first went away; he does not realish my Sitting down to write, because it imposes a restraint upon him; I calld him just now to come to me. he replid, Grandmamma, what You call me for when You writing? he is very talkative and amusing.— this page is for Mamma, as well as Pappa— Your Brother wrote you last week and Your Father too I think, so I did not feel anxious least you should not hear from us— last Evening I received your Letter of Dec^{br} 30th I shall deliver Your Message to Your Brother when he returns from Dedham and do not doubt but that he will pay due respect to Your recommendation.[1] the General Court meet on wednesday next.

Your Father used to say that N Englanders were always the Dupes of the Southern states. I conjecture they are so now, as it respects the motion made, or the recommendation to appropriate Eight or ten Millions to purchase the Floridas— it is suspected that the measure would be unpopular, and, our wise Men are ready to take the odium upon their own shoulders or may be; they are desirious of making as good a speck out of the purchase; as it is said the Chancelor, and Joel Barlow Swan, Parker and others have done out of the 15 Millions—[2]

Sunday Jan^{ry} 12th—

an interruption has retarded my pen, and delayed my closing my Letter. George dinned with me to day in good health and desires me to tell his Pappa and Mamma that he is very well, and a very good Boy; but that Thomas and John make him very wild and Noisy.[3] John is So happy to See George, that their weekly meeting is quite an entertainment John is however much more manageable alone; we shall all get too fond of him; he is so easily reasoned into doing right, that very little authority controuls him.—

I have not had an opportunity Yet to make Such an inquiry of Mr storer respecting the House which was that owned by mr Sewal, as to enable me to write satisfactory upon the Subject— the House owned by mr Fairweather is also to let, and you know that it is a large and Handsome House.[4] Dr Waterhouse has mentiond it to Your Father.— You may however procure one nearer Boston I suppose, but it is like the Rent will be much higher, for an inferiour House— Mr Ames, I

January 1806

very much fear will not accept the appointment; some of his Friends flatterd themselves that he would, as the Nomination was universally approved, but last week he fell down, either in an apopletic or an Epileptick fit. he has recoverd his Senses again; but it will no doubt affect his spirits, and be considerd by him as an objection to entering upon so arduous an office— You have not mentiond Your own Health; how is it? Your Friends write me that You do not look so well as when You first arrived and they think that the walk twice a day is too much for you[5] in the morning when the weather is fine it might not be an injury to you; but when; exhausted by attention, or perplexd by Buisness; or vext by ignorance or stupidity, a tedious long walk with an empty Stomack is very unhealthy you may depend upon it. it serves to irritate the whole nervous System; which wants Soothing and calming with the oil and wine of comfort and consolation, instead of ploding along on foot a three miles trudge— beside the very look of it will be attributed to a cause which has no foundation some will call it Parsimony, others will call it odity, but all this I should not heed so much as the real injury I conceive it will be to your Health— pray assure me that you will ride in all bad weather—and I shall be easier in My Mind, and go to rest more tranquil at night.—

I would write Seperately to Mrs Adams, but writing to one is writing to Both, and we have so few subjects either novel or amuseing that I should scarcly be able to fill a page to her; I could tell her that mr whitney has had the good luck to have an other of his sisters married in Town to a son of mr James Brackets, a likely young Man, and that the Eldest sister of the whole, has come to Quincy to make a visit.[6] we know not where to find a Husband for her, unless she would take the Major; but we would be cautious of making the proposal, and wish the Lady better Luck—

with my best regards to the whole family / I am my Dear Son your truly / affectionate Mother   Abigail Adams

RC (Adams Papers); endorsed: "My Mother 9. 12 Jan[y:] 1806. / 20. Jan[y:] rec[d:] / 25. d[o:] Ans[d:]."

[1] JA's and TBA's letters to JQA have not been found. In his letter to AA of 30 Dec. 1805, JQA expressed his concern for GWA's health and requested more frequent updates. He also commented on the debate in Congress around purchasing the Floridas and additional territory in Louisiana and described a visiting delegation of Native Americans. His message for TBA was to bring a motion forward in the Mass. General Court supporting the federal government's actions for protecting the nation "against the outrages of *Spain* and *Great-Britain*" (Adams Papers).

[2] The Americans engaged in business or speculation in France included Robert R. Livingston, who helped negotiate the Louisiana Purchase, poet and former diplomat Joel Barlow, and merchants James Swan and Daniel Parker (vols. 5:464, 11:109, 12:95, 13:xii, 15:xii).

[3] That is, Thomas Boylston Adams Norton,

son of Elizabeth Cranch and Rev. Jacob Norton (vols. 13:480).

[4] For the property formerly owned by Stephen Sewall, see AA to JQA of 17 Dec., and note 3, above. Cambridge merchant Thomas Fayerweather (1724–1805) purchased a home on Brattle Street in 1774 and lived there until his death. The house today is part of the Longfellow House–Washington's Headquarters National Historic Site (vol. 8:174; *An Historic Guide to Cambridge*, 2d rev. edn., Cambridge, 1907, p. 110–111).

[5] LCA expressed concerns about JQA's health in her letter to AA of 6 Dec. 1805, above.

[6] Sarah Whitney, a sibling of Rev. Peter Whitney Jr. and Elizabeth Whitney, was married on 6 Jan. 1806 to Lemuel Brackett (1780–1869), son of Mary Spear and James Brackett (vol. 14:141, 618; Frederick Clifton Pierce, *Whitney: The Descendants of John Whitney*, Chicago, 1895, p. 162; Sprague, *Braintree Families*).

Abigail Adams Smith to Francisco de Miranda

Sir   New York jany 13th 1806

in the conversation that passed on Saturday upon the subject of my Sons going with you, it was not mentioned, what Station he was designed to fill in your family. it would be sattisfactory to me to have it defined by you Sir[1]

and he is solicitous to know what services may be required of him, as well as to be informed whether (Short as the time is) there is any preparation upon his part, that he can make to render himself usefull and acceptable to his General   A. Smith

RC (National Academy of History, Venezuela:Miranda Archives, VI:220).

[1] Miranda was preparing to launch an expedition to liberate Venezuela from Spanish rule and agreed to take with him AA2 and WSS's son William Steuben Smith, for which see Descriptive List of Illustrations, No. 2, and Introduction, Part 2, both above.

John Quincy Adams to John Adams

Washington 14. January 1806.

I received some days since your kind favour containing the account of your occupations and amusements; and I have this day that of my brother dated at the close of the last and commencement of the present year—[1] I have occasionally forwarded such public documents to you, as I supposed would be worthy of your perusal, together with the Journals of the two Houses— That of the Senate will I hope furnish you some excuse for my delays in answering the letters of my friends— We have now for several days been seriously engaged in business, and that which is preparing and maturing in select Committees is already more considerable and daily accumulating.[2]

Though from observations I have occasionally heard you make, I have concluded that your opinion of Tacitus is not so favourable as

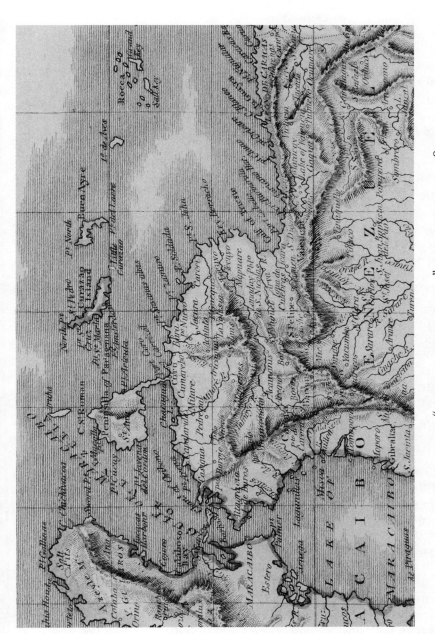

2. DETAIL FROM "CARACCAS AND GUIANA," BY JOHN MOFFAT, 1817

See page x

my own, yet I have no doubt you derived much pleasure from the very attentive perusal you gave him with a constant comparison of the original with Murphy's translation— I have never been much pleased with this translation; for although from his extreme conciseness, and his elliptical style, he is perhaps the most difficult of all the antient prose-writers to translate into a modern language, Murphy appears to me to go into an opposite extreme, and to be unnecessarily diffuse and verbose.— The Dialogue on Eloquence, I have never duly studied, and from the comparison of styles, have not supposed to be the work of Tacitus.

Your ploughing in December, is an occupation which I need not say to you, is much more agreeable than labouring at the political plough— The Season here has been in all respects uncommonly mild, untill within these few days, and the world of parties and legislation as moderate as the temperature of the atmosphere— But as the new-year advances, the weather grows cold, and we grow warm— We are very much perplexed what we shall do to manifest our valour without hazarding our persons, and after spending a long Session in discussing the subject we shall in all probability finish without doing any thing of importance— At least I have already seen enough to convince me that we shall do nothing good— For the protection of our Territory or of our Commerce we shall do nothing; but we may very possibly prepare for the abandonment of the first; and contribute our share to the sacrifice of the last— We shall perhaps enter into the unprofitable contest, with Great-Britain, which can do the most harm, *not* to the other but to ourselves; in this emulation of mischief, I am far from being certain but that we shall bear the palm.

Reports are in circulation that all our differences with Spain are already settled, entirely to our advantage; but if not we shall try again to *trade* with her for land—[3] We shall perhaps offer her almost all our province of Louisiana, for the Florida's; or if she likes it better, more money—fighting her we have almost done even talking of.

Captain Landais particularly desires me to present his respects to you— I have sent you the report of the Secretary of State on his petition or memorial— The papers are curious, and Count Bernstorf's letter in Answer to the application of D^{r:} Franklin, is amusing, as it shews the old Gentleman's embarrassment between the alternate pressure of England on one side, and France on the other— He appears to have understood that his most effectual means of extricating himself was to drown his outrage against the United States in a flood of personal adulation to their Minister.[4]

January 1806

Our Tunisian and Indian visitors are still the principal objects of curiosity we have to entertain us— Many of the Indians who were here are gone, but others have come to take their places, without any invitation, and they are so numerous as to occasion some uneasiness among the inhabitants of this neighbourhood— They are sometimes troublesome by introducing themselves unexpectedly to private houses, and their habits of intemperance sometimes make them uncomfortable companions.

M: Giles and M: Bayard have not yet taken their seats this Session. I suppose they will arrive nearly together— Their absence leaves both sides of the house in a manner without leaders, and a great degree of unsteadiness and languor hangs over our proceedings, in consequence of this circumstance— We find great reason to regret the loss of our late President.

We are here all well— With my duty and affection to the family in its various branches I remain faithfully yours.

RC (Adams Papers); internal address: "J. Adams Esq.."; endorsed: "J. Q. Adams / Jan. 14. Ans^d 29 / 1806." Tr (Adams Papers).

[1] JA to JQA, 23 Dec. 1805, above; TBA's letter to JQA has not been found.

[2] On 9 Jan. 1806 JQA wrote a resolution requesting information from the president about "new principles in the law of nations" and documents related to Anglo-American diplomacy. The resolution came out of a committee that included JQA and was tasked with considering a memorial from New York merchants introduced in the Senate on 6 January. The merchants sought the "immediate interposition of Congress" to address possible effects on the U.S. economy of rulings by the British Admiralty Court. JQA met with committee members on 9 Jan., and the resulting resolution was passed by the Senate the following day. During debate, Robert Wright of Maryland questioned whether the Senate had a compelling reason to request such information and was the only senator to vote against it. JQA may also have been referring to a bill to institute a voluminous code of conduct to govern the U.S. Army, which on 13 Jan. was referred to a committee on which he served. The Articles of War were signed into law on 10 April (*Annals of Congress*, 9th Cong., 1st sess., p. 45, 47; JQA, *Diary*, 9, 10, and 13 Jan.; U.S. Senate, *Jour.*, 9th Cong., 1st sess., p. 19; *U.S. Statutes at Large*, 2:359–372).

[3] On 4 Jan. newspapers began reporting that issues between Spain and the United States had been "amicably adjusted," including boundary disputes and spoliation claims. See, for example, the Boston *Columbian Centinel*, 4 Jan.; New York *Evening Post*, 9 Jan.; Philadelphia *United States Gazette*, 10 Jan.; Alexandria, Va., *Daily Advertiser*, 13 January.

[4] Capt. Peter (Pierre) Landais (ca. 1731–1820), a French naval officer who served on behalf of the United States during the American Revolution, petitioned the House of Representatives in Dec. 1805 seeking prize money for his capture of British vessels during the war. The House referred the request to the secretary of state, and on 31 Dec. James Madison reported on Landais' capture of British ships and their subsequent seizure in Norway by Denmark, which returned them to their owners. Madison enclosed several documents, including correspondence from 1779 and 1780 between Benjamin Franklin, then an American peace commissioner at Paris, and Count Andreas Peter von Bernstorff (1735–1797), the Danish foreign minister. Congress awarded Landais $4,000 in 1806 (Madison, *Papers, Secretary of State Series*, 10:697–699; Soren Jacob Marius Peterson Fogdall, *Danish-American Diplomacy, 1776–1920*, Iowa City, Iowa, 1922, p. 13; Franklin, *Papers*, 31:261, 32:75–76).

Abigail Adams to Louisa Catherine Adams

Dear Mrs Adams   Quincy Jan'ry 19th 1806

Your Letter of Jan'ry 6 I received last Evening.[1] your Children are very well, and very well taken care of, so do not give yourself any anxious solisitude about them. I believe they are much better off than they could have been at any boarding House in Washington, where [th]ey must have been confined in some degree; or have mixd with improper persons; with respect to John, the Child enjoys perfect Health, as I see to him myself, and he is always with me, never left to the care of any domestick unless when I go to meeting. I know that he has every thing which is proper for him, and nothing which can prove injurious; I never knew him either ask for pork, or eat a mouthfull, except one day, which was previous to your going from here. I agree with you that it is too grose food for a child inclined to be so fleshy as John— with regard to George if you will write to mrs Cranch she will give you all the information respecting him which You can desire I can only say that every person who has a young Child for which they are particularly anxious think themselves peculiarly fortunate if they can place it under her care— ask mrs Quincy if she does not consider herself So? that you should wish to hear often from them, is natural and highly proper— I have seldom mist a week in writing unless mr Adams has written to his Brother when I know he has mentiond the Children— there cannot be any thing more dissagreable than transporting young Children twice a year, either by water, or in crouded Stages at such a Distance, and however reluctant you might feel, at being seperated from them, I should suppose that your own judgement experience and good sense would have convinced You of the propriety of the measure without compulsion— I have experienced seperations of all kinds from Children equally dear to me; and know how great the sacrifice & how painfull the task—but I considerd it the Duty of a parent to consult the interest and benifit of their Children.

when You see Mrs Quincy present my Love to her and tell her her little sophia is very well grows finely and is very lively and sprightly—

I do not know but you are still Blooming at washington, but here we have winter in good earnest—not much snow; but intensly cold and that for six days Successively, again it is snowing:

I am glad to learn that your family are all well and hope Eliza has got rid of her cough. I hope she will be more attentive to her person, and not be guilty of self Murder. the savages cover their persons with

January 1806

oil and Brick dust which is a great security against the cold. nay frown not Eliza if your sister reads this to you

> "And still to make You more my friend
> I strive your Errors to amend"[2]

My Love to mr Adams when he is at leisure to take a lesson I have one for him— Remember me to your Mother. let me hear frequently from you, and I shall not be defficient in writing to you or to my son. George and John both Send Duty to their Parents, tho John never like to see me write—

affectionatly Yours   Abigail Adams—

RC (Adams Papers); addressed: "Mrs Louissa Adams / Washington"; notation by CFA: "To the Same." Some loss of text due to placement of the seal.

[1] In her letter to AA of 6 Jan., LCA expressed her relief at receiving news of her children and requested that AA not serve them salt pork (Adams Papers).

[2] AA quoted Edwin Moore, "The Panther, the Horse, and other Beasts," lines 11–12, but replaced the word "less" with "more."

John Quincy Adams to Thomas Boylston Adams

Washington 20. January 1806.

Your letter closing the last and commencing the present year, has been several days in my hands, and has hitherto remained without reply, from a variety of causes; but the want of time has been the principal one.[1] Business is thickening upon us very fast, and notwithstanding your injunction to me at the time when I was getting into the Carriage to come here, I have not been able to keep myself sufficiently unconcerned with what is going forward, to reserve much of my time—

Your opinion that the Merchants of this Country have more reason to dread the *protection* of their own Government, than the outrages of any other will I presume before the close of this Session be confirmed in its fullest extent— Measures of such a Nature are in contemplation, that it is time for all those who have property afloat upon the Ocean to take such care of it as they can, themselves. The principle lately revived by the British Government proscribing all commerce between neutral Nations and the Colonies of their Enemies, is in my opinion wholly unwarranted, and what we ought firmly and coolly to resist.—[2] But instead of that we shall take ground which we never can maintain, and of course maintain nothing— I have yet strong hopes that we shall avoid a War; but it is because I believe the fortunes of the War on the Continent of Europe, will compel the British Government again to relax from the rigour of her new System.— We have a large pamphlet on this subject said to be the work of the Secretary of State, entering very largely into the discussion of the question, and written with all his ability—[3] I have not had time to peruse it through, but from what I have seen of it, he appears to me, to undertake proving rather too much; and not to confine himself to the single question in controversy.

I think if you could imagine one half the pleasure you give us in writing that our children are in good health, you would confer that satisfaction upon us two or three times where you now send it once— For we have scarcely had the information long enough to enjoy it properly before we want again to have it— I hope when you reproved George for his confession of lying, that you had an appearance of real seriousness rather more effectual than you can always command, when you cover your jokes with a sober Mask.

You are unwilling to mark the exact degree of your contempt for my project to compare the climates of Washington and Boston or Quincy, by the thermometer— But when you have once got well engaged in the practice you will find your taste for it rapidly increasing; among other things you will feel the superiority it gives you over the rest of the world, to have always in your possession the most correct information on that very important topic of conversation the weather— And when you hear a person in the shades of ignorance presuming to say it was colder or warmer yesterday than to-day, with how much self-complacency will you be able to correct the mistake— Indeed Sir you are mistaken it is colder to-day, by 2 degrees— I shall send M^r: Shaw my projected mode of exhibiting in two parallel columns, the state of the thermometer at the same hour, in Washington and Boston, and hope he has taken care to keep the record from the commencement of this Month—so as to begin with the year— It will be a very good monthly page for the Anthology.[4]

We had some days since a little incident occurr'd in the family where I reside, of a nature partaking of Tragedy and Comedy, though by its conclusion its character has been fixed to the latter description— After being much disturbed one Night by a great noise and bustle in the house, on going down to breakfast, I enquired whether any body in the house was ill; and was informed that Betsey the Maid-Servant— But stay, M^r: Dana of the House of Representatives is not here to discuss the same in Greek to you; and the Comte de Mac Carthy is too far distant to put it in Latin— So you must e'en take it in rhyme; and here you have it on a separate slip of paper, that you may burn it after having read it—⁵ For as the adventure was followed in the course of a few days by a wedding and a christening, all improper breaches were repaired, and the Lady being again an honest woman must be respected in her reputation.

I propose to write as soon as possible to M[r:] Shaw, and forward to him the answers to the questions he some time since sent me—⁶ By your extract of a Letter from Cambridge, I find that the House which was M[r:] Fayerweather's is to be rented— I will thank M[r:] Shaw to make enquiries at what rate? I am waiting to hear from him on the other houses concerning which I formerly wrote you—⁷ I much lament the prospect of losing M[r:] Ames as President, and fear it will be very difficult for the College Government to make another choice so universally acceptable.

Nothing material has occurr'd here, except the numerous secrets not worth knowing, which you will infer from the occlusion of the doors of both Houses of Congress, so often and during such a length of Time— M[r:] Quincy, M[r:] Cranch and their families are well; as are ours.— This letter I presume will find you engaged in *your* Legislative labours, which I hope you will find more agreeable than ours.

Yours faithfully

RC and enclosure (Adams Papers); internal address: "T. B. Adams Esq[r.]"; endorsed: "J. Q Adams Esqr / 20[th:] Jan[y] 1806 / 31[st:] D[o] Rec[d] / 2[d:] Feb[y] Answ[d]."; enclosure filmed at 12 Jan. 1806.

¹ Not found.
² In May 1805 the British Admiralty Court shifted its policy toward U.S. shipping when it condemned the American ship *Essex*, which had been seized by a British privateer in Oct. 1800. The decision reinstated the "Rule of 1756," a policy developed during the Seven Years' War that held that trade closed to neutrals in time of peace could not be opened in time of war. The policy had been largely ignored in peacetime and was blunted by an 1800 ruling that allowed a neutral ship to trade with British adversaries after an interim stop in a neutral port, as the *Essex* had done. The 1805 Admiralty decision dealt a devastating blow to the U.S. economy by threatening the re-export trade, which had grown from $2 million in 1792 to $53 million in 1805.

This new aggression, paired with the continued British impressment of American seamen, prompted Congress to act. On 29 Jan. 1806 Andrew Gregg of Pennsylvania introduced a bill in the House of Representatives that would become the Non-Importation Act of 1806. Gregg proposed a blanket ban on the importation of British goods until a settlement was reached on impressment. Debate moved between proponents of retaliatory measures and those who feared war. The House passed a more moderate version of the bill on 25 March, and the Senate took it up on the 27th. On 10 April JQA voted with the majority in favor of sending the bill to a third reading, despite being "the only federalist who have voted for it in either house." The Senate passed the legislation on 15 April, with JQA joining the majority; Thomas Jefferson signed it into law on the 18th.

A product of compromise, the act met the aims of neither side. While it banned the import of many British goods, it excluded important products such as textiles and metals. A provision also delayed enforcement until 15 Nov. to give time for U.S. envoys to attempt a negotiated settlement, for which see LCA to JQA, 5 May, and note 5, below. Ultimately, the act did little more than further inflame Anglo-American relations. The law was effectively superseded by the Embargo Act of 1807, for which see TBA to JQA, 27 Dec. 1807, and note 3, below, and the Non-Intercourse Act of 1809, for which see JQA to LCA, 8 Feb. 1809, and note 5, below (Wood, *Empire of Liberty*, p. 640, 644, 649–650; Lance E. Davis and Stanley L. Engerman, *Naval Blockades in Peace and War: An Economic History since 1750*, Cambridge, Eng., 2006, p. 74, 75; Howard Jones, *Crucible of Power: A History of American Foreign Relations to 1913*, Lanham, Md., 2009, p. 66; Donald R. Hickey, *The War of 1812: A Forgotten Conflict*, rev. edn., Urbana, Ill., 2012, p. 10–11; New York *Mercantile Advertiser*, 21 Sept. 1803; *Annals of Congress*, 9th Cong., 1st sess., p. 412–413, 841–842; JQA, *Diary*; U.S. Senate, *Jour.*, 9th Cong., 1st sess., p. 68, 79–80, 86; *U.S. Statutes at Large*, 2:379–381).

³ James Madison, *An Examination of the British Doctrine, Which Subjects to Capture a Neutral Trade, Not Open in Time of Peace*, Washington, D.C., 1806, in which the secretary of state argued that British attacks on neutral shipping violated the law of nations (Madison, *Papers, Secretary of State Series*, 11:36–162).

⁴ For JQA's temperature record, which was not published in the *Monthly Anthology*, see JQA to William Smith Shaw, 27 Dec. 1805, and note 8, above.

⁵ JQA enclosed a poem dated 12 Jan. 1806 and titled "The Misfortune," which related the circumstances of a domestic servant in the Hellen household. He began, "Poor Betsey was a maiden pure / Declin'd in years, but so demure / That *Man* was her aversion" and concluded, "The wonder to unravel.— / . . . Poor Betsey!—was—IN TRAVEL!!" In addition to his allusion to Samuel Whittlesey Dana, JQA referred to Comte Justin de MacCarthy-Reagh (1744–1811), an Irish bibliophile residing in France (Christopher de Hamel, *Meetings with Remarkable Manuscripts: Twelve Journeys in the Medieval World*, N.Y., 2016, p. 419).

⁶ See JQA to Shaw, 27 Dec. 1805, and note 3, above.

⁷ JQA previously wrote to his brother about Cambridge rental properties on 2 Jan. 1806. The news that Thomas Fayerweather's house might be available for lease was also noted by AA in her letter of 9 Jan., both above.

John Quincy Adams to Abigail Adams

Washington 25. January 1806.

The first thing I look for in all the letters I receive from Quincy, is that which relates to our children, who cannot speak for themselves; and both of whom we left indisposed, and when I find that they are well, I feel myself relieved thus far, and only hope that the rest of the letter may contain information equally pleasing, of all the other persons in whose welfare I am so deeply interested— Nothing could gratify me more then than your kind favour of the 9th: and 12th: where you give me so good an account of them both.— I rejoyce that George has been so well as to be able to attend his school so constantly, and that he has had the benefit of a school during the Winter— I am sure you will tell them that I always think of them when I write to you, and that above all things I hope they will be good and behave themselves so as to have Grandmamma's approbation.

As New-England has so long been in the practice of being the dupe of her Southern Neighbours, it is to be expected she will not very soon

January 1806

change it— Certainly if she is now a dupe in this respect, it is her own fault, as she is a most willing dupe— The measures now in contemplation are pretty well known to be the measures of New-Englandmen; who are brought forward as the ostensible leaders, and perhaps are flattered with the opinion of having taken the management of affairs completely out of the hands of Southern Men— Under this system The responsibility as well as the burden of our national affairs will rest upon New-England, however hostile they may prove to *her* interests— But what can be said or done, when New-England most eagerly lavishes her confidence upon those very characters who are the readiest to promote other interests at the expence of her own?— So long as she chuses to be made the beast of burden to the Union, who can object against it?

On the subject of the business done and to be done with closed doors, it is of course not proper for me to say any thing abroad. But the most important of our public deliberations, relates to the State of our affairs with Great Britain— We have certainly great reason to complain of the conduct that Government is now pursuing towards us; and the principles she is advancing are such that if we submit to them without resistance, it will be equivalent to a total abandonment of all rights of neutral Commerce— I feel no disposition for my own part to abandon those rights; and I believe by a firm and determined opposition to her pretensions, at present we can bring her to relinquish them— But I am not without apprehensions that the temper with which our own Executive and Legislature *have* managed, and will *continue* to manage *these* controversies, will throw us into difficulties of a much more pernicious nature, and perhaps finally reduce us to the necessary abandonment even of the rights to which we are entitled— We commenced the Session with an apparent vigour and energy far beyond the tone which had for some years been in fashion. The public expressions of the Message were strong against Great-Britain, and much stronger against Spain—[1] But the general tendency of our public policy has uniformly been from the first day of the Session to this, to let down the chain of resentment against Spain, and to wind up that against Britain— The Result of our proceedings will probably shew in a striking light this variation in the phases of our policy— The Hurricane of Animosity and of hostility against Spain, will gradually subside and die away, untill scarce a distant murmur of it will be heard; while the moderate breeze which first blew against Britain, will freshen to a gale, untill the tempest will try the strength of our timbers to a degree which I cannot look forward to without concern— You will see a Bill we have now before us; a Bill, the title of which is for the protection and indemnification of American Seamen— Of its contents I need say nothing; if you will take the trouble barely to read it, you will draw your own conclusions as to the present State of our feelings respecting Great-Britain— I have not a spare copy that I can send you; but it will unquestionably be published in the newspapers; it will probably not pass in its present shape, but whatever modifications it may receive, I know not what *basis* it affords for any measure upon the subject, that can avail us for the accomplishment of the promise in the title of the Bill.[2]

I have also enclosed together with many other papers, a bill for the classification of the Militia, which is of considerable importance, and which perhaps my father may be curious to see—[3] I have some doubts whether this or any thing much like it, will pass the two Houses of Congress— The Militia is a delicate subject to touch; and any valuable regulations concerning it press upon so many *Constituents*, that their *Representatives* will be cautious how they meddle very seriously with them.

The increase of the Navy, of which there has also been much talk since we met, has already become a desperate hope— Though one of the President's friends this day told me, that we must now have a Navy; for that the President was made an Admiral last week— On asking an explanation of his meaning, he told me that the President had been with some of his Indian visitors last week on board one of the frigates *rotting* in the Eastern Branch (these were his own words) and at the moment when he ascended the ship's sides, Captain Murray displayed the *Admiral's flag*, in full luxuriance; and when the President left the Ship it was immediately struck—[4] The inference of my informer that the 74's must be built to support the dignity of the Admiral's flag, may be correct, but I have still some distrust of the opinion.

We have had a few days of cold weather here, but it is now again very moderate and fine— The Season has been remarkably mild throughout the Continent— My Register of the Thermometer I still keep very regularly—from the 9$^{th:}$ to the 20$^{th:}$ of this month was the only time during which we have had the usual severity of the Winter.

M$^{r:}$ Bayard yesterday took his Seat in Senate; the first time this Session— M$^{r:}$ Giles would probably have made his appearance at the same time; but on his way was overset, and broke his leg in a manner which is said to be very dangerous—[5] Probably therefore we shall not see him this Session— General Jackson of Georgia is here, but lies very ill, said to be of a dropsy in the chest.—[6]

January 1806

My own health remains pretty much as when I left you— Sometimes improving; at others feable— But in every State, well or ill, I am ever faithfully your's.

RC (Adams Papers); internal address: "M^rs: Adams."; endorsed: "J Q Adams / Jan^ry 25 1806." Tr (Adams Papers).

[1] Public response to Thomas Jefferson's 3 Dec. 1805 message to Congress echoed concern about U.S. relations with Great Britain and Spain. The Washington D.C., *National Intelligencer*, 9 Dec., expressed apprehension about continuing conflicts with Spain over the disputed border with the Floridas, but took solace in the fact that Spain could inflict only "trifling" damages on the United States while "that which we can do her is almost unlimited" since Spain's colonies were not protected from U.S invasion. The Boston *Repertory*, 17 Dec., expressed surprise that the president's address was not as forceful in discussing relations with Great Britain (*Annals of Congress*, 9th Cong., 1st sess., p. 11–16).

[2] On 20 Jan. 1806 Robert Wright of Maryland introduced a bill in the Senate that would declare anyone impressing an American seaman under orders of a foreign power "a pirate and felon," who "on conviction shall suffer death." The bill authorized seamen to employ lethal force in repelling impressment and further encouraged such resistance with a $200 bounty. JQA voted against each variation of the bill's language. On 10 March the Senate tabled the bill until the following session (Boston *Repertory*, 31 Jan.; JQA, *Diary*, 20 Jan.; U.S. Senate, *Jour.*, 9th Cong., 1st sess., p. 40, 44–45, 50, 55).

[3] On 22 Jan. Samuel Smith of Maryland introduced a bill in the Senate that would require all able-bodied free white male citizens between the ages of 18 and 45 to register for the federal militia, excluding only seamen. The bill was another response to Jefferson's call for military preparedness. Debate began on 17 Feb., and on the 25th the bill was defeated by a majority that included JQA (*Annals of Congress*, 9th Cong., 1st sess., p. 69–70; U.S. Senate, *Jour.*, 9th Cong., 1st sess., p. 6, 24, 25, 26, 40, 43, 45, 47; JQA, *Diary*, 25 Feb.).

[4] On 8 Jan. Jefferson toured the U.S. frigate *John Adams* at the Washington Navy Yard with Capt. Alexander Murray (1755–1821), his secretaries of war and navy, and Native American leaders. The ship was decorated for the visit and a salute was fired. The *Philadelphia Gazette*, 13 Jan., reported that the Native Americans "were highly pleased with this mark of attention" but elicited "little, if any emotion, at the spectacle or the firing" (S. Putnam Waldo, *Biographical Sketches of Distinguished American Naval Heroes in the War of the Revolution*, Hartford, Conn., 1823, p. 247, 339).

[5] William Branch Giles broke his leg when he was thrown from his carriage on the way to Washington, D.C., in January. He did not return to the Senate until 1 Dec. 1806, the first day of the second session of the 9th Congress (Richmond, Va., *Enquirer*, 23 Jan.; Dice Robins Anderson, *William Branch Giles: A Study in the Politics of Virginia and the Nation from 1790 to 1830*, Menasha, Wis., 1914, p. 101; *Annals of Congress*, 9th Cong., 2d sess., p. 9).

[6] Gen. James Jackson (b. 1757), a senator from Georgia, died on 19 March (*Biog. Dir. Cong.*).

John Adams to John Quincy Adams

My dear Sir   Quincy Jan. 29. 1806

The Mail of Yesterday brought, me, the Documents and in the Evening I received from Boston your favour of the 14th. By the Journals of the Senate I See, that you have Work enough, to excuse you from private Correspondences. By all that I read in the Documents Journals, and Newspapers, it Seems to me that the reigning Principle is to crouch to france & Spain and be very terrible to Britain. This

System will Succeed with neither: but the reign of Chaos will come again in consequence of it, among ourselves. It will affect the Revenue, the public debt, the public faith, the Bank Stocks of all the innumerable kinds, the Insurance Companies, the Corporations of all Sorts the fortunes of individuals, the Commerce Fisheries, Agricuture, and every other Interest. I know We can go through Such a Scæne of distraction and Confusion for We have done so once before, But I think all this ~~was unnecessary~~ might have been avoided.

Do you remember the Motto over the Door of the Hotell de Valentinois, or the basse Court de M. Le Ray de Chaumont, where the illustrious and immortal Franklin and the obscure and mortal John Adams lived together as American Ministers to the Court of Versailles. I think it was "Si Sta bene non Se move."[1] While our Government were allowed to maintain their Neutrality We Stood well. But when the Republicans Sacrificed me to Mr Jefferson and Mr Tallerand, and the Fœderalists Sacrificed me to Mr Hamilton and Mr Pitt, all went wrong and here We are. If I had not more compassion for the distresses of the Merchants of New York Philadelphia and Baltimore than I have resentment for their past follies and Injuries to me, their Scrieches would be Musick in my Ears. But the Subject is too Serious and I indulge no resentments. To commit the command of their Commerce to Virginians was to commit the Lamb to the Guardianship of the Wolf.

Brotier and Murphy are full in the opinion that the Dialogue, concerning the Causes of the Corruption of Eloquence, was written by Tacitus. Indeed who could have written it? Pliny and Velleius Paterculus were the only Writers in or near that age, who had taste and Elegance enough to compose this Dialogue. Velleius was too much a Slave, and Pliny would have filled it with Vanity. Considering it as written in youth, and in Dialogue, and that his History and Annals were written in old Age or a least in mature Manhood, the difference between the Styles is not so great as to be an argument of much Weight against Tacitus. The Historical Style of Tacitus is exquisite, consummate Clock Work. Every Period must have cost him a day, to turn it and file it, and polish it, and burnish it.

Two or three of the Speeches in the Dialogue are lost: and these unfortunately were the most interesting, because they were directly on the Subject of the Causes of the Corruption of Eloquence. Brotier has attempted to Supply them and has Said Something very clever: but this will never Satisfy like the original. He begins with Ovid and proceeds to Seneca as Corrupters of Eloquence, &c[2]

January 1806

Those Parts which remain of the Dialogue are very beautifull and of great Value.

We are apt to Set up the ancients as Standards of Taste, and Models indeed they are: but as no Model perhaps deserves imitation in all parts, We ought to exercise our own Reason, before We follow them implicitly. Good Sense is the foundation of all good Writing. There is a passage in Plato, which is called a Description, or Definition or Picture of Man. Longinus calls it a divine passage. Not all the Authority of Plato and Longinus together, can make me think it any thing but a Monster: a puerile Sport of a trifling Imagination. It is ten times worse than Ciceros Play upon the Punishment of Parricide.[3]

To return for a minute to our public affairs. I expect to be Stripped by the conduct of our Rulers, of all the little income I have, except the produce of my Farm. The Labour upon this costs me all my revenue and more. In case of a War they will tax me annually more than all the produce of my farm and compell me to pay incalculable bounties to hire Men for the service. All this however does not terrify me. But all this is for nothing but visionary Whims weak partialities and little passions.

I Speak of War, as a thing to be expected. Embargoes, and Non Intercourse Laws, if We could Observe them, would not divert Britain from the Judgments of their Admiralty Courts. Our Commerce may all fall into their hands: and We have no resource but reprisals. I Should rather begin with this. If I once voted for an Embargo on Merchant ships, I would let loose all the Privateers and Vessels of force at the Same time to prey upon the British Commerce. If I tryed to do harm I would endeavour to do as much as possible at once. for the most We can do would be, by a sudden Enterprize at the first onsett.

Our People have been wrought up to such an enthusiastic opinion of the Omnipotence of France and of the near approach of the ruin of England that they think they shall be Safe under the Wing of the former, and may use what Liberties they will with the latter. These Notions are both erroneous, dangerous and pernicious.

I expect daily to hear that the trade to St. Domingo is prohibited. What Mandate will come next.? a requisition for a Subsidy, and I Suppose it will be as humbly obeyed. I blush for the humiliation of my Country. But We have purchased the Jealousy and terror of France and Spain too as well as England, at an expence of fifteen Millions of Dollars and We must meet it as well as We can. My Love to all the branches of our Connections. your Sons are very well, and very fine Boys.   J. Adams

RC (Adams Papers); internal address: "J. Q. Adams Esq."; endorsed: "My Father 29. Jan^y: 1806. / 9. Feb^y: rec^d: / 11. D^o: Ans^d:."

[1] JA resided with Benjamin Franklin at the villa of Jacques Donatien Le Ray de Chaumont (1725–1803) while they served as American peace commissioners at Paris in 1778 and 1779. JA translated the Latin phrase, "If you stand well do not move" (vols. 3:xxiii–xxv; 6:84–85; JA, D&A, 4:41–43).

[2] JA continued the discussion of Arthur Murphy's translation of Tacitus' "A Dialogue concerning Oratory, or the Causes of Corrupt Eloquence" for which see his letter of 23 Dec. 1805, and note 2, and JQA's reply of 14 Jan. 1806, both above. JA also referenced Gabriel Brotier's edition of Tacitus' *Opera Supplementis, Notis et Dissertationibus*, 7 vols., Paris, 1776, a copy of which is in JA's library at MB, in arguing that neither Pliny the Younger (ca. 61–ca. 112) nor Roman historian Velleius Paterculus could have authored the text. Murphy (8:127–129) discusses Brotier's attribution of the "Dialogue" to Tacitus (Hoefer, *Nouv. biog. générale*; *Catalogue of JA's Library*; Oxford Classical Dicy; Tacitus, *Works*, transl. Murphy, rev. edn., 8 vols., London, 1805).

[3] Plato offered an extended characterization of humankind in *Timaeus*, sect. 65c–85e, which Athenian rhetorician and philosopher Cassius Longinus (ca. 213–273) called "divinely" inspired in his essay *On the Sublime*, ch. 32, sect. 5. JA also referenced Cicero's allusions to the Roman stage from his legal defense of Sextus Roscius the Younger during his trial for patricide, *Pro Sexto Roscio Amerino*, ch. 16, sect. 46–47 (Cassius Longinus, *On the Sublime*, transl. W. H. Fyfe and Donald Russell, Cambridge, 1995; Oxford Classical Dicy.; Cicero, *Pro Sexto Roscio Amerino*, transl. John Henry Freese, Cambridge, 1930).

Abigail Adams Smith to Francisco de Miranda

New York jany 29th 1806

we are about to commit to your charge a Son the natural object of a Parents affection it is impossible, and would be improper to divest ones self of the feelings fears and anxious solicitude that exist upon this occasion, he is young and inexperienced and will require advice and caution his disposition is amiable and mild, and I hope he will be found worthy the station in which he is placed, and that his conduct may be such as to merit your approbation, and regard

I hope he will endeavour to imitate the example he has before him, and that under your guidance and protection he may cultivate a taste for Study, and application to such objects of knowledge as it is necessary for him to acquire

from the long friendship that has existed between Coll^n Smith and yourself, and from my own observations, I can say that I do not know any person to whom I could with so much confidence entrust him— permit me to wish you a pleasant passage, and success, in the object of the enterprise / and to subscribe myself with great / respect your Hum^ble servt

A Smith

RC (National Academy of History, Venezuela:Miranda Archives, VI:221).

Abigail Adams to Ann Harrod Adams

My Dear Nancy   Quincy Feb^{ry} 2^d 1806

Miss Ann Beal deliverd me your Letter this morning at meeting. you will see by my Letter of fryday Evening how much the President was dissapointed both by the travelling and Weather.[1] we adjournd the club on purpose. to day the travelling is better than since the Snow fell— I have lookd up the articles you requested, and judging others by myself, that a kind turn will not be considerd as a burden, I venture to send the Bundle by mr Beals, and am half tempted to add one for mr shaw, as I know he must want. if I do, will Your sister oblige me by Sending her Boy with it— I have an other much larger, but that I shall try to send Some other way—

I need not say how much I miss Your companionable qualities—tho some times a little too low spirited, yet we could talk of that—and reason about it— what a contrast I have between the loquasity of Susan, and the Taciturnity of Louissa—apathy what art thou?

> Absence of occupation is not rest;
> A mind quite vacant, is a mind distress'd—[2]

I have only been twice out since you went away, once to the funeral and once to sister Cranch's—[3] I have been troubled with a pain in my stomack, but am better to day— Susan is quite well, and regreets your absence daily— John talks of you constantly—rides to see you—and inquires how all your Family do.—

My Love to your Sister if the weather should be pleasent & the travelling good I may run in some day in the week, but you know I have many hinderences—so do not expect it till you see me— I have not sent the other stockings because the dryed yellow in spots—

John Greenleaf George & John, have been prateing about me all the time I have been writing—[4]

affectionately Your Mother   A Adams

I see a mr Whitwell is selling of his Hard ware at the corner of union street[5]

RC (PHi:Dreer Collection); addressed: "Mrs Ann Adams / Boston."

[1] AHA's letter has not been found. She was early into a monthlong visit with her sister Frances Harrod Foster (1782–1872) in Boston, while TBA attended the Mass. General Court. Writing to AHA on 31 Jan. (private owner, 2019), AA noted that she missed her daughter-in-law but was "better Satisfied to have you in Town, because I think you feel happier." She reported that visiting Boston would be difficult because of current traveling conditions

and enclosed $2, requesting the purchase of a coffeepot, buttons, and cotton (Treat, *Treat Family*, p. 270; AA to SSA, 23 Feb., below).

[2] William Cowper, "Retirement," lines 623–624.

[3] AA was referring to the 29 Jan. funeral of Elisha Turner (b. 1762) of Quincy, who died on 24 January. Turner was the husband of JA's niece Mary Adams Turner (vol. 9:22; *New-England Palladium*, 28 Jan.).

[4] That is, John Greenleaf Jr., son of Lucy Cranch Greenleaf. AA sent her niece a gift and a brief note on 9 March (MHi:Adams Papers, All Generations).

[5] Boston hardware merchant Samuel Whitwell advertised in the *New-England Palladium*, 31 Jan., that he was closing his business at the corner of Union and Ann Streets and selling his inventory at reduced prices.

John Quincy Adams to Thomas Boylston Adams

Washington 5. Feby: 1806.

Your favour of the 19th: of last Month, has been several days in my hands—[1] I have enclosed you the two sheets which were wanting to complete your files of the Journals of the House, but I cannot find a spare copy of the first sheet of the Senate's Journals— I send most of the public documents to Shaw, because he wants them more than you, and because you will always have the first perusal of those among them which you will think it worth your while to read.

In the intimation I gave you in a former letter to your mother, of my wish that you would bring forward a certain Resolution, I had at once in view what I thought would be a useful public measure, and what it appeared to me would be creditable to yourself—[2] Your present situation is one in which as your warm friend and well-wisher, I am desirous to see you *bring yourself forward to the public eye*— You are fully competent to appear as an active and influential member of the body to which you belong; and you cannot shew yourself there to advantage, without at the same time rendering yourself useful to your Country— You have always in your choice the topic upon which you may commence operations, and to possess yourself fully of a subject, before you make it a material for legislative discussion;—and if you do not like the one I intimated, think of some other—

I did not fully understand your wit upon the subject of yankey grain and salt-pork; but I find something on the same subject in other letters from Quincy, which has made it intelligible—[3] I have as you well know no antipathies either to pudding or pork, and I have no doubt but my children would fare as well upon them as upon any thing more delicate or luxurious.— The more thoroughly they are made to be Yankeys in Heart and Soul the more comfort I am sure they will afford to me.

It is true, as you have observed that the Senate have hitherto during the Session, more frequently thought proper to place me upon Committees than at former Sessions, and your inference from it is naturally enough a pleasing one— But on the one hand you must not draw your conclusions too extensively from a circumstance of merely an equivocal nature; and on the other you will perceive that it brings an additional load of business, requiring a still closer application than I have heretofore given to the subjects which occasionally come before us for discussion— Our Committees are all appointed by ballot, and a plurality of votes forms the choice— Hence it often happens that a member gets upon a Committee who would not obtain a majority— And this body has already manifested by majorities, some jealousy of its own elections by pluralities, in the course of the present Session— in all probability, arising from the very circumstance which you have observed with pleasure— You will find for instance that three successive Committees, one of five members, and the two others of seven, have been appointed upon what is substantially one and the same subject— One upon a Memorial from the Merchants of New-York, a second upon a part of the President's Message, and a third upon a memorial from the Merchants of Philadelphia—[4] Yet when the ballots were taken; all the members on the first were again placed upon the others with the addition of two members on the second and third— I presume you remarked the appointment of these three Committees on the Journals, and without this explanation must have thought it somewhat extraordinary— I have this day enclosed to your father a Report from one of these three Committees, consisting of three Resolutions upon which I wish you to *pause* and *ponder*. The first and second of these Resolutions are in substance mine— All three were drawn up by me—the third was not *my measure*, for I had in contemplation a very different one; but from a Spirit of accommodation I acquiesced in the proposal of another, modified as it stands— I shall probably vote for it eventually; but it is doubtful whether that or either of the others will be adopted.—[5]

This Subject has engaged much of the Time we have to spare in the intervals between our daily Sessions— The Committee have met every day for many days past— Several other of the Committees on which I am placed, are of considerable importance, and require much labour of investigation; both in Committee, and at home preparatory for meeting in Committees—so you see that I whom you have charged with too anxious an attention to the public business, heretofore have double duties put upon me by the frequent assignment of this Committee-service to me.

I lament exceedingly the disaster which has happened to you by the loss of your thermometer; but I hope Shaw has contrived to have a record kept in Boston— I hoped before this time to have sent him my register for the month of January; but I have not yet had time to copy it off.— I will thank you to ask him whether he ever ship'd for this place a box of macaroni which I left at Whitcomb's, to be sent me, and which Shaw promised to put on board the first vessel that should come from Boston to Alexandria or Georgetown.

We have as yet the prospect of a long Session. Upwards of two months have elapsed since we met, and no one subject of material importance has yet been brought to a conclusion— Many of the most important have scarcely got fairly before either house for discussion— I have little expectation of reaching home earlier than May; if it should extend to the middle of June, I should not be surprized.

You will find by the multitude of Resolutions and Motions in both Houses pointed against Great-Britain, which will come to your knowledge, that we are in a towering passion with her: but we shall temper our valour with discretion— You must not be alarmed at our sounding words— In all probability we shall content ourselves with talking big; and then we can boast as much of our heroism, as we have done in relation to our affairs with the Barbary Powers.[6]

The Supreme Court of the United States should have been in Session this week; but I believe there are not enough of the Judges present to form a Court— Judge Chase is ill at Baltimore; and Judge Cushing is unwell here, so that he has hitherto been unable to attend.[7]

We are all in tolerable health— Farewell.

RC (Adams Papers); endorsed: "J. Q Adams Esqr / 5[th:] Feb[y] 1806 / 18[th:] Rec[d:] / Ans[d]."

[1] Not found.
[2] See AA to JQA, 9 Jan., and note 1, above.
[3] See AA to LCA, 19 Jan., note 1, above.
[4] Since the 1st session of the 9th Congress began on 2 Dec. 1805, JQA had been named to committees to consider a treaty with Tripoli, for which see note 6, below; examine an act that would form a government for the Northwest Territory; regulate foreign currency; report on a petition on New Orleans land titles; assess a treasury report; and consider Senate rules changes. In addition, he served on committees to consider statements in the president's annual message on "violations of neutral rights"; a memorial from New York merchants who feared economic disruption from restrictions on Anglo-American trade, for which see JQA to JA, 14 Jan. 1806, and note 2, above; and a like memorial from Philadelphia merchants that was introduced 15 Jan. and urged that all diplomatic means available be employed to stop British depredations (U.S. Senate, Jour., 9th Cong., 1st sess., p. 3, 8–9, 13, 15, 16, 18, 21, 22, 29, 50; U.S. Senate, Exec. Jour., 9th Cong., 1st sess., p. 4; Amer. State Papers, Foreign Relations, 2:737–741).

[5] The enclosure sent to JA was probably JQA's [Feb. 1806] transcription of three Senate resolutions on Anglo-American relations (Adams Papers). The first resolution called the British capture and condemnation of U.S. vessels "a violation of their neutral rights, and an encroachment upon their national independence." The second called on the president to demand that the practice cease and seized property be restored, and the third

called for a suspension of British bank transfers in the United States until the issue was resolved. The first passed unanimously on 12 Feb., followed by the second on the 14th. The third, which JQA attributed to Samuel Smith of Maryland and Joseph Inslee Anderson of Tennessee, was not brought forward for a vote (*Annals of Congress*, 9th Cong., 1st sess., p. 90–91, 104–112; JQA, *Diary*, 12, 13, 14 Feb.; *Biog. Dir. Cong.*).

[6] The Tripolitan-American Treaty of Peace and Amity of 4 June 1805 was submitted by the president to the Senate on 11 Dec. 1805, and on the 16th it was referred to a committee comprised of JQA, Smith, and Uriah Tracy. On 23 Dec. the committee recommended, without other comment, that the Senate give its advice and consent. Further action was delayed more than three months over opposition to the payment of a tribute to Tripoli and the U.S. treatment of the ousted pasha, Hamet Qaramanli, who was the brother of the current pasha, Yusuf Qaramanli. The United States had provided arms to Hamet, but before he could use them to attack his brother, the United States negotiated the treaty and withdrew its support of his efforts, though it included in the treaty a provision calling on Yusuf to release Hamet's family whom he was holding hostage. At the president's urging, Congress appropriated $2,400 for Hamet's support in exile, despite a long speech by JQA questioning the payment. On 8 April 1806 opponents were unsuccessful in delaying ratification of the treaty until the United States obtained proof of the hostages' release, a pledge Yusuf eventually fulfilled. JQA was part of a majority approving the Senate's consent on 12 April. The United States ratified the treaty on 17 April and proclaimed it on the 22d. The treaty and a $60,000 tribute to Tripoli ended the First Barbary War (vol. 15:280–281, 353; U.S. Senate, *Exec. Jour.*, 9th Cong., 1st sess., p. 3, 4, 9, 28, 31–32; Miller, *Treaties*, 2:529–535; Frank Lambert, *The Barbary Wars: American Independence in the Atlantic World*, N.Y., 2005, p. 165–169; *Annals of Congress*, 9th Cong., 1st sess., p. 14, 48–50, 185–188, 211–224; 10th Cong., appendix, p. 2330–2337; *U.S. Statutes at Large*, 6:62).

[7] The U.S. Supreme Court, with justices John Marshall, Bushrod Washington, William Paterson, and William Johnson present, convened its session on 10 Feb. and handed down decisions in 28 cases before adjourning on 5 March. Samuel Chase, who was afflicted with gout, did not attend the session. William Cushing recovered from a fever and joined the proceedings on 19 Feb. (Cranch, *Reports of Cases in the Supreme Court*, 3:237; Anne Ashmore, "Dates of Supreme Court Decisions and Arguments," p. 5–6, U.S. Supreme Court, www.supremecourt.gov; Melvin I. Urofsky, ed., *Biographical Encyclopedia of the Supreme Court*, Washington, D.C., 2006; Hannah Phillips Cushing to AA, 28 April, below).

Abigail Adams to John Quincy Adams

My Dear Son   Quincy Feb'ry 9th 1806

I begin my Letter by announcing the Health of your Children, that Your mind and that of their Mothers may be at ease & "they cannot Speak for themselves it is true," but there are Mothers who are not less anxious for those who can speak for themselves; and it is with much pain that I learn from your Friends that Your Health does not appear to have been Mended by Your journey, or change of residence. Mrs Quincy who never fails writing every week to your Aunt Cranch, Seldom omits informing me how you are; that You do not gain flesh is ~~not~~ to be expected, for your mind must suffer from the prospect before you, and the perplexed state of our publick counsels so contrary to your own Ideas of sound policy.

The sentiments exprest in Your Letter of Jan'ry 25th upon the subject of our foreign Relations and connections So perfectly accord with those of your Father, that it might have been conjectured you had as formerly, sat down together by our fire side and canvassed the Subjects together.— that Great Britain is wrong, a common understanding may discover from reading the statements of the Merchants to the Secretary of state Mr Gore's Letter, and Mr Madisons.— altho I am not for adopting mr Wrights Resolutions, I would make a firm and resolute stand against the unjust assumption of any Nation;[1] I would propose what was just honorable, dignified and energetic— Such measures as were practicable, from which there should be no receeding but if the Chief Majestrate of the Nation is capable of such duplicity as he is accused of—but which I am loth to believe; we are indeed, and in very Truth, in a helpless state, and no one can Say where the evils will terminate What ever may be the conduct of the Head of a Nation, those who are accredited are received by him as Representitives from foreign Powers: ought out of respect to the Nation, to treat him with decency and good Manners in both which I think a certain Marquiss deficient.— I have heard and seen specimins of his politeness upon former occasions, and at the time despised his littleness.—[2] Your Father has written You a Letter in which he has exprest to you his opinion upon some ~~parts~~ of the Subjects in Your Letter to me;[3]

My Love to mrs Adams to whom [I will] write next. if I do not write every week, you must not think that Your Children are unwell. George visits me always once a week, sometimes oftner, but for the last Month, we have had neither good Riding or walking except a few days together.

You write to your Brother respecting a House[4] do you expect that congress will rise as early as May? I wish whenever you return you would consult Dr Rush upon the state of Your Health. I have a good opinion of dr Mays practise. Your dijestion is defective— Your food does not nourish You. You do not derive spirits or strength from it— I would recommend to you to eat a hard Bisquit, and 3 figs daily, between meals, make the experiment, add a Glass of wine—and tell me after one Month if You do not feel the benifit of it—

I am sorry for mr Giles misfortune— poor Shadow of Randolph— has he worn out his Lungs in a good cause? tis said he has been Rational this Session. What a pitty that closed doors should have deprived the public from witnessing So novel a Spectacle—

Your Brother and sister have been in Boston for this fortnight past. he returnd last Evening to attend some town affairs, but will go again on tuesday. tell mr Quincy his little Girl was very well to day— mrs cranch has quite a family of little ones, but she devotes herself to them, tho she says they craize her upon a Stormy Day, when they cannot go to School—

with the sincerest Love and affection / I am Your Mother

Abigail Adams—

RC (Adams Papers); addressed by TBA: "John Q Adams Esqr / Senator of the US / City of Washington"; endorsed: "My Mother 9. Feb^y: 1806. / 20. Feb^y: rec^d: / March Ans^d:"; notation by Richard Cranch: "Quincy Feb: 10$^{th.}$ 1806. Free." Some loss of text where the seal was removed.

[1] A memorial from Boston merchants published in the Boston *Repertory*, 31 Jan., was presented to the Senate on 3 February. The memorial outlined "great injuries sustained by the aggressions of the belligerent Powers" and suggested the Jefferson administration send a special mission to Great Britain. This followed an 18 Nov. 1805 letter from Massachusetts attorney Christopher Gore to James Madison that described British policies as "peculiarly injurious to the merchants." Madison followed with a report to Congress of 25 Jan. 1806, calling Britain's claim of broad powers to blockade ports, and its unauthorized searches of foreign vessels and impressment of American sailors, "important deviations from the code of public law" (*Annals of Congress*, 9th Cong., 1st sess., p. 72–73, 81, 777–778, 843–854, 890–899; New York *Commercial Advertiser*, 3 Feb.). For Senator Robert Wright's 20 Jan. bill on impressment, see JQA to AA, 25 Jan., and note 2, above.

[2] Carlos Martínez, Marquis Casa Yrujo, Spanish minister to the United States, on 6 Dec. 1805 sent a letter to Madison objecting to the president's comments on Spain in his 3 Dec. annual message to Congress. Receiving no response, Yrujo communicated the letter to colleagues on 21 Jan. 1806, and it was printed in the Philadelphia *United States Gazette* on 27 January. The Federalist Boston *Repertory*, 7 Feb., seized on the dispute, claiming that either "Spain has been very unjust, insulting and overbearing" or Thomas Jefferson was "guilty of foul misrepresentation." Madison replied by releasing to the press recent correspondence with Yrujo in which he explained that the diplomat received no response to his Dec. 1805 letter because Jefferson did not consider him a representative of the Spanish government after he had requested Yrujo's recall in April. Despite Jefferson's stance, Yrujo remained in his diplomatic post until he was replaced by chargé d'affaires Valentin de Foronda on 7 July 1807 (vol. 15:443–444; Madison, *Papers, Secretary of State Series*, 10:621–626; 11:185–186, 196–198, 205–206; *Repertorium*, 3:445; Boston *Repertory*, 25 Feb. 1806).

[3] In a 5 Feb. letter to JQA, JA considered Anglo-American relations, expounding on the right of neutral nations to ship authorized goods without threat of the impressment of their seamen on the open seas (Adams Papers).

[4] JQA to TBA, 20 Jan., above.

Abigail Adams to Hannah Carter Smith

my Dear Friend   Quincy Feb'ry 14th 1806.

If the sympathy of Friends could alleviate the sorrow of an afflicted Heart, deeply wounded by the loss of a Dear child, how readily would I strive to pour the balm of consolation into Yours. Your trial has been great, whilst you Sat in speechless anguish over the languid and decaying Form of your Departed Mary, Striveing to obtain that Submission to the Divine Will, which religion teachs, and which I trust you have not sought in vain.[1]

> Hope looks beyond the Bounds of time
> when what we now deplore
> Shall rise in full immortal prime
> And Bloom to fade no more[2]

Tho Your former wounds are opened affresh, he who sees fit to wound can heal

> Insatiate Death! stern Messenger of pain
> Thy darts flew twice and twice thy peace is slain[3]

The ways of Providence are never more inscrutable to us, than when we See the early promising Blossom witherd, and cut of in its early Bloom—e'er it reach maturity. We are ready to inquire, wherefore it is? whilst Many who to us appear as cumberers of the ground are left to fill up the measure of their iniquity— Yet it becomes us weak feeble short sighted beings, to consider all events as under the controul and direction of a supreem all wise and benificent Being— who knows what is best for his Creatures—and whom we are assured does not willingly afflict his Children. whom the Lord Loveth, he chastneth—[4]

in the Multitude of your thoughts may the comforts and consolations of Religion delight Your soul, and as your trials are may, your graces and virtues Shine with increasing Lusture.

That the remainder of Your flock may be spaired to you, and reward all your anxious cares, and solisitude for them, by virtuous lives, fillial respect—Duty and affection—is the sincere and ardent wish / of Your sympathizing Friend   Abigail Adams

RC (MHi:Smith-Carter Family Papers); addressed: "Mrs Hannah Smith / Boston"; endorsed: "A. Adams / Quincy, 1806."

[1] Mary Carter Smith, the seven-year-old daughter of William and Hannah Carter Smith, died on 10 February. AA wrote to AHA on [ca. 11 Feb.] that she had read of the death, which was noted in the *New-England Palladium*, 11 Feb., adding that the child's mother had been "arming her mind for the fatal issue" (Adams Papers, filmed at [April 1797]).

[2] Anne Steele, "On the Death of a Child," lines 17–20.

[3] AA was quoting a poem, "Resignation," lines 9–10, by "E.," that was published in the *Port Folio*, new ser., 1:63 (1 Feb. 1806), though she changed "thrice" to "twice" in the second quoted line.

[4] Hebrews, 12:6.

Abigail Adams to Louisa Catherine Adams

my Dear Mrs Adams   Quincy Feb'ry 15th 1806

I shall begin my Letter by putting Your mind at ease respecting Your children, who are both very well; George I saw Yesterday quite in Rap-

February 1806

tures; his uncle Cranch had made him a little sled with a small box upon the top; similar to one which Dexter had made John; and which employs half his time, Sometimes to Draw about Miss Juno, who Seems to like the ride very well, and sits in it as grave and demure, as tho she could never skip, and play. he has his Hammer, and his shovel, sometimes mimicks Jobe in shoveling the snow and at other times Hammers stoutly enough.— at other times uses his needle and sews away with Susan— he is also a Great rider, but it must be in a Sleigh or carriage— I devote my chamber where I sit to him, and it is pretty well litterd from morning to night.— whilst as a Mother you must be anxious to hear frequently from Your Children; you will still bear in mind that they are Mortal: and that no Solisitude or care can at all times sheild them from the common lot of Mortals.— poor Mrs smith is now mourning over the Remains of her dear Mary, who is this Day to be committed to the silent Tombe— 12 weeks she has languished in a decline a slow fever, which has been fatal to many children the last Season, was her first complaint. no medicine could remove it. it fixed upon her Lungs. she fell into a consumption, which in 12 weeks terminated her Life, during which time Mrs smith has held her in her Arms.— she would not be prevaild upon to lie upon the Bed in the Day time— M^{rs} smith has been nearly worn out, and the anguish of her mind has prey'd upon her health and spirits.—

I am not a little concernd for the Health of My dear son— the cold weather used to brace him up—but I learn from his Friends at Washington that he looks pale, thin, and slender.— I know his anxiety upon the state of our public affairs will wear him, and harrass his mind I wish he had less reason for it;

we have had some severe cold Weather and plenty of snow. I presume you must have had some taste of it at Washington; how is Your Mother this winter. has Eliza got rid of her cough? is caroline well have You heard from Your Brother— does he like Norfolk and his own situation?—[1]

we all send our Regards to all our inquiring Friends. what shall I say to Mamma John I am writing to her? say little Johns good Boy. what shall I say to Pappa. that little John is roleing upon the Carpet— playing with Juno;

affectionatly Yours

A Adams

RC (Adams Papers); notation by CFA: "To the Same."

[1] Thomas Baker Johnson's activities in Norfolk, Va., are unknown except that they were "so little lucrative" and void of any "idea of promotion" that his sister Eliza wrote to James Madison on 3 Sept. requesting a position for him in the State Department or another gov-

ernment office. Eliza Johnson also raised the idea of a post in New Orleans, and it is there that her brother relocated by early 1808, for which see Thomas Jefferson to LCA, 8 Aug. 1807, and note 1, below (Madison, *Papers, Secretary of State Series*, 12:270–272).

Abigail Adams to Ann Harrod Adams

my dear Nancy   Quincy Feb'ry 16 1806

I expected to have heard from you by mr Beal, but his comeing to dine Yesterday with the club I presume Prevented. the snow has left us so far that we went in the carriage to meeting to day. we are all well and wish to see you

Dexter was in Town one day. I directed him to call, but he said the Town was so full, and so crouded that he could not leave his team; does mr Adams intend comeing out this week: I should be glad to get his Linnen and shaws who has not sent his out the last week—

~~Mrs~~ Sister Cranch is much afflicted with her Leg. the Humour has increased to an allarming degree, so as to confine her, And make her quite sick.[1] I feel very anxious about her. how is Your own Health?

we have not had ~~any~~ but one Letter from Washington since You left us.[2] have you received any further commission? John inquires daily if Aunte is not comeing home. I have not been a visiting since you went away except once to see Mrs Norten, and to See Mrs cranch. My Ideas are confined pretty much to my own fire side. sometimes pleasent, sometimes anxious—sometimes painfull.— who is without their share of all this. who that thinks and reflects can avoid it. this state is a state of trial; whether we glide on under a full sail of prosperity, or are driven by adverse Winds upon a tempestuous coast, adversity calls forth more graces and virtues, than prosperity usually exhibits. the prayer Agur discoverd a mind fully sensible of this truth—[3]

Let me hear from you and be / assured of the affection / of your Mother   Abigail Adams

My Love to Mrs Foster Susan desires to be rememberd to both—

RC (Adams Papers); addressed: "Mrs Ann Adams / Boston."

[1] In a [*Feb. 1806*] letter to AHA, AA reported Mary Smith Cranch's recovery and offered to send laundered items if TBA was in need of clean clothes (MBBS).
[2] JQA to AA, 25 Jan., above.
[3] Proverbs, 30:7–9.

February 1806

John Quincy Adams to Thomas Boylston Adams

Washington 17. Feb^{y:} 1806.

Your favour of the 2^{d:} inst^{t:} enclosing a copy of the judiciary Bill which was before you for consideration came to hand some days since—[1] As your legislative occupations employ you only three hours a day, I can readily conceive that you can find little time for private correspondence; for as an Antient Orator was wont to say that he had not time to make his speech short, so I have often found by experience, that the more leisure I have the less time I can spare for any particular duty—[2] My punctuality to correspondents therefore is generally proportioned to the multiplicity of my avocations, and is never greater than when I have not a moment I can call my own—

I am glad to find that your lawyers of both parties are agreed in supporting the plan for an improvement in the Judiciary.— The opinion of young M^{r:} Story is in my mind of peculiar weight—[3] I should recommend to you to cultivate an acquaintance with this Gentleman, who is certainly possess'd of considerable talents, and will I hope make a valuable public character— His *popular* propensities must be regarded with indulgence; because it is the sin which most easily besets all young men of aspiring genius, and strong minds— When they have radical principle at the heart, their overweening democratic passions wear away as they advance in years, and rise in the world— Many of our most distinguished men have begun their career with the same enthusiasm of popularity as M^{r:} Story has manifested— And he has already given ample proofs of various kinds that he is not to be ranked with the vulgar herd of demagogues—

The report which you received from the newspapers of an Extraordinary Embassy to the Courts of London and Paris, had I believe no other foundation than the wishes of certain partizans of the person who was named as having received the appointment— It was perhaps meant as a hint to the President—whether he will be inclined to take it or not, I cannot tell—but I do not believe the late Vice-President will on the present occasion be sent with a diplomatic character either to France or England—much less do I imagine that the two missions will be united in him.[4]

The indignation which you remark as having been excited by the mandatory letters of Talleyrand and Turreau, is not exactly the sentiment occasioned by them here— At least indignation is not the operative principle which will arise from them— There is another feeling quite as efficacious which those papers have produced with us; and that is *fear*—And one of its infallible consequences will be the prohibition of the S$^{t:}$ Domingo trade— Since the appearance of those letters, the very members of the Senate, who had most strenuously opposed the prohibition (myself only excepted) have become the most zealous favourers of the measure—So that I find myself on this subject deserted by the most powerful of my original co-operators— War with France however is considered as inevitable, unless we submit to these rough requisitions, and accordingly submission is avowed as the principle for the government of our measures. The prohibitory Bill has not yet pass'd this branch of the Legislature, but undoubtedly will, and probably in the course of the present week.[5]

I sent your father last week the copy of a Bill which I have introduced to prevent the abuse of the privileges and immunities of foreign Ministers—it has been twice read and is referred to a select Committee of five Members, but I have not much expectation that it will finally pass—[6] The difficulty on this as on all similar cases is that the measure proceeds from a quarter which must not be encouraged— So convinced have I been that this principle will predominate upon every proposition I can bring forward that I have been as unwilling to originate business as you are; though not absolutely from the same reason. On this occasion however, as no other person did propose any legislative provision, and as I believed some provision highly expedient, I ventured to ask leave to bring in this Bill— I supposed that although the point would probably not be carried *now*, yet a basis would be laid upon which something useful may be done at a future time—And I thought some benefit might be derived from presenting to the consideration of the *public* out of Congress, what I deem the proper remedy for a grievous evil.

Of the three Resolutions reported by the Committee of Senate, upon the subject of our differences with Great-Britain, a copy of which I sent you last week, the two first, being those which I informed you were originally drawn up by me, have been acted upon, and adopted by the Senate—[7] The first *unanimously*— The second by 23 yeas to 7 nays— The third only remains for discussion; but I doubt very much of its adoption. I have told you that this was not my measure— I contemplated something more effectual, more practicable, and less mischievous to ourselves—But being convinced from a variety of circumstances that it could not be carried down, I thought it best not to bring it forward— I acquiesced in the third Resolution as reported, but am not yet clear how I shall vote upon it after discussion.

February 1806

I have received from Mr. Shaw the monthly Anthology for January— And mean to write to him in the course of a few days— I am well satisfied with this number of that work; excepting that in the Review of the British Pamphlet entitled "War in Disguise" there appears to me too much of *neutrality* in the reviewer, upon the main question in controversy—[8] Indeed he professedly declines the expression of an opinion upon this point, alledging his own *incompetency* to its decision— Yet a Reviewer of the British Pamphlet ought to have been able to refute its sophistries, and detect its injustice under all the splendor of its diction, and the fascinations of its style— I hope not only that we shall see no defenders of the British doctrine, but that we shall have no *doubters* of its injustice nay—not even any lukewarm believers in our own rights upon this subject— It was from a strong sentiment on my own mind of the necessity there is for pledges of unanimity in *our* opinions on this topic, that I drew up the first of the three Resolutions; and I was accordingly gratified by the unanimous adoption of that Resolution, in Senate— I am also very glad that the subject has been so thoroughly and so ably investigated in this Country, as it has been in the various memorials from our Seaports, and by several other very able pamphlets, recently published— They have completed the demonstration of the Justice of our Cause, and have swept away every atom of argument on the side of our Opponents.

We are all tolerably well— Remember me kindly to your wife— I hope she will duly receive a letter from mine which I enclosed to you last Week.[9]

Your's affectionately.

RC (Adams Papers); internal address: "T. B. Adams Esqr."; endorsed: "J Q Adams Esq{r:} / 17th Feby 1806 / 27{th:} Recd / Ans{d} March."

[1] TBA's 2 Feb. letter and enclosure have not been found.
[2] Blaise Pascal, *Lettres provinciales*, Letter XVI.
[3] Attorney Joseph Story (1779–1845), Harvard 1798, represented Salem as a Democratic-Republican in the Mass. General Court from 1805 to 1807. Story served on a joint committee that in Jan. 1806 recommended a bill to give state judges greater latitude in interpreting laws. The bill, which was widely seen as an attempt to empower the judiciary at the expense of juries and the legislature, failed in the house of representatives on 15 Feb. by a vote of 118 to 91 (*Biog. Dir. Cong.*; R. Kent Newmyer, *Supreme Court Justice Joseph Story: Statesman of the Old Republic*, Chapel Hill, N.C., 1985, p. 56, 57; Boston *Independent Chronicle*, 17 Feb.; Boston *Columbian Centinel*, 18 Jan.).
[4] The New York *Daily Advertiser*, 25 Jan., printed a false report that Aaron Burr had been appointed as a U.S. envoy to Great Britain and France. The report was reprinted in New England, including in the *Providence Gazette*, 1 Feb., and the *Boston Commercial Gazette*, 3 February.
[5] Despite regulations passed by Congress in 1805 to stem private U.S. arms sales to revolutionary forces in Haiti, for which see JQA to JA, 3 Nov. 1804, and note 7, above, trade continued unabated. Responding to a 27 Dec. 1805 request by the Senate, Thomas Jefferson on 10 Jan. 1806 submitted to Congress letters

sent from Aug. 1805 to Jan. 1806 by French foreign minister Charles Maurice de Talleyrand-Périgord to U.S. minister to France John Armstrong Jr. and by French minister to the United States Louis Marie Turreau de Garambouville to James Madison. France demanded stronger action from the U.S. government to curb the trade, which it claimed nourished "rebellion and robbery." Congress approved legislation on 28 Feb. that banned the arms sales (*Amer. State Papers, Foreign Relations*, 2:725–727; *Annals of Congress*, 9th Cong., 1st sess., p. 117–138; *U.S. Statutes at Large*, 2:351–352; Arthur Scherr, "Arms and Men: The Diplomacy of U.S. Weapons Traffic with Saint-Domingue under Adams and Jefferson," *International History Review*, 35:633–637, 647 [June 2013]).

⁶ For JQA's unsuccessful bill reducing diplomatic immunity for foreign ministers, see his letter to AA, 14 March, and note 4, below. JQA enclosed the bill in his letter to JA of 11 Feb., for which see JA's reponse of 26 Feb., and note 2, below.

⁷ See JQA to TBA, 5 Feb., and note 5, above.

⁸ British lawyer James Stephen in his influential pamphlet *War in Disguise; or, The Frauds of the Neutral Flags*, London, 1805, characterized the countenancing of neutral commerce in wartime as an "indulgence" that helped Great Britain's enemies and threatened its security. An unsigned review in the *Monthly Anthology*, 3:47–53 (Jan. 1806), withheld an opinion on Stephen's claim, endorsed Anglo-American peace efforts, and argued that Britain had no interest in war with the United States. Gouverneur Morris published a response in February, *An Answer to War in Disguise; or, Remarks upon the New Doctrine of England, Concerning Neutral Trade*, N.Y., 1806, arguing that Britain did not have the right to abrogate the longstanding tenet of neutrality (Joseph Eaton, *The Anglo-American Paper War: Debates about the New Republic, 1800–1825*, N.Y., 2012, p. 42; Madison, *Papers, Secretary of State Series*, 11:297–298; Morris, *Diaries*, 2:xxx, 426; Willem Theo Oosterveld, *The Law of Nations in Early American Foreign Policy*, Boston, 2016, p. 256).

⁹ Not found.

Thomas Boylston Adams to Thomas Cadwalader

Dear sir. Quincy. 19th: February 1806.

I have just now, upon my return from Boston, found your letter of the 9th: instant, disclosing to me an enterprize in which you contemplate embarking, as an Associate with Dr Rose, a Gentleman of whom you have heretofore spoken advantageously in your letters to me. At the same time you have proposed to me an Agency to obtain for you in this quarter, purchasers and settlers of the land which is offered to your choice.¹ As I have not given myself sufficient time to deliberate upon this proposition, I shall now only acknowledge the receipt of your letter, and after thanking you for this mark of confidence, endeavor to suggest such crude opinions as may present themselves upon the first intimation of a subject so entirely novel to me. It may be proper for your satisfaction to premise, that you shall have all the aid of my attention and enquiry to ascertain how far your project can be advanced in the New England states, and you may calculate upon a speedy communication of every fact that may come to my knowledge in furtherance of your views.

As to myself, I am free to declare that I am utterly incompetent to give you any information upon this subject, which deserves the least weight; but having the means of access to members of our Legislature

February 1806

now in Session, it may be in my power to acquire such intelligence as will serve to regulate your future operations.

It is well known to you already, that the Province of Maine has within a few years past offered a *cheap Assylum* to the surplus population of the Massachusetts Bay. Large tracts of that Country still remain unsettled and unlocated which, nevertheless, from the rapidity of population in that region promise considerable profit as well to owners as settlers. In order to encourage the settlement of that new Country the Legislature of this Commonwealth to which much of it belonged have made grants of considerable tracts by way of endowment of Academies and schools; these are sold with all possible dispatch for active funds and consequently very cheap, but the object intended by the Legislature has been in some measure effected by turning the tide of enterprize and speculation into that channel. Our people, who emigrate for the most part go *down East*, as they parsimoniously call it; but the people of Connecticutt principally emigrate to the Northward & Westward; I should therefore imagine that your hopes ought to rest chiefly upon them for Cultivators and purchasers. The people of Connecticutt also, if I am correctly informed are of a more roving disposition than those of the other N.E. states, owing to their superabundance of population.[2] I will converse with some Gentlemen whom I believe to be competent judges of the subject of your letter and without betraying your secret, avail myself of their intelligence, when you may expect to here further from me.

I am now so much in haste that I can only reciprocate your good wishes, and with best remembrance to your Lady[3] subscribe / Your friend
T B Adams.

RC (PHi:Cadwalader Collection); addressed: "Thomas Cadwalader Esqr / Philadelphia"; internal address: "Thomas Cadwalader Esqr"; endorsed: "Quincy. M$^{tts.}$ 19. Feb. 1806 / T.B. Adams Esq / rec$^d.$ 27."; notation by Richard Cranch: "Quincy. Feb: 20$^{th.}$ 1806. Free."; and by JA: "J. Adams."

[1] Cadwalader's letter has not been found. Philadelphia physician Robert Hutchinson Rose (1776–1842) was preparing to purchase vast tracts of land in Susquehanna County, Penn., to offer as lots for sale through agents. TBA wrote to Cadwalader again on 6 Dec. (PHi:Cadwalader Family Papers), responding to a renewed request for advice on finding New England buyers (Madison, *Papers, Retirement Series*, 2:250; William H. Egle, *History of the Commonwealth of Pennsylvania*, 3d edn., Phila., 1883, p. 1099; Emily C. Blackman, *History of Susquehanna County, Pennsylvania*, Phila., 1873, p. 32, 76, 445–446).

[2] The population of Massachusetts grew from 100,000 in 1700 to 1 million in 1800, fueling migrations to Maine, New Hampshire, Vermont, Canada, and points west. Population densities in southern New England states in 1800 ranged from 52 to 64 people per square mile, while the average in Maine territory was just over 5. Laws passed in 1805 and 1806 by the Mass. General Court helped to spur the population shift. On 16 March 1805 an act was approved establishing an academy at Bath, Maine, and granting to its trustees a six-mile-square tract to be divided for settlement. A like amount of land was granted two days ear-

lier to the trustees of an existing school in Hallowell, Maine. A week after TBA wrote this letter, the legislature also passed a law clearing title to settlement lands granted earlier to the trustees of an academy in Lincoln, Maine (Joint Economic Committee of the U.S. Congress, *New Dimensions in Rural Policy: Building Upon Our Heritage*, Washington, D.C., 1986, p. 72, 73; David Hackett Fischer, *Albion's Seed*, N.Y., 1989, p. 17; Mass., *Acts and Laws*, 1804–1805, p. 199–201, 381–382, 664).

[3] That is, Mary Biddle Cadwalader, for whom see vol. 15:414.

Abigail Adams to Sarah Smith Adams

my Dear Daughter   Quincy Feb^{ry} 23^d 1806

Your Letter of Feb'ry I duly received, and should sooner have replied to it, but I wished to consider the subject of it maturely, and to give you the best advise in my power—[1]

If you have a prospect that you can be supplied with a number of Boarders in the spring, it will be adviseable for You to continue your House, but you certainly cannot make it answer with one only. commencing in winter when you must necessarily consume more wood, renderd housekeeping more expensive:

I will remit you a Hundred Dollors the present Year for Abbes Board, and this I shall take from the income of half a Farm left me by my Father. You are not a Stranger to the embarressment we were plunged into by, the failure of the House of Bird and savage. expecting them to have been secure, Money was taken from where it was Safely lodged drawn into their hands, and there sunk by their failure at the Same time Your Father had made a purchase of a Farm which required that money to pay it. concequently he has been obliged to take what he had at interest, and fullfill his engagements as fast as he could— there is still a considerable sum due, and he is Struling to get through it—[2] this has kept us so short of ready Money, that I some times experience great mortifications in concequence of it— it is in vain to complain of a Life devoted to the public, and of services renderd a country, who are blindly and wantonly throwing away those blessings obtaind for them—

My interest will not be due untill April, when I will remit you 50 dollars. I wish it was in my power to do more for You; You must not get discouraged. I trust You will finally Succeed.

Charity is making Money from her Indian Medicine, and her, nostrums:[3] I really think if she possessd common prudence She might do very well, but she is no sooner Successfull, than her head is turned, and she becomes such a boaster that She ruins all her plans— Several persons have applied to her from this town, in consumptive cases—by which means I have heard more of her than I should otherways. she cannot help Making daily boasts of the money she acquires— she has ten dollors for every Mess, but if the patient dyes before the Medicine is expended she returns part of the Money. in Some instances her Medicine has been successful—and I do not doubt but that she has acquired a good deal of property by it.— she says her House is thronged from morning till Night. She undertakes to cure the most inveterate Deafness—but she should remember the Hen who laid the golden Egg, by aiming at too much, she may lose the whole

Your Friends here all desire to be rememberd to you— I am quite alone now, save Susan and little John— Mrs Adams has been in Boston this Month with her sister. Mr Adams is attending the Gen'll court— Louissa is with her sister who is very unwell. we have many fears least she is in a decline—

My Love to Abbe from your / affectionate Mother   A Adams

RC (NIC:Johnson Family Papers); addressed: "Mrs Sarah Adams / Newark."

[1] Not found.
[2] For the financial losses sustained by the Adamses with the failure of the London firm Bird, Savage, & Bird and JA's land purchases, see vol. 15:x–xi, xvii, 284.
[3] Charity Smith Shaw, sister of WSS and wife of Benjamin Shaw of Boston, began selling "Indian Medicines" from a shop on Chambers Street in May 1805, advertising widely and claiming they would cure a broad array of illnesses, including dysentery, cancer, consumption, tapeworm, whooping cough, fever, and dropsy. After encountering financial difficulties in Boston, Shaw moved to New York in Sept. 1806. She continued her business until 1821, becoming celebrated as an early nineteenth-century marketer of patent medicines (vol. 8:321, 323; Jason Peter Zieger, Rise of the "Indian Doctors": Charity Shaw and the Marketing of Indian Medicine, College of William & Mary, M.A. thesis, 2008, p. 5, 52–55, 67–68; Boston *Independent Chronicle*, 27 Feb. 1806; *New-England Palladium*, 28 Feb.).

Elizabeth Smith Shaw Peabody to Abigail Adams

Atkinson. February 24th 1806.

I will not, I dare not, stop to think how long it is, since I have written to my Dear Sister,[1] but hope she has been favoured with as good a state of health, through this winter, as she enjoyed in the course of the former part of the year, & that each dear & valuable branch of her household, have had a large Share of a blessing, which those who are deprived of health, espicially, know to be inestimable.

We have had a large portion of Sickness in our Family, in the last year, but thanks to heaven, Death has not deprived me of any branch. Though his ebon wand has been held over us, yet we have been hitherto spared—[2] How melancholly the houses of our Neighbours look? when they have been bereaved of any of its inhabitants, whether they be young, or the aged—

Mr Vose has lost his youngest Child, it was indeed a beautiful little Creature—one year & half old— Just as the tender leaves were opening, the cruel Spoiler comes, & blasts the promised joy—

The last week their fears were again renewed by their Eliza's being taken in the same sudden manner, but it has happily ended in a lung fever, & her symtoms have much abated—[3] By the Papers I have seen, & sincerely regret the loss of another little Mary Smith— When I was at Mr Smiths I really thought she was a lovely Child— And now, she is safely "lodg'd above these rolling Spheres;

> The baneful Influence of whose giddy dance
> Sheds sad vicissitudes on all beneath"—[4]

I often in imagination place myself in your domestic Circle, & fancy that you are very happy in each others Society, in a constant interchange of parental, fillial, & friendly offices; not but I must suppose, that many things intervene as alloys, but few I hope, as could reasonable be expected, under existing Circumstances, & those by *your good dispositions* made easy as possible, for I have found, that what evils cannot well be avoided, had always better be cheerfully & patiently borne— they serve to refine humanity from its dross, & makes it better prepared to Join the Society of pure & perfect Spirits.

I have had but little Intelligence from Boston, or Quincy this winter— I hope my dear Son enjoys health, & has a comfortable share of Employment to defray his necessary expences— I feel very anxious for him, because I know they must be great, & I am perfectly willing to help him all in my power— I have knit him three pair of white woollen Stocks, & have been waiting for a good conveyance— I must apply to you my dear Sister, to tell me whether he does not want very much, linnen Shirts, & cotten & linnen drawers— Abby has been so sick this winter, that I have not thought for, or done for him, what I intended— She recovers slowly, sometimes she has had the Rheumatism in her Stomach, as you used to have—but is better of that, & then Miss White burned her foot, & she was obliged to keep it in a Chair for a fortnight—& many troubles the poor girl has in her youth—[5] She has been so well for this year or two, that I thought her quite firm but she has had a severe fever, now, & it is hard for such Constitutions to recover— The Dr says she wants nothing but air & excercise, & high living— If she is well enough I must send her as soon as the weather will permit, to the Salt water again— She wants much to visit her Aunts at Quincy, but I believe she sometimes is fearful, she shall not

February 1806

be well enough— But I hope she will, though it is very discouraging to be so long confined—

I hope your Absent Children, & Grand Children are well— And if their deserts or my wishes could make them so, they would be surrounded with the Sunshine of Prosperity—

How is Cousin Louisa this winter, & Sister Smith— I can hear nothing of Mrs Foster, I wish she loved to write as well, as two or three of my little Boarders— Louisa would write a letter every hour in the day if I would let her— So would Henry, & John— I am affraid absolutely to oppose strenuously lest they should, when grown, never love to write, when they well know how happy it would make their friends to have a Letter, even one in three months—

I hear Mr Harrod has been to visit his Children at Boston & Quincy—[6] I wish I had known it— I would written

Please to let me know how Phebe does—&ccc room only for—

E Peabody

RC (Adams Papers); endorsed: "Mrs Peabody / 22 Febry 1806."

[1] Peabody's last extant letter to AA was of 16 April 1804 (vol. 15:357–360).
[2] William Mason, "Musaeus: A Monody to the Memory of Mr. Pope," line 43.
[3] The child who recently died was Mary Vose (b. 1804), the youngest daughter of Atkinson Academy preceptor John Vose and his wife, Lydia Webster. Elizabeth Quincy Vose (1801–1827) was their elder child (Ellen F. Vose, *Robert Vose and His Descendants*, Boston, 1932, p. 191, 192, 322).
[4] Edward Young, *The Complaint; or, Night Thoughts*, Night I, lines 187–189.
[5] Possibly Mary White (1784–1836) or her sister Anna (1786–1878), siblings of Daniel Appleton White of Haverhill, Mass. (vol. 14:110; Daniel Appleton White, *Descendants of William White, of Haverhill, Mass.*, Boston, 1889, p. 32).
[6] For AHA's parents, Haverhill innkeeper Joseph Harrod and Anna Treat Harrod, see vol. 9:25.

Abigail Adams to William Smith Shaw

Dear William

Quincy Febry 25th 1806

I have found the account and inclose it to you. I wish you to inquire of our Tennant whether the House must be removed, and at what price he would undertake to do it? whether any fence will be necessary, and whether the place would not be benifitted by planting out a Young orchard and a number of fruit trees. I think Mr Teel agreed that he would dig a new cellar & remove the house for 200 dollors. I should be willing to expend as much as that in improveing the place and rendering it still more Valuable. I think we have lain out of our property long enough—and we must finally lay at the Mercy of those who chuse to make property of us— but if we cannot help ourselves we must settle it so—for settle it, we had better even so than it should lay as it has done for Years.— You will converse with Mr Adams about it—[1]

I have a number of documents for you which I will Send by the first good opportunity— have you heard lately from Your Mother. how was Abbe I am anxious to learn. Yours affectionatly

Abigail Adams.

RC (OClWHi:Western Reserve MSS).

[1] Enclosure not found. Benjamin Teel was the tenant of the Medford farm that AA and Elizabeth Smith Shaw Peabody inherited from their father. For TBA's involvement, see his letter to Shaw, 24 April 1805, and note 1, above. In a [13 May 1806] letter (Adams Papers), AA advised JQA that workmen had moved the farmhouse, installed new fencing, and planted an orchard (vol. 15:453).

John Adams to John Quincy Adams

Quincy Feb. 26 1806

My Exordium must inform you that George is and has been a long time in perfect health. John has been as plump and gay and hardy and hearty as you could wish him, till Yesterday when he looked a little paler or rather a little less ruddy than usual but he worked and played as usual all day; but this morning he discovered Symptoms of qualms in his Stomack and puked a little, but a Tea Spoonfull or two of Some of his Grandmammas Remedies I suppose will restore him to his usual Activity and appetite, in a few hours.

I believe the prohibition of the Trade to St. Domingo is without Example. If a nation has a Country under its dominion, it has Power as well as right to prohibit the commerce of other nations with it. They may Seize, make Prize, confiscate, any Vessels or Cargoes concerned in Such illicit trade. But to require other Nations to make Laws to restrain their own Subjects from Such Intercourse, I believe is as new as it is arbitrary and imperious. If I mistake not there is in Belshams Memoirs of the reign of George the first, Some Account of Such peevish requisitions of Spain, to induce England to prohibit their People from trading with the Spanish Main: but they were treated with more than contempt by the house of Commons.[1]

The Power and Resources of France, have been exaggerated in the Minds of our People, for thirty Years past, and Since the revolution more than ever. The Weakness and danger of England, have been as much misrepresented on the other hand. When I received your Letter, I was very far from your opinion that the Continent of Europe was prostrate at the feet of France: but Since that time news has ar-

February 1806

rived of a very different Complexion.² The particulars are not yet Stated from Authentic Sources. But I cannot believe that France will derive any Solid Addition of Power or reputation from this Campaign. There is no Country under her Power, that is not full of discontent; and revolutions in a contrary direction may Suceed each other, much sooner and more rapidly than We imagine.

In all Events, I know that Submission to unreasonable demands from France, is not the Way to Secure ourselves against her Grasp.

I perceive no Signs of any Warm Passions among the People or of more Decision or Unanimity, than there is in Congress. They are all at a gaze: and know not what to do. Parson Moodys Doctrine was that "it is the Duty, of a Person or a People, in difficult times when they know not what to do, to be very *carefull that they do not do, they know not what.*"³ a good Lesson for Some of the bold Men at Washington.

Negotiation is the only measure in which all Men Seem to agree. But the exclusive System of confining all appointments to a Party, which Seems to be adopted by the present Administration with more Severity than it was by the Federalists, though by them it was carried too far, will prevent the nomination of any Man in whom the great body of the People will confide. And therefore I expect that no measures will be adopted, which will give Satisfaction to the public. Our Rulers have Shackled themselves. They obtained their power by professions of a Sordid Œconomy, and are more afraid of their own constituents, than of their opponents. Mr Macon and Mr Early by Some of their Speeches have let Us See into the hearts of the Party more clearly than they intended, though they expressed themselves with curious caution and ingenious Address.⁴

I am Sorry that Mr Randolph has made his motion to make the Judges more dependent on the Legislature.⁵ The Nature of our Government being more than half federative, renders a perfect Independence of the Judges more necessary here than it is in England. I hope it will not pass Congress, and if it should, I hope it will not be accepted by the States.

You have indeed Business and studies enough in Senate, and I wish not to interrupt you: but if you can find a moment I wish you would ask Dr Mitchell in my name whether, the Plant which is called Soda, Kali, and Barilla, has ever been found in America and if it has, in what part of it, and whether any Seeds of it have been imported, to try the Experiment, whether it will grow here.?⁶

I have read your Bill. What the Corps Diplomatique, will think of it, I know not.— It is a dangerous and delicate Subject. But Something

Seems necessary to be done, to prevent too much Petulance and impertinence.

RC (Adams Papers); internal address: "J. Q. Adams."; endorsed: "My Father 26. Feb:y 1806. / 8. March rec:d." Tr (Adams Papers).

[1] William Belsham, *Memoirs of the Kings of Great Britain of the House of Brunswic-Lunnenburg*, 2 vols., London, 1793, 1:154–155, 208–209, 257–258.

[2] On 11 Feb. JQA wrote to JA on the Senate's views on U.S. relations with Great Britain and France, declaring, "Unqualified submission to France, and unqualified defiance of Great-Britain, are indeed the two pillars upon which our measures are to rest" (Adams Papers). The *New-England Palladium*, 25 Feb., carried an unconfirmed report of Napoleon's 2 Dec. 1805 victory at Austerlitz, Austria, for which see JQA to AA, 14 March 1806, and note 5, below.

[3] This had been a favorite anecdote of JA's since a 1774 dinner conversation in York, Maine, in which Mass. General Court representative Jonathan Sayward attributed the quotation to York parson Rev. Samuel Moody. Both JA and AA repeated it in letters, and AA quoted it at the end of her last in-person conversation with Thomas Jefferson in Jan. 1801 (vols. 1:116, 121; 7:394, 396; 14:542; JA, *D&A*, 3:307, 313).

[4] In a transcript of a 23 Jan. 1806 debate in the House of Representatives, the Philadelphia *United States Gazette*, 29 Jan., reported that Democratic-Republican representative Peter Early (1773–1817) of Georgia broke with Jefferson and other members of his party by arguing that more information was needed before a bill to bolster defenses along the U.S. coast was put to a vote. Speaker of the House Nathaniel Macon supported Early's assessment despite Jefferson's call for congressional action: "I am not sent here to obey the mandates of the president; but to examine and judge concerning publick good; and this I will do let who will be president" (New York *Evening Post*, 31 Jan.; Boston *Independent Chronicle*, 3 Feb.; Hartford *Connecticut Courant*, 12 Feb.).

[5] On 7 Feb. John Randolph introduced a bill to make justices of the U.S. Supreme Court and all other federal judges removable by the president upon a joint petition of both houses of Congress. Randolph first introduced the measure at the end of the previous session on 1 March 1805, but no action was taken. The House took up the measure on 24 Feb. 1806 but postponed it again (*Annals of Congress*, 8th Cong., 2d sess., p. 1213–1214; 9th Cong., 1st sess., p. 446, 499–508).

[6] JA sought information from Samuel Latham Mitchill on barilla, a plant found in Spain, Sicily, and the Canary Islands and imported to the United States for use in the manufacture of soda, soap, and glass. Varieties of the plant are now established as invasive species in New England and other parts of the United States (*OED*; Sergei L. Mosyakin, "A Taxonomic Synopsis of the Genus Salsola (Chenopodiaceae) in North America," *Annals of the Missouri Botanical Garden*, 83:387, 389 [1996]).

Abigail Adams to John Quincy Adams

my Dear Son   Quincy March 5th 1806

I fear Your Father may have given You unnecessary anxiety; I told him at the time it was not best to mention an indisposition so slight as John's was, but he said if he wrote; he must tell all.[1] I had observed for Several days about noon a high couour in his cheeks, and at that time, he was unusually irritable. some other Symptoms indicated a redundancy of Bile, which proved to be the case for the first time, since he has been with me. I gave him a little medicine and it relieved him. he was quite well the next day, and I took him with me to Boston,

February–March 1806

where he both gave, and received much delight; he is very fond of his Aunt Adams, and the meeting between them is always a very joyous scene after a little absence. I told him to day that I should write to you. he is never willing to see me take my pen; it requires a little more silence from him than he likes, but when I tell him I am going to write to you, or his Mamma, he is more reconciled to it. to day he requested me to say that he was a good Boy, and added of himself— ask Pappa to come home. George spent March meeting Day with him, and is very well. I thought I perceived upon his face a few of the old pimples returning, and advised his Aunt to give him some of the black powders, which she will do. it is about the season when he was so afflicted the last Year—

I rejoice to learn, as we have by a Letter from mrs Quincy that Mr Cranch is appointed Chief Justice of the District of Columbia— the appointment will do honour to mr Jefferson, a thing very necessary to him, nor can I believe as some persons do, that he did it reluctantly—[2] I have More pity for him than Many others, more compassion for his errors and some of his frallties— ill treated as some of My Friends have been—I never could, or did receive any Satisfaction from the oblique cast upon ~~him~~ his Character.

what a strange Buisness is this in which Miranda has engaged.? When I saw the first account in a New york paper, it struck Me as something in which the administration must have some concern and knowing the enterprizing Character of Miranda I thought it probable that he might be engaged in some secret progect, particularly as so much secrecy had been preserved in congress—and so much buisness done with closed doors—but the sensation which has been, since his sailing excited and the Queries which have been made to mr Madison have given me not a little uneasiness—least an innocent and amiable Youth may fall a Sacrifice. the first intimation I ever had respecting him—was in a Letter which I received last week—in which it was Said, You know his mind has been long intent upon the sea. an opportunity offering which was considerd advantages, he has gone a voyage. I no sooner read it, than I drew the conclusion, and tho not an other syllable has been written upon the subject, I conclude the Query in the paper to be true. I this day received a Letter from the same quarter, but the Subject is not even mentiond.[3] I dare not say all I fear or half I apprehend; you know in what light it will be considerd here by his . . . and how execrated.—[4]

a strange coalition is taking place in NewYork—[5] what a medly?

I hope the buisness of congress will be well Matured dijested, sifted, purified refined— If you can accomplish a shield for the President, you will shew the world, that you can requite evil with good, the most honorable and glorious victory in My estimation which can be obtaind over our Enemies— bless them who curse You. do good to those who despightfully use you—[6]

with my Love to Mrs A / I subscribe affectionatly / Your Mother
Abigail Adams—

RC (Adams Papers); endorsed: "My Mother. 5. March 1806. / 14. March rec$^{d:}$."

[1] See JA to JQA, 26 Feb., above.

[2] Eliza Susan Morton Quincy's letter to AA has not been found. William Cranch had served as an assistant judge of the U.S. Circuit Court of the District of Columbia since 3 March 1801. On 21 Feb. 1806 Thomas Jefferson nominated Cranch to replace William Kilty as chief justice, and the Senate confirmed the appointment on the 24th. Cranch remained in the post for almost half a century. Several newspapers reported the appointment without comment, while the Richmond, Va., *Enquirer*, 30 May, claimed Jefferson's nomination was in line with his stated intention of promoting from within the courts and that criticism of the elevation of a Federalist in this case was "a mite converted into a mountain" (vol. 15:1–2; *ANB*; U.S. Senate, *Exec. Jour.*, 9th Cong., 1st sess., p. 21, 22; *Philadelphia Gazette*, 3 March; New York *Commercial Advertiser*, 3 March; Boston *Columbian Centinel*, 8 March).

[3] These letters to AA have not been found. The New York *Commercial Advertiser*, 21 Feb., reprinted a piece questioning the roles of the U.S. government and WSS in Francisco de Miranda's expedition against Venezuela, for which see JQA to WSS, 16 April, and note 2, below. The article suggested that William Steuben Smith's participation, for which see Introduction, Part 2, above, constituted evidence that his father assisted Miranda in his capacity as surveyor for the port of New York.

[4] Ellipsis in MS.

[5] The Boston *Repertory*, 4 March, asserted that New York Democratic-Republicans had splintered anew after supporters of Aaron Burr "formed a new coalition" with those favoring DeWitt Clinton. The newspaper suggested that Morgan Lewis would be challenged by a candidate to be chosen by the new coalition.

[6] Matthew, 5:44.

Abigail Adams Smith to Hannah Carter Smith

My Dear Madam New York March 12th 1806

I have intended a long time since to write to you but have been prevented by various avocations. sincerely have I sympathized with you in your late affliction and you have been frequently in my remembrance.

the various trials we meet with in this Life, are perhaps necessary to give us a true Idea of its inefficacy to ensure our happiness and to teach us to place our affections and direct our views towards another to which we are all hastening, and few of us are reconciled to the thoughts of quiting this, altho our paths may not have been strewed with roses, very few that do not find Stong ties and attachments yet remaining; amidst the greatest trials, we have many blessings to be gratefull for, and we never aught to distrust the care and protection of Providence your mind my Dear Madam is I know much better impressed upon thease Subjects than I can pretend to be your reason and religion will direct it in the right path,

however severe the Stroke it is our duty to submit and to resign our nearest friends when they are taken from us

my mind can easier reconcile itself to such events as appear to be the dispensation of providence, than such as result from our own imprudence, and want of judment, altho thease may often be the means, to affect the object

you will have heard before this time that we have parted with our Son William for some time. I did not expect when he went away that his excursion would have excited Such a Spirit as it has amongst us— or that he would have been made of so much consequence as to excite such various conjectures and Surmises. many of them time and events will contradict I presume—

we received a letter from Mr Smith with the articles that he sent on by Water which we received Safe and are much obliged by his attention to them[1]

I must apologise to you for not having sent your Cap before this time. my eyes were so weak for some weeks that I could not work upon muslin and this must be my excuse for Sending it unfinished the lace work is not done as I know your Daughter excels in this kind of work I must request her to fill it up.[2]

it may I hope serve to remind you of one who highly respects and esteems you, and who with pleasure subscribes herself your friend

A Smith

be so good as to remember me to Mrs Welch and the young Ladies tell Hariet I often wish for her—

RC (MHi:Smith-Carter Family Papers); endorsed: "A. Smith / N.Yk. 1806."

[1] Not found.
[2] That is, Smith's eldest daughter, Elizabeth Storer Smith.

John Quincy Adams to Abigail Adams

Washington 14. March 1806.

It is so long since I have had one hour of leisure that I could appropriate to correspondence with my friends at Quincy and Boston, that I am fearful you will impute to some other cause the length of the interval between my letters— My health however has been gradually improving ever since I left you, and on the whole has been better through the Winter, than for two years before.— A variety of public business has so occupied my time and attention that for the last three weeks I have not been able to snatch even during the sitting of the Senate a moment to thank you and my father for the kind letters I have repeatedly received from you and him.

Yet after all the toil and trouble I have taken, there is but little satisfaction in the issue of any business we have had before us— My opinions on every subject of moment which occur, are eventually the opinions overruled, and for any purpose of public benefit to be answered, a tenth part of the time and anxiety which I give to the public affairs would be attended in all probability with the same issue—

The newspapers will inform you that in the House of Representatives the complexion of public debates has assumed a singular and unexpected hue— The debate upon M$^{r:}$ Gregg's Resolution for a non-importation Act, from Great-Britain has discovered principles, opinions and fears which were very unexpected—[1] As I have been so much confined to the Senate-chamber, that I could not attend in the House of Representatives while these debates have been held, I am not able to state them with the correctness or the minuteness which they will obtain in the public prints— You will see that in the midst of the important business of the Nation now before Congress, a very sharp electioneering campaign has commenced, and is carrying on with great violence—for an election nearly three years distance—[2] If common report and something more be credited, the antient dominion is divided against itself—and the question between the two candidates has already excited a strong spirit of party between their respective partizans.

It is probable that Congress will rise about the 15$^{th:}$ of next Month— For any good they have done or will do they might have risen on the 3$^{d:}$ of December— Much harm they have done, and how much more they will do I am not competent to determine.

I hope to see you by the last of April, and perhaps some days sooner— My wife will probably remain here; being in a condition which would make it dangerous for her to venture on so long a journey— If she should be able in the course of the Summer she will follow me home—

Among the other strange adventures of these times, is the mysterious expedition of Miranda, in which I am very sorry to see a connection of ours so much implicated. How far the Government here are also implicated will appear hereafter— That the President and Secretary of State had certain propositions made to them by Miranda, is true—[3] At least he himself told me so, without hinting of what nature

March 1806

they were— The degree of assent, of acquiescence or of negation they may have given them, is altogether unknown to me.

My bill respecting foreign Ministers was rejected on two grounds— One side contending that the President has the power it proposed to give him; and the other that he has it not, and ought not to have it— Neither federalists nor their opponents favoured it, and the principal opposition to it in debate was from a federal quarter— I still believe that some provision of the kind must at one day or another be made— The subject was not a new one to me; for I had been obliged to consider it in 1793 and 1794 at the time of the contests with Genet—[4]

A Peace it appears is in all probability made on the Continent of Europe— The English Accounts of the Actions on the 2^d: of December and the following days, have always borne to me a very suspicious appearance— The facts prove as I have all along thought they would that the career of French victory has been uninterrupted—[5] I am very sorry for it.

Most affectionately yours.[6]

RC (Adams Papers); endorsed: "Mr J Q Adams / March 24th 1806."

[1] Press coverage of congressional debate of the Non-Importation Act of 1806, for which see JQA to TBA, 20 Jan., and note 2, above, fell largely along party lines, with Democratic-Republican newspapers calling it a necessary response to British aggression and the Federalist press depicting it as ruinous to the U.S. economy. The Boston *Democrat*, 15 March, endorsed sponsor Andrew Gregg's contention that the measure was needed to address the "outrages, insults and oppressions of Britain," while the Boston *Repertory*, 21 March, claimed the bill would not bring Great Britain to terms, and queried, "Would it not be better to pursue the old honest path of negotiation; make a commercial treaty, and have done with it" (Joanna Cohen, *Luxurious Citizens: The Politics of Consumption in Nineteenth-Century America*, Phila., 2017, p. 52–59).

[2] Lines were being drawn as the 1808 race for the presidency took shape. "Plain Facts" in the *Washington Federalist*, 3 Feb. 1806, criticized Thomas Jefferson's foreign policy. In commentary reprinted in the Boston *Repertory*, 21 Feb., the writer opined that the president's stance was driven by a desire for reelection. Eugenius in the Washington, D.C., *National Intelligencer*, 21 Feb., took the opposite tack, supporting Jefferson and calling on readers to remember that he was elected by a majority of the American people. See also LCA to AA, 24 Jan. 1808, and note 3, below.

[3] For the purported role of the U.S. government in the Miranda expedition, see JQA to WSS, 16 April 1806, note 2, below.

[4] JQA introduced a bill in the Senate on 13 Feb. to reduce the full diplomatic immunity enjoyed by foreign ministers resident in the United States and make them subject to the nation's laws for personal conduct. In a 3 March speech, which was printed in the *Monthly Anthology*, 3:266–280 [May 1806], JQA reasoned that "immunities of a nature so extraordinary cannot, from the nature of mankind, be frequently conferred, without becoming liable to frequent abuse. Ambassadors are still beings subject to the passions, the vices, and infirmities of man." Only three other senators joined JQA in voting in favor on 7 March, with 24 in opposition (*Annals of Congress*, 9th Cong., 1st sess., p. 92–94, 145–161, 165–166). For French minister to the United States Edmond Charles Genet's 1793 extralegal attempt to circumvent U.S. neutrality and his recall for pursuing the strategy, see vol. 9:442, 446, 462.

[5] On 2 Dec. 1805 French forces under Napoleon routed a combined Russian and Austrian army at Austerlitz, Austria (now Slavkov u Brna, Czech Republic). In the early stages of the engagement Napoleon ordered his troops to leave no enemy soldier alive—

whether they surrendered or not—resulting in 15,000 Russian and Austrian dead to 1,350 on the French side. The New York *Commercial Advertiser*, 15 Feb. 1806, reprinted an account from London that mistakenly reported the engagement as a French defeat and claimed that allied forces launched a successful offensive the next day. The Baltimore *Telegraphe and Daily Advertiser*, 13 March, correctly reported the French victory and that the decimated allied army was suing for peace (Schom, *Napoleon Bonaparte*, p. 413; *Philadelphia Gazette*, 17 Feb.; *Portsmouth Oracle*, 1 March).

[6] AA answered JQA on 24 March, commenting on congressional news and speculating on partisan election strategies. She also advised her son on health and grooming. "I hope you never appear in Senate with a Beard two days old, or otherways make, what is calld a shabby appearance," AA wrote. "Seriously I think a Mans usefullness in Society depends much upon his personal appearance— I do not wish a Senator to dress like a Beau, but I want him to conform so far to the fashion, as not to incur the Character of Singularity; and nor give occasion to the world to ask what kind of Mother he had? or to Charge upon a wife neglegence and inattention when She is guiltless" (Adams Papers).

William Stephens Smith to John Quincy Adams

D.r Sir—   Newyork March 23.d 1806.

I am informed that M.r P. A Schenk is nominated as Surveyor of this port, and of course I am to be superceeded as is expressed in the public papers, for my secret connection with Gen.l Miranda[1] can it be possible that I am to be condemned unheard— Will my frinds in the Senate consent that I shall be sacrificed & my Wife and Children deprived of bread, to shelter men in higher station for their want of consistancy, political integrity and firmness of mind? if this must be submitted to at least let the office be given to my Brother Justus B. Smith, that my family may not suffer, for my immaginary Crimes— let me hear from you

Yours &c   W: S: Smith

RC (Adams Papers); internal address: "J. Q. Adams Esq.r"

[1] In a letter to the Senate of 17 March Thomas Jefferson nominated merchant Peter A. Schenck as surveyor of the port of New York, effectively dismissing WSS. The Senate confirmed the appointment on the 21st and Schenck served until 1815. The *New-York Gazette*, 22 March 1806, reported the change for the reason stated by WSS. Earlier reports rejected WSS's contention that his actions were justified because the expedition was sanctioned by the Jefferson administration. The Baltimore *Telegraphe and Daily Advertiser*, 7 March, for example, argued that the president did not approve the plan and WSS's claim "only proved, and that most conclusively, that colonel Smith has been the *dupe* of Miranda" (U.S. Senate, *Exec. Jour.*, 9th Cong., 1st sess., p. 30; JQA to WSS, 26 March, below; Walter Barrett, *Old Merchants of New York City*, 2d ser., N.Y., 1863, p. 91–92; New York *Commercial Advertiser*, 3 March; *Philadelphia Gazette*, 4 March).

March 1806

Abigail Adams to Eliza Susan Morton Quincy

my dear Mrs Quincy   Quincy March 24th 1806

I have contemplated writing to You for Some time; and thanking you for the information which I have received through You respecting my son's Health.[1] when he writes himself, he is too much occupied with public cares, and too inattentive to himself, to give me such information as I am desirous of obtaining upon a subject, which has given me, many anxious hours—

there are Some malidies so deep rooted, that the most delicate hand dare not probe. the attempt might fix an incureable wound. a depression of Spirits I am certain has been the chief cause of his low state of Health. it gave me particular pleasure when You informed me through my sister that he appeard in better Health, and Spirits, than when he arrived in Washington.

Your little sophia is a very fine Child and grows rapidly. I need not add, that She is as attentively attended too, as you could desire were You present. my little Charge I think a lovely Boy, possest of an engageing temper, and disposition. the least refractory of any child I ever met with, of his Age. so lively and Sensible as he is, he has been quite an amusement to me this winter. I hope I shall not have any cause to regreet that I undertook the care of him.—

Your good Husband my Friend has been fully initiated into the areana of politicks this Session I presume, tho closed Doors have precluded the *Masters* from knowing what their *Servants* were transacting.— aya it was not so *in my Day*. what the federalists dared to do, they dared to avow. tho secrecy is sometimes necessary, and the fate of a Nation may be involved in a disclosure of measures, Yet such was the Clamour of the Democrats and there adherents, under the former Administrations, that closed doors for any length of time was a Novelty. when we have been permitted to hear mr Quincy upon any Subject, we have been much pleased and entertaind, and have to regreet that the one half has not been told us—

I have been mortified to see such confusion in counsels as have marked every period of the present Session Such a timid time serving Wavering policy. such a deficiency in tallent amongst the Ruling party, excepting mr Randolph, who uses the whip and scourge like a true Virginian. we do not read any thing which would circulate the Blood, or quicken the pulse a single Stroke, and he appears like a Lunitick, more than a wise Man legislating for a Great Nation. if he is right upon one subject, he is totally wrong upon others. tho he pretends a respect for the constitution when it suits his purpose, he would break and Scatter it like Chaff before the wind when it militates with his purposes. witness his exultation upon the illegal acts past in the Seventh Congress.[2] he reminds Me of a woman in this place, who lost her Reason for many years, when she saw and held converse with innumerable invisible Spirits. after a lapse of Some years, she recoverd her faculties, and transacted buisness in a rational manner; So that a person unacquainted with her, would never have supposed her otherways—but touch upon the subject of her spirits—and she instantly became wild, and frantic. I have thought that the Judges were Randolphs Spirits— his late and former persecution of them, cannot be considerd the ospring of sound intellects. a sensible writer observes, that there are certain Epoch's in the History of every Country, when the best and brighest Men are overwhelmd by a general combination in favour of stupidity, avarice or faction.[3] in Such cases it is vain to look for much patriotism in individuals. Let us look into the Democratic Majority, and contrast them with the federal Majority of the former Administrations where will they find a Murry, Harper, Dexter or Ames? and many others who bore a conspicuous part in Legislation in those Days.— They had a Maddison, the best and most sensible Man of their Party. they also had a Giles, and many others who could clamour— but what will the journals of the Ninth Congress present to Posterity? if it were possible for me to rejoice in the degradation of my country, I should have a compleat triumph. when the federalists permitted the passions of envy and jealousy, to rule their reason, and judgement, they Signed the Death Warrent of their own influence, and concequence the ambition of one Man, now no more, contributed to this Catastrophy and has left a stain upon his Memory which will descend to Posterity nor can all the Eulogys bestowed upon him wash it out.

"Heaven from all creatures hides the Book of fate."[4]

What is to be the destiny of our country time must disclose. at present clouds and thick darkness hang over it—

Present me kindly to mr Quincy, and to Miss Susan.[5] tell my Nephew the Judge that I rejoice in his advancement; no one who knows him will Suspect any change in his principles. he rose by regular succession—independant of his Merrit. I would also hope that the conscience of a Great man may be disposed to make Some attonement for the injury he has done the constitution and his country by displaceing many worthy and respect Men.

My best regards to Mrs Cranch and family. I have ever considerd her as one of those Virtuous women described by King Soloman, who will do her Husband good and not evil all the days of her Life, so that the heart of her Husband may safely trust in her—[6]

when you see my good Friend Mrs Cushing, be so kind as to present my best regards to her.

I anticipate Your return to Quincy with much pleasure, and hope the Day not far distant when you may fold Your Dear ospring to your Maternal Bosom receiving them in Health and safety from the Friends to whose care you committed them—

I am my dear Mrs Quincy / affectionately Your Friend

Abigail Adams

FC (Adams Papers); notation by AA: "Mrs A to Mrs / Quincy 1806."

[1] For Quincy, see Descriptive List of Illustrations, No. 7, above.

[2] AA was referring to the 1802 repeal of the Judiciary Act of 1801 by the 7th Congress and the resulting removal of several federal judges by Thomas Jefferson, for which see vol. 15:165–166. The *New-England Palladium*, 14 March 1806, printed a 24 Feb. speech in which John Randolph expressed support for Jefferson's actions.

[3] AA referenced Joseph Dennie Jr.'s 1803 gloss on comments in a 27 Dec. 1757 letter from Oliver Goldsmith to Daniel Hodson, in which Dennie sought reasons for Goldsmith's obscurity in Ireland and claimed a similar lack of interest in literature in the United States (*Port Folio*, 3:93 [19 March 1803]; William C. Dowling, *Literary Federalism in the Age of Jefferson: Joseph Dennie and* The Port Folio, *1801–1812*, Columbia, S.C., 1999, p. 76).

[4] Alexander Pope, *Essay on Man*, Epistle I, line 77.

[5] That is, Quincy's daughter Eliza Susan Quincy.

[6] Proverbs, 31:10–12.

John Quincy Adams to William Stephens Smith

Dear Sir. Washington 26. March 1806.

I received last Evening your favour of the 23$^{d:}$— The appointment of M$^{r:}$ Schenck had been two or three days before confirmed by the Senate— I most sincerely lament your removal from the Office of Surveyor; but this act is exclusively within the power of the President, and the only notice he usually gives to the Senate of a removal is by a new Nomination to the Office— Such was the case in the present instance— The first intimation I had of your being suspended was the nomination of the new Officer. Neither have the Senate, or, I believe, any of your friends in this body, any influence which could affect a nomination in favour of your brother, or in opposition to that which was made.

With respect to your connection with General Miranda, or the knowledge which the President or Secretary of State had of his projects, I know nothing but what is to be collected from the Newspapers; never having had any communication from you, from Miranda, or from the Executive on this Subject. If you were induced to believe that it was the President's intention to countenance any purpose of hostility to Spain, I very much regret both the fact and its consequences— That he had no such intention is obvious from the course of policy which has prevailed, and has always appeared evident to me, from the time when I had last the pleasure of seeing you at New-York—Of the grounds you may have had for a different inference I am unable to judge; not knowing what they were.

I am, Dear Sir, with sincere attachment, yours'.

LbC (Adams Papers); internal address: "Col[l:] Willliam Stephens Smith— New-York."; APM Reel 135.

John Adams to John Adams Smith

My dear Child,   Quincy March 27th: 1806

I am much pleased with the temper and spirit of your Letter of February 28th:—[1]

The subjects of your future Examination, are judiciously chosen and I hope you will acquit yourself to your own satisfaction as well as that of your Instructor's

I know of no Characteristic of a weak head a dull discernment and superficial reflection more remarkable than the opinion you mention of many young Men, who disregard a degree at College as non essential. The simplest common sence is so sufficient to see and foresee the innumerable benifits of it, that I should think it an ill compliment to your Understanding to enumerate them in detal. A few particulars, nevertheless, may be mentioned. A Diploma from an University is to an honest and discreet Man a Passport through the civilized World. Without it your Contemporaries of College and even your own Classmates will never acknowledge you to be on an equal footing with them. The Government of the University will never pride themselves in your Virtues, Talents and Name as they would have done if you had been enrolled in their records as one who had received there honours and done honour to them. The Men of Science and Learning in the World will with much more difficulty be induced to acknowledge you as one of their Body. But I forbear: your own Reflections will suggest more Advantages from a Degree than it is necessary for me to particularize.—

Your Brother has gone upon his Travails without a Degree, and I do not say that there are not cases in which Advantages may present themselves, sufficient to justify a young Gentleman in relinquishing the honor and advantage of a degree. Whether his Case is one of these I know not as the whole history of the rise, progress and termination of the Business is wholly a Mistery to me. I am wholly ignorant of every Thing relating to it—

When I arrived at Bourdeaux in April 1778 I found an Anecdote in every Man's mouth concerning the Marquis De la Fayette. A Marshall of France had said, when he first heard of the Marquise's Adventure to America "C'est le premier page dans l'histoire, d'un grand homme." "It is the first page in the history of a great Man."[2] Whether your Brother's Enterprize resembles in any degree that of the Marquis, or not, I know not: but in any honest supposition I wish he may be more fortunate in Life than the Marquis has been. I can only commit him to his Almighty Protector. I do not wish you to write me any thing concerning him, except it be intelligence of his health and safety—

I believe a great proportion of the present dominant Party among the People at large as well as in the Administration and in both Houses of the Legislature begin to repent of some of their Obloquies and persecutions against me: for it is very obvious, that they now see, my System of foreign affairs to be the only one in which there can be honor or safety to their Country. I am, your affectionate &C

J. A.

LbC in TBA's hand (Adams Papers); internal address: "J. A. Smith"; APM Reel 118.

[1] Not found. This is the first extant letter from JA to one of his grandchildren.
[2] JA repeated this reference in his autobiography, there noting that the family of the Marquis de Lafayette, which contained "no less than six Marshalls of France," convened and chose him to represent its ranks in America (JA, D&A, 4:83–84).

John Quincy Adams to William Smith Shaw

Dear Sir.   Washington 31. March 1806.

Since I wrote you last I have not heard directly from you although an interval of several weeks has elapsed— I sent you receipts for Gurley's & Delille's Rent, which I presume you have received—[1] On this Idea, I have now to desire that you would enquire whether any dividend on the Stock of the Fire and Marine Insurance Company was made on the first of this Month— And if there was I will thank you to pay my father from the monies of mine in your hands, a sum equal to the dividend upon *forty shares* of the Insurance Stock.²

I continue to send you from time to time the most important public documents as they are published— I expect that our Session will close in about a fortnight, and hope to see you by the end of the next Month.

Last Friday the Senate pass'd an Act for a compromise with the Georgia-Land Claimants—19 ayes 11. Nays— And on Saturday the House of Representatives 62 to 54 determined to *reject* the Bill at the first reading—³ So there is an end of that business for this time.

I remain with invariable regard and esteem, truly yours.

John Quincy Adams.

RC (MWA:Adams Family Letters); addressed: "William Smith Shaw Esq[r] / Boston. / Massachusetts."; internal address: "W. S. Shaw Esq[r.]"; docketed: "J. Q. Adams / 1806"; notation by JQA: "*Free* / John Quincy Adams. / S.U.S."

[1] In a 19 Feb. letter, JQA requested that Shaw collect rents on his Boston properties and commented on the *Monthly Anthology* (MWA:Adams Family Letters).

[2] The Massachusetts Fire and Marine Insurance Company was the first insurance company incorporated in the state, operating from 1795 to 1848. JQA purchased twenty shares of the company's stock on 17 April 1802 and additional shares on 21 Jan. 1803, eventually holding forty shares in his name for the benefit of JA. In a letter of 18 June 1807 (Adams Papers), JQA informed JA that the company would make a capital repayment in the form of Boston Bank stock. JA responded on 20 June (MHi:Winthrop Family Papers) that he would retain the stock rather than sell it (Moses King, *King's Hand Book of Boston*, 9th edn., Boston, 1889, p. 278; JQA, *Diary*).

[3] For the congressional failure to settle Yazoo land claims, see JQA to Shaw, 3 Feb. 1805, and note 3, above.

Eliza Susan Morton Quincy to Abigail Adams

My dear M[rs] Adams—   Washington April 6[th:] 1806.

By the last mail, I had the honour, and the pleasure, to receive your most acceptable letter—¹ To be indeed remembered by you, and with so much distinction, was what I had rather hoped, than expected. Yet it was an hope, so flattering to my pride, and so grateful to some *better* feelings, that it had been fondly cherish'd, and had served to brighten many of the hours since we parted. I was made very happy by the assurance that I had been instrumental in conveying some satisfaction to you, about your Son, thro' the medium of M[rs:] Cranch.

If I had been aware that you derived any comfort, or additional information, upon that subject, from my communications I should have found much pleasure in making them more circumstantial than they have been.— I have now the power to assure you, my dear Madam, that M[r:] Adams is in much better health, and spirits, than when he first arrived here—indeed we think that he has been improving in both respects, for some time past. We met him in church to day, at the Capitol, and brought him home with us to dinner. He staid all the afternoon and is just gone— Mr. Quincy has gone with him to accompany him half way. We cannot have the pleasure of seeing him as often as we anticipated—As we are placed at the very extremities of the City from each other. I believe it is not less than four miles, from this, to M{r:} Helen's.²

Your Son, my dear Madam, I presume keeps you fully informed of every thing relating to the affairs of the political world, which can be curious or interesting to you— The state of parties here, is "confusion, worse confounded"—³ Your view of the democratic majority, is indeed, for the honour of our country, too just a picture—but to be a perfect likeness, you ought to be on the spot, and draw from the *life*. Then, if you could rejoice in the degradation of your country, it would be indeed a triumph to you to contemplate the difference between the federal majority of former Administrations, and the one which M{r:} Jefferson has selected from the American Nation!— But he is already suffering a righteous recompence for all his wicked devices, and evil deeds.— Having succeeded in excluding all men of worth, probity, and talents from the councils of the nation—and in introducing such as he thought would serve well enough for tools to be applied by his master hand, he now finds them wholly incapable of defending him, or themselves, against the violent attacks of a counter revolutionary party. He has not a single man to oppose to Randolph, who carries every thing before him—and who seems to be determined to stop at nothing, short of the destruction of Mr. Jefferson, and his party— At the last trial of strength, Randolph gain'd a compleat victory, in getting a majority in favor of taking off the *injunction* of *secrecy*—a measure which was known to be entirely hostile to the wishes of M{r:} Jefferson.⁴ The Administration, are certainly, in a very unpleasant situation Their party dividing into opposite factions—their Treasury empty—and Randolph successful in throwing in their way every obstacle that the most ingenious malice can invent— As for Randolph himself—as you justly observe—nothing that is good, or consistent can be expected from *him* He, undoubtedly, has his own personal objects in view, which are probably as wide from the *true* interests of his country, as are those of the Man he now persecutes— He is a true Virginian, incapable of an enlarged or liberal policy—and fit only for his *present* employment to be a "scourge for the fools back."—⁵ During these contests between the ruling party—the little band of federalists have judged it most politic and expedient to keep aloof and let them fight it out—useing their influence on the best side, as the case might be; and in this way, have often held the ballance between them, and enjoyed the satisfaction of preventing evil—the nobler pleasure of producing good, is at present beyond their power— What is to be the future state of our country, is indeed a mystery—but from the prospect we already have, we can have no doubt that the event is *mercifully* conceal'd from our view— "For forward, tho' we cannot see; we guess, and fear."—[6] My husband is so little delighted with his "*initiation*," or the prospect it has given him of future gratification, that he is equally anxious with myself to return to the happy shelter of our home at Quincy— We have found from experience, how much more pleasant it is, "thro' the loop-holes of retreat, to peep at such a world" than to be engaged in its bustle, and anoyed by a contact with its depravity, and vice.[7]

This wilderness-city affords little to amuse, less to interest, and nothing to gratify us, who have been too long used to drink at the fountains of good-principles, society, literature and religion, to be satisfied, with these shallow streams, which mock the lip that approaches to taste them.— We look to the end of our banishment with an impatience which you, my dear Madam, can easily imagine—for I am sure of your sympathy in our feelings upon the subject of this most painful seperation from our children, and our friends— I am greatly obliged to you for your notice of my dear little babe— I have indeed no doubt of her being as tenderly regarded as I could wish, by the dear & valuable friend to whom I entrusted her—but yet every additional testimony of her health and well-being, is like "oil, and balm" to my longing anxious heart.—[8] We are very highly gratified, my dear Madam, by your kind expression of a wish to see us again at Quincy— Be assured that next to the happiness of folding our dear little ones in our arms, we anticipate the pleasure of returning to your neighbourhood, and the enjoyment of your society. Your worthy relations Judge & M^(rs:) Cranch present their best regards to you. M^(rs:) Cushing left this place many weeks ago. M^(r:) Q. unites with me in offering to you, and M^(r.) Adams, the assurance of our sincere and affectionate attachment. I fervently hope, that the day is not far distant when I may again take you by the hand, and have the pleasure to see you and yours in the enjoyment of health—and to express my warm regard for / you.—
                                                                E S. Quincy—

RC (Adams Papers); endorsed: "Mrs J Quincy April / 1806."

[1] AA to Quincy, 24 March, above.
[2] Quincy and her husband, Josiah Quincy III, boarded with William and Anna Greenleaf Cranch during the 9th Congress, at this time at the Cranches' home at the corner of Pennsylvania Avenue and G Street SE near the Capitol and later at their residence on Greenleaf's Point south of the city (vol. 14:495; Edmund Quincy, *Life of Josiah Quincy*, 6th edn., Boston, 1874, p. 82, 105; William Cranch to Richard Cranch, 17 Aug. 1804, MHi:Christopher P. Cranch Papers).
[3] Milton, *Paradise Lost*, Book II, line 996.
[4] John Randolph in his ongoing feud with Thomas Jefferson over the dispute with Spain appealed to the House of Representatives on 5 March 1806 to unseal journals of recent secret sessions in which Floridas policy was debated. "They dare not come out and tell the nation what they have done," Randolph declared, prevailing on 31 March when the House voted to make the journals public. For the political consequences of releasing the information, see Descriptive List of Illustrations, No. 1, above (Jackson, *Papers*, 2:93; *Annals of Congress*, 9th Cong., 1st sess., p. 566; U.S. House, *Jour.*, 9th Cong., 1st sess., p. 458).
[5] Proverbs, 26:3.
[6] Robert Burns, "To a Mouse," lines 47–48.
[7] William Cowper, "The Winter Evening," *The Task*, Book IV, lines 88–89.
[8] Shakespeare, *Troilus and Cressida*, Act I, scene i, line 91.

William Stephens Smith to John Quincy Adams

Dr. Sir—   Newyork April 6th. 1806.

my son John Graduates at this College the next Commencement— I am so occupied and shall continue so for some time to come, in the final arrangement of my affairs, that I shall not be able, and sufficiently composed, to give him the aid that he may require, in composing an English oration for him to deliver on that day—

Will you do me the favour to write one on such a subject, as will instruct, suited in some degree to the situation of our Country, such as will stamp on his youthfull mind the first Principles of Patriotism and public Virtue,—[1]

Give a Lesson to statesmen capable of varying their pursuits, at the frowns of a Tyrant, and base enough to barter the freedom of their Country and their own fame for filthy lucre or the tinsel charms of an empty title—

do this & he will do honor to its author he is a good speaker and a very promising firm young man— The family are all well

Your friend & Humble Servt.   W. S. Smith

RC (Adams Papers).

[1] For John Adams Smith's Columbia College commencement ceremony, see JQA to LCA, 9 July, and note 2, below.

Thomas Boylston Adams to John Quincy Adams

Quincy 9th: April 1806

Supposing that you will be at Washington long enough to receive a letter from this place before your departure, I shall venture to acknowledge the receipt of your favor of the 19th: ult: to inform you of the health of both your children, as also of your friends at Quincy, who are looking with pleasure for your return, and who hope the cause of your leaving your wife behind you, will terminate in an happy issue.[1] By this post I shall send, at my wife's request a packett for Mrs: A— to the contents of which I am a stranger, except that the stuff of which the chief material consists is oil cloth— There is doubtless an use for it, and on such occasions men folks should not be too inquisitive.

During the past week and some part of the present, we the people have been very busy in making our Governors for the ensuing year. You know the principal ingredients in this electioneering mess, are 1st: A plenty of slander defamation and detraction, commonly, among the craft, called *billingsgate*, which is *grossly* defined—foul language or abuse. 2d: Some thousand copies of pamphlets, got up, on each side, with ~~great~~ high taste & low style to suit the vulgar. 3d: Local lies, adapted to small Towns & districts, and unceasing efforts to set neighbours at variance on questions of interest or reputation, in order that the bad passions may all be enlisted in the service of Democracy and its leaders, on election days. 4th: Some preaching on Fast days, to tell the people, that, for their sins, during the past year, they have richly merited the displeasure of Heavenly Majesty, and that unless they begin a reform by voting for good, pious, christian rulers, they will all be damned together. We have just got through with the first course of the entertainment for the current year, and the plates & dishes are now changing for the second. It has been found by the federalists that *organization* is your only weapon of defence against organization— So, not to be outdone by our neighbours, we organized in Quincy, as the Jacobins had already done, and having held their Caucus first, they cheated us out of half a dozen of our votes— The Federal Caucus was numerously attended—nearly seventy assembled upon one day's notice, and after hearing the federal Circular, contrasted with the Jacobin Circular, with such comments, (upon the recommendation therein to the people of Massachusetts to chuse Governors who would harmonize with the National Executive), as

April 1806

the moment suggested; after reading the Report of your Committee of the senate on the subject of Hamet ex Bashaw with suitable remarks, the vote was taken will you support Strong or Sullivan for Governor and carried by unanimous acclamation— Accordingly on Monday we mustered 106 votes for Strong and 47 for Sullivan— The returns already received from 62 Towns give Strong a majority of 1455—but "Our General" out-runs M[r.] Robbins in many towns and will probably be chosen.[2] Eleven Federal Senators are already known to be chosen.[3]

This is all the information I have now time to communicate / Sincerely your's

RC (Adams Papers); internal address: "J. Q. Adams."

[1] JQA in his letter of 19 March wrote that he expected to depart for Quincy in mid-April and that owing to her pregnancy LCA would spend the season with her family. He also reported on Senate business and advised TBA to ignore political pressure in making his decisions as a state legislator, writing, "I do not like retreating from a vote of Constituents for fear of being deserted by them" (Adams Papers).

[2] Electioneering efforts in advance of the 1806 Massachusetts gubernatorial election included the Boston *Democrat*, 1 March, calling on voters to support Democratic-Republican challenger James Sullivan. The *Boston Commercial Gazette*, 31 March, urged support of incumbent Caleb Strong, arguing that Federalists in state government should not be replaced by Jefferson allies. Strong narrowly defeated Sullivan, a result that Democratic-Republicans in the Mass. General Court unsuccessfully challenged, for which see JQA to LCA, 8 June, and note 4, below. Maj. Gen. William Heath defeated incumbent Federalist lieutenant governor Edward H. Robbins, but Heath declined to serve and the office was left vacant for a year. TBA accurately reported the Quincy vote for governor. A federal issue was raised in the state campaign when the *Boston Commercial Gazette*, 31 March, attempted to tarnish the standing of local Democratic-Republicans by blaming the party for the Jefferson administration's treatment of Tripolitan ally Hamet Qaramanli, for which see JQA to TBA, 5 Feb., and note 6, above (A New Nation Votes).

[3] Democratic-Republicans wrested control of both houses of the Mass. General Court from Federalists for the first time in 1806, winning a narrow majority of 21 to 19 in the senate (Sean Wilentz, *The Rise of American Democracy: Jefferson to Lincoln*, N.Y., 2005, p. 120; A New Nation Votes).

John Quincy Adams to William Stephens Smith

Dear Sir.   Washington 16. April 1806.

I have within these few days successively received your two letters, one of them containing the relation of the circumstances respecting General Miranda's projects, and your relations with him while he was in this Country; and the other containing the request that I would write an Oration for your Son John—[1] On the first of these subjects, I trust that in the trial of the Cause, on the Bill found by the Grand-Jury, of which I have seen an Account in the New-York prints, you will have competent proof to produce that you have not violated the

Laws of the United States.—² As to the conduct of the President and Secretary of State, whether they said too much to Miranda, or whether he inferred from what they said or did more than he was warranted to infer, I am at present very incompetent to determine— That he misunderstood or misrepresented their real intentions I have no doubt. Where the mistake originated must remain for the present a matter of opinion.

My own occupations so fully engross my time, that I fear it will not be in my power to write the Oration; and I have so much confidence in the genius and acquirements of your Son, that I believe him able to honour himself more by writing his own performance at his Commencement, than by depending upon a friend for the production. I have an high opinion of his good sense, discretion and application, and am perswaded he will acquit himself very creditably without any assistance from abroad.

Congress are to adjourn next Monday the 21st: They break up under a variety of unpleasant and unpromising circumstances. I propose to leave this place about the 25th: and hope to have the pleasure of seeing you before the last of the Month— My wife remains here for the present, and probably will remain here through the Summer.— I am, Dear Sir, every truly your's—

LbC (Adams Papers); internal address: "Coll: William S. Smith— New-York."; APM Reel 135.

¹ WSS's letters were of 29 March, for which see note 2, below, and 6 April, above.

² A grand jury indicted WSS and New York merchant Samuel G. Ogden on 7 April on charges that they violated federal law by helping to organize and fund a military action against Venezuela, which as a Spanish colony was at peace with the United States. Both men pleaded not guilty in U.S. Circuit Court in New York on 10 April, and on the 11th Judge Matthias B. Tallmadge set a trial date of 14 July. John Swartwout, U.S. marshal for the District of New York, viewed the trial as political grandstanding and packed the jury with Federalists who would likely favor the defendants. Ogden's role in supplying the vessel and WSS's actions as surveyor of the port of New York in facilitating the vessel's clearance were key points in their trials. The prosecution contended that the ship's manifest was falsified to conceal the arms it carried. WSS denied any misconduct at trial and also in a letter to JQA of 29 March (Adams Papers), claiming that customs collector David Gelston cleared the vessel without his input. "I never was on board of this Ship," he wrote to JQA. "I never contemplated to have, neither have I, any connection with her Owner. . . . I never supplied nor paid for any of the component parts of her Cargo.— I appointed as usual, an Officer of the Customs to attend her exportation, who never made any report." The proceedings ultimately pivoted on the defense's assertion that Thomas Jefferson and James Madison verbally approved the plan. When neither appeared in court to dispute the contention, the jury acquitted WSS on 22 July and Ogden on the 26th (Thomas Lloyd, *The Trials of William S. Smith, and Samuel G. Ogden*, N.Y., 1807, p. vi–xi, xvii, xviii, xxi, xxiv, 101, 125, 222, 242, 249, 287; Robert L. Jones, "Finishing a Friendly Argument: The Jury and the Historical Origins of Diversity Jurisdiction," *New York University Law Review*, 82:1067, 1069 [Oct. 2007]).

April 1806

Abigail Adams to William Smith Shaw

Dear William   Quincy April 19th 1806

The Bill which our Tennant has presented must I presume be allowd him; the repairs were necessary I have not any doubt. he ought not however to do these things without consulting us. have You leazed him the place an other Year? does he comply with the terms of his lease?[1] I wish You to keep the Rent you receive always seperate from any other Charges. I have devoted it the years past to the assistance of Sally to pay the Board of Abbe: Make out the account which you have against Your uncle and bring it up with you when you come. Charge in the Br Frothinghams account.[2] you know you paid me last summer thirty dollors— credit me therefore for 17 & /2 return to you of the sum I then had,—that you know is the sum I left in Your hands of the last quarters Rent to pay Frothingham— I have since thought it best that his account should be charged, and I either made debtor only for 12 /2 dollors or given me for 17 /2 returnd. do which you please. allow the Tennant my half of the repairs and hold the remainder subject to my order—

I am anxious about Your Sister who I hear is very unwell. I wrote your Mother to let her come and try the air of Quincy.[3] I hope she will— you must come to Quincy before you go to Atkinson—

Poor Mrs Smith and family are in great trouble— never were such arbitary preceedings heard of before in a free country— the Grand jury presented a Bill against the Judge for his conduct[4]

I am yours &c   Abigail Adams

RC (DLC:Shaw Family Papers); addressed: "William S Shaw / Boston"; endorsed: "Mrs Adams / rec 19 April." and "Apl 19 1806."

[1] See AA to Shaw, 25 Feb., and note 1, above.
[2] Brothers Thomas and Nathaniel Frothingham were Boston coachmakers who maintained shops on West Street. The Adamses purchased a carriage from Nathaniel in 1801 (vol. 14:524; *Boston Directory*, 1806, p. 53, Shaw-Shoemaker, No. 50652; William Richard Cutter, comp., *New England Families Genealogical and Memorial*, 4 vols., N.Y., 1913, 1:50–51).
[3] AA's letter to Elizabeth Smith Shaw Peabody has not been found.
[4] See Hannah Phillips Cushing to AA, 28 April 1806, and note 2, below.

Abigail Adams to Ann Harrod Adams

My dear Nancy   Quincy April 28th 1806

we forgot half doz pound of Chocolat which Mrs Adams sent for amongst the articles she wanted. if you have not purchased the cambrick Muslin omit it, as I wish You to get every thing for her which she Sent for— I see in the paper Ticknor advertizes currents, and Baker real shear Book Muslins. No 1 state street.[1] I do not know what price currents are at; if not more than 1/6 I would like to have half a dozen pd for myself.— with Love &c / yours affec'ly   A Adams

~~PS~~

RC (MHi:Adams Papers, All Generations); addressed: "Mrs Ann [Adams] / [Boston]"; docketed: "1806— / Mrs Abigail Adams." Some loss of text due to a torn manuscript.

[1] Boston grocer Elisha Ticknor advertised in the *New-England Palladium*, 25 April, that fresh currants were available at his store at 42 Marlborough Street, while merchant Ebenezer Baker announced in the Boston *Independent Chronicle*, 24 April, that "real India Shear Book MUSLINS" could be purchased by the piece or yard at his shop at 1 State Street.

Hannah Phillips Cushing to Abigail Adams

My Dear Madam   Scituate April the 28th. 1806.

We are again permitted to return home in good health, after having passed as pleasant a winter as the times would permit. Mr Cushing was confined to his room three weeks with a great cold, attended with a slight fever, but his spirits were good even at that time, & he saw company every day. He attended Court 19th. Feby & on the 22nd. sat near seven hours without once leaving the bench, with as little fatigue as any one.

We came in five days to Phila.. two days less than we ever came before; the roads being very good. Through Jersey they were very bad. According to Judge Livermores definition, they were truly democratic.[1] We were at New York some days the begining of this month, I called to see Mrs Smith several times. She was in good health & better stirits than I expected. She related to me some circumstances relative to the Star chamber proceedings, which have been since published in the Herald.[2]

Conl. Smith had crouds of company every day. He was not anxious as to the event of the Leander business, as it respected himself. But the loss of his Office I do most sincerely regret. I hope to have the pleasure of seeing & conversing with you the 15th. of May if the weather be good; we shall endeavour to be at Quincy by 12 OC.[3] I shall send by the Stage tomorrow some Scions of the Pumkin sweetings, which we brought from Cont.. They are in perfection in Der. & Jany. If you have not any of the kind I think you will be pleased with them. Also some Scions of the high Sweetings from our Orchard.

April–May 1806

which are excellent for baking the last of Aug$^{t.}$ Will you my dear Friend be so good as to send some of the Scions of the St Germain to Judge Cranches, for him to give to the Stage driver to bring to me. The Plymouth Stage that leaves Boston Mon^{ys}, Wed^{ys}, & Fri^{ys}, passes our house. The other Stage passes on five miles from us. I will be much obliged to the Judge if he will take the trouble of attending to them. Please to give my regards to him, & Mrs Cranch. Mr Cushing joins me in best respects to the President, & yourself, & compliments to M^r, & Mrs Adams, & Miss Smith.

Your Affectionate   H Cushing

Mrs Cushing will be much obliged, if Mrs Adams will send her two or three Scions of the Trowbridge apple.[4]

RC (Adams Papers); internal address: "M^{rs} A Adams."

[1] Possibly Samuel Livermore, for whom see vol. 9:324.

[2] The New York *Herald*, 9 April, reported the 7 April indictment of WSS and Samuel G. Ogden, for which see JQA to WSS, 16 April, and note 2, above. WSS was interrogated by a judge without counsel present for six hours prior to the handing down of the indictment, the newspaper reported; his attorney later called the interrogation "tyrannical and unjust." The newspaper concluded by characterizing the proceedings as a "worse than Star Chamber court."

[3] On 15 May the Cushings dined at Peacefield, with JQA and TBA also on hand (JQA, *Diary*).

[4] The preceding sentence is in William Cushing's hand.

John Quincy Adams to Louisa Catherine Adams

My dearest Louisa.   New-York 1. May 1806.

Untill this day, I have been from the moment when I left you, in such continual motion that I have not had a moment of leisure to perform the promise I made, of writing to you on my way home— We had a rainy day from Washington to Baltimore, where I parted with Mess$^{rs:}$ Tracy and Dana, on the moment of our arrival— M$^{r:}$ M'Henry having taken them both to his House— They were to come on two days after, but whether they persevered in this intention or remained longer at Baltimore, I have not been informed. Sunday Morning I embarked in the French-town Packet, and after a tedious passage of more than twenty-four hours reached French-town— We were however more fortunate in ascending the Delaware, and arrived at Philadelphia Monday Evening about 10. O'Clock. The next Morning I proceeded in the Diligence Stage, and cross'd the ferry at Paulus Hoek yesterday, about noon—[1] There is a Packet going for Providence this afternoon, in which I shall take my passage, unless my Sister should conclude to go on with me, which I have invited her to do, and upon which she had not come to a final determination last Evening. In that case I shall wait, untill she can send for her daughter Caroline, who is in the Country, and whom she will take with her—

Mr: Gilman kept company with me as far as Philadelphia, and in the Stage from that place I met Mr: Cadwalader, who came on with us to Brunswick.—² I stop'd at Newark a few minutes and there saw Mrs: Charles Adams and her daughter— Mrs: Smith (the old Lady) and Nancy are at Philadelphia, and have been there all Winter— I met between Newark and Paulus Hoek, Mr: Justus Smith and the Coll's: son John, going on to Philadelphia to visit them—

The Coll's: situation here I suppose you know— I cannot dwell upon it— That of his family, is very distressing— I have therefore, as I mentioned before invited my Sister to go on with me, and take her daughter; and to pass the Summer with me, either at Quincy, or if I can procure a suitable house, at Cambridge— She has not yet determined what to do— They have heard indirectly from William, as late as the 15th: of March, when he was well— Most heartily do I wish he was returned— The Coll: keeps up his Spirits, with apparent cheerfulness; and still seems to flatter himself with prospects, which to my eyes have not so much rational foundation as a fairy tale.

I am lodged at the City-Hotel—³ Yesterday I dined with Mr: King, and spent the last Evening at Coll: Trumbull's— The City of New-York is in the greatest bustle I ever witness'd— This is the universal moving day, and about half the inhabitants are changing their places of abode— They are also in the midst of a warmly contested Election, for members of Congress and of their State Legislature— The federalists for the first time these two or three years have run Candidates of their own, and though they do not much expect to carry the Election, there is no doubt but they will come very near succeeding—⁴ Besides all this there has been great agitation in the City, from an unfortunate occurrence on Saturday last— The British ships Leander and Cambrian are lying off this port, and a shot fired from the first of them, kill'd a man on board a coasting vessel coming from the Delaware— All communication with the ships has been since cut off, and two or three of their Officers are on shore, and cannot get on board— The Grand Jury of the City and County have found a bill of Indictment against the Captain of the Leander for Murder, and a representation of the facts has been sent on to the President at Washington, where I [hav]e no doubt you will hear much of this Event—⁵

I feel a great and con[tinu]al anxiety to hear from you, and by the time I reach home, hope to find a letter ready to receive me— Let me know you are well—at least as well as you can expect, and with my kind remembrance to your Mamma and all the family be assured that you are ever in the thoughts & affections of your faithful friend.

John Quincy Adams.

RC (Adams Papers); endorsed: "J. Q. Adams / Rec. May 4th. / Answer'd May 5." Some loss of text where the seal was removed.

[1] JQA departed Washington, D.C., on the Baltimore stage early on 26 April, without LCA but in the company of Uriah Tracy and Samuel Whittlesey Dana. The trio met former U.S. secretary of war James McHenry in Baltimore before JQA left the city on the 27th, arriving at Philadelphia late on the 28th and New York City on 30 April. Leaving aboard the packet *New York*, Capt. Williams, on 1 May, he arrived at Providence, R.I., on the 3d, took a stage to Dedham, Mass., and arrived in Quincy that afternoon (JQA, *Diary*).

[2] Nicholas Gilman (1755–1814) of Exeter, N.H., represented his state in the U.S. Senate from 1805 until his death (*Biog. Dir. Cong.*).

[3] The City Hotel operated at 115 Broadway in New York City from 1788 until the mid-nineteenth century (Henry Collins Brown, *Glimpses of Old New-York*, N.Y., 1917, p. 149; CFA, *Diary*, 1:16, 17).

[4] In May 1806 congressional elections, only 2 Federalists were among 17 candidates elected to serve New York in the House of Representatives. None of the 32 elected to the state senate and only 18 of the 100 voted into the assembly were Federalists (A New Nation Votes; New York *American Citizen*, 15 May; Jabez D. Hammond, *The History of Political Parties in the State of New-York*, 4th edn., 2 vols., Cooperstown, N.Y., 1846, 1:237).

[5] On 25 April the British warship *Leander* fired on the sloop *Richard* after the American merchant vessel was slow to obey an order to lay by, killing seaman John Pierce. The incident angered the U.S. press and New York citizens, who paraded Pierce's coffin through the city and threatened violence against British nationals. Thomas Jefferson responded with a 3 May proclamation (DLC:Jefferson Papers) calling on the British government to recall and court-martial *Leander* captain Henry Whitby and ordering British ships *Leander*, *Cambrian*, and *Driver* from U.S. waters. The British government complied and Whitby was recalled on 22 June, but he was acquitted at a court-martial trial in April 1807 (Madison, *Papers, Secretary of State Series*, 11:507; Heather Carlquist Walser, "Mourning a Murder: The Death of John Pierce, Local Politics, and British-American Relations," *JER*, 43:35, 36, 37 [Spring 2023]; Bradford Perkins, *Prologue to War: England and the United States 1805–1812*, Berkeley, Calif., 1970, p. 107–108; LCA to JQA, 5 May 1806, below).

Louisa Catherine Adams to John Quincy Adams

My beloved friend.   Washington May 5. 1806

After a couple of days of anxious solicitude I last night recieved your very affectionate letter from New York which revived my half drooping spirits by affording me the delightful certainty of your being in health and having arrived thus far in safety—[1]

I am rejoiced to hear that the Col. still supports his misfortune with cheerfulness and sincerely wish he may yet find a more pleasing termination to his difficulties than we at present have reason to hope I admire the plan of your Sisters going to pass the Summer with and should much regret her declining your invitation as it was what I desired to propose before you left this place but the uncertainty in which we remain as to your future residence ~~made~~ induced me to wait untill I heard farther from you I request you to make my affectionate love to M$^{rs.}$ Smith and tell her how much I regret not being able to join you and pass the Summer in her Society— your Sisters company will I am sure prove a great benefit to yourself as I trust it will prevent a too intense application to business of which I at present confess I am extremely apprehensive for my sake my beloved friend and for that of our dear little ones let me entreat you to attend to your health and beware of again reducing your strength as you did the last year or your constitution will be materially injured—

M$^{r.}$ Hellen has been in Baltimore since the Thursday after you left as he was called as a witness on a trial for defamation between Govr Mercer[2] and M$^{r.}$ Bay an englishman with whom M$^{r.}$ H. has had some very unpleasant dealings—

Mama has had a letter from M$^{r.}$ Thorpe in England making bitter complaints of M$^{r.}$ Maitlands conduct who it seems has at length discover'd his real character and excited some suspicion of his honesty it appears from Mr T.'s letter that the late remittances made by Mr Cook which became due at certain periods have not been paid to the creditors which has occasioned doubts as to the other property in M$^{r.}$ M's hands[3] Taylor & Stroud have filed a bill in Chancery and got letters of administration in which he endeavor'd to be joined which they absolutely refused and the affair must now take its course Mr Pinckney who has been here was very anxious to see you before he sailed for England he has offer'd to do any thing for Mama in this business and seems to think that the notes may be of use in England Mama wished to know your opinion as she thought it would be imprudent to trust the original notes out of her hands—

This New York affair makes a great noise here the President has issued a proclamation which I have not seen but it does not seem to be generally approved he leaves town tomorrow for Monticello[4] I do not hear a word of news excepting that it is said Mr Monroe is to return and M$^{r.}$ Pinckney is to remain as minister in england[5] Mr Wright I suppose you have heard is appointed Attorney general of the state of Maryland in Mr Pinkneys place[6] in all probability you will have less talking in the Senate next Session—

Adieu my best beloved Kiss our little darlings for me repeatedly and remember to impress upon their young minds that they have a mother whose every wish in this world centres in them and you and whose heart untill it ceases to beat will throb with every sentiment of love and affection.   L. C. Adams

May 1806

P.S. I will thank you to pay Mrs. Adams for the purchases she has made for me and deduct it from my next quarter— I paid Mr. Hellen 150 Dollors as you he said he did not know what it was for you carried away the Book which you had made for the Thermometer I beg you will send it at as soon as possible I have been very attentive to since your departure and am up at Sun rise every morning to look at it.— Adieu

RC (Adams Papers); addressed: "John Q. Adams Esqr"; endorsed: "Louisa—5. May 1806. / 10. May rec^{d:} / D^{o:} Ans^{d:}."

[1] JQA to LCA, 1 May, above.
[2] John Francis Mercer served as governor of Maryland from 1801 to 1803 (vol. 9:322; *Biog. Dir. Cong.*).
[3] The letter from Johnson family friend Samuel Thorp to Catherine Nuth Johnson, not found, concerned the activities of speculator John Maitland, whom LCA blamed for the financial difficulties encountered by her father before his death. Attorney William Cooke was one of those charged with collecting debts owed to Wallace, Johnson, & Muir, Joshua Johnson's former company (vol. 15:199–200, 389; LCA, *D&A*, 1:52, 53; Papenfuse, *Pursuit of Profit*, p. 228–231).
[4] Thomas Jefferson departed Washington, D.C., for Virginia on 6 May 1806 and returned on 7 June (*Jefferson's Memorandum Books*, 1:liii).
[5] Jefferson nominated James Monroe and William Pinkney on 19 April as joint commissioners to Great Britain, a mission that resulted in the unratified Monroe-Pinkney Treaty of 31 Dec., for which see JQA to LCA, 19 Feb. 1807, and note 2, below. James Madison provided Pinkney instructions dated 17 May 1806 enclosing a joint commission and letter of credence dated the 12th. Pinkney departed Baltimore on the ship *Diana* on 22 May and arrived in Liverpool on 20 June. Rumors in the press that Monroe might leave the negotiations to Pinkney and return to the United States to become a presidential candidate proved unfounded (Alexandria, Va., *Daily Advertiser*, 24 April; U.S. Senate, *Exec. Jour.*, 9th Cong., 1st sess., p. 35; Madison, *Papers, Secretary of State Series*, 11:576, 590; New York *Evening Post*, 24 May; Baltimore *Telegraphe and Daily Advertiser*, 16 Aug.; *Newport Mercury*, 26 April; Portsmouth *New-Hampshire Gazette*, 29 April).
[6] Senator Robert Wright of Maryland was appointed state attorney general in April to replace Pinkney. Wright declined the appointment and John Thomson Mason assumed the post in his stead (*Biog. Dir. Cong.*; Kenneth L. Carroll, "The Court Inquires about a Ghost," *Maryland Historical Magazine*, 55:40 [March 1960]; *Maryland Manual*, 126:104 [1915–1916]).

John Quincy Adams to Louisa Catherine Adams

My dearest Louisa.   Boston 10. May 1806.

I wrote you last Sunday, the day after my arrival at Quincy, and gave you an account of the progress and termination of my Journey from New-York.[1] On Tuesday I went with my father to Cambridge to attend the inauguration of the new President of the College, M^{r:} Webber.— The ceremonies of the day were sufficiently dull— The performances mostly in Latin, with a comfortable proportion of English in the Idiom, to make it intelligible— There was however a young Gentleman, just out of College, who knew more about *making* Latin, as they call it at school than the rest, and pronounced a sort of complimentary Oration, which would have pleased me very well, but for a little prophetical sally, in which he told them what wonders of Eloquence they were to perform when the new Professor should come—² My turn will be next, and as there is no installation without a Speech, I have asked the privilege, of pronouncing it in a language which I can write and the hearers can understand—³ I expect to be indulged; though some of the adherents to the Old School are very tenacious of the immemorial usage and abhorrent of innovation— I suppose my induction to Office will be the week after next.

On Thursday I came to this Town, and am lodged for the present at Whitcomb's— I dined yesterday at M[r:] T. C. Amory's and this day at M[r:] G. Green's—⁴ I am seeking for a place to lodge and board, for the Summer, but know not yet whether I shall fix in Boston or in Cambridge. At M[r:] Amory's I met Sir Isaac Coffin, a British admiral, who has just arrived from England, and is going to take the naval Command at Halifax— He tells me that M[r:] Merry is recalled and a Lord Selkirk appointed in his stead—⁵ This Lord Selkirk is said to be a great *philosopher*, and perhaps may be of great use to you know whom, in helping to *make a Moon*.

There are two boxes of things for which you had written waiting for a passage, and I see in the newspapers a vessel up for Alexandria to sail in a few days— Her name I think is the rambler—⁶ I have desired M[r] Shaw to open one of the boxes, and put in the Cotton, which according to your order I procured for you at Providence, and which I hope you will find such as you wanted. It was compared with the two specimens you gave me, and purchased at the same Shop where I went with you before— By the way, I found on opening my trunk a piece of Silk which you put up with my clothes; but either you forgot to tell me the purpose of sending it, or I have forgotten what you told me— I conjecture your object was to have it dyed, but for better certainty will thank you to write me word.

I have this day received with great pleasure your kind letter of the 5[th:] inst[t:]— And although you tell me nothing of your health, I flatter myself, from your *early* attention to the Thermometer, that it is at least tolerable— I hope however that neither for the thermometer, nor for any other consideration, you will let it suffer, by depriving yourself of your rest— The observation at 8 or 9 in the morning will answer the purpose quite as well as at 6.— The book which I made for you must have got somewhere mislaid, for I do not find on looking over my trunk of papers, that I took it with me— I did indeed in the hurry of departure take the *case* of the thermometer with me, so that if you

May 1806

should remove to another house it will be necessary to take it in the hand— I have not yet commenced my observations here, but intend to, as soon as I get settled; I find upon the comparison for the twenty days that my brother kept the register at Quincy, untill his instrument got broken, with the same dates and hours at Washington, a very good commencement for an estimate of the difference between the two Climates.

The 150. dollars which I left with you for M^{r:} Hellen, was for the purpose of settling with him on account of our Expences, from the time of the last payment I had made him, untill I came away— The other 80 dollars was for my part of Cookendorfer's bill—[7] In both these instances, as in all the former, as M^{r:} Hellen has always declined mentioning any precise sum, I have been obliged to measure it by an estimate or guess of what would be proper & satisfactory to him—As an indemnity for all positive expence—but not for that invariable kindness and attention both from him and M^{rs:} Hellen, to you and to me; for which I shall always feel and acknowledge the obligation.

I suppose the Notes from M^{r:} Maitland will be important to the Administrators in England, to shew the nature of his connection in business with your father, and much of the subsequent correspondence to shew the State of Accounts between them— Maitland's Answer to the Bill in Chancery must be given upon Oath— If he gives it with *truth*, it appears to me there must be a large balance for which he will be compelled to Account— If he should prevaricate, the notes, Accounts, and especially the rectification of the heavy charges of payment to the Captain of the Indian Chief, which he never made, will be very important to the Administrators— M^{r:} Pinkney may safely be entrusted with the Notes, to make use of them if he should judge it expedient— And it does [not see]m probable they will ever be of importance in this Country— If however your Mother [. . . co]nclude to send them, it will be prudent to keep copies well attested, to prevent accidents.

[Your] dear Children are both in perfect health, and both anxious for Mama to come home— John especially talks of you continually, and is as charming as when we went away last November— He is not so fat as we left him, but has grown in Stature, and his Countenance has lengthened a little, like George's— He is the Delight of all the family, and my father thinks he has *more ideas* than any child of his age that he ever knew. I have abandoned the hope of having either of them with me, this summer, and this deprivation sharpens the severity of that which I feel in the absence of their mother— The ensuing year will I hope be more propitious, and bring a consolation for the necessary sacrifices of the present.— I do not find that Sister T. B. would be under any such necessity of staying behind if he were called away; but I have not ventured to ask the question, and I am not Connoisseur in shapes enough to decide upon external inspection.[8]

Dearest Louisa, I send you *les plus tendres baisers de l'Amour.*

RC (Adams Papers); addressed: "M[rs:] L. C. Adams. / at M[r:] Hellens / Washington City."; endorsed: "J Q Adams / Rec[d.] May 16 / Ans[d.] do. 18." Some loss of text where the seal was removed.

[1] On 4 May JQA wrote to LCA and confirmed that AA2 elected not to accompany him to Quincy. He also described the rest of his travels from New York to Quincy and reported that JA2 did not immediately recognize him when they were reunited (Adams Papers).

[2] Hollis Professor of Mathematics and Natural Philosophy Samuel Webber was installed as president of Harvard College on 6 May. The *Massachusetts Spy*, 14 May, noted JA's and JQA's presence at the ceremony. The young Latin orator was Samuel Cary (1785–1815), Harvard 1804, who was ordained as pastor of King's Chapel in Boston on 1 Jan. 1809 (vol. 15:443; Henry Wilder Foote, *Annals of King's Chapel*, 2 vols., Boston, 1896, 2:407, 408, 415).

[3] For JQA's installation as Boylston Professor of Rhetoric and Oratory at Harvard, see JQA to LCA, 15 June 1806, and note 1, below.

[4] For Tilly Whitcomb's businesses, see JQA and GWA to LCA, 18 May, and note 6, below. JQA dined first at the home of Boston merchant Thomas Coffin Amory and second at that of Boston merchant and banker Gardiner Greene (1753–1852) (vol. 15:369, 408; George Chandler, *The Chandler Family*, Worcester, Mass., 1883, p. 224).

[5] British rear admiral Sir Isaac Coffin (1759–1839), who was born in Boston, served as the resident commissioner of the royal dockyard at Halifax from 1799 to 1800. In 1798 the British Treasury patented to him the proprietorship of the Îles de la Madeleine. He visited the Quebec island group in 1806 to curb its use by French and American fishermen. Coffin told JQA that British foreign secretary Charles James Fox had recalled Anthony Merry as British minister to the United States and replaced him with Thomas Douglas, 5th Earl of Selkirk (1771–1820). After Selkirk declined the post, the appointment went to David Montagu Erskine, later 2d Baron Erskine (1776–1855). Erskine presented his credentials to Thomas Jefferson on 3 Nov. (*Dicy. Canadian Biog.*; *Instructions to the British Ministers to the United States, 1791–1812*, ed. Bernard Mayo, Washington, D.C., 1941, p. 220, 224; LCA, *D&A*, 1:264).

[6] The *Rambler*, Capt. Hezekiah Lombard, advertised freight carriage from Boston to Alexandria, Va., in the *New-England Palladium*, 9 May, and sailed on the 13th (JQA and GWA to LCA, 18 May 1806, below; Boston *Columbian Centinel*, 14 May).

[7] Probably Leonard Cookendorfer, who offered carriage services in Washington, D.C. (*Jefferson's Memorandum Books*, 2:1171).

[8] AHA was then pregnant; see TBA to William Meredith, 30 July, and note 2, below.

Elizabeth Smith Shaw Peabody to Abigail Adams

My Dear Sister,   Atkinson May 10[th.] 1806—

It has been a cold backward Spring, & Abby could not get abroad as I wished, she has a great deal of pain in her side yet, but I think her feverish habit abates, if her appetite was but good I should be greatly encouraged, & hope she would soon be as well as ever— I am rejoiced to hear Mrs Foster has a Daughter, & comfortable, from what you wrote, I was greatly concerned about her.[1] Mrs Norton & our

May 1806

other Nieces, make up in full I think, for *all* our families defficencies, & we may say with propriety, as Gad did of old, "behold, a Troop cometh"—[2] As to Mr Peabody, he fears his family will be quite extinct, for his Daughter has no little Ones, & his Son can find no twin-born Soul,[3] no yoke fellow willing to share with him a decent competence, & "bless the dear bondage"—[4] We expect Mrs Webster in June at our Election, to make us a good long visit—

The accounts which we have had in the news Papers relative to the Leander, & Col. Smith, have given us all much pain, & regret.[5] Whether Mirandas motives were any better those of Cortez, or the first Mexicon Adventurers, I cannot pretend to say, but History informs us, that Ambition, Pride & Avarice have rivitted the Chains of more millions, than ever Humanity, Benevolence, & Patriotism emancipated— But what we most regret is, that at the Presidents, & your period of life, that you, or any of your dear Children, should be involved, & tormented with Evils, which your many Virtues, seem as if they should have prevented, & secured you from; But this world my Sister is not the state of Retribu[tion] Happy for us, that we can look upward, & humbly hope, for that time, when human affairs will be adjudged in Righteousness, where Hypocrisy, will be unvieled, & each receive their Just Reward—

I wish you would be so good as to ask my Son, if he has not received a letter from his *only* Sister, & whether he does not think it merits a reply—

By Mr & Mrs Quincy Sister will the pleasure of hearing, particularly from Son, & family, which must be next to seeing them herself— My love to her & hers, tell her Abby longs to be well enough to ride as far as Quincy, & I hope she will soon be able My kindest regards to our Nancy, may heaven bless, preserve, & smile propitious. ~~upon all~~ I am pleased to hear that Cousin Louisa enjoys better health— but those events, are all under divine Government—& tranquility & contentment with allotted Blessings is the way to enjoy them, & be happy—

Notwithstanding my anxieties, & multiplied Cares, my health is better than it was last Spring— For this, & innumerable other favours, gratitude should warm the heart of your Sister

Elizabeth Peabody—

PS— Mr Peabody presents his best respects— A member of Congress writing to Mr Peabody, said, Randolph had told *"damning Truths"*—[6]

RC (Adams Papers); addressed: "To Mrs A. Adams"; endorsed by Richard Cranch: "Mrs Peabody / May 10th 1806." Some loss of text where the seal was removed.

[1] Louisa Catherine Smith Foster (d. 1860), daughter of Elizabeth Smith Foster and James Hiller Foster, was born on 6 April (CFA, *Diary*, 5:394; Boston City Registrar:Deaths, 1860, record 1285).

[2] Genesis, 30:11.

[3] Mary Peabody Webster and her husband, Stephen Peabody Webster, never had children. Stephen Peabody Jr. did not marry until 1810 but ultimately had five children (vols. 7:3, 11:51; Selim Hobart Peabody, comp., and Charles Henry Pope, ed., *Peabody Genealogy*, Boston, 1909, p. 38, 72; William C. Todd, *Biographical and Other Articles*, Boston, 1901, p. 82).

[4] Isaac Watts, "Few Happy Matches," line 33.

[5] The Miranda expedition and WSS's involvement received ample coverage in the local press, including reports on 11 March 1806 of WSS's arrest (*Haverhill Museum*, 11, 18 March; *Newburyport Herald*, 4, 11 March, 15, 25 April, 9 May).

[6] The *Washington Federalist*, 12 April, reported that John Randolph "thundered damning truths against the administration" during debate on whether to make public the transcripts of closed debates on the Floridas. Several newspapers reprinted the piece, including the New York *Evening Post*, 18 April, and the Hartford *Connecticut Courant*, 30 April.

Louisa Catherine Adams to Abigail Adams

My dear Mother   Washington May 11th. 1806

A few days since I recieved your very obliging letter in which you mention having procured the articles I wrote for and for which I return you many thanks[1] I am much distressed at the idea your letter seems to convey of want of respect or attention to Mrs. Cranch it has ever been my most ardent desire so to conduct myself to every branch of your family as not only to merit their esteem but their affection that I have not always succeeded has been more my misfortune than my fault and I sincerely regret that Mrs. Cranch could possibly imagine that my silence proceeded from neglect or inattention as I concieve myself under obligations both to her and you which I shall never have it in my power to repay Mrs. Cranch never having said a word to me on the Subject before I left Quincy I did not feel myself authorized to write to her and feared that my addressing her unasked would betray a troublesome solicitude for the welfare of my Child who I very well knew would recieve every tender care and attention which the tenderest mother could desire my education and the misfortunes which have pursued my family from the moment of what I may stile my entrance into the world (I mean my marriage) may have given a harshness to my character which does not naturally belong to it and render'd me cold and fearful of forcing attentions were they might not prove acceptable and the least appearance of unkindness or dislike acts so powerfully upon my feelings as to destroy every desire of pleasing or rendering myself agreeable where I have once percieved it. you will therefore not be surprized at my using the word which gave you such offence and which I could not concieve to have any allusion to you whatever as Mr. A. was very well assured that nothing but compulsion would have induced me to leave them and swore in Philadelphia on my way to Boston that they should not accompany me again the letter which you wrote in answer and which I had determined not to have said any thing about certainly gave me pain as it obliquely insinuated a reflection on my family who have perhaps degraded themselves from a kind motive to your Son and me. excuse me my dear Madam for mentioning this circumstance which I meant to obliterate forever from my memory as it is my earnest desire to cultivate by every means in my power your good opinion—

The loss of Mr. Adams's society is to me irreparable his tenderness and affection to me throughout this winter have been inexpressible and I have enjoyed almost perfect happiness I already look forward to his return with the most anxious impatience and should it please heaven to spare me and my Infant anticipate with delight the moment when I shall present it to recieve a fathers blessing. He is very desirous of taking George to reside with him and it is my most ardent wish as the care of the Child would cause a degree of relaxation from his studies to which otherwise I am sure he will devote himself to the prejudice of his health—

I am sorry John is become subject to feverish complaints I fear my dear Madam you are too indulgent to his appetite and would wish him to live as simply as possible during the hot months as I have a great terror of billious disorders particularly for Children they so often prove fatal—

Adieu my dear Mother make my affectionate love acceptable to all the family and permit me again to offer my thanks for the present which you have so kindly sent but which I am fearful I shall not be able to get worked as I do very little in this way myself and the Girls are busily employed for my Sisters and believe me your very affectionate daughter   L. C. Adams

RC (Adams Papers); addressed: "M^{rs:} A. Adams / Quincy near / Boston"; endorsed: "Mrs L Adams / May 11th 1806."

[1] Not found.

John Quincy Adams and George Washington Adams to Louisa Catherine Adams

My dear Louisa. Quincy 18. May 1806.

The Children are both in perfect health; both contented with their situations, and both beloved by all around them— George appears to have lost none of his sensibility, but has a placidness and ease of temper, which must have come to him I think from some of his *Remote* Ancestors— He reads tolerably well, and still prides himself as much as ever in his learning. He agrees very well with his companions Thomas Norton and John Greenleaf who are still there; and always enquires whenever I see him why his Mamma does not, and when she will come home? He has not grown so much as I should have expected; but his countenance continues to grow longer, and he resembles you more than formerly— Not however so much as John, who seems a little miniature of yourself— Our friends here think him more like your Sister Eliza, but in this I do not altogether concur— The alteration in him from what he was when we left him is not so great as in George. His face is only not so round; but his dimples when he smiles are deeper— He is by no means a troublesome child; but not quite so manageable as his brother— The family are all very fond of him, and very attentive to him.— It is I assure you with the greatest reluctance that I forego the pleasure of having them with me this Summer, but instead of being able to find lodgings where I could get them duly attended to, I have found it extremely difficult to procure any for myself at Cambridge— I have finally been obliged to engage a couple of chambers, which I must furnish, myself, and to board, untill I can procure better accommodations, at the tavern—[1]

My installation is not to be so soon as I expected when I wrote you last—[2] Next Wednesday, there is to be a vacation at the College which will continue a fortnight, and I suppose it will be a week or fortnight after that before they Seat me— My State in the mean time will be very unsettled— Here, at Boston and at Cambridge, as Occasion shall serve.

The day after my last Letter, I dined with M[r:] Payne in Boston— His wife expects a further increase of his family— The two boys are well, but from the difference of their growth you would suppose a year's difference in their age—[3] M[r:] & M[rs:] Gore were there—and Admiral Coffin, who the next day went for Quebec— I was mistaken in

May 1806

writing you that he comes to take the command of the naval Station at Halifax— He has only a leave of absence on his private concerns.

Tuesday I dined with M^r: D. Sears—I believe you know him—there I met M^r: Lowell, who has just returned from Europe with his family, and was very full of his travels—[4] Much disgusted with England; high in admiration of France; and especially of Buonaparte— This has occasioned some surprize among his friends, because something of a Revolution from his former opinions.

Wednesday Evening I pass'd with the old Club, to which you remember I used to belong—[5] There I met M^r: Quincy, who had arrived at Boston with his Lady a few days before— They are still at Boston, but propose coming out here in a fortnight or three weeks.

Thursday morning I came out from Boston, and have pass'd the succeeding three days here— To-morrow morning I shall return— I lodge comfortably enough at Whitcomb's; but it has the double inconvenience of being a public house, and a dancing-school— Else I should perhaps conclude to keep my lodgings for the Summer there.— M^rs: Whitcomb, I suppose will keep pace with you—At least she looks nearly as far advanced— Her children are both well; and Caroline begins to go to school—Not a little to her Annoyance.—[6] As to my brother's wife, it seems to me impossible that her prospects should be so near at hand as you conjecture— Indeed from her appearance, I should not suspect her to be in that way at-all.— M^rs: Norton last Wednesday produced another daughter; and her Sister at Cambridge, M^rs: Greenleaf had one about a month ago—[7]

Thus much for births— As to Marriages—I can only tell you of two in return for those of Miss Murray and Miss Stoddert mentioned in your kind letter of the 11th: which I received yesterday—[8] The one is of M^r: Jonathan Mason's daughter of Boston, to a M^r: Grant, an Englishman I believe; at least a very handsome young Man; whom I met at M^r: T. C. Amory's.— The other is Miss Hetty Newcomb, who is to be married to M^r: Page—[9]

I enclose you the bill of lading for the barrel and two boxes sent you by the Rambler, Captain Lumbard— You will find in one of the boxes that short as my stay at Providence was, I did not forget your Cotton— The Plumb-Cake will not go by this opportunity; but the materials are procured, and the Cake will be immediately made— I will send it by as early an opportunity as possible.

The report of the king of England's death which you mention was, I apprehend, a mistake— For we have information here later than the appointment of Lord Selkirk, and I have heard nothing of the other event but from your letter— A report has been circulated here of a War between England and Prussia, but I find no authentic source of that—[10] There have been several arrivals at different Ports, bringing accounts from Barbadoes and Martinico, that Miranda had affected his landing in the Caraccas and met with some success, but I have no faith in them.[11]

It is not yet ascertained who is to be the Governor of Massachusetts for the year ensuing— M^{r:} Strong has a majority of about 600 votes out of 75000. but some of the returns are said to be irregular and may be set aside, in which case, Mr Sullivan will come on— The Lieutenant Governor, and a decided majority of both branches of the Legislature will be democratic.[12]

It is possible that the Book for keeping the Thermometer which I made for you may have been thrown inadvertently by me into the great Trunk of Books and Papers which is to come round by water; but I certainly did not bring it with me— I will however send you a sheet prepared for the time you will want it, with this letter If I can prepare it in time—[13] If not, by my next.

George is now sitting by my side, and asks me what I am writing to you?— He says he wants Mama to come home, and to go and live at the house where we lived last Summer— John calls it Papa's *beauty* House—and last Summer it certainly deserved that character— For if it had nothing else in it, there was as much *beauty* at least as in any dwelling House in New-England—[14] John's turn for Mimicry now and then breaks through all the discouragement of sober faces—

Remember kindly to all the family your ever affectionate

John Quincy Adams.

Dear Mama

George sends his duty written with his own hand—

RC (Adams Papers); endorsed: "J Q Adams / Rec^{d.} May 25 / Ans^{d.} do do."

[1] JQA boarded with Israel Porter, who in 1796 took over the former Blue Anchor Tavern on Boylston Street (now John F. Kennedy Street) between Mount Auburn Street and Harvard Square in Cambridge (JQA, *Diary*, 12 May 1806; *An Historic Guide to Cambridge*, 2d edn., Cambridge, 1907, p. 36, 38).

[2] JQA to LCA, 10 May, above.

[3] On 11 May, JQA dined with William and Lucy Gray Dobell Payne, whose twin sons, Edward William and William Edward, were then two years old. Just under a year after the date of this letter, on 8 May 1807, Lucy delivered a second set of twins, Christopher Gore and Ellis Gray Payne (vol. 15:357; Whitmore, *Families of Payne and Gore*, p. 23).

[4] Boston merchant David Sears had offices at 14 Central Wharf and a home on Beacon Street. Boston lawyer John Lowell Jr. and his wife, Rebecca Amory Lowell, traveled in Europe from Sept. 1803 to April 1806. The tour cost $20,000 and prompted the family to sell assets to cover their debts, including some real estate purchased by JQA, for which see his and GWA's letter to LCA, 24 May, and note 3, below (*Boston Directory*, 1806, p. 109, Shaw-

Shoemaker, No. 50652; Chaim M. Rosenberg, *John Lowell Jr. and His Institute: The Power of Knowledge*, Lanham, Md., 2021, p. 35, 36, 37).

[5] For Boston's Wednesday Evening Club, see vol. 15:168.

[6] Tilly Whitcomb ran a coffeehouse and hosted William Turner's Dancing Academy four days per week. Tilly Churchill Whitcomb (d. 1807), son of Tilly and Elizabeth Epps Whitcomb, was baptized in Boston's Trinity Church on 22 June. The couple's older children were Catherine Louisa Whitcomb (1802–1883), for whom JQA and LCA served as godparents, and a son born in 1804 (vol. 15:369, 431; *Boston Directory*, 1806, p. 124, 133, Shaw-Shoemaker, No. 50652; Boston *Columbian Centinel*, 19 April 1806; Andrew Oliver and James Bishop Peabody, eds., *The Records of Trinity Church, Boston, 1728–1830*, Col. Soc. Mass., *Pubns.*, 56:130, 138; A. C. Thompson, *Eliot Memorial: Sketches Historical and Biographical of the Eliot Church and Society, Boston*, Boston, 1900, p. 437–438).

[7] Lucy Ann Norton, eighth child of Elizabeth Cranch and Rev. Jacob Norton, was born on 13 May, and Mary Elizabeth Greenleaf, fifth of Lucy Cranch and John Greenleaf, arrived on 13 April (*History of Weymouth*, 4:444–445; Greenleaf, *Greenleaf Family*, p. 223–224).

[8] In her letter of 11 May (Adams Papers), LCA reported two Washington, D.C., betrothals. The intended marriage between widower John Wayles Eppes and Catherine Elizabeth Murray (1783–1854) did not take place. Elizabeth Stoddert, daughter of former naval secretary Benjamin Stoddert and Rebecca Lowndes, married naval surgeon Thomas Ewell on 3 March 1807 (vols. 8:108, 15:374; Thomas Jefferson to Eppes, 24 May 1806, CSmH:Thomas Jefferson Coll.; Peter Hedlund and others, eds., *Encyclopedia Virginia*, www.encyclopediavirginia.org; LCA, *D&A*, 1:261; Monroe, *Papers*, 7:438; Jefferson, *Papers, Retirement Series*, 12:475; Donald C. Pfanz, *Richard S. Ewell: A Soldier's Life*, Chapel Hill, N.C., 1998, p. 5).

[9] Anna Powell Mason, daughter of Jonathan Mason Jr. and Susannah Powell Mason, married London banker Patrick Grant on 1 Oct. 1807. Mehitabel Newcomb, the daughter of Jerusha Adams Newcomb and shoemaker Charles Newcomb of Braintree, wed on 9 Nov. 1806 Capt. Benjamin Page, a carpenter from New Bedford, Mass. (vol. 8:375; "Alexander Grant to Patrick Grant, 1840," MHS, *Procs.*, 3d ser., 52:31 [Nov. 1918]; Boston, *30th Report*, p. 248; John Bearse Newcomb, *Genealogical Memoir of the Newcomb Family*, Elgin, Ill., 1874, p. 476–477).

[10] The Boston *Repertory*, 16 May, reported a Franco-Prussian alliance against Great Britain and that "England appears to be preparing for a firm, defensive war." The rumors were caused by the signing of the Franco-Prussian Cooperation Treaty on 15 Feb. in Paris, in which formerly neutral Prussia pledged cooperation with France. The nascent alliance went no further, however, as Prussia broke with France in October and joined the allies to form the Fourth Coalition in a renewed offensive (Schom, *Napoleon Bonaparte*, p. 420, 451).

[11] The Boston *Independent Chronicle*, 8 May, and other newspapers erroneously reported that Francisco de Miranda's vessels had been joined by British forces in landing at Caracas, Venezuela, and that after taking several towns Miranda "proclaimed the independence of the province" (Boston *Repertory*, 9 May; *New-England Palladium*, 9 May).

[12] For the results of the Massachusetts gubernatorial election, see TBA to JQA, 9 April, and note 2, above.

[13] Four forms in JQA's hand with temperature readings in LCA's hand are in JQA's Diary No. 49. LCA recorded readings from 26 April—the day JQA departed the capital—until 24 July. The Diary also includes a page with readings in JQA's hand that ceased on 25 April (JQA, *Diary*, 1, 26 April, 1 May, 1 June, 1 July; JQA to LCA, 1 May, note 1, above).

[14] That is, the John Quincy Adams Birthplace.

Louisa Catherine Adams to Mary Smith Cranch

My dear Aunt   Washington May 18 [1806]

Had I had an idea that my writing could have afforded you one moments satisfaction I should certainly have taken a much earlier opportunity of addressing you and offering my thanks for your kind attention to my darling boy I now entreat you to believe it was not owing to any inattention or neglect ~~on my part~~ and that nothing but a conviction on my part that you did not desire it could possibly have induced me to delay it on you entirely it depends though you will not gain much by so poor a correspondent I am confident I have hitherto lost considerable pleasure & improvement from not having earlier besought it from you—

I congratulate you on the birth of another granddaughter of which M$^{rs.}$ Adams informed me in her last letter[1] and am happy to hear that M$^{rs:}$ Greenleaf has got well through her confinement I wish it was my case it is not a pleasant thing in anticipation—

I regret much that the distance renders so impossible for me to enjoy more of M$^{r.}$ & M$^{rs.}$ Cranchs society our houses are unfortunately at the very extremities of the City and the distance of five miles without a Carriage almost entirely debars everything like social intercourse I sincerely rejoice in his new appointment in which he is perfectly calculated to shine and to which he will do honor—

I beg your acceptance of the enclosed cap which I wish was handsomer but being the work of one of my Sisters I hope it will not prove unaceptable

Make my best respects to M$^{r.}$ Cranch and remember me affectionately Kiss my little darlings for me and believe me your ever gratefully obliged and affec$^{te.}$ L. C. Adams

RC (Adams Papers); addressed: "M$^{rs:}$ Cranch. / Quincy"; endorsed: "M$^{rs.}$ L C. Adams."

[1] Not found.

John Quincy Adams and George Washington Adams to Louisa Catherine Adams

My dearest Louisa. Quincy 24. May 1806.

I wrote you this day week, last Sunday that I intended to return to Boston the next morning—But I did not go untill Tuesday.[1] I have been chiefly there untill ~~this~~ yesterday afternoon when I came out in the Stage, and found the family here all well; and particularly both the children— The first thing John said to me was to enquire whether I had sent a kiss for him to Mamma— I cannot stay many days absent from them without feeling an irresistible desire to see them again; and when I do see them I feel with double severity the separation from them and you too— But I see no prospect of a present remedy, and must reconcile myself as well as I can to my fortune.

May 1806

Wednesday I went to Cambridge to attend the sale at Auction of a House and Land, belonging to M$^{r:}$ Pearson—[2] My intention was to have purchased it, if it had gone at a reasonable price— The House would be a very convenient one for us during the Summer Season, for the remainder of the term that we are to spend the Winters at Washington, and the situation is such that its value will in every probability rise in the course of three years so that I could dispose of it advantageously whenever our convenience would suit— But M$^{r:}$ Pearson rated it so high, that he found no bidder, and the place was not sold— I did not regret the circumstance, because I knew you had no partialities in favour of Cambridge, and supposed you would willingly dispense with the purchase of any house there at-all— Perhaps I may yet agree to take it for two years from next March; in which case it will answer all my purpose, as it still remains my intention at the expiration of my term of public Service, to return to Boston.— While I was at Cambridge, I gave up the two chambers for which I had spoken— Principally on account of the great inconvenience to which I should be subjected in having to furnish the chambers, and at the expiration of five Months, to remove the furniture again.— I have now determined to remain for the present at Boston, and to take lodgings wherever a convenient opportunity shall offer them— As yet I am at Whitcomb's.

I am at this moment in Treaty for the sale of my house in Half-Court-Square, the one that Whitcomb formerly had, and which is now rented by the frenchman Delille— I expect in the course of this week to send you a deed of it, for you to sign and seal— I shall sell it advantageously, though upon a long credit— But I shall have a mortgage of the place itself as security for the payment— On the other hand I am also treating with M$^{r:}$ John Lowell for the purchase of his two houses which he built some years since, opposite M$^{r:}$ William Foster's, just below the bottom of the Mall—[3] I do not mean the houses where the old hay-market Theatre stood, but those somewhat lower down the Street—[4] I believe you will recollect them— One of them will I think answer our purpose to reside in when we return to Boston; better than any other house that I know of within the compass of our means—And both in a situation where they can easily be rented, as long as we may wish— I can obtain the two for little more than I am to receive for Delille's place, and the exchange will I hope be a beneficial one for our interest, as well as for the purpose of securing a dwelling house for ourselves whenever we shall want it— I mention all these things to you because your wishes as well as your particular interest are much concerned in them— As it is landed Estate, you have your right of dower in it, and this is one reason why in selling it I concluded to vest the money again in the same species of property— The situation of the house in half-Court-Square is a very advantageous one for business; and it now rents for 900 dollars a year— But the house is old, and will want constant repairs; and it will be difficult to keep so high a rent at its present standard— The other two houses rent for 500 dollars each—they have not been built more than four years, and will require no considerable repairs for a long time— They cannot probably rise much in value, but they promise fair to keep at the standard, and will be easier to rent, the sum for each of them being within the reach of greater numbers of persons— I wish it had been in my power to consult you before concluding the bargains, but the first proposition for the purchase of my house was made me last Thursday, and Lowell intends to sell his houses at public auction next Thursday, unless I take them previously off his hands— So I must presume upon your approbation, and I certainly should not have determined upon either of these steps, had I not believed that you would approve them.

There is another thing upon which I shall have time to receive your advice, and have therefore to request it— The situation of Col$^{l:}$ Smith and his family is known to you— My Sister determined not to leave him, and I think she was right— But it is probable that in the course of a short time he may be released, and in that case he will seek his fortune where he can— His family will be to be provided for by their friends— M$^{rs:}$ Smith and her daughter, I suppose will come here— But my proposition regards his son John; who is to take his degree at the College this Summer, and who will then want three years more to finish his education— My wish is to make him the offer to take him to live with us during that Time, in the Summer, while we keep house— And when we go to Washington in the Winter, he can come and stay here— He can in the mean time be entered as a Student either with me, or with my brother— He will thus be enabled to complete his education without cost to himself or his father; and unless he has some such assistance his situation will be really distressing— I say I ask your advice about making him this offer, though I know so well the generosity of your Nature, that I have not a doubt but it will meet your assent— It will no doubt occasion some expence, and will in some respects be inconvenient to you; but I am convinced the pleasure which it will carry with it, will in your mind overbalance every thing

May 1806

else. I wish you however to let me know your sentiments on the subject.

I have not heard yet of the arrival of Lord Selkirk, which is something extraordinary, as he must have sailed more than two Months since from England— His matrimonial projects I am suspicious will prove to be deeper in the heads of others than in his own heart— And I am of M^rs: Merry's opinion—It is not the fashion for Lords, not even for democratic or philosophical Lords, to come to America for their wives; and our Ladies have as great an antipathy to being *Countesses*, as M^rs: Orby Hunter.[5]

Your plumb-cake is made, and ready to be ship'd whenever an opportunity for Alexandria shall offer— Perhaps the vessel by which the trunk is coming will return; in which case I will send it by her— I hope you will receive it in Season for the occasion, when it will be wanted— I shall pay due attention to all your other commissions— I have hitherto regularly received your letters every Saturday, and they have become a necessary of life to me— I did not get your last (enclosing the bill of lading) untill I came out here last Evening; and I had felt a craving void for it from the morning.[6] I have written with equal regularity, and am glad to find you receive my letters with the same punctuality— I shall wait with anxious and hourly calculation for the time you are expecting; which cannot now be far distant— In the mean time believe me to be with invariable and ardent affection your faithful husband.   John Quincy Adams

Dear Mamma.

George says he can write to-day as well as last Sunday— He sends his duty to you, in his-own hand-writing.

RC (Adams Papers); endorsed: "J Q Adams Esq. / Rec^d May 31 / ans^d· June 2."

[1] JQA and GWA to LCA, 18 May, above.

[2] Eliphalet Pearson on 21 May auctioned a house and orchard adjacent to the Cambridge Common near the present-day intersection of Massachusetts Avenue and Cambridge Street. Receiving no bids, Pearson later sold the property to Rev. Abiel Holmes (Boston *Independent Chronicle*, 28 April; Boston *Repertory*, 20 May; Cambridge *Harvard Crimson*, 27 Jan. 1956).

[3] On 1 June 1806 Boston lawyer Andrew Dexter Jr. paid JQA $15,000 for the Half-Court Square house that JQA had purchased on 6 Nov. 1802. LCA attested to her release of dower on 9 June 1806 in Washington, D.C., and the deed was recorded in Boston on 14 July. On 20 June JQA paid the same amount to John Lowell Jr. for two structures at the corner of Frog Lane and Nassau Street. Boston tobacconist William Foster resided across Nassau Street from the property (vol. 15:316; Suffolk Co. Registry of Deeds, Boston:Suffolk Co. Deeds, 216:152–153, 160–161; John and Rebecca Lowell to JQA, deed, 20 June 1806, Adams Papers, Wills and Deeds; *Boston Directory*, 1806, p. 51, Shaw-Shoemaker, No. 50652).

[4] From 1796 to 1803 the Haymarket Theatre stood at the corner of Tremont and Boylston Streets in Boston (Winsor, *Memorial History of Boston*, p. 363, 365).

⁵ LCA wrote to JQA on 18 May 1806, reporting that in addition to his appointment as British minister to the United States, the Earl of Selkirk's purpose for crossing the Atlantic Ocean was a "matrimonial expedition" to court Philadelphia socialite Sarah Lukens Keene, for whom see JQA to LCA, 1 Feb. 1807, and note 6, below. LCA may also have referenced Elizabeth Orby, daughter of Sir James Orby, Baronet of Croyland Abbey, who married Gen. Robert Hunter (d. 1734), the untitled colonial governor of New York (Bernard Burke, *A Genealogical and Heraldic History of the Landed Gentry of Great Britain & Ireland*, 9th edn., 2 vols., London, 1898, 2:1574–1575).

⁶ The bill of lading was for the shipment of a trunk (LCA to JQA, 18 May 1806, Adams Papers).

Louisa Catherine Adams to John Quincy Adams

Washington May 25 1806

The pleasure I recieved on reading your account of our charming Children my best beloved friend you can more readily concieve than I describe¹ I can believe that George grows like me but Johns round face and deep dimples must I think be infinitely more like his father who has ever been celebrated for this to *me* fascinating beauty the delight I feel at learning that they still talk of me is exquisite but I dare not flatter myself with a hope that they will have the slightest recollection of my person when I return either the pinions of Time have been terribly clipt or the total inactivity into which I am sunk makes him lag most ~~petiably petious~~ tediously even my approaching hours of pain hold out some prospect of relief from this dreadful insipidity and I really anticipate it with pleasure you I presume are so fully occupied in preparations for the approaching ceremony in which you are to shine preeminent as to be altogether unable to judge of the vacuity I complain of but after having been accustom'd to the cares of a family it is difficult to find a substitute for such an employment one of my disappointments and not the least is the being so far from you on this occasion as I proposed to be present and expected great gratification from hearing you speak in Public which is a pleasure I have hitherto been deprived of I shall feel some degree of anxiety untill it is over though I entertain no doubt whatever of your giving general and unlimitted satisfaction in any language—

Mrs: Mason is at length confined (after a miscalculation of five weeks) and has a Son.² Daughters appear to be the fashion among you Mrs Norton does well I think which of the Mrs. Foster's is it that has a daughter we are all well here excepting little Walter who I am fearful is much more unwell than his parents are aware of was he mine I should be apprehensive of a gradual but almost imperceptable decline Mr. Hellen has return'd from Baltimore some of his friends have recommended a new fashion'd medecine with which he has been dosing himself untill he has made himself quite sick he remains very uncertain about the House the agents refuse to let it for any time.

He has been very fortunate in the Sales of the Tobaco he shipped last year should he be as successful the present and he has purchaced very largely at a very low price he will make a fortune—

Mon amie I fear you will think I teaze you but I wish you would suffer me to buy the piece of Sheeting we talked of getting once a year I am much in want of them here and have leisure enough to make them 30 Dollars was the sum we intended to devote to this purpose— I wish if you can find such a thing as very fine small tooth comb you would send it me for my infant I cannot procure one fine enough here or in Baltimore The way in which you are going to live really makes me unhappy and I cannot concieve but what [. . . m]ight find some place in Boston much more [. . .]able and more suitable than the plan you have adopted I have always supposed it was very easy to find houses to board in in Boston and cannot imagine what can be your difficulty particularly as you do not take the child—

Adieu my beloved friend Kiss my sweet Boys and remember me affectionately to all at home most sincerely do I wish I was at Johns beauty house I thank you for Georges first attempt in writing which does him and his dear papa infinite credit— I can but repeat how tenderly and unalterably attached remains ever your

L. C. Adams

Direct your letters M^{rs} J Q Adams

RC (Adams Papers); addressed: "John Quincy Adams Esq$^{r.}$"; endorsed: "Louisa. 25. May 1806. / 31. May rec$^{d:}$ / 1. June Ans$^{d:}$." Some loss of text where the seal was removed.

[1] JQA and GWA to LCA, 18 May, above.
[2] Eilbeck Mason (d. 1862), the sixth child of Anna Maria Murray Mason (1776–1857) and banker John Mason (1766–1849) of Georgetown, D.C., was born on 20 May (vol. 12:535; ViLoGH, "The Mason Web: The Mason Descendants Database," www.gunstonhall.org).

Louisa Catherine Adams to John Quincy Adams

My best beloved friend   Washington June 2^d 1806

I write you a few lines although with difficulty having been for some days extremely ill and still remaining too unwell to be able to attend to any-thing my illness was I believe occasion'd by walking though a very small distance and nearly threaten'd a premature confinement I am so much better that I trust I have escaped the danger and make no doubt I shall get through very well your charming letter did more towards my recovery than all the Doctors perscriptions and would my strength permit I would answer it fully[1] as it is I can only say that all you propose meets my entire approbation and thanks and I only feel mortified that you should have thought it necessary to mention your intentions regarding John Smith as it must ever be a pleasure to me to concur in every thing that can afford your family either comfort or advantage and it shall be my study to render my house as agreeable to him as I possibly can I feel myself under too many obligations to you as it regards your kindness to my Sisters ever to have it in my power to repay them—

Adieu my best and dearest friend should it please heaven to spare me to you and our dear children it shall be my chief delight and endeavour to return by every tender and affectionate mark of gratitude the deep sense I entertain of your unmerited kindness to your sincerely devoted wife   L C Adams

RC (Adams Papers).
[1] JQA and GWA to LCA, 24 May, above.

John Quincy Adams to Louisa Catherine Adams

My dearest friend.   Quincy 8. June 1806.

Yesterday was the first Saturday since I arrived here, which passed over without bringing me a letter from you; and although I am willing to hope that it may be owing to some delay at the Post-Office, or to some accident which prevented your writing at the usual time, I cannot help feeling some degree of uneasiness least the omission should have been caused by the state of your health— Indeed the Saturday itself has scarcely been gone before I begin to feel impatient for the next, and when even that fails to bring me the tidings of your health, I strongly feel the disappointment.

When I closed my last letter to you, I was just coming out here; which I did—but returned the next morning to Boston, where I have again pass'd the week—[1] Yesterday I came out with my mother; and expect to return to-morrow morning to Boston— I am still lodged at Whitcomb's, and having a chamber to myself, am as well situated as I should be at a private house— But next Thursday is the day upon which I am to be made a Professor, and for the convenience during the heat of the summer of being near at hand I have concluded to take a chamber at Dr Waterhouse's untill Commencement—[2] That is, untill the last week in August— A vacation of four weeks immediately

June 1806

follows after that, and when the Collegiate duties recommence, the Autumn will be so far advanced that I shall find no difficulty in going from Boston to Cambridge twice a week for the performance of my duties there— In which case I shall resume my chamber at Whitcomb's, untill the period of my departure for Washington— Such is at present the prospect before me— It is to be sure that of a very unsettled life; but so mine must be untill the close of my public life; which has now little more than two years to run.— My temptations to break off from my connections with public affairs and resume the practice of the law, are even now so strong that if you were here, and as willing as I am, I believe I should renounce my official character at once. The time is peculiarly auspicious for commencing practice at the bar— The two most eminent men of the profession, in this State being just at this time removed— One to be Governor of the State, and the other to be Chief Justice of its Supreme Judicial Court.[3]

M[r:] Sullivan will undoubtedly be Governor— M[r:] Strong had indeed a full majority of all the votes returned— But as the Senate and House of Representatives, decide upon the *validity* of the returns, and as there is a majority in both Houses, opposed to the Governor, they have appointed a committee who reported to *reject*, as not legally returned just votes enough to take the complete majority from Strong— Then the Election is to be made by the Legislature, and of course M[r:] Sullivan will be chosen— The Senate have already accepted the report of the Committee and it goes to the House of Representatives for discussion to-morrow—[4] The issue is foreseen, but it has already taken up almost as much time as our Legislature generally sit at this Season of the year— I dined yesterday with M[r:] Strong, at Sheriff Allen's— His niece Miss Allen, whom you well remember, was married a few days since to Governor Strong's eldest Son.[5]

I hope you have received the deed which I enclosed to you last week, and that you will send it back to me, executed, as soon as possible— It is necessary to enable me to finish not only that business, but also Lowell's houses— He has given me substantially satisfaction with respect to the difficulties of title which I hinted to you— But there are some little irregularities of form in the conveyances to him, which he has engaged to have corrected, before we finally execute the deeds— I consider the matter as settled, and feel no small satisfaction at the circumstance of having an house ready for us to go into, whenever we shall find it expedient. There are tenants at present in both of them; but they hold only from quarter to quarter, and either of them will go out with a quarter's Notice.

I have yet said nothing to you of the children, because when I began my letter I had not seen George— He is now here to dine, and as well as his brother is very well— His complexion is darkened by the power of the Sun, and I think he will grow up, not very fair— I brought them out last Sunday the presents from you—A book for George, and a horse for John— They were both highly delighted with them, and thank Mamma, a thousand times.

The weather is this day excessively warm, and we have had a very few other days and parts of days; but the season in general has been cold and dry to excess— Only one rain of half a day since I came home— The vegetation more backward than I ever remember— Strawberries just now but in blossom, and not a pea, yet to be seen.

The Hawk is not yet arrived with my trunk from Alexandria, neither can I hear of any vessel going either there or to Georgetown— I have been looking anxiously for an opportunity to send you the plumb-Cake, which has been made sometime and is all ready to be sent.[6] I shall according to your directions have the silk dyed, and will get your net handkerchief hunted up, and also dyed as you desire— I hope to get the comb, and forward it by the time you will want it, though it will probably not be in my power to procure any so fine as those you formerly had.

You have complimented me rather too soon upon my future performance; and in one respect I shall be glad that you will not be here; because it will save you the mortification of a disappointment— In another I regret very much your absence, for I am sure I should do better, if I could enjoy the advantage of reading my discourse to you, before I speak it— In former instances I had that benefit, and know how useful it was to me; most especially in the hints of passages to be struck out— I much want an adviser for that purpose now— The object and the occasion, are of little consequence, nor is much expected in such cases— Yet I feel a foolish uneasiness about me, from an idea that too much expectation will be formed by the hearers, and from the knowledge that it will not be gratified. There will probably be however little company, and I shall get through as I can.

Your's ever affectionately—   John Quincy Adams[7]

RC (Adams Papers).

[1] JQA wrote to LCA on 1 June, alerting her that recent newspaper reports of the death of "Ann Adams" did not refer to AHA. He also reported the results of Massachusetts legislative elections and enclosed a deed of sale for a Boston property, which he asked her to sign and return (Adams Papers).

[2] Harvard College professor Dr. Benjamin

Waterhouse and his wife, Elizabeth Oliver Waterhouse, lived in a house that still stands at 7 Waterhouse Street on the Cambridge Common. He had assisted JQA in 1785 with his entrance to Harvard (vol. 4:33; JA, *Papers*, 17:35–36). For JQA's installation as the college's Boylston Professor of Rhetoric and Oratory, see JQA to LCA, 15 June 1806, and note 1, below.

[3] On 5 June Theophilus Parsons informed Gov. Caleb Strong that he would accept appointment as chief justice of the Mass. Supreme Judicial Court. Parsons served until his death in 1813 (JA, *Legal Papers*, 1:cvi; Theophilus Parsons Jr., *Memoir of Theophilus Parsons*, Boston, 1861, p. 228).

[4] After Strong narrowly defeated James Sullivan to win reelection in April 1806, the Democratic-Republican majority in the Mass. General Court challenged the election results, appointing a joint committee to examine ballots from across the state. In a 5 June report the committee recommended that slates from several majority-Federalist towns be disregarded because town clerks had abbreviated candidates' names on the ballots, a step that would throw the election to Sullivan. The state senate voted along party lines to accept the committee report, while six Democratic-Republicans in the house of representatives joined a Federalist minority in opposition. The actions of the majority party provoked a severe public backlash, with the *Boston Commercial Gazette*, 9 June, calling it "the utmost breach of faith, and an outrageous stretch of prerogative." A lengthy protest signed by nineteen senators was printed in the Boston *Columbian Centinel*, 11 June, and characterized the plan as "an open usurpation of the power of the people." Democratic-Republicans backed off on 11 June, announcing that because the slates of other towns were also defective Strong was the victor. He was sworn in to a new term on 12 June (A New Nation Votes; Edward B. Foley, *Ballot Battles: The History of Disputed Elections in the United States*, N.Y., 2016, p. 61–69, 395; Boston *Repertory*, 13 June).

[5] Theodore Strong (1779–1855), Yale 1797, married on 3 June Martha Allen of Lynn, Mass., a niece of Boston sheriff Jeremiah Allen (vol. 9:342; Benjamin W. Dwight, *The History of the Descendants of Elder John Strong of Northampton, Mass.*, 1 vol. in 2, Albany, N.Y., 1871, 2:1189; [James Allen], *Letter Relating to the Estate of the Late Jeremiah Allen, Esq.*, [Boston, 1824], p. 2).

[6] See JQA to LCA, 15 June, and note 4, below.

[7] JQA wrote again to LCA on 10 June, noting his relief at learning of her improved health. He also reported that he would appear as counsel in U.S. Circuit Court in Boston and described the progress of AHA's pregnancy (Adams Papers).

John Quincy Adams to Louisa Catherine Adams

My dearest Louisa. Quincy 15. June 1806.

I pass'd the day yesterday, in anxious expectation of having a letter from you again, but it did not come— The fear that your illness should have continued or returned to prevent your writing, heavily weighs upon me; and the only probable contingency that my Imagination offers me to account for your omission again to write at the usual time is that you received my letter enclosing the *deed* on Saturday; that you could not execute it so as to send it back to me untill Monday, and that you delayed writing untill you could send the deed with your letter— I shall feel uneasy however untill I hear from you again— If, as may be already the case you find an inconvenience in writing, ask one of your Sisters to write in your stead, barely to inform me how you find yourself—a few days more, and I hope you will be lightened of your burden; and though it be an exchange only of one charge for another, yet that the one which succeeds will compensate for its troubles by its pleasures.

I went into Boston last Monday Morning, and pass'd the week there— On Thursday afternoon at 5 O'Clock, the installation took place— The time fixed for the purpose was half-past three; but a heavy thunder gust came up exactly at that time and delayed the performances nearly two hours— It also prevented the attendance of many persons, and the company was very small— The heat was excessive, and I suffered much from it— The auditory were I believe in general well satisfied with my discourse, which was very short—[1] I returned the same Evening to Boston— This week I expect to go to Cambridge, and to reside there three or four Months— I am to have a chamber at D^{r:} Waterhouse's.

The great political question who should be Governor is at length settled; and M^{r:} Strong is in for one year more— He had a clear majority of all the votes returned; but an attempt was made, and push'd with an unusual violence of party Spirit, to reject a number of votes sufficient to prevent him from having a majority of the whole number; a Committee of the two houses of the Legislature, five Demo's against two federalists, did accomplish the object as far as depended on them— They contrived to reject just votes enough to leave the Governor short of the complete majority by 14— And it is amusing to observe the expedients to which they resorted for that purpose— The Senate after long and warm debates accepted the report of the Committee in all its parts; but the members of the minority, entered a protest against the decision, which has appeared in all our newspapers, and shews the grounds of controversy— When the Report however pass'd down to the house of Representatives, many of the party began to stagger— The general Sentiment abroad was much against them, and their own partizans were ashamed to support what they were doing— All of a sudden they bethought themselves to reject the votes of two towns *more*, by which means the majority was restored to M^{r:} Strong; they immediately declared him to be chosen— And when I left Boston, on Thursday to go up to Cambridge, all the Bells were ringing for joy that he was having the Oaths of Office administered to him— He is however the only federalist left in the Government— The Legislature have changed all the Officers, annually elected by them, and the Governor's Council is completely altered.[2]

We are in expectation of a *total* Eclipse of the Sun to-morrow morning— This is a very rare occurrence, and has never been known to happen in Boston, since the settlement of the Country— There is indeed

June 1806

some little question whether it will be total here even now, as there are two Calculations—one of which makes it less than total by about a minute and a half— At Washington you will see it very large, but the Sun will not be wholly eclipsed by nearly one twelfth— The little Society which you remember I once belonged to in Boston, have made some preparations for observing it with some attention, and are provided with glasses for the purpose— I have agreed to meet with them— in M^r: Bussey's Garden, which he has offered them to take their observations.³

The children are both well— M^rs: T. B. Adams took John to Boston with her on Thursday; but she did not go up to Cambridge— They stayed that Night in Boston and returned here on Friday— John was quite impatient to come home.

I enclose you a comb which is the finest I have been able to procure for you— The Cake is now in Boston, packed up in a long wooden box, and has been sometime waiting for an opportunity of conveyance— I intend to have it put on board the schooner *Silvia*, Captain Daggett, I think it is—address'd to the care of M^r: Henry K. May at Alexandria— She was advertised to sail this day, but will not go untill the day after to-morrow. I hope the box will arrive in due Season— I believe I mentioned to you that the Hawk had arrived—and I have received the trunk—⁴ It was bound round with ropes, but the latch into which the bolt of the lock turns was broken off, and the lock itself was also broken— Whether this happened before the shipment of the trunk, at Washington or since I do not know— There appeared to be nothing missing from the trunk.

We are all well here except my father who has a very severe cold— He thinks it the influenza, which is very frequent here at present— Abby Shaw is here— She came with me yesterday in the Stage from Boston—

The most interesting matrimonial news I have is that M^r: Wales & Miss Beale, appear at the Meeting-House posted up together, as intending *better acquaintance*.⁵

Best remembrance to all the family, from your's unalterably

RC (Adams Papers); endorsed: "J. Q. Adams / Received 21st. June / Answer'd 22 June."

¹ JQA was installed as the first Boylston Professor of Rhetoric and Oratory of Harvard College on 12 June. At the Cambridge ceremony he delivered an English-language oration in which he declared public speaking to be the greatest art: "It is by the means of reason, clothed with speech, that the most precious blessings of social life are communicated from man to man, and that supplication, thanksgiving, and praise, are addressed to the Author of

the universe." The Boston press lauded the address; the *Boston Commercial Gazette*, 16 June, wrote that it abounded "in fertility of illustration, force of delivery, and originality," while the *New-England Palladium*, 17 June, praised JQA's "free, strong and perspicuous outline of the nature, history and practice" of oratory. On 1 July the oration was published both in the *Monthly Anthology*, 3:288–295 [June 1806], and as a pamphlet.

The appointment had been many years in the making. The position was endowed in 1771 by a £1,500 bequest from Nicholas Boylston, a maternal cousin of JA's. The university took no action until 1801, when Ward Nicholas Boylston threatened to sue if his uncle's wishes were not fulfilled and also proposed JQA for the professorship. The Harvard Corporation did not move forward until 24 June 1805, when it voted unanimously to offer the post to JQA. He initially expressed reservations and over several months negotiated changes to the parameters of the appointment, including the removal of a requirement that he reside in Cambridge. In December JQA accepted the position.

Between 11 July 1806 and 28 July 1809, JQA delivered 36 lectures, numbered I to XXXVI, repeating the course through Lecture XXIV beginning in the fall of 1808 after the first set of students graduated. When college was in session, he spent one hour each week delivering a lecture and a second teaching the class, although his Diary for the period records hours of preparation. He required substitutes only three times in three years. An incomplete bound set of JQA's drafts of the lectures are in the Adams Papers (M/JQA/37, APM Reel 231; M/JQA/38, APM Reel 232). The lectures were published in a two-volume edition in 1810 (vol. 4:342–343; Donald M. Goodfellow, "The First Boylston Professor of Rhetoric and Oratory," *NEQ*, 19:372–381, 384–385 [Sept. 1946]; JA, *Papers*, 17:388; JQA, *Diary*, 26 June 1805; JQA, *Writings*, 3:123–129; JQA, *An Inaugural Oration, Delivered at the Author's Installation, as Boylston Professor of Rhetorick and Oratory, at Harvard University*, Boston, 1806, Shaw-Shoemaker, No. 9800; JQA, *Lectures on Rhetoric*, 1:14–15).

[2] The Democratic-Republican majority in the Mass. General Court elected John Bacon to replace Harrison Gray Otis as senate president and Perez Morton to succeed Timothy Bigelow as Speaker of the house. The nine Federalist members of the governor's council were also turned out in favor of Democratic-Republicans (*Manual for the Use of the General Court*, Boston, 1903, p. 240, 242; A New Nation Votes).

[3] As early as 1800 scientists predicted that a solar eclipse would be visible from Boston to Richmond, Va., on the morning of 16 June 1806. JQA gathered with members of Boston's Society for the Study of Natural Philosophy in the garden of merchant Benjamin Bussey's home at 5 Summer Street. JA later claimed to be among those who accurately calculated the timing of the eclipse. The four-minute event began just after 11 A.M., a few minutes earlier than the time predicted in a pamphlet published in Boston in May (vol. 15:158, 160; JQA, *Diary*; Alan Hirshfeld, *Starlight Detectives: How Astronomers, Inventors, and Eccentrics Discovered the Modern Universe*, N.Y., 2014, p. 21–22; *Boston Directory*, 1806, p. 28, Shaw-Shoemaker, No. 50652; Jefferson, *Papers*, 34:172; JA to David Sewall, 4 Nov. 1821, LbC, APM Reel 124; [Andrew Newell], *Darkness at Noon; or, The Great Solar Eclipse*, Boston, 1806, p. 7).

[4] The schooner *Sylvia*, Capt. Joseph Lewis, was advertised in the Boston *Columbian Centinel*, 14 June, as sailing the next day, but its departure from Boston was not reported until the 19th. JQA corrected the name of the captain in a letter to LCA of 18 June (Adams Papers), also enclosing $50 for expenses and updating her on his Boston real estate dealings. Henry K. May was an Alexandria, Va., merchant. LCA shipped JQA his trunk aboard the sloop *Hawk*, Capt. David Starbuck (*Boston Commercial Gazette*, 19 June; Alexandria, Va., *Daily Advertiser*, 8 May).

[5] Ann Beale, daughter of Capt. Benjamin Beale Jr., married her cousin Thomas Beale Wales in Quincy on 9 July (vol. 14:173–174; Sprague, *Braintree Families*).

June 1806

Louisa Catherine Adams to John Quincy Adams

My best friend   Washington June 15 1806

To hear from you and to write you are the greatest pleasures I am at present capable of enjoying and even this is in a great measure restricted by the almost total loss of the use of my thumb which I fear will yet teaze me three long weeks my sincere desire to prevent your feeling any uneasiness on my account urges me to use every possible exertion and I must rely on your indulgence for every due allowance both for the writing and diction: harrassed by a sense of pain our thoughts (spite of philosophy) will not flow easily and unconstrain'd and we cannot help becoming tedious by an involuntary recurrence to our sufferings my last letters have I fear been of this nature and [. . . .] feel greatly relieved as it regards my general [. . .] I reproach myself for having occasioned you a degree of anxiety which might have been spared and which could not possibly benefit me had not the life of a dear little being been at stake believe me nothing on earth could have induced me to relinquish the delight of seeing my beloved children and enjoying your society which is all I most value in this world and I am now ready and willing to leave this place as soon as I am up from my confinement and to unite with you in any plan that you may think prudent or adviseable as to your future mode of life. you well know that my inclinations have ever pointed to the line which you now tell me is open'd to you as the least unstable of any you can adopt although it is perhaps the most laborious and the least gratifying to a mind form'd as yours has been for a more brilliant sphere yet my beloved friend I do not feel myself qualified to become an adviser on a question of such importance as your resignation of your public duties in which you are so eminently calculated to shine and to be of real and essential service to your Country self and family comfort must sometimes be sacrificed for the general good and though I am consious how much this sentiment must operate against myself still I feel irrisistibly impelled to express it from an ardent desire to see at least some men of respectability and talents adorning public stations and to save them while I had the power from sinking into total disgrace which though it may perhaps be but for a short space still promotes the pleasing reflexion of having exerted every ability to delay the ruin which could not be prevented think not that this desire proceeds from a foolish and weak ambition which at the present crisis of affairs can hold forth but a poor compensation for the unsettled and divided life we at present lead if I know my own heart it springs from the purest motives which banish every interest but the public welfare which in my simple opinion has already been much injured by a want of just reflexion on this very important subject and a too close adherence to private interest nature produces very few really great men interest and the world corrupt many of those few we are therefore bound when we possess the means to use them and to use them greatly— After what I have written you must act as you think most proper I dare not indulge my favorite wish and I never will be the ~~means~~ cause of your doing that which you might ever after repent it is certainly the right and the glory of every wife to enjoy the confidence of her husband but it is likewise her duty to use her influence with caution and to make his interest and prosperity her chief study and this my dearest and best friend I trust I shall ever be proud to do excuse my prolixity I thought myself called upon to reply very fully to your last letter and am prepared to learn your decision—[1]

Mr. Hellen saw Mr Wagner a few days since and had some conversation with him upon the New York business Mr. W. insinuated to him that the G. were much shocked at the conduct of the judge and meant as soon as the trial was over to do something for the gentlemen who had certainly been treated very improperly[2] I wish this may be true the heads of department are obliged to attend and leave this place shortly for that purpose the President is here and it is said never was in better spirits or health he remains here untill the middle of July—[3]

Adieu Kiss my lovely babes for me and tell George I will buy him a Sister as soon as I can I am glad to hear he is so attentive to the Ladies it is a good sign and bespeaks a good heart—

if I were with you I would make you sensible how much you are beloved by your affectionate   L. C. Adams

The Vessel is arrived safe[4]

RC (Adams Papers); addressed: "John Q Adams Esqr" and "at Dr. WaterHouse's / Cambridge / J.W."; endorsed: "Louisa— 15. June 1806. / 24. June recd: / 29. June Ansd:." Some loss of text where the seal was removed.

[1] JQA to LCA, 8 June, above.

[2] State Department chief clerk Jacob Wagner was among the federal officials who, following Thomas Jefferson's directions, declined to travel to New York to testify in WSS's trial, for which see JQA to WSS, 16 April, and note 2, above. Gov. Morgan Lewis made no move to assist WSS with state employment after his trial (Thomas Lloyd, *The Trials of William S. Smith, and Samuel G. Ogden*, N.Y., 1807, p. 2, 6–7).

[3] Jefferson arrived in Washington, D.C., from Monticello on 7 June and remained in the capital until 21 July (*Jefferson's Memorandum Books*, 1:liii).

[4] See JQA to LCA, 10 May, and note 6, above.

John Quincy Adams to Louisa Catherine Adams

Dear Louisa.   Cambridge 22. June 1806.

Here I am at length, established as an intimate, in the family of D^r: Waterhouse; but from a variety of delays I did not come from Boston, untill the Evening before last— And being once here I concluded to adhere a sufficient time to get habituated and reconciled to my new Situation before I would absent myself from it— This prevented me from going out yesterday to Quincy, according to my custom, and it deprives me of the pleasure of seeing our dear children for one week— It must be a strange necessity indeed that will stay me the next Saturday— Another comfort too of which I feel the want, as a customary enjoyment of that day is a letter from you— I should not indeed have had much right to expect one had I remained at Boston or gone out to Quincy yesterday; because I had so recently received your's of the 9$^{th:}$ enclosing the deed, and because besides the interruption which I must of course anticipate in your correspondence arising from your present condition, you have prepared me to meet with such disappointments occasionally, without feeling so much anxiety for the cause, as I have felt hitherto—[1] The days are now very near at hand which come to the period of your own calculations—those calculations which some of your friends thought so far behind the reality— I presume you will not go beyond your time, and still have the expectation that you will be relieved some days short of it— Perhaps at the very moment when you receive this letter

My conjectures respecting M$^{rs:}$ T. B. A. were indeed quite erroneous— She is now in daily expectation of confinement, and in all probability will be beforehand with you—So at least I am informed— But even now her external appearance, even when she is most inclined to discover the secret, does not make it known so obviously, as yours did when you was most disposed to conceal it, before I left Washington— M$^{rs:}$ Whitcomb is getting quite well.

I just mentioned to you, in a line which I wrote you on Wednesday,[2] that I had with a company of philosophers observed the Eclipse in M^r: Bussy's Garden— It was indeed a very remarkable sight— The principal part of it you must have witness'd at Washington; but many of the most curious phenomena, were those which arose from the total obscuration of the Sun— His face was *entirely* covered at Boston, about four minutes and a half.— The darkness was such that it would have been impossible to read a small print, and I was obliged to use a lanthorn to observe the state of my thermometer— The fowls roosted— The lowing herd wound slowly o'er the lea.—³ The western horizon, with a sky perfectly serene, looked as if it had been charged with one of the heaviest thunderclouds— The moon appeared like a patch of court-plaister upon the face of Heaven, and all round the edges of her disk was a luminous border like that which you sometimes see round the edges of a dark cloud— Just before the Sun came out the edge of the moon on the side from which he was to proceed assumed a deep crimson colour; but never since my existence have I seen any thing like the brightness of the first beam, which he shot forth upon his return— The naked eye could not bear it for an instant, though for several minutes before his face was entirely closed in, he suffered us to look at him— I know not the philosophical reason why the first rays of reviving splendor should be so much more dazzling than the last beams of expiring glory, but such was the fact.— From the commencement of the eclipse to the time of the total obscurity the thermometer fell eleven degrees—and by the time the moon fully disappeared, it had risen again, about as much; being all the time in the shade.

I have seen in the Newspapers an account of the Death of Mr George Wythe, a Judge of the Court of Chancery in Virginia, and a man much distinguished during an important period of the American Revolution— He was at one time an intimate friend of my father, who once address'd to him a letter on the subject of Government, which has often been published— Of late years he like so many other persons of the revolutionary times had forgotten antient friendships, and had fallen into another political scale; yet he had not lost his place in my father's regard, and I am sure he has been much affected at this incident—particularly as by a paragraph in the Richmond Enquirer, it appears there were suspicions that Mr Wythe's Death was not in the ordinary course of Nature— On whom the suspicions have fallen the papers do not say; but probably as it is in your neighbourhood, and as he was a man of so distinguished a character you may have heard— If you have, let me know how the circumstances are told.⁴

I have been here so short a time th[at] I can yet only tell you in general terms that I am as well satisfied with my situation as I could possibly expect— My serious privations, that is, of my wife and children are the same here that they were in Boston— There however I had a source of dissipation in the succession of my fellow-boarders, as they came and went, and with whom I associated at breakfast dinner and supper— In this I found, as in everything else, some good and some evil— The good was that by varying the scene & the company before me, it enlivened the time which hung most heavily upon me— The evil was that sometimes the companions were not agreeable, and that always the time spent with them was diverted from studies to which I ought to devote every moment of my present leisure, and to which I have not half time enough to devote— Here, my Society is as yet perfectly ~~at leisure~~ agreeable, but I have more time for meditation and composition— The scene will be so uniform that I am afraid you will find my future letters duller than ever— At least I hope they will prove that my heart whether in the City or the Village, in the crowd or the solitude is ever equally devoted to you—

John Quincy Adams.

RC (Adams Papers); endorsed: "J Q Adams Esq[r] / Rec[d.] June 30[th.] / Ans[d.] do do." Tr (Adams Papers). Some loss of text due to placement of the seal.

[1] In her letter to JQA of 9 June, LCA related that she was in moderate health, sought information on AHA's pregnancy, and communicated reports about the Miranda expedition (Adams Papers).

[2] JQA to LCA, 18 June, for which see his letter of 15 June, note 3, above.

[3] Thomas Gray, "Elegy Written in a Country Churchyard," line 2.

[4] George Wythe (b. ca. 1726), a judge and educator from Richmond, Va., died on 8 June. JA and Wythe had served together in the Continental Congress. An [April 1776] letter from JA to the Virginia jurist, not found, was reprinted as JA's *Thoughts on Government*, for which see JA, *Papers*, 4:65–73, 86–93. The *Salem Gazette*, 20 June 1806, reported that his death was being investigated. Suspicions were raised when Wythe and two free African American servants, Lydia Broadnax and Michael Brown, became ill after dining on 25 May. Wythe's great-nephew, George Wythe Sweeney Jr., attempted to cash a check with the judge's forged signature two days later, leading Wythe to suspect that Sweeney had poisoned them and prompting him to remove a bequest to him from his will before his death. LCA recounted to JQA on 30 June (Adams Papers) rumors that Sweeney had put arsenic in coffee served to the victims. Sweeney was tried for Wythe's and Brown's murders in Richmond District Court in September and acquitted. The press blamed the verdict on Virginia's prohibition on testimony by African Americans against defendants of European descent (Encyclopedia Virginia, www.encyclopediavirginia.org).

Louisa Catherine Adams to John Quincy Adams

Washington June 24 1806

I still continue as well and better than we could reasonably expect my best beloved friend and shall write two or three lines merely to announce this I know to you pleasing intelligence my milk as yet gives me no trouble and I hope I shall escape without the usual difficulties and I have had no fever whatever my time was a very bad one and lasted 20 hours twelve hours more would have terminated an existence which though of little use I flatter myself is of some consequence to you—[1]

Adieu write me often and permit me to come to you as soon as my health will permit D[r.] May and M[r] Winne are both going on soon[2] I can take one of these opportunities to reunite myself to all I hold dear in this world in which desire I hope soon to learn that you join your truely affect^{n.} L. C. Adams

Kiss my precious treasures as usual
I shall not write again for some days unless I should not be so well—

RC (Adams Papers).

[1] On 22 June LCA gave birth to a stillborn son. She later blamed the event on a walk she made on 21 June to and from the home of her sister Harriet Johnson Boyd: "I walked home at eight or nine o clock in the Evening and at 3 oclock in the afternoon of the next day under circumstances of the most imminent danger gave birth to a dead Child with the Thermometer at a hundred and neither Father or Children near me to console me for my sufferings" (LCA, D&A, 1:xxx, 235–236).

[2] U.S. Navy purser Timothy Winn (1773–1836), Harvard 1795, of Woburn, Mass., served in the Mediterranean before settling in Washington, D.C. (Edmund Janes Cleveland and Horace Gillette Cleveland, comps., *Genealogy of the Cleveland and Cleaveland Families*, 1 vol. in 3, Hartford, Conn., 1899, 3:2443; Boston *Columbian Centinel*, 2 March 1805; Washington, D.C., *National Intelligencer*, 14 April 1806; Boston *Independent Chronicle*, 6 April 1807).

Louisa Catherine Adams to John Quincy Adams

My very best friend   Washington June 29 [1806]

My health continues to mend rappidly and the prospect of soon rejoining you and my little darlings supports my spirits and enables me to bear the dreadful stroke that has befallen me with more fortitude than otherwise I fear I should have done—

I can safely assure you that this misfortune was not caused by any imprudence on my part Dr. Weems is satisfied that the Child had been subject to violent convulsions sometime before he died and had he lived the probability is that he woud have been all his life subject to fitts[1] much as I suffer for the loss of this lovely Infant I could not desire its life upon terms so painful—

I am in the greatest anxiety to hear from you two days have passed over the accustomed time and I feel a degree of terror lest some sickness or accident should have prevented your writing Oh my best beloved friend should any thing have happen'd to you or the Children I do not think I could live over it my spirits are very weak and my frame more so they tell me it is fortunate I have no child to Nurse—

John Randolph has challenged T. M. Randolph for his speech in the house which was supposed to be made up and they are to fight shortly the P. has made such arrangements as to be able to quit Washington as soon as the duel takes place We learn this from M^{r.} & Mrs. *Mad.* therefore you may rely on the truth of it[2]

June 1806

A horrid circumstance took place here yesterday Mr. Mason sometime ago whipped one of his negroes whom he had the greatest confidence in the man swore to be revenged and before day break yesterday morning when the family were all asleep at their house on the Island which you know to be of wood laid fire—at each end of the roof of a sort of wide passage which forms the Centre of the building and comunicates with each wing the Centre and one of the wings were entirely consumed and the whole family would have been destroyed had the wretch not been betrayed by one of the Women Servants he was immediately secured by the Constables his hands tied and put into a Boat to be convey'd to Prison he however threw himself overboard and was drown'd before any assistance could be obtain'd his body was found late in the evening—[3]

Adieu my best friend M^{r.} & Mrs. Cranch have been to see me she looks very well and tells me Mrs. T. B. Adams expects to be confined every day I most sincerely wish she may be more fortu[nate] than I have been Caroline will accompan[y me to Bo]ston and I shall take the opportunity [. . . .] with Dr. May or Mr Winne who I un[ders]tand are going shortly Kiss my lovely boy a hundred times for me and remember me—to all the family and believe every thing that is tender and affection from her whose delight is to sign herself your grateful and sincerely attached Wife   L. C. Adams

RC (Adams Papers); addressed: "John Quincy Adams Esqr."; endorsed: "Louisa. 29. June 1806. / 7. July rec^{d:} / 9. d^{o:} Ans^{d:}." Some loss of text where the seal was removed.

[1] That is, Georgetown, D.C., physician Dr. John Weems, for whom see vol. 15:353.

[2] During a 21 April House of Representatives debate on an import duty on salt, a dispute arose between John Randolph and his cousin and fellow Virginia congressman Thomas Mann Randolph after John glanced at another colleague and his cousin, seated nearby, interpreted it as a slight directed at him. The challenge resulted from a subsequent altercation on the floor marked by "great trepidation and excessive rage." Tensions simmered into June, but, due in part to a 23 June letter from Thomas Jefferson to Thomas Randolph exhorting him not to fight, no duel took place (Monroe, *Papers*, 5:498; Alexandria, Va., *Daily Advertiser*, 26 April; Jon Meacham, *Thomas Jefferson: The Art of Power*, N.Y., 2013, p. 665–666).

[3] The summer home of John Mason on Analostan Island in the Potomac River opposite Georgetown, D.C., was destroyed by fire on 28 June. Press accounts mentioned nothing about arson or the involvement of an enslaved servant, instead reporting $3,000 in damages and praising neighbors' efforts to save the family's furniture. Jefferson provided an account similar to that of LCA but attributed the fire to arson by a servant "who wished the family to go back to Georgetown" (Washington, D.C., *National Intelligencer*, 2 July; *New-York Gazette*, 4 July; *The Family Letters of Thomas Jefferson*, ed. Edwin Morris Betts and James Adam Bear Jr., Charlottesville, Va., 1995, p. 286).

John Quincy Adams to Louisa Catherine Adams

Cambridge 30. June 1806.

My dearest and most affectionate friend.

You will receive I presume at the same time with this a letter from me written yesterday at Quincy, in the ardour and satisfaction of Hope—[1] This morning on my coming into Boston, your letter of the 23$^{d:}$ so lovely by its tender sensibility, so admirable by its resignation and fortitude, yet so distressing to me by the affliction in which it was written, and the marks of suffering apparent even in the hand-writing that I have no words to express how much it has affected me, was put into my hands—[2] I was engaged with M$^{r:}$ Boylston upon some business when Shaw gave me your letter—[3] On perusing it, I was barely able to preserve that appearance of tranquillity which could conceal the immediate impression upon my heart; I hurried hither to the retirement of my own chamber, where I could indulge the weakness, which the bitterest of sorrows is forbidden to discover to the world—[4] And the first moment I have obtained a sufficient command over myself for any exertion of my faculties I devote to thank you for the most excellent though the most painful letter I ever received from you. If the tears of affliction are unbecoming a Man; Heaven will at least accept those of gratitude from me, for having preserved you to me through the dangers of that heavy trial both of body and mind which it has called you to endure— When you receive this I hope that both your health and Spirits will be so far recovered that it will impart to you only so much of my feelings as can testify to you the tenderest and most sympathetic affection—

I hope you will now soon recover your health, and there is yet so much of the Summer before us, that if you can meet with any opportunity of a companion coming this way, you will find it probably promotive both to your health and Spirits to come on— In that case I would engage the house of which I wrote you yesterday, and which stands next door to Doctor Waterhouse's where I now write— By engaging it for one year from the beginning of August or September, you might come and spend a couple of months here before the Session of Congress commences, and have a home to return to next Spring for three or four months after we shall come back— If you should find it upon trial not agreeable, I should have the year before me to look out for another— I hope your health will be sufficiently confirmed to enable you to travel by the first of August—in which case you might get

June–July 1806

here by the twentieth. If you conclude to come however be extremely careful not to let your impatience hasten your departure too soon— Should you not leave Washington, untill the middle of August (now only six weeks distant) and could find a friend coming only so far as New-York, I may then have it in my power to go thus far to meet you for as Commencement here is the last week in August, after which there is a vacation of four weeks, I should be at liberty by the 25$^{th:}$ of August, and in three days could go to New-York— Let me know by the return of the mail or as soon as you can whether this plan suits you; and if it does I will make all necessary arrangements to carry it into Execution— But do not overstrain your strength to write before your time— Take, my dearest friend, I intreat you the most scrupulous care of yourself, and preserve the greatest of blessings to your ever affectionate husband. John Quincy Adams.[5]

RC (Adams Papers); endorsed: "J Q Adams Esqr / Rec$^{d.}$ July 5 / Ans$^{d.}$ do 6."

[1] JQA's letter to LCA of 29 June stated that he did not intend to resign his Senate seat but expected to be replaced when his term expired. He also reported on the Waterhouse family, his search for a Cambridge home, and his anxiety about his duties at Harvard (Adams Papers).

[2] LCA's letter of 23 June has not been found. On 1 July, JQA received LCA's 24 June letter, above, along with a 22 June letter from Walter Hellen, not found, that included "a few lines from my dear wife, written on the 22$^{d:}$ the day of our misfortune" (JQA, *Diary*).

[3] Ward Nicholas Boylston was being assisted by JQA in a protracted attempt to recover compensation for the brig *Mary*, Capt. Jonathan Titcomb, a vessel leased by Boylston when it was captured and taken to Brest, France, in Aug. 1794 (JQA, *Diary*, 30 June 1806; Boylston to JQA, 9 Nov. 1805; JQA to Elias B. Caldwell, 30 June 1806, both MHi:Boylston Papers; JQA to Boylston, 11 Dec. 1805, LbC, APM Reel 135; Monroe, *Papers*, 3:156–157).

[4] After learning of the stillbirth of his son, JQA recorded in his Diary: "The mercy of Heaven has compensated me for all those sufferings by my two boys, who promise all that a parent's Heart can wish from children of their age— I had given up my Heart to Hope, and Joy in the Hope of a third— It is gone" (JQA, *Diary*, 30 June 1806).

[5] JQA wrote to LCA again on 2 July of his continuing efforts to come to terms with their loss: "I have endeavoured to gather resignation under the hand of Heaven in this Calamity, and with you I turn my thoughts to the inexpressible blessings yet left us in our remaining children." He also refined travel plans for her return to Massachusetts when she fully recovered (Adams Papers).

John Quincy Adams to John Adams

My dear Sir. Cambridge 4. July 1806.

I enclose you a letter, which I received last Monday, and by which you will learn the distressing misfortune which has befallen me—[1] I have not communicated it to you before, from the wish that it might not come to the knowledge of my brother's wife, at a moment when it might too much affect her— I have another letter from Washington, one day later than the one enclosed; my wife was then as well as she could expect after the danger she had so narrowly survived—

181

You will readily conceive I have no inclination at this moment to mingle in high festivities: though I heartily wish that of this day may be agreeable to you— Independent of my own feelings, my present duties require my unremitted attention, and every *day*, is important to my studies— I am afraid I shall also be obliged from the same cause to intermit my weekly visit to you at Quincy to-morrow— But I hope to come out the next week— The Corporation have consented that the Sophomore Class should attend my Lectures, from the first—[2] And this day week, my birth-day, I hope with the blessing of Heaven to begin—

I am in all duty and affection, your Son.

John Quincy Adams.

P. S. If W: S. Shaw gives you a copy of my Inaugural Oration, I hope he will take care it be one of those in which the Greek motto is printed *correctly*.[3]

N. B— Please to preserve the enclosed letter to return to me—[4]

RC (Adams Papers); addressed: "John Adams Esq[r] / Boston."; docketed by JA: "J Q A / July 4 1806."

[1] JQA enclosed LCA's letter of 23 June, not found.

[2] An undated set of institutional guidelines governing JQA's Harvard College professorship specified that lectures would be delivered only to the "two senior classes" (MH-Ar:Records Relating to the Founding of the Boylston Professorship of Rhetoric and Oratory). On 26 June JQA met with Harvard president Samuel Webber and asked that sophomores be allowed to attend the first six lectures, so they did not have to join the course late when they became juniors in a few weeks' time. Webber denied the request, and JQA appealed to the Harvard Corporation in a letter of the same day. On 3 July Webber informed JQA that the corporation agreed to his request (JQA, *Diary*; JQA, *Writings*, 3:148–149).

[3] JQA, *An Inaugural Oration, Delivered at the Author's Installation, as Boylston Professor of Rhetorick and Oratory, at Harvard University, in Cambridge, Massachusetts, on Thursday, 12 June, 1806*, Boston, 1806, Shaw-Shoemaker, No. 9800. The title page featured a quotation in Greek from Homer's *Iliad*, Book IX, line 441, which translates as "To be both a speaker of words and a doer of deeds" (transl. A. T. Murray, London, 1928). Two versions of the publication are extant, one with the first Greek word misspelled and one with it corrected.

[4] The second postscript was written vertically in the left margin.

Louisa Catherine Adams to John Quincy Adams

My most affectionate friend   Washington July 6[th.] 1806

I last night recieved your truely tender and kind letter[1] words cannot describe the feelings with which I read it my heart swelled with gratitude and love and I almost ceased to think the stroke so bitter which proved to me how dear I am to your heart—

Your plan is so perfectly agreeable that I beg you will take the house and if possible have it prepared and my Children with you by the time

July 1806

I arrive which I hope will be by the middle of next month if not before Dr. May will accompany us all the way to Boston I shall therefore not be under the necessity of troubling you to meet me at New York I propose to go by water from Baltimore as the least fatiguing mode of Travelling at this season of the year shall rest one day at Philadelphia and one at New York I shall write you a line from that place that you may if possible be ready to meet me in Boston as I do not wish to go to Quincy untill I have seen you and my darling Babes and I do not think my spirits equal just yet to the meeting Mrs. T. B. A. with her infant the mind I am convinced my beloved friend partakes insensibly of the weakness of the frame and there are times when we require the utmost indulgence to enable us to attain a proper degree of fortitude you will therefore I am sure excuse and gratify this request and only pity a weakness which I trust you will not condemn— I should think Mrs. Waterhouse or Mrs. Greenleaf might perhaps hear of a woman and engage her before my arrival or you may perhaps find some one at Quincy that would suit us if not Mrs. Whitcomb might be able to procure one in Boston you had better enquire of each though I fear to give you too much trouble—

Should you not be able to meet me in Boston let Shaw look out for us at Concert Hall and give us your directions that I may know how to proceed immediately if Dr. May is ready I shall leave this place the 23^d of this month you must therefore write as soon as possible or I shall not recieve your letter and send it to Town or it is two days longer coming—

It is reported that Jerome Buonaparte is taken by the English[2] I am reading the Secret Memoirs of St Cloud I wish you could see them.—[3]

Adieu my best beloved and most affectionate friend may every blessing await you and my lovely Children and may we soon find comfort in a happy meeting for our past severe affliction is the ardent prayer of your   L C Adams

RC (Adams Papers); addressed: "John Quincy Adams Esqr" and by JA: "Cambridge"; endorsed: "Louisa. 6. July 1806. / 21. July rec^{d:}"; notation by JA: "J. Adams"; and by Richard Cranch: "Quincy July 17th. 1806. Free."

[1] JQA to LCA, 30 June, above.
[2] The Baltimore *American and Commercial Daily Advertiser*, 3 July, carried a report that Jerome Bonaparte had been captured by the British while serving with a French squadron in the Caribbean under Rear Adm. Jean Baptiste Willaumez. The report may have stemmed from Bonaparte's decision to sail the ship *Vétéran* north in search of bounty without informing Willaumez. Bonaparte managed to seize or destroy several British ships and to avoid a hurricane that struck the rest of the squadron, resulting in his being the only vessel of the fleet to return to France later in the

year (Alexander Mikaberidze, *The Napoleonic Wars: A Global History*, N.Y., 2020, p. 460–462).

[3] LCA was reading Lewis Goldsmith's pseudonymous depiction of Napoleon's court, Mr. Stewarton, *The Secret History of the Court and Cabinet of St. Cloud in a Series of Letters from a Resident in Paris to a Nobleman in London*, Phila., 1806, Shaw-Shoemaker, No. 11412.

Abigail Adams to John Quincy Adams

My dear son   Quincy July 9th 1806

I sympathize with you in the loss you have sustained, and rejoice that the event did not prove fatal to the mother, as well as Child. let me hear from you when You get a Letter from Washington.

your affectionate / Mother   A Adams—

RC (Adams Papers); addressed: "Honble J Q Adams / Cambridge."

John Quincy Adams to Louisa Catherine Adams

My dearest Louisa.   Cambridge 9. July 1806.

I was just going to account as well as I could for your having been two days over the accustomed time, without receiving my first letter from this place, dated the 22d: of last month, of which delay you complain in your's of the 29th: when receiving that of the next day, I rejoyce to find in it, that you had been relieved from your anxiety and received my letter— A new Post-Office seldom fails to occasion some delay; but I hope you have regularly received all my later letters— The last I wrote you was this day last week;[1] for on Sunday last an occasional occupation engrossed so completely the whole day, that I had not so much as a quarter of an hour for writing a line to you— It was not you may be sure an ordinary call, to which I could sacrifice any of the time appropriated for you, and you have a right to know what it was. My Nephew John Smith takes his degree at New-York the 6th: of next Month; and is to deliver an English Oration— Sometime last Winter his father wrote to request that I would write his Oration for him; but I thought he would do better to write one himself, and supposed I should not have the Time, so that I then declined— Last week, however I received a letter from my Sister, in which *she* renewed the request, and I found it utterly impossible to refuse her— This then was the purpose to which I devoted the Sunday, and I have now sent him his Oration—[2] I had no other day which I could borrow; for I am oppress'd with the composition of Lectures which I am to deliver once a week, and each of which it takes me a week of very close assiduity to compose.

July 1806

I have invited John Smith to come and reside with us; and if he accepts the invitation he will perhaps be ready to accompany you by the time you reach New-York. The 4th: of July was celebrated in Boston with unusual brilliancy— There was a federal dinner of five hundred persons at Faneuil-Hall, to which I was invited, but felt no inclination to go—³ I therefore spent the day coolly and studiously, upon the occupations which my present duties require, without going out of Cambridge. Neither could I spare the time to go out to Quincy on Saturday— For I find that this visit nearly deprives me of three days— The Saturday to go; the Sunday there; and the Monday to return— So that I shall be obliged to content myself for the future with going out once a fortnight.

I most sincerely hope your Sister Harriet will yet preserve her child.— As you have said nothing in your late Letters of little Walter, I hope he has quite recovered from his indisposition.

I heard last evening from Quincy, by Mr: Greenleaf, who dined there yesterday, and who brought me a line from my Mother—⁴ Our dear children, are both perfectly well. Mrs: T. B. Adams is not yet released from her *burden*.

This *word* brings to my mind a circumstance which may divert you— A few days after I came home, I took George by one hand, and John by the other to walk with me in the Garden— Come said I; *great burden* on this side, and *little burden* on that— It set them both a laughing, and ever since, it has been a by-word between them— George says, "I am Papa's Great Burden,["] and John "I am Papa's little burden." John goes regularly to Meeting, every Sunday— About a fortnight ago the Minister, who was a Mr: Bradford of Roxbury, preach'd a Sermon, contrasting the characters of Herod, and of JOHN the Baptist.⁵ After meeting, returning home, John says "Grandmama the Minister preached all the time about ME."— The name of *John*, so often repeated in the Sermon, had caught his attention, and he concluded it must mean him.

Next Saturday, I intend going to Quincy; and as I shall have no Commencement Oration to write, I hope on Sunday, to give you some further account of myself and of your darlings— Mean time I am ever affectionately your's.⁶

RC (Adams Papers); endorsed: "J.Q. Adams / Recd 19 July / Ansd 20 July."

¹ For JQA's letter to LCA of 2 July, see his of 30 June, note 5, above.
² John Adams Smith and eighteen other students of Columbia College received bachelor degrees in commencement ceremonies on 6 August. LCA and AA2 attended the event at New York's Middle Dutch Church. Smith spoke sixth, according to the New York *Com-*

mercial Advertiser, 12 Aug., offering "A discourse On the Instability of National Greatness" that was delivered "with a degree of correctness and propriety which gave energy to the neatly expressed and delicate sentiments that distinguished the composition." AA2's letter has not been found.

[3] JA was a guest of honor at the Federalist dinner at Boston's Faneuil Hall on 4 July, one of several celebrations in the city. The former president introduced visiting Tunisian minister Sidi Soliman Mellimelli and offered the following toast: "May the Trident of Neptune ever protect the Independence of Nations, and defend the Liberty of mankind." JA's toast was the subject of a subsequent newspaper debate, with the Boston Independent Chronicle, 7 July, stating that "if Mr. Adams looks to old Neptune to become the guardian of his country's liberty, by the magic power of his trident, we must be for many years in a state of servitude." The Boston Columbian Centinel, 9 July, responded that the rival paper "would have extolled Mr. ADAMS to the stars" if he had instead toasted a "Monticellonean sentiment" (Boston Columbian Centinel, 5 July; New-England Palladium, 8 July).

[4] AA to JQA, 9 July, above.

[5] Rev. John Bradford (1756–1825), Harvard 1774, was pastor of the Second Church of Roxbury from 1785 until shortly before his death (Centennial Celebration of the Wednesday Evening Club, Boston, 1878, p. 44–45).

[6] JQA wrote to LCA again on 13 and 28 July 1806. In his letter of the 13th, he described walking from Cambridge to Boston the previous morning and then to Quincy. He also discussed Virginia politics and reported that AA2 and WSS had received a letter from William Steuben Smith in the Caribbean, which disproved press reports that he had been captured while on Francisco de Miranda's expedition against Venezuela. In the 28 July letter, JQA informed LCA that because he was unable to secure a house in Cambridge they would reside in the John Quincy Adams Birthplace for the summer (both Adams Papers).

Louisa Catherine Adams to John Quincy Adams

Washington July 11th. 1806

Accept my best beloved friend the sincere congratulations of your wife whose prayers are humbly offered to the author of all good for your happiness and to grant you many *many* happy returns of this day that it may be the last which we may pass in affliction and separated—

This day poor little Archibald was consign'd to the earth close by our dear little babe and poor Boyd and his wife are in the deepest affliction[1] how much this second stroke has renew'd my grief you may readily imagine and my impatience to reach home increases every hour I strive my best friend to attain fortitude but nature will prevail and there are moments in which I find it nearly impossible to conceal the feelings of my heart nothing but the sight of you and my darling children can alone restore me to happiness—

We have just heard of the death Aunt Cook—[2]

Mon Amie my spirits are so much depressed I feel almost incapable of writing Kiss my little cherubs God bless you and grant that we may soon meet to part no more. L. C. Adams[3]

I send you the Bill of Lading for the things

RC (Adams Papers).

[1] George and Harriet Johnson Boyd's infant son Archibald died on or about 11 July, which years later LCA mistakenly recollected as having occurred a day before she delivered her stillborn son (LCA, D&A, 1:235–236).

[2] LCA's aunt Elizabeth Johnson Cook of New Market, Md., died on 23 June (vol. 15:408; Robert W. Barnes, "Vital Records Abstracted from the Frederick-Town Herald 1802–1815," *Maryland Historical Magazine*, 67:190 [Spring 1972]).

[3] JQA replied to LCA on 20 July, conveying his condolences to the Boyds and reporting on his activities in Cambridge and Quincy (Adams Papers).

John Quincy Adams to Abigail Adams

My dear Mother. Cambridge 29. July 1806.

By the last Letters I have received from my wife I expect she will reach Boston by the last of this week, or the beginning of the next—[1] The House in which M^r: Ware lives will not be vacant untill after Commencement, and M^r: Pearson, proposing to sell his declines letting it—[2] He is indeed in Treaty now, for the sale of it.

I have therefore concluded to go in to my House at Quincy again for the remainder of the Summer— I shall have to come to Cambridge not more than two or three times before Commencement; and then the vacation will carry us to the last of September—

I will thank you, if you can to have such little things done at my house this week that we can go into it immediately— The materials I presume are all there— Newell's father, ask'd me some time ago to take his son *Charles*—[3] I should be glad now to engage him immediately— If possible, procure me also a woman, for cooking &c— At any rate I wish to go in to the House next Monday— I shall be gratified in spending the rest of the Summer, again in your neighbourhood—

The enclosed for my father is from Judge Dana.[4]

Your affectionate Son John Quincy Adams.

RC (Adams Papers); addressed: "M^{rs}: Abigail Adams / Quincy."; endorsed: "J Q Adams / 29 july 1806."

[1] LCA's most recent letter to JQA was dated 20 July, in which she lamented that his Harvard duties were keeping him from seeing their children in Quincy. She reported her improved health and travel plans for her return to Massachusetts (Adams Papers).

[2] Rev. Henry Ware became Hollis Professor of Divinity at Harvard in 1805, having served as pastor of the First Church of Hingham since 1787. When JQA was a Harvard student in 1786, he boarded briefly with Ware, who was then a Cambridge schoolteacher (vol. 7:91, 92, 130).

[3] See JQA to AA, 9 Aug. 1806, and note 3, below.

[4] Enclosure not found.

Thomas Boylston Adams to William Meredith

My dear Sir. Quincy July 30th: 1806.

Your very friendly letter of the 8th: instant came to hand on the 16th: and I have with some impatience waited the arrival of a little Stranger, whose advent has been delayed *a full month*; that I might have the pleasure, in my reply, of announcing to you & your good lady similar tidings to those communicated by you.[1] I have a Daughter for your son, provided you should approve the Alliance, and provided all the parties should concur in it of their own accord. After a severe conflict of nearly twenty-four hours, and at the dead-watch of night, the little *urchin*, broke loose from its thraldom and adventured an expedition into the regions of Day— I know what it is to be a father, and am not amid the joys of this new title, unconscious of the additional weight of duty, which necessarily attends it. This joyful event happened, at one minute before twelve oClock, on Tuesday night the 29th: July AD 1806—[2] Chronology bear Witness! The Mother & child are *reasonably* well.

Your determination to educate your eldest son at Harvard gives me great pleasure. I think the advantages to be enjoyed at that seminary, yield to no similar institution upon the Continent; but the age of Boyhood should be nearly past, before a youth should be sent to that College. I know, experimentally, that the age of fourteen is too green, at least by two years, and that the branches of Science taught, during that period, at the University, would be much more perfectly attained in preparatory discipline. This seems to be the opinion of the *faculty*, or as we used to term it, the *government* of the College, since the attainments required of a candidate for admission are much more considerable than they were in my time.

The new Professor has entered upon the duties of his Office and already delivered three public lectures, of which I hear favorable mention.[3] It has been fashionable, with a few of his friends, to resort to his lectures, and I know not, but in process of time, we may look up to him as the founder of a new sect of Rhretoricians.

The Annual Commencement at Cambridge will be held on the 27th: of August. I should think you might devote sufficient time to recreation for the sake of attending this Jubilee of the Muses. I have no share in the exercises of that day, but on the succeeding day, I am designated as the chief spokesman to a Society denominated the ΦBK. and I

Abigail Smith Adams, born July 29th 1806 — was carried to meeting and christened by Mr Whitney when she was five weeks old. The day she was eight months old her first tooth came through. She spoke several words distinctly at eleven months and walked alone when she was a year and a fortnight old. She was inoculated for the Kine Pox when she was sixteen months old by Dr. Waterhouse. The sixth day she began to look pale and heavy — and for the three succeeding days her fever continued to increase her arms were very sore but no eruptions appeared on any part of her body.

3. FAMILY RECORD, BY ANN HARROD ADAMS, 1806–1825
See page x

should feel emboldened rather than abashed in the discharge of such an office, having so partial a friend as yourself present at the exhibition.[4]

Present me to M[rs:] Meredith and your family with much kindness; and if the plannet Dennie be visible, give him friendly salutations from / Your assured friend   T. B. Adams—

RC (PHi:Samuel Washington Woodhouse Coll.); addressed: "William Meredith Esq[r] / Att[y] at Law / Philadelphia"; internal address: "William Meredith Esq[r:]"; endorsed: "Tho[s.] B. Adams / July 30[th:] 1806— / Rec[d.] Aug[t.] 6. 1806 / Ans[d] —— 23[d.]"; notation by JA: "J. Adams"; and by Richard Cranch: "Quincy, Aug[t:] 1[st.] 1806. Free."

[1] Meredith's letter has not been found, but it announced the 5 July birth of Samuel Ogden Meredith (d. 1877), the sixth child of William and Gertrude Gouverneur Ogden Meredith of Philadelphia. TBA previously wrote to William on 27 June (PHi:Samuel Washington Woodhouse Coll.), correcting a false rumor of AHA's death. He also reported that William Smith Shaw would investigate a financial matter as Meredith requested (William Ogden Wheeler, comp., *The Ogden Family in America*, Phila., 1907, p. 195).

[2] Abigail Smith Adams, the first child of AHA and TBA, was born on 29 July, for which see Descriptive List of Illustrations, No. 3, above.

[3] JQA on 11 July delivered his first lecture as Boylston Professor of Rhetoric and Oratory, telling his Harvard College students of the importance of brevity: "The art of speaking well embraces in the fewest possible words the whole compass of the subject." JQA wrote that Lecture I was "well received" and if "the issue of the whole course would but bear a *proportion* to the effect of this introduction, I should be fully satisfied." In Lecture II on 18 July he spoke on "Objections against Eloquence Considered" and on the 25th delivered Lecture III on the "Origin of Oratory" (JQA, *Diary*; JQA, *Lectures on Rhetoric*, 1:38, 53, 73; M/JQA/37, APM Reel 231).

[4] For TBA's oration before the Phi Beta Kappa Society, see his letter to Meredith of 2 Sept., and note 5, below.

Louisa Catherine Adams to John Quincy Adams

My best friend   New York August 3[d] 1806

I arrived here yesterday after a very fatiguing journey but find my health tolerably good Your Sister is in charming health and spirits and I think looks better than I ever saw her Capt Hull on his arrival here recieved new orders and is uncertain about going on to Newport however as M[rs.] Smith insists on our staying here untill after Commencement I hope we shall if he should not proceed be able to find some person going that way under whose protection I can place myself[1] I have not yet seen John or the Col. but your Sister says he will not go on as he wishes to pay a visit to his Uncle Smith before he leaves this part of the Country—[2]

I am much disappointed in the alteration in your arrangements but it cannot be helped so I must make the best of it—

Young M[r] Duer of this place travel'd with us from Washington he is a young man of very promising talents is lately from New Orleans and perfectly enthusiastic in its praise[3] I never met with so much politeness and attention in my life from any person and regret very much that I cannot introduce him to you as I am sure you would be much pleased with him and might gain considerable information respecing that Country—

I do not think it would be worth while to take a stage to Quincy I shall therefore go on to Boston which will be much less expensive I shall however be cruelly disappointed if I do not meet you there indeed I wish if it were possible you could meet in Providence but I do not ask it as I know it would be attended with great inconvenience as soon as the time for my departure is fixed I will write that you may know when to expect me you do not mention the Children I hope however they are well Kiss them for me and teach them to expect me I left directions respecting any letters that might arrive Adieu as I approach the Place which contains all I hold most dear my impatience encreases to clasp you to the heart of your devoted wife   L. C. Adams

I presume the Vessel will be arrived with the things I will thank you to tell Mr Shaw to enquire for the Dog I sent of the Capt.

RC (Adams Papers); addressed: "John Q. Adams Esqr / Boston"; endorsed: "Louisa— 3. Aug$^{t:}$ 1806— New York. / 9. Aug$^{t:}$ rec$^{d:}$."

[1] LCA reported to JQA on 30 July (Adams Papers) that she departed Washington, D.C., on 26 July and arrived in Philadelphia on the 30th. She visited AA2 in New York until 8 Aug., and then traveled to Boston via Providence, R.I., reuniting with JQA on the 10th. Her companion on the first part of her journey was U.S. Navy captain Isaac Hull, who had recently returned from Mediterranean duty to supervise gunboat construction at naval yards on Long Island Sound and the Chesapeake Bay (vol. 13:412; JQA, *Diary*, 10 Aug.; LCA to JQA, 20 July, Adams Papers; *ANB*).

[2] Probably WSS's brother Justus Bosch Smith, who resided in Lebanon, N.Y. (vol. 12:289).

[3] William Alexander Duer (1780–1858), who later served as president of Columbia College (LCA, *D&A*, 1:237).

Thomas Boylston Adams to William Smith Shaw

Dear William   Quincy 3$^{d:}$ August 1806

I have received a letter from my friend D$^{r:}$ Chapman, informing me of his intention to compile in a series of volumes the best of the modern Orations, both forensic and parliamentary with brief remarks illustrative of each case. He wishes to know if my father's library contains the Speech of the late Lord Littleton on the Canada-bill—Charles Townshend's on raising a Revenue in America, so highly praised by Burke—And the Speech of L$^{d:}$ Chatham wherein he makes the *florish* about employing the Savages. For the supply of these documents he promises a set of his work, and he only waits my reply, to announce the contents of the first volume. Does your collection contain all or either of these Speeches, and would you undertake to transcribe & forward them for the sake of *the Reward*. If you know who owns a parliamentary Register in Boston, you can doubtless obtain the loan of it, and if you will search out the Specified harrangues and furnish me with them, I will undertake to get them copied.

The D^r promises a prospectus of his work in a short time and asks what Speeches are in my *father's collection*, both foreign & American, which would suit him.[1] You know what answer I must make to this enquiry better than I do— My belief is there are none, and if I were about to make such a compilation I should rather take my chance among your collection than any that I know of—

Answer me speedily and send your letter by the Mail if no private opportunity offer tomorrow—

I suppose the fame of my Daughter has long since reached your ear and that you have given her all the celebrity that the Town Crier could have done in the same space of time— The Young Miss Abigail Adams is about as likely & promising a Maiden as any stirring— She has not yet been decorated with her best bib & tucker to be carried out to get a good name, nor will She be until the Mother is able to stand sponser for her in person. The Grandparents are so earnest for the Christening, that I dont know whether they wont carry it out themselves— I am afraid of being tedious on this subject, otherwise I could descant for a page or two in praise of my Daughter's genteel shapes—her jetty-locks & *darkling* eyes—the perfect symmetry of her *nose—just like her father* her dimpled cheeks, plump as a partridge—her becoming forehead, neither rising too high nor yet too low compressed—the sweetest mouth—distilling nectar— In short, not to be tedious—the girl is well enough for aught I can see, but in no wise extraordinary—

With usual good will, truly Yours   T. B. Adams—

RC (MWA:Adams Family Letters); addressed: "William S. Shaw Esqr / Boston"; internal address: "W. S. Shaw:"; endorsed: "Thom B Adams."

[1] Dr. Nathaniel Chapman was collecting material for *Select Speeches, Forensick and Parliamentary*, 5 vols., Phila. 1807–1808, Shaw-Shoemaker, No. 12281, the prospectus for which was *Proposals by I. Watts, for Publishing by Subscription, Select Speeches, Forensic and Parliamentary, with Illustrative Remarks, by N. Chapman*, Phila., 1806, Shaw-Shoemaker, No. 11819. The publications Chapman sought were Thomas Lyttelton, 2d Baron Lyttelton, *The Speech of Lord Lyttelton, on a Motion made in the House of Lords for a Repeal of the Canada Bill, May 17, 1775*, London, 1775; a 26 Jan. 1767 speech by Charles Townshend introducing the Townshend Acts, which Edmund Burke on 19 April 1774 in Parliament called "a brilliant harangue"; and an 18 Nov. 1777 speech in which William Pitt the elder, 1st

Earl of Chatham, declared that the British had "lost the affection" of the Americans "by spiriting up the savages of America to scalp them with the tomahawk." None of the works are in JA's library at MB, though the speeches are included in the 1792 printings of collected works of Burke with JQA's bookplate and Pitt with CFA's bookplate in the library at MQA. Chapman included the speeches by Burke (1:27–91) and Pitt (5:379–392) in his work (*ANB*; Namier and Brooke, *House of Commons*, 3:547; Burke, *Speech of Edmund Burke Esq. on American Taxation, April 19, 1774*, London, 1775, p. 24; Burke, *The Works of the Right Honourable Edmund Burke*, 3 vols., London, 1792, 1:507–580; Pitt, *Anecdotes of the Life of the Right Hon. William Pitt, Earl of Chatham . . . with his Speeches in Parliament*, 2 vols., London, 1792, 2:162; Catalog of the Stone Library).

John Quincy Adams to Abigail Adams

My dear Mother.   Boston 9. August 1806.

I left Cambridge yesterday, after having finished my weekly performance, to come here and meet my wife whom I expect hourly here—[1] I received this morning letters from her, dated one at Philadelphia 30. July—and one at New-York 3. August—[2] She was with my Sister, who was well and in good Spirits— She intended to stay over Commencement which was last Wednesday, and then come on as soon as possible— I have therefore concluded to remain here, instead of coming out to spend Sunday with you at Quincy— Though if she comes we may yet perhaps see you before Monday—

Last Sunday, I called on Mr: Micajah Adams to enquire if he would let me have his son Charles, as he had proposed to me some weeks before— He said he must consult his wife, who was not then at home—[3] I desired him to send his answer within a day or two, to you—which he promised— If he is engaged, and also the woman whom you mentioned to me, I will be obliged to you, to give them notice, to be ready by Monday Morning to go into the house.

If it should so happen that my wife should not arrive here before next Wednesday, (which is the day of the Academy's meeting at Cambridge) and my father should go to Cambridge, I will thank him, if it be not inconvenient to come through Boston, and take me with him—[4] In that case, if you can send me a clean shirt, pair of stockings, and pocket and neck handkerchief, I shall thank you— My little Stock of linen, is in the trunk which I have sent already to Quincy, and I have with me only a single change— Adieu my dearest Mother; tell my children, I am sorry not to be sure of seeing them to-morrow; but that they will see Mama the next time I come— Caroline Johnson is with her—

Your's affectionately   J. Q. Adams.

RC (Adams Papers); addressed: "Mrs: Abigail Adams. / Quincy."

[1] On 8 Aug. JQA delivered his Lecture V on "Cicero and His Rhetorical Writings," encouraging his students to "open an unobstructed avenue between the beauties of Cicero and your own understandings" (JQA, *Diary*; JQA, *Lectures on Rhetoric*, 1:117, 118; M/JQA/37, APM Reel 231).

[2] For LCA's letter to JQA of 30 July, see hers of 3 Aug., note 1, above.

[3] JQA's cousin Micajah Adams (1769–1843) and Alice Hayward Adams (1771–1809) of Quincy were the parents of JQA and LCA's former servant Micajah Newell Adams (1794–1873), known as Newell, and Charles Adams (1795–1877), who began serving the Adamses on 11 Aug. (Sprague, *Braintree Families*; JQA, *Diary*).

[4] JQA went to Quincy on 13 Aug. and accompanied JA to a meeting of the American Academy of Arts and Sciences at Harvard. After dining he delivered his father back to Quincy and returned to Boston, writing, "The day has been lost to my occupations" (JQA, *Diary*).

Elizabeth Smith Shaw Peabody to Abigail Adams

My Dear Sister,   Atkinson August 11th. 1806

Last week I went to Newbury-port to accompany Capt Peabody,[1] when I returned a Letter from my Sister Cranch was handed me, which announced the joyful tidings of the birth of your Grandchild— Most sincerely I congratulate you, & the Parents, who by this circumstance I suppose, are made completely happy— I long to clasp my dear Thomas & Nancy's little Bantling to my bosom, I hope it will live, & be a blessing to its connections—& I trust I shall this Fall make a visit to Quincy, & then I shall see what a charming Mamma she makes—

I was happy to see by the Papers, that Col. Smith was honourably acquited—[2] His dear Wife must have gone through many distressing Scenes— I remember what our sagacious mother used to predict, "that she was born to exhibit great Virtues"—& she has had an unusual call for there Exercise— I hope Col Smith will be restored to his Office, I think it the least compensation the Heads of Government can make— Col Smith appears through the medium of the news Papers, to have conducted agreeably to the Dignity becoming his rank, & Character I hope we shall yet see our dear amiable William & all rejoice together—

But in this life, how quick are the successions of Joy, & Sorrow— While I am rejoicing with you, upon the birth of a new-born Infant & the safety of your ~~family~~ House, I cannot forbear to mourn with you, & the distressed family, the sudden loss of two worthy members of your Neigbourhood—by an accidently Death— Such Events are indeed shocking to the human heart—& is more than near relatives are able to ~~support~~ bear, unless supported by the "Widows God"—may she find present help, now her "lover & friend is put far away"— The loss of Mr Mitchel, must be an interruption to the Presidents Agricultural arrangements—for a capable honest Tenant, is a valuable acquisition

& the bereavement in such a sudden manner very affecting, & unfortunate—³

I am very glad to hear my Abby is in better health— Debility seemed to be her disorder, & the Salt air has hitherto been favourable— I hope she will see her Aunt Goodwin in Boston, if she, (as she frequently comes to commencement),⁴ should happen this year to be in Town,— I wish Abby may be fortunate enough to know it—that she may pay her respects to her Fathers only Sister—⁵ I wish her Brother would enquire—

I fear Abbys visit has been so long, that she will tire her friends— I believe her Father will go to Cambridge in a Chaise, & she can come home with him— Last week as I was gone, my letter to her d[id] not go on by the mail, I suppose she looked sober that she did not recieve one from Mamma She has been a good Girl, & has written to me often—

I must close with best respects, & love where due, from your / Affectionate Sister   Elizabeth Peabody

Excuse the badness of the writing, I fear the mail will pass on—

RC (Adams Papers); addressed: "Mrs Abigail Adams / Quincy—"; endorsed: "Mrs Peabody / August 11th 1806." Some loss of text where the seal was removed.

¹ Peabody's brother-in-law was Capt. John Peabody (1732–1820) of Bridgton, Maine (Selim Hobart Peabody, comp., and Charles Henry Pope, ed. *Peabody Genealogy*, Boston, 1909, p. 37, 38).

² The *Newburyport Herald*, 5 Aug., reported WSS's 22 July acquittal in U.S. Circuit Court in New York. The newspaper claimed Thomas Jefferson's decision to replace WSS as surveyor of the port of New York before the trial was prejudicial and that the proceedings were undertaken for partisan purposes.

³ Quincy husbandman James Mitchel, age 38, and Peter Hardwick, age 14, drowned on 29 July. Peabody quoted Samuel Bourn, *The Christian-Family Prayer Book*, London, 1737, p. 43, 217, and Psalms, 68:5, 88:18 (JQA, *Diary*, 3 Aug.; Boston *Independent Chronicle*, 14 Aug.; Quincy City Clerk:Records of Deaths in the Town of Quincy, 1800–1844, p. 14).

⁴ Closing parenthesis editorially supplied.

⁵ Ruth Shaw Goodwin (1744–1825), wife of Gen. Nathaniel Goodwin of Sandwich, Mass., was the only sister of Rev. John Shaw, Elizabeth Peabody's first husband and father of Abigail Adams Shaw (*Sibley's Harvard Graduates*, 2:427; *Vital Records of Bridgewater, Massachusetts, to the Year 1850*, 2 vols., Boston, 1916, 1:289; *Boston Daily Advertiser*, 16 Feb. 1825).

Thomas Boylston Adams to William Meredith

Dear Sir.   Quincy 2d: September 1806.

Accept my best thanks for the Volume of Moore's fugitive poems, which accompanied your letter of the 23d: ult: It is the more acceptable, as it completes my set of his works, the former of which, were presented me, by S. Ewing.¹ As specimens of perfection in the Style of printing books, in your City, they are far superiour to any I have ever seen; but of their contents, I am truly not sufficiently possessed, to pass judgment upon their merits. Of M$^{r:}$ Moore I have a very favorable opinion, as a Poet and a Schollar. No man ever read Greek so currently as he does, without being a luminary of Science. The Greek language really seems to possess the faculty of inspiration. It is the oil that feeds the Lamp of learning, and there is nothing in my esteem more enviable than a facility of conversing with "the most illuminated people on earth" (as Cumberland calls the Greeks) in their own tongue—[2] But Alas! the labour I never did so understand that magic language as to be able to read it with ease, and it is not very probable I ever shall, though my father is often encouraging me to buckle too and master it. After thirty years preaching, he says he has made a convert of my brother to his belief in the importance of the Greek language, and perhaps he may not despair of drilling me, in as short a time, into Greecian discipline.

Moore's preface to his fugitive pieces might have been spared. I know the meridian for which he published required no less than that he should offer a deliberate affront to the Americans, and instead of softening the sauciness of his remarks, by any bland expression, that he should say "just enough to offend." He probably read our Newspapers and saw too much of Virginia. I cannot help being *piqued* at a sneer and hurt at a frown upon my Country and its inhabitants; but soberness of reflection generally adds the double mortification, that there is too much truth in the libel. This however ~~takes~~ detracts nothing from the force of the sentiment, for who has philosophy enough to be taken to task and ridiculed for his faults & imperfections, in the face of the world, without taking offence at the familiarity? Moore was himself offended by the rude familiarity of Democracy and Republicanism, and he revenges himself by giving a specimen of Monarchical satire, which about balances the account. I suppose, "M$^{r:}$ Dennie and his friends," of whom he speaks with such distinction, feel some complacency towards him, and it proves perhaps no more than this, that upon more intimate acquaintance his exceptions would have been more numerous.[3]

Our Commencement at Cambridge was uncommonly brilliant.[4] The exercises were not altogether equal to those of the last year, though very reputable to the College. Of one of the performances on the succeeding day, it becomes not me to speak.[5] The company was much *more select*, as it usually is, than on the day preceding and more numerous than on any former *occasion*. For the accommodation of the audience—perhaps I should say spectators, the Society convened

September 1806

in the Meeting house, a building capable of receiving more than double the number of the *Church* where we used to convene— I had graduated my voice for the lesser building, and, of course, was but imperfectly heard in the larger. My discourse was so exclusively designed for the entertainment of my brethern; at whose request it was delivered, that I very well knew *the Ladies* would think it *monstrous dull*, as in truth it was; but my credit suffered less from them by their not being so situated as to hear— The dear creatures gave me credit (*for aught I know*) for an intention to please them, than which nothing was further from my subject or my thoughts.

The Poem was pronounced with a louder voice and more rhapsody & of course, was better suited to *the Sex*— I hope it will be published, and if it should be, I will send you a copy— The Poet was my Classmate and an intimate friend—[6] I am partial perhaps to his merit; but it has always appeared to me that his poetry was the best of all American specimens—

Give my *love* to "M." whose sagacity in detecting blunders I have often had occasion to remark—[7] Nevertheless—under favor I would ask if the "dead-watch of night," be not the nearest approach to the ["]dawning of day." If so, why then the "little urchin aforesaid," adventured out of one region into another, both extreemly dark no doubt; as the absence of light is apt to produce that effect; and the distinction between night & morning, being only nominal and arbitrary— immagination surely has a better claim to sport with names than time with seasons. So that I cannot retract my expression without more cogent arguments than the Stanza of "M."

> Darkness 'tis true obscured my sight
> Yet led me not astray—
> For tho' *the region* was not light
> *Old time* pronounced it day.

The pleasure of visiting Philadelphia, at some future period, is, I very sincerely hope, in reserve for me and my Wife; but it is quite out of my power to foretell the time when. Your meditated excursion to Niagara will probably soonest happen, and you know that the town of Quincy is in the way to the Lakes; so that I expect a visit from you ere you have one from me. At all events there is much comfort in the anticipation.

My Wife, of whom I am not very apt to talk *even now*; but who concentrates all my best thoughts, has lately found out that I hold a correspondence with people in Philadelphia, with whom she has no acquaintance, and as this circumstance might lead to unlucky surmises, I have taken some pains to introduce her to you and your lady; since which she has expressed a desire to be better acquainted. She wonders what I have written about her daughter, which could have produced a sort of birth-day Ode already, and insists upon knowing and reading in future all I write upon the subject. This is so reasonable a demand, that I cannot refuse her the gratification; so that in future you may calculate upon my taking the same liberty with your letters, as you have taken with mine.

With kind remembrance to all friends I am truly yours

T. B. Adams.

RC (PHi:Meredith Family Papers); addressed: "William Meredith Esq[r:] / Philadelphia"; internal address: "W. Meredith Esq[r]."

[1] Meredith's letter of 23 Aug. has not been found but was accompanied by Irish poet Thomas Moore's *Epistles, Odes, and Other Poems*, Phila., 1806, Shaw-Shoemaker, No. 10898, for which see note 3, below. Moore's three earlier works were: *Odes of Anacreon*, London, 1800; *The Poetical Works of the Late Thomas Little, Esq.*, London, 1801; and *The Fairies' Revels*, London, 1802.

[2] Richard Cumberland, *The Observer*, 2d edn., 3 vols., London, 1787, 1:182.

[3] Moore traveled in the United States in 1804, and the preface of his 1806 collection of poems was highly critical of American culture for its "rude familiarity of the lower orders, and indeed the unpolished state of society in general." He criticized Democratic-Republicans for "exhibiting a vulgarity of rancour" and Federalists for being "so forgetful of their cause as to imitate" but praised time spent with Joseph Dennie Jr.'s Tuesday Club as "the only agreeable moments which my tour through the States afforded me" (vol. 15:392; Moore, *Epistles*, p. x-xi, 198; Kaplan, *Men of Letters*, p. 171).

[4] Harvard College conferred degrees on 42 graduates in ceremonies at Cambridge on 27 Aug., which featured a Latin oration by recent graduate David Tenney Kimball before an audience that included Gov. Caleb Strong (*Harvard Quinquennial Cat.*, p. 182, 183–184; Boston *Independent Chronicle*, 28 Aug.).

[5] On 28 Aug. TBA delivered an oration at the First Church of Cambridge to mark the thirtieth anniversary of the Phi Beta Kappa Society. "A Disquisition upon the Philosophy of the Ancients" discussed the texts of Socrates, Plato, and Aristotle in a "ramble without reserve in the pleasant fields of Philosophy." A review in the Boston *Columbian Centinel*, 30 Aug., declared that TBA's oration "honorably maintained the reputation of the family from which he is descended." LCA, who attended the event, found TBA's "manner always good but his voice not loud enough." The oration was published in the *Monthly Anthology*, 3:505–513 (Oct. 1806) (LCA, *D&A*, 1:240).

[6] Augusta, Maine, lawyer Benjamin Whitwell (1772–1825), Harvard 1790, presented his poem "Experience; or, 'Folly as it Flies,'" which included the lines, "Beyond the grasp of Time, immortal Fame / Unite to WASHINGTON's her ADAMS' name." The poem was published in the *Monthly Anthology*, 3:477–484 (Sept. 1806) (James W. North, *The History of Augusta*, Augusta, 1870, p. 435–437).

[7] That is, Meredith's wife, Gertrude Gouverneur Ogden Meredith, a writer and contributor to *Port Folio* (vol. 15:336).

John Quincy Adams to William Smith Shaw

Dear Sir. Quincy 3. September 1806.

I now enclose you the auctioneer's Bill and will thank you to make out the list of the Books, *by their titles*, with the prices fixed against them, and get the receipt of the auctioneer upon it, as *received of me*—which will be necessary for me as a voucher— There are only two volumes (Mason on Elocution, and Carey's Pocket Atlas),[1] which I purchased for myself, and are not to be included in the list— I have put them apart at Wells's— The others are all in a trunk— Be kind enough to have the Set of the Historical Society's publications also ready at Wells's, for ~~Publica~~ packing up with the rest as soon as possible.[2]

Your's truly. J. Q. Adams.

RC (MHi:Guild Library); addressed: "W. S. Shaw Esqr / Boston."; internal address: "W. S. Shaw Esq$^{r.}$"; endorsed: "Quincy / J Q Adams."

[1] Closing parenthesis editorially supplied.

[2] JQA agreed on 31 March to purchase books in Boston for the Library of Congress, while other agents did the same in New York and Philadelphia. He departed the capital with $494 in federal funds and spent the summer collecting books. In a 10 July letter to Shaw (MWA:Adams Family Letters), he requested a Boston auction catalog and on 24 July attended an auction and made purchases for the library. The titles he acquired for personal use and stored at the 6 Court Street shop of bookseller William Wells were John Mason, *An Essay on Elocution*, London, 1748, and Mathew Carey, *Carey's American Pocket Atlas*, Phila., 1796, Evans, No. 30161. On 10 Oct. JQA and Shaw packed the books for shipment to the library in Washington, D.C., dividing them between the schooner *Mary and Eliza* and another vessel. Most were lost when the *Mary and Eliza* foundered on 15 Oct., though JQA received credit for the loss and in 1807 made additional purchases for the library (JQA, *Diary*, 31 March 1806, 24 April, 24 July, 10 Oct., 22, 24 Dec.; 4, 20 March 1807; Boston *Repertory*, 9 Sept. 1806; *Boston Directory*, 1806, p. 129, Shaw-Shoemaker, No. 50652; JQA to LCA, 17 Dec., Adams Papers).

Abigail Adams to Ann Harrod Adams

my dear Nancy Quincy Sep'^{br} 20 1806

Having finishd my Farm House avocations I sit down to inquire how you are, and how my dear little Girl is after your journey. the fog of the morning I feard would prevent your sitting out early, and make it late before you reachd the much longed for Paternal Habitation. I could enter into all Your sensations upon approaching it, and meeting again a kind and affectionate Mother after a long Seperation, in a new Character, and with a little darling to present to her— I hope all your expectations are realized, and that after the first joy of meeting and the How do ye's & How do yes are over, You will find time to answer all my questions. The morning after You left me—You know I had to receive the cavalcade which I presume you met, tho upon inquiry of mr Shaw he could not give any account of you, but mrs Harper inquired if the Lady had an infant with her, and my replieing that she had, she said, she met a very pretty Lady in a chaise, & wonderd who she was—[1] no Sooner was the visit over than I had to undress myself and take to my Bed having been seazed most voilently with the disorder common to the Season. in a few Hours it weakned me to such a degree, that I was obliged to Send for the Dr— a terrible pain in the Head, and fever came on—so that for three Days, I kept my chamber the applications relieved me, but that and the extreem Heat So debilitated me that untill this day upon the change of weather I have not strength to write you a line—

Mr Adams returnd on Wednesday Evening for some papers, complaind much of the Heat, went again in the morning, and this Day have sent mr T Greenleaf to bring him home I learn that he has been very successfull this week in obtaining his causes—[2]

Mrs Cranch has just sent me Your Letter of the 18[3] I rejoice to learn that You and the Baby are well I hope the pig may prove benificial, but if the Mother would not eat of a pig when it was sit before her; why should the child want it— only a pig is to cure all longings. well if we can believe Such vagaries, why should we laugh at those who believe in Faries Witches &c Anatomist tell us that the inward parts of a Hog resemble those of the Humane species more than any other animal but I never heard of any peculiar virtue in the Brains of a pig.—

your sister Foster is still—as the country folks say, stirring about— I wish I could hear she was well abed—least she should lose her Nurse— unless Mrs Minot should follow the ten Months fashion—[4]

Susan desires to be rememberd to you, and the little Girl— little John continues unwell yet— the rest of the family are well— I hope to get Well enough to go to visit Judge cushings next week.— I shall write to you when I return. adieu my dear Nancy take good care of your Health and my little Girl who I hope will fatten upon the native soil of her Mother— Mrs Quincy came yesterday to see us, and desired to be kindly rememberd to you—

My kind regards to your Mother and Love to Betsy—[5] tell her she must not be too witty upon my little Girl: tho it made us all laugh Heartily a Ladys writing is often call'd pot Hooks and trammels— mine I think bears a near resemblence to them but it requires not the aid of fine Writing to say that I am / most affectionatly your / Mother

A Adams

RC (Adams Papers); addressed: "Mrs Ann Adams / Haverhill"; notation by ECA: "Abigail Smith / Adams— / first Grand / daughter named / for Grand Mother."

[1] The guests to Peacefield were Catherine Carroll Harper and her husband, Robert Goodloe Harper, of Baltimore, who were visiting Boston, along with Catherine's sister, Mary Carroll Caton, and two of Caton's daughters, probably the eldest, Marianne, and Elizabeth. Among those joining them on the Quincy excursion were Isaac P. Davis, Daniel Denison Rogers, William Smith Shaw, and William Sullivan (JQA, *Diary*, 17 July, 15 Sept.; LCA, *D&A*, 1:241; Boston *Columbian Centinel*, 20 Sept.; Arthur Meredyth Burke, ed., *The Prominent Families of the United States of America*, London, [1908], p. 412; *Boston Directory*, 1807, p. 58, 130, Shaw-Shoemaker, No. 12180).

[2] A notation in an unknown hand appears here noting that AA meant "T.B.A.," who attended a session of the Norfolk County Court of Common Pleas in Dedham, Mass., from 15 to 20 September. Among the cases scheduled to be heard were a petition by landowners seeking to dredge Stony Brook and a request for the division of an estate. The person sent to retrieve TBA was Thomas Greenleaf Jr. (1788–1817), son of Thomas and Mary Deming Price Greenleaf (JQA, *Diary*, 15, 18, 20 Sept.; Boston *Columbian Centinel*, 2 Aug., 27 Sept.; Sprague, *Braintree Families*).

[3] Not found.

[4] AHA's sister Frances Harrod Foster on 14 Oct. gave birth to Charles Phineas Foster (d. 1879), who was later CFA's Harvard classmate. Foster's nurse was Thomazine Elizabeth Fielder Bond Minot (ca. 1778–1864), a relation of Richard Cranch and wife of John Minot of Dorchester, who gave birth to John Cranch Minot on 25 Oct. (vol. 12:263; Pierce, *Foster Genealogy*, 1:270; CFA, *Diary*, 1:158; First Church of Dorchester:Baptisms, Deaths, Communions, and Covenants, 1729–1845, p. 301; *The Correspondence of Henry D. Thoreau*, ed. Robert N. Hudspeth, Princeton, N.J., 2013– , 1:50).

[5] That is, AHA's sister Elizabeth Marston Harrod (vol. 10:449).

John Quincy Adams to Louisa Catherine Adams

Washington Friday 28. November 1806.

My dear Lousia.

From the moment when I left you untill the present, I have been so constantly in motion, that I have not been able to write you, on the road— Nor have I put pen to paper, except to direct a couple of pamphlets which I purchased for M$^{r:}$ Shaw, at New-York. I came on as far as New-Haven by Land—Then embarked in a packet and landed at New-York last Sunday morning— After passing that day at Col$^{l:}$ Smith's, I came on the next morning to Philadelphia, which I reached on Tuesday— Wednesday morning at eight, embarked again at Philadelphia, and in twenty-hours landed at Baltimore— There I stop'd only a few hours, and arrived here last Evening; just two days sooner than I expected, on leaving you— The shortness of my passage from Philadelphia was the occasion of my getting here before my time— There is a new line of Packets and Stages established on that road; and the competition between the two makes them unusually expeditious—[1] The wind also favoured us much, both on the Delaware and Chesapeak, so that we accomplished the passage, in a shorter time than it was run by the mail Stage, which travell'd all night.

I found your mother and all the family here, well, excepting little Walter, who has a fever and sore mouth, much like that of our John in the Autumn— M^rs: Boyd has a fine boy, and is very well— The child was born about a week since, and you will be informed of it before this letter can reach you—²

I travell'd almost the whole way, with a succession of members of Congress, who had the same destination as myself— The first day about 30 miles this way from Boston, we took up M^r: Hastings, who came on with me as far as Philadelphia, and then parted, to come on by the way of Lancaster and Frederick— At Hartford we found M^r: Taggart, with whom we came to New-York; whence he proceeded in a different line of Stages— At Middletown, half way between Hartford and New-Haven we were joined by M^r: *Dana*, whose first salutation to me was a compliment upon the two young gentlemen I had been *educating*, since last Winter, upon my *cheeks*— He kept us company as far as New-York, and there much to my regret stop'd a day later than I did— He is not yet arrived here, and will probably not get here untill to-morrow Evening— At New-Haven M^r: Pitken, and M^r: Dwight of Connecticut, with M^r: Thompson of New-Hampshire took passage with us in the Packet; but parted from us again; the two first at New-York and the last at Philadelphia— From New-York I came on with a new Stage load of members, though none I believe of your acquaintance; and at Philadelphia, I embarked again with another company of them— From Baltimore I came here with M^r: Ely—M^r: Gilman, and M^r: Hough—³ So that at different times I have been associated with more than twenty of them; though I have not come with any one more than half the way—

The last letters Col^l: Smith and my Sister had received from William were of 16. September—dated at Aruba, and written in a tone of despondency respecting their Success;—he expected to come home in the course of the Winter, as I hope he will—⁴ Since that time Miranda has been driven off and obliged to take refuge in one of the British Islands— I consider William Smith, as having a very sorry prospect before him for his future life—Bred to nothing—possess'd of nothing— Having Nothing to expect— This quixotic adventure at the outset of life, is just calculated to make him fit for nothing upon this Earth— The Col^l: with manifest efforts keeps up an appearance of Spirits— My Sister feels the difficulties of her situation and struggles against them with fortitude—But her prospects are dark, and threaten to be still more so— I hope she will go on with me in the Spring— The Col^l:

November 1806

seems still to flatter himself with the hopes of an appointment— I know not why—

At Philadelphia, I called on D^r: Rush, M^r: Hopkinson and M^r: Meredith, but found neither of them at home— I met M^r: R. Rush in the Street; and he with M^r: Ewing called on me in the Evening, at my lodgings— But I did not see them; being a-bed before they called— D^r: Rush has moved away from the house where he formerly lived; and now resides at a short distance from it in the same Street.[5]

Though I arrived at Princeton after 8 O'Clock in the Evening, and left it again before 6 the next morning, I could not forbear calling upon D^r: Smith, the President to thank him and his Lady for their kind attentions to you last Summer—[6] They made particular enquiries with regard to the state of your health.

I sent the two parcels, which you had carried on to New-York, for M^{rs}: Whitewood—[7] John Smith carried them himself, and found one of the Ladies to whom the parcels were directed— He left them both there; for both the ladies had lived in the same house; though one [. . . .] now gone to France.

I have called this morning upon the President and M^r: Madison; the latter of whom was not at home— The President has his arm in a sling; from some accident which he says lately happened to one of his fingers—[8] He appears in other respects to be very well.

M^r: & M^{rs}: Merry have left Washington— He is going immediately to England; but she intends passing the winter in this Country—at Alexandria— M^r: Erskine has taken the same house; but is now at Philadelphia.[9]

I am very anxious to hear from you; to learn that your own health, and that of Caroline and the children is well— I hope you still remain satisfied with your lodgings, and that you have found a good school for the children— I write you no politics yet—but I have not forgotten either of my promises— At present I have little to write— Next week I suppose we shall have a budget.[10]

Your's affectionately   John Quincy Adams.

RC (Adams Papers); addressed: "M^{rs}: J. Q. Adams. / Boston."; endorsed: "J.Q. Adams Esqr. / R. 6. Dec$^{br.}$ / Ans$^{d.}$ 8." Some loss of text where the seal was removed.

[1] JQA departed Boston on 19 Nov. and arrived in Washington, D.C., on the 27th. Joshua and George Ward launched a new line of packets and stages between Philadelphia and Baltimore in September, advertising that their route required less time on packet boats, while William McDonald advertised that his established route necessitated fewer miles by stage (JQA, *Diary*; Baltimore *American and Commercial Daily Advertiser*, 18 Sept.).

² John Quincy Adams Boyd (d. 1831), the son of Harriet Johnson and George Boyd, was born on 21 Nov. (LCA, D&A, 1:261, 2:590).

³ JQA's various traveling companions were mostly members of the House of Representatives. They were Seth Hastings (1762–1831), Samuel Taggart (1754–1825), and William Ely (1765–1817) of Massachusetts; Samuel Whittlesey Dana, Timothy Pitkin (1766–1847), and Theodore Dwight (1764–1846) of Connecticut; and Thomas Weston Thompson (1766–1821) and David Hough (1753–1831) of New Hampshire. He was also joined by Senator Nicholas Gilman of New Hampshire (vols. 7:170, 13:377; *Biog. Dir. Cong.*).

⁴ Not found.

⁵ Benjamin Rush had moved from his former home at the corner of Fourth and Walnut Streets in Philadelphia to 98 South Fourth Street (vol. 15:87; *Philadelphia Directory*, 1808, p. [262], Shaw-Shoemaker, No. 15911).

⁶ When LCA passed through Princeton, N.J., on her way to Massachusetts on 29 July, she was hosted by Princeton president Samuel Stanhope Smith and his wife, Ann Witherspoon Smith (1749–1817), both of whom treated her with "every kind attention" (LCA, D&A, 1:237; Joseph Bailey Witherspoon, *History and Genealogy of the Witherspoon Family*, Fort Worth, Texas, 1973, p. 103).

⁷ Midwife Elizabeth Whitewood (d. 1809), of Washington, D.C., attended LCA during her most recent pregnancy (LCA, D&A, 1:232; District of Columbia Probate Court:Elizabeth Whitewood will, 1809–460).

⁸ Thomas Jefferson had lost the nail of his middle finger (Jefferson to Anne Cary Randolph, 8 Dec., CSmH:Papers of Thomas Jefferson).

⁹ British minister to the United States Anthony Merry presented his letter of recall to Jefferson on 3 Nov. and sailed from Alexandria, Va., on 6 December. His wife, Elizabeth Death Leathes Merry, remained in Alexandria until sailing for England from New York in June 1807. Merry's replacement, David Montagu Erskine, for whom see JQA to LCA, 10 May 1806, and note 5, above, moved into the Merrys' former residence on K Street in Foggy Bottom (vol. 15:308; Malcolm Lester, *Anthony Merry Redivivus: A Reappraisal of the British Minister to the United States, 1803–6*, Charlottesville, Va., 1978, p. 118, 119).

¹⁰ On 8 Dec. Albert Gallatin delivered to the Senate a treasury report on federal revenue, spending, and debt. The Senate passed an 1807 federal budget with the concurrence of the House on 3 March 1807 and it was signed into law the same day. Government revenues for 1807 amounted to just under $16.4 million, while spending totaled $8.3 million (*Amer. State Papers, Finance*, 2:204–206; *U.S. Statutes at Large*, 2:432–436; U.S. Senate, *Jour.*, 9th Cong., 2d sess., 4:171; U.S. House, *Jour.*, 9th Cong., 2d sess., 5:643; U.S. Department of Commerce, *Historical Statistics of the United States, Colonial Times to 1970*, 1 vol. in 2, Washington, D.C., 1975, 2:1104).

John Quincy Adams to Louisa Catherine Adams

My dear Louisa.   Washington 2. December 1806.

I have been expecting to hear from you these two or three days, and begin to feel some anxiety to learn how you all have been since I left you—

Yesterday was the day at which the Session of Congress commenced, and a Quorum of both houses appeared— The President's Message has just been read, and is very long— But it gives no information on the subjects of the highest importance to the Nation—the state of our affairs with England & with Spain— There is much talk about expeditions undertaken by individual citizens against Spain, without naming any body, and a dissertation upon projects against the United States, which *might* be some where concerting— Recommendations to repeal the Salt-tax—and to make an Amendment of the Constitution to apply the revenue, which we shall soon have without knowing what to do with it, to some scientific purpose; or Academy for Education.[1]

The family are all as well as when I wrote you last—[2] Little Walter is yet unwell— Adelaïde and your brother still have occasional returns of the fever and ague; but not with regularity.

Remember me kindly to Caroline, and kiss the dear Children for their and your / affectionate   John Quincy Adams.

RC (Adams Papers).

[1] The 2d session of the 9th Congress convened on 1 Dec. and adjourned on 3 March 1807. Thomas Jefferson submitted his annual address to Congress on 2 Dec. 1806, reporting that there was little news on the special missions to Great Britain and Spain and expressing hope that he would have news on the negotiations with Britain by the end of the session. The president also touched briefly on U.S. relations with the Barbary States and Native Americans, reported on the expedition by Meriwether Lewis and William Clark, and called for an end to the African slave trade. He also proposed that Congress eliminate an impost on salt but continue existing taxes on luxury imports to fund public education (U.S. Senate, *Jour.*, 9th Cong., 2d sess., p. 105, 106–109, 169, 178).

[2] JQA to LCA, 28 Nov., above.

Louisa Catherine Adams to John Quincy Adams

Boston Dec$^{br:}$ 7th 1806

I am all impatience to hear from you, my beloved friend, and cannot concieve the reason, of your not having written from New York, according to your promise. there are some reports about, that have occasioned me ~~some~~ much uneasiness and I wish very much to learn, that our friends there are *all well*, not a line having been recieved here. I have sent your Bank book, &c, as you desired, and have not yet hear'd any thing from Osgood—[1]

M$^{r.}$ Shaw was here to day, and took George to meeting and to pay several visits, where he made him read french; I do not like to refuse Shaw, but I fear it will be of no service to the Child, as he already possesses a degree of Vanity, very unusual in a child of his age, and it makes him fancy that he has already learnt enough— I am sorry to say that I much fear, he will not benefit from my instructions, he having sense enough to draw comparisons, between your skill and mine, in the art of tuition— however I will do my best, and if he loses, you must make due allowance. John can repeat la Cigale, he is very anxious to get the Rocking Horse.[2]

Dec^br. 9th.

I have just recieved your letter, my beloved friend, but cannot concieve why you sent it to Quincy.³ most sincerely was I rejoiced to learn, that Col. S. was in New York, as it was here confidently asserted, that he had gone to the westward, which caused great anxiety to your family—⁴

Your Journey must have been amusing, at least, if as we are told, "variety is charming." it would however, have been much more so, had your very pleasant companion not quitted you so early.⁵ but being *free*, and *unshackled* as you now are, must certainly add considerably to your enjoyment—

We go on here as well as I expected, Sally however could not support the what she termed, *horrors* of the situation. after quitting me, and living one week with M^rs. G. (who promised her 9 Shillings a week, and gave her 7 & 6) went of to Quincy, where she expects to live with your Mother. she has however condition'd to return to me, in the Spring.⁶ I have got a very good Girl from Groton, and I believe I shall be a gainer by the exchange. Caroline has been very sick but is now much recover'd.—

I have been visited by a few ladies, M^rs: George Blake sat with us near an hour.⁷ your Brother & Sister were in Town yesterday, and your father came to see us last Saturday was a week. We spent thanksgiving alone, it was a very disagreeable day. by the by, the Seats are so very high at Lowels meeting house, I have not ventured to take one. I think therefore it would be better, to take th[e o]ne in Brattle Square.⁸ Mr Shaw tells me the [. . . .]⁹ at present, pays you rent for it. I wish [. . . .]¹⁰ let me know if we can have it, as [. . . .]¹¹ the Children go. I know you will smile at the request, but this is a subject upon which I cannot dwell. as it is one upon which I much fear, you and I can never agree—

Adieu, my best beloved friend, remember me to all who enquire after me, and believe me most sincerely yours   L. C. A.

I have sent the Box by a Baltimore Vessel¹² your Boots are in it— The bills for the articles I enclose for M^r. Hellen with a request to forward the money as soon as convenient it must be here by Xmas

RC (Adams Papers); addressed: "The Honble: / John Quincy Adams Esqr. / S. U. S. / City of Washington"; endorsed: "Louisa. 9. Dec^r: 1806. / 16. Dec^r: rec^d: / 17. d^o: Ans^d:." Some loss of text where the seal was removed.

¹ For Boston stonemason Peter Osgood, see LCA to JQA, 7 Jan. [1807], and note 2, below.

² Aesop's fable "The Grasshopper and the Ant."

3 JQA to LCA, 28 Nov. 1806, above.

4 WSS remained in New York State in the coming months, writing from Albany to Gov. Morgan Lewis and the N.Y. Council of Appointment on 3 Feb. 1807 in an unsuccessful bid to solicit the post of sheriff of New York City and County (NjMoHP).

5 JQA wrote in his Diary that when LCA saw him off on the stage in Boston on 19 Nov. 1806, he joined only one other traveler, "a young woman who came only as far as Mendon." LCA quoted a line from an English folksong, "I'm in Love with Twenty," that since 25 Jan. had been used by Joseph Dennie Jr. as the title for a regular column of literary miscellany in *Port Folio* (JQA, *Diary*; *The Blackbird: An Elegant Collection of Well Chosen Songs*, Doncaster, Eng., 1777, p. 70–71; *Port Folio*, new ser., 1:44 [25 Jan.]).

6 Probably Sarah "Sally" Jones Cleverly (1758–1847), who worked for Mary Bancroft Gulliver, the wife of LCA's landlord Benjamin Gulliver. Cleverly then worked for AA during the winter and after receiving a poor recommendation from her did not return to LCA's household (Sprague, *Braintree Families*; Boston, 30th Report, p. 491; LCA to JQA, 1 Jan. 1807; JQA to LCA, 1 Feb., both below).

7 Rachel Baty Blake (ca. 1773–1807) was the wife of George Blake, U.S. attorney for the District of Massachusetts (vol. 10:45; *Boston Commercial Gazette*, 16 Nov.; Madison, *Papers, Presidential Series*, 6:634–635).

8 Rev. Charles Lowell (1782–1861), Harvard 1800, was ordained as pastor of Boston's West Church on 1 Jan. 1806. The pew in Boston's Brattle Street Church was leased by JQA to merchant Rufus Davenport. JQA agreed to LCA's request that he approach Davenport about ending the lease but stated a preference to purchase a pew in Rev. William Emerson's First Church (Samuel A. Eliot, ed., *Heralds of a Liberal Faith*, Boston, 1910, p. 46; JQA to LCA, 17 Dec., Adams Papers; LCA to JQA, 21 Jan. 1807, below; Paige, *Hist. of Cambridge, Mass.*, 1:182).

9 Three words missing.
10 Three words missing.
11 Four words missing.

12 LCA shipped goods to JQA aboard the schooner *Sally*, Capt. Israel Brayton, which advertised that it would depart for Baltimore on 16 Dec. 1806 and reached its destination on the 24th (Boston *Repertory*, 2 Dec.; Boston *Columbian Centinel*, 10 Dec.; *Baltimore Price-Current*, 25 Dec.).

John Quincy Adams to Louisa Catherine Adams

My dear Louisa   Washington 8. Dec^r: 1806.

Last Evening I received with heart-felt pleasure your letter of the 25$^{th:}$ ult$^{o:}$ which was the first line I had from you since my departure—[1] It has been a long time on the road, and should have reached me sooner—

The information respecting the children was delightful— George's reluctance at his french lesson he must overcome— No French—no Horse— I am glad John has begun seriously upon his studies— He too must learn his French, so as never to be troubled with it, when grown up— Every hour of toil now will save them precious days hereafter—

Eaton's story about the offers made him by Burr, has now been served up in all the newspapers— Burr's Story we have not yet heard— Eaton himself would have been wiser had he been more silent— The amount of his narrative is that he advised the President to send Burr upon an important embassy, BECAUSE!!! he had discovered the said Burr to be a *Traitor to his Country*.

I send you some documents to read, or to dispose of as you please—

Wilkinson's letter is a curiosity, as perfectly characteristic.—² Tis Don Adriano de Armado the second.

After our Snow Storm last week we have had some very cold weather— This morning my thermometer stood at 17.

We are all tolerably well at Mr: Hellen's and Mr: Boyd's— Little Walter is getting better— Eliza has been unwell.

The last Paragraph of your letter I do not fully understand—³ I will not say I can neither live with you or without you; but in this cold weather I should be very glad to live with you.

Kiss the dear—dear children for me—And Caroline too— And ever believe me your's affectionately   John Quincy Adams.

RC (Adams Papers).

¹ See note 3, below.

² Aaron Burr spent eight months traveling through the Mississippi River Valley at the close of his vice presidency in March 1805. The tour was a prelude to a later expedition, one that Burr claimed was aimed at establishing a settlement from which he would lead a private army into Mexico if the United States went to war with Spain. Burr and dozens of recruits departed for the lower Mississippi in Aug. 1806. The expedition was cut short in Feb. 1807 with Burr's arrest on a charge of treason after allegations surfaced that his true aim was to establish a western empire and overthrow the United States.

Increasingly strident press coverage leading up to Burr's arrest prompted several associates to distance themselves, including Gen. James Wilkinson and Gen. William Eaton (1764–1811). Eaton unsuccessfully proposed to Thomas Jefferson that he remove Burr from the west by dispatching him on a diplomatic mission to Europe. The Washington, D.C., *National Intelligencer*, 5 Dec. 1806, reported Eaton's allegation that Burr tried to recruit him for a military attack on the U.S. Treasury. The same newspaper printed extracts of four letters and related documents from Wilkinson, who had assisted Burr before the charges emerged but turned on him in a series of letters to Jefferson and other officials. The letter JQA likely referenced was written on 24 Sept. to Texas governor Manuel Antonio Cordero y Bustamante. In it Wilkinson pledged that his troops would not attack Spanish forces unless attacked (vol. 12:403–404; Isenberg, *Fallen Founder*, p. 268–269, 271–272, 279, 282, 303, 304, 311–312, 314, 315, 321–322, 331; David O. Stewart, *American Emperor*, N.Y., 2011, p. 9–12; Jefferson, *Papers*, 42:392). For more on Burr's expedition, see JQA to AA, 3 Feb. 1807, and note 2, below.

³ LCA's letter to JQA of 25 Nov. reported on their children's schooling and recounted Boston social calls. She also sought news on William Steuben Smith's participation in the Miranda expedition. The last paragraph was a single sentence: "Adieu my best beloved friend I already long for your return though not in a situation to make this desire dangerous but so it is I can neither live with or without you and am sincerely and affectionately L. C. A." (Adams Papers).

Louisa Catherine Adams to John Quincy Adams

Boston Decbr. 14 1806

I have just recieved your letter of the 5, my beloved friend, and can only lament, that the extreme irregularity of the Mails, should have caused you unnecessary anxiety. I have written to you twice, and trust ere this, your mind is perfectly at ease on our account.¹ I am sorry

December 1806

however, to be obliged to tell you, that George has a very bad Cough, and that I am very unwell with a Sore Throat, and Cold. the weather is excessively severe, and as usual very trying to my *foolishly delicate* constitution. this house is one of the Coldest I ever lived in, it leaks in almost every part of it. the time is short which we have to remain in it. and I dare say we shall make out very well. George goes on with his french, but as I have already told you, it is out of my power to make him speak, it, nor will he repeat his fables. I hear him read morning, and evening, regularly. and nothing has hitherto caused us any interruption. you must remember mon Amie, that he is *fourteen months* younger than John, and that he has not had the advantage of a *good Shool* like his ~~brother~~ Cousin. M^(rs.) Lee is severe, but I believe perfectly understands her business.[2] George according to your desire, has begun writing but I do not at all approve of his present teachers method, though I make no doubt it is proper. she pencils letters, & then Guides his hand over the pencil marks— John to my great astonishment is very fond of School; and extremely anxious to get the Rocking Horse. he already repeats la Cigale. very prettily, and says it to every body that comes to the house. it is something new, and I fear wont last long. I am told he sits in the middle of the room at School, with the old lady's Rod, and if any of the Boys, dont spell well, (as he says), he ~~give~~ corrects them. from this you may judge what a favorite he is. should he retain his fascinating powers, I fear, he will cause many a serious heart ache. George has just return'd from meeting with M^(r.) Shaw, and *Miss Scollay* has lent him, two Vol. of l'Amie des Enfans.[3] I wish you would get it for him, if you can meet with it in Philadelphia. he is quite delighted with them, this Subject is never ending—

I thank you for the *Message*. though it required some exertion, and perseverance, to peruse it.[4] I should suppose the original copy, must be nearly destroyed from frequent use & really think it cannot last another year.—

I was at a large party, a few evenings since at M^(rs.) Heards.[5] there were two rooms open, and both very well filled. my old acquaintance, really gave me so warm a welcome to Boston, that I felt more pleased, and gratified, than I have felt before on such occasions, for many years. very kind enquiries were made after you—

Offer my best love to all, likewise to M^(r.) Tracy. who you have not mention'd in your letters. I hope his health is better than it was last winter. To yourself my best friend, I will only say that I *think* I never will part with [my] bed fellow again in the Winter. I am absolutely obliged to [. . . .]d, and even then am so cold, that I expect [. . . .]

befo[re . . . .]ng. I anxiously anticipate your return, [. . . .] alone can reanimate, your sincerely affectionate W[ife]   L. C. Adams

P. S. I have not hear'd from Quincy, since I last wrote. Tomorrow I shall make my first payment to M$^{r\cdot}$ G.[6] they have not yet got a Cook, & dont intend to get one—

RC (Adams Papers); addressed: "The Hon$^{ble:}$ / John Quincy Adams Esq$^{r:}$ / S. U. S. — City of Washington"; endorsed: "Louisa— 14. Dec$^{r:}$ 1806. / 21. Dec$^{r:}$ rec$^{d:}$ / 22. d$^{o:}$ Ans$^{d:}$." Some loss of text where the seal was removed.

[1] JQA's letter to LCA of 5 Dec. (Adams Papers) reported that Congress had yet to do any substantive work. He also described a snowstorm that struck Washington, D.C. LCA's letters were those of 25 Nov., for which see JQA to LCA, 8 Dec., and note 3, above, and 7 Dec., above.

[2] GWA had attended the school of "Mrs. Lee" since Nov. 1804 (JQA, *Diary*, 1 Nov.).

[3] LCA was referring to one of the four elder daughters of Boston apothecary William Scollay and Catherine Whitwell Scollay: Catherine (1783–1863), Lucy Cushing (1788–1883), Mary (1793–1882), or Anna Wroe (1794–1845). The publication was Arnaud Berquin, *L'ami des enfans*, 24 vols., Paris, 1783–1784, an anthology of children's literature (Alexander S. Porter, "The Scollays," Bostonian Socy., *Pubns.*, 1st ser., 5:44–45, 52 [1908]; Samuel C. Clarke, *Records of Some of the Descendants of William Curtis*, Boston, 1869, p. 22).

[4] For Thomas Jefferson's 1 Dec. 1806 message to Congress, see JQA to LCA, 2 Dec., and note 1, above.

[5] Susan Oliver Heard (ca. 1780–1863) and her husband, attorney John Heard Jr., resided on Bowdoin Street in Boston (Charles Collyer Whittier, *Genealogy of the Stimpson Family*, Boston, 1907, p. 52–53; Boston *Massachusetts Ploughman*, 24 Oct. 1863; *Boston Directory*, 1806, p. 64, Shaw-Shoemaker, No. 50652)

[6] LCA paid rent to Boston merchant Benjamin Gulliver for apartments on Poplar Street in Boston, which JQA leased for her use during the winter. JQA informed William Smith Shaw on 6 Nov. (MWA:Adams Papers) that they would take a lower room and furnish it themselves and that Gulliver would supply candles and enough wood to keep two fires constantly burning (*Boston Commercial Gazette*, 29 Sept.; JQA, *Diary*, 19 Nov.).

John Quincy Adams to Louisa Catherine Adams

My dear Louisa.   Washington 19. Dec$^{r:}$ 1806.

I wrote you yesterday that little Walter had been again very ill the night before; but was better—[1] He continued so untill the Evening— D$^{r:}$ Weems had been sent for the night before last; but was gone to Alexandria, to attend M$^{rs:}$ Merry, who is ill of a fever— On his return he came to M$^{r:}$ Hellen's, and pronounced that the child had the hives, but did not think him in any danger— He was so well that your Mamma, and the girls all spent the Evening at D$^{r:}$ Thornton's, where I attended them—[2] When we got home last Night, we found that D$^{r:}$ Weems was there: and the child in great danger— The D$^{r:}$ remained with him the whole Night; but could procure no relief for him— When I came to the Capitol this morning, he was barely living, and I am apprehensive he has ere the moment I am now writing been released from all his

December 1806

sufferings— The distress of M^r: & M^rs: Hellen, as you readily conceive is great.— I can only add that I am ever faithfully your's.

John Quincy Adams.

5. O'Clock P. M.—

As long as a possibility remained of a favourable turn, I kept my letter open— The child has just expired, almost without a groan—³ Your Mamma is at M^r: Boyd's, with M^rs: Hellen's infant—⁴

Adieu my dearest friend—

RC (Adams Papers).

¹ In his letter to LCA of 18 Dec., JQA also commented on Washington, D.C., society. He had written another letter on 17 Dec. and discussed GWA's progress in learning French, the hiring of servants, and the possible purchase of Boston church pews, and he mentioned the state of politics in the federal capital (both Adams Papers).

² That is, Washington, D.C., physician and architect William Thornton (vol. 13:187).

³ Walter Hellen Jr. died on 19 December. The infant was interred the next day at Rock Creek Cemetery on the grounds of St. Paul's Episcopal Church in Washington, D.C. (JQA, *Diary*; Robert Benedetto, Jane Donovan, and Kathleen DuVall, *Historical Dictionary of Washington, D.C.*, Lanham, Md., 2003).

⁴ The Hellens' other child, under the temporary care of Catherine Nuth Johnson, was Mary Catherine Hellen, designated as MCHA in *The Adams Papers*, who was born on 10 Sept. and would marry JA2 in 1828 (LCA, *D&A*, 2:781; CFA, *Diary*, 7:90).

Louisa Catherine Adams to John Quincy Adams

My best beloved friend   Boston 21st [*December*] 1806

I this morning recieved your favor of the 12 which afforded me the satisfaction of knowing that you were well & regret very sincerely the strange ~~delay~~ remisness of the Mails for which I can no way account—¹

I made my first payment to M^r· Gulliver as you directed M^r· Shaw inform'd me to day he should bring me the money from Mr Bradford in the course of a Week² he is so much occupied in attending poor Walter who is hourly expected to quit this world of trouble that I seldom see him and when I do it is only for a few minutes³

I went last evening to take tea at M^rs· Paynes a few minutes after I left home a Candle which was standing on my Drawers, owing to a sudden curent of air set fire to a towel which was thrown over a Basket and in a few moment was in a blaze fortunately it was soon extinguished although I lost several articles of Cloathing which I must tax your Pocket to replace you will perhaps wonder at my mentioning this circumstance so lightly but when I know that five minutes would have render'd it impossible to save the house I humbly bow to the God of all mercies with thanks for thus protecting us in this moment of danger and feel the blessing too sincerely when I look at my darling Boys to be sensible of my trifling loss 30 Dollars however would hardly repair the mischief some mischance seems always to threaten me when absent from you and I could almost *swear* never to quit you again I have no faith in presentiments but my dread of fire since I have lived in this house has been continual and I have *continually* endeavourd to guard against it but it all would not do and the accident has happen'd our Quincy affair was a sort of Warning I think—[4]

I met a M:r: Picman last night at M:r: Paynes I do recollect the one who used to visit us this however is a very pleasant man—[5]

Adieu my best belov'd friend do not I entreat you feel any alarm on our account I shall certainly be more cautious than ever in regard to fire and every other circumstance and feel more impatient than ever for the hour which is to return you to the arms and heart of your

L C Adams

Remember me to all our children are well The french as usual

RC (Adams Papers); addressed: "The Hon:ble: / John Quincy Adams Esq:r: / S. U. S / City of Washington"; endorsed: "Louisa— 21. Dec:r: 1806. / 29. Dec:r: rec:d: / Same day Ans:d:."

[1] JQA in his letter to LCA of 12 Dec. discussed a recent snowstorm and remarked on the capital social scene, including his attendance at a tea party with dancing (Adams Papers).

[2] Boston merchant Joseph Nash Bradford (1770–1818) leased one of the houses at the corner of Frog Lane and Nassau Street that JQA purchased on 20 June (JQA, *Diary*, 12 July; JQA and GWA to LCA, 24 May, and note 3, above; Frederick S. Sherman, *Ancestry of Samuel Sterling Sherman and Mary Ware Allen*, Oakland, Calif., 2017, p. 116).

[3] William Smith Shaw's good friend and Harvard classmate Arthur Maynard Walter died in Boston at age 26 on 2 Jan. 1807 (vol. 13:334; Felt, *Memorials of William Smith Shaw*, p. 237; Boston *Independent Chronicle*, 5 Jan.).

[4] The earlier incident took place at Peacefield on 17 Nov. 1806 when a coal from a fireplace was knocked under a chair and burned a floorboard (LCA, *D&A*, 1:245; JQA, *Diary*).

[5] LCA met Boston merchant William Pickman (1774–1857), a brother of Salem, Mass., merchant Benjamin Pickman Jr. with whom JQA socialized when both studied law in Newburyport (JQA, *Diary*, 27 Feb. 1785, 5 March, 25 April 1803, 13 Sept.; *Boston Directory*, 1806, p. 99, Shaw-Shoemaker, No. 50652; Essex Inst., *Hist. Colls.*, 15:286–287, 303 [July, Oct., 1878]).

John Quincy Adams to Louisa Catherine Adams

My dear Louisa.   Washington 22. Dec:r: 1806.

Last Evening I received your's of the 14:th: which makes me anxious to hear from you again— Your sore throat and George's cough will keep me upon thorns untill I hear better tidings of you— I am perhaps the more susceptible on this subject from the heavy calamity so recently befallen the family here.— It is vain to lament or to anticipate—and would be vain to attempt expressing what I feel.

The weather I hope has ere this mitigated its severity with you as it has here— The River which was frozen over is again open, and the Snow has almost disappeared from the ground— We had last week and the week before as much and as bitter cold weather nearly as was experienced through the whole of the last Winter.

I have given as you desire your *best love* to M[r:] Tracy, who thanks you for your kind remembrance, and is peculiarly gratified by it— His health is I think better than at any time since I have known him, but still infirm

Your Mamma desires me to tell you that the reason of her not writing, is that she has a sore finger on the right hand— Catherine says she is not to write untill she has answers to her two last Letters to Caroline.

On Saturday we committed the remains of poor little Walter to the grave at Rock-Hill-Church— M[r:] & M[rs:] Hellen are yet in deep affliction—but well in health.

Heaven bless you, and my dear boys—   John Q. Adams.[1]

RC (Adams Papers).

[1] JQA wrote to LCA again on 26 Dec., expressing anxiety about her health and reporting the loss of the shipment of books for the Library of Congress. He also relayed rumors about Aaron Burr's activities in the west and described Thomas Jefferson hosting Osage visitors at a "Rope Dancer's Show" (Adams Papers).

Louisa Catherine Adams to John Quincy Adams

My dearest & best friend   Boston 24 Dec[br.] 1806

I last evening recieved your almost unkind letter which was brought me by your brother & M[r] Shaw[1] the latter came to town to attend Selfridges trial which I understand commenced yesterday[2] he looks very well and says our friends in Quincy are all in good health I have not seen them since my residence in Town Caleb is so bad a Driver they cannot send for us

I am really hurt at the stile of your last letter which appears to insinuate that it is owing to my negligence that you have been disappointed in hearing from me believe me when I tell you I have written four or five different times and I can no way account for the loss of my letters I shall send this to M[r.] Shaws office and hope it will prove more successful—

Adieu my beloved friend be assur'd that I love you too sincerely *to wish* to cause even a momentary uneasiness I too well know what I suffer'd myself during my painful separation from yourself & my darling Children willingly to occasion you one such heart rending pang and I flatter myself you are too well convinced of my affection after the proof I gave you in the Summer when my mind & my body were equally afflicted to suppose it possible— remember me affectionately to all the family & tell Adelaide I will answer her kind letter as soon as my health which is very indifferent & my Spirits which are worse will admit³ George is so unwell I have thought it adviseable to keep him from School that he may take such remedies as may prove of service I await with impatience the arrival of your next letter which I hope will restore peace to the heart of your affectionate Wife

L. C. Adams

RC (Adams Papers).

¹ On 15 Dec. JQA wrote to LCA that he was impatient to hear from her and could no longer attribute the lack of letters to the poor weather: "I have imputed the delay of your letters to this as long as I could— But we have now here Boston Newspapers to the 8th: of this month." JQA also described the continuing cold temperatures and reported on the deteriorating health of Walter Hellen Jr. (Adams Papers).

² For the Boston murder trial of attorney Thomas Oliver Selfridge, see LCA to JQA, 1 Jan. 1807, and note 2, below.

³ Not found.

Louisa Catherine Adams to John Quincy Adams

Boston Decbr. 28 1806

Your letters of 17th 18th 19th were brought me on Friday,¹ the information they contain'd, must plead my apology, my best friend, for not writing immediately. but the Shock was so great, I felt totally incapacitated for the exertion, which it required. Your Mother & Father came to see us yesterday, having hear'd of our loss. Alas my beloved friend, three times in the last twelve months, as it pleased Heaven, to visit us with severe affliction. and our wretched family seem indeed, doomed to bear, every "blasting calamity.["] in that time I have severely suffer'd from the same cause. and too well do I know how to participate in their grief. my own loss weak, and selfish, as I am again recurs forcibly to my imagination, and my heart bleeds for Nancy's, which is so much more painful. I know, and feel, how unnecessary it is, to urge you to offer all the consolation, in your power. but there are numberless little attentions, trifling in themselves, which it is in our power to offer on such occasions, & which afford the greatest consolation, to the unhappy. forgive, my friend, this observation. I know how much your mind is occupied, and how *almost impossible*, it is for you, to attend to such circumstances. but I likewise know the goodness of your heart, and am sure you will not feel offended at this suggestion. Nancy from a doubt of the strength of her *mind*, has repeatedly said, she was convinced you thought her too insignificant, to pay her any sort of attention. Our sex in general, I am convinced, however great their pretentions, can be objects of very little importance to a mind like yours. but my friend, as heaven has made us a part of the Creation, and ordain'd that men even of the *greatest abilities*, should pass the greatest proportion of their lives *with us*; as we are form'd of *such materials*, that even *seeming unkindness bitterly affects us* it aught, (even if it only proceed from a motive of compassion in your sex), to render you *anxious* to offer us those little civilities, which by raising us in our own esteem, inspires us with gratitude, and thereby render us anxiously solicitous, to return by every means in our power, those sweet, and flattering attentions, which form the basis of mans happiness— I know not where my pen has strayed, but I have done—

The Children are well, John went to Quincy yesterday and I fear will forget his french. Adieu my beloved friend, heaven bless you I am now suffering so acutely with a *bad head* ache that I can only subscribe myself sick or well ever affectionately yours

L. C. Adams

P.S. Selfridge was acquitted the day before yesterday I enclose the bills[2] I [will an]swer your letter as soon as [I am ab]le

RC (Adams Papers); addressed: "The Hon[ble:] / John Quincy Adams Esq[r.] / S. U. S. / City of Washington"; endorsed: "Louisa. 28. Dec[r:] 1806. / 5. Jan[y:] 1807. Rec[d:] / 6. D[o:] Ans[d:]." Some loss of text where the seal was removed.

[1] For JQA's letters of 17 and 18 Dec., see that of 19 Dec., and note 1, above.
[2] The enclosures have not been found, but were likely the receipts JQA requested in his 18 Dec. letter (Adams Papers).

Mercy Otis Warren to Abigail Adams

Plymouth, M[s.] Dec[r.] 28[th.] 1807 [1806]—[1]

It is a long time since I have had a line from a friend who for many years I have cordially loved, and have been grieved that in so many of them, the intercourse has been seldom.— It is true I have by me an excellent letter of yours which has lain too long unanswered;—but the great debility which has long afflicted my eyes has & still deprives me of the use of my own pen, nor is it easy to express the effusions of friendship, or the sensibilities we feel on any other occasion, when we borrow that of another.—[2] This with the death of very many of my best correspondents, has almost broken off the habit of Letter-writing in which I once, so much delighted;—but while I live, I shall love the friends of youth, of maturer age, and those few, who may be carried with myself, to that advanced period, when no hopes or fears, "no jarring, dissonant, ungrateful string" ought to cause any disquietude to beings, who stand on the marge of two worlds.—[3]

I sometimes transiently hear that Mrs. Adams is very much out of health, and again by a similar transient report, I hear that both Mr Adams & herself, enjoy the blessing of health in a high degree. The last time I saw Judge Cushing & Lady, they informed me that you had both recently made them a visit at Scituate;—had you extended your journey to Plymouth, it would have been a pleasant circumstance to your friends resident there.— This ancient town you have often visited with pleasure;—the recollection of those visits, calls back a thousand ideas that may lay dormant but can never be erased.

Past recollections would animate me to the indulgence as usual when writing to you, of expatiating on a variety of subjects, which would give equal pleasure to my own mind, as in those days you mention, when *"thought met thought, and a happy union of sentiment endeared our friendship."*—[4] It has always been my opinion, that no variation of sentiment with regard to subjects which make up the great bustle of the world, ought to dissever the hearts of true friendship.— I may censure your politics, yet love you as ever,—you may renounce mine, without losing your esteem and affection;—men nor women were not made to think alike on all subjects,—it cannot be;—yet equal probity may be viewed by the eye of him who searcheth all hearts.—

One half of our lives has been a period of the most remarkable revolutions that time has recorded. . . .[5] Should I ask Mr Adams what he thinks the Emperor Napoleon was made for?— I presume he would not tell me.— Should he ask me the same question, I should give my opinion without the smallest reserve.—

My unreserved and social habits, with a good degree of chearfulness and equanimity, have accompanied me through a long life, notwithstanding the changes I have seen in politics, in families, in manners, and even notwithstanding a circumstance nearer my heart, the death of the most valuable friends and children.— *Death* is a familiar word;— it is daily seen in every neighbourhood, yet we understand not nor can comprehend the extent of the term and its effects, until called to realize it by our own experience.— May we my dear friend, meet a joyous explanation, when we have quitted these mortal scenes, and passed through the dark valley!—

When did you see your daughter?— Mrs Smith may have forgotten her aged friend, but I have loved Nabby Adams too well, not to feel an interest in her happiness.— Does she yet know whether her absent son is still an inhabitant of this earth?— With respectful Compliments to Mr Adams I presume he will rejoice to hear, as will you, that your worthy friend, General Warren enjoys vigor of mind, strength and animation of sentiment at the age of fourscore, though his bodily health is somewhat impaired.—

I am my dear M^rs. Adams, as usual, / Affectionately Your Friend,

Mercy Warren[6]

RC in James Warren Jr.'s hand (Adams Papers); internal address: "M^rs. Adams—" Filmed at 28 Dec. 1807.

[1] The dating of this letter is based on AA's response of 9 March 1807, below.
[2] AA to Warren, 16 Jan. 1803 (vol. 15:255–257).
[3] William Kenrick, "Epistles to Lorenzo," Epistle III, lines 186–187.
[4] Alexander Pope, "Eloisa to Abelard," line 95.
[5] Ellipsis in MS.
[6] Signature in Warren's hand.

John Quincy Adams to Louisa Catherine Adams

My dear Louisa. Washington 29. Dec^r: 1806.

I have as little faith in presentiments as yourself—but the anxiety which I have felt for this whole week on your account has been such, that on receiving this morning your two letters of the 19th: and 21st:— I opened them with a trembling hand and heart—[1] I lay this morning an hour before day-light, torturing myself with the fancy that some calamity of FIRE had befallen you or the children; and when I broke the seals of your letters, your sore throat and George's cough, and the dread of fire, were all mingled in a sort of confusion in my mind, which was relieved only by getting through both your letters; and by an ejaculation of inexpressible gratitude to Heaven on finding that nothing but your clothes had been burnt— Had your loss been six times as great, I should still have bless'd Heaven that it was no worse— I shall henceforth feel easier with respect to the danger of fire; because I am convinced that the accident you have met with will sharpen your caution— That you will attend not only to the fires in the chimnies; but to what is infinitely more dangerous the candles upon your tables and drawers— Let me intreat you my dearest friend, never to suffer a candle to be LEFT burning in your chamber, when there is nobody there;

and if you could keep all cotton and linen articles of Cloathing so ranged as not to be crowded and cluttered upon drawers where candles are placed your life and that of your children would be more secure—

On the morning when I left you my dear friend, you remember I asked you for a promise—which was, that you would *take care of the children*— You seemed to think that the request was almost equivalent to a reproach— I had no such intention— I knew your *heart* would always take the tenderest care of them— But what I wish'd to impress upon you was continual reflection—if possible to prevent a *thoughtless* moment— I knew you would always do right when you gave yourself time *to think*.— I have seen by the newspapers an account of *three* children burnt to death in New-York the week before last, by their Cloaths catching fire— Their Cloaths were of Cotton, and the paper cautions against the use of Cotton for the winter cloathing of children.—[2] Ours I presume have no Cotton about them— But let us extend the lesson further, and learn in all cases to keep Cotton cloathing from the fire.

The loss of poor little Walter has not only made *me* more susceptible of alarm than before— M[r:] and M[rs:] Boyd feel the same increase of sensibility in regard to their little boy— He has been unwell for some days, though they know not exactly what ails it— They have had recourse both to Doctors and Doctresses for its relief; but I hope the child is not so ill as they fear— Their House is so cold and damp that they cannot live in it any longer— They are about to move into one of the six buildings—[3]

I have an invitation to dine with the President on Wednesday—the last day of the year— We are still doing nothing in both Houses of Congress.

You say nothing of Caroline—But I see a letter enclosed in your's from her to Kitty— My love to her, and to the dear children— I have not yet had one line from Quincy—

Ever your affectionate   John Quincy Adams.

RC (Adams Papers).

[1] LCA's letter of 21 [*Dec.*] is above. In her letter of 19 Dec., she assured JQA that she had written often and reported on the health and schooling of their children. She also remarked on Massachusetts politics (Adams Papers).

[2] Three children died in New York the previous week from their clothes catching fire, according to the *New-York Gazette*, 17 Dec., which also called for a ban on cotton clothing for children.

[3] The "Six Buildings" was a row of attached townhouses on the north side of Pennsylvania Avenue between 21st and 22d Streets NW that was begun by James Greenleaf and completed by Isaac Polock by May 1800 (Lee H. Burke, *Homes of the Department of State, 1774–1976*, Washington, D.C., 1977, p. 27).

December 1806 – January 1807

John Quincy Adams to Louisa Catherine Adams

My dear Louisa.   New-Years' day 1807.

I cannot suffer this day to pass without wishing you and our dear children many and many happy returns of it though my fingers are almost too numb to write— The year has introduced itself with great severity; though with delightful weather— My thermometer this morning stood at 9. which is precisely the lowest point to which it descended through the whole course of last Winter.

The Senate adjourned over this day, and I have been with your Mamma, and Sisters to the President's Annual levee— It was crowded as usual, and in addition to the customary Indian visitors had two Squaws with three children of the Mandan tribe brought by Captain Lewis—[1] They are the most distant, and whitest Indians that have ever been seen here— The children are of a lighter complexion than most Spaniards or Italians; and ruddy as Milkmaids.

I dined yesterday at the President's— Captain Lewis was there; more altered in manners and appearance, from what he was when we saw him before than I ever beheld any man— I did not know him again, though I expected to meet him— I must add that his alteration is to my judgment inexpressibly for the better— But he looks fifteen years older—

Your Mamma's things, together with my boots have arrived safe. M:r: Buchanan received and forwarded them immediately—It was very fortunate they were not sent with my boxes of books, neither of which has yet arrived

M:r: Boyd's child is still quite unwell, though they scarcely know what ails it— All the rest of the family here and there are well.— Adieu My dear friend; may every happiness [atten]d you through this and many many succeeding years— So prays again your ever affectionate husband.   John Quincy Adams.

Do not forget to give my love and kindest wishes to Caroline— I do not know whether you can read my letter— My fingers are all but frozen—

RC (Adams Papers). Some loss of text due to wear at the fold.

[1] At the conclusion of the Lewis and Clark expedition, Meriwether Lewis traveled to Washington, D.C., with a small group from the Mandan Nation headed by Chief Sheheke and his wife, Yellow Corn, for whom see Descriptive List of Illustrations, Nos. 4 and 5, above.

4. SHEHEKE, BY CHARLES BALTHAZAR JULIEN FÉVRET
DE SAINT-MÉMIN, 1807
See page xi

5. YELLOW CORN, BY CHARLES BALTHAZAR JULIEN FÉVRET DE SAINT-MÉMIN, 1807
See page xi

Louisa Catherine Adams to John Quincy Adams

Boston Jan^{ry.} 1st. 1807

To offer you, the kindest wishes of the season, my best friend, is almost unnecessary; my happiness, & felicity, in this world, is so interwoven with yours, that I fondly believe, the one cannot be sensible of a joy, or a pain, which is not sincerely participated by the other. to say that I hope each revolving year, may produce additional felicity, is poorly to ~~express~~ describe my feelings; and I must leave it to your own heart, to suggest *all* that *my pen* is inadequate to express—

I scarcely know what I wrote you on Sunday;[1] the distress of my mind, and the dreadful headache I suffered almost incapacitated me from writing at all, but the fear of occasioning you a moment of painful anxiety, induced me to attempt it, and I fear my pen ran away with my reason, of which I can seldom boast—

The acquital of Selfridge, seems to have given great & serious offence to some people. Mrs. Carters House, was surrounded by a mob a few nights since, which they threatend to pull down, and to day, they hung Mr. S. in Effigy in the Mall, which roused the anger of some others, who cut the figure down. Mr. White, the Son of a Carpenter in Boston was almost killed in the attempt.[2] I cannot actually vouch for the truth of this story, but this was told me at noon. It is pity things should be carried such lengths—

I am very anxious to hear from you, though I thank you a thousand times, for devoting so much *more* of your precious time to me, than I could reasonably expect. I think George improves in his french, but am almost afraid to say so. I devote the greatest part of the day to him, but cannot prevail on him to speak it. he frequently asks when you mean to return, and is really impatient to see you. John is at Quincy, where I think it is probable he will stay, great part of the winter. I am reconciled, as your Mother cannot live without him. She looks remarkably well, and was in good spirits. She gave me such an account of *Sally*, that I cannot think of permitting her to return[3] it seems she has so powerful a propensity to liquor, she is seldom sober, where she can possibly find the means of gratification. I have partly engaged the Boy we now have to live with us this Summer, but it remains for you to decide. his father is a violent Demo', I do not know how far this might prove an objection; he is intelligent and tinctured with the modern principles, if we engage him he is to have victuals & cloaths while he stays—

January 1807

Adieu my best friend, I regret much the loss of the Books but am happy it does not fall upon you. the Vessel in which I sent the Box, is called the Sally, Capt Brayston, master. I sent Mr. Buchanon a bill of Lading, with a request he would forward it as soon as possible—

Once more, my friend, farewel, give my love & best wishes to all, and that the choicest blessings of heaven may a[ttend] you, is [the] ardent Prayer of your tenderly affectionate, w[ife]

L. C. Ad[ams]

Papa I wish you many happy years[4]

RC (Adams Papers); addressed: "The Honble. / John Quincy Adams Esqr. / S. U. S. / City of Washington"; endorsed: "Louisa— 1. Jan^{y:} 1807. / 8. d^{o:} rec^{d:} / 9. d^{o:} Ans^{d:}." Some loss of text where the seal was removed.

[1] LCA to JQA, 28 Dec. 1806, above.

[2] A political dispute between Benjamin Austin Jr. and Federalist attorney Thomas Oliver Selfridge erupted into violence on 4 Aug. when Selfridge encountered Austin's eighteen-year-old son, Charles, on a Boston street. The teenager berated his father's adversary and struck him with a cane, prompting the lawyer to fire his pistol, killing him. Selfridge was tried for manslaughter in the Mass. Supreme Judicial Court from 23 to 26 December. Attorney General James Sullivan headed the prosecution, while Christopher Gore and Samuel Dexter represented the accused. The jury determined that Selfridge had acted in self-defense and returned a verdict of not guilty. Democratic-Republicans took to the streets in the nights following, surrounding the boardinghouse of widow Catherine Crafts Carter (ca. 1754–1822) on Southac's Court where Selfridge resided. Among those caught up in the protests was probably a son of one of two Boston housewrights, Luther White or Ebenezer White. TBA attended most sessions of the trial, he reported in a 28 Dec. letter to JQA, writing that the defense by Dexter was "unrivalled as a specimen of bar eloquence." JQA responded on 13 Jan. 1807 and 10 Feb. (all Adams Papers), disputing Dexter's contention "that a man *of honour*, may kill for the defence of his reputation against the *disgrace* of a beating." Nevertheless, he wrote, the verdict confirmed that "the purity of Juries" is often fairer than "the firmness of *Judges*" (Wood, *Empire of Liberty*, p. 334; John D. Lawson, *American State Trials*, 17 vols., St. Louis, Mo., 1914–1936, 2:547–551; *Newburyport Herald*, 30 Dec. 1806; Boston *Repertory*, 9 Jan. 1807; Boston *Democrat*, 4 April; *Boston Directory*, 1807, p. 47, 156, Shaw-Shoemaker, No. 12180; Ann Smith Lainhart, "John Haven Dexter and the 1789 Boston City Directory," *NEHGR*, 140:49–50 [Jan. 1986]; *Boston Commercial Gazette*, 12 Dec. 1822).

[3] That is, Sarah Jones Cleverly, for whom see LCA to JQA, 7 Dec. 1806, and note 6, above.

[4] The postscript is in GWA's hand.

John Quincy Adams to Thomas Boylston Adams

My dear Brother. Washington 5. Jan^{y:} 1807.

On new year's day I received your very agreeable Letter of Dec^{r:} 21^{st:} which I should have answered immediately;[1] but it was not *sitting* day; and I find no time for my correspondence but while we are in Session— The reason of which is that having become a Jack of so many trades, I employ all the time I have to spare at *home*, in preparing for my business at Cambridge next Spring— I have therefore been more buckled down to business since the commencement of this Session, than ever before, though we have yet done nothing of a public nature, and the Senate have not been upon the average in Session one hour a day.— Happily I have enjoyed and still enjoy better health than I have known these fifteen years.— Another cause however why I did not answer your letter was that the next morning I received one from my wife with such an account of her health, and that of my dear boy George, that it has kept me in a state of alarm and suspense, so distressing that I was in no situation to answer with that pleasantness which a due return to your letter required— I have been this morning relieved by information from my wife that the children are both well; and you have been long enough a Parent to know how much joy that must have given me.[2]

I have been witness here, and in some degree a partaker of the distress which the loss of an infant child must occasion— M^r: and M^{rs}: Hellen have lost their youngest boy, a charming child just turn'd of two years old— His disorder was the same of which M^r: W. Smith's son John so lately died— They call it here the Hives.[3]

I congratulate you upon the success of your Causes at the Norfolk Common Pleas.— I do not suppose the question of right respecting the Sea-weed could be settled on the question whether the Special pleas should be filed, but whenever that hopeful idea of more than rank jacobinism shall be duly brought before a Court of Justice, I trust it will meet with the fate which it so richly deserves— I hope the worthy town of Quincy, will act as correctly upon every attempt to draw them into wickedness and absurdity as they have done, and never countenance such profligate combinations against private property, as are this and the half-moon controversy both—[4]

I have continued to forward you our Documents, though hitherto few of much consequence have been printed— I have also two or three times I think written a few lines to my father with the enclosures; and ought to have written to my dear Mother—[5] She will accept as my apology the same cause which I have alledged to you at the beginning of this letter— I knew she would learn by the receipt of the documents and by my frequent letters to my wife, how we are here; and that she would excuse my omission of writing specially to her on knowing what has really oppress'd me with business here— When Pope undertook the Translation of Homer, he used to dream that he was toiling upon a Journey, to which there was *no end*—[6] My Lectures for Cambridge, haunt me Night and Day, in the same manner, and not a week passes without my dreaming about them— I hope by the blessing of

January 1807

Heaven at some day to find *an end* to the Journey they have opened to me; but they must give me *unremitting* labour for years yet to come.

With respect to my farm I shall be satisfied, with what you will do concerning it— My expectations now are not quite so sanguine as when I left you— Time, absence and Reflection have cooled down the ideas, which the anxiety of Vesey and the other applicants had excited, and I remember again what a *farm* yet is— I rely with perfect confidence on your good-offices and discretion— I am very sorry to hear of Mʳ: Briesler's illness, and hope he has ere this recovered— I presume he will have no money to pay over to you— I owe him a year's interest upon a note of hand, which I ought to have paid him before I came away— I desired him if he sold the Cattle to deduct the amount I owed him ($74:30) and credit it upon the note— And I promised him if he could not sell to send him a check for it from here— I will thank you therefore to ask him whether he has paid himself the year's interest, and given me credit for it upon the note; or whether he expects I should send him the check—[7] If he wishes this, I will send it immediately on receiving your answer.

Your project of purchasing the house and land of the Vesey's appears to me a very good one; nor should I suppose $4000 by any means a high price for them— They would in every respect suit you better than your place at ~~Quincy~~ Braintree—[8] I would purchase this of you myself, if I could command the means—

The sculls of our members in the House of Representatives have not yet been cracked *externally*— Their alarm has furnished some merriment to the wits, and I wonder it has not furnished much more— Yet I believe there was real danger—and they did actually sit with something worse than a *dagger of lath*[9] suspended over their heads.

Mʳ: J. Randolph if we judge from present appearances, is put upon his good behaviour— It appears to me that in the lapse of ages his name must have gradually changed, and that in the days of Jack Falstaff it was *Bardolph*:—the same of whom the fat knight says, that he would not *swagger* against a Barbary-Hen, if her feathers turned up, with any shew of resistance.

I hope Buonaparte will never undertake to teach him *french*, as he did the poor king of Prussia— I pity this unfortunate Gentleman too— but the young Dace, must be a bait for the old pike—[10] There was no help for it— Like his brother of Austria, he fell because he could not stand— Prince Louis was not the king's brother— He was a son of Prince Ferdinand; or rather he was one of those of whom Mirabeau says that Count Schmettau was the *pere indubitable*— Schmettau too, according to the papers was killed in that butchery of Jena; and if so he was a heavy loss.— I have always been of opinion that the Prussian army would never again *fight*— Möllendorff had still a soul in his body worthy of old Frederic— But he was turned of 80—and he was all— I knew personally almost every man high in command in the Prussian Armies— I pretend to know nothing of military character— But the conclusion I *had* drawn from my own observation was that take off *Möllendorff*, *Schmettau*, and Tempelhoff, (I do not see him mentioned in these late accounts) and there was nothing in the Prussian army left but muskets—Artillery—and UNIFORMS.[11]

I do most cordially congratulate you and rejoyce with you, at the health and growth of your dear little girl— Heaven grant that she may continue to grow, and thrive, and always be not only as the Hebrew idiom says a *desire to the eye*—but also a delight to the heart of both her Parents—[12] Remember me affectionately to all the family, and particularly to your wife. / *Adieu*

RC (Adams Papers); endorsed: "J Q Adams Esq[r] / 5[th:] January 1806 / 15[th:] Rec[d] / Answ[d]."

[1] Not found.

[2] LCA to JQA, 24 and 28 Dec. 1806, both above. JQA responded to LCA's letter of the 24th on 2 Jan. 1807, apologizing for earlier comments about the laxity of her correspondence and attributing them to his anxiety about her health and that of their children (Adams Papers).

[3] John Clarke Smith (b. ca. 1801), the son of William and Hannah Carter Smith, died of croup in Boston on 23 Oct. 1806 (Boston *Columbian Centinel*, 25 Oct.; JQA, *Diary*; LCA, *D&A*, 1:244).

[4] TBA was apparently litigating a case pertaining to a shore-property question under debate in Norfolk County about whether it was legal to collect seaweed for agricultural use from shoreland owned by other people. A landmark New York court decision in Aug. 1807, *Emans v. Turnbull*, largely settled the question in favor of property owners and served as precedent for a later similar ruling in Massachusetts. JQA also alluded to a second issue that arose in a Quincy town meeting in April 1806 when local fishermen attempted to codify a right of the public to use Half Moon Island for fishing and fowling as per local custom. JA, who acquired the island by inheritance and purchase in 1801, successfully defended his right to control the use of the property, drafting an [1806] memorandum that provided evidence of his claim and asserted that owners of shore property had an exclusive right to both its use and the seaweed that washed onto it (vol. 15:139, 140; JA, *D&A*, 1:141–142; JA, Memorandum on the Legal Status of Half-Moon Island in Quincy Bay, [1806], Adams Papers; Mitchell W. Feeney, "Regulating Seaweed Harvesting in Maine," *Ocean and Coastal Law Journal*, 7:340 [2002]; William Johnson, *Reports of Cases Argued and Determined in the Supreme Court of Judicature . . . in the State of New-York*, 20 vols., N.Y., 1807–1823, 2:313).

[5] JQA's letters and enclosures to JA have not been found.

[6] William Lisle Bowles, ed., *The Works of Alexander Pope*, 10 vols., London, 1806, 7:313–314.

[7] John Briesler Sr. resided in the John Adams Birthplace and managed that and the John Quincy Adams Birthplace. JQA settled accounts annually until Briesler vacated the property in 1807. On 22 March JQA paid off the note (vol. 15:343; JQA, *Diary*, 5 Oct. 1805, 22 March 1807, 3 May).

[8] No evidence has been found that TBA purchased or built a house; instead he resided at Peacefield with AHA and their children until 1810. Property abutting JA's land was for sale by brothers Mottram Veasey and Ebenezer Veasey Jr. (1759–1816), who were selling

family property in a series of transactions following the 5 May 1806 death of their mother, Mary Miller Veasey. TBA did not buy the property, though JQA purchased a right-of-way from the estate. TBA owned three acres near the Neponset River bridge that he purchased from Joseph Phinney for $350 on 27 Feb. (vols. 10:357–358; 13:336; 15:314; Kirsten Holder, James Bertolini, and Jaime R. Young, *Cultural Landscape Report for Adams Birthplaces*, Boston, 2014, p. 46, 47; Norfolk County Registry of Deeds, Dedham, Mass.:Norfolk County Deeds, 25:54; 27:89, 113, 243; JQA, *Diary*, 15 Nov.; Sprague, *Braintree Families*).

[9] Shakespeare, *Twelfth Night*, Act IV, scene ii, line 136.

[10] Shakespeare, *King Henry IV, Part II*, Act II, scene iv, lines 107–109; Act III, scene ii, lines 356–357.

[11] After France defeated Austria at Austerlitz, Emperor Francis II of Austria signed the Treaty of Pressburg and on 6 Aug. renounced the title of Holy Roman Emperor. The French Army under Napoleon on 14 Oct. routed Prussian forces under King Frederick William III at Jena, Saxony. Four days earlier, Ludwig (Louis) Ferdinand, Prince of Prussia (b. 1772), a son of August Ferdinand, Prince of Prussia (1730–1813), and a nephew of King Frederick II, was killed in a preliminary engagement. The battle and the death of the prince received extensive coverage in the Washington, D.C., *National Intelligencer*, 31 Dec., and prompted JQA to ruminate on his time in Berlin. In questioning Ludwig Ferdinand's paternity, JQA quoted a similar indictment of Friedrich Wilhelm, Count von Schmettau (1742–1806), by Honoré Gabriel Riquetti, Comte de Mirabeau, in his *Histoire secrète de la cour de Berlin; ou, correspondance d'un voyageur françois*, 2 vols., Alençon, France, 1789, 2:192. Schmettau was injured in the Battle of Jena and died a few days later. Another casualty was Richard Joachim Heinrich, Count von Moellendorff (1724–1816), who was wounded and taken prisoner but survived. Maj. Gen. Georg Friedrich Ludwig von Tempelhoff (1737–1807) was an artillery officer in the Prussian ranks (George F. Nafziger, *Historical Dictionary of the Napoleonic Era*, Lanham, Md., 2002, p. 20; Alexander Mikaberidze, *The Napoleonic Wars: A Global History*, N.Y., 2020, p. 214, 220; LCA, *D&A*, 1:56, 58; Princess Louise, *Forty-five Years*, p. 427–428, 437, 438, 446; Peter Hofschröer, *Prussian Staff & Specialist Troops, 1791–1815*, Oxford, Eng., 2010, p. 23).

[12] The idiom JQA referenced derives from line 16 of a poem by Renaissance poet and translator Joseph Sarfati, which was printed at the beginning of the *Biblia Rabbinica*, Venice, 1525 (Ann Brener, "A Poem by Joseph Sarfati in Honor of Daniel Bomberg's *Biblia Rabbinica*, Venice 1525" in Chanita Goodblatt and Howard Kreisel, eds., *Tradition, Heterodoxy, and Religious Culture: Judaism and Christianity in the Early Modern Period*, Be'er Sheva, Israel, 2006, p. 263, 268, 272).

John Quincy Adams to Louisa Catherine Adams

My dear Louisa. Washington 6. Jan$^{y:}$ 1807.

I received yesterday your letter of Dec$^{r:}$ 28$^{th:}$ with the enclosures to M$^{r:}$ & M$^{rs:}$ Hellen, and to your Mamma— I enclosed to you last Evening a letter from her to yourself; and one for Caroline, but not having received them untill my return from the Capitol which was late, I was obliged, to save the last Evening's Mail to defer answering your letter untill this morning—[1]

I take in kind part your observations upon my neglect to pay proper *little attentions* to M$^{rs:}$ Hellen; in which I perceive with pleasure your tender affection for your Sister— I submit cheerfully to the voice of reproach from you, when I remember that it was dictated by your love for her— That my heart has bled with the purest sincerity, for her, in this affliction is true; but might perhaps be of no use for me to assert—

That I would have done any thing to which my powers of body or of soul are competent to avert the misfortune, or to alleviate her suffering under it, is alike true, though I neither claim nor expect any credit for it; but ~~most~~ equally true it is, that I do not know what are the *trifling attentions*, by which the heart of a mother can be comforted upon the death of a darling child, and from this ignorance, I am afraid that I have been as deficient in paying them on this occasion as your letter apprehends—

I lament that M^{rs:} Hellen should ever have entertained the opinion that my want of attention to her has proceeded from an unjust depreciation of her strength of mind— I have always felt a proper sense of her kindness to us, however unfortunate I may have been in expressing it— Of her strength of mind, and genuine Fortitude, I have had at this time the most convincing proof— It has impress'd itself forcibly upon my observation, and has a full share of my respect and admiration— I should certainly be very far from deserving those compliments which you make to the goodness of my heart, if my inattention to the little Chesterfieldian graces of life, proceeded from an overweening, presumptuous confidence in my own *abilities*, or from a pedantic and foolish overrating of my own *occupations*—

For your sake and for that of your Sisters I have often wished that I had been that man of elegant and accomplished manners, who can recommend himself to the regard of others, by *little attentions*— I have always known however that I was not, and have been sensible that I could never be made that man— It has perhaps been natural that my deficiency should be imputed to a deeper, and more inexcusable Cause—to a want of proper sensibility—to an unfeeling heart— If the general tenor of my conduct does not authorize persons disposed to kind construction, to ascribe my imperfections to the lighter-shaded fault, I know they must impute it to the darker— If such imputation must befall me, I hope it is erroneous—

I have said thus much, My dear friend, to reply, as far as I am able, and in the Spirit of kindness, to a complaint, which in the moment of your distress for your Sister, you conceived proper to make against your husband.

I hope the head-ache under which you laboured while you were writing your letter did not out-last the day; and that you have ever since enjoyed uninterrupted health— Your letter before the last had alarmed me for George; and although you only say in your last that *the children* were well, without mentioning him particularly[2] I hope his cold and cough have been subdued by your care in keeping him

January 1807

from school to take proper remedies; I rejoyce that you took that precaution, and hope he will have no return of the cough—

We are here all tolerably well— M^{rs:} Boyd's child is quite recovered— I never saw two children more contrasted than this little boy, and M^{rs:} Hellen's daughter, Mary— The boy is *pepper*— The girl is *oil*— Both charming children— Mary is very large for her age, and the sweetest tempered child I ever saw.

Adieu my Dear Friend; I cannot continue writing without making the family wait for dinner— My love to Caroline & the children.

Affectionately your's   J. Q. Adams.

RC (Adams Papers); endorsed: "J. Q. Adams Esqr / Rec^{d.} 15 Jan^{ry} 1807 / Ans^{d.} 16." Tr (Adams Papers).

[1] LCA's letter to JQA of 28 Dec. 1806 is above; her correspondence with Walter and Ann Johnson Hellen and Catherine Nuth Johnson has not been found.
[2] LCA to JQA, 24 Dec., above.

John Adams to John Quincy Adams

My dear Son   Quincy January 7. 1807

I have regularly received the Journals and Documents you have been So good as to inclose and two Short Letters for which I thank you. I have rec^d also the Economica of Mr Blodget for which I pray you to thank him.[1] It is I presume a Work of merit and Utility. I have not been able as yet to attend to it, very carefully.

I have not written to you before, because I had nothing to write, unless it were about Law Suits and Town Meetings of which I Suppose your Brother has informed you. The Town has now three times rejected the importunity of certain uneasy Spirits and at present there is an apparent tranquility.[2]

My old Friends are dropping off very fast. Old Mr Vernon of Newport once a Member of the Navy Board and Father of your fellow Traveller in 1778 died last Week and I expect to Attend, tomorrow the Funeral of the Treasurer of Harvard Colledge, who ascended to Heaven as easily as the Prophet;[3] I was never more busy in my Life. Hallicarnassensis, is not quite abandoned, I hope:[4] but your Advice and that of Some other of my Friends, have prevailed upon me, to renew my former Attempts to put Some of my papers in order, and make a few comments upon them.[5] The Extent of the Business will not I hope again discourage me from pursuing the plan as far as the time left me will allow. But this you know is between You and me.

Your Family is well and John is with Us, as gay as a bird. I go to Town but seldom but have visited your Family as often as I have gone. Their Situation is wholesome and pleasant and the more So I should think, for being a little out of the Way of the Noise and Smoke and Bustle of the multitude.

Mr Burr is the Subject of all Conversation. But the most dark misterious and unaccountable Business it is, that ever was heard or read. For my own part I am determined to wait with patience for the ultimate devellopement before I venture a conjecture upon the Object or the motives of all the movements beyond the mountains. Many People this Way begin to Suggest Suspicions and even opinions, that one or more foreign Powers are at the Bottom. If this is true We Shall hear more of this project before it is over, nor will the defeat of this prevent another and another. They talk of a Connection between this Enterprize And Mirandas.[6] But I can See no probability nor Scarce a possibility of that.

Of one thing however I am very certain that south America has been So much arroused and alarmed, by the Conquest of Buenas Ayres, by Mirandas Expedition, by the Purchase of Louisiana, by the Exploration of the Missisippi the Missuri and the red Rivers and above all by the discovery of a passage by Land to the Columbia River and the pacific Ocean, and the Attention of all Europe has been turned by all these means so much to this quarter of the World that We shall e'er long be obliged to turn our Thoughts to some means of preservation and defence.

After a little more Sleep, a little more Slumber, and a little more folding of the hands to Sleep, We shall awake to terror and dismay. The World around Us on every Side is in too unsettled a State for Us to Sleep always in Security.

Whether our General Court, now in session will Address Mr Jefferson to Stand a Candidate of the next Election, is a problem or theorem.[7] Some think they Will—others say no, because it will excite a disagreable debate. I know not how it will be decided. and indeed am not much interested in the question. If We are to have no national power of a Navy an Army a militia or a Revenue, of what importance is it whether Mr Jefferson or Mr Madison, Weilds the Scepter? or Mr John Randolph?

I wish you a good night,   J. Adams

RC (Adams Papers); internal address: "J. Q Adams Esqr"; endorsed: "My Father 7. Jan^{y:} 1807. / 17. Jan^{y:} rec^{d:}." Tr (Adams Papers).

[1] JQA's letters to JA have not been found. The publication was Samuel Blodget Jr., *Economica: A Statistical Manual for the United States of America*, Washington, D.C., 1806, a

copy of which is in JQA's library at MQA (Catalog of the Stone Library).

[2] See JQA to TBA, 5 Jan., and note 4, above.

[3] Newport, R.I., merchant William Vernon Sr. (b. 1719), who served on the Navy Board of the Eastern Department in Boston from 1777 to 1781, died in Newport on 22 Dec. 1806. His son, merchant William Vernon Jr. (1759–1833), voyaged to France with JA and JQA on the Continental frigate *Boston* in the winter of 1778. Longtime Harvard College treasurer and distant Adams kin Ebenezer Storer died on 6 Jan. 1807; his funeral took place at his home on Sudbury Street in Boston on the 9th (vols. 3:130; 4:124; 5:ix; JA, *Papers*, 21:339, 384; JA, *D&A*, 2:271; Morris, *Papers*, 1:190; "The Trumbull Papers," MHS, *Colls.*, 7th ser., 2:429–430 [1902]; *Princetonians*, 3:120, 125; Boston *Columbian Centinel*, 7 Jan.).

[4] JA had long recommended the study of *Dionysiou Halikarnasseōs*, a history of early Rome by the Greek historian Dionysius (vol. 9:130).

[5] After laying the project aside for more than a year, JA began part two of his autobiography, "Travels, and Negotiations," on 1 Dec. 1806 and completed it in early 1807. He then began part three, "Peace," breaking it off to devote his energies to refuting his depiction in Mercy Otis Warren's *History of the Rise, Progress, and Termination of the American Revolution*, for which see Warren to AA, 11 July, note 4, below (JA to JQA, 30 Nov. 1804, and note 3, above; JA, *D&A*, 4:1, 270).

[6] Conflicting reports abounded in the Boston press on Aaron Burr's activities in the Mississippi valley, for which see JQA to LCA, 8 Dec. 1806, and note 2, above. The Boston *Repertory*, 19 Dec., reported rumors that Burr was preparing an expedition with an unknown goal. The Boston *Democrat*, 3 Jan. 1807, declared that Burr was intent on dismembering the union, while an article in the *Boston Commercial Gazette*, 5 Jan., characterized the former vice president's activities as "Western Rebellion." The Boston *Columbian Centinel*, 24 Dec. 1806, counseled caution, claiming that Burr's alleged force of a thousand men in fact numbered only twenty. The same newspaper, on 3 Jan. 1807, reported concerns that the expedition had foreign backing. The press also reported on Francisco de Miranda's activities in the Caribbean, though without suggesting a connection between the expeditions (Boston *Repertory*, 30 Dec. 1806; *New-England Palladium*, 6 Jan. 1807).

[7] The possibility that the Democratic-Republicans in control of the Mass. General Court would address Thomas Jefferson was proposed by a writer in the Boston *Repertory*, 19 Dec. 1806. In Jan. 1807 the legislature approved a memorial dated 26 Jan. that informed the president that although Massachusetts was "behind most of our sister states in this justly deserved, and highly becoming tribute of approbation," the legislature was moved to declare its esteem for "the wisdom and rectitude of your administration." Jefferson responded on 14 Feb., praising "the progression of sentiment" in the state and anticipating future support from its "enlightened people." The Boston *Repertory*, 10 March, condemned the exchange, opining that the legislature engaged in "the most charming condescension" and the president in response "resolved not to be outdone in this barter of molasses" (Hudson, N.Y., *Bee*, 10 Feb.; *Massachusetts Spy*, 4 Feb.; Boston *Repertory*, 27 Feb.).

Louisa Catherine Adams to John Quincy Adams

Boston ~~Dec^{br.}~~ Jan^{ry.} 7 1806 [1807]

I have impatiently waited for letters, my best friend, having recieved none, since last Thursday[1] I sincerely lament, having mentioned Georges Cough, which though it still continues, will I fervently hope, not be attended with any bad consequences. I take every possible precaution to prevent it, and by Dr. Welsh's advice, do not suffer him to go out of the House, unless the weather is very mild. he may perhaps lose a little time by it from school, but his Lungs have never been strong, since he had the Whooping-cough, and what he loses in English, he perhaps may gain in French—

I am sorry to inform you that Deacon Storer was yesterday found Dead in his bed I never hear'd of it untill just before dinner when Shaw called to let me know it and to bring me the Book which M^r. Duer sent the Funeral is to take place on Friday your Father & Mother are expected in town to attend. which I shall do likewise—

M^r. Osgood as sent an estimate as you requested I know not whether to send it on or send you a copy I believe the latter will be best as I can enclose it in my next if you desire it[2]

Estimate[3]

"Carpenters bill including painting & Glazing	$7000
Masons bill including all other charges	6895.
	13895.

Messrs Clap & White have intimated to me that they will pay one half of the expence of the partition wall between you & their building[4] which will be about $400
The materials of the old building will be worth   400
                                                             800

Which deducted from the first Sum leaves   13095

N. B. We calculated for Slated Roof Plaistering the two first Stories the Silhs of the Shop excepted & the Ceilings of the two upper do—["]

The expence will be somewhat greater than you expected but the advantage would still be great arising from it should you be able to rent it for what you mention'd to me when the idea first occur'd of building

Adieu my best beloved friend tell Mama how anxious I am to hear from her & the Girls give my love Boyds & Hellens families & believe most sincerely yours—   L. C. Adams

J[ohn is] still at Quincy & well

RC (Adams Papers); addressed: "The Honble: / John Quincy Adams Esqr / S. U. S / City of Washington"; endorsed: "Louisa. 7. Jan^y: 1807. / 14. Jan^y: rec^d:." Some loss of text where the seal was removed.

[1] Probably JQA to LCA, 22 Dec. 1806, above.

[2] JQA planned to employ Boston stonemason Peter Osgood to expand his house on Court Street. When he received this estimate he deemed the project too expensive and decided not to proceed (JQA to LCA, 1 Feb. 1807, below; *Boston Directory*, 1807, p. 116, Shaw-Shoemaker, No. 12180).

[3] This word was written in the left margin.

[4] Bookseller Samuel Clap and stationer James White shared a store on Court Street adjacent to JQA's house (Boston *Independent Chronicle*, 3 April 1805, 6 Nov. 1806, 18 June 1807; *New-England Palladium*, 20 March).

January 1807

John Quincy Adams to Louisa Catherine Adams

My dear Louisa.   Washington 14. Jan^y: 1807.

The last Letter I have received from you was that of the 1st: instt: which I answered last week— I then mentioned to you that I had written some lines to Mrs: Hellen, in consequence of your observations in a preceding letter—and that I would send you a copy of them— They are accordingly now enclosed—[1] Of their merit or demerit, a part belongs to yourself, as they were instigated by your remarks; and with a view to shew *some* of that attention which I am sensible is too often neglected by me— It is indeed an attention *in my own way*; and I know not whether it is of a such a nature as you alluded to— However I hope it will give you satisfaction, as Mrs: Hellen was pleased with it.

Saturday Evening, I was with your Mamma and Sisters at a large party at Mr: Madison's— There was a supper, at a small table in one of the lower Rooms, to which the company successively retired by turns in portions sufficient to fill it— The supper *I heard* was very good; for I was not let in to the secret, untill after we got home— Upon which your Sisters enjoyed a good laugh, at my expence.

Sunday, we dined at Mr: Boyd's; whose child I wish I could say was better— We are all very uneasy for it; and it appears to me to be in a situation very similar to that of my brother's child, as you remember it was for three months after it was born, before it took the Dysentary. It is attended by Dr Weems, and one Mrs: Lytle a Quaker woman in high repute as a doctress for children— I believe you know quite as much on the subject as she does— The child seems to be in constant pain—In the Night time particularly, and has kept them up now for many Nights— Mrs: Boyd herself, suffers much in her health, by the fatigue and anxiety she endures— I am suspicious that the child has not sufficient sustenance, and wants *feeding*— This they are very reluctant at believing, and have not hitherto given it any other subsistence— I still hope the child will do well, but am much concerned for it.

We have hitherto had no business to occasion debate; but the House of Representatives have again pass'd a bill for a bridge over the Potowmac; which is now before the Senate, and has already been two or three times postponed— The parties on both sides are warmer than they have ever been before, and I expect we shall have a very animated discussion of the question— The time now fixed for it is next Monday. The General Assembly of Maryland have pass'd a Resolution instructing their Senators to use their influence against it; and Mr: Giles, who is here takes a very strong interest against it— But M$^{r:}$ Bayard and M$^{r:}$ White are quite as zealous in its favour; and as far as I can judge the opinions in Senate are very equally divided—[2] The probability seems to me that the bill will pass—

This day there is a subscription dinner given at Stelle's to Captain Lewis, of which and of its toasts I suppose the newspapers will give account— I shall not be present, though I think Captain Lewis deserves much more than a dinner—[3] Indeed I have no opinion of this species of payment for public services—

Kiss my dear boys for me, and believe me ever affectionately yours

J. Q. Adams.

RC and enclosure (Adams Papers). Tr (Adams Papers).

[1] JQA answered LCA's letter of 1 Jan., above, on 9 Jan. (Adams Papers), reporting on capital social life, discussing finances, and including a paragraph written to his children in French. JQA also commented on the death of Walter Hellen Jr., acknowledging LCA's 28 Dec. 1806 criticism that he be more solicitous of her sister. In this letter of the 14th, he enclosed a transcription of an original eighty-line poem, "To M$^{rs:}$ Hellen. on the 19. Sept$^{r:}$ 1803. and 19. Dec$^{r:}$ 1806." In the poem JQA evoked a scene of Ann (Nancy) Johnson Hellen's deceased children, Washington and Walter Jr., in the presence of a "throne of living light" in heaven: "Oh! Nancy! be that solace thine: / Let Hope her healing charm impart; / And soothe, with melodies divine, / The Anguish of a *Mother's Heart*." The poem was dated 10 Jan. 1807, the same day he sent an original, not found, to his sister-in-law. LCA in a response of 26 Jan. (Adams Papers) reported that the editors of the *Monthly Anthology* were so persistent that she agreed to its anonymous publication as "Lines, Addressed to a Mother, on the Death of Two Infants" (JQA, *Diary*; *Monthly Anthology*, 4:39–40 [Jan. 1807]).

[2] In early 1806 petitions for and against the construction of a bridge across the Potomac River from Washington, D.C., to Virginia occasioned a study by a committee of the House of Representatives. The committee reported on 21 Jan. 1806, recommending approval as a boon to commerce and arguing that placing a draw in the middle of the span could address concerns of opponents who feared it would block passage of merchant vessels to Georgetown, D.C. The legislation was tabled until the next session that began in December, by which time the Md. General Assembly passed a resolution calling on the state's senators to oppose the project. On 29 Jan. 1807 JQA joined William Branch Giles and the majority in voting to table the issue until the 10th Congress, narrowly defeating a bloc in favor that included Delaware senators James Asheton Bayard and Samuel White. A year later, on 22 Jan. 1808, JQA was part of the minority that opposed a bill approving construction, which became law on 5 February. The bridge was completed in 1809 at a cost of almost $100,000 (*Amer. State Papers, Miscellaneous*, 1:437–439; Alexandria, Va., *Daily Advertiser*, 8 Jan. 1807; U.S. Senate, *Jour.*, 9th Cong., 2d sess., p. 134–135; 10th Cong., 1st sess., p. 222–223; JQA to LCA, 1 Feb., below; *U.S. Statutes at Large*, 2:457; Kapsch, *Building Washington*, p. 13).

[3] A dinner in honor of Meriwether Lewis was held at Stelle's Hotel on 14 Jan., after it was delayed several days in unfulfilled expectation of William Clark's arrival in the capital. Lewis was fêted as a "favorite of fortune, who has thus successfully surmounted the numerous and imminent perils of a tour of nearly four years," according to the Washington, D.C., *National Intelligencer*, 16 January. More than two dozen toasts were offered to Lewis, Thomas Jefferson, the expansion of the United States, and the visiting Mandan delegation, for which see Descriptive List of Illustrations, Nos. 4 and 5, above. Joel Barlow read a poem at the dinner that JQA later parodied, for which see JQA to William Smith Shaw, 17 Feb., and note 1, below.

January 1807

Abigail Adams to John Quincy Adams

My Dear Son   Quincy Jan'ry 16th 1807

I think it is full time to take my pen and inquire after Your Health, and to assure you that I should not have been thus long silent if I had not known that Mrs Adams was a constant and punctual correspondent, and would inform You of the welfare of herself and Children.— John has made me a visit of a couple of weeks; on Saturday I brought out George in hopes that a change of air; and a little medicine would cure him of a cough which has been troublesome to him for some time: I think it is better already; he is a very good Boy, and reads well. John went home on monday with the promise of returning when George had made his visit— the situation of Mr Gullivers is very cold and bleak. in summer I think it must be very pleasent. the greatest inconvenience I experience, is that it is so much out of the way of a call, that I cannot hear from them so often as I Should be glad to—

We have enjoyed very good Health through the Winter, which has been in general mild and pleasent, without Snow, a few days of severe cold excepted;

Mr storers family have Sustaind a severe shock by his sudden death.— they were quite overpowerd by the event, Yet both to himself and family it may be esteemed a blessing. his sight was almost extinguishd, and he daily deprecated becomeing useless— he was strongly imprest with the belief that he should not live untill the spring, and said that day: Charles will come too late—[1] he had expected him for several weeks—

Mr shaw has lost his friend Walter which has affected him like the loss of a Brother. he was with him through his Sickness, which was rapid. the bursting of a Blood vessel was supposed to be the cause of his Disease— his death is a loss to Society as he was a Young man of correct Morals, of Genius and Tallents

Mr Burr has occupied much of the public attention. he has led the administration into a labyrinth out of which not even the clue of Adriana will extricate them Mr Jefferson was So much blamed for countanancing Mirandas Wild enterprize, that I cannot but suspect he has committed himself equally by crying ~~the Wolves~~ the Wolfs; when no harm was intended—

I have many unhappy hours upon Mrs smiths account— I fear her situation is more necessitous than She make me acquainted with— I know her prudence and her desire to Economize, that she will make a little go far, but still she must have some means; when you return I should wish you to inform Yourself as fully as you can without wounding her feelings any more than such an inquiry necessarily must—

Your Brother and Father have both written to You repeatedly.[2] I wonder you have not received their Letters— when you See mr Quincy tell him his little daughter is very well, just recoverd from the chicken pox— our little Girl grows finely, and is as playfull as a kitten—

Remember to mrs Johnson and family and be assured of the unabating affection of / your truly affectionate / Mother

Abigail Adams

RC (Adams Papers).

[1] Charles Storer resided in Bellows Falls, Vt., where he raised sheep and served as clerk of a local canal company (vol. 5:ix–x; JQA, *Diary*, 29 Aug. 1833; Patricia and Edward Shillingburg, *The Dering Letters*, 3 vols., Shelter Island Heights, N.Y., 2014, 3:59–61; Lyman Simpson Hayes, *History of the Town of Rockingham, Vermont*, Bellows Falls, Vt., 1907, p. 285–286).

[2] JA's most recent letter to JQA was that of 7 Jan. 1807, above; for TBA's letter of 28 Dec. 1806, see LCA to JQA, 1 Jan. 1807, note 2, above.

Louisa Catherine Adams to John Quincy Adams

Boston Jan$^{ry.}$ 16$^{th.}$ 1807

Your letter of the 6th and the enclosures, arrived safe last evening. I was a little surprized at your appearing *so angry* at the observations made in my letter. I merely meant to insinuate that by now & then addressing *her* particularly in conversation, and leading her to partake of it, she would feel herself highly flatter'd. this my testy friend was all I required, and you must really think me mad, if you supposed that by *little attentions*, I could possibly think of *Chesterfieldian graces*. any one really possessing them, would laugh at the Idea. be good humour'd my friend, and dont imagine, that any thing has been written to me on the subject. on the contrary, all the letters are filled with your praises, but enough on this (to you) very disagreeable subject—

Last night the Columbian Museum, was destroyed by fire. they had been commemorating the last misfortune, which took place three years ago, and owing to some accidental circumstance it caught fire.[1] It is the first serious alarm this Winter I hope it will be the last—

I supp'd at Dr Howards a few nights since where I met all the Sargent Family the old Lady spoke very highly of you and said she regretted that circumstances had arisen to check your former intimacy; hower to use her own words, (do not think me vain,) she was so fascinated with *me*, that she should avail herself of that evening in-

January 1807

troduction, and take the earliest opportunity, to visit me. (dont laugh mon Ami.) Harry is going to be married immediately to little Hannah Wells. and I suspect Daniel who by the by looks very old, is to be married shortly, to Harriet Frazer, this I do not know positively, but M^rs. Sargent told me *two* of her Sons would shortly lead their young Brides to the alter—² She tells me that M^rs. Gardner is her Sister, who resides in your house, that they do not wish to move from your house, but that owing to a *gentleman*, having purchaced a house which is the receptacle of every vice, she is under the necessity of changing her situation.³ they are in hopes you will undertake to *remove* this nuissance, it will not be a very *agreeable* undertaking—

George is still at Quincy with his Grand Mamma, and much better, John is with me, very well. he has nearly forgotten the little french he had acquired, but as you will take him as soon as you return, he will then acquire it very rappidly, I have no doubt—

The Thermometer was below five the day before yesterday, and rose thirty degrees yesterday, these violent changes cannot be good I am sure. Your friends are all well. Joe Hall has been much alarm'd, by a complaint in his lip, which has been for some time thought of a cancerous nature.⁴ it is at length pronounced not to be so to the great relief of his mind—

Adieu, Heaven bless you make the best of the dreadful evils under which you labour and remember you took me for better for worse and if you have so much the worst of the bargain I am sorry for it I have vainly wished to render you happy and it is still and ever will be the most ardent wish of your really affectionate wife   L. C. Adams

P.S. I never knew what Harriet had called her Child till last night the letter you wrote proves that the name is appropriate to the character you gave him I have just heard that seven men lost their lives by the falling of the wall of the Museum during the fire—

Papa John sends his duty says he is a very good Boy⁵

I see by the Papers the Attorney General is dead— write me who is to have his place—⁶

RC (Adams Papers).

¹ The Columbian Museum on Tremont Street in Boston, a gallery of art and curiosities with an associated theater, caught fire early in the morning of 16 January. The fire was attributed to flammable chemicals stored for use in an upcoming show. The tragedy was compounded later in the day when the south wall of the ruined theater fell into the abutting King's Chapel Burying Ground, killing six bystanders ranging in age from eleven to twenty and injuring several others ("Broadsides, Ballads, &c. Printed in Massachusetts,

1639–1800," MHS, *Colls.*, 75:392 [1922]; Boston *Repertory*, 16, 20 Jan.).

[2] LCA dined at the home of Boston physician John Clarke Howard and conversed with Mary Turner Sargent (1743–1813), mother of Boston merchant Daniel Sargent (1764–1842), whose late wife Mary Frazier Sargent JQA had once courted. Daniel's brother, artist Henry Sargent (1770–1845), married Hannah Welles (1779–1841) of Boston on 19 April. Daniel did not marry his sister-in-law, Harriet Frazier (1779–1819) of Newburyport, and LCA in a letter to JQA of 29 Jan. (Adams Papers) reported her mistake (vols. 11:497, 15:419; John H. Sheppard, *Reminiscences of Lucius Manlius Sargent*, Boston, 1871, p. 7, 32, 39; Albert Welles, *History of the Welles Family*, Boston, 1874, p. 117; *Vital Records of Newburyport Massachusetts to the End of the Year 1849*, 2 vols., Salem, Mass., 1911, 1:148; *Gravestone Inscriptions and Records of Tomb Burials in the Granary Burying Ground Boston, Mass.*, Salem, 1918, p. 102).

[3] The Adamses' tenant was Sarah Turner Gardner (1747–1809), sister of Mary Turner Sargent and wife of Boston merchant Henry Gardner (1747–1817) (Harrison Ellery and Charles Pickering Bowditch, *Pickering Genealogy*, 3 vols., Cambridge, 1897, 1:184; Sheppard, *Reminiscences of Lucius Manlius Sargent*, p. 39).

[4] That is, Boston attorney Joseph Hall Sr. (vol. 15:312).

[5] The preceding sentence was written by JA2.

[6] John Breckinridge of Kentucky served as U.S. attorney general from Aug. 1805 until his 14 Dec. 1806 death, which was reported in the *Boston Commercial Gazette*, 15 Jan. 1807. Also on 15 Jan. Thomas Jefferson nominated Caesar Augustus Rodney of Delaware to replace him, and the Senate confirmed the appointment on the 20th (*Biog. Dir. Cong.*; U.S. Senate, *Exec. Jour.*, 9th Cong., 2d sess., p. 48).

Louisa Catherine Adams to John Quincy Adams

Boston Jan[ry.] 21st 1807

How shall I express my gratitude, my thanks, my *admiration*, of your very beautiful lines,[1] my best beloved friend you have more than answer'd my every wish and evidently proved how little trouble it costs you to gain the hearts of all those you wish to please you may smile mon ami but a fond and tender Mother & every human being who possesses real sensibility must feel affection for a man whose heart so truly sympathizes in the afflictions of his fellow creatures; and who can thus delicately offer consolation from the only source from whence it can be found my tears flow every time I peruse them & my heart is filled with sensations utterly impossible to express, but your heart will understand what I cannot describe—

Caroline has had a letter from Buchanon he has not actually offer'd himself but made a sort of insinuation that he shall be happy to meet with an opportunity to do so when they meet should not some favor'd Bostonian become sensible of her worth before that time and seize the invaluable prize.[2] do not mention the circumstance to the family as they would only laugh at her & perhaps disconcert her quite on such subjects she is very tenacious—

I. P. Davies who is at Washington it is here reported is going to be married to Miss Susan Jackson of Philadelphia who passed the last

January 1807

Summer at M^rs: Quincy's to the astonishment of all the World³ Professor Ware likewise finds it impossible to live any longer without a Rib and is going to marry the Widow Lincoln poor Miss Bose—⁴

There has been a Pew advertized to be sold at M^r. Emmerson's for some time had you not better commission Shaw to purchace it if reasonable the meeting house at Cambridge-port is now open M^r. Davenport I suppose will give up the Pew he has at Thatchers—⁵

I understand they are growing quite gay at Quincy & have established a Dancing subscription Assembly your Brother is the leading man in the business⁶ George is still there and very well I tremble for the french John is at home and always asking when march will come he says he wants to see papa as he used always to keep the best Apples for him at Quincy and he was *a very good Papa*— since his return from Quincy it has been impossible to prevail on him to go to school your mother says it is of no consequence and you know I am too much inclined to agree with her in opinion—

Adieu my most sincerely loved friend, I fear I caused you some uneasiness, in what I said concerning our living, I have spoken to M^r. Gulliver and we now go on very well therefore I beg you will not think any thing about it—

That every blessing may await you is the ardent prayer of your tenderly affectionate though I fear undeserving Wife

L. C. Adams

I am much distressed at the indispostion of Harriets Child and still more at their again employing two people physicians I mean to attend tell her the best thing⁷ is to change the air take it to Nancy's for a little while and feed it in very small quantities upon very light food and to wrap it well up in Flannel and not suffer its feet to be exposed to the cold air tell her that your Sister's child was wash'd from head to foot in hot brandy and a broad flannel steep'd in the same kept round its body it must be fresh dip'd twice a day tell her I have seen the good effects of this. otherwise I would not recommend it your Sister child was fed on Arrah Root with a little magnesia stir'd into it once a day while its Bowels were weak give my affectionate love to all and compliments to M^r. Tracy. who is I hope recover'd—

RC (Adams Papers); addressed: "The Honble. / John Quincy Adams Esqr."

¹ For JQA's poem of condolence to Ann Johnson Hellen, see his letter to LCA of 14 Jan., and note 1, above.

² Baltimore merchant Andrew Buchanan (1766–1811) was a widower and father of three daughters with his first wife, Anne McKean. Buchanan and Carolina Virginia Marylanda Johnson were married by Rev. William Emer-

son of the First Church of Boston on 21 July. AA and AA2 attended, and LCA and JQA hosted a reception at their home (LCA, *D&A*, 1:33, 250; CFA, *Diary*, 1:4; Cornelius McKean, *McKean Genealogies*, Des Moines, Iowa, 1902, p. 122; JQA, *Diary*).

[3] Boston attorney Isaac P. Davis (1771–1855) and Susan Jackson (ca. 1785–1867) married in Philadelphia on 12 June. Jackson was the daughter of Susan Kemper Jackson and Philadelphia physician David Jackson and a cousin of Eliza Susan Morton Quincy (CFA, *Diary*, 3:223–224; Beverly Wilson Palmer, ed., *The 1833 Diary of Anna Cabot Lowell Quincy*, Boston, 2003, p. 21, 25; Philadelphia *Democratic Press*, 15 June; Edmund Quincy, *Josiah Quincy*, p. 53–54).

[4] On 9 Feb. Rev. Henry Ware married Mary Otis Lincoln, widow of Benjamin Lincoln Jr. The bride died just eight days later, on 17 February. Her sons from her first marriage were Benjamin Lincoln III and his younger brother, James Otis Lincoln. Ware married again on 18 Sept., to Elizabeth Bowes (1776–1850), daughter of Nicholas and Rebecca Wendell Bowes of Boston (vol. 15:350; Emma F. Ware, *Descendants of Robert Ware of Dedham, Massachusetts*, Boston, 1887, p. 26; Boston *Columbian Centinel*, 18 Feb.; *Sibley's Harvard Graduates*, 7:457).

[5] Pew 45 in Rev. William Emerson's First Church was advertised for sale in the *New-England Palladium*, 13, 20 January. Rufus Davenport was instrumental in the establishment of the Cambridgeport Meeting House, which was dedicated on 1 Jan. (Paige, *Hist. of Cambridge, Mass.*, 1:182–183).

[6] For the Quincy dance assemblies, see LCA to JQA, 20 Feb., and note 5, below.

[7] The remainder of the postscript is written on the fourth page, horizontally through the address.

John Quincy Adams to Louisa Catherine Adams

My dear Louisa.   Washington 1. February 1807.

The Potowmac Bridge question is at last postponed untill the next Session of Congress, after seven days of as warm and close debate as I ever witness'd in the Senate— The postponement was carried by a single vote 17 to 16, and in all probability had the question on the Bill itself been taken, it would have prevailed— I have been so constantly engaged upon it, that I could not find time for writing even to you, more than two very short letters in the last fortnight, and my letters from my mother and brother yet remain unanswered.[1]

The Bridge is for the present dismiss'd; but king Burr furnishes a topic of no less interest and agitation in its stead— Two of his agents *Bollman* and *Swartwout*, who were employed to seduce General Wilkinson and the army, and whom the General seized and sent here, have been committed upon a charge of high Treason; but I suppose they must be sent back to New-Orleans for trial— At least they cannot as I believe be tried here—[2]

I am much obliged to you for the copy you sent me of M[r.] Osgood's estimate of the expence which it would cost to build the place I contemplated in Court Street—[3] The amount is so much higher than I had expected, that I shall be obliged at least to postpone the Execution of the Plan— For although I might possibly borrow money to pay the bills, yet the chance of making it a profitable undertaking is so much lessened by the amount of the sum to be expended that I think it best not to embarrass myself with a heavy debt upon a prospect of remuneration which at best must be uncertain— I shall therefore not abandon the design, but reserve it for an opportunity if it should ever present itself, when I can engage in it, with safety, and without getting too much involved.

I have received in one of your late Letters Riggs's Bill, which together with the other you mention shall cheerfully be discharged—[4] I am sorry that any thing in this matter has given you pain, and once more assure you that so long as I have a dollar in the world it shall always readily be devoted to any thing which in your own Judgment can contribute to your comforts.

I rejoice to learn that upon speaking to M$^{r:}$ G—— you have been better accommodated in the Article of diet—[5] I was indeed much mortified and chagrined at hearing that you had any reason to complain in that respect, and hope it will not happen again— The time is now fast approaching when I hope to return, and to go into our own house— I presume M$^{r:}$ Shaw has informed M$^{r:}$ Bradford that we shall want it at the expiration of his present quarter— You mentioned sometime since that you had a boy with you, who you thought would answer our purpose there— If you still continue of this opinion I wish you to engage him—And also to procure in Season if you can a woman as Cook; for after what we hear of Sally, we must not think of taking her— M$^{r:}$ Bradford's quarter expires I think the 17$^{th:}$ of March; by which day I hope to be in Boston; and I would have you be ready to move without the loss of a day, as soon as the house shall be empty— The inconveniences of the neighbourhood mentioned to you by M$^{rs:}$ Sargent are to be regretted, and certainly I shall use my best endeavours to have them removed.

I thank you sincerely my dearest friend for mentioning the pew for sale at M$^{r:}$ Emerson's; if it can be purchased at a *reasonable* price, I wish Shaw would bespeak it for me— My personal friendship for M$^{r:}$ Emerson concurring with other impressions on my mind induce me to be desirous of *not leaving him*, when I reside in Boston, though as a temporary object the pew which M$^{r:}$ Davenport now holds in the Brattle Street Church would suit me sufficiently.

Within the last fortnight I have dined both at M$^{r:}$ Erskine's and Gen$^{l:}$ Turreau's; and have pass'd Evening's at Miss Lee's, Georgetown, and M$^{r:}$ Erskine's & M$^{r:}$ Madison's in the City— M$^{rs:}$ Lenox and Miss *Keene* are here—[6] The latter a beauty of the most dazzling pretensions— We heard her perform the other Evening on the Tambourine, with all the confidence and all the graces of a gypsey— Her dress is as much admired as her person and manners; and in the poetical vein of D[r:] Thornton[7]

> On her breast she wears a dart
> Which I warrant will make the heart
> Of many a fine Gentleman *smart*.

This morning as I was going to the Treasury to hear M[r:] Laurie[8] I met M[r:] Hopkinson, and M[r:] Hare, who told me that he saw you about three weeks ago, though he did not say where. They are here to attend the Supreme Court, which is to sit to-morrow.[9]

I called at M[r:] Boyd's, and gave Caroline's letter to Eliza. They were all at Breakfast so that we had the anecdote of D[r:] Spring & his patient without going through the indirect course of M[rs:] and M[r:] Boyd before it came to me—[10] I am going there again, to dinner, which obliges me to shorten this letter, that I should else certainly carry through the other page— M[rs] Boyd's child continues at intervals very ill—but is this day more easy— What its name is I never told you because I have not understood that it was finally fixed upon— I heard talk of its being called by *my* name, but never either from its father or mother— Be it called what it may, I pray God it may recover and do well.—

Your's ever affectionately.   J. Q. Adams.

Kiss my dear John for his remembrance of Papa—And George too if he has returned—[11]

RC (Adams Papers). Tr (Adams Papers).

[1] JQA wrote to LCA on 19 Jan., commenting on congressional activity and the extreme cold, advising her on interactions with their landlord, and seeking information on the family's health. He wrote again on the 26th, apologizing that Senate business kept him from frequent correspondence and describing the health of the Johnson family (both Adams Papers). AA's letter of 16 Jan. is above. TBA's letter, not found, was dated 18 Jan. (JQA to TBA, 10 Feb., Adams Papers).

[2] For the arrests of Aaron Burr associates Justus Erich Bollmann and Samuel Swartwout, see JQA to AA, 3 Feb., and note 2, below.

[3] See LCA to JQA, 7 Jan., and note 2, above.

[4] In his 9 Jan. letter to LCA (Adams Papers), JQA enclosed a bill, not found, and asked her to confirm its accuracy. The bill was from Elisha Riggs, a dry goods merchant in Georgetown, D.C. (JQA, *Diary*, 19 Jan. 1808, 2 Sept.; Washington, D.C., *National Intelligencer*, 28 Jan. 1807).

[5] LCA in her letter to JQA of 11 Jan. commented on the quality of food supplied to her under an agreement with landlord Benjamin Gulliver (Adams Papers).

[6] JQA visited on 24 and 29 Jan. the British minister to the United States, David Montagu Erskine; on 30 Jan. James Madison; and on the 31st the French minister to the United States, Louis Marie Turreau de Garambouville. On 21 Jan. he had played cards at the home of Anne Lucinda Lee (1791–1835), daughter of former attorney general Charles Lee, who argued a case before the U.S. Supreme Court on 16 February. He also socialized with Tacy Lukens Lenox (d. 1834) of Philadelphia and her niece Sarah Lukens Keene (d. 1866) (JQA, *Diary*; C. F. Lee Jr. and Joseph Packard Jr., "Descen-

dants of Col. Richard Lee, of Virginia," *NEHGR*, 26:67 [Jan. 1872]; Washington, *Papers, Presidential Series*, 17:26; Madison, *Papers, Secretary of State Series*, 10:496).

[7] LCA later noted that William Thornton was known for his "admirable buffoonery" (LCA, *D&A*, 2:438, 455, 508, 534).

[8] Rev. James Laurie (1778–1853), University of Edinburgh 1800, was a clerk of the U.S. Treasury Department and held services in the treasury building from 1803 until the Associated Reformed Presbyterian Church opened later in 1807 (Sprague, *Annals Amer. Pulpit*, 4:314–316).

[9] The U.S. Supreme Court issued decisions in nineteen cases between 2 Feb. and the 28th (Anne Ashmore, "Dates of Supreme Court Decisions and Arguments," p. 5–6, U.S. Supreme Court, www.supremecourt.gov).

[10] JQA was possibly referring to Marshall Spring (1742–1818), Harvard 1762, a Watertown, Mass., physician who in February was appointed by the Mass. General Court to the board of directors of the Union Bank (Convers Francis, *An Historical Sketch of Watertown, in Massachusetts*, Cambridge, 1830, p. 119–120; Boston *Columbian Centinel*, 14 Feb.).

[11] The postscript was written vertically in the left margin of the third page.

John Quincy Adams to Abigail Adams

My dear Mother.   Washington 3. Feb$^{y:}$ 1807.

I have hardly been able to reconcile it to my own conscience for some weeks that so much time had elapsed since the Commencement of this Session, and that I had not written directly to you— The occasion of my silence has been explained in my letters to my father and my brother, which you have certainly seen—[1] Your favour of 16. Jan$^{y:}$ has been these ten days in my possession, but this is the first time I have found a moment for replying to it.

Our foreign Negotiations are in a state of *suspension*, concerning which a degree of apathy prevails here, not very creditable to our foresight— France and Spain, are obviously waiting *only* for a moment of leisure, to push us with claims and pretensions which when they come will make themselves felt, and the Treaty with England is broken off upon a pretension on our part to which G. Britain will never concede, as I believe, and to which I doubt much whether we ought to require her to concede— How this policy of sleeping on the edge of the precipice will eventually terminate, I hardly dare to enquire; but we must put our trust in Providence much more than in the wisdom or the fortitude of man.

The projects and the transactions of M$^{r:}$ Burr, are giving rise to an extraordinary course of our public affairs— On the one hand we are assured that his conspiracy is altogether impotent; without means; and without resources—while on the other we adopt the most violent and extraordinary measures to counteract them— the President pledges all his responsibility to a state of facts, exhibiting M$^{r:}$ Burr at the head of an expedition to sever the western States and Territories from the Union, *by force*, with the intention to seize New-Orleans and plunder the Bank there, as a preliminary step; and yet he tells us that there is no danger to New-Orleans— At the same time General Wilkinson establishes de facto martial law in New-Orleans, denounces one of the judges, as an accomplice in the conspiracy—seizes and ships off three Citizens of the United States, on the ground that they cannot be safely tried, or even suffered to remain there—And two of these three Citizens upon application to the Judges of this District, have been committed by their order to prison, without bail or mainprize, as upon a charge of *high-treason*. The Senate suspend the privilege of Habeas Corpus, by an Act pass'd in one day: and without a division— At the same time the House of Representatives reject the Bill at its first reading by an almost unanimous vote—[2] By the last accounts Mr: Burr was at the mouth of Cumberland river *encamped* with four or five hundred men—[3]

I have not heard directly from my Sister since I came through New-York— Of her situation then she said not much to me, but I know it was distressing— The Coll: had no occupation, and no rational project or prospect of occupation, and was still flattering himself with the idea of a new Office from the Government— I was gratified however by receiving from him a most positive and unqualified assurance that he had no knowledge of Mr: Burr's purposes against the Union— On my return home I shall make the enquiries you desire, and shall again propose to my Sister to go on with me; if as I apprehend must be the case their situation will make it impossible for them to remain at New-York, keeping house—

I have been once at Mr: Cranch's, and only once since the Commencement of the Session— Their Residence is in a situation much more pleasant than where they were last Winter, though so much more retired that Mrs: Quincy does not like it so well— They are all as well as circumstances admit; and yesterday Mrs: Cranch brought a son in addition to the family.[4]

The Supreme Court yesterday commenced their Session— Judge Cushing and his Lady have been here this fortnight, and are very well—[5] We are also well in the family where I reside, and my own health has been hitherto so unusually good, that I am afraid I shall fatten into laziness—

I remain ever affectionately your's.   John Quincy Adams.

Best remembrance to all the family—And Love to my boy, if either of them be with you.

RC (Adams Papers); endorsed: "J Q Adams / Febry 3 1807."

¹ JQA wrote to JA on 27 Jan., apologizing for not writing sooner owing to "an excessive press of business." He noted that the heavy Senate calendar included debate of a bill to prohibit the importation of enslaved people into the United States, for which see JQA to William Smith Shaw, 17 Feb., and note 3, below. He also discussed court action relating to the Aaron Burr case and described his study of Greek literature (Adams Papers). JQA's most recent extant letter to TBA was dated 13 Jan., for which see LCA to JQA, 1 Jan., note 2, above.

² Thomas Jefferson sent a 22 Jan. message to Congress laying out the case that Burr was engaged in treasonous activities on his western expedition, based largely on accounts from Gen. William Eaton and Gen. James Wilkinson, for which see JQA to LCA, 8 Dec. 1806, and note 2, above. While the president acknowledged that the evidence was "a mixture of rumors, conjectures, and suspicions," he alleged Burr was "the prime mover" in a conspiracy aimed at a rogue attack on Mexico and "the severance of the Union of these States by the Alleghany mountains." The case gained momentum when Wilkinson accused New Orleans judge James Workman (d. 1832) of complicity and arrested four alleged Burr co-conspirators: German physician Justus Erich Bollmann; Burr aide Samuel Swartwout (1783–1856) of New York; and merchant Peter V. Ogden (1785–1820) and attorney James Alexander, both of New Orleans. The four were sent to the federal capital, where on 23 Jan. 1807 the Senate took up a bill calling for a three-month suspension of the writ of habeas corpus in treason cases. A committee that included JQA recommended approval, and the bill passed unanimously the same day. The House took up the bill on 26 Jan. and, after lengthy debate in which opponents argued a suspension was unwarranted, defeated it by a vote of 113 to 19. At the president's urging, District of Columbia district attorney Walter Jones Jr. then sought a writ of habeas corpus before a three-judge panel of the U.S. Circuit Court headed by William Cranch, which granted bail on 30 Jan. to Ogden and Alexander but despite Cranch's dissent ordered Bollmann and Swartwout held without bail. The U.S. Supreme Court took up the case as Ex parte Bollmann in February, issuing a preliminary ruling on the 13th and a decision on 21 Feb. that threw out the case and freed the defendants, thereby setting precedents in defining treason and limiting the power of the executive to order detentions (vol. 11:152; Isenberg, *Fallen Founder*, p. 313–314, 350; U.S. House, *Jour.*, 9th Cong., 2d sess., p. 544–547; Jefferson, *Papers*, 35:670, 44:449; Jackson, *Papers*, 6:29; Clay, *Papers*, 6:1082; Hamilton, *Papers*, 26:218; U.S. Senate, *Jour.*, 9th Cong., 2d sess., p. 130–131; *Annals of Congress*, 9th Cong., 2d sess., p. 401–402, 423–424; R. Kent Newmyer, *The Treason Trial of Aaron Burr: Law, Politics, and the Character Wars of the New Nation*, N.Y., 2012, p. 49, 50, 56, 61–65; JQA to AA, 13 Feb., below). For Burr's trial for treason the following summer, see JQA to LCA, 19 Feb., and note 4, below.

³ The Washington, D.C., *National Intelligencer*, 2 Feb., reported that Burr's expeditionary force numbered "three or four hundred men."

⁴ For the Quincy family's boarding with the Cranch family, see Eliza Susan Morton Quincy to AA, 6 April 1806, and note 2, above. Anna Greenleaf Cranch gave birth to her seventh child, John Cranch (d. 1891), on 2 Feb. 1807 (Greenleaf, *Greenleaf Family*, p. 222; *New-Church Messenger*, 96:242 [14 April 1909]).

⁵ JQA called on the Cushings on 25 Jan. and dined with them at the Cranch home that evening (JQA, *Diary*).

John Quincy Adams to William Smith Shaw

Dear Sir.   Washington 5. February 1807.

I received some days since your favour of the 19. January, and thank you for the information it contains, and for the trouble you have taken in my individual concerns;¹ I should have been happy to hear *frequently* from you; but I have been sensible that the multiplicity of your usual occupations, and the extraordinary call upon your time and attention, by the illness and decease of your excellent and lamented friend Walter, were amply sufficient to justify your silence— I have continued to enclose to you all the public documents; though having also sent a copy of them to my father, I may sometimes have sent a double set to him and none to you— This may have arisen from the hurry with which I am sometimes obliged to make up the packets, and will easily be rectified by yourself on examining the papers received at Quincy.

I am sorry that you have been unable to accomplish the purchase which I was desirous of making when I left Boston— M$^{rs:}$ Adams has written to me that there is a pew in the first Church (M$^{r:}$ Emerson's) advertised for sale— I now regret very much that I sold that I had there; for being determined to resume my residence in Boston, I wish to return to the same place of worship which I have always frequented since my establishment in Boston in the year 1790. My friendship and esteem for M$^{r:}$ Emerson, is a decisive consideration for inducing me to return there now—[2] If the pew advertised is to be had on reasonable terms, I will thank you to *engage* for me the refusal of it— I hope to be in Boston by the middle of next month, when I can come to a final arrangement upon the subject.

M$^{r:}$ Bradford I presume understands that my intention is to go into the house which he now occupies, at the expiration of his present quarter— This I think will be the 15th—(or the 17th) of next month— If it should so happen that I do not arrive in Boston by that day, I shall rely on your goodness for assisting my wife and family in their removal.

I have observed by the Boston papers that the reading-room has been opened, and I hope that the subscribers, and you who have taken so much interest in the establishment, have found it as useful and satisfactory as you have anticipated—[3] I have not received any of the numbers of the Anthology this Winter, nor would I wish you to take the trouble to forward any of them to me; I shall have the pleasure of perusing them after my return— I have seen in the Boston Gazette, some lines upon Walter's death, said to be taken from the Emerald, and with which I was much pleased. My brother writes me that they were to be republished in the Anthology.[4]

M$^{r:}$ Burr and his conspiracy have made so much noise, and fill'd all the newspapers throughout the Union to such an extent that I imagine I can tell you nothing new concerning it— His accomplices Bollman and Swartwout are imprisoned here upon a charge of Treason— But it appears that they cannot be tried here; and there is a great doubt whether they can be convicted of Treason any-where.

There is an application before Congress from the Corporation of

February 1807

the Chesapeake and Delaware Canal Company, requesting that a quantity of the public Lands (about 200,000 acres) be appropriated to purchase shares for the public in that Company— M^r: Bayard has just closed an eloquent speech in favour of this measure— M^r: Giles has just risen in answer to him— I doubt whether the measure will or ought to pass.[5]

The Supreme Court of the United States are in Session, but I have not been able to attend, and learn what they are engaged upon— The whole Court is here; but Judge Cushing has been indisposed and unable to attend—[6] We have pass'd a Bill in Senate to add a seventh Circuit consisting of the three Western States, to the Courts of the United States, and for the appointment of an additional Judge of the Supreme Court— It is now before the House of Representatives—[7]

If you see my brother, I will thank you to tell him I have received his letter of 21. Jan^y: and shall answer it in the course of a few days—[8]

With great regard & esteem, I remain, Dear Sir, truly yours.

J. Q. Adams.

RC (MWA:Adams Family Letters); endorsed: "Washington 5 feb / John Q Adams"; docketed: "1807 / Feby 5."

[1] Not found.

[2] JQA had attended Boston's First Church since Rev. William Emerson took over in Jan. 1802. JQA and LCA's marriage in England was retroactively recorded in the church's records, and GWA and JA2 were both baptized there. JQA purchased a pew in the church on 30 July but sold it after fielding inquiries about its availability shortly before his departure for Washington, D.C., in Oct. 1803 (vols. 8:172–173, 15:160, 473; JQA, *Diary*, 6 Sept. 1787, 10 Jan. 1802, 30 July, 8 Sept. 1803; CFA, *Diary*, 3:14).

[3] The Anthology Society advertised in the *New-England Palladium*, 2 Jan. 1807, that its library and reading room were open in temporary quarters in Joy's Buildings on Congress Street. More than 160 subscribers paid a $10 annual subscription, allowing them and their guests access to more than 1,000 volumes in the collection. Shaw's name was included on a list of eleven trustees. On 13 Feb. an act of the Mass. General Court incorporated the society as the Boston Athenæum, which continues to operate at 10 1/2 Beacon Street (Hina Hirayama, *The Boston Athenæum and the Origin of the Museum of Fine Arts, Boston*, Boston, 2013, p. 17–18, 32, 34).

[4] A lengthy unsigned poem in the short-lived Boston journal the *Emerald; or, Miscellany of Literature*, 1:22–24 (10 Jan.), marked the death of Arthur Maynard Walter. The *Boston Commercial Gazette*, 12 Jan., reprinted the memorial, but the *Monthly Anthology*, 4:88–89 (Feb. 1807), published another unsigned poem eulogizing Walter.

[5] In 1804 the Chesapeake and Delaware Canal Company began construction of a canal to connect the Chesapeake and Delaware Bays, thereby reducing a 500-mile voyage by water to 21 miles. Construction was halted owing to cost, and the company petitioned Congress in Jan. 1806 to publicly fund the project. The proposal was tabled, then brought forward again in Jan. 1807 as a bill that would exchange public land for company stock. JQA opposed the measure, arguing that it was a revenue bill that could not legally originate in the Senate. Tabled again, the bill passed in the Senate in Feb. 1808 but failed in the House of Representatives. Construction of the canal ultimately resumed in 1824, and it opened in 1830 (U.S. Army Corps of Engineers, *Chesapeake and Delaware Canal . . . Environmental Impact Statement*, Phila., 1996, p. 4–40; David P. Currie, "The Constitution in Congress: Jefferson and the West, 1801–1809," *William and Mary Law Review*, 39:1496–1499 [May 1998]; JQA, *Diary*, 10 Feb. 1807).

[6] William Cushing attended the first day of

the U.S. Supreme Court session on 2 Feb. but that night fell ill with fever. Hannah Phillips Cushing reported to AA on 25 April that the justice was severly ill for nearly three months but slowly recovered and was finally able to walk unassisted the day before she wrote the letter (Adams Papers).

[7] The Seventh Circuit Act of 1807 was signed into law on 24 February. The additional circuit covered the states of Kentucky, Tennessee, and Ohio, which at their foundings had been excluded from the circuit system. The law also expanded the Supreme Court from six to seven members, with a requirement that the new member reside within the new circuit. Thomas Jefferson's 28 Feb. nomination of Thomas Todd of Kentucky as the new justice was confirmed by the Senate on 2 March (Michael C. Blumm, Kate Flanagan, and Annamarie White, "Right-Sizing the Supreme Court: A History of Congressional Changes," *Case Western Reserve Law Review*, 72:25-27 [2021]; Thomas E. Baker, *A Primer on the Jurisdiction of the U.S. Courts of Appeals*, Washington, D.C., 1989, p. 5; U.S. Senate, *Exec. Jour.*, 9th Cong., 2d sess., p. 53, 54).

[8] Not found.

Thomas Boylston Adams to John Quincy Adams

Dear Brother   Quincy 8th: February 1807.

When Sunday comes I usually enquire whether I have any arrearges to make up with my correspondents; if I have, it is to me the most convenient season for discharging such debts. Though I have, at present, no letter unacknowledged, I have a variety of documents and journals from you, which deserve mention, because they serve as a substitute in some degree for letters, which we know you have not leisure to write.

I wrote you, in my last, that I had not formed an opinion as to the design of the Ex-Vice President, in his movements to the Westward.[1] We had not then received the Messages of the President, in which he discloses the additional information from that quarter. These go a great way in assisting me to make up my mind; and, if I were called upon now, to give an opinion, as to the views and intentions of Mr: Burr, I should say with Mr: Wood, the Editor who first denounced him, that I believe him *"an innocent man."*[2] What single act has he done of which any legal evidence yet appears of a criminal nature? Did he write that cyphered incoherent scrawl to Wilkinson?[3] And if he did, is it treason or rebellion or insurrection? Our Chief Magistrate and a majority of his Constitutional advisers must have been haunted by the Ghost of General Hamilton to excite this hue & cry against Col: Burr. There never was, in any Government, or in any Country that I ever heard of, such ado about nothing as this whole affair now appears to me. If the reward or price set upon Burr's head were worth stopping the descent of his boats a single day, I have little doubt but he would voluntarily surrender himself. Ten boats and sixty men going to market down the Ohio, produced a bill in the senate of the United states to suspend the privilege of the Habeas Corpus. This

February 1807

beats all the Ocean Massacres and Tub bottom plots, which caused so many sarcasms a few years ago.

But this is not the language of the Presidents adherents. The Proclamation has knocked the treason in the head, and the Commander in chief of the Army has arrested the chief abettors of the illegal combination; the Militia posted on the Ohio & *its waters* have stopped the ammunition boats, and "the most formidable conspiracy, (late or present) of any we know of in history," has thus most providentially been nipped in the bud.[4]

You have heard so much on this subject, that you would willingly dispense with my crude comments. But you will remember that I am only amusing myself, at the publick expense, and attempting to give you some faint idea how happily adapted the recent measures of our Rulers at Washington are to excite mirth; "making that Ideot laughter keep men's eyes, and strain their cheeks to idle merriment."[5]

The proceedings in the Circuit Court for the District of Columbia, upon the motion of M^r: Jones have but one precedent, that of Judge Tallmadge in New York.[6] I expected Judge Cranch would think and act right, as I believe he did.

Your Wife and family have been with us a few days and are in good health; they will return some time this week to Boston.

Since I wrote last, I have agreed with M^r: Frederick Hardwick to let him your Quincy Meadow for five years, at $50 per ann:[7] I prefered this to taking the chance of a tenant at Auction, as I have a good opinion of M^r: Hardwick's circumstances and character. He takes the land unconditionally for that price, which neither of the other applicants would. M^r: Faxon has requested to take back his offer for the Salt-meadow, and to take his chance at Vendue. I consented to it, believing we shall get more for it in that way.

It is not improbable that I shall become your tenant in the house you left—say the old Mansion house in which we were born. I shall be willing to take my chance as a bidder and if the house should be struck off to me, I can dispose of the land adjoining, unless I should want it for some purpose of my own. It is not long since this project was contemplated, and I have embraced it more earnestly on account of some recent letters from our Sister at New York, which make it probable that she will come here this Spring.[8] I shall be, on many accounts better satisfied to live by myself, with my own little family, than as I have done hitherto; though I have every reason to be grateful for the kindness & indulgence I have so long experienced from our parents. If I had sooner determined upon this step I should have communicated it to you; but I had another plan in view, which I think cannot be so readily accomplished. If any objections occur to your mind, as to the fitness of this measure, I beg you to mention them without reserve. It will not be too late to change my purpose, if I hear from you by return of Mail.

With best remembrance to all friends / I am truly Your Brother
T. B Adams

RC (Adams Papers); addressed: "John Q Adams Esqr / Senator of the U S. / City of Washington"; internal address: "J Q Adams Esqr"; endorsed: "T. B. Adams 8. Feb^y: 1807. / 23. Feb^y: rec^d: / 24. D^o: Ans^d:."

[1] TBA's most recent letter to JQA, not found, was dated 28 Jan. (JQA to TBA, 10 Feb., Adams Papers).

[2] John Wood's Frankfort, Ky., *Western World* was a main source of the allegations that Aaron Burr had treasonous intentions in his western expedition, charges that were reported in the Boston press during the summer and fall of 1806. Wood recanted the allegations when called as one of seventeen witnesses in a Frankfort grand jury investigation of Burr in November. The testimony was included in a pamphlet that Wood published on 9 Jan. 1807. The Boston *Independent Chronicle*, 12 Jan., reported that the grand jury not only declined to issue an indictment but went further to "on their oaths, in the heart of the country where he is said to be carrying on his enterprize, declare him innocent!" (Isenberg, *Fallen Founder*, p. 306; Boston *Independent Chronicle*, 25 Aug. 1806; Boston *Repertory*, 14 Oct.; Wood, *Full Statement of the Trial and Acquittal of Aaron Burr, Esq.*, Alexandria, Va., 1807, p. 34–35, Shaw-Shoemaker No. 14235; Alexandria, *Daily Advertiser*, 9 Jan. 1807).

[3] A key piece of evidence against Burr that Gen. James Wilkinson sent to Thomas Jefferson was an undated letter in cipher that was alleged to be a communication from Burr to Wilkinson in which Burr described plans to raise an insurrection in New Orleans, to invade Mexico and West Florida, and to establish an independent nation in the west (ICN: Graff Coll.). Wilkinson curated the information by altering the contents and retaining the cipher code, and it was his transcription that was widely reprinted, including in the *New-England Palladium*, 3 Feb. (Isenberg, *Fallen Founder*, p. 310–315).

[4] The Washington, D.C., *National Intelligencer*, 30 Jan., reported on a skeptical military officer who detained Burr and his recruits on the Ohio River and found "nothing on board that would even suffer a conjecture more than a man bound to market." The newspaper also reported the 26 Jan. House of Representatives debate on whether to temporarily suspend the writ of habeas corpus in treason cases, noting that members described Burr's plans as "formidable, extensive and threatening" and said the conspiracy was "of greater magnitude than any we know of in history."

[5] Shakespeare, *King John*, Act III, scene iii, lines 45–46.

[6] TBA was alluding to Jefferson's refusal to testify before U.S. Circuit Court judge Matthias B. Tallmadge in WSS's trial for abetting the Miranda expedition, for which see JQA to WSS, 16 April 1806, and note 2, above.

[7] Frederick Hardwick was a Quincy cordwainer (vol. 11:234).

[8] Not found.

John Quincy Adams to Louisa Catherine Adams

My dear Louisa.   Washington 9. February 1807.

Since I wrote you last, when we were in the midst of a hurricane from the Northwest, untill this moment, we have had the coldest spell of weather I ever knew in this place— On that day as I wrote you, the windows were blown in and broken down here at the capitol—[1] Houses,

February 1807

or at least one House was unroofed— Carriages were overset; and Mr: Quincy undertaking to walk home was so much overpowered by the gale, that he became faint and dizzy; and but for assistance to carry him home, might have perished on the way— My old Cap however did me its usual service on such occasions; and I walk'd home without suffering more from the cold, or wind than a walk in Winter must always expect— The weather having been so severe here, I am not unconcerned, to hear what it must have been with you— If the cold, or the violence of the Storm was as much greater there than here, as the usual difference of the climate imports, I hardly know how the houses themselves could stand— Since Friday the thermometer has every night been nearly or quite as low as o, but this day the wind has come round to the Southward, and the weather has become comparatively moderate— We had very little snow, which fell the night before the tempest came on; but it is all blown away— The sky has been the whole time clear as a Bell—

I received last week a letter, bearing the Post-mark of *Frankfort, Kentucky*. which upon opening, I found dated Paris 3. Septr: 1806. in french—quite a long, and a remarkably kind letter, without signature, but from its contents I knew it must be from *Pichon*— He speaks with much affectionate esteem of your family, and desires the remembrance of his wife to you— How it got to Frankfort in Kentucky, I cannot imagine— He refers me for information respecting himself to a Mr: *Giraud*, of whom he speaks, as the bearer of the letter—[2] It was originally address'd to me on the back, *at Boston*— But Boston is struck out, and *Washington City*, written in its stead; in a hand-writing which looks to me like *Whitcomb's*— I have suspected that this Mr: Giraud must be in Boston; living at Whitcomb's, and that learning I was here he had given the letter to Whitcomb, to be forwarded, and he made the alteration in the direction— But still I know not how the letter could have got into a Kentucky Post-Office before it came here.

I received on Saturday your letter of 29. Jany: and most heartily rejoyce to learn that you were all well; which I with equal ardour wish you may still remain and hereafter continue.— Mrs: G—— was rather late in her doubts respecting her own condition, and I am glad to learn they were eventually solved to her satisfaction—[3]

Yesterday I dined at Mr: Boyd's; where they are all upon the whole well, though the child is not in confirmed health— We are also well at Mr Hellen— The enclosed from your mamma is for Caroline, to whom as to my dear boys, remember me with the tenderest affection
Your's J. Q. Adams.[4]

RC (Adams Papers).

¹ In a letter to LCA of 6 Feb., JQA described alarmed senators fleeing the chamber when a window was blown in by the storm. He also wrote of support in capital society for the jailed Samuel Swartwout and enclosed a poem satirizing women's fashion. JQA wrote previously on 4 Feb., reporting on the health of family members and recounting developments in the Burr case (both Adams Papers).

² The 3 Sept. 1806 letter (Adams Papers) to JQA from Louis André Pichon, former French chargé d'affaires to the United States, congratulated JQA on his academic appointment but lamented that he would devote less time to politics. Pichon also discussed Franco-American relations and commented on a publication by JA. The letter bears a postmark of Lexington, Ky., 18 Jan. [1807], and was carried there by Marc Antoine Alexis Giraud (1748–1821), French consul at Boston from 1798 to 1815, who spent the winter of 1807 in Lexington (vol. 15:153; JQA, *Diary*, 11 Aug. 1810; François Alphonse Aulard, ed., *Recueil des actes du comité de salut public*, 28 vols., Paris, 1889, 1:392; James Cheetham to Thomas Jefferson, 18 Oct. 1806, DLC:Jefferson Papers).

³ LCA in her letter to JQA of 29 Jan. 1807 (Adams Papers) described a thaw that made icy Boston streets treacherous for pedestrians and commented on the behavior of their children, noting that they looked forward to JQA's return in March. She also reported that Mary Bancroft Gulliver gave birth to a son on 27 January.

⁴ JQA wrote LCA again on 11 Feb., reporting on the health of the Johnson family and forwarding mail, explaining that he mistakenly broke the seal on one letter. He also reported on recent federal appointments (Adams Papers).

John Quincy Adams to Abigail Adams

My dear Mother.   Washington 13. Feb^{y:} 1807.

I have received your kind letter of January; and shall particularly attend to your directions at Philadelphia, respecting the flour—¹ It is at present my intention to leave this place the 4^{th:} of next month; but the winter and the roads are now breaking up; so that I know not whether the roads will at that time be passable—

The termination of this Congress will leave our public affairs in a singular Situation; threatened with War on all sides, external and internal, yet disarming ourselves of all force both of arms and of Revenue— We have now nothing to do— Or rather we do nothing— But I think there must be a special call of the next Congress before December.

We have no further news from M^{r:} Burr since the paper I enclosed to my brother two days ago—²

The Supreme Court have this day decided after long argument that they *have* the power to issue an *Habeas Corpus*, and have accordingly issued the writs for Bollman and Swartwout returnable next Monday— Neither of the Judges, Cushing or Chase, was present.³

I remain in duty and affection, your's.   J. Q. Adams.

RC (Adams Papers); addressed: "M^{rs:} A. Adams— / Quincy / Massachusetts."; docketed: "Feb. 1807"; notation by JQA: "*Free* / John Quincy Adams. / S. U. S."

¹ On 29 Jan. AA wrote to JQA, reporting on visits to Quincy by GWA and JA2 and proposing medicines for use by LCA's family. She also inquired about JQA's opinion on the Burr

case and asked him to settle her flour account with Thomas Allibone as he passed through Philadelphia on his return home (Adams Papers).

[2] In a letter to TBA of 10 Feb., JQA concurred with TBA's uncertainty about Aaron Burr's motives. He enclosed the Washington, D.C., *National Intelligencer*, 11 Feb., which printed a 13 Jan. letter from Mississippi Territory acting governor Cowles Mead to Henry Dearborn reporting that Burr contacted him and maintained his innocence. For Burr's surrender to Mead, see JQA to LCA, 19 Feb., and note 4, below.

[3] For the U.S. Supreme Court decision in Ex parte Bollmann, see JQA to AA, 3 Feb., note 2, above.

Louisa Catherine Adams to John Quincy Adams

Quincy Feby. 15 1807

Being apprehensive that you may be uneasy at not hearing from me my beloved friend I write from your mother's where we have been the last fortnight and where I think we seem likely to remain sometime longer although I at present expect to go into Boston tomorrow Louisa has been very sick and Sister T. B. is confin'd with a bad Breast her Baby grows finely and is one of the prettiest creatures I ever saw still not so handsome as our John who retains his beauty in its highest perfection—

Your Father was for a considerable time much concerned about the bill which passed so rappidly through the Senate and still cannot account for the Vote of a *certain friend* of mine. it never caused me the slightest anxeity as I know your opinions to be generally form'd upon mature reflection and deliberation and almost always correct. he has tax'd me once or twice upon two of your former votes as if he suspected my having been concern'd in the subject, which makes me smile. no woman certainly ever interfer'd less in affairs of this kind than I have, and *if I ever* possess'd any influence, I certainly have never exerted it. however these two Votes, he says, he never can forgive, and I suspect he has since included the last among the number.[1] Is it fair mon Ami, for a man, thus to condemn, without knowing upon what grounds you have acted? I think not, but my judgement is apt to be erronious—

The Boy I mention'd, has left Mr. Gulliver, and is not to be had. his father intends to keep him at School. I do not know where to look for one, but will make enquiries, before you return. I have some time been enquiring for a Girl, and hope I shall be able to procure one who may answer our purpose— I shall be ready to remove the moment you return, which I most anxiously anticipate. they all here endeavor to alarm me, a little by assuring me that the Senate will be detain'd some months after the Session expires. but this I will not believe, it would make me too unhappy. nothing but the period of your absence being limitted, to a short time, could possibly have induced me to stay. I should be too severely punish'd for doing so, if your time is lengthen'd—

You will see by the papers, how much we are like to shine the next Election, two such bright constellations as Judge Sullivan, & Levi Lincoln, cannot fail to add lustre, to the bright hemisphere of Massachusets—[2]

The deposition of Judge Inis, affords a topic of conversation at present, and not a little astonishment. he certainly must be a very profound & learned Judge, to require ten years deliberation, before he could decide how he should conduct himself in such a situation[3] I always thought untill now, that a J. should possess strict integrity, firmness, and decision of char[acter . . .] idea I presume is obsolete—

Adieu my best belov'd friend the Children a[re] both well, John has been quite sick but is entirely recover'd. the Thermometer since I have been here has been as low as 11 in the entry between your Fathers and Sister T. B.s room, and as low as 15 below nought out of Doors. it is now very mild and has raind heavily since yesterday before Sun Rise. every thing is overflow'd, even the bridge by Mrs Blacks. if it continues I think poor Neponset, will be washed away—[4] present my best love to all the family, and believe me most sincerely, & affectionately yours,

L. C. A.[5]

Bring Mrs. Smith home with you if possible Your Mother hopes you will take no denial as it regards John—

The Col. is building a house at Shenang to which Mrs. Smith intends going in the Summer[6]

RC (Adams Papers); addressed: "John Q Adams Esqr."; endorsed: "Louisa. 15. Feb^{y:} 1807. / 1. March rec^{d:} / D^{o:} Ans^{d:}." Some loss of text where the seal was removed.

[1] JA disapproved of JQA's support of the Senate's 23 Jan. bill to temporarily suspend the writ of habeas corpus in treason cases. The Federalist *New-England Palladium*, 13 Feb., shared JA's view, criticizing the bill as giving unbridled license to federal officers to make arrests without evidence of wrongdoing. JA offered only muted criticism of JQA in an 8 Jan. 1808 letter (Adams Papers) that reflected on his son's Senate career and singled out two earlier bills for negative comment: a measure funding the construction of U.S. naval gunboats that passed the Senate unanimously on 18 April 1805, for which see JQA to William Smith Shaw, 27 Dec., and note 7, above, and the Non-Importation Act, passed on 15 April 1806, for which see JQA to TBA, 20 Jan., and note 2, above. While lauding JQA's independence in voting for them, JA called the aims of the bills "ridiculous" and "mere compliments to the silly humours and ignorant Notions of the People" that would ultimately "do little good or little harm" (Robert R. Thompson, "John Quincy Adams, Apostate: From 'Outrageous Federalist' to 'Republican Exile,' 1801–1809," *JER*, 11:176 [Summer 1991]).

[2] The *Boston Courier*, 12 Feb. 1807, was one Boston newspaper that called on Democratic-Republicans "who venerate the *glorious principles of '75*" to elect James Sullivan governor and Levi Lincoln lieutenant governor. Both were victorious in the April gubernatorial

election, with Sullivan unseating incumbent Federalist governor Caleb Strong by a wide margin (Boston *Democrat*, 14 Feb.; Boston *Independent Chronicle*, 19 Feb.; A New Nation Votes).

³ Kentucky federal judge Henry Innes provided a deposition in a trial of fellow judge Benjamin Sebastian for allegedly accepting a bribe from a Spanish official. Innes' deposition reported that in 1797, he, Sebastian, and two Kentucky lawyers were offered $100,000 to help facilitate the creation of a western empire under Spanish control. The deposition was widely published, including in the Boston *Columbian Centinel*, 21 Jan. 1807, and drew the interest of the Adamses owing to Innes' claim that he and an associate kept the offer secret for a decade because neither supported JA's administration, believing that the president "kept a watchful eye over our actions" and was "disposed upon *the slightest pretext* to send an army to this State." Sebastian was convicted and forced to resign. The House of Representatives investigated Innes in April 1808 but declined to issue articles of impeachment (W. E. Beard, "Colonel Burr's First Brush with the Law: An Account of the Proceedings Against Him in Kentucky," *Tennessee Historical Magazine*, 1:13 [March 1915]; W. H. Perrin, J. H. Battle, and G. C. Kniffin, *Kentucky: A History of the State*, 7th edn., Louisville, Ky., 1887, p. 299–300, 578; Washington, D.C., *Universal Gazette*, 8 Jan. 1807; *Salem Gazette*, 16 Jan.; *Amer. State Papers, Miscellaneous*, 1:922–934; Madison, *Papers, Presidential Series*, 6:236).

⁴ Floods caused by the thaw resulted in "immense damage" across southern New England, sweeping away bridges in several towns in Massachusetts and Rhode Island (*Newburyport Herald*, 20 Feb.).

⁵ LCA also wrote to JQA on 17 Feb., thanking him for "the sauciest lines I ever perused" in his poem satirizing women's fashion. She also discussed the hiring of servants for the household (Adams Papers).

⁶ This sentence was written vertically in the left margin of the third page. WSS built a home in Smith's Valley near the Chenango River in central New York. The property was in the town of Lebanon, near the homestead established earlier by his brother Justus Bosch Smith (vol. 12:289; JA, *D&A*, 3:183).

John Quincy Adams to Louisa Catherine Adams

My dear Louisa. Washington 16. Feb[y:] 1807.

The enclosed lines were written as a tribute of my affectionate remembrance, of your birth-day— But though begun upon that day they were not finished untill the next, and the necessity of copying them fair, has delayed their transmission, untill this time.

I have not heard from you of a later date than the 1[st:] of this month; nor have I later letters from any of my friends at Quincy—[1] We have had great changes of weather—rapid and frequent successions of very mild and very cold weather— The *glassy-floor* of the Potowmac mentioned in my Stanzas is already converted into a liquid surface— And we have now a degree of cold sufficient in two or three days to convert it into glass again—

M[r:] Boyd's child continues in frail health, and Eliza has a very severe cough; which however does not confine her from attendance at the parties; of which as the Winter draws to a close the number has become almost oppressive— I have been however almost free from engagements for a fortnight untill last Saturday evening, when we were at Gen[l:] Mason's, at Georgetown— To day I am to dine at the President's and this Evening there is a party at Captn: Thompson's—To Morrow, a Ball at M^rs: Erskine's—Wednesday, Dinner at M^r: Tayloe's—Thursday the Assembly Ball—and Friday, dinner at M^r: Duvall's.— The Assembly I shall escape, and I should much prefer an escape from the rest.²

The Senate this day barely met and adjourned, the Vice-President not attending— His Daughter who is here with him has lain several weeks at the point of Death, and will probably not survive this week.³

We had last Evening a visit from Judge Livingston, Genl: *Van Cortlandt*, and M^r: Verplanck—⁴ They all made obliging inquiries after you; as most of your acquaintance whom I meet always do.

As the Armistice between France and Prussia is concluded I suppose the Peace will soon ensue; but what a terrible intrenchment upon the Prussian army and Monarchy, since we were there— The vicissitudes of this world have reached many of our old acquaintance there; and that beautiful and thoughtless queen, whom we were accustomed to see so splendid has been brought to dance something less delicious and more vivid than a waltz.— I was much affected at an anecdote in the newspapers respecting Prince & Princess Hatzfelt, with Buonaparte—⁵ I suppose that it was one of the french theatricals, but I rejoice that it so happened, that Napoleon that day preferr'd a farce to a Tragedy.

Our Supreme Court are now in Session with Bollman and Swartwout before them; brought in by Habeas Corpus; upon a motion to admit them to Bail.

Adieu, my dear Friend; write me one line in answer to the enclosed, which I may receive before I leave this place— In the meantime I remain affectionately your's.

J. Q. Adams.

ENCLOSURE

Louisa's Birth-day 12. *Feb^y:* 1807.

A Winter's Day.
To Louisa.

1.

Friend of my bosom! wouldst thou know,
How, far from thee, the days I spend?
And how the passing moments flow?

February 1807

To this short, simple tale attend—
When first emerging from the East
The Sun-beam flashes on my curtain,
I start, from slumber's ties releas'd
And make the weather's temper certain.

2.

Next, on the closet's shelf I seek
My pocket Homer, and compel
The man of many wiles, in Greek,
Again his fabled woes to tell.
How true he paints the scenes of life!
How sweet the Poet's honest prattle!
Far sweeter than fierce Ilium's strife
And never-ending fields of battle.

3.

At Nine, comes Moses to my door,
And down stairs summons *me*, with ease;
But on my neighbour calls before,
And knocks,—"Miss Kitty—Breakfast—Please."
Again he louder knocks, and stronger;
Till Kitty answers—"coming, Moses."
And then, in half an hour or longer,
Comes Kitty, just as breakfast closes.

4.

Then forth I sally for the day;
And musing Politicks or Rhyme,
Take to the Capitol my way,
To join in colloquy sublime.
There, with the Fathers of the Land
I mix in sage deliberation;
And lend my feeble voice and hand
With equal Laws to bless the Nation.

5.

The labours of the Senate o'er,
Again with solitary pace,
Down to Potowmac's glassy floor,
My Morning footsteps I retrace.

And oft, dejected or elate,
With painful, or with pleas'd reflection,
In thought, renew the day's debate,
And canvass votes by retrospection.

6.

At home, I find the table spread;
And dinner's fragrant steams invite:
But first the two-fold Stairs, I tread
My atmospheric tale to write—
Then, seated round the social board
We feast, 'till absent friends are toasted—
Though sometimes *my* delays afford
The beef or mutton *over-roasted*.

7.

In bounces Johnson from his school,
A dog's ear'd Webster in his hand—
Repeats his daily-studied *Rule*,
And next his mother takes his stand—
With looks of pure maternal bliss
Mama says—"John, wilt have an Apple?"
And on his cheek imprints a kiss—
His cheek, which rose and lily dapple.

8.

Soon, little Mary too they bring;
And now, we practice every wile;
And clap the hands, and laugh, and sing,
To catch that Heaven, an infant's smile.
Meantime, an apple-paring, whirl'd
Thrice round the head, with mystic ditty,
And forthwith on the carpet hurl'd
Foretells her future Lord to Kitty.[6]

9.

As Eve approaches, I ascend,
And hours of Solitude ensue—
To public papers I attend,
Or write, my bosom's friend, to you.

February 1807

Gaze at the fire, with vacant stare,
Suspended pen, and brow contracted;
Or, starting, sudden from my chair,
The chamber pace, like one distracted.

10.

I see the partner of my Soul,
I hear my darling children play;
Before me, fairy visions roll
And steal me from myself away.
Not long the dear delusions last—
Not long these lovely forms surround me—
Recover'd eyes too soon I cast,
And all is Solitude around me.

11.

My heart, a short depression feels;
And throwing straight aside my pen;
I take the volume that reveals
Their duties and their hopes to men—
Yes! wherefore should I not confess,
This book of sacred inspiration,
Yields to my bosom in distress
Both Fortitude and Consolation.

12.

Anon, the Supper's bread and cheese
Begins, with grave and solemn face;
Till Silence, yielding by degrees,
The festive Spirit takes its place.
Good-Humour comes, with waggish mien
And shakes his sides, with laughter hearty;
And Satire's face, is not unseen
Reflected from the last Night's party.

13.

At last, dispersing, we retire—
Again, the glass's state I learn—
Then, for the Night compose my fire,
And to my lonely Couch return.

There—for my wife—my boys—my friends,
Imploring blessings without number;
E'en while the vow to Heaven ascends,
My sense dissolves in peaceful slumber.

14.

Thus, in succession pass my days,
While Time with flagging pinion flies;
And still the promis'd hour delays,
When *thou* shalt once more charm my eyes.
Louisa! thus remote from thee
Still something to each *Joy* is wanting;
While thy AFFECTION can, to me
Make the most dreary Scene enchanting.

RC and enclosure (Adams Papers). Tr (Adams Papers).

[1] In a brief letter of 1 Feb., LCA reported to JQA on the health of the children and their plans to visit Quincy (Adams Papers).

[2] JQA spent the evening of 14 Feb. at the home of John Mason. On the 16th he dined with Thomas Jefferson, then attended a party at the home of U.S. Marine Corps paymaster James Thompson (1769–1856). On the 17th illness kept him from a gathering at the home of Frances Cadwalader Erskine (1781–1843) and her husband, British minister to the United States David Montagu Erskine. The next night he dined at the home of Col. John Tayloe III, then, as he suggests in the letter, he declined to attend the Washington Dance Assembly ball of the 19th. On 20 Feb. he joined a gathering hosted by comptroller of the U.S. Treasury Gabriel Duvall (1752–1844) (JQA, Diary; Georgetown, D.C., *Independent American*, 7 July 1810; LCA to JA, 29 Nov. 1820, Adams Papers; Thompson to Jefferson, 16 May 1808, DNA:RG 59, Letters of Application and Recommendation; Washington, D.C., *Daily Union*, 18 Oct. 1856; Charles H. Browning, *Americans of Royal Descent*, 2d edn., Phila., 1891, p. 139; LCA, D&A, 1:219, 230; 2:414; *Biog. Dir. Cong.*).

[3] Cornelia Clinton Genet, the daughter of Vice President George Clinton and Cornelia Tappen Clinton and the wife of former French minister to the United States Edmond Genet, died of tuberculosis on 23 March 1810 (vols. 8:273, 275; 10:ix; North Callahan, *Thanks, Mr. President: The Trail-Blazing Second Term of George Washington*, N.Y., 1991, p. 54).

[4] JQA was visited by Brockholst Livingston, a recently appointed U.S. Supreme Court justice, and Gen. Philip Van Cortlandt (1749–1831) and Daniel Crommelin Verplanck (1762–1834), two U.S. representatives from New York (vol. 11:464–465; LCA, D&A, 1:230, 2:418; *Biog. Dir. Cong.*).

[5] The Washington, D.C., *National Intelligencer*, 13 Feb. 1807, reported that an armistice between France and Prussia was signed at Berlin on 16 Nov. 1806 following the Prussian defeat at the Battle of Jena a month earlier, for which see JQA to TBA, 5 Jan., and note 11, above. JQA was premature in his prediction of peace, however, as Frederick William III refused new demands by Napoleon after the armistice and fled east with Queen Louise Auguste Wilhelmine of Mecklenburg-Strelitz. Prussia formed a new alliance with Russia in April and continued the war until the coalition capitulated in June and agreed to the Treaty of Tilsit. The press also carried a report of Friederike Karoline, Princess von Hatzfeldt (1779–1832), wife of Prussian diplomat Franz Ludwig, Prince von Hatzfeldt, with whom JQA and LCA had socialized in Berlin. The account claimed Napoleon spared the prince's life after a personal appeal by his wife (Clive Emsley, *The Longman Companion to Napoleonic Europe*, N.Y., 2014, p. 10–12; Christopher Clark, *Iron Kingdom: The Rise and Downfall of Prussia, 1600–1947*, Cambridge, 2006, p. 307–308, 312; New York *Public Advertiser*, 5 Feb.; LCA, D&A, 1:129; Deutsche Biographie, www.deutsche-biographie.de).

February 1807

⁶ An American folk tradition holds that the peel of a whole apple swung around the head and thrown to the floor will form the letter of a future spouse's first name (Fletcher Bascom Dresslar, "Superstition and Education," *University of California Publication in Education*, 5:16 [15 July 1907]).

John Quincy Adams to William Smith Shaw

Dear Sir.　　　　　　　　　　Washington 17. February 1807.

I received in proper time from you, a copy of Selfridge's trial, and also the Anthology for January, for which you have my best thanks; and in return for which I now send you a blossom for the next month's basket— I hope your council of Literary botanists will not be of opinion that some of its petals are too rank for the sense; however it is entirely at your and their disposal.—¹ You must shew it to M^(rs:) A— before the publication, as she has a right to see every thing of the production of this soil; but if she should in return shew you another, though a more fragrant flower, which I sent her yesterday, you will perceive that that cannot be fit for publication—

Bridge-fighting, which has been as much in fashion here this winter as at Boston, has subsided for the Session—² The slave bill has almost pass'd the two houses of Congress; and there is nothing else to detain us here, excepting the custom of staying here untill 3. March—³ But the Supreme Court are *full* of business— Bollman and Swartwout are now before them on return to a writ of *Habeas Corpus*, and two motions in their behalf are under argument; one to discharge them; and the other to *Bail* them for appearance at the Court in New-Orleans— The Senate have pass'd a Bill to regulate the summoning of Grand-Jurors, which will excite *your* attention— But it has not yet pass'd the house of Representatives.⁴

Your's with the greatest regard & esteem.

RC (MWA:Adams Family Letters); addressed: "William S. Shaw Esqr / Boston / Massachusetts."; internal address: "W. S. Shaw Esq^(r:)"; endorsed: "John Q Adams"; docketed: "1807"; notation by JQA: "*Free* / John Quincy Adams. / S. U. S."

¹ JQA enclosed a poem he had written the evening before, which parodied a poem by Joel Barlow on the Lewis and Clark expedition. Barlow's work appeared in the Washington, D.C., *National Intelligencer*, 16 Jan., after it was read at a 14 Jan. banquet in Meriwether Lewis' honor. In it Barlow extolled the explorer's "soaring genius" and proposed that the Columbia River be renamed for him. JQA, who did not attend the banquet, suggested in his parody that Lewis had no expectation of such a tribute and, in a barb aimed at Thomas Jefferson, compared it to renaming Sally Hemings "Isabella." The board of the Anthology Society approved publication of JQA's poem at a 26 Feb. meeting, and it appeared anonymously in the *Monthly Anthology*, 4:143–144 (March 1807), accompanied by commentary making it clear that Barlow rather than Lewis was the target (Albert Furtwangler, "Captain Lewis in a Crossfire of Wit: John Quincy Adams v. Joel Barlow," in James P. Ronda, ed., *Voyages of Discovery: Essays on the Lewis and Clark Expedition*, Helena, Mont., 1998, p. 237–

238; JQA, *Diary*, 14 Jan., 16 Feb.; Mark Antony DeWolfe Howe, "The Capture of Some Fugitive Verses," MHS, *Procs.*, 43:239 [Jan. 1910]; *Journal of the Proceedings of the Society Which Conducts the Monthly Anthology & Boston Review*, ed. Mark Antony DeWolfe Howe, Boston, 1910, p. 104–105; JQA to LCA, 14 Jan., above).

² The Mass. General Court in February debated a petition calling for the construction of a second bridge from Boston to South Boston north of an 1805 bridge across the same channel. The plan pitted South Boston developers against merchants whose wharves would be cut off by the new bridge. The proposal was presented annually from 1806 until 1811 when a riot put it to rest for more than a decade. The bridge was finally constructed in 1828 (vol. 15:330; *Boston Commercial Gazette*, 29 Jan. 1807; *New-England Palladium*, 3 Feb.; Nancy S. Seasholes, *Gaining Ground: A History of Landmaking in Boston*, Cambridge, 2018, p. 243–244). For congressional debate of a proposed bridge over the Potomac River, see JQA to LCA, 14 Jan., and note 2, above.

³ On 8 Dec. 1806 Stephen Row Bradley of Vermont introduced a bill in the Senate to ban the transport of enslaved people into the United States. The action followed Jefferson's call for such a measure in his 2 Dec. annual message to Congress, for which see JQA to LCA, 2 Dec., and note 1, above. The president's recommendation anticipated the expiration of a clause in the U.S. Constitution that delayed implementation of a ban until 1808 and paralleled current debate in Parliament of a prohibition of the British slave trade that received royal assent on 25 March 1807. After Senate debate on 15 and 16 Jan., the measure passed on 27 Jan. "without a division." JQA twice observed House debate on the bill, which passed on 13 Feb. by a vote of 113 to 5. Jefferson signed the Slave Importation Act on 2 March. Effective on 1 Jan. 1808, the law also outlawed the outfitting and financing of slave trade vessels in U.S. ports and set punishments for violators of up to $20,000 in fines and jail terms of up to ten years. The milestone legislation stemmed direct international trade to the United States from Africa even as many U.S. traders continued to operate as middlemen, smugglers, and traders under the flags of other nations and the domestic slave trade continued (JQA, *Diary*, 8, 23 Dec. 1806; 15, 16, 26, 27 Jan. 1807, 10 Feb.; Hugh Thomas, *The Slave Trade: The Story of the Atlantic Slave Trade: 1440–1870*, N.Y., 1997, p. 550–552, 556; *Annals of Congress*, 9th Cong., 2d sess., p. 32–33, 35–36, 47, 486; *U.S. Statutes at Large*, 2:426–430; Leonardo Marques, *The United States and the Transatlantic Slave Trade to the Americas, 1776–1867*, New Haven, 2016, p. 56–72).

⁴ On 6 Feb. JQA was appointed to a committee to draft a bill that would require district attorneys to obtain judicial approval before summoning federal grand juries. A resulting bill passed the Senate 12 Feb. but was rejected by the House on 3 March (U.S. Senate, *Jour.*, 9th Cong., 2d sess., p. 141, 147; U.S. House, *Jour.*, 9th Cong., 2d sess., p. 642; U.S. Senate, *A Bill to Regulate the Summoning of Grand Jurors*, Washington, D.C., 1807, p. 1–2, Shaw-Shoemaker, No. 13875).

John Quincy Adams to Louisa Catherine Adams

My dear Louisa. Washington 19. Feb^{y:} 1807.

Since I wrote you last[1] I have been a little affected with the rhumatism in my shoulder, so that I did not attend at M^{rs:} Erskine's Ball— I had also something of a cold, and was disinclined to be out so late at Night as a Ball necessarily imports— Your Mamma and the Girls were there; the company was numerous and the party very agreeable.

We have this day received a Message from the President, containing letters from our Ministers in England, from M^{r:} Armstrong, and from the Secretary of the Mississippi Territory— The first mentions that they have fully agreed upon all the points of Negotiation with the British Commissioners, and had nothing further to do but to draw up

February 1807

and sign the Treaty, which would be done in a few days, and would be satisfactory to our Government.[2]

The letter from M[r:] Armstrong encloses his correspondence with the french Minister of Marine respecting the Imperial Decree, declaring the British Islands in a State of Blockade— The Minister assures M[r:] Armstrong that our navigation will be as far protected as our Treaty with France has provided.[3]

The letter from M[r:] Meade, informs that M[r:] Burr and his party, about a hundred men, and boys, had surrendered himself; and was under confinement for trial.—[4] As you enjoined me to write you politicks, I take the first moment to inform you of this very important intelligence.

The Supreme Court have bailed Swartwout and Bollman untill tomorrow—when they are to decide finally whether they shall be discharged or bailed.— Your's ever affectionately.   J. Q. Adams.[5]

Love to Caroline and the boys.

RC (Adams Papers). Tr (Adams Papers).

[1] JQA to LCA, 16 Feb., above.

[2] On 19 Feb. Thomas Jefferson submitted to Congress a 27 Dec. 1806 letter from James Monroe and William Pinkney in London announcing they had that day signed an Anglo-American trade treaty. The U.S. diplomats negotiated with Henry Richard Vassall Fox, 3d Baron Holland, and William Eden, 1st Baron Auckland, from 27 Aug. to 31 December. Great Britain agreed to drop opposition to the lucrative U.S. re-export trade between France and the French West Indies, accept a more favorable definition of contraband, provide official notice of port blockades, and reduce duties on U.S. imports. In exchange the United States agreed to observe a moratorium on new trade restrictions against Britain, accept new restrictions on trade with the British East Indies, and maintain a neutral stance toward Britain. When the treaty arrived in Washington, D.C., on 3 March 1807, it met with the president's disapproval because it was silent on impressment and included a provision giving tacit U.S. sanction to British retaliation against France, which Jefferson viewed as deal-breakers. The president informed a joint committee of Congress the same day that he would not submit the treaty for consideration, and it never took effect. Instead, Anglo-American tensions continue to rise as the United States instituted the Embargo Act of 1807, for which see TBA to JQA, 27 Dec., and note 3, below (Washington, D.C., *National Intelligencer*, 20 Feb.; Donald R. Hickey, "The Monroe-Pinkney Treaty of 1806: A Reappraisal," *WMQ*, 3d ser., 44:65–67, 73–74, 78 [Jan. 1987]; JA, *Papers*, 18:56; U.S. Senate, *Jour.*, 9th Cong., 2d sess., p. 152; Monroe, *Papers*, 5:554–561).

[3] Jefferson on 19 Feb. submitted to Congress a 24 Dec. 1806 letter from U.S. minister to France John Armstrong Jr., enclosing two letters exchanged with the French minister of marine Denis Decrès regarding Napoleon's 21 Nov. Berlin decree. The order commenced France's Continental System by closing all European ports to British ships and neutral vessels that traded with Britain and declaring that any neutral ship adhering to British trade policy was liable to seizure by France. On 10 Dec. Armstrong inquired if the decree applied to U.S. vessels, and on 24 Dec. Decrès replied that in his view it did not represent a change in policy toward U.S. shipping, citing the Franco-American Convention of 1800. Britain responded to Napoleon's decree with an Order in Council of 7 Jan. 1807 prohibiting neutral trade to all enemy ports (*Amer. State Papers, Foreign Relations*, 2:805–806; David S. Heidler and Jeanne T. Heidler, *The War of 1812*, Westport, Conn., 2002, p. 25–27; Wood, *Empire of Liberty*, p. 646; Hoefer, *Nouv. biog. générale*).

⁴ Cowles Mead, Mississippi Territory acting governor, wrote to the secretary of war Henry Dearborn on 19 Jan. announcing he had negotiated Aaron Burr's surrender. A Mississippi grand jury convened on 2 Feb., and while it declined to return an indictment, Burr was ordered to remain on hand. Instead he fled and was arrested on 19 February. On 5 March Burr was sent under guard to Washington, D.C., but rerouted to Richmond, Va., where he arrived on 26 March. A U.S. Circuit Court grand jury considering treason charges returned indictments on 24 and 25 June. Burr's trial, presided over by John Marshall, began on 3 August. Testimony centered on Burr's intentions, with prosecution witnesses claiming he made treasonous statements and defense witnesses testifying that the charges were exaggerated. On 1 Sept. the jury returned a verdict of not guilty, finding that Burr's actions did not constitute an "overt act of war." The prosecution raised the possibility of charging Burr in Ohio or Kentucky, but Marshall ruled on 20 Oct. that there were no grounds for further charges, ending Burr's legal jeopardy but leaving the former vice president disgraced and deep in debt (Isenberg, *Fallen Founder*, p. 319–324, 335–337, 346, 349, 350–352, 362, 363, 367–368, 498).

⁵ JQA wrote again to LCA on 27 Feb., reporting that the impending close of the congressional session required unrelenting work. He also commented on capital society and the spring weather (Adams Papers).

Louisa Catherine Adams to John Quincy Adams

My best friend   Boston 20 Feb$^{ry.}$ 1807

Tomorrow week being the 1$^{st.}$ March I presume this must be the last letter I address to you at Washington supposing you will set off on your journey home the earliest opportunity after the Session closes—

I yesterday recieved your favor of the 9$^{th.}$ and was rejoiced to find that you supported the extreme severity of the Cold with so much philosophy Poor Quincy, what would he have done here when even the *Wells* at Quincy were frozen and a Bottle of spirit of Heartshorne standing on the Chimneypiece in my Chamber were a fire is constantly kept was frozen solid¹ I have already told you the Thermometer has been more than once at 15 below no 0 and frequently at ten— I hope you will take every possible precaution to guard against the Cold when you travel—

The melancholy circumstance which took place in Cambridge has no doubt reached you ere this letter will arrive poor M$^{r.}$ Ware what a dreadful situation for his family this marriage astonish'd every person who was acquainted with the parties and this dreadful termination has been too convincing a proof of the justness of their apprehensions it is supposed that the violent opposition of her eldest Son to the marriage and the agitation caused by the change in her situation brought on one of her fits of insanity in which she so Violently put an end to her existence—²

I was much surprized at the letter you mention and cannot concieve how it could possibly get to Kentucky unless the Gentleman intended upon quitting Boston going to Washington and from thence

February 1807

to Kentucky, but having changed his plan forwarded it by the post. this is mere conjecture and if it carries the Boston post mark a very erronious one—

I am however very happy to hear of the welfare of that family they were always very interesting to me more particularly Madame who I thought a lovely woman[3]

Do write me if a certain family were ever invited to the great House this Winter[4] the extreme anxiety expressed last Season has induced me to ask the question—

Mon Ami, I count the hours till you return. your Brother tells me, your absence has produced great alteration in my looks Dancing three or four dances at the Quincy Ball so perfectly exhausted me I was sick two days. your poor Aunt Cranch will never get over the shock she has recieved she takes infinite pains to convince all the wicked persons concern'd in this sinful business that dancing is absolutely forbidden in Sripture and exhorts them to give up the idea of having any more but it is in vain I find there is to be another on Wednesday fortnight in spite of Mr. Norton and Mr Strong two ministers who have thought proper to preach publicly against them this appears to have produced its usual effect and acted as a spur[5] Breisler is going to take Mr. James Bracketts house to build a Ball room over the Shop and to open an *Hotel* for the benefit of recieving company in the Summer Season and Sleighing parties in the Winter all this upon a *large scale*—[6] I understand Mr. Obadiah Thayer wishes to take your house his Lady desires to have a *handsome habitation* in the Country—[7]

God bless you my best beloved fr my heart Throbs to behold you the Children are as anxious as myself for your return and we all anticipate the hour which brings you back with delight, but none so sincerely as your very affectionate wife   L C Adams

George is going to Atkinson with Shaw on a visit to his Aunt—

RC (Adams Papers); addressed: "John Q Adams Esqr."; endorsed: "Louisa. 20. Feb^{y:} 1807. / 3. March rec^{d:} / 8. D^{o:} Ans^{d:} Philadelphia."

[1] Spirit of hartshorn is a liquid ammonia solution used as smelling salts that is derived from the horn of the hart (*OED*).
[2] For Mary Otis Lincoln Ware's death, see LCA to JQA, 21 Jan., and note 4, above.
[3] That is, Alexandrine Émilie Brongniart Pichon, wife of Louis André Pichon (vol. 15:153).
[4] For the strained social relations between Thomas Jefferson and former British minster to the United States Anthony Merry and his wife, Elizabeth Death Leathes Merry, see vol. 15:318.
[5] LCA attended the subscription dancing assembly with TBA and AHA and found the "very long Country dance" particularly fatiguing. Mary Smith Cranch's opposition to dancing dated to at least 1771 when she and Richard Cranch told JA that they would not send their children to dancing school. The pastors

in opposition were the Cranches' son-in-law Rev. Jacob Norton of Weymouth, and Rev. Jonathan Strong (1764–1814) of the First Church of Randolph (LCA, D&A, 1:247; JA, Diary, 2:46–47; JQA, Diary, 17 Jan. 1786; Sprague, Annals Amer. Pulpit, 2:275–276).

[6] Capt. James Brackett, a third-generation tavern keeper, operated a public house at the corner of Elm and Hancock Streets in a building constructed after 1795. Brackett rather than John Briesler Sr. appears to have embraced the plans; in 1809 he opened a Quincy hotel with a ballroom on Hancock Street near the Neponset River (vols. 12:328; 14:139, 216; Sprague, *Braintree Families*; Pattee, *Old Braintree*, p. 168–169; Herbert I. Brackett, *Brackett Genealogy*, Washington, D.C., 1907, p. 550).

[7] Probably Boston merchant Obadiah Thayer (b. 1766) and wife Elizabeth Thayer Thayer, who had family connections to Braintree (*Boston Directory*, 1806, p. 120, Shaw-Shoemaker, No. 50652; *New-England Palladium*, 1 Jan. 1805, 7 April 1807; Sprague, *Braintree Families*).

Abigail Adams to John Quincy Adams

My dear son   Quincy Feb^{ry} 27 1807

I fully designd writing to you so that my Letter Should have reachd you at washington, but ten days of very severe Sickness has prevented me from holding a pen, and now I do it against many expostulations. I duly received Your two kind Letters, and thank you for them.[1] Mrs Adams caroline and the two Boys made me a very pleasent visit of a fortnight. I enjoyd their Society in my usual health, but a day or two after their return to Town, I was most Seriously taken very sick with a kind of Influenza very prevalent at this time, which brought on a racking cough and all my old Rheumatic complaints. so here I am fastned to one chamber, and Nancy to the other with a Broken Breast; but hope lives Eternal and we both hope soon to be better— my present intention in Writing, was not to give you this history which might well have been spared, but to express to you my extreem anxiety respecting your Sister, and to request you to converse freely and fully with her, and to prevail with her to break up Housekeeping as I have written to her, and come and spend the summer with us—with her Children She has written a Letter to Your Father, which from the best motives and intentions I did not give him, but requested her to write an other[2]

I could say many things to you which would not be proper to write, and your own mind will furnish You with some of them— there are delicacies to be observed towards those who are in distress which every person You know does not feel I need not add any thing further. your family were all well yesterday—

I am my dear son Your / affectionate Mother   Abigail Adams

RC (Adams Papers); addressed by TBA: "John Q Adams Esq$^{r:}$ / New York"; endorsed: "My Mother 27. Feb$^{y:}$ 1807. / 12. March rec$^{d:}$— New York."

[1] JQA's letters to AA of 3 and 13 Feb. are both above.
[2] The letters from AA to AA2 and AA2 to JA have not been found.

Louisa Catherine Adams to John Quincy Adams

Boston March 6th. 1807

I write you my beloved friend in the hope that half your journey will be perform'd when you recieve this letter and that it may be the last I may have occasion to write.[1] my impatience to see you is becoming so great, minutes seem hours, and days years. Though I endeavour to laugh at my folly, but even my dreams partake of this folly, and after passing the night in idea with you I wake mortified and depressed at finding it nothing but an *illusion* the dread of a disappointment hangs upon my mind and half destroys the sweets of anticipation. how shall I thank you my friend for the beautiful lines I recieved from you[2] did I possess the talents of Sapho I would answer you but alas the Muses never smiled on me and I can only attempt to express my gratitude and affection in bad prose and trust to the heart that so sweetly expresses its own feelings to understand and justly appreciate mine—

Mon Ami I am sorry to have unpleasant news to communicate Mr. Bradford refuses to quit your house and has grossly insulted Shaw in the Street who was fortunately prevented from knocking him down.[3] having engaged Servants as you desired I know not what to do and anxiously wait your return Mr. Gardner intends to remain in the other and we are all at a stand it is strange conduct in this man as Shaw gave him notice when he paid his last quarter if you should be here on the 15 you may perhaps be able to do something with him yourself— This news of Shaws and not hearing from you has so completely depressed me that I am not able to write any thing that can give you one moments pleasure

Your Mother has been very ill but is now quite recover'd Sister T. B. A. is still very sick and I fear will have a long confinement The Children and Caroline are well and I shall be well when I have the happiness of clasping you once more to the heart of your tenderly / affectionate Wife   L. C. Adams

RC (Adams Papers).

[1] JQA departed Washington, D.C., for Baltimore by stage on 5 March, reporting to LCA from Philadelphia on 8 March (Adams Papers) that he had arrived there by packet the day before. He then traveled to New York by boat and stage. In New York he suggested to AA2 that she, John Adams Smith, and Caroline Amelia Smith travel with him to Massachusetts for an extended visit. She accepted, and they departed by packet on 15 March, ar-

riving in Providence, R.I., on the 17th and traveling by stage to Boston on 18 March. Upon arrival the travelers discovered that LCA and her children had moved two days earlier from their rented quarters to one of JQA's houses at the corner of Frog Lane and Nassau Street. AA2 and her children went to Quincy on 19 March and remained in Massachusetts until 11 Jan. 1808 (JQA, *Diary*, 9, 10, 11, 12 March 1807; JQA and GWA to LCA, 24 May 1806, note 3, above; AA to AA2, 14 Jan. 1808, below).

[2] JQA to LCA, 16 Feb. 1807, and enclosure, above.

[3] Joseph Nash Bradford did not vacate JQA's second house at Frog Lane and Nassau Street until 16 May (JQA, *Diary*, 15, 16 May).

Abigail Adams to Mercy Otis Warren

My Dear Mrs Warren   Quincy March 9th 1807

To your kind and friendly Letter I fully designd an immediate replie,[1] but a severe attack of a Rheumatick complaint in My Head has confined me to My Chamber for several weeks and renderd me unable to hold a pen. tho recovering from it, my head still feels crakd; Shatterd I am sure it is— You will therefore pardon any inaccuracy I may commit. My Health which You so kindly inquire after, has been better for two years past, than for Many of those which preceeded them. I am frequently reminded that here I have no abiding place. I bend to the blast. it passes over for the present and I rise again.

Your Letter my dear Madam written so much in the stile of Mrs Warrens ancient Friendship, renewed all those Sensations which formerly gave me pleasure, and from which I have derived sincere and durable gratification, and I anticipate a still closer and more cordial Union in the World of Spirits to which we are hastning, when these Earthly tabernacles shall be moulderd into Dust.

If we were to count our Years by the revolutions we have witnessed, we might number them with the Antediluvians. so rapid have been the changes; that the mind tho fleet in its progress, has been outstriped by them, and we are left like statues gazing at what we can neither fathom, or comprehend.

You inquire what does Mr Adams think of Napolean? If you had askd Mrs Adams, she would have replied to you in the words of Pope—

> If plagues and Earthquakes break not heavens design
> Why then a Borgia or a Napoline?[2]

I am Authorized to replie to your question, What does mr Adams think Napoleon was made for? "My answer shall be as prompt and frank as her question. Napoleons Maker alone can tell all he was made for. in general Napoleon was, I will not say made, but permitted for a catoninetails, to inflict ten thousand lasshes upon the back of Europe as divine vengeance for the Atheism Infidelity Fornications, Adulteries Incests, and Sodomies, as well as Briberies Robberies Murders Thefts Intrigues and fraudelent Speculations of her inhabitants—and if we are far enough advanced in the career—and certainly we have progressd very rapidly—to whip us for the Same crime's—and after he has answerd the end he was made, or permitted for—to be thrown into the fire— now I think I have merritted the answer from Mrs Warren which she has promised me to the Question, What was Napoleon made for?"[3]

May I ask mrs Warren in my turn, what was col Burr made for? and what can you make of him or his projects? enveloped in as many Mystery as Mrs Ratcliffs castle of udolphus?[4] how he mounted to power we know, and a faithfull historic page ought to reord, and after he had answerd the end for which he was permitted, we know how he fell. what is yet left for him to perform, time must unveil.

I thank You My dear Madam for Your inquiries after my Daughter— She was well a few days Since. She had Letters from her son dated in Nov'br he was then at Trinidad where he expected to pass the Winter.[5] a don Quixot expedition which could never have met with his Grandfathers or My assent or consent, if it had been known to us before he had saild.[6] it has been a source of much anxiety to us, and to his Mother.

I cannot close this Letter, without droping a sympathizing tear with you over the remains of Your beloved Neice, and my valued Friend.[7] She was from her Youth all that was amiable Lovely and good, the youthfull companion of my daughter. I always saw her with pleasure, and parted from her with regreet. she was endeard to me by the misfortunes of her Youth which from her Strong Sensibility, and dutifull affection, I was frequently made the depositary of her sorrow and tears— She always exprest for me a sincere Regard. when I learnt her new engagement, knowing the delicate state of her Health, I feard she might find it too arduous for her, but her companion She had long known, esteemd and valued as his Many virtues deservd[8]

Heaven spared her to act well the Mothers part towards her sons, to whom she devoted herself and having reared them to Manhood, for wise ends, which we cannot comprehend—took her out of Life—[9] what can we say, but that the ways of Heaven are dark and intricate—[10]

I pray You to present mr. Adams's and my regards to Gen'll Warren— we both of us rejoice to hear that he enjoys so much health at his advanced period of Life. we shall always be happy to hear of the welfare of Friends whom we have loved from our early Years and with whom we have past many, very many social hours of pleasing converse, in unity of Bond and Spirit.

With Sincere Regard / I Subscribe Your Friend

Abigail Adams

RC (MHi:Warren-Adams Papers); endorsed by James Warren Jr.: "M^rs. Adams & Answ^r / Mar 1807"; notation: "No 24." Dft (Adams Papers).

[1] In the Dft, AA continued, "but it so happend that my house was then and for a fortnight after full of company to which I was obliged to attend." Warren's letter is that of 28 Dec. [1806], above.

[2] Alexander Pope, *Essay on Man*, Epistle I, lines 155–156. AA wrote in the Dft, "cataline," reflecting the language of Pope's original.

[3] JA separately drafted a response to Warren's query (JA, Comments on Napoleon, [9? *March 1807*], Adams Papers), which AA copied into the text here with minor changes.

[4] Ann Radcliffe, *The Mysteries of Udolpho*, 4 vols., London, 1794. In the Dft, AA instead completed this paragraph: "it looks like tweedle dum & tweedle dee—like the tale of the Tubs—and many other unfathomable Mysteries—that there must be more penetration to see through a mill-stone than I am possesst of, to give a shape and coulour to his transactions—a Man like cain pursued by his own conscience—and a wounded spirit who can bear."

[5] Not found.

[6] In the Dft, AA instead finished this paragraph: "it has made his Mother unhappy, and the concequences to the family are such as any person of common Segacity might have foreseen."

[7] In the Dft, AA continued, "like a daughter I loved her," in reference to the death of Mary Otis Lincoln Ware. A mark at the end of the seventh paragraph refers to a note at the bottom of the third page: "M^rs J O B. Lincoln—daughter of James Otis."

[8] In the Dft, AA added: "I hoped she would find the happiness she anticipated."

[9] In the Dft, AA continued, "it could be no act of her own— she was a woman who feared God and walked uprightly."

[10] Joseph Addison, *Cato*, Act I, scene i, line 45.

Elizabeth Smith Shaw Peabody to Abigail Adams

Atkinson March 9th. 1807

It is a long time my Dear Sister, since I have written to you;[1] but I consider it a priviledge that we can *think* of our Friends, animate our Souls by a view of their useful lives, & refresh ourselves by a retrospect of past scenes, when we cannot find one leisure moment to visit them, or impress our Ideas upon paper.—

Ever since Thansgiving we have had one, or other of our Family sick in bed, or confined to their Room. We have had a large Family all winter, & we ought to be grateful to heaven, that we are continued in Being, while so many of our dear Friends in the course of the last year, are numbered among the Dead. My eldest Brother Oakes Shaw, I see by the publick Papers, has finished his ministry on Earth, & is now, I hope, joined the redeemed of the Lord—[2] Every valuable Connectition taken from us, should increase our Zeal in the service of our heavenly Master And when we see that *our Day* is far spent, may

March 1807

we be found with our Lamps trimed & burning, ready to attend our final Summons. It was painful to me, that I could not see you last Fall. Oh! how rejoiced I should have been, to have had the President & my Sister made us such a friendly visit, as they kindly intended, but though we were dissappointed of that honour, I hope, it will be put into your hearts, to make us a visit this Spring,—Perhaps, the weather may be more salubrious, & much more pleasant when the days are growing longer, & when Nature assumes her most mild & charming Aspect,—than when the falling leaves lie whithered upon the sable ground, & Earth with a mournful face, sees the Herald of the shortest Days, when she must be buried in cold, & ice—& Snow—

All the Ideas respecting the advanced age of our friends had fully impressed my mind, before I received your last letter—& the uncertainty of life, & of ever seeing each other again are often in my thoughts—But hope, is the balm of Life, & the pleasure of seeing each others Face, I fondly cherish—[3]

My Son was very unfortunate in the time of his visit here— My help were all sick, & I could not speak scarcely one word, Lydia has had a disorder, a humour in her feet, which has for six weeks disenabled her from walking, & Nabby Leach was sick a bed—[4] And Abby had just got about house— I pitied myself, & him too, poor little George, will never want to come again— Though I was relieved at my Lungs so as to speak by monday, though it hurt me, that I dare not say much— George appeared very fond of my Son—& he is really a fine Child— He had two new hankercheifs, which Abby hemed, marked one, but had not time to mark the other— If miss Susan will mark it for him I will thank her—

Mr Peabody was at Haverhill, & heard that Miss Adams was very sick— You my Sister have suffered greatly in the same way, & know how to pity h[er]

My Love, & tender regards to all your family, & my Brother & Sister Cranch—

The Stage calls, & I can only add what I always am, your affectionate / Sister   Elizabeth Peabody

RC (Adams Papers); addressed "To Mrs Adams—"; and by Stephen Peabody: "Honble. John Adams Esqr / Quincy"; docketed: "Mrs Peabody / 1807." Some loss of text where the seal was removed.

[1] Peabody's previous extant letter to AA was of 11 Aug. 1806, above.
[2] Rev. Oakes Shaw (b. 1736), Harvard 1758, pastor of the West Parish Church of Bridgewater, Mass., and brother of Peabody's first husband, John Shaw, died on 11 Feb. 1807 (JQA, *Diary*, 18 April 1787; Frederick Freeman, *The History of Cape Cod*, 2 vols., Boston, 1858, 1:587; *Newburyport Herald*, 27 Feb. 1807).
[3] AA's letter has not been found.

[4] In addition to the illness of servant Lydia Springer, Peabody reported the indisposition of Abigail Leach (b. 1791), daughter of Benjamin and Abigail Harriman Leach of Haverhill (F. Phelps Leach, *Lawrence Leach of Salem, Massachusetts, and Some of His Descendants*, 3 vols., East Highgate, Vt., 1924–1926, 3:141).

Abigail Adams to Elizabeth Smith Shaw Peabody

My dear Sister   Quincy June 10th 1807.

If I had written to You my dear Sister half as often as I have thought of you, and contemplated writing, you would have had a Letter by every Mail for these two months: I have to acknowledge the receipt of two kind Letters from You, since I have made you any return the last bearing date May 29th, which came last week to hand,[1] and to which I should have replied yesterday by a Young Man who lives with us who was going home for a week, and has promised me to call and tell you how we do: and bring me word of your welfare; I attempted writeing to you yesterday, but the weather had become so suddenly so intencely hot, that my feeble frame sank under it, and renderd me wholy unfit for any exertion of body or mind; To day an Easterly wind has given me new Life and spirits, and I determined, no longer to delay returning you thanks for Your kind favours which always do my Heart good; tho they are so spareingly bestowed that I have frequently to regret, that talents so brilliant and powers so harmonious and touching, should not more frequently be displayd for the improvement, and edification of those who know how to appreciate their value.

I know You can plead a thousand cares and avocations which necessarily devolve upon you; surrounded as you are by your numerous family, in which you are continually doing good, and communicating it to others, knowing so well as you do, that we live not to ourselves.[2]

My own Family when collected together consists of 21 persons. Mrs Smith, John & Caroline have been these three weeks in Boston upon a visit to my son J Q Adams, who with his family are residents in Boston. I say residents, because they mean to take their flight in the fall like the Birds of passage to the southward— I shall inform Mrs smith of your kind invitation to her and her children— she is a woman of great firmness of mind you know, from her youth up— she has had ample Scope for the excercise of it, in the visissituted of fortune which have attended her. to herself are confined her troubles. she never makes them a subject of complaint to her most intimate Friends—but they evidently wear upon her spirits, and produce many a silent tear— her present Situation is painfull to her. her future prospects . . .[3] we see but a little way into futurity—"Or who could Suffer Being here below"?[4]

This world we are told is our school may we all of us improve aright, the usefull Lessons we are taught.

I hope Lydia has recoverd, and that you will make us a visit soon. we are now, all in pretty good health. I have recoverd from the disorders which confined me, from the first week in Feb^{ry} untill the middle of April. I was threatned with a Lung fever for many days, which finally terminated in an Eruption upon the skin, which with its dissagreable qualities gave me one pleasure—that of Scratching—

Mrs T B Adams hopes you will come before she makes her visit to Haverhill, or not untill her return. She will go there the first week in july. my little name sake is a sweet Child—pretty enough I think— I have little John with me too— Susan is grown to the stature of a woman before she is in her teens—a great misfortune to have the Body out grow the mind— I never saw two children more different in their turn of mind behaviour and tempers than Caroline Smith and Susan— I sometimes think of what mr Joseph Dyar, used often to say to me when I was young and very wild, Nabby you will either make a very bad, or a very good woman—[5] Caroline is soft in her manners compliant in her temper and disposition, yealding to the opinions of those whom she considers her superiours—and every way engageing— a thread would govern one, a cable would be necessary for the other— Yet time is doing, much for her—and reason and argument begin to take hold, and make impression which give hopes that a very good woman may be made from seeds sown. If you had been near me, I should have sent her to you long ago; but the distance has been an obstacle— she has a strong mind and a generous, temper. she is not proud haughty or envious—but an ardent temper, and a spirit of contradiction odious in Youth— You have had a variety of tempers and dispositions to deal with— how would you manage one, upon whom you could not impress any subordination—any true defference to age, or relation or Rank in Life?

how hard it is to rule the spirit and govern the tongue—

Brother and sister Cranch are well. Mrs Norton looks very thin— She is indeed Multiplied in children— I hope she will live to see them a comfort to her, and reward her for all her toil and trouble

Your son is well—envoloped in science a promoter of literature with all his Heart and soul and strength— no man engages more Zealously, or is more persevering. there is some talk of his sacrificeing to the

Graces— he will not however acknowledge it yet I belive he has his favorite—and in time will make it appear so, if other circumstances are favorable— I have at length prevaild upon him to get him a peice of linnen, and Mrs Smith with susan & caroline have made it up; and a very good peice it was—but he wants a care which neither you or I can help him to—a stich in time—and a care of his own things, and indeed a knowledge of them— a Man whose mind is So engrosed with great objects—cannot descend to the minutiea of an odd sock—a raggid ristband &c &c—

My Love to my dear amiable Neice I hope she will accompany You. my best respects to mr Peabody in which we all join— I shall tell John Smith what you have written respecting him. he is the Same in mind and Manners that he early presaged—

Pray my dear Sister do not let it be long e'er you make us all happy by seeing and embraceing you with that sincere and tender affection which has ever subsisted between us—and which still burns with undiminished fervour / in the bosom of your Sister

Abigail Adams.

RC (DLC:Shaw Family Papers); addressed: "Mrs Elizabeth Peabody / Atkinson."

[1] Peabody to AA, 9 March, above; the 29 May letter has not been found.
[2] Romans, 14:7.
[3] Ellipsis in MS.
[4] Alexander Pope, *Essay on Man*, Epistle I, line 80.
[5] Weymouth yeoman Joseph Dyer (1731–1807) was AA's childhood neighbor (*History of Weymouth*, 3:213; Norfolk County Probate Court, Canton, Mass.:Norfolk County Probate, 14:350).

Abigail Adams to Ann Harrod Adams

[*post 6 July 1807*][1]

commit this hasty scratch of My pen to the flames my dear Nancy. it is written more to shew you how much I bear you in mind, and how tenderly I love you than to afford you any entertainment—a mere chit chat Scrible—not half so Elegant so refined so sentimental as my dear Daughters to her ever affectionate / Mother   Abigail Adams—

Present me kindly to all your family. Mrs smith caroline John and susan all send a thousand Loves & kisses for our dear Babe— even juno & Theatis would embrace her

RC (private owner, 2021); addressed: "Mrs Ann Adams / Haverhill."

[1] The dating of this letter is based on AHA's July visit to Haverhill, departing on the 6th and returning prior to the 21st (AA to Elizabeth Smith Shaw Peabody, 10 June, above; JQA, *Diary*, 5, 21 July).

June–July 1807

Mercy Otis Warren to Abigail Adams

Plymouth M^s: July 11th: 1807.—

Though your last Letter was not immediately answered, I offer no apology but my own frequent infirmity.[1] It was, my dear Mrs Adams, a very pleasant circumstance to me, to receive an account from your own hand, of your appreciated health, nor did I find in your late letter, any marks of the shattered condition of your head, of which you complain.— Indeed, I think the bough that bends to the gale, and rises again, is sometimes invigorated and prepared to meet a fresh blast.— So, our feeble constitutions, may be renewed and strengthened, after the storms that assail us have passed by.— Certainly, the head of my friend appears as intelligent as before her late attacks, and I have no doubt her heart is as firm and sincere as ever.— These combined, I hope will long delight your correspondents and improve the moral feelings in the circle of your associates.—

I am glad to hear your daughter has had agreeable tidings from her son;—no one can more easily conceive than myself, the anxiety of a mother for a beloved son drawn into danger and distress, by the deception, the cruelty, or the weakness of men.— But, the stricken deer may be silent, though she can never cease to weep.—[2] What a variegated scene has my long page of life exhibited!— The fate of my amiable neice, is one of those inscrutable events, which at once surprizes the beholder and admonishes to silent adoration and submission, while it ought to inspire a lively sense of our dependence on that Being who lends both reason and life, and has a right to resume his blessings in what time and manner he sees fit.— Dear hapless child of sorrow!— She long struggled with the storms of life, but "the winds were not always tempered to the shorn lamb."—[3]

I thank Mr Adams for his prompt reply to my question relative to Napoleon:—when replying, methinks I saw his brow, his air, his manner, exactly as I have usually seen it in the days of our more frequent intercourse.— Long used to hear the free expression of his opinions, it seems like a revival of old habits to which age sometimes recurs with the same relish that in youth, it tasted its cakes and sugar-plumbs.—[4]

The *permission* of Bonaparte to execute judgment upon sinners, Mr Adams has displayed with energy,—but when he ceases to be the scourge of kings and of nations, I hope he is not to be *thrown into the fire himself*.—

What may be the result to the civilized world, of the conduct of the

Emperor Napoleon, is beyond the ken of human sagacity.— This singular man acts undisguised in the full face of meridian day, prompted by an ambition & by designs that are bounded by no horizon.— Yet he may be an agent in the divine hand finally to ameliorate the condition of mankind, when they have been sufficiently punished for their cruelty and crimes, to bring them back to reason and justice.—

Mr Adams asks me what I think of Col$^o.$ Burr?—a full reply to this question might lead to a longer page than he has leisure to read;—yet I will observe that I think him *permitted by his Maker* to exhibit to the world another instance of the abuse of superior talents.— But I will not attempt to draw his character—the fibres and cords of the heterogeneous materials which compose it are so entangled, and the tints which are discovered on the surface require a finer pencil and a more dexterous adept in the researches of human intellect, human depravity, and the capacity for virtuous improvement in the human soul, to delineate with just precision.— He is now arraigned at the bar of justice and of law, where the intricacies of his intrigues will doubtless have a clear developement;—then some *faithful historic page* may record his rise and his fall, and give a just portrait of his character, and an ample detail of his abilities and his crimes, of his perfidy and his fate.—[5]

Mr Warren with myself, at all times reciprocate the expressions of regard and respect from our friends at Quincy.— I sometimes amuse myself with the fanciful idea of listening to a long political conversation between the two venerable sages, your husband and mine;—but it seems to me to resemble the fabulous dialogues of the dead.—

I am glad to see the name of your son on the conspicuous list that has determined to support the measures of Government against the insults & aggressions of the old inveterate foe of America.—[6] Make my Compliments to him—tell him I wish him success in the honorable pledge he has given, to maintain to the last the independence of his country which his father had so considerably shared in obtaining.

I am, my dear friend, as ever, / Y$^{rs.}$ Mercy Warren[7]

RC in James Warren Jr.'s hand (Adams Papers); endorsed: "Mrs Warrens / Letter july 1807."

[1] AA to Warren, 9 March, above.

[2] Mary Pilkington, *Rosina: A Novel*, 5 vols., London, 1793, 3:150.

[3] Laurence Sterne, *A Sentimental Journey through France and Italy. By Mr. Yorick*, 2 vols., London, 1768, 2:176.

[4] The long friendship between the Adamses and Warrens, tested by political differences over the years, further frayed after Warren's portrayal of JA in her *History of the Rise, Progress, and Termination of the American Revolution*, 3 vols., Boston, 1805, which JA believed

6. THE *CHESAPEAKE* AND THE *LEOPARD*, BY IRWIN JOHN DAVID BEVAN, CA. 1875–1940
See page xii

misrepresented his views on monarchy, his diplomatic missions in Europe, and his demeanor as a statesman. On the same day that Warren wrote this letter to AA, JA wrote the first of a sixteen-letter exchange with the author, declaring, "I am not about to write a Review of it. . . . But as in those Passages which relate personally to me, there are Several Mistakes. I propose at my Leisure to point out Some of them to you, in the Spirit of Friendship." In a 16 July response, Warren wrote that while she anticipated "criticisms of great and little men" she had "uniformly endeavoured to write with impartiality, to state facts correctly, and to draw characters with truth and candor." JA wrote to her again on 19 Aug., comparing her writing to "magpie chatters" containing "egregious Errors," and criticizing James Warren's political career. Mercy Warren closed the exchange on 27 Aug., charging JA with engaging in "rancour, indecency, and vulgarism" and demanding an apology if their correspondence was to continue (JA to Warren, 11, 20, 27, 28 July, 3, 8, 15, [17], 19 Aug., all MHi:Warren-Adams Papers; Warren to JA, 16, 28 July, 1, 7, 15, 27 Aug., all MHi:Mercy Otis Warren Papers). No further letters were exchanged until AA wrote to Warren in Dec. 1809, for which see AA to AA2, 8 Dec. 1808, and note 6, below.

[5] For Aaron Burr's trial, see JQA to LCA, 19 Feb. 1807, and note 4, above.

[6] On 10 July JQA served on a committee of Boston citizens that drafted a resolution condemning the attack by the British warship *Leopard* on the U.S. frigate *Chesapeake*, for which see Descriptive List of Illustrations, No. 6, above (Boston *Democrat*, 11 July).

[7] Signature in Warren's hand.

Thomas Jefferson to Louisa Catherine Adams

Madam   Monticello Aug. 8. 07.

I have duly recieved your letter of the 28th. of July expressing a wish that your brother could find some emploiment in New Orleans in which his knolege of the French & Spanish languages might be made useful.[1] it would have been pleasing to me to have been able to point out such an emploiment, & more so to add that any such was within my powers of appointment, but the only appointments I make there, or in any department, are of the highest officers. they alone appoint to all subordinate places under them. in N. Orleans the Governor, Collector, Naval officer & Surveyor of the port are of my appointment: but each of them appoints those under them; and being responsible for their underagents, are left uncontrolled in their choice as is just. I can do no more therefore than indicate the true sources of appointment there to which your brother should apply. I tender you at the same time the assurances of my high respect & consideration.   Th: Jefferson

FC (DLC:Jefferson Papers); internal address: "Mrs. L. C. Adams."; docketed by Jefferson: "Adams L. C. Aug. 8. 07."

[1] LCA's letter has not been found. Thomas Baker Johnson had relocated to New Orleans by March 1808. He continued to seek a federal post, requesting but not receiving an appointment as commissioner of the territorial land office from James Madison on 10 March and earning a recommendation from Orleans Territory governor William Charles Cole Claiborne in a 14 Dec. letter to Albert Gallatin (vol. 10:346; Madison to Johnson, 10 March, ViU; Clarence Edwin Carter, ed., *The Territorial Papers of the United States*, 28 vols., Washington, D.C., 1934–1975, 9:812; LCA, *D&A*, 1:196; 2:461).

July–August 1807

John Quincy Adams to Catherine Nuth Johnson

Boston 18. August 1807.
Quarter past nine O'Clock in the Morning.

My dear Madam.

I take the first moment of self-possession that I have to inform you that my dear wife at half-past eight this morning presented me a third son.— The labour which commenced about 2 O'Clock this morning was extremely severe, and the child and mother both suffered so much in the birth as to give us great concern—[1] We had at first little hopes of the child's life; but it is now and M^{rs:} Adams also as well and better than we could have expected.— I hope in the course of a few days that she herself will give you a favourable account of both; and in the mean time with our affectionate regards to M^{rs:} Hellen, M^{rs:} Boyd and the families remain, Dear Madam, ever truly your's

John Quincy Adams.

RC (Adams Papers); addressed: "M^{rs:} Johnson. / Washington."; internal address: "M^{rs:} Johnson."

[1] Charles Francis Adams (d. 1886), designated as CFA in *The Adams Papers*, was born on 18 Aug. (Sprague, *Braintree Families*).

John Quincy Adams to Catherine Nuth Johnson

Dear Madam.   Boston 20. August 1807.

As the account I gave you the day before yesterday may occasion you some anxiety on ~~her~~ my wife's account, it gives me the most cordial pleasure now to inform you that she is as well as under the Circumstances could possibly be expected, and the infant remarkably hearty and Strong— My Sister Smith came in from Quincy the morning of the child's birth and has been with M^{rs:} Adams constantly since.

I remain, Dear Madam, ever-faithfully your's.

John Quincy Adams.

I write a few lines to say that I am doing very well and that the little Gentleman is likely to do so too he is born to be lucky as you say having come into the World as Harriet did—[1]

RC (Adams Papers): addressed: "M^{rs:} Johnson / Washington City."; internal address: "Mrs. Johnson."

[1] LCA added the preceding paragraph.

Abigail Adams to
Louisa Catherine Adams and John Quincy Adams

Dear Children   Quincy October 25th 1807

I address you jointly and congratulate You upon the fine weather we have had since you commenced Your journey I hope e'er this day, You have reached Washington ~~in safety~~ with Your Dear little Boy, for whose safety, I was not a little anxious through so long and fatigueing a journey. We had the pleasure to receive a Letter from You, informing us of Your arrival at New york—[1]

The week after You left us, Your Father and I undertook a visit to Atkinson to carry George— it really appeard as formidable as a journey to Philadelphia used to, when we were accustomed to make it Annually. we found our Friends all well, and desirious of making Master George happy. it was vacancy and mr & Mrs Vose were gone a journey. there are two lads from Baltimore one of them near George's age with whom he will be very companionable, and what you will consider more fortunate, there is a very geenteel Young French Gentleman of about 17 who attends mr vose to learn the English Language; who was quite pleasd, to find George speaking French, I requested that he would Speak always French to George; by which means I hope he will not lose what he has already acquired— I could not but admire to see how readily George enterd into all the rules, & regulations, of the Family, appeard quite at home, and attachd himself to Mr Peabody as if he had always lived with him. When we left him, he did not express any desire to return, only desired that I would write to you that he determined to be very good, One of the best Boys in School.

John I sent to his Aunt Cranch's he goes to School every day, but is not quite so well weaned from Grandmamma as George. to day being sunday I brought him home to dine but he could not consent to go to meeting, without I would promise to take him home with me to night; So here he lies upon the cushing in My chamber eating an apple very happy. When he does not see me he is quite content— I told him I was writing to you, and he desires I would say that he is a very good Boy.—

our Family are all getting over their great colds. News we have not any to communicate, but are waiting to hear what the Great counsels will do & say when they assemble— Let us hear frequently From you—

and remember me affectionatly to your Mother and other connextions—

Your affectionate / Mother   Abigail Adams

RC (Adams Papers).

[1] See JQA to AA, 27 Oct., and note 1, below.

John Quincy Adams to Abigail Adams

My dear Mother.   Washington 27. October 1807.

I wrote a line to my father, from New-York, enclosing a letter for Mr: Shaw, and informing you of our safe arrival thus far, upon our Journey.—[1] We stopp'd at New-York two days, and then proceeded with as much expedition as we found practicable, untill we reached Baltimore. We stopp'd only one Night at Philadelphia, and had no opportunity to visit any of our acquaintance there— We came on in the water Stage by the Newcastle and Baltimore Packets, and although, not at all favoured by the winds travell'd with less fatigue and as much dispatch as we could have done by land.— At Baltimore we spent a couple of days with Mr: and Mrs: Buchanan, and found Mrs: Johnson there on a visit to her daughter— She returned with us to this place, where we arrived on Saturday Evening, much fatigued, but thanks to Heaven all safe, and in good health—[2] The child appears to bear his travels to a charm, and has been less troublesome than we had found either of his brothers before him.

Yesterday the Congress assembled— In the House of Representatives appeared one hundred and eighteen Members— In the Senate, twenty-five—a greater number of both houses than I have known to be here on the first day of the Session, at any former period.

Mr: Varnum was chosen Speaker of the House, without much competition, Mr Macon the former Speaker not being here; and Mr: Nicholas of Virginia who was expected to be a candidate, being likewise absent— Mr: Magruder was elected Clerk of the House, after numerous ballots, and some electioneering debate.[3]

We have this day the President's Message, of which I shall if possible enclose a copy by the Mail of this Evening—[4] Its character is that of caution rather than of ardour; and by the dispositions which I have as yet been able to discern among the members, the *fear* appears very much to predominate over the *desire* of War.

The Employment of the present week I suppose will principally consist of attendance upon the *Races*.⁵

We long to hear from our friends at Quincy, and from both our boys— We have yet had nothing since we left Boston.

Affectionately your's   John Quincy Adams.

RC (Adams Papers); addressed: "M⁽ʳˢ⁾ Abigail Adams. / Quincy."; internal address: "M⁽ʳˢ⁾ A. Adams—"; endorsed: "J. Q. Adams / 1807."

¹ JQA's letter to JA of 17 Oct., not found, enclosed one for William Smith Shaw of the same date, where JQA reported on his travels and the health of his family and asked Shaw to ship them items mistakenly left in Boston. JQA wrote again to Shaw on 28 Oct. and 7 Nov. (all MWA:Adams Family Letters), seeking assistance with his financial affairs (JQA, *Diary*).

² JQA, LCA, and CFA departed Boston on 10 Oct. by stage to Providence, R.I. The trio embarked by packet for New York on the 11th but owing to faint winds did not reach the city until the 16th. The trip then proceeded as JQA described, with the travelers reaching Washington, D.C., by the Baltimore stage on 24 Oct. (JQA, *Diary*).

³ The 1st session of the 10th Congress convened on 26 Oct. and did not adjourn until 25 April 1808. In the absence of Nathaniel Macon of North Carolina and Wilson Cary Nicholas of Virginia, Gen. Joseph Bradley Varnum of Massachusetts was voted Speaker of the House with 59 votes. Former Maryland representative Patrick Magruder was elected clerk of the House of Representatives, also with 59 votes, a post he occupied until 1815 (*Annals of Congress*, 10th Cong., 1st sess., p. 9–10, 382, 781–782, 783–785, 2284; *Biog. Dir. Cong.*).

⁴ The central topic of Thomas Jefferson's 27 Oct. 1807 annual message to Congress was the 22 June *Chesapeake-Leopard* Affair, for which see Descriptive List of Illustrations, No. 6, above. Noting that in a proclamation of 30 July he called on Congress to convene early to consider a response, the president declared, "On this outrage no commentaries are necessary. Its character has been pronounced by the indignant voice of our citizens with an emphasis and unanimity never exceeded." Jefferson also noted that on 2 July he had issued a proclamation ordering coastal defenses bolstered and expelling armed British ships from U.S. waters. In concluding his annual message he called on Congress to fund a standing army, create a maritime militia force, and appropriate funds for warship construction (*Annals of Congress*, 10th Cong., 1st sess., p. 9, 14–18; *Amer. State Papers, Foreign Relations*, 3:23–24).

⁵ The annual Washington Jockey Club horse races took place from 27 to 29 Oct. and were attended by some in the Adams and Hellen households (*Washington Federalist*, 28 Oct.; JQA, *Diary*).

Louisa Catherine Adams to Mary Smith Cranch

Washington Nov. 3ᵈ 1807

Having at length recover'd from the fatigue of a very unpleasant journey I take the liberty my dear Aunt of writing to solicit the favour of your correspondence although I know your avocations to be so numerous I almost fear to trespass upon your time—

It was with the greatest regret I found myself obliged to leave Boston without seeing you as I wished much to converse with you concerning John who has appear'd two or three times this Summer to be threaten'd with a dreadful complaint which is known by the name of

Hives of which I feel a continual apprehension owing to its being so sudden in its consequences I will therefore my dear Madam simply mention the remedies made use of in this part of the Country where the disorder is common. It generally at first comes on with a hoarseness and difficulty of breathing the least symptom of which must be immediately attended to by giving Onion juice prepar'd in this cut a large Onion into slices and lay as much Brown Sugar between as will extract all the strength of the Onion to be taken a teaspoonful at a time frequently and not to be exposed at all to a damp air if this does not take effect an Emetic to be givin immediately and the feet and Stomach rub'd with Goose Oil—

You will I am sure excuse my writing you on this subject as it is a complaint which even the Physicians in Boston are very little acquainted as D^r· Welsh inform'd me and the loss my Sister met with last Winter as render'd me more than usually anxious I am fully persuaded that under your protection he is perfectly safe and happy which is a source of comfort and happiness to / Your affectionate and grateful Neice L C Adams

P S Remember me affectionately to my Mother and tell her how anxious I am to hear from her likewise to the President and all the family.

RC (Adams Papers); addressed: "M$^{rs:}$ Cranch"; endorsed: "Letter from / Mrs John Q. Adams / Nov 3^d 1807."

John Quincy Adams to Abigail Adams

My dear Mother. Washington City 4. Nov^r: 1807.

Last Evening I had the pleasure of receiving your favour of 25$^{th:}$ ult$^{o:}$ which contained the first information we had received from you or from our children since we left Boston—and for which we began to be very anxious. I am glad to hear that George is so well satisfied with his situation and promises so well— If the french Gentleman will allow him to chatter with him according to his own propensities he will maintain his French at least where it is, and I hope another Summer will get over all the difficulties he will ever have to encounter for the mastery of *that* Language.— John has been so much more with you and has experienced so much of your tenderness and indulgence, that I am not surprized he should hanker a little for it now and then— But

I feel so perfectly easy with regard to the affection and kindness with which he will be treated and such entire Confidence in the Management he will be under, that I am satisfied he will be perfectly reconciled to his situation, and be content with occasionally visiting you on holidays.

We have hitherto been doing as little more than Nothing as imagination can conceive, to form a distinction— The Message *advised* us to wait for news from abroad before we should do any thing decisive, and the disposition is universal to take the advice— Our friends in Boston were afraid that the measures of Congress would be warlike— I did not expect so myself and I now know from personal observation that the national Representative pulse never has beaten so *slow* as it does at this time— The *Cotton* of the South is a great peace-maker— The great Sentiment which appears to me predominating in the minds of Congress-Men at present is the dread of *their* own valour— Every man seems to tremble least he should do something rash— We *feel* less than the People do— We shall want a spur more than a rein.

M^{r:} and M^{rs:} Cranch called upon us last Sunday— Both very well, with their family— M^{rs:} Cranch has grown quite fat— I am doing the same thing untill I am afraid of growing lazy too— My wife and child, and all the family we are with are well— We pass'd a couple of days at Baltimore with M^{r:} & M^{rs:} Buchanan who are also very well.

Your's ever affectionately   John Quincy Adams.

RC (Adams Papers); addressed: "John Adams Esqr / Quincy / Massachusetts."; internal address: "M^{rs:} Ab: Adams."; docketed: "J Q A. / 1807."

Thomas Boylston Adams to John Quincy Adams

Dear Brother   Quincy 5^{th:} November 1807.

Your letter from Washington of the 27^{th:} ult: to our dear Mother, came to hand this day, and as she was in Boston, we had the first perusal of it. We learn from it with much pleasure your safe arrival at the end of your journey and that you and yours are in good health. In return for this intelligence I am happy to be able to acquaint you with the health of all our friends here and your children in particular. Little John is here this afternoon with his Aunt and he stays with us regularly on Sunday's though he seems perfectly contented at his place of abode. From George we have heard but once since his Grandparents left him. He was quite at home before they came away and I have no doubt he will recommend himself very soon to the favour of the

November 1807

good people among whom he lives. His aptitude to learn and his inquisitive turn of mind will gain the good graces of the old parson, who will stuff him chock full of stories so as he but listen to his tediousness. I shall endeavour to see him when I go to keep *Thanksgiving*, as we are wont, with our friends at Haverhill[1] Our sister is still with us and I think will not leave us this Winter; at least I hope not, for I think there cannot be suitable accommodations for her at Hamilton. We have had no news of John since he was at Albany, though letters are expected from him every day. William is very desirous of obtaining a situation in a Compting-house in Boston, but has not yet made any direct application to any Merchant. I shall render him all the aid in my power towards the attainment of his wishes, but whether the terms on which he would be admitted are such as he can comply with, I am yet to enquire.

I presume that our good Uncle Cranch has communicated to his Son the result of the law suit in which he was engaged in the Circuit Court. M$^{r:}$ Blake thought proper to become non-suit, for default of evidence though he ascribed it to the Plaintiffs marriage, which he acknowledged to be the fact, notwithstanding we had taken no advantage of it in our plea. Miss Penelope Alias M$^{rs:}$ (I dont know who) is said to have torn herself from the embraces of her newly acquired husband and is gone to the West Indies in search of evidence of her birth & parentage, with which she threatens to come back and overwhelm us. We shall wait with patience her return. The Baxters very probably will be glad to see their Dollars back again rather than the lady.[2]

The only news I have of importance to communicate is that on Tuesday last His Excellency the Governor of the Commonwealth, accompanied by his trusty and well-beloved Jerry High Sheriff &$^{ca:}$ paid a visit in due form and ample style, at Quincy; I was in Boston and he saw none of the family but your father, who received him, I presume, with due respect.[3] The Governor & his Council are yet twain. They pull different ways, but measures go with the greater number; so that we are generally thought to have nine Governors in lieu of one. The winter Session of the General Court will determine who shall be our next Governor.[4] Either his Excellency or the Honorables in Council must yield their sharp points, or there will be serious divisions among the dominant sect. This is the opinion of some folks, but I have not sufficient knowledge of the matter to make any conjectures of my own.

If you Should take the new paper which we hear is established at

Washington, we shall be glad to receive it instead of the Intelligencer, provided the debates are reported in it.[5]

With best love and regards to all friends at Washington, I am / Your's affectionately

Thomas B Adams

RC (Adams Papers); internal address: "J Q Adams Esq[r:]."

[1] On 16 Oct. Gov. James Sullivan declared 26 Nov. a day of thanksgiving throughout the state (Boston *Independent Chronicle*, 19 Oct.).

[2] TBA represented Richard Cranch in a case heard by the U.S. Circuit Court in Boston in late 1807. The case involved a claim on the estate of the Quincy family in Braintree by Penelope Verchild Markham (b. 1757), a granddaughter of James Verchild of St. Christopher (now St. Kitts). Verchild died in 1769 a few weeks after arriving in Boston from the West Indies and after having purchased a portion of the Quincy estate. This included the house later occupied by Richard and Mary Smith Cranch. Verchild's death left the status of the property unsettled, as he did not mention it in his will. Earlier attempts by Verchild heirs to claim the property resulted in an agreement by the Cranches to pay rent. Markham asserted a new claim in 1803 and joined by Capt. Daniel Baxter of Quincy sued Richard Cranch. TBA succeeded in having the case dismissed and in Jan. 1808 informed Baxter that he would seek repayment of the cost of the suit as awarded by the court. The Cranches remained in the house. Markham married John Barton in Boston on 21 April 1807 (vols. 7:255, 10:363; "Markham of St. Christopher," *Caribbeana*, 4:73–74 [1919]; Salem *Essex Gazette*, 19 Sept. 1769; Cranch to TBA, 16 July 1803, 7 Jan., [Jan.] 1808, all NAII:Cranch-Greenleaf Papers; *New-England Palladium*, 16 May 1806; Boston, *30th Report*, p. 234).

[3] The governor was joined in his visit to JA by Benjamin Clarke Cutler (1756–1810), who served as Norfolk County sheriff from 1798 until his death. On 13 Oct. 1807 JA accompanied the two men and other dignitaries in reviewing the county militia at the Neponset River bridge (William T. Davis, *Bench and Bar of the Commonwealth of Massachusetts*, 2 vols., Boston, 1895, 2:56; Horatio Gray, *Memoirs of Rev. Benjamin C. Cutler, D.D.*, N.Y., 1865, p. 2; Boston *Columbian Centinel*, 21 Oct.).

[4] For the results of the 1808 gubernatorial election, see TBA to JQA, 24 March 1808, and note 2, below.

[5] Richard Dinmore's weekly *Washington Expositor*, which featured detailed reports of congressional activity, was published in the federal capital from 13 Nov. 1807 to 6 Jan. 1809 (Clarence S. Brigham, "Bibliography of American Newspapers, 1690–1820," Amer. Antiq. Soc., *Procs.*, 23:359–360 [Oct. 1913]; *Washington Expositor*, 21 Nov. 1807).

Louisa Catherine Adams to Abigail Adams

My dear Mother   Washington Nov 11[th.] 1807

Your very kind letter has eased my heart of a load of anxiety, on account of our dear George, whose health appear'd to me to be in a very indifferent state.[1] and I could not have quitted him with any satisfaction, had I not placed him under your protection. recieve my dear Madam our united thanks for your extreme kindness in taking him to Atkinson which journey I sincerely hope proved beneficial both to the President and yourself—[2]

I have nothing to write worthy your attention Washington is worse than Dull at present M[r.] Randolph has commenced the Session by making a violent attack upon the administration condemning it severely for not having called Congress together immediately after the affair of the Leopard.[3] many of the Members have not yet arrived— I have not seen the new Room for the Representatives but am told that it is extremely Elegant—[4]

Mr. Erskin has not left Philadelphia but is expected shortly—[5]

Do my dear Mother write soon, if you can possibly spare the time and tell us if Mrs. Smith is with you & if she stays with you this Winter. at any rate give my best love to her and request her to write to me remember me kindly to all, particularly to Louisa Smith. Kiss my darling John for me. Charles grows finely he is the very image of his father who is thank God more fleshy and in better health than I ever knew him—

I passed two days with Mrs. Buchanon she had been very sick but was much recovered she requested me to offer her best respects to yourself and family and I remain dear Mother your very affectionate daughter L. C. Adams

RC (Adams Papers); addressed: "Mrs: A. Adams / Quincy near / Boston"; endorsed: "Mrs L Adams / Novbr 11 1807."

1 AA to LCA and JQA, 25 Oct., above.

2 JA in a letter to JQA of 12 Nov. recounted his and AA's recent trip to deliver GWA to the care of Rev. Stephen and Elizabeth Smith Shaw Peabody in Atkinson, N.H. He also discussed his reading and conveyed Quincy social news (Adams Papers).

3 On 10 Nov. John Randolph in the House of Representatives criticized Thomas Jefferson's response to the *Chesapeake-Leopard* Affair, claiming that the president should have recalled the U.S. minister to Great Britain and demanded immediate redress. If that demand was not met, he said, Jefferson should have invaded Canada or Jamaica in retaliation. Randolph declared that while he did not relish war with Britain, neither did he wish to "sink into that vile and supple thing, an humble follower, a pliant tool" (Washington, D.C., *National Intelligencer*, 20 Nov.).

4 After four years of construction overseen by architect Benjamin Henry Latrobe, a new House chamber opened in the south wing of the Capitol on 26 October. Glare from unshaded skylights immediately proved a nuisance and they were successively covered with canvas, prompting new complaints that the hall was too dark. While the addition of a central lantern was contemplated, no alteration was made (William C. Allen, "Remembering Paris: The Jefferson-Latrobe Collaboration at the Capitol," in Cynthia R. Field, Isabelle Gournay, and Thomas P. Somma, eds., *Paris on the Potomac: The French Influence on the Architecture and Art of Washington, D.C.*, Athens, Ohio, 2007, p. 53).

5 British minister to the United States David Montagu Erskine spent the summer in Philadelphia, the birthplace of his wife, Frances Cadwalader Erskine, arriving there by 13 May and returning to Washington, D.C., by 31 Oct. (Charlene M. Boyer Lewis, *Elizabeth Patterson Bonaparte: An American Aristocrat in the Early Republic*, Phila., 2012, p. 72; Erskine to James Madison, 13 May, DLC:Madison Papers; 31 Oct., DNA:RG 59, Notes from Foreign Legations, Great Britain).

Abigail Adams to Louisa Catherine Adams

my dear Daughter   Quincy Nov^br 30th 1807

I received your favour of Nov^br 20th and rejoiced to learn that you reachd Washington in safety with your Young Charge.[1] it is an important undertaking to travel such a distance with so young a Baby, by land and by water, but you have been accustomed to it, and therefore feel less embarressd with it than others would be— the little fellow seems to be Born for deeds of greater hardihood than his Brothers—

John grows very fat. he is as thick as he is long is very well, but that Gasping for Breath always attends him when he grows fleshy. I know not what to attribute it to. I hope he will out grow it— he is very well, sleeps quietly and is quite Gay and happy. he is fonder of me than ever, thinks it a great priviledge to tarry with me a day or two at a time, which he frequently does, and looks for Sunday with much earnestness— yet when he is at his Aunts, he is quite content— he amused Me much a few days since with his Reasoning. he was sitting on my lap—when he began, Grandmamma, I know who made me, God made me, and made me to be happy— Well are you not happy? after a pause of some moments, Grandmamma Elizabeth had a peice of toast this morning, and I had two peices, but Elizabeths one peice was larger than both mine—[2] now that did not make me happy— altho he was very serious, I could not refrain from bursting into a laugh.

I heard from George a day or two since he was very well and quite content— his Aunt writes, that he is a very good Boy, and not more trouble than Children of his Age usually are—[3]

Mrs smith William & Caroline are still with us, and will pass the Winter here— I cannot think of her going into the Wilderness at this season of the year— William wishes to go into a store to qualify himself for a voyage to the East Indies—but the State of uncertainty in which our public affairs are involved, are a Bar and obstical to his getting into a merchantile House at present— his engageing Manners, and pleasent temper & disposition are qualities which will recommend him. he has also a Strict sense of honour and integrity— we have not heard from John but once since he left Quincy, which was from albany.[4] Mrs Smith is very anxious and uneasy in concequence of it— he was always so punctual to write, and so anxious himself to get Letters, that we know not what cause to attribute it to—

Mr and Mrs T B Adams are gone to celebrate Thanksgiving at Haverhill when her sister Betsy is to be married[5] I have scarcly ever been able to collect my Family together tho So small a Number at these Annual festivals— they have been Scatterd over the Globe— I had the largest collection of them together the last Sunday you dinned with us—all my Children, & all but one of my Grandchildren—which have ever met before— it is a pleasing and gratefull Sensation to parents to See them thus assembled like olive plant round about the table.— yea to See as the psalmist expresses it, to see our childrens, Children—[6]

By the Journals of Senate I perceive mr Adams is like to have his share of Buisness—but congress never get their Blood in motion untill after Christmass.— I was quite amused to see how reluctantly the Truth came out, that the Administration had been obliged to have recourse to those very measures, which their ignorance and folly had led them to censure under Washingtons— under the last, there was not any Money applied, but what had been previously appropriated— yet Such will frequently be the exigency of the country, that such a measure must be resorted to for its immediate safety, and security, but that was a Jeffersonian trick to catch popularity; of which he ought now to be asshamed, to make the people believe that he was so tender & carefull of their money, that not a shilling should be expended, but what they had voted to a particular purpose—[7] I do seriously believe that the greater part of Mankind from the days of Adam to this hour were designd to be dupes and tools—and they have most admirably answerd the End of their creation to this blessed hour as all history proves from haughty Nimrod to the tyrant ~~Bo~~ Napolean—

Quincy December 3^d

My Letter has lain by for several Days, unfinishd— I have only to add that the family are all well—and desire to be rememberd to yours. Louissa desires me to present her Love to you & Mrs Buchannan whose Sickness we hope is not of a very allarming nature— the weather is very fine, tho we had one severe snow storm in Nov^{br}—

My Love to my son I am glad to learn that he grows fat, as well for his looks as his Health—

Whilst you nure I do not expect you will be Burdend— Remember me kindly to your Mother and sisters ask Eliza if She has Sown wild oats enough to become the sober solid dame of a parsons wife?— she had better persuade her swain to think of some other profession—[8]

Mrs Smith caroline susan and Mrs Adams / all present their best Love to which I join that of your / affectionate Mother

Abigail Adams—

RC (Adams Papers); addressed: "Mrs Catharine Louissa Adams / Washington"; notation by CFA: "To the same—"

[1] No letter from LCA to AA of 20 Nov. has been found; AA likely meant that of 11 Nov., above.

[2] That is, Elizabeth Norton (1802–1869), daughter of Rev. Jacob and Elizabeth Cranch Norton (*History of Weymouth*, 4:445).

[3] Not found.

[4] Not found.

[5] Elizabeth Marston Harrod married Boston printer Chester Stebbins in Haverhill on 28 Nov. (Treat, *Treat Family*, p. 270; *New-Bedford Mercury*, 4 Dec.).

[6] Psalms 128:3, 6.

[7] In Thomas Jefferson's 27 Oct. annual message to Congress, the president stated that the urgency of the *Chesapeake-Leopard* Affair caused him to expend funds in excess of those previously appropriated for national defense. Jefferson expressed certainty, however, that Congress would retroactively approve the expenditures. Congress quickly did so, passing a bill that was signed into law on 24 Nov. (U.S. Senate, *Jour.*, 10th Cong., 1st sess., p. 186–189; *U.S. Statutes at Large*, 2:450).

[8] LCA's sister Eliza Johnson was being courted by Rev. Samuel Ripley (1783–1847), Harvard 1804, who was born in Concord, Mass., and served as a tutor in Washington, D.C., before relocating to Cambridge in 1807. For LCA's assessment of the match and her role in breaking it off, see LCA, *D&A*, 1:275, 282.

Louisa Catherine Adams to Mary Smith Cranch

My dear Aunt   December 13th. 1807

I recieved your very kind Letter for which I return many thanks[1] I hope you will pardon the anxiety which my last expressed concerning my darling John who is I am well aware safer with you than with me but the continual apprehension his father and I suffer'd when he visited us last Summer induced me to write so particularly. We are sincerely thankful for your kindness to our Children and I shall ever feel happy in expressing my gratitude for your goodness—

There is nothing new stirring here We hear of nothing but War The P—— however has no idea of anything of the Sort which gives me great hopes that the Negociation may terminate amicably. war is certainly to be deprecated by either side, the mischief resulting from such a step, must be nearly equal to both Countries—

Mr. Adams is just come in from his Walk I must therefore resign my seat but must first request you to give my most affectionate love to my Mother and all the family with best respects to Mr. Cranch and a thousand kisses for John of whom I am delighted to hear so good an account Charles grows in proportion to what he was when you saw him. he is a lovely Baby! he has two Teeth nearly through with the wishes for your health & happiness I with pleasure subsribe myself your affectionate Niece   L C Adams

P. S I have seen Mr. & Mrs. Cranch but once they were in good health She is grown very fleshy

RC (Adams Papers); addressed: "M^rs: Cranch / Quincy near / Boston"; endorsed: "M^rs. L. C. Adams. / Decr 13. 1807"; notation by JQA: "*Free* / John Quincy Adams. / S. U. S."

[1] Not found.

John Quincy Adams to Thomas Boylston Adams

Washington 14. Dec^r: 1807.

Your's of the 3^d: inst^t: came to hand the night before last; I am perfectly satisfied with your sales of my wood—[1] I had a little kindness for the grove in the rear of the brook, and if circumstances should carry me back to the house of our nativity, shall miss the prospect which it furnished; but your reasons for disposing of it are substantial, and I suppose a young growth will come up, instead of that which is now to be removed.

I have enclosed the Journals and Documents of the present Session from time to time, to your father, though not with so much regularity as heretofore— I have been so much engaged, while in Senate, as well as at home, that I have not so frequently enclosed the papers, as they appeared, but have suffered them to accumulate too much— And I have not enclosed Newspapers, as I take only one published here, which during the Session I keep on file—for the purpose of referring to it—[2] I will however endeavour to get you a Newspaper, and forward it as often as I can.

Your questions to the great land-animal are more than he will answer— But his magnificent projects of Conquest, are like Hodge's Razors, made to sell— You will see that he has many other plans equally wise and splendid with that for the reduction of Jamaica, without either navy or army—[3] Thus he is about to enrich all the indigent heroes of our Revolution—to arm the whole body of the militia, and to provide a formidable train of field Artillery, all by the magic of his Eloquence, without the application of the usual physical means— It is all a strife of grandiloquence; for which many others besides him are contending, but of which he continues to bear away the palm.

M^r: Quincy and myself yesterday presented the Boston petition for the modification, suspension or repeal of the non-importation Act— A Petition from Philadelphia for the repeal had been refused a reference in the House of Representatives, for some unlucky hints of the sentiments entertained by the petitioners respecting the general policy of the Administration— But the Boston Petition was so guarded and so reasonable, that it was referr'd to a Committee in Senate, not on my motion, but on that of Gen^{l:} Smith of Maryland;—without a division— And after that the Petition from Philadelphia was referr'd to the same Committee—[4] I believe the Administration would be well satisfied if the Act could be made to vanish from the memory of Mankind, as easily as it can be torn out of the Statute-Book— But there it is, and how they can get rid of it, without seeming to shrink from their own measures is the difficulty— I presume the act will be modified, but not repealed—

The attack upon the Chesapeake has been disavowed, and all pretensions to search a *National ship* for deserters disclaimed in terms as explicit as the English Language can afford, by M^{r:} Canning in his correspondence with M^{r:} Monroe— I feel some satisfaction at this, because I have been subjected to no small obloquy, and have been written AT in almost all the newspapers in Boston, and in pamphlets too for maintaining that principle against *Americans*!!—[5] But I am not prepared to put the fortunes of this Country upon the die of War, for the unqualified pretension of protecting all *men* without exception on board our merchant vessels— Still less for the pretence of protecting Deserters from foreign Ships public or private— Yet for this we must wage war now if any thing; the great question of the search of the Chesapeake being abandoned by Britain, and therefore taken from under us.

The British Proclamation brings indeed very near to an issue the general question of impressment from our merchant vessels— How, or whether we shall parry it I am not yet informed— There may be a question *in fact*, still more ~~dissolution~~ difficult of solution—[6] The Revenge before and after her mission to England touched at *Brest*.—[7] Here has been all along the hook in my opinion, upon which our ultimate policy would depend, and I have some reason to say to you that our Peace or war with G. B— now rests neither upon the British nor upon the American Government— It will be settled by him who settles every thing.

Love and duty to all friends—

RC (Adams Papers); endorsed: "J. Q. Adams Esqr / 14th December 1807. / 25^{th:} Rec^{d:} / 27^{th:} Answ^d wrote again 24th Jan^y."

[1] TBA's letter of 3 Dec. has not been found. TBA wrote to JQA on 15 March 1808 (Adams Papers) and reported that he had received payment of $160 for forty cords of wood taken from a lot near the Mill Pond. The purchasers were probably JQA's tenants Noah Curtis (1772–1856), a Quincy shoemaker, and Ebenezer Adams (Laurel A. Racine, *Historic Furnishings Report: The Birthplaces of Presidents John Adams and John Quincy Adams*, Charlestown, 2001, p. 45; Sprague, *Braintree Families*).

[2] JQA regularly consulted the Washington,

D.C., *National Intelligencer* and sent issues to Quincy (TBA to JQA, 5 Nov. 1807, above).

³ John Randolph had spoken in the House of Representatives on 5 March 1806 against the Non-Importation Act, comparing the United States to "a great land animal" and Britain to a shark. If the "great mammoth" wades into the sea for battle, he declared, "let him beware that his proboscis is not bitten off in the engagement" (Washington, D.C., *National Intelligencer*, 21 March; *Speech of the Hon. J. Randolph on the Non-Importation Resolution*, N.Y., 1806, p. 7, 26, Shaw-Shoemaker, No. 11246). For Randolph's suggestion that Thomas Jefferson should have responded to the *Chesapeake-Leopard* Affair by invading Jamaica, see LCA to AA, 11 Nov. 1807, and note 3, above.

⁴ On 14 Dec. JQA in the Senate and Josiah Quincy III in the House introduced a 1 Dec. memorial signed by about 900 Boston merchants in response to the Non-Importation Act of 1806, for which see JQA to TBA, 20 Jan. 1806, and note 2, above. The act had come into effect on 15 Nov. 1807. The merchants declared that while they would be "among the last to interfere" with the actions of Congress, the anticipated economic impacts of enforcement prompted "a strong wish that some modification, suspension, or repeal of the said act may be made." The memorial was referred to committee in both chambers, in the Senate on a motion by Samuel Smith of Maryland. A similar memorial from Philadelphia merchants contained more incendiary language and was tabled in the House after two unsuccessful attempts to refer it to committee; in the Senate it passed to committee by a narrow margin but went no further. Congress did not repeal the Non-Importation Act of 1806. On 22 Dec. it added new restrictions to block exports with the passage of the Embargo Act of 1807, for which see TBA to JQA, 27 Dec., and note 3, below (U.S. Senate, *Jour.*, 10th Cong., 1st sess., p. 197, 203; U.S. House, *Jour.*, 10th Cong., 1st sess., p. 74–75, 76–82; Boston *Columbian Centinel*, 23 Dec.; Philadelphia *United States Gazette*, 30 Nov.).

⁵ On 8 Dec. the president delivered to Congress recent correspondence between U.S. and British diplomats in London on the *Chesapeake-Leopard* Affair. Among the documents considered by Congress in closed-door session were seven letters written by British foreign minister George Canning (1770–1827) to James Monroe between 25 July and 10 October. In the initial letter Canning expressed his nation's "deepest regret" that American lives were lost and pledged compensation if Britain was found to be at fault. Later letters codified negotiations between Canning and Monroe and William Pinkney about possible reparations. Articles in the Boston press in early December blamed JQA for congressional measures taken in response to the *Chesapeake-Leopard* Affair, which New England Federalists feared would lead to war. The Boston *Commercial Gazette*, 3 Dec., ascribed to JQA a committee recommendation that Congress empower the president to order the interdiction of foreign vessels in U.S. waters, an action the Boston *Repertory*, 4 Dec., called a prelude to war (JQA, *Diary*, 8 Dec.; U.S. Senate, *Exec. Jour.*, 10th Cong., 1st sess., p. 62–63; Monroe, *Papers*, 5:650–653; Jefferson, *Papers, Retirement Series*, 1:170; LCA, *D&A*, 2:539; *Amer. State Papers, Foreign Relations*, 3:187, 188, 197–201, 203).

⁶ On 16 Oct. King George III issued a proclamation ordering home all British seamen in foreign service and giving British captains official license to impress sailors from neutral merchant vessels (*Amer. State Papers, Foreign Relations*, 3:268). For JQA's view of the proclamation, see TBA to JQA, 27 Dec., and note 3, below.

⁷ The U.S. schooner *Revenge* was sent by the Jefferson administration soon after the *Chesapeake-Leopard* Affair to deliver dispatches to Monroe in London. It returned to New York with dispatches from U.S. diplomats on 12 Dec., having passed through a British blockade to stop at Brest, France, on both legs of its voyage, prompting the *New-England Palladium*, 8 Dec., to question whether the stops unnecessarily raised tensions (Paul A. Gilje, *Free Trade and Sailors' Rights in the War of 1812*, N.Y., 2013, p. 182; *New-York Gazette*, 6 July; Alexandria, Va., *Daily Advertiser*, 17 Dec.). For the dispatches to Monroe, see TBA to JQA, 27 Dec., and note 6, below.

Thomas Boylston Adams to John Quincy Adams

Dear Brother   Quincy 27th: December 1807

I returned from Dedham on Friday morning, and found your letter of the 14th:. The Court of Common Pleas dispatched business rather faster than usual, on account of Christmas; but there was business enough left unfinished to have occupied a day or two more.[1]

I am glad to find you are satisfied with my sale of your wood— I believe, no body has done better since, though sundry lots have been disposed of at publick sale. If Congress should declare war against GB. the price of wood, in the vicinity of Boston, would doubtless be considerably higher, than it is or has been, but, as I could not *absolutely* calculate upon such an event, I am, as yet, well pleased with my private bargain for the Grove.

The information you gave us on political topicks, was, in some particulars, a confirmation of opinions entertained here, especially as to the influence of the Corsican; but the rumour of yesterday, brought by *express* was, that the Secret Session had been held in consequence of dispatches from our Minister in France, which confirmed the declaration that there should henceforth be no Neutrals; that *the Decree* should be rigidly enforced against us in common with others, and that any Nation, having a Minister at the Court of GB, should be considered enemies at war with France.[2] So much for rumour—which also reported an act to have passed both houses of Congress laying an Embargo throughout the U.S.[3] If all this should be true!! What then? I am sure I can't tell, or even *guess* from the complexion of your Congress, what effect any external occurrence will produce there. Some say the Senate are unanimous for war with France & the House of Representatives nearly so, for war with GB. A Committee of conference ought to decide the question between you, since the *venerable* President is so neutral. Alas! We learn from his own pen, his wish to retire from the Aræna of political contention, that he may enjoy the security of domestic scenes, while the furies of war and discord, which he has let loose, are striving which shall do the most harm; not to a foreign enemy, but to our own dear Country.[4] In critical times he has been known to call on the Mountain to cover him,[5] and I hope the same friendly retreat may be reserved for him again. It is generally believed that for himself he has no idea of fighting, and is not a little surprised to find that any body should think him in earnest. Mr: Monroe is said to be astonished at the hue & cry for war so prevalent here;

December 1807

doubtless because his instructions were of a more pacifick tenor than the publick have been taught to believe.⁶ A language official and a language confidential has been heard of under a former Administration.

We have received the documents and a file of Newspapers; but I have not yet had time to read much of the debates. The Gun-boat system has undergone a tedious investigation, and there I think it would be best to leave it.⁷ But I speak after the manner of Men—having little knowledge of the subject, any more than common sense teaches, and what Peter Pindar says on *the same*, "Fleas are not Lobsters G–d-damn their souls."⁸

I shall be glad to receive your instructions as to the disposition of so much of your Real Estate in Quincy, which was leased for one year & which will expire on the first of April. If I can let the house and all the land together would it not be preferable to dividing it among many tenants? But if no person should apply for the house and farm, how shall I dispose of the land? I do not like Mr: Cook for a tenant, *at any rate*, and shall give him seasonable notice to quit.⁹ Shall I sell your fresh and Salt hay soon or wait till Spring? The Spring chance for a price being fairest, but I am afraid of Cooks horse or some one's else being in great straits for food before the Winter is over— There is but a small quantity of fresh hay to steal or sell and the Salt hay is safe enough.

My wife & daughter are well and send love to Mrs: A— Give mine into the bargain. Your boy John is well and passed the day with us— My little daughter has just recovered from the Kine-pock, which she had very severely by the *instrumentality* of your friend the professor.

If you read the Col: Centinel, you need no private hints on the subject therein discussed between my two worthy and highly esteemed friends, the Doctors; Who shall decide when Doctors disagree?¹⁰ This is a very trite quotation, but it suits my purpose to a tittle. I wish them *well* through with the scuffle, but will have no hand in prescribing for either.

We are all well. The young Col: is teaching our youth the discipline of angles & parrallelograms—¹¹ He is one of my chusing, being myself on the sub-school Committee. I like him well— So do all who know him, and I refrain from odious comparisons—

Compliments of the Season to every friend I have in Washington. / Your's

RC (Adams Papers); addressed: "John Q Adams Esqr / Senator of the U. S / City of Washington"; internal address: "J Q Adams Esqr"; endorsed: "Adams— T. B. 27.

Dec^r: 1807. / 8. Jan^y: 1808 rec$^{d:}$"; notation by Richard Cranch: "Quincy Decr. 28th. 1807 Free."

[1] Norfolk County Court of Common Pleas sessions at Dedham, Mass., began on the third Monday in December, which in 1807 fell on the 21st (Mass., *Acts and Laws*, 1805–1809, p. 79–80).

[2] For John Armstrong Jr.'s correspondence regarding France's Berlin decree, see JQA to LCA, 19 Feb., and note 3, above. The Boston *Columbian Centinel*, 26 Dec., suggested that Napoleon would extend enforcement of the decree to U.S. shipping despite previous assurances that American vessels would be exempt. While confirmation had not yet reached the United States, Napoleon had already done so with the issuance of his 17 Dec. Milan decree that declared all neutral ships that had contact with Great Britain subject to French confiscation. The latest decree was in response to Britain's 11 Nov. Order in Council that escalated the trade war between the two powers by placing blockades on the ports of both enemies and neutral countries that traded with enemies. JQA wrote to William Smith Shaw on 18 Dec. (MWA:Adams Family Letters), reporting rumors of the new French maritime restrictions (David S. and Jeanne T. Heidler, *The War of 1812*, Westport, Conn., 2002, p. 25–27).

[3] The Boston *Columbian Centinel*, 26 Dec., reported the passage of the Embargo Act of 1807, which Thomas Jefferson signed on 22 December. In an 18 Dec. message to Congress the president proposed the passage of a law halting the shipment of U.S. products to foreign ports as a means to protect U.S. ships, seamen, and merchandise from being plundered by British and French ships. On the same day the Senate referred the message to a five-member committee that included JQA, who had "very strong doubts" about the proposal owing to the "utterly inadequate" documentation accompanying the president's message, which included the 16 Oct. proclamation of George III authorizing the impressment of sailors from neutral merchant vessels. When no other committee member voiced opposition, JQA "finally acquiesced" and joined other members in recommending the embargo's passage. He also joined the 22 to 6 majority in passing the bill with virtually no debate also on 18 December. The House of Representatives debated the bill in closed session on 21 Dec., passing it by a margin of 82 to 44 after adding a provision permitting U.S. fishing vessels to travel to international waters. The Senate concurred on 22 Dec., and the House followed with a vote to make its earlier actions public.

Jefferson endorsed the measure at the suggestion of James Madison and over the objections of Albert Gallatin in the hopes that stopping the flow of U.S. goods would pressure Europe's warring powers to halt harassment of American ships. The embargo, however, was ineffective as an instrument of diplomacy and proved catastrophic to the U.S. economy, cutting exports from $108 million in 1807 to $22 million in 1808. British ships still carried goods into the United States, subject to the restrictions of the Non-Importation Act of 1806. Until its repeal in 1809, for which see JQA to LCA, 8 Feb., and note 5, below, the embargo was widely unpopular, especially among Federalist merchants (*U.S. Statutes at Large*, 2:451–453; *Annals of Congress*, 10th Cong., 1st sess., p. 50–51, 52, 1217–1223, 1228; JQA, *Diary*, 18 Dec. 1807; Wood, *Empire of Liberty*, p. 649–652; J. Van Fenstermaker and John E. Filer, "The U.S. Embargo Act of 1807: Its Impact on New England Money, Banking, and Economic Activity," *Economic Inquiry*, 28:165 [1 Jan. 1990]).

[4] In 10 Dec. letters from Jefferson to the Penn. General Assembly and other state legislatures, the president declared that due to declining health he would retire at the end of his second term (Boston *Columbian Centinel*, 26 Dec.; Jefferson to the New Jersey legislature, 10 Dec.; Jefferson to the New York legislature, 10 Dec., both DLC:Jefferson Papers).

[5] Luke, 23:30.

[6] After four years of diplomatic service in France, Spain, and Great Britain, James Monroe returned to the United States. His return coincided with Britain's determination to send a special envoy to the United States to negotiate a settlement of the *Chesapeake-Leopard* Affair, for which see LCA to AA, 24 Jan. 1808, and note 2, below. Monroe arrived in Norfolk, Va., aboard the *Augustus*, Capt. Howe, on 13 Dec. 1807 and traveled soon after to the federal capital. The *New-England Palladium*, 25 Dec., reported that the returning diplomat was surprised by concerns about war in the United States "as the government and people in England were so averse to a war with us." Monroe had received new instructions dated

6 July from James Madison that ordered him to continue emphasizing a U.S. "disposition to maintain faithfully every friendly relation" (Monroe, *Papers*, 5:xxiii–xxiv, 660–661; Easton, Md., *Republican Star*, 8 Dec.; *Amer. State Papers, Foreign Relations*, 3:183–185).

[7] Secretary of the navy Robert Smith requested that Congress finance the construction of gunboats for the protection of the U.S. coast. A bill was introduced in the Senate on 20 Nov. and passed unanimously on 3 December. The measure passed with little opposition in the House on the 11th and was signed into law on 18 Dec., authorizing the expenditure of $852,500 for the construction of 188 gunboats (Washington, D.C., *National Intelligencer*, 2, 9, 14 Dec.; JQA, *Diary*, 19, 20, 25 Nov., 3, 10 Dec.; U.S. Senate, *Jour.*, 10th Cong., 1st sess., p. 200; U.S. House, *Jour.*, 10th Cong., 1st sess., p. 72–73; *U.S. Statutes at Large*, 2:451).

[8] Peter Pindar, "Sir Joseph Banks and the Boiled Fleas," line 84.

[9] The tenant was possibly Nathan Cook or Thomas Cook from Cape Cod, who both resided variously in Quincy from 1807 to 1815. JQA sought a tenant for the John Adams Birthplace after it was vacated by John Briesler Sr., and in 1808 Briesler's daughter and son-in-law, Elizabeth Briesler Arnold and Joseph Arnold, leased the property and a large portion of JQA's Penn's Hill farmland (Sprague, *Braintree Families*; JQA to TBA, 5 Jan. 1807,

and note 7, above; Laurel A. Racine, *Historic Furnishings Report: The Birthplaces of Presidents John Adams and John Quincy Adams*, Charlestown, 2001, p. 44–45).

[10] Dr. Benjamin Waterhouse vaccinated sixteen-month-old Abigail Smith Adams against smallpox, about which AHA reported that on "the sixth day she began to look pale and heavy—and for the three succeeding days her fever continued to increase her arms were very sore but no eruption appeared on any part of her body." Waterhouse and Boston physican John Clarke Howard were then engaged in an extended newspaper war in which disagreements over the efficacy of vaccination techniques descended into personal attacks (M/AHA/1, APM Reel 284; John B. Blake, *Benjamin Waterhouse and the Introduction of Vaccination: A Reappraisal*, Phila., 1957, p. 51–53, 65, 72, 92; Boston *Columbian Centinel*, 16, 23 Dec.).

[11] William Steuben Smith served as an assistant to John Whitney (1785–1850), brother of Rev. Peter Whitney Jr., who taught at the Quincy town school for three years beginning in late 1807 (LCA, *D&A*, 1:280; Pattee, *Old Braintree*, p. 329; Sprague, *Braintree Families*; Franklin Clifton Pierce, *Whitney: The Descendants of John Whitney*, Chicago, 1895, p. 295; AA to SSA, 20 Jan. 1808; LCA to JQA, 26 Feb. [1809], both below; JQA, *Diary*, 26 March 1809, 23 July).

Elizabeth Smith Shaw Peabody to John Quincy Adams

My Dear Nephew,   Atkinson. Jan^{ry.} 10th. 1808.

Mr Peabody, & your Aunt, were much gratified last Fall, by a visit from your venerable Parents, who presented me with a Letter from you, requesting our parental care & attention to your eldest Son.[1] With heartfelt pleasure, I received the precious Charge, considering it as a pledge of your regard, & former affection; & of the Opinion you still entertain of my Integrity, in discharging the important Offices, incumbent upon those, to whom the Education of Youth is committed.—

Every day, I am more convinced that the very earliest periods of Life, are the best time to check the turbulent Passions, to sow the seeds of Knowledge, Virtue, & Religion; to impress upon their infant minds, that the great Object of Life, was to do good; that our beneficent Creator, did not send us here, merely to walk the Earth, to gaze, & draw fresh air, but gave us Time & Intellects to improve, great & important buisness to perform; & that the Ultimate view of Instruction, was to render them Useful & happy.—

Your Son is a lovely Child— He appears to have more regard to truth, & justice, than is common to One of his age.— Many things which he says, appear to be the result of thought, & principle; which to me, is peculiarly pleasing, for half the Evils we suffer, are because we do not accustom ourselves to thought & reflection.

Master George claims my promise, that when he had commited the English Accidence to memory, & began to Pars, I would write, & inform you, & his Mother of his proficiency.—[2] He really learns very well, is fond of reading, & often comes home from the Academy, delighted by the encomiums of his Preceptor, when he tells him, he learns like a *Hero*—for he is charmed, with everything martial.—

I have frequently written to your Mother, & requested her to inform you, respecting your Sons Health— But I presume, it will not be an unpleasant Task to hear particularly from your Son, by a letter, from an absent Aunt, who always loved you as her Nephew, & Friend; revered you, for clasical & scientific Knowledge, which you have early devoted to your Country, & which claims your Talents as a Statesman, a Philosopher, & a Patriot. And, while you view with contemplative Eye, the Causes, by which Empires rise, & fall, you cannot but breathe a Sigh, responsive with the Fathers of Columbia, & weep over the fair Edifice of virtuous Liberty, which has lost its "*stability*," & now totters to its Base.—

May Heaven preserve us, from the envenomed arrows of civil Discord,—may the sword never be unsheathed but for the *defence* of our *natural Rights*—never, to aggrandize a fellow Worm—to monopolize Wealth, or to extend dominion over a vast Territory.—

And, may the cloud which now darkens our Horison, & casts a deep gloom over every Face, be dispelled, by the energies of *united Wisdom*; & Peace, still, extend her Olive Branch, over an happy Nation.—

You will be so kind as to present my Affectionate regards, to my much loved Nephew, Judge Cranch, & his Family,—& to Mr Quincy, who appears an able & zealous advocate for his Constituents.—

Master George begs you would accept of his dutiful love, he cannot Yet write well enough, to tell you himself—but hopes to very soon, he wishes me to tell his Mamma he is well, & very happy.— My Daughter pays great attention to him, & he is good Lydia's Favorite.— We have

January 1808

a post Office very near, & if you could sometimes be good enough to send a Washinton news paper, it will please both him, Mr Peabody / & your Aunt, who with esteem, & affection, / Subscribes,

Elizabeth Peabody—

RC (Adams Papers); addressed: "Hon. John Quincy Adams / City of Washington"; endorsed: "Peabody— Elizabeth. 10. Jan^{y:} 1808. / 6. Feb^{y:} rec^{d:} / 10. Ans^{d:}."

[1] JQA's letter to Peabody has not been found. GWA remained in the Peabody household and attended Atkinson Academy through 1812 (AA to JQA, 30 Dec. 1812, Adams Papers).
[2] John Trusler, *An English Accidence; or, Abstract of Grammar*, London, [1790].

Abigail Adams to Abigail Adams Smith

my Dear Daughter   Quincy Jan'ry 14th. 1808

Your departure was so sudden that I had scarcly time to think of it, or realize that You could be about to leave me and when you was really gone I felt the full force of Your absence and sat down without a wish to move from my chair the whole day or to see any one; I had fully believed that you would pass the winter with me, yet when the col came for You, I could not but approve of Your determination; knowing as I do Your fixed resolution to make every Situation in which You are placed as agreable to Your Self and Friends as You can, by a cheerfull compliance and a ready acquiescence in all circumstances, times and places; I shall try to reconcile myself to what was demed best, and think it most prudent, weighing all things in their proper balance that you should have acted as you have done; I hope you will be prosperd in your Basket and store, and if you have not the Elegancies You will have the comforts of Life.

I rose the morning after you left us, fearfull that rain was suddenly comeing and would retard your journey but the clouds dispersed and we had a fine day, rather too warm but not enough so to greatly injure the travelling. yesterday was much colder, and I traveld on with you very successfully, but this day, thursday, by ten oclock a snowstorm commenced and has continued through the day, damp, threatning to end in rain— You cannot get on—yet I know not where to place you. your road is out of My track, that beyond Northhampton I am a stranger to—

You must write Me all your adventures, and how you and caroline Employ yourself, how Your House is and you must be sure to plant out Some trees and call them after your names— I am rejoiced that you are to have Mrs St Hilliar with you.[1] I know how cheerfull she used to be, and I have always considerd her as a heroine her Life and history, a Romance—her attachment, her patience her fortitude her affection through trials and sufferings unabated.— I really look at her History so far as I have known it with supprize and astonishment

I shall write to you as soon as I hear from you. Love to My dear Caroline whom I Miss not a little— My Love also to the col whose good spirits served to enliven Mine, and made us all regret that his stay with us was so short. I have got the Cambrick for Williams shirts and Louiss is putting it on

Most tenderly your / affectionate Mother   Abigail Adams

RC (private owner, 2008); addressed: "Mrs Abigail Smith / Albany."

[1] WSS's sister Margaret Smith de St. Hilaire resided for an extended period with her brother and AA2. Her husband, Felix Leblond de St. Hilaire, who engaged in central New York land speculation with WSS and advertised his services as an art and dance instructor, had likely recently departed on a visit to France from which he returned in the summer of 1809 (vol. 11:39, 249–250; AA to JQA, 30 Sept., Adams Papers).

Elizabeth Smith Shaw Peabody to Abigail Adams

My Dear Sister—   Atkinson Jan. 15th 1808—

I received your kind letter,[1] with the sum enclosed for Mr Little— Butter has, since yours was engaged, fallen to fifteen Cents pr pd— but *we* have had none yet, under a shilling— It is very mortifying to the Farmers to bring their produce so many miles, & have to take a quarter less than they expected— An high price, has for many years sweetened their Labour,—& their heavy toils have been lightend, by increasing Wealth—

Every Class of People seem to be hanging their Harps upon the Willow, suffering, or foreboding Evil—[2] But none feel distress more immediately, than those who do buisness upon the mighty Waters, & have ploughed the Deep, to get their bread— Totally unaccustomed to fell the lofty Forrests, or to dig, the Earth—& sow the grain, how shall they gain subsistance for their dependant Families.— Was there *just Cause* for War, was it to *defend* virtuous Liberty, our natural Rights, our Country,—with pleasure, I could see our Sons, gird on the Sword, martial their Hosts, & like Cornelia, I would contribute my *all*, for their Support— But now—how puerile, how weak, how impolitic the pretext,—Alas! what can feeble Woman do, to avert the uplifted Sword, but ardently petition Heaven, to "Send forth the *saving Virtues* round the Land, In bright Patrol"—[3]

January 1808

I find Your eldest Son shares the same fate with his predecessors in public Office, that is, have his best motives misconstrued— But I trust his integrity will uphold him, & his knowledge of National Interests, eventually convince all, that he is not actuated by sinister motives, but that their best good, is his ~~great~~ Ultimate Object— Mr Quincy is very eloquent in Congress, & appears to be an able advocate for his Constituents—[4]

The above has lain this fortnight for Time, to give me one kind favourable moment, to finish what I had to say at present, & send it on Post haste— Since your last Letter, we have had Cold, & Wind, & a dreadful Storm—enough to satisfy all the "Croakers," that Winter would not perish in the Sky—& that the serene, pleasant Sunshine, was only the Halcyon Days, which we too often find the prelude to dark, & tempestous Seasons,—both in the natural & moral World—

I am very glad to hear Cousin William is with you, as he had not opportunity given him to finish his Collegiate course, he can now take hold of them, perhaps, to greater advantage, under the Patronage of his venerable learned Grandfather, than he could, even, at the best University— I am fully convinced the advantages My Son, received from a like situation, under your parental beneficent roof, priviledged with the best Society, & the best of Books were more than he obtained the whole four years he spent at Cambridge— It is true, that I believe, he looks back, with regret, & thinks his Time & opportunities might have been *much better improved*—"have borne to heaven more welcome tidings— It is greatly wise, to talk with our past Hours," & I hope he does not neglect this important duty—[5] Nor would I have him *forget, to look forward*, & secure a prudent, virtuous, sensible, partner, to partake of his Joys, & of the Sorrows, which are inevitable, in this Vale of [tears] How does our distressed Phebe do? I have thought much of her, in this cold weather— When she leaves this, I hope she will arrive at a better Country—where pain, & sorrow never reach—

Master George is well—sends duty, & Love. When it is weather he cannot attend in the Academy he studies at home, Abby assists him in parsing, & is very fond of him—

We had a few days of fine travelling, & we were full of company all the time, since that we have had bad colds, & one of my family taking with puking, & incessant sickness of the Stomach which lasted four days, & to day, is full of pain, & fever— This must apologize for my not writing before, & sending Mr Little's Bill to you—

With sincere love, & affection for you all of both dear families, I am ever yours—   E— Peabody

RC (Adams Papers); addressed: "Mrs Abigail Adams / Quincy"; endorsed by Richard Cranch: "Mrs Peabody / Jan 15th 1808." Some loss of text due to a torn manuscript.

[1] Not found.
[2] Psalms, 137:2.
[3] James Thomson, *The Seasons*, "Summer," lines 1603–1604.
[4] The *Newburyport Herald*, 4 Dec. 1807, reprinted criticism that JQA had received in the Boston press for his part in a proposal to grant the president expanded powers to respond to foreign aggressions, for which see JQA to TBA, 14 Dec., and note 5, above. The same newspaper on 25 Dec. lauded Josiah Quincy III for his advocacy of the memorial from Boston merchants, declaring "Mr. Quincy does himself and constituents honor."
[5] Edward Young, *The Complaint; or, Night Thoughts*, Night II, lines 376–378.

Abigail Adams to Sarah Smith Adams

my dear Daughter   Quincy Jan'ry 20th 1808

I will not delay a single hour to replie to your Letter of Jan'ry 8th just received, and to acknowledg the receipt of yours of Nov'br which ought not to have lain so long unanswerd.[1] since mrs Smith has been with me, I have not been in the habit of writing much, and when ever a reluctance to the pen commences, it increases with time, untill it becomes urksome. I know I ought to have written to you, but if my pen has not performd its Duty, My Mind has been occupied about you and Yours, and your future prospects: equally, tho not perhaps So anxiously; as for Mrs Smith and her Family; now destined to the Wilderness: altho from her natural disposition[2] she will be disposed to consider the Wilderness blossomeing as the rose,[3] and determined to accommodate her mind to her situation, her Friends cannot view it, in any other light; than a deprivation, and Sacrifice, of social enjoyment; and a seclusion from the world. her good humour and that of your sister, who is to accompany her, will mitigate every sacrifice, and serve as a Panacea to heal all the wounds the Rubs and scratches which they receive in passing through this rough world. Patience and fortitude will make a smooth road where the pickaxe has never levelled the inequalities, as it will Soften the Mattrass, and make a pillow of down to the contented mind—[4] I strive to reconcile myself to the seperation but find it a very hard task.

If you have received susans Letter,[5] You will find that Your Brother came on to Quincy with the first Snow and took Mrs Smith and Caroline with him to   [6] it was so late in the Season before the house was compleated, that I thought it best that mrs Smith Should pass the winter with me, and go in the Spring. I had prevaild upon her to write thus, but your Brother came as far as Albany and wishd her to meet him there, but I could not consent that She should go on in the stage at this Season. it was much better that he took advantage of the first snow, and came himself for her— when that was the case, I could do no otherways than consent to her going. I would have done so Myself under similar circumstances, tho you may easily Suppose how Sensibly I feel their absence[7]

William remains with us. John left us in October— William is engaged for the winter Months as an assistant to mr Whitney not *to preach*, but in his School to teach arithmetick which will qualify him to go into a Merchants Counting House in the spring; which he is very desirous of doing, if buisness should revive and peace continue. William is an amiable modest engageing Youth, and I hope and trust will make his way through the world with honor and integrity: through the unsuspecting credulity of his Father; he has been placed in a perilous Situation, and his Father deprived of the means of supporting himself and Family, nor can he hope or expect to be any way employd under the present administration. he has therefore pursued the wisest course left him to follow, withdrawn to the wilderness, there with his own hands, and by the Sweat of his Brow, determined to earn his Bread. may Success crown his honest endeavours. he appears in good Spirits, pleasent & happy, and assured Me that he did not feel a wish to quit his Situation

I have had a very large family through the Summer, seldom less than twenty two, and you know to whose lot it falls to provide for, and attend to them. I have been blest with more health than usual; and have enjoy'd my family as much as I could consistant with the anxiety I have felt for their future subsistance.

I ask not why the world has delt thus hardly with us. we have lived in perilous times—and tho we reap not the full Harvest we have earned—I trust future Generations will feel the benifit of the sacrifices we have made; and do justice to the Memory of those, who have sufferd much, and endured much for their benefit—[8]

I rejoice that you have a kind Sister, and that you can be mutually benificial to each other— I hope she has quite recoverd her health from the dangerous sickness which threatned her Life and that she will not be unmindfull of the hand which healed her. the world looks very different to us when surrounded with its pleasures and allured by its temptation[9] to what it does when the world of spirits opens to our view, then all things and objcets are as nothing before us.

> "O time how few thy value weigh;
> How few will estimate a day"[10]

Susan is very well. she does not attend any School now. she has Made a considerable proficiency in arithmetick which she continues at home under the direction of her Grandfather. she has also some knowledge in drawing. My greatest difficulty is to convince her of the utility of order Method and diligence towards improvement. She May properly be call'd an out sizd Girl. she is already as tall as her cousin Louissa, & almost as large, *and a Woman* tho not yet [12 years of age. all these things are] a dissadvantage to her, because the Maturity of years, and discretion are expected from a Girl not yet in her Teens. I think she is improveing.[11] Caroline whom you know is a fine figure; has been of much service to her[12] in stimulating her to hold herself properly. she will never have half so handsome a face as Abbe, but I think her form will be Majestic— I hope time will fashion her Manners, and dispotion to My mind, but she does not possess those femenine graces, that soft and yealding disposition which some children do. I hope it will be compensated to her, in strength of mind and sound judgment

She will write to you soon—as I shall and Make you a remittence, which I should have done now; but that I wish'd to assist mrs smith all I could when she left me—

amongst Your acquaintance in Philadelphia I would recommend to you to cultivate that of dr Rush & family. you will find them most amiable and agreable— if you meet any of My old acquaintance who retain a regard for me, present mine to them

Mrs Cranch Mrs TB Adams and Louissa all desire to be kindly rememberd to you. I hope you will make us a visit when the spring comes; whether you bring with you, a stranger, or not

Be assured I shall always cherish for you / a sincere and affectionate Regard / as your Friend and Parent[13]   Abigail Adams

RC (NIC:Johnson Family Papers); addressed by Louisa Catharine Smith: "Mrs Sarah Adams / Philadelphia"; docketed: "Abigail Adams / 1808 / character of different / Members of the family / &c." Dft (Adams Papers). Text lost due to wear at the fold has been supplied from the Dft.

[1] Not found.

[2] In the Dft, AA wrote and canceled: "to submit with cheerfullness to whatever situation She is calld to share and participate with her family."

[3] Isaiah, 35:1.

[4] AA paraphrased a 26 Feb. 1762 letter of Lady Mary Pierrepont Wortley Montagu that was published in the *Monthly Anthology*, 4:649 (Dec. 1807).

[5] Not found.

[6] Blank in MS. In the Dft, AA wrote here "Chenang."

[7] In the Dft, instead of the preceding two words, AA wrote, "her loss and that of Carolines who is a most amiable child."

[8] In the Dft, AA inserted and canceled: "at present they seem disposd to sacrifice all the blessing of Independence."

[9] In the Dft, AA instead concluded this par-

agraph: "we pass headless on, in sickness we feel our dependence and our obligations."

[10] Thomas Scott, "The Importance of Time," lines 1–2.

[11] In the Dft, AA continued: "I have been distresst least she Should be crooked for she would stoop in spight of constant admonition & run out her head, which gave her a very awkerd appearence."

[12] In the Dft, AA finished this sentence, "and she has improved in her Shape for the last Six months."

[13] In the Dft, AA added, "My Love to my dear Abbe / from her affectionate Grandmother."

Abigail Adams to Caroline Amelia Smith

My Dear Caroline: Quincy, January 24th, 1808.

To-morrow will be a fortnight since you left me; I have watched the weather with much solicitude, and when we had snow, as we had the Thursday after you set out, I hoped it might speed your journey, provided there should not be too great a quantity; although the storm was severe and cold on Saturday, it was pleasant sleighing. I flattered myself we should enjoy it for a week or ten days, but so changeable the season that on Monday we had a partial thaw. If you have had similar weather I fear you have not reached your journey's end. We were rejoiced to hear from you at Worcester, and afterward at Northampton.[1] A letter from a travelling friend is a great treat to those who sit by their firesides, compassionate their toils, sometimes fancying that they must suffer from the cold, from the snow, from the rain, hard beds, scanty clothes, small pillows, &c. But patience, my dear girl, will make a smooth road where the pick-axe has never levelled the inequalities, and soften the mattress and the pillow.

You will find new scenes opening before you; in the venerable oaks, you must fancy you see the image of those grandparents you have left behind, and every tree of the forest you must picture some friend or acquaintance, even to our little A., who daily calls for you. You must write me how you spend your time, what are your daily occupations and amusements, what acquaintance you make with the quail, the partridge, and the pheasant. If you find sufficient amusement in the winter, the spring will give you new employment, and new pleasures.

> "You must mark how spring the tended plants,
> How Nature paints her colours, how the bee
> Sits on the bloom extracting liquid sweets."[2]

I shall fancy you flitting about among the trees gathering the sweets of the season. Your friends were all much surprised at your sudden flight, and regret that they had not the opportunity of bidding you adieu. I shall send my regards to uncle Justus, and congratulate him on the acquisition of his female friends; tell him they will make the wilderness blossom like the rose, and add much comfort, I hope, to his domestic happiness. He deserves, I think, all they can bestow.

I think of you more on Sunday than on any other day. If you cannot attend public worship, you can spend your Sabbaths in a useful manner, as Mr. W. told us to-day, every moment should be devoted to some useful purpose, that we might ask the moments as they passed, what report they bore to Heaven—that the more we cultivated and improved our intellectual powers, the more capable we should be of enjoyment in a higher and more perfect state of existence; the nearer we should be allied to angels, and the spirits of just men made perfect; and that in order to cultivate our faculties to advantage, we must have order and method in all our affairs.

I am called to close my letter, yet I have not said half I intended; take it as it is, warm from the heart of your affectionate grandmother,

A. Adams.

MS not found. Printed from AA2, *Jour. and Corr.*, 1:209–211.

[1] Not found.
[2] Milton, *Paradise Lost*, Book V, lines 21–22, 24–25.

Louisa Catherine Adams to Abigail Adams

My Dear Mother							Washington Jan 24th. 1808

I have delay'd answering your very kind letter owing to my Baby's having been very seriously sick and requiring all my attention during a fortnight.[1] he is now entirely recover'd and has two teeth—

I much fear it will be a long time before I shall be permitted to see you as every thing appears to be in such a state of confusion and hostility that it is impossible to form any idea of the time that Congress may remain in Session since Mr Rose's arrival the cry for War seems to redouble, and it is generally supposed impossible to avoid it with one or other of the contending Powers—but the present system so evidently inclines to France the Negociation with G. B. is not likely to terminate very amicably of this however very little has transpired and it is only from ~~rumour~~ common report that we hear any thing on the subject—[2]

The Presidential Election is a subject which likewise furnishes a large proportion of our present conversation parties are becoming extremely violent and there is a decided opposition between Clinton and Madison which I think is likely to produce a complete division of

January 1808

the present Party there are now evidently four distinct parties of which Mr M's is undoubtedly at *present* much the strongest.³ it appears to me in the present desperate situation of Public affairs it will not prove an enviable station as the path is so thickly strew'd with thorns that the few flowers with which it is decorated only serve to conceal the poison by which it is surrounded— Our situation here this winter is not very pleasant as it is universally believed your Son has changed his party and the F., are extremely bitter ~~about~~ his talents are of too much real importance for them to venture publickly to throw him off but in private they circulate reports very much to his disadvantage⁴ he bears it with great fortitude and keeps up his health & spirits surprizingly indeed our time is now so short that I myself do not feel very anxious although I almost impatiently anticipate the moment of our release—

We are very solicitous to hear from you. Sister T. B. must I think be confined ere this, and I wish much to know how my dear Mrs Smith is, and if she, and her family, are still with you— I will thank you to make my love to all and particularly to Louisa tell her that Mrs Buchanan has had a *misfortune* so she need not beg[in] part of the work she promised though I dare say it will not be long before it is wanted Mrs B. has nearly recover'd her health but is still delicate

I hope my dear Mother as I am conscious of not shining very much in the art of letter writing that you will confine the perusal of this to yourself Kiss my lovely Boy remember me to Mrs Cranch and believe me very respectfully and affectionately   L. C. Adams

RC (Adams Papers); addressed: "Mrs A Adams"; endorsed: "Louissa Adams / Jan^ry 24 1808." Some loss of text where the seal was removed.

[1] AA's previous extant letter to LCA was that of 30 Nov. 1807, above.

[2] After British envoy George Henry Rose (1771–1855) arrived in Washington, D.C., on 13 Jan. 1808 to negotiate a settlement of the *Chesapeake-Leopard* Affair, the capital press carried rumors of impending war and expressed skepticism over Rose's mission. The Washington, D.C., *Universal Gazette*, 14 Jan., printed a resolution of the Va. General Assembly lamenting the "groans of murdered citizens" aboard the *Chesapeake* and pledging the state's support should the United States go to war. The *Washington Federalist*, 16 Jan., predicted that Rose's mission would "prove an idle errand." Rose and James Madison met from 1 to 25 Feb. and exchanged letters in March, for which see TBA to JQA, 10 April, and note 1, below. By mid-March the negotiators reached an impasse over Great Britain's demand that prior to any agreement the president rescind his 2 July 1807 proclamation prohibiting armed British ships from U.S. waters. Rose left the capital on 22 March 1808 and returned to London without an agreement (Jackson, *Papers*, 2:181; JQA, *Diary*; Monroe, *Papers*, 5:696; Madison, Notes on Negotiations with George Henry Rose, 1 Feb., DLC:Madison Papers; *Washington Expositor*, 26 March).

[3] Thomas Jefferson's announcement of 10 Dec. 1807 that he would not seek a third term as president set off a frenzy of electioneering to position a Democratic-Republican successor. Jefferson made it clear that his choice was Madison, who with Jefferson's backing and Dolley Payne Todd Madison's campaigning became a front-runner for the nomination. In opposition, John Randolph attempted to form

a "Tertium Quid" coalition of moderate Federalists and Democratic-Republicans to support the nomination of James Monroe. Jefferson's rejection of the Monroe-Pinkney Treaty combined with resistance from Federalists doomed the effort. A possible challenge by DeWitt Clinton of New York was forestalled by a move to advance Clinton's uncle and Jefferson's vice president, George Clinton. Congressional Democratic-Republicans held a nominating caucus on 23 Jan. 1808, where anonymous straw polls yielded 83 votes for Madison to 3 each for Monroe and George Clinton. Clinton received overwhelming support as the vice-presidential candidate. For JQA's attendance at the caucus, see his letter to TBA of 6 Feb., and note 4, below. The Federalists held the first national political convention in New York on 15 Aug., nominating a ticket of Charles Cotesworth Pinckney and Rufus King (D. D. McBrien, "Thomas Jefferson and the Question of Presidential Tenure," *Historian* 6:11 [Fall 1943]; Allgor, *Perfect Union*, p. 124–129; Robert Allen Rutland, *The Presidency of James Madison*, Lawrence, Kans., 1990, p. 3–5; Harry Ammon, "James Monroe and the Election of 1808 in Virginia," *WMQ*, 3rd ser., 20:34–35 [Jan. 1963]; John P. Kaminski, *George Clinton: Yeoman Politician of the New Republic*, Madison, Wisc., 1993, p. 280; Samuel E. Morison, "The First National Nominating Convention, 1808," *AHR* 17:753, 760–761, 762 [July 1912]). For the results of the presidential election, see JQA to LCA, 8 Feb. 1809, and note 4, below.

[4] JQA also ruminated on his political situation in an end-of-year summary in his Diary. "On most of the great national questions now under discussion, my sense of duty leads me to support the administration, and I find myself of course in opposition to the federalists in general," he wrote. "My political prospects are declining, and as my term of Service draws near its close, I am constantly approaching to the certainty of being restored to the situation of a private citizen." Years later LCA reflected on her and JQA's status on the capital social scene at this time: "Politics were growing very hot and Mr. Adams was very busy and very anxious— The Whigs began to be jealous of him, and the old Federalists hated him: so that we were fast getting into hot water" (JQA, *Diary*, Dec. 1807, Day entry; LCA, *D&A*, 1:264).

Thomas Boylston Adams to John Quincy Adams

Dear Brother   Quincy 24th: January 1808.

You have been lately gratified with such copious communications from this quarter, that I have been the more remiss in mine, not wishing to encumber you with too much matter at once.

We have read your Report to the Senate in the case of Mr: Smith, and the printed documents together with Mr: Smith's vindication; but the volume of evidence communicated by the President I have not seen, and am not competent to pronounce upon the correctness of the opinions expressed in the Report so far as they are grounded upon facts. I have no doubt but the Committee felt themselves justified in submitting their Report to the consideration of the Senate, but I confess that I am not able to discern the participation of Mr Smith in Burr's conspiracy, by any evidence I have yet seen. The testimony of Peter Taylor & Elias Glover has been so ably *chastised* by Mr: Smith that very little credit is due to either of them.[1] I *allow* them both, to use Peter's favourite expression, to be rogues or blockheads;[2] and if Smith should be able to fortify his own story, by other evidence than his own, I think he will retain his seat. The language and style of the

Report has undergone some criticism, but it generally passes for *elegant* composition. This is *my* opinion of it at least, and I had occasion soon after it reached Boston to express myself to that effect in answer to an objection made by a friend of ours, who said it was astonishing that a man who had written so much as you have should be so very incorrect in his *metaphors*. Why SHAW said I, you are a d——d fool: Do you pretend to criticise the professor of Rhetorick? He laughed very heartily at my civil rebuke and there it rested.

You see by the Boston papers what a fuss is made about the embargo. I suppose it is the same with all the great Sea port towns, though our Boston Scribblers are generally the most clamorous of any, when measures of Government happen to touch their tender feelings. The expectation of many is that it will be raised before March, but they ~~expect~~ hope to know more about it when the Senate shall have acted upon your motion.[3]

It may look foolish, ~~in me~~ to tell you what is said to me by some of the quidnuncs whom I happen to meet in Boston streets, on the subject of your reported nomination as a Candidate for the Vice-President's office. I was in town the day that the letter from Washington was published, in which the report was stated, and before I had seen the Newspaper, one man accosted me thus. ["]Well! Your brother is to be our next Vice President. Ah! How does that appear? Published in this day's Palladium & comes from Washington. Messrs Madison & Dearborn are held up by the Demo's & Monroe & JQA—in opposition.[4] What! then he belongs to Monroe's party said I? Yes, have you any doubt of him? Oh no, not the least, and do you mind his weather-cock said I, if you want to know when the wind will set in the right quarter." Exeunt— Not long after—the Honble Speaker overtook me, and after usual salutes—"Your brother John runs high for the Vice presidency on our Mountain."[5] "Oh yes, He is going to cut some of *you* out." I suppose so said he, & we turned off at right angles. One or two more such street-walking dialogues took place, but this specimen must suffice.

Our Genl Court have been in Session two or three weeks. The Governor Speechified both-houses, but only one branch has deigned a reply.[6] The Senate is dumb as a fish— I suppose their organ is out of tune or some of the pipes are missing. At any rate, no sound has yet reached the publick ear from that body.

We are all well & hope you are so. My visible family as yet consists of only three; but prospects increase. Faithfully yours

T. B. A—

PS. A letter from you to J. G W. Neale in our Post Office causes some speculation—[7] Your old would be pupil, is itinerant—though for aught I know he continues his old trade of wool-gathering—

RC (Adams Papers); internal address: "J Q. Adams Esqr."

[1] The fallout from Aaron Burr's treason trial, for which see JQA to LCA, 19 Feb. 1807, and note 4, above, included a Senate resolution introduced on 27 Nov. by Samuel MacLay of Pennsylvania. It called for consideration of Ohio senator John Smith's expulsion for his support of the Burr expedition and was prompted in part by the voluminous dossier of evidence in the Burr trial that the president submitted to the Senate on 23 November. The resolution was referred to a committee chaired by JQA, which recommended on 31 Dec. that a trial be held. JQA's committee report was printed as *Report of the Committee Appointed to Inquire into the Facts Relating to the Conduct of John Smith*, Washington, D.C., 1808, Shaw-Shoemaker, No. 16592. Smith answered the charges in *Queries Addressed by the Committee, 9th December, 1807, to Mr. Smith, with His Answers as Finally Given*, [Washington, D.C.], [1808], Shaw-Shoemaker, No. 16542. The pamphlet that TBA had not yet seen was *Evidence Reported to the Senate, by the Committee Appointed to Inquire into the Facts Relating to the Conduct of John Smith*, [Washington, D.C.], 1807, Shaw-Shoemaker, No. 13900.

The crux of the case against Smith lay in the testimony of gardener Peter Taylor and Cincinnati, Ohio, attorney Elias Glover (d. 1811), who both claimed that the senator had knowledge of Burr's allegedly treasonous plans. The full Senate held hearings from 13 to 20 Jan. 1808 then delayed proceedings until 1 April. In a four-hour speech on 8 April, JQA detailed the case against Smith, arguing that the defendant's own testimony and that of his confederates revealed collusion with Burr that merited expulsion. JQA joined eighteen others in voting for expulsion the next day, but a coalition of four Federalists and six Democratic-Republicans led by William Branch Giles of Virginia was enough to save Smith's seat. Smith, however, resigned on 25 April (JQA, *Diary*; *Biog. Dir. Cong.*; *Annals of Congress*, 10th Cong., 1st sess., p. 39–42, 170, 237–265, 324; *Amer. State Papers, Miscellaneous*, 1:486–645, 701–703; Isenberg, *Fallen Founder*, p. 356; Jefferson, *Papers, Retirement Series*, 1:643; Lebanon, Ohio, *Western Star*, 12 Oct. 1811; Anne M. Butler and Wendy Wolff, *United States Senate Election, Expulsion and Censure Cases, 1793–1990*, rev. edn., Washington, D.C., 1995, p. 18–21). For the political ramifications JQA faced for his role in the Smith case, see AA to AA2, 8 May 1808, and note 1, below.

[2] William Cobbett, *Porcupine's Works*, 12 vols., London, 1801, 6:83, 85, 86.

[3] The Boston press split along party lines in its views of the Embargo Act of 1807. The *Independent Chronicle*, 31 Dec., called it "wise and prudent" and dismissed the outcry from merchants: "the more the Tories roar, the better for the country." The Boston *Repertory*, 1 Jan. 1808, took the opposite tack, charging that the embargo required Americans "to submit to the most distressing privations—many to absolute ruin." The Boston *Democrat*, 20 Jan., also reported that JQA had introduced a resolution on 11 Jan. inquiring into when the embargo would be lifted and merchant ships allowed to arm "*to resist Foreign Aggressions*." The news had not yet reached Boston that on 21 Jan. the Senate defeated passage of the resolution without debate (JQA, *Diary*).

[4] The *New-England Palladium*, 19 Jan., reported JQA and Henry Dearborn as vice presidential candidates, claiming, "both parties feel the necessity of cultivating the interests of the Northern States."

[5] That is, Perez Morton, Speaker of the Mass. house of representatives.

[6] Gov. James Sullivan addressed the Mass. General Court on 8 Jan., calling on the legislature to encourage national unity and a negotiated end to the crisis with Great Britain. "It is time that we had become one people; without invidious distinctions, having no appropiate appellation, but that of American citizens," Sullivan declared. The house replied on 14 Jan., endorsing "a generous confidence in our rulers, and an inviolate obedience to their authority." The senate response was published on 30 Jan., expressing agreement but adding that the state must "be prepared for the worst events" (Boston *Democrat*, 9, 16, 30 Jan.).

[7] The letter from JQA to James G. W. Neale, not found, was likely related to Neale's desire for a military commission. On 26 Aug.

1806 Neale wrote from Quincy to the president (PHi) seeking a commission and offering JQA as a reference, though he stated that they were not well acquainted and were of opposite political parties. On 2 Jan. 1808 JQA visited Henry Dearborn and provided him with a letter from Neale, not found, seeking patronage. Meanwhile, on 5 Jan. Neale enlisted as a U.S. marine at the Charlestown Navy Yard. He sought patronage again in June but none was forthcoming (JQA, *Diary*; Charlestown Navy Yard muster roll, May 1808, DNA:RG 127, Records of the U.S. Marine Corps; Neale to Jefferson, 18 June; Jefferson to Neale, 15 Dec., both DLC:Jefferson Papers).

John Quincy Adams to John Adams

My dear Sir.   Washington 27. Jan$^{y:}$ 1808.

I have already written you a very long letter in answer to your favour of the 8$^{th:}$ inst$^{t:}$—and after writing it, upon reading it over concluded the best disposition I could make of it would be to burn it— Accordingly the flames have consumed it, and I must begin again.

Your answers and observations upon my inquiries respecting the impressment of our seamen by the British are of the highest interest—[1] But this general question has been absorbed by the new decrees of the great contending belligerent powers— Right and wrong are no longer subjects of discussion in our concerns with the European Nations— They appear to be agreed in the determination that there shall be no more neutrality, and our only choice is, which of the two we will resist.

I am very sensible of that situation in which you consider me to stand, and that being now wholly unsupported by any great party, the expiration of my present term of service will dismiss me from my public Station— By this Event my vanity may be affected; but in every other respect it will be a relief— Deeming it inconsistent with my duties ever to shrink from the service of my Country, I have always adhered to the principle that I should not solicit any of its favours— The present time, and the prospects of the Nation are such that a seat in the public Councils, cannot be an object of my desire— My literary profession and the Education of my children will occupy all my time in a manner which will furnish me duties enough to discharge— I shall also resume the practice of the Law, as far as that will resume me, and although this is a business for which I know myself to be indifferently qualified, I shall still pursue it as far as my circumstances will admit.

Notwithstanding the critical situation of the Country, the two Houses of Congress are acting very much at their leisure, and from their present proceedings one would imagine we were in a state of profound peace— The Presidential Election engrosses the principal attention of the Members— About one half the members of both houses here, have declared in favour of M^r: Madison; and to re-elect the Vice-President.— In the Legislature of Virginia also the friends of M^r: Madison have outnumbered those of M^r: Monroe nearly three to one— I understand that by way of making a temporary provision for M^r: Monroe, he is to be chosen Governor of Virginia.

I think you mentioned to me before I came on here, that there were two of the notes due at Hingham, which you would wish to have discharged the next Spring— I will therefore if it is agreeable to you enable and request M^r: Shaw, at the end of the present quarter (which will be I think the 22^d: of March) to pay you so much of the debt I owe you, as will reduce it to 4000 dollars— It is now a little more than 6000.— Of course he will pay you upwards of 2000 dollars of the principal, which will be sufficient to discharge two of the Notes, as far as I recollect—[2] If this arrangement should suit you, I will thank you to let me know, as early as convenient—That I may give directions in season to M^r: Shaw.

I remain, Dear Sir, ever faithfully yours.   J. Q. Adams.

P.S. My wife and child have been afflicted with colds, but are now well, and present their duty— The boy has two teeth— We received two days ago a letter from my Mother, to whom we offer our best affections.[3]

RC (Adams Papers); endorsed: "J. Q. A. ans^d Feb. 19."; docketed: "J. Q A 1808." Tr (Adams Papers).

[1] In reponse to a 27 Dec. 1807 query by JQA, JA wrote to JQA on 8 Jan. 1808 providing an extended legal discussion of armed resistance to impressment, drawing on recent cases and his knowledge of maritime law. He concluded that the United States was on firm legal ground, and that while Great Britain had the military might to impose its will, a "want of Power takes away no right." He also advised JQA on responding to the political backlash that followed his recent vote for the Embargo Act of 1807: "You are supported by no Party. You have too honest a heart, to independent a Mind and too brilliant Talents, to be Sincerely and confidentially trusted by any Man who is under the Dominion of Party Maxims or Party Feelings,: and where is there another Man who is not.?" (both Adams Papers).

[2] See JA's 19 Feb. reply, and note 1, below.

[3] Not found.

John Quincy Adams to Thomas Boylston Adams

My dear Brother.   Washington 6. Feb^y: 1808.

I am indebted to you, I believe for two letters; but there is so much in the last, of what parson Gardner in one of his Sermons said was called in the barbarous jargon of modern times *quizzing*, that I hardly know how to answer it at-all—[1] For the use or abuse of my name in the newspapers, whether from friend or foe, in good or in evil I hope I shall not be held accountable— Neither do I suppose any of my friends, nor even the nearest of my relations can expect or wish that for every malicious or every silly paragraph which either federalists or republicans can find a motive for pointing at me, I am bound to explanation—to admission—or to denial.— Because a certain portion of federalists have thought fit to connect the fortunes of their Cause with that of Admiral Berkley, and with that of Emperor Burr, and because in these two hopeful projects of theirs, I have thought it my duty not only to abandon them but to take a part active and decided against them, I am not at-all surprized to see the whole pack of their blood-hounds opening upon me— I expected it, and am as well prepared for it as I could be for any trial of that description— But I did suppose that I had friends in the world who had knowledge of my general character and confidence in the stability of my principles enough to be satisfied that my course of conduct as a public man never was and never would be regulated or governed by any base motive or any selfish consideration.

The Coalition of the *Berkley-ites* and the federalists, at the commencement of the present Session of Congress was highly exasperated against me, for what was termed *my Bill*—² They began immediately to shew their teeth, but had generally the wit to restrain their rage for that time— My vote upon the embargo increased their virulence, but they still thought some measures with me were to be kept— They knew perfectly well that with regard to that measure I was responsible for much more than my *vote*—for all the influence, and all the exertions I could use— But they still reserved much of their resentments in *petto*.

The Coalition of the *Burrites* and of the federalists, which is nearly the same with the other, but which includes some individuals of consequence who dared not pledge themselves quite so far, was driven to the last extremities by my report on the case of John Smith— Since then, they have avowedly excluded me from the ranks of federalism— have endeavoured by sly insinuations in Congress, and by open denunciations in the public prints to impute every false and atrocious motive to my conduct, and among others of their ingenious devices, have bent no small portion of their anxiety to inform the world that I am professor of Rhetoric and Oratory at Cambridge— They have attacked my Report for its style—for its principles—for its argument—for every thing that it did, and for every thing that it did not contain— They have amused me with insulting anonymous letters, and are very assiduous in the common routine of slander and invective, by which a man's character is hunted down by these doughty champions of order and good Government.³

All this as I have before told you is no more than I expected— But this very *Berkleyan—Burrite—Federal* violence against me, has produced a counteraction, which I believe years of mere public service, would never have obtained— It has made their opponents not only willing to number me on their side, but to give me a puff upwards for every blast downwards of their antagonists— It has given me a standing of Consideration in the Senate, certainly more distinguished than I ever before possessed; and has even led some of them in newspapers and Caucuses, to talk about me for Offices to which I have neither pretension, expectation nor wish.

You have seen, and by the manner in which you mention the Circumstance, it seems to have given you pain if not suspicion, newspaper intelligence from supposed Caucuses here; in which it was asserted that the Monroe party talked of linking me, for the Vice-Presidency with him, as President—and this in opposition to Madison, with Gen[l:] Dearborn— I have also seen these newspaper Publications, and I know nothing more of them than you do— I never received the most distant intimation from any one of M[r:] Monroe's friends, that could warrant a supposition that such an idea had ever been entertained by them— I did attend, by invitation the Caucus or Convention of Members which recommended Madison for President & Clinton for Vice-President, and voted at it—⁴ But in other respects I took no part in the proceedings— I was a mere Spectator and Hearer— You may be assured that if any suggestion of connecting my name with that of M[r:] Monroe upon this occasion had been made to me, I should have discountenanced it without hesitation, and in the most pointed manner— I do not think that he ought to be chosen President, and I have made no scruple of saying so at any period of the present Session—

Intimations from other quarters (not from either of the candidates) I have received— It is unnecessary for me to say any thing more to you about them than this— I have explicitly declared that in any support which I have given or may hereafter give to this or to any other administration, I have no personal views or expectations whatsoever—Nothing to *ask*—nothing even to *wish*— That the only reason upon which I have supported or may support the Administration, is a conviction that they are struggling to maintain the best interests and *rights* of the Country— Whether this answer was satisfactory or not, is unimportant— You may perhaps hear less of my prospects for the Vice-Presidency, or for any thing else, than you have hitherto, but you

February 1808

may rely that I neither am nor ever will be *pledged* to any thing but to the interest of my Country.

The laborious part of our public business, in the Senate, is now chiefly transacted in Committees, and there have been but two Committees on any subject of national importance yet raised this Session, of which I have not been a member—[5] The time I have spent in the Committee-Room has I believe exceeded in quantity that in which the Senate has been sitting, and the time employed in my own chamber upon the subjects discuss'd in Committee has perhaps been more than either— I have therefore had very few moments that I could have devoted to the canvass of election had it been a sort of occupation congenial to my taste— But I am observing not inattentively the attack and defence, the mines and countermines of the political combatants, and I find in them ample materials for reflections upon human nature and human Events, as well as considerable insight into the recesses of individual character— In this respect I am a mere by-stander, and without taking a hand myself find amusement and instruction in overlooking the Cards.

The subject for the last four or five days which has engaged the deliberations of the House of Representatives has been a proposal of M^{r:} Sloan for removing the Seat of Government to Philadelphia—[6] It is not yet decided, but the probability seems to be that the project will not succeed. I suspect its real and principal object is to produce an effect on the Election— We had also two days ago a new *Yazoo* Petition—from New-York—presented in Senate by D^{r:} Mitchill, who has heretofore always voted against those claimants— Warm debate on the question whether the petition should be *received*—taken at last by yeas and nays— You have seen in the newspapers how the memorial from the Massachusetts Legislature was treated in the other house—[7] Perhaps the New-York Legislature may take it up next— Congress may refuse to hear those People, untill they will find inducements to listen stronger than the naked sense of Justice.— It is now one of the most powerful electioneering Engines that has yet been brought into play. The Extinguishment of the State Balances has also been worked for the same purpose, but that was at length dismiss'd from the Senate by a bare majority—[8]

The Negotiation with M^{r:} Rose is said to have been suspended, and nearly broken off ten days ago, by his requiring as a preliminary the repeal of the President's interdicting Proclamation— His legation certainly then did talk of going home immediately, and the *Berkleyans* in Congress were writing paragraphs for publication at home charging our Administration with the rupture of the Negotiation— The rumour of departure has since subsided, but it is said M[r.] Rose is negotiating with others besides M[r.] Madison— I believe there is foundation for the report.[9]

My wife and child are well— I hope the same of yours, and ask affectionate remembrance / to the whole *fire-side*. / Your's.

P. S.— If you should discover in this Letter an unreasonable number of metaphors too incorrect for the *Professor of Rhetoric*, get Shaw [to] ask the favour of the Anthology-Reviewer of the pamphlet called the British Treaty to correct them.[10]

RC (Adams Papers); endorsed: "J Q Adams Esq[r.] 6[th.] Feb[y] 1808 / 18th Rec[d]." Some loss of text due to an ink blot.

[1] TBA's most recent letters were those of 27 Dec. 1807 and 24 Jan. 1808, both above. JQA was referring to his friend John Gardner (ca. 1769–1825) of Boston (vol. 13:410; *Boston Patriot*, 25 April 1810; JQA, *Diary*, 20 May 1808; Boston, *21st Report*, p. 373).

[2] For JQA's role in a bill authorizing the president to interdict foreign vessels in U.S. waters and the backlash JQA faced, see JQA to TBA, 14 Dec. 1807, and note 5, above. Adm. George Cranfield Berkeley (1753–1818), commander of Great Britain's North American Squadron, based in Halifax, Nova Scotia, was recalled for issuing the orders that were the catalyst to the *Chesapeake-Leopard* Affair. Some New England Federalists rejected the near-universal condemnation of Berkeley, fearing that reprisals would bring further economic consequences and countering that Thomas Jefferson's policies provoked British actions. The Boston *Columbian Centinel*, 30 Dec., argued that calls to punish Berkeley provoked Anglo-American discord that would only benefit France (*Dicy. Canadian Biog.*; Bradford Perkins, *Prologue to War: England and the United States 1805–1812*, Berkeley, Calif., 1968, p. 140–144).

[3] The New York *Herald*, 27 Jan. 1808, attacked JQA's committee report recommending Senate consideration of John Smith's expulsion, for which see TBA to JQA, 24 Jan., and note 1, above. The newspaper, edited by William Coleman (1766–1829), condemned the "reprehensible" report and lambasted JQA as a *"professor of Oratory in Massachusetts"* whose writing was imbued with "more the declamation of a Grecian sophist than the chastened dignity of a Roman Senator." JQA was also attacked in a [23 *Jan.*] letter from a "Supporter of the administration of John Adams" (Adams Papers), which dismissed the Smith case as politically motivated and enclosed clippings from the *Herald*. The writer called on JQA to "think of your former reputation already sinking in the eyes of those men whose good opinion is alone worth having— Think of the reputation of your Worthy father & pause before it be too Late" (TBA to JQA, 19 Feb., below; Jay, *Selected Papers*, 7:206).

[4] JQA attended the 23 Jan. Democratic-Republican presidential nominating caucus at the invitation of Vermont senator Stephen Row Bradley. His presence and the single vote he received as a vice-presidential candidate enraged Federalists. William Jackson in his Philadelphia *Political and Commercial Register* published an anonymous letter claiming that JQA snuck into the caucus uninvited and that the vote for him "excited universal surprise" and on examination "was found to be in John Q. Adam's own hand writing." The Boston *Democrat*, 10 Feb., reprinted the report and labeled it "crimination and villany" and lauded JQA for standing "unshaken by the roaring blasts of federalism" (JQA, *Diary*, 20 Jan., 23 Feb.; Bradley, Letter to Republican Members of Congress, no imprint, 19 Jan., Adams Papers; Robert R. Thompson, "John Quincy Adams, Apostate: From 'Outrageous Federalist' to 'Republican Exile,' 1801–1809," *JER* 11:180 [Spring 1991]; Salem *Essex Register*, 16 Feb.).

[5] The journals of the Senate session to date record 37 instances of committee reports by JQA and referrals to committees of which JQA was a member, including those considering a response to the *Chesapeake-Leopard* Affair, reviewing memorials from U.S. merchants,

drafting the Embargo Act of 1807, and considering the treaty with Tripoli. These duties were in addition to chairing the committee considering Smith's expulsion (U.S. Senate, *Jour.*, 10th Cong., 1st sess., p. 190, 191, 192–193, 194, 196, 197, 198, 200, 201–202, 203, 205, 208, 210, 211, 212, 214, 217–219, 221, 223, 224, 226, 227; U.S. Senate, *Exec. Jour.*, 10th Cong., 1st sess., p. 59, 66; JQA to TBA, 14 Dec., and note 5; TBA to JQA, 27 Dec., and note 3; 24 Jan. 1808, and note 1, all above; JQA, *Diary*, 16 Dec. 1807, 5 Jan. 1808).

⁶ On 2 Feb. James Sloan of New Jersey introduced a resolution in the House of Representatives to move the federal capital to Philadelphia owing to the "meager and wretched appearance" of the District of Columbia. A 9 Feb. vote to advance the bill failed and the measure was tabled (*Annals of Congress*, 10th Cong., 1st sess., p. 1531–1532, 1542–1543, 1549–1550, 1595–1596; *Biog. Dir. Cong.*).

⁷ On 5 Feb. Samuel Latham Mitchill of New York introduced a memorial in the Senate from speculators seeking to resolve Yazoo land claims, for which see JQA to William Smith Shaw, 3 Feb. 1805, and note 3, above, by placing the case before the U.S. Supreme Court. Although JQA viewed the action as an electioneering ploy by George Clinton's backers, he joined a 22-to-3 majority in approving the memorial's reading. No further action was taken. A similar memorial from Gov. James Sullivan and the Massachusetts legislature was presented in the House on 4 Jan. 1808, claiming that residents had invested heavily in the lands in good faith and seeking a speedy resolution of their claims. Viewed by the press and in the House as an attempt to advance questionable claims, the memorial was referred to committee in the House, and on 12 Feb. a resolution to further consider the memorial failed and no further action was taken (*Biog. Dir. Cong.*; U.S. Senate, *Jour.*, 10th Cong., 1st sess., p. 228; JQA, *Diary*, 5 Feb.; *New-England Palladium*, 15 Jan., 16 Feb.; *Boston Commercial Gazette*, 22 Feb.; *Newburyport Herald*, 19 Jan.). For JQA's role in a later U.S. Supreme Court case on the Yazoo claims, see JQA to LCA, 5 March 1809, and note 1, below.

⁸ Samuel White of Delaware on 30 Oct. 1807 introduced in the Senate a resolution calling for a committee to study whether debts owed the United States for funds advanced to states for the fortification of coastal defenses should be forgiven. A recent report showed one of the outstanding debts was an 1801 advance of $222,810 to New York. A bill to extinguish the debts was reported from committee but tabled until the following December after a 21 Jan. 1808 motion by JQA was approved by a single vote (*Biog. Dir. Cong.*; U.S. Senate, *Jour.*, 10th Cong., 1st sess., p. 190, 191–192, 218, 222; *Amer. State Papers, Finance*, 2:163–164).

⁹ For the unsuccessful negotiations between British envoy George Henry Rose and James Madison, see LCA to AA, 24 Jan., and note 2, above. Rose was also consulting with Timothy Pickering, who blamed Madison and French influence for the failure of the talks (Gerard H. Clarfield, *Timothy Pickering and the American Republic*, Pittsburgh, Penn., 1980, p. 236–238).

¹⁰ The *Monthly Anthology*, 4:563–570 (Oct. 1807), included a review of *The British Treaty*, [Phila.?, 1807], an anonymous pamphlet attributed to Charles Brockden Brown. The review endorsed the pamphlet's support of Jefferson's rejection of the Monroe-Pinkney treaty and effusively praised the author as "a man, who evidently possesses so much genius and information" (p. 564).

Abigail Adams to John Quincy Adams

my dear son   Quincy Feb'ry 15 1808

I take it for granted that You will neither in public or private Life do any thing which you are unwilling to own, or to affix Your Name. I write to ask You if uninvited You attended the Caucus at washington of which mr Bradley was President.?

It is not the Scandolous publication in Jacksons Register at Philadelphia, which has induced me to ask this question, but because I have considerd it as inconsistant both with Your principles, and your judgment, to have countananced such a meeting by Your presence, the Constitution having expresly excluded any Representative or Senator from being an Elector.¹ I should suppose delicacy would forbid their presumeing to dictate to their constituents in a matter of such high importance, and consider it, as an infringment upon the *freedom* and *purity* of Elections, if I may apply such words to our Elections at the present period. in the next place I should not have expected, that You would have been an invited Guest, much less, that You would have appeard there an unvited Spectator.

my Solisitude to know the truth, arises from Some persons giving credit to the report, whom I know to be Your Friends, and have staggerd my beleif. If You was present, I can only say, thinking as I do, I can never cease to regreet it,—as I shall most sincerely a decision in favour of the Removal of the judges, by a petition from both Houses of congress.² If through Age or imbecility, some judges may continue upon the Bench, longer than the powers and faculties of their minds are equal to their situations, is it not a less Evil, than would result, from making them dependent upon Legislative power.?

You must have considerd this subject upon a larger scale than I have; Yet I have been taught to consider an independent judiciary as our surety against arbitary power, our ~~only~~ best security for Life Liberty and property. I regret that Death has deprived You of so valuable a Friend as Mr Tracy, without supplying his place.³ to confer freely with a confidential Friend, gives strength and confidence to opinions, of which we may be doubtfull. King Solomon sanctiond this Sentiment when he declared that two were better than one—⁴

The abuse thrown out against You, and so liberally bestowed in anonymous publications in newspapers, or private Letters, some of which I have seen, particularly from Newyork—where it is presumed Burr Yet has Friends, and an English party powerfully prevails. I would pay no further attention to them, than to See if any truth was containd in them, which might prove usefull as admonition or reproof, never refuseing to profit even by the advise of an Enemy.

It is said of Fabius in the Roman history that he patiently sufferd the most injurious and unmerited reproach; saw his reputation torn in peices; and exposed himself to universal censure and reproach, for observing the only conduct capable of preserving the state; saw the most important Services repaid with the most cruel ingratitude by an whole people, Yet he departed not from his plan or his Duty in the midst of so many, and so sensible subjects of discontent.⁵ This adds the Historian must be confessd to be the effect of a force constancy

February 1808

and nobleness of Sentiments much above the common. this Love of the public good was the Soul of his actions and continually inspired him with that inflexible firmness and constancy for the Service of his Country, against which he never deviated into the least resentment, what ever injury he received from it—

This is a Character Worthy of imitation, which cannot fail to transmit itself to futurity, and receive from ages to come the just applause it deservedly merits, tho the spirit of party may now obscure its Lusture, and envy through over it her darkest shade.

Altho You may differ from some of Your nearest and best Friends in your judgment, and opinions upon important subjects I should much sooner suspect the soundness of their judgments, than the purity and uprightness of Your intentions— So long as You live, may You hold fast Your integrity, is the sincere and / fervent prayer of / Your affectionate Mother A Adams

RC (Adams Papers); addressed by TBA: "J Q Adams Esqr / City of Washington"; endorsed: "My Mother. 15. Feb^y: 1808. / 24. Feb^y: rec^d: / D^o: Ans^d:."

[1] For the attack on JQA in William Jackson's Philadelphia *Political and Commercial Register*, see JQA to TBA, 6 Feb., and note 4, above. The U.S. Constitution, Art. II, sect. 1, prohibits federal officeholders from serving as electors.

[2] Senator Edward Tiffin of Ohio on 5 Nov. 1807 introduced a proposed constitutional amendment to limit federal judicial appointments to an unspecified number of years and make judges removable upon a two-thirds vote of both houses of Congress. The proposal was one of six introduced during the congressional session, part of a series of unsuccessful attempts to limit judicial tenure advanced between 1807 and 1812 by state legislatures, including those of Massachusetts, Vermont, and Pennsylvania. The final one considered in the present session was prompted by a 2 March 1808 resolve of the Mass. General Court instructing its congressional delegation to introduce a proposed amendment making judges removable on a vote of a majority of the House and two-thirds of the Senate. JQA introduced the resolution on 12 April and it was referred to committee. The Mass. General Court repealed the instructions in the next session and no further action was taken (Herman V. Ames, "The Proposed Amendments to the Constitution of the United States during the First Century of Its History," Amer. Hist. Assoc., *Ann. Rpt. for 1896*, 2:149–151, 328; Mass., *Acts and Laws, 1806–1810, Resolves*, p. 118–119; *Biog. Dir. Cong.*; JQA, *Diary*; *Annals of Congress*, 10th Cong., 1st sess., p. 21–22, 331).

[3] Senator Uriah Tracy of Connecticut died in Washington, D.C., on 19 July 1807, and he was the first member of Congress interred in the new Congressional Cemetery (*Biog. Dir. Cong.*; Rebecca Boggs Roberts and Sandra K. Schmidt, *Historic Congressional Cemetery*, Charleston, S.C., 2012, p. 24).

[4] Ecclesiastes, 4:9.

[5] AA paraphrased historian Charles Rollin on the fortitude of Quintus Fabius Maximus Verrucosus in adhering to his principles and ignoring public censure while opposing Hannibal (Rollin, *The Roman History from the Foundation of Rome to the Battle of Actium*, 3d edn., 10 vols., London, 1768, 3:448).

John Adams to John Quincy Adams

My dear Son　　　　　　　　　　　　　　　　Quincy Feb. 19. 1808

In Answer to your Letter of the 27 of January I request you to make Provision for Advancing me, by Mr Shaw one thousand one hundred and twenty five dollars and fifty Cents, or thereabout, which is the amount of an obligation I owe to Miss Thaxter, ~~or if you choose~~ and I think there is but one remaining due to that Family.[1]

your Mother has written you on the Subject of Caucus's.[2] I am not of her opinion. Among the Romans the Patricians often held Caucus's, the Senators had Caucus's and So had the Plebeians. The Town of Boston has held Caucus's time out of mind and So have all other popular assemblies. They cannot be avoided. Bradley to be Sure made too much Pomposity of it, and therby exposed it to criticism. I blame not your Attendance nor your Vote. You ought to go on with your System. You will be instructed to vote for the alteration in the Tenure of the Judges offices, and I cannot blame you for obeying your Instructions, tho I Sincerely lament them. The dinner given in London to Mr Munroe, will not give him in my opinion the preference to Mr Madison.[3] If this latter Gentleman is chosen he will not continue more than four Years. He will be turned out as I was. one System cannot last more than twelve years. The present System will not Shine in History. Its measures have not been wise, nor its morals pure nor its Religion divine, if it has had any. I apprehend it will not redound to your Popularity or mine to Support it. But it must be Supported, however unpopular it may be hereafter. We have no other Way to defend ourselves against the Sharks and Panthers.[4]

Mr Madisons bias towards the French has always been too great but I never Suspected him of Corruption. On the contrary the bias of all the Federalists to my certain Knowledge, even of my friend Mr Jay is too Strong against France and in favour of England.

If I were Alexander the great and had absolute Power like him I would declare War against England France and Spain all at once and Soon have the Floridas and Mexico too, and have Commerce by Sea at least by captures. That River ~~Louisiana~~ Missisippi I fear will cost Us much blood. I always expected it would involve Us in War. It is the very nettle that tingles in the veins of England. and that of France and Spain too. But it is ours and We must defend it.

May the divine blessing attend you, fortify your heart against the rude blasts you must endure, and conduct you and your Country into a Safe harbour. So prays your affectionate Father

John Adams

RC (Adams Papers); internal address: "John Quincy Adams Esqr." Tr (Adams Papers).

[1] JQA owed JA for real estate he purchased after the family's losses in the 1803 failure of London banking firm Bird, Savage, & Bird. JQA wrote to William Smith Shaw on 18 Feb. 1808, asking Shaw to pay JA $290 out of dividends received on JQA's shares of stock in the New England Insurance Company and the Boston Bank. In response to JA's request he wrote to Shaw again on 7 March (both MWA: Adams Family Letters), asking him to make a payment to JA of $1,081 of the principal and $91 in interest. JA's debt was to Hingham residents Celia and Elizabeth Thaxter, nieces of the late Norton Quincy, for 29 March 1802 notes that were part of JA's acquisition of Mount Wollaston Farm (vol. 15:x–xi, 140; Cotton Tufts to JA, 20 April 1803, Adams Papers; *History of Hingham*, 3:232–233).

[2] AA to JQA, 15 Feb. 1808, above.

[3] "Merchants trading to America" hosted a public dinner in London for James Monroe on 10 Oct. 1807 shortly before his return to the United States. The Federalist *Massachusetts Spy*, 13 Jan. 1808, reported the event, noting that attendees toasted a continuing friendship between the two countries (*Mississippi Herald and Natchez Gazette*, 31 Dec. 1807).

[4] JA echoed popular motifs that cast Great Britain as a shark and France as a panther (JQA to TBA, 14 Dec., note 3, above; Colin Jones, "French Crossings: III. The Smile of the Tiger," *Transactions of the Royal Historical Society*, 22:17 [2012]).

Thomas Boylston Adams to John Quincy Adams

Dear Brother.   Quincy 19^{th:} February 1808

I received, yesterday your favor of the 6th instant, for which I thank you. The letter, which upon mature consideration, I burnt, as I informed you in the cover of a letter from my Mother, sent a few days ago,[1] was on the subject of the proposed alteration of the Constitution, as to the tenure of judicial Offices; but my ideas upon paper suited me less than when they were revolving in my mind, and as there appeared to be no originality in them, I concluded to frank them, up the Chimney, with a blaze, instead of *illuminating* your thoughts, by sending them in the Mail. After the paper on which they were written had taken fire, a sudden draught of wind took the sheet at once out of sight and I never expected to hear or see more of ~~them~~ it; but, to my great surprize and alarm, two or three days from the time when they were committed to the regions of soot & smoak, while I was sitting quietly by the fire, down came the half burnt and lacerated dispatch, covered with a quantity of the chimney ingredients, the weight of which had caused its unexpected descent. I thought it was the Ghost of the Judiciary that had so long haunted my imagination, and by the colour and general complexion I took it to be a pretty correct representation of the features of our National Judiciary, as they will appear whenever two thirds of the States shall have sanctioned the scheme of removing the Judges upon the address of both houses of Congress— Smoak-dried—discoloured and be sooted as it was; here a dark stain, there a spot more luminous & legible, interspersed with a few yawning holes, where the voracious element had entirely consumed its texture, I examined it for an instant, in a state of suspence, ruminating whether, should I send it to its original destination in that doleful plight, it would not present a more perfect picture of my true reflections than in its first estate. A second thought impelled me to complete the work of destruction, and I have the satisfaction now to confirm the once premature tidings of its total consumption. I believe that a fertile fancy might have wrought these materials into an instructive Allegory, but to me it is not given to weave a web, like the brain-born Goddess. I shrink from the experiment lest mine should be the fate of the fabled Arachne.

I am aware of the difficulties under which you labour in your political career; the envy, malice and humiliated pride of furious partizans must find a vent somewhere, and you will be covered with the sparks of their effervescence. For any of our family to aid the measures of the present Administration, however congenial those measures may be with the true interests of the Nation, will be looked upon as damnable heresy, by those who call themselves federalists; and to be accused of apostacy, time serving and treachery is the least that can be expected from them. Selfish views and interested motives are ascribed without exception to every man who takes pains to distinguish himself in publick life. In our virtuous Republick, these are the wages of preferment, and yet how many are eager to receive this salary and to prize it in proportion to the quantity of gilding with which it is surrounded. I was fully convinced before I had the assurance from you, that you had never encouraged the Association of your name with that of M^r: Munroe, for any purpose whatever. Nor did I believe, that you had attended the Caucus and voted for yourself as *Vice President in your own hand-writing*, as the immaculate Major Jackson would have it in his Register. I did not believe you thought so meanly of yourself as to ~~give~~ put in for Vice President, when there was a poll open at the same place for President. Nor, *some how or other*, did I believe, that you would have assisted, at all, at such a Caucus. But herein I reckoned without mine host, and upon a little self-examination I began to doubt whether I might not have attended, through curiosity, and have been called a Jacobin, as I did on another

February 1808

occasion, when you were appointed to Office, and baptised at the same time. Now, it seems, that the old Spanish proverb, that a man is known by the company he keeps, applies to all who are seen within the walls of a Caucus Room, notwithstanding there may be some spies & some interlopers among them. I remember, one or two instances of federal Caucuses, when suspicious members gained admittance— Much staring and whispering— Is he a Fed? Who knows that man? And many more such questions flew round the Room, when, at last, somebody who knew him and could vouch for his political creed, being interrogated, instantly dispelled the gloom of jealousy, and appeased the dismay of suspicion. It is supposed, that there will be a considerable division among the *Republicans*, in consequence of M$^{r:}$ Munroe's pretentions to the Chair. It will be a laughable coincidence of circumstances, should Monroe be supported by the Tories, the Burrites and Federalists. But what can *we* do? We must have a candidate. Clinton has some friends, but he is too old for ~~some~~ many; and the general opinion appears to be that he must stay where he is, or decline a re-election. There will be twelve States, at least in favor of Madison for President, unless a change should take place before the fall. New York, if we may judge by the behaviour of their Representation in Congress, is displeased at the preference given to youth, talents and activity, in the person of Madison, to the humiliating exclusion of their favourite old General.[2] I should give my vote for Madison sooner than any Candidate that has been mentioned or thought of; but I should prefer John Jay to any man in the Union. He is out of the question, as much as if he had been dead for a Century.

I have read some of the attacks in the New York papers upon your report. The criticism in Coleman's Herald has been ascribed to a man, once of Senatorial rank, and upon comparing it with a review of the Declaration of Independence, which was published some years ago in the Gaz. U. S. I have concluded that the same hand produced them both. Among a few sound remarks in this last performance there is an abundance of malignant and illiberal severity. *Our writers*, in Boston have only talked about it queerly.[3] Friend S—— when I shall shew him your postscript will understand it, perhaps, better than I do. The Review you mention I have since read in order to take your meaning; but, saving that it appears to be from a british patriot, I can discern no clue to your allusion.

My wife & *children* are well. I presume you will learn the news of an increase of our family from some quarter or other, before this will inform you. My daughter Elizabeth will be a fortnight old, on Tuesday.[4] With best love to your wife and all our Washington friends, I am truly yours. T. B. Adams.

RC (Adams Papers); addressed: "J. Q. Adams Esqr / Senator of the U S. / City of Washington"; endorsed: "Adams— T. B. 19. February 1808. / 2. March. rec{d:} / 12 Ans{d:}."

[1] JQA's letter of 6 Feb. is above. The note that TBA included with AA's letter to JQA of 15 Feb., above, has not been found.

[2] For the electioneering in New York by a faction advancing Vice President George Clinton as a presidential candidate in the 1808 election, see LCA to AA, 24 Jan., and note 3, above.

[3] Democratic-Republican commentators in Boston newspapers generally lauded JQA's report on the John Smith expulsion case, with the *Independent Chronicle*, 21 Jan., calling it "masterly" and the *Boston Courier*, 14 Jan., declaring that it was "couched in energetic and impressive language, and will command the universal attention of the American people." For the attacks on JQA by the New York *Herald*, see JQA to TBA, 6 Feb., and note 3, above.

[4] Elizabeth Coombs Adams (d. 1903), designated as ECA in *The Adams Papers*, was born on 9 Feb., for which see Descriptive List of Illustrations, No. 3, above.

John Quincy Adams to Abigail Adams

My dear Mother. Washington 24. Feb{y:} 1808.

I have just received your affectionate letter of the 15{th:}—and do not a moment delay to answer your question— I did attend the meeting of members at the Capitol on the 23{d:} of last Month—but not without invitation— I received the same invitation, which was given to the other members—And besides that I was also personally urged to attend, by another member of the Senate— I did not attend without due reflection upon what was proper for me to do— That it should have met your disapprobation I can never cease to regret—But I cannot see the force of the objection against the Constitutionality of this proceeding.

The Constitution has forbidden members of Congress from being *Electors*—but it has not forbidden them from giving their votes for Electors— They enjoy in this respect the common right of their fellow-Citizens, nor can any provision in the Constitution, excluding an individual from a privilege possessed by the community in general, be extended by argument and inference beyond the force of the excluding terms. Members of Congress cannot be *Electors*; but they are not forbidden as I conceive, from having their opinions, or from expressing them with regard to the person whom they think, best fitted, for the Office of President, or upon whom at a difficult and dangerous period, it is most expedient for the National welfare that the election should fall.— The question I believe has never before been raised; and in the years 1792–1796—and 1800 the right was I believe practiced by the federal members of Congress, as well as by their opponents.

February 1808

I am sensible that there are objections of principle against *all* Caucusing, previous to Elections— Yet the difficulty of effecting a concert of opinions, and a combination of efforts—of *harmonizing* the will of great numbers of individuals actuated by the same public principles, in any other manner, has perhaps produced the necessity of resorting to measures of this kind—they are constantly resorted to by all parties, and with some inconveniences they have the advantage of rendering Elections less tumultuous, and more peaceable than they would be without such preparatory precautions.

I do not consider a recommendation to the *people*, made by a number of their public Servants—made professedly in their individual capacities, as the result of a comparison of sentiments among themselves, on a subject important to all, as an attempt to *dictate* to the People, whom they shall choose— The People will certainly choose as Electors, whom they please—excepting that they cannot choose those who make the recommendation—

It is undoubtedly to a certain extent the exercise of influence, but being merely advisory, I cannot think it more unconstitutional, than for the father or mother of a Member of Congress to advise him and express their wishes to him how he shall vote upon important questions, in his official situation.— The influence of a Parent upon a Son, must certainly in the heart and mind of every man who feels as I do, be much greater than that of a Senator or Representative over the vote of his Constituent; yet I think myself obliged to my Parents for their advice upon any subject upon which I am to deliberate and vote; nor do I think it unconstitutional to admit any influence they think fit to exercise upon my will, as far as my own sense of duty can be made reconcileable with it.

Having said thus much, I must now add that the numerous newspaper Publications, which have been directed against me since the present Session of Congress, were not unexpected to me— My situation has been difficult—my conduct, governed by my best judgment, under a deep conviction of the perilous State of the Nation, and of my own duties in the Station where I have been placed— I could wish to please my Country— I could wish to please my Parents— But my duty, I *must* do— It is a Law far above that of my mere wishes.

The proposal for an Amendment to the Constitution making the judges of the United States removable by Address of the two Houses, has been recommended by the Legislatures of five or six States, but not yet as far as I know by that of Massachusetts— I do not expect that it will pass in Congress by the Constitutional Majority, the present Session—when it comes to deliberation I shall certainly give the subject all the attention that I can bestow upon it, and shall eventually vote, as upon all other questions, according to my sincere and imperious sense of duty.

I write you in the midst of an important debate, upon M^r: Giles's Treason-Bill—[1] I am afraid my letter will partake of the broken attention, which this Circumstance occasions—But I could not delay even till Night an answer to your letter— My wife and child are well— I will answer my father's letter, as soon as possible.[2]

With unchanging duty and affection, I remain ever yours'.

RC (Adams Papers); endorsed: "J Q A / 24 Febry / 1808." Tr (Adams Papers).

[1] In response to a request for treason law reform in Thomas Jefferson's 27 Oct. 1807 message to Congress, the Senate on 16 Jan. 1808 named JQA and four others to a study committee. Chair William Branch Giles reported on 11 Feb. with a bill defining a list of specific crimes as treason and making it punishable by death. Debate centered on whether the delineation would encourage or discourage prosecution. JQA joined a minority voting against the bill when it passed in the Senate on 6 April, but the measure failed to win acceptance in the House and went no further (JQA, Diary, 23 Jan., 12 March, 6 April; Annals of Congress, 10th Cong., 1st sess., p. 86, 108–109, 135–149; U.S. Senate, Jour., 10th Cong., 1st sess., p. 261; Dice Robins Anderson, William Branch Giles: A Study in the Politics of Virginia and the Nation from 1790 to 1830, Menasha, Wisc., 1914, p. 116–119).

[2] JA wrote to JQA on 12 Feb. of his alarm over the proposed constitutional amendment on judicial impeachment, adding, "I am grieved to see that you favour the Amendment!" Judicial independence, he wrote, "is fortified in our national Constitution beyond all former Example. . . . It is the only Security of our Lives, and Liberties." JA also wrote extensively on federal debt policy (Adams Papers).

John Quincy Adams to Thomas Boylston Adams

My dear Brother.   Washington 12 March 1808.

I begin by congratulating you upon the birth of your daughter Elizabeth, of which I had never heard, untill I received your letter of 19$^{th:}$ ult$^{o:}$ although we had been three or four weeks in daily expectation of receiving the news, and as this is intelligence of peculiar interest to the Ladies, there was scarcely a day pass'd, but upon my return home, my wife's enquiries were, of advices from Quincy, and the increase of the family— I pray that this newcomer together with her elder sister, may prove a comfort to your succeeding years, and in due time the happiness of another's youth, and the promise of succeeding generations.

Your alarms and anxieties on the subject of the judiciary, are more earnest than the occasion requires— I refer you, for my sentiments to a long letter, which I wrote a few days since to your father—[1] My faith in the theory of judicial Independence has been somewhat staggered, by the batteries of experience; but I have not yet abandoned it altogether, and I am willing to try the experiment a little longer— This disposition is also felt by so many members of both Houses of Congress, that no Judges will be unseated during the present Session— What the next will bring forth, is not given to me to say.

Your reasoning upon the report, transmitted by Major Jackson's Correspondent, that I had voted for myself, at Bradley's meeting was very sound as far as it went— If I had been capable of voting for myself, I should hardly have had the modesty to wait untill the second ballot— The truth is that I did attend the meeting, but not without invitation—that I did vote, but not for myself— Who it was that put in the ballot bearing my name, I am utterly ignorant, as well as of his motive— Who was Major Jackson's Correspondent I do not absolutely know, but I can shrewdly conjecture— His motives I understand tolerably well; and thereby hangs a tale—[2]

M^{r:} Bradley's printed circular to convene the meeting was dated the 19^{th:} of January— On the 20^{th:} he address'd one of them to me, and delivered it personally to me— I read it—asked no questions; and told him I would attend.— I knew not who else was invited, or whether other federalists besides myself were included in it under the denomination of Republican members— Between that day, and the 23^{d.} (when the meeting was held) I heard more than one federal member *ask* M^{r:} Bradley for an invitation, in a jocular manner indeed, but apparently with an inclination to obtain it, and with obvious disappointment, at his eluding the solicitation— The disposition to favour M^{r:} Madison's election was not even concealed in this courtship of invitation; but I know not wherefore— It did not succeed— Some days after the meeting, when it was generally known, that I had been the only federalist invited, I asked M^{r:} Bradley why he had invited me— He said it was because I had received marks of confidence from the Republicans among my own Constituents, and referr'd immediately to the meeting at the State-House in Boston last Summer, and to my name appearing on the Committee appointed upon that occasion—

Jackson's Correspondent I take to have been one of these Gentlemen, who had asked invitations for themselves—they too had enquired of Bradley, why they should not receive an invitation, since he had SENT one to *me*— Bradley, to get rid of their importunity, said to one of them that he had not SENT me an invitation; and although the person to whom this was said knew very well, what Bradley meant, yet on these words, he wrote to Jackson that I had attended, without invitation— The rest of the Story, about my vote in my own handwriting, was all of his own invention.

In the Gazette of the United States there appeared a contradiction of this miserable slander, in reply to which Jackson's Correspondent took the field again— I know not who was the writer of the piece in Bronson's paper, and knew nothing of it untill its appearance in print—³ You will observe the bullying style of the reply, and the readiness which the writer professes to maintain his words *like a Gentleman*— Now the distinction upon which this *Gentleman*, insists upon his charge that I attended the meeting without invitation is this— Bradley told him that he had not SENT me an invitation; but he added, or at least the *Gentleman* knew, that Bradley had delivered the invitation to me himself. But he takes post at the word SENT, to charge me with attending the meeting without invitation, and finding this contradicted, renews the charge, affirms that Bradley told him he had not SENT me an invitation; that I attended without SUCH invitation, and that he is ready to exchange names with Bronson's Correspondent; whom he has reason to believe to be me, or rather Bradley, at my instance— Whether this itch for shooting me down in a duel, would have stood the test of a determination on my part to gratify it, is perhaps not perfectly clear— The same dueling itch in a bad cause, and probably *in the same person*, has cost Gardenier, all but his life— For Gardenier as I am well informed would not have fought, but for a stimulus from the same quarter—⁴ However this may be, upon the best reflection I could give the subject, I concluded to take no notice of the publication.

You may perhaps think it extraordinary, that on an occasion of so little significancy, and where my only real offence against this valiant federalist was, that I HAD received an invitation to Bradley's meeting, which *he* could not obtain, even by asking for it, there should have arisen a malignity so absurd, and so rancorous in his mind against me. To explain this, it would be necessary for me to give you the history, of at least the last and the present Session of Congress, and also of some secret and personal history, which I am not at liberty to tell— There are *federalists*, who in the present state of Affairs, are anxious to *negotiate* themselves into favour with Mr: Madison and his friends— They have been very desirous to obtain admission into the corps of his supporters— Now according to their mode of reasoning, an invitation to Bradley's Meeting was the *test* of this Admission, and when they found *me* thus admitted, and themselves excluded, if you will

March 1808

trace the workings of certain passions, upon souls at once aspiring and groveling, you will discover the key to the letters from Major Jackson's correspondent— They fancied that I too had been negotiating for the same purpose as themselves, and they were stung to the heart, at the thought that my negotiation had succeeded, while theirs had failed— They found selfish motives at the bottom of their own system of public conduct, and they imputed them to me— They knew themselves; but they did not know me— The truth is, that while they were *making* advances, I was *receiving* them— While they were *soliciting* pledges of personal support and local influence, I was *rejecting* them—while they were offering themselves *to Market*, I was explicitly declaring, that in any support I might ever give to this or any future Administration, I had no personal views whatsoever— Nothing to *ask*— nothing to *wish*. This Answer I was giving, to overtures of no equivocal nature.

I have sent you the newspaper, containing the *protest*, against Mr: Bradley's Convention, and against the nomination of Mr: Madison, signed by seventeen members of Congress, four of whom are from Virginia, six from Pennsylvania, six from New-York, and one from South-Carolina— The stamp of the composition is that of Mr: John Randolph, and it is understood to be the signal of a coalition between the supporters of Messrs: Clinton and Monroe—[5] There are some other facts and some rumours in circulation connected with the appearance of this protest; which I shall now mention for your amusement, and which I commit to your discretion—

The lieutenant-governor of Virginia, Mr: M'Rae, one of the principal friends of Mr: Monroe is here—deputed (as is said) for the purpose of forming the coalition—[6] The first proposition (as alledged; though I can hardly credit this) was that Mr: Clinton should agree to serve as Vice-President, Mr: Monroe to be substituted instead of Mr: Madison for the Presidency— This however, if made, was rejected, and ultimately the order was reversed— Mr: Clinton to be supported, for the *great-house*—and Mr: Monroe to come in as Vice President— This point however seems to be conditionally conceded; and the protest is in the nature of a manifesto, proclaiming the principles of the association— The proscription of federalists, and of any yazoo compromise, are to be the fundamental articles of the compact— It is remarkable that about three weeks since, a Yazoo Petition, came for the first time *from New-York*, and was presented in Senate by Dr: Mitchell— The Vice-President then in conversation with me, express'd himself fully in favour of a compromise of this claim, as he had often done before— Whether the protest is to pledge him against it, Time will perhaps discover— It is also known as a fact, that hitherto, much of M^r: Monroe's expectation in *Virginia*, has been of support from federal assistance; which Madison's canvassers have used as a heavy engine against Monroe— The inference then seems to be, that the Monroe party in Virginia, having abandoned all hopes of success in running him for the Presidency, are now resolved to put up with the second place for him, and entirely to discard that federal assistance upon which they had previously relied.

The inveteracy between the Monroites and the Madisonians in Virginia, is great and daily increasing. M^r: Monroe is to publish a Book— A view of the conduct of the Executive, *number two*.— This is to open the eyes of the Nation to the faults of M^r: Jefferson's administration of late years, in relation to foreign Affairs— It is to shew that M^r: Monroe was compell'd to sign the obnoxious Treaty of 31. Dec^r: 1806. because nothing better could be obtained—[7] That nothing better could be obt[ained] because at the critical moment, when M^r: Monroe was on the point of getting every thing we could [want a col]league was sent out to defeat him; and that the colleague was sent out to defeat him, by M^r: Madison's influence, and for the purpose of getting the start of Monroe, in the race of popularity, which was to terminate in the presidential chair—

The Coalition, if really settled and understood, to the extent, which I have some reason to believe it is, will constitute a formidable phalanx against M^r: Madison's election— One of its first effects must be to compel Madison's friends, to change their candidate for the Vice-Presidency— Else they might be placed in a very perplexing dilemma— For if they vote for M^r: Clinton as Vice-President, while his own friends vote for him as President, and Monroe as Vice-President, unless Madison should obtain a majority of the whole number of Electors, M^r: Clinton may become at once one of the three candidates from among whom the house of Representatives must select the President, and one of the two from whom the Senate will have to chuse the V.P.— and by declining the latter, may leave Monroe to the certainty of being Vice-President, and oblige the house either to prefer him to Madison for the Presidency, or to have both the Offices at once fill'd by Virginians— This is a thing so manifestly contrary to the *intent* of the Constitution, that I have always thought it expressly prohibited; which however it is not.— The Madison men are now confident of a full majority of the Electors; but of this I have my doubts— I question whether they will trust to it themselves— Yet they cannot drop their

March 1808

nomination for Vice-President without inconsistency—nor without weakening their canvas for the Presidency.

I know not whether Shaw, will have understood my reference to the Anthology-reviewer, any better than yourself—[8] But my meaning was this— That a Report of a Committee, might ask indulgence for incorrect metaphors, nearly as much as a familiar letter— That such papers were written *currente calamo*, and that their *style*, was a circumstance usually suffered to pass without notice— I did think it probable that Shaw's very microscopic scrutiny into the accuracy of the metaphors in my Report was in its origin Anthology Criticism; and that it proceeded from a disposition so much displeased with the substance, as to be ready to nibble more than was necessary at the form— It was the same disposition, which at New-York, thought to degrade the Report, by proclaiming that the Author was a *Professor of Oratory*.— The real fact is that in the composition of that Report, I paid scarcely any attention to the *style* at-all— It was written at short intervals of leisure from a most laborious investigation of the facts, and of the principles upon which it was founded— Written at different times, and printed from a rough draft, with scarcely a correction other than several erasures—Yet the style was very designedly unusual— My purpose was to command attention— To make the Report *be read*; and I knew so well the character of the American reading public, that I was sure nothing would contribute so much to get readers, as here and there a flash of declamatory lightening— A mere dry logical state paper would have pass'd uncensured, and unread— This object I believe was very effectually obtained— But as to the correctness of the metaphors, I must abandon that to the critics; for I never stop'd to examine one of them.

M^r: Rose is not yet gone, but is said to be upon the wing— There are so many false reports in circulation respecting the progress and termination of his mission that I scarcely can tell you any that is near the truth— You see the federalists in and out of Congress storming the Executive for information—papers—foreign correspondence—M^r: Armstrong's letters—&c &c &c— You and I know what it is, for American Ministers abroad to have all their official communications liable to be divulged to all the [. . .] a call of papers from Congress— M^r: Jefferson holds a tighter hand upon foreign papers than was possible [. . . .] I am glad he does— If what he has communicated were published, it would aid him more than it would his anglo-federal enemies; but I believe his real apprehension is that it would exasperate the people *against* England more than he yet wishes to see them.[9]

I think Congress will adjourn in the course of next month— The members are becoming very impatient to go home—nothing keeps them together but the wish before they go to repeal the Embargo— They might indeed give the President a discretionary power to remove it during the recess, but he does not chuse to have it.[10] The Senate have pass'd a bill for raising six thousand men; with two brigadier-generals and no commander in chief.[11]

Affectionately yours'.

RC (Adams Papers); endorsed: "J.Q. Adams Esqr: 12th March 1808. / 21st Rec^d: / 24th: Answ^d"; notations: "J Q A"; and by ECA: "*I E C A still live—* / *to 1895!*" Some loss of text where the seal was removed.

[1] JQA's letter to JA, which was begun at the end of February and finished on 6 March, has not been found but was praised by JA as "luminous" (JA to JQA, 18 March, Adams Papers; JQA, *Diary*, 28 Feb.).

[2] The anonymous correspondent who attacked JQA in the Philadelphia *Political and Commercial Register* hinted that he was a member of Congress. JQA considered approaching colleagues to seek the writer's identity "but concluded, after some reflection that it would be giving him too much consequence." He also decided not to answer the charges in the press, reasoning, "The danger of once undertaking to answer newspaper falsehoods, is of involving yourself in a sort of obligation always to answer, which would be endless" (JQA, *Diary*, 23 Feb.).

[3] Enos Bronson's Philadelphia *United States Gazette for the Country*, 11 Feb., published a defense of JQA calling the suggestion that he voted for himself at the Democratic-Republican nominating caucus "an arrant falshood" and a product of "sheer malice."

[4] In the House of Representatives on 20 Feb. New York Federalist Barent Gardenier (1776–1822) accused Tennessee Democratic-Republican George Washington Campbell (1769–1848) of being subservient to France in his advocacy of strong measures against Great Britain. JQA was in the House gallery and wrote in his Diary that the "very vehement and inflammatory" rhetoric prompted talk of a duel. The pair attempted to duel on 27 Feb. but were stopped by magistrates after a large crowd gathered to watch. They met again on 2 March. Gardenier was seriously wounded but survived (JQA, *Diary*; LCA, *D&A*, 1:268; *Biog. Dir. Cong.*; Bernard S. Katz and C. Daniel Vencill, eds., *Biographical Dictionary of the United States Secretaries of the Treasury, 1789–1995*, Westport, Conn., 1996, p. 50).

[5] Seventeen Democratic-Republican members of Congress signed a 27 Feb. address "To the People of the United States" expressing disapproval of their party's 23 Jan. presidential nominating caucus, which endorsed a ticket of James Madison and George Clinton. The address, printed in the Washington, D.C., *Universal Gazette*, 10 March, called the caucus a "gross assumption of power" and claimed that those objecting to it had been unfairly labeled "enemies of liberty." In attacking Madison as indecisive and "unfit to fill the office of President," the address also furthered John Randolph's attempts to rally support for James Monroe as a presidential candidate, for which see LCA to AA, 24 Jan., and note 3, above (*Biog. Dir. Cong.*).

[6] Alexander McRae (ca. 1765–1840) was the lieutenant governor of Virginia (Monroe, *Papers*, 4:539; Harry Ammon, "James Monroe and the Election of 1808 in Virginia," *WMQ*, 3rd ser., 20:42 [Jan. 1963]).

[7] JQA reported on 13 Feb. that he encountered William Branch Giles in the Capitol, and Giles appeared upset by a rumor that Monroe would soon publish "an Electioneering Book, to defeat Madison's Election & promote his own." The defense of his role in the negotiation of the Dec. 1806 Monroe-Pinkney Treaty, for which see JQA to LCA, 19 Feb. 1807, and note 2, above, would constitute a sequel to Monroe's earlier defense of his diplomacy in France under George Washington, *A View of the Conduct of the Executive, in the Foreign Affairs of the United States*, Phila., 1797. Monroe did not publish such a work (vol. 12:345; JQA, *Diary*; Monroe, *Papers*, 5:704–705; Daniel Preston, ed., *A Comprehensive Catalogue of the Correspondence and Papers of James Monroe*, 2 vols., Westport, Conn.,

2001, 1:198, 199; Washington, *Papers, Retirement Series*, 2:169).

⁸ See JQA to TBA, 6 Feb. 1808, and note 10, above.

⁹ Thomas Jefferson submitted a series of documents to Congress in March regarding U.S. diplomacy with Britain and France. Those included dispatches from Monroe during his mission to Britain and from U.S. minister to France John Armstrong Jr. on his conversations with French officials. Although Jefferson marked Armstrong's dispatches confidential, they were read in open session of the Senate and later published by order of the House of Representatives (*Letters from the Secretary of State to Mr. Monroe*, Washington, D.C., 1808, Shaw-Shoemaker, No. 16454; *Letters from the Secretary of State to Mr. Monroe . . . Part II*, Washington, D.C., 1808; *Letters from the Secretary of State to Messrs. Monroe and Pinkney . . . Part III*, Washington, D.C., 1808; *Papers Relative to French Affairs Communicated by General Armstrong to Mr. Monroe*, Washington, D.C., 1808, Shaw-Shoemaker, No. 16536; JQA, *Diary*, 26 Feb.).

¹⁰ While Congress did not repeal the Embargo Act of 1807 before adjourning on 25 April, it passed three bills modifying the embargo's parameters that were all signed into law. An act signed on 12 March suspended duties on goods intended for export but held back by the embargo. A second authorizing the president to raise the embargo during the congressional recess was signed on 22 April. Then the third act, signed on 25 April, laid out procedures for enforcement of the Embargo Act and enacted penalties for violations (JQA, *Diary*; *U.S. Statutes at Large*, 2:473–475, 490, 499–502).

¹¹ Jefferson and Secretary of War Henry Dearborn on 25 Feb. called for enhancements to national defense, prompting the Senate on 9 March to pass a bill providing for the raising of the military force described by JQA. The bill was overwhelmingly approved in the House on 7 April and signed into law on the 12th (*Amer. State Papers, Military Affairs*, 1:227–228; U.S. Senate, *Jour.*, 10th Cong., 1st sess., p. 246, 264; JQA, *Diary*, 26 Feb.; U.S. House, *Jour.*, 10th Cong., 1st sess., p. 255–256; *U.S. Statutes at Large*, 2:481–483).

Hannah Phillips Cushing to Abigail Adams

My Dear Madam　　　　　　　　Washington March the 17$^{th.}$ 1808.

We were blessed with fine weather & roads from Providence to Phil$^{a.}$, where we staid a fortnight; & from thence here as good as usual in Jany. My Husbands health daily increasing, & my own entirely restored from the anxious & destressing winter, & summer, I had just passed through, also having heard as late as the 26$^{th.}$ Novr of the welfare of our dear Relatives at New Orleans, my spirits were revived, & I was pleasing myself with the hope of having an agreeable winter, when lo we had been in this our pleasant Chamber but five days when the sudden death of my beloved & only Brother, came as a faithful monitor, to warn us of the frailty of all human enjoyments.¹ But blessed be Heaven since the first day & night my mind has been wonderfully composed & resigned, being fully persuaded that his days were then numbered & finished, that, that was the way ordered by the great Ruler of the Universe for him to depart out of this World, into I hope & trust a Heavenly region. I have mentioned him but seldom to you my bosom Friend, but he was very near my heart, & if I could have ransomed him from death a few years longer, by living on bread & water the remainder of my days, I would most cheerfully have done it. His heart was truly benevolent, for the milk of human kindness flowed around it. He took no delight in speaking ill of any one, & the tongue of slander he put far from him. He has left a bright example of patience, & fortitude, under great trials, & reverse of fortune. Often have I viewed him with astonishment & delight rising superior to them all, & labouring hard for his daily bread; at the same time my heart has been sorely grieved for him, & if I had been possessed of a fortune, with how much satisfaction would it have been bestowed. While I lament & bewail the departure of one so deservedly dear to all his connexions, I reverence the hand which inflicted the blow, & bow with submission to the will of the most High; Believing that there is a time to come when we shall be reunited where no revolutions of nature shall ever separate us more. The excellent sentiments contained in your good letter, which I received in May last at Phil$^{a.}$, often occur to solace me in this great affliction, & I have not yet expressed to you how much satisfaction the receipt of it gave me.[2] I have a propensity often, when most obliged to say the least. I have received a letter from my dear afflicted Sister Phillips. She is under very great affliction, but strives to be submissive. Religion seems to be her all & only consolation, & it is in that all Balm of comfort, that I must resort to for the healing of this & every other sorrow, that Heaven sees fit to inflict upon me. I will endeavour all in my power to fulfil what would have been his last worldly wish could he have expressed it, Do what you can my Sister for my Wife, & two darling Children. The eldest is not eight years old. Court finished yesterday.[3] My Husband sat six weeks daily, two days excepted. They went in at 11OC & sat till 4, generally, which was trying to a feeble constitution; & last sabbath after we came from the Capitol He was taken with chills. I sent immediately for Dr May who recommended a dose of six Lockyer Pills, which had a good effect. We had intended a visit to Mount Vernon to see Mrs Judge Washington. She too has had great affliction since we parted in Nyork last June, having lost her Father, & a Son of her Brothers, whom the Judge & her self had adopted for their own, also a Son of her Sisters, & a Miss Washington, Niece of the Judges.[4] The last three were buried in less than three weeks by the side of each other. Notwithstanding I am so strongly drawn by the cords of nature, & love, to hasten my return to my dear & sorrowing Sisters, to sympathize with, & console each other, for the death of our dear departed Brother; yet it is with heart felt regret that I relinquish the idea of first seeing Mrs Washington, & also some dear Friends in Alexandria. But Dr May advises us to set our faces to the

March 1808

North without delay, & my own fears coincided, least we should have the same scene to go through as that of last winter. The D[r] request me to give his best respects to you & the President. Judge & M[rs] Cranch have just called to see us; they are both in good health. It is some days since I saw M[rs] Adams, but presume that She, & M[r] Adams, are well.

Baltimore the 20[th.] Sunday.

We came to Rosses 9 miles the 18[th.] & yesterday reached here.[5] The roads never were better, having had remarkable fine weather for some time. Vegetation is coming on rapidly. It is three weeks since the buds of the Lombardy Poplars began to swell. I have seen or heard but very little of what has been going on in the City this winter. Having neither dined or taken Tea out of my room once. Contrary accounts have frequently circulated respecting M[r] Rose, & it was confidently asserted ten days since that the Negotiation was at an end, But I called to see M[rs] Madison yesterday week, who told me it was not so; That M[r] Madison had finished his part of the Buisiness, & that it remained for M[r] Rose to close it. That when it was committed to paper which was nearly done, it would be immediately laid before the Public. She observed that to be sure She was not let into the secret, yet as the Negotiation was going on in her drawing room, (M[r] M[s.] ill health not permitting him to leave it) She could not help hearing more than she wished. I told her that is was said M[r] Rose only had power to settle the Chesapeak affair. She said that was not true. My Husband whose veneration & respect, with mine will be as lasting as life for you, & The President, wishes to be respectfully remembered to you both, also to Judge & M[rs] Cranch. I often think of M[rs] Adams, & Miss Smith, & wish to be mentioned to them with esteem. I have delayed writing to you my bosom Friend, much longer than I intended; My dear Connexions being separated, & residing in so many different places, & all of them anxious to hear often from us, engrosses 'most all my time that I have for writing. We hope to be in Middleton by 10[th.] of April; a letter from you my Dear Madam will be gratefully received by your Friend H Cushing

RC (Adams Papers); internal address: "M[rs] Adams."

[1] Capt. Thompson Phillips (b. 1752), Cushing's only living brother, had recently "drowned at New-Orleans, by the upsetting of a boat." His widow was Abigail Cheeseborough Mumford Phillips (b. 1767), and their children were Abigail (b. 1800) and Anne Duryee (b. 1803), the younger of whom would spend significant time in the Cushing household after her father's death (vol. 15:280; Middletown, Conn., *Middlesex Gazette*, 28 Jan.; James Carnahan Wetmore, *The Wetmore Family of America*, Albany, N.Y., 1861, p. 498–501;

James Gregory Mumford, *Mumford Memoirs*, Boston, 1900, p. 222–223; Ct:Connecticut Church Records, State Library Index, vol. 70, part 2, p. 429; Richard Jay Hutto, *The Kaiser's Confidante: Mary Lee, the First American-Born Princess*, Jefferson, N.C., 2017, p. 12–13).

[2] Not found.

[3] The U.S. Supreme Court session began on 1 Feb. and ended on 16 March, with the justices hearing arguments in 27 cases and handing down decisions in 32 (Anne Ashmore, "Dates of Supreme Court Decisions and Arguments," p. 6–7, 8, U.S. Supreme Court, www.supremecourt.gov).

[4] Julia Ann Blackburn Washington, wife of Supreme Court justice Bushrod Washington, lost her father, Col. Thomas Blackburn (b. ca. 1740) of Rippon Lodge, on 27 Oct. 1807. Her siblings were Richard, Thomas, Catherine, Sarah, and Mary. "Miss Washington" who died in 1807 was Jane Mildred Washington (b. ca. 1793), a daughter of Bushrod's brother Corbin Washington (vol. 15:405; Horace Edwin Hayden, *Genealogy of the Glassell Family of Scotland and Virginia*, Wilkes-Barre, Penn., 1891, p. 601–603, 633–638; Justin Glenn, *The Washingtons: A Family History*, 2d edn., 10 vols. in 14, El Dorado Hills, Calif., 2015, 1:79; Sarah Blackburn Craufurd to Dolley Payne Todd Madison, 23 Oct. 1808, *Dolley Madison Digital Edition*).

[5] William Ross ran a tavern in Bladensburg, Md., nine miles north of Washington, D.C. (Washington, D.C., *National Intelligencer*, 21 March; Washington, *Papers, Retirement Series*, 1:53–54).

Abigail Adams to Abigail Adams Smith

my dear Daughter   Quincy March 18th 1808—

William has been so punctual in writing to you every week, that I have been more remiss. I cannot write in an Evening. the only time in which I feel a disposition to use my pen is the forenoon; you know how buisily that is generally occupied, and more so now Louissa is in Boston; and the Farm buisness is just commencing. Mrs Dexter is going to housekeeping.[1] I know not where to Supply her place, but her family increases mine, and the Embargo distresses us all. yet is it a measure that I am convinced was the ~~most~~ best calculated to avert the horrors of war, of any which prest on all Sides as our Government were, could have been resorted to, cruel & oppressive as it appears, and hard as it is to be borne. we had better suffer temporary privations, than the calamities of war, which when once commenced no one can calculate or estimate. You have expresst, Your surprize that Your Brother attended the caucus at Washington. William has coppied a Letter and inclosed to You in replie to one which I wrote under the same impression which you felt at the report;[2] as he says he weighd well the subject before he went, I presume he considerd mr Madison the fittest man upon that Side of the Question, and one of the most sensible and candid of Virginians, a moral Man unexceptionable in Private Life. in the present state of our Country, union is essentially necessary to our very existance, and So Small is the federal weight in the political scale that there is not the least probability of their succeeding in any federal Character they might nominate, to obtain the Best and least exceptionable on the other side is a desirable

March 1808

object. these were the reasons I have not a Doubt which induced Your Brother to attend the caucus which has subjected him to So much falshood and calumny from the federal party; for they could always perform their part, not quite So hardily however as the Antis.

In a Letter of late date, March 9th he says, I have no partialities in favour either of Britain or France.[3] I do not believe that either of them is fighting the battles of the world, or sacrificing itself for the Liberties of Mankind— During the present war the first aggression against Neutral Rights was committed by Great Britain She it was, who by her pretended rule of the War of 1756 undertook to interdict the trade of neutrals with her Enemies colonies—for the purpose of Monopolizing it herself.[4] Scarcly two years have elapsed Since Congress was besieged with petitions and memorials from all the Merchants of the united states against this usurpation upon the most unquestionable Neutral rights. a Resolution of the senate *unanimously* declared it, ["]an unprovoked aggression upon the property of our Citizens, a voilation of their Neutrals rights an encroachment upon our national independence,". it was in consequence of a memorial from Boston on this Subject that a special mission was sent, to England— That special mission you know has failed— It terminated in a *treaty* so *derogatory* to our *Rights* that the President did not even lay it before the senate. A *Treaty* which would ["]in substance have surrenderd to Great Britain the whole of her principle against which we had so formerly, and so justly protested"

with respect to foreign influence he observes thus—the Speculative opinions and personal feelings of the President & Secretary of state, have perhaps always inclined too much towards France; as the opinions and feelings of other Statesmen equally distinguished have inclined too much towards England— there are few, very few indeed, in this great political conversion of the World whose *Hearts* have not taken a side in the struggle; but it has been, and still is my candid opinion, that so far as relates to public conduct, and official acts, the neutrality of the present administration has been as fair and impartial as it was under either of those which preceeded, and during the former war— The administration is and must be charged with the duty of asserting, and maintaining the Rights of the Nation; but this Duty it can never discharge, unless the Nation itself give it countenance and support in its measures.—

"Speaking of the embargo, he writes, I consider it as the last anchor of our peace, and if it can preserve us that Blessing, heavily as it bears upon our country, I shall always rejoice at my vote in its favour, as contributing to the extent of my power to the best interest of the Nation— there is no smart like that which is felt, that we may have no opportunity to compare by this Scale of actual feeling the sufferings, of war with those of Embargo—I do most fervently wish, but if we should, I have no doubt of the result. The little finger of war, will be heavier than the loins of Embargo."

I wish I could transcribe the whole of the Letter, but do not feel at Liberty to, as it is written to mr Hall, and only lent to me. it Breaths through the whole a spirit of candour impartiality, and integrity which is the true Character of the Man, and which is a source of never failing satisfaction to me.

with respect to mr Rose's negotiation, I do not believe from the statement given, that it can terminate to the Satisfaction of the Government— He says, I told mr Roses principle companion, (who was an old acquaintance of mine at Berlin) that if he & I had the negotiation to conduct, and I had unlimited powers—I would ask of him one single word, and give him *Carte Blanche*—[5] The word was *Reciprocity*, but great Britain has no Idea of that.

I know how much you feel interested in whatever affects the Characters of those nearly connected with You—and I could not so ably defend your Brothers against the base attacks made upon it, by attributing to him views which never enterd his mind, and conduct which he scorns, as by transcribing his Letter, and giving you fully his sentiments— you can form an opinion by what is before you—

william this day has finishd his school much to the satisfaction of his employers— his attention has been unremitting and his success will speak his praises— he appears averse to the Law. the Embargo is an obstical to all commercial enterprize. the Army seems to be his object, and his Grandfather has told him that he should not have any objection to writing both to the President and mr Madison & the secretary of war— I have also told him that I would write to the President. Several young Gentlemen have gone from Boston to washington for the purpose of engageing in the service. upon this Head, he will consult both his Father and you— I feel loth he should leave us, but know not what to advise him to do—

Tell caroline I will attend to her commission to her Brother, and that I shall write soon to her Mrs Adams has had a fine getting up, scarcly Sick a day. her little Girl grows finely and is quiet. they both went to meeting last Sunday, Elizabeth Coombs is its Name— Abbe grows daily more and more interesting—dresses herself up and shakes her hand with a good by Mamma, by Grandmamma, go and see aunt

March 1808

Miff and caroline, which She has now learnt to pronounce— she is very fond of the Baby, call it precious sister—and teazes it so with her carresses that her Mamma cannot keep her with her— My paper is almost full, yet I have many more things to say. Your Father had a Letter from John this week who was well.[6] Susan has written to caroline, what kind of a Letter I know not as she would not let me see it— I inclose it however.[7] Pheby is so much better that she hobbles about House— with Love to all—I am your truly affectionate / Mother—[8]

RC (MHi:De Windt Family Papers).

[1] Longtime Adams servants Rebeckah Tirrell Dexter and Richard Dexter married at Peacefield in 1804 and had children Edward (b. 1805) and Caroline (b. 1807) (vol. 15:425; Sprague, *Braintree Families*; AA to AA2, 8 May 1808, below; Elizabeth Smith Shaw Peabody to AA, 13 Nov. 1810, 11 Nov. 1811, both Adams Papers).

[2] William Steuben Smith's transcription has not been found but was of JQA's 24 Feb. 1808 letter to AA, above.

[3] AA included substantial extracts from JQA's 9 March letter to Boston attorney Joseph Hall Sr.; see TBA to JQA, 24 March, and note 6, below.

[4] For Great Britain's reinstatement of the "Rule of 1756," see JQA to TBA, 20 Jan. 1806, and note 2, above.

[5] Justinian Casamajor (d. 1821) was secretary to British envoy George Henry Rose and had earlier served as secretary to diplomat John Joshua Proby, 1st Earl of Carysfort, in Berlin and socialized with JQA and LCA there (JQA, *Diary*, 19 Jan. 1808, 21 March, 21 Oct. 1815; Vere Langford Oliver, *The History of the Island of Antigua*, 3 vols., London, 1894–1899, 2:29; LCA, *D&A*, 1:138, 154, 267).

[6] Not found.

[7] Not found.

[8] AA wrote to AA2 again on 27 March 1808, alerting her that William Steuben Smith had departed three days earlier to join his family in central New York. She also reported on local agriculture and neighborhood news, commented on European politics, and relayed greetings from friends in Boston (MHi:De Windt Family Papers).

Thomas Boylston Adams to John Quincy Adams

Dear Brother   Quincy 24th: March 1808.

Although I have recently written you a letter of some length,[1] I will not therefore refrain from a prompt acknowledgment of your favour of March 12th: which particularly deserves my thanks for the variety of intelligence it contains, of a nature not to be derived from any other source. The detail you have given of the various intrigues supposed to be in operation at head quarters and elsewhere for the accomplishment of particular objects, is amusing to those who consider themselves only as lookers-on, and purposely avoiding to take any part in the plot. You know how strong the prejudice of the federal party in New-England generally, and in this State in particular, always has been against a Virginia President, since the time of Washington, and though the Democrats have yielded the precedence to the antient dominion and supported the Administration of Mr: Jefferson, with great zeal, it may be questioned whether there will be equal unanimity among them in the choice of a Successor. I rather incline to think that M:̲ Clinton would obtain more votes for President than M:̲ Madison, at present, through the N. England States, but how it may be six months hence is another question. It is to be presumed that a pledge will be required of the Electors to support some one of the Candidates and to this end care will be taken to select *fit* men for Electors. Much of the success of any Candidate will depend upon the state of the Country at the moment of chusing Electors— If we have war, it is understood that the present incumbent will be *forced* to continue; and if we have peace, it is my humble opinion that the party will, for fear of accidents, persuade him to stand another poll. I do believe that the sentiments expressed by the Protestors against Bradley & C⁰ and their nomination, will create such divisions among the Democrats, that the Federalists may yet prove a more formidable phalanx than the protestors themselves are willing to admit. The votes of Connecticutt and Delaware may yet turn the scale against the favourite Candidate, and there is no doubt of their being thrown into that which would disappoint the greatest number of the Democratick party.

We are to be drummed up, once more, in this State, to show our teeth against Gov:̲ Sullivan. I have been nine years constantly voting and making myself busy in the cause of Federal against Democratick Governors. What shall I do this year? This is more than I can tell. I cannot vote for M:̲ Sullivan, for *several* reasons, and though I am personally friendly to M:̲ Gore whose character is altogether unexceptionable, so far as I know, I am well persuaded he cannot be elected.² The Circular letter alone would be sufficient to defeat the prospect of his success, though it is expected to produce most wonderful effects in the Sea ports— *In Boston it will not do* to express a doubt as to the success of the Federal ticket— I am not disposed to defeat it, and if silence on the subject will do any good, I am content to hold my peace. But in opposition to this it seems to be the opinion of some of your best friends, that *you* ought not to keep your peace. The Letter from the "Venerable," has stirred up some old-blood, which at times circulates with considerable rapidity—³ I need not particularize . . .⁴ The conclusion seems to be, that you must act your own sound discretion, as to the expediency of communicating, any information you may possess, relative to our foreign relations, directly to your Constituents. There is a disposition in many to think & act right, but they want information; not as the clamourers for correspondence in Congress want it, for the sake of mischief, but honestly, for *conscience*-sake. This class however is not very numerous, for between those whom no information would satisfy, and those who want none to be satisfied with the conduct of the Administration, the men of influence are generally divided. On your return home you must expect to find yourself in a strange land. The sour looks & spiteful leers will not be few, that you will have to encounter, but they will be seen on the faces of those, who have long harboured a secret heart-malignity against yourself as well as against your father. By relying on the efficacy of the "Venerable's" prescription, at this particular crisis of our National malady, the Junto will most inevitably fail in their expectations of a cure. The address from the federalists of Boston in this days paper is but an Echo of the Senatorial Manifesto— It condemns the Embargo as a "desperate remedy" and declares that no other probable ground or motive, than to gratify the wishes of the Emperor of the french, is competent to account for that measure.[5] As no electioneering purpose would be promoted by an address from you before your return, I have thought fit to suggest such a step for your consideration, rather as a borrowed than an original idea of my own— though I have some recollection of having urged it upon you a year or two ago. By Governor Sullivan's curious replications to your Colleague, you will observe that his Excellency tells the Venerable that his view of National affairs and yours are widely different, as "the world knows." Now the world has not seen your view of National affairs, but only a few individuals, unless the summary of the substance of your letter to H— which got into the Chronicle should pass for such.[6] This would be an injustice to yourself, as the Chronicleers have only selected what they thought useful to their purpose. Indeed, neither the federal nor the Democratick presses would be pleased to imprint *all* your sentiments, but I would undertake to make the same types subservient to a letter of your-writing, as were employed in the *first* Epistle of Timothy. This will be fighting the Junto with their own weapons.

I thank you very kindly for your congratulations upon the birth of my daughter. It had escaped my memory, having informed you of the fact; so you will find the intelligence repeated in my last letter. We are all well, and I presume you will see us on your return, still members of the same family & under the same roof, which I very much regret, as it is induced by necessity rather than choice. If I remove at all, it will be to my own farm, but to this there are so many obstacles, in addition to my own aversion to the place, that I must submit to be a pensioner for a time to come. Our nephew William, having completed the term of his School engagement, has left us to join his parents. His views are for the Army, in which he would accept a Commission if it can be obtained. The Miranda discipline has not, I trust, disqualified him for the service of his Country, though it may possibly prove some impediment to his obtaining a desirable rank. If the men are to be raised, which you mention as having been voted in Senate, I wish you would feel the pulse of the Secretary of war, on the subject of a Commission for the *young Col*; If he were personally known to me I should have no hesitation in making application for a youth of So much real merit, as I know he possesses.

Present me very kindly to your wife and all our friends at Washington. We shall not look for you till the last of April, by which time the Roads will be fit for travelling with pleasure & dispatch. Our friend Shaw is dolefully mortified that I betrayed to you his sapient criticism upon the metaphors— I took some little delight in his *fidgeting* because he is too easily wrought upon by the *last speaker*, upon most subjects. His Associates, literary and political are full of *Boston notions*; a very partial, prejudiced, self sufficient & locally attached set of people, with pretentions to a character & reputation the very reverse of all this. I never held and never shall hold much communion with them.

I am truly your's.

RC (Adams Papers); internal address: "J Q Adams Esq^{r:}"; endorsed: "Adams— T. B. 24. March 1808. \ 3. April rec^{d:}."

[1] TBA wrote to his brother on 15 March (Adams Papers), reporting on ECA's baptism, summarizing his management of JQA's properties, and voicing his belief that war with Great Britain loomed. He also commented on Timothy Pickering's opposition to the embargo, for which see note 3, below.

[2] On 4 April Massachusetts voters reelected incumbent governor James Sullivan over Federalist challenger Christopher Gore (*New-England Palladium*, 5 April; A New Nation Votes).

[3] With New England Federalists seething about both the embargo and JQA's support of it, Massachusetts' "venerable" senior senator, Timothy Pickering, drafted a letter to his constituents in February. Directed to Gov. Sullivan for presentation to the Mass. General Court, Pickering's letter argued that the embargo was pushing the United States and Great Britain toward "a war absolutely without necessity." He also called for what amounted to sectional resistance to the law by merchants and seamen and alleged that the Jefferson administration was purposely withholding from the public critical information relative to Franco-American relations. Pickering's letter became public on 10 March, after another Federalist, George Cabot, had it published as a pamphlet. The publication was an opening salvo in a public exchange with the state's Democratic-Republican governor that lasted through April. By the time TBA wrote this letter on 24 March, Sullivan's initial reply of 3 March, Pickering's 9 March response, and Sullivan's final contribution of 18 March had additionally been published or extracted in the city's press. The letter of 18 March and Pickering's final reply of 22 April would also appear as a pamphlet in May.

Sullivan's initial reply of 3 March returned Pickering's missive as more appropriately directed to one of the secretaries in the legislature. When Pickering replied on 9 March, he challenged the governor's refusal to act as a conduit to the legislature and insisted on the need for Massachusetts' citizens to weigh the embargo's effects on the state. In his response of 18 March, Sullivan condemned Pickering's intentions as "seditious" and "disorganizing." He also brought JQA into the conversation by pointing to the senator's two votes in favor of the embargo (Bemis, *JQA*, 1:143–144, 145; *New-England Palladium*, 15 March, 3 May; Pickering, *Letter from the Hon. Timothy Pickering . . . Exhibiting to His Constituents a View of the Imminent Danger of an Unnecessary and Ruinous War*, Boston, 1808; *Boston Commercial Gazette*, 10 March; Boston *Independent Chronicle*, 14, 24 March; Boston *Repertory*, 15, 22 March; *Interesting Correspondence between . . . Governor Sullivan and Col. Pickering*, Boston, 1808, p. 5, 7, Shaw-Shoemaker, No. 16269). For JQA's reaction, see William Smith Shaw to JQA, 9 April, and note 1, below.

[4] Ellipsis in MS.

[5] The *Boston Commercial Gazette*, 24 March, carried a resolution from local Federalists that called for the election of candidates who would oppose the embargo and "restore to our unhappy Country the blessings of *free and uninterupted Trade*."

[6] TBA was referencing JQA's recent correspondence with Boston lawyer Joseph Hall Sr., from whom letters of 6, 10, 23, and 29 March are extant in the Adams Papers and generally report on local reactions to the embargo and Pickering's open letter to the governor. In his 23 March letter, Hall noted that the contents of JQA's recent letter induced him to share it with several men without taking the additional step of publishing it. Hall encouraged JQA to make a public statement, believing it would influence the forthcoming state election in favor of Democratic-Republicans. The letter he referenced was dated 9 March, and although neither it nor any of JQA's other replies to Hall in this period have been found, AA included a substantial extract in her letter to AA2 of 18 March, above. The summary of JQA's letter appeared first in the Boston *Democrat*, 19 March, and then the Boston *Independent Chronicle*, 21 March. In it JQA described British envoy George Henry Rose's mission to the United States as a delaying tactic by Britain, and he praised the Jefferson administration's conduct toward the European powers as impartial and appropriate. The summary further reported that opposition to the embargo was waning in Congress but that what remained grew more virulent as support dwindled.

Elizabeth Smith Shaw Peabody to Louisa Catherine Adams

My Dear Niece,   Atkinson March 24th. 1808

Your Letter did not reach me untill several Weeks after it was written, & as I had a few days before addressed a letter to Mr Adams, I presumed upon the reception of that, your minds would be rendered less anxious,[1] but notwithstanding this, I should immediately have replied to your polite friendly letter, & to your questions, respecting Master George, if we had not been so unhappy as to have a number in our family taken sick one after another, with fevers, & my duty called me to unremitted attentions to the beds of Sickness, & to do all in my power to soften the pillow of distress— You need not my dear Niece have made the lest appology for writing to One, under whose care a "Darling Child" had been placed. He is in fine health & spirits, & is indeed a lovely Boy— His mind is strong, & penetrating, with great facility he commits things to memory, & applys them with uncommon Judgment— The other day he was playing with one of his mates who endeavoured to deceive, & cheat him— He soon perceived his design, & said, "William I have somewhere read in a Book, that he who endeavoured to cheat *Others,* cheated *Himself.*"—²

His Father observed he had some propensities which ought to be checked. Where the soil is fertile, we may expect to see the "weeds & flowers promiscuous Shoot," & it requires a most skillful, judicious hand, to know what to erase, & what we should permit to flourish;³ for flowers have sometimes poisonous qualities, as well as Weeds, & Virtues, if not rightly directed, may degenerate, & grow into Vice.

Master George reads, parses, & spells well, but he learns to write very slow— He wished to write to his Father, I gave him paper, he soon came to me, & read a very affectionate letter, with his duty to you, & love to his little Brother Charles—hoped he should soon see you all in Boston— I looked at it, but could not read a word, he wondered what could be the reason, for he met with no difficulty himself—

Congress has had a long Session. The conduct of some of the Members, have not escaped many unfavourable remarks.— But the *Integrity* of Mr Adams, was in *my Mind, unquestionable*— I firmly believed, that he was not actuated by sinister motives, nor party Spirit, but would think, judge, & act, from a sense of the highest Duty—

My Dear Nephew & Niece may be assured, that both Mr Peabody, & your Aunt, will tenderly watch over your Child, & do all in our power to make him good, that he may be a Blessing—

With esteem & affection / Your / Aunt, subscribes

Elizabeth Peabody—

FC (DLC:Shaw Family Papers); internal address: "To Mrs Louisa C. Adams / at the City of / Washington."

[1] LCA's letter to Peabody has not been found. JQA received his aunt's 10 Jan. letter, above, on 6 February.
[2] Montesquieu, *Persian Letters,* Letter LII.
[3] Alexander Pope, *Essay on Man,* Epistle I, line 7.

Abigail Adams to Hannah Phillips Cushing

my dear Friend [*post* 24 March 1808]¹

Your Letter begun at Washington and finishd at Baltimore I received a few days since read and wept over it, most tenderly Sympathizing in the sorrow which have harrowd up the Bosom of my Friend since we last parted.² I had heard of your safe arrival at Washington and found from the papers and from private Friends that the Judge had been so well as constantly to attend court.³ this was so much beyond my fears and expectations, considering the low state he was in the

March 1808

last season, that I flatterd myself you would enjoy as pleasent a winter as the aspect of our public affairs would permit You to. I knew you must in common with every friend of the country experience a degree of anxiety at the allarming situation in which our once happy country is involved. I know You to be too purely American to feel any partiality but such as reason & Justice would justify—and that you must view with equal Eye the Arbitrary conduct of Both the Great contending powers towards us, whilst the measures pursued, or rather not pursued by our own Government in leaving us so defenceless when menaced and threatned upon all sides, excites the most anxious fears for our individual Security and Safety— but I was to learn from your Letter the ~~domestic~~ private affliction of My Friend in the Death of a beloved Brother, ~~whom tho I knew not personally, yet from~~ whose Character drawn by the affectionate pen of a Mourning Sister, I can unite in lamenting, and beseeching that Being by whose hand Life and death are lodged, to afford the consolations promised in his word. We are told that at the Death of Lazeres jesus wept.[4] if possesst with the power of raising him from the dead as we are assured he did, he wept as a proof of his affection and sorrow. surely he must look with compassion upon those of his Creatures from whom he sees fit to take the nearest and dearest connextions, with the assurrence only that they shall rise hereafter— by his example we are permitted to shed the tears of sorrow to ease the swoln heart; and we must be less than humane Beings not to feel the hand which strikes us.

> Teach us the hand of Love divine
> In evils to discern
> Tis the first lesson which we need
> The latest which we learn
>
> Is resignation's lesson hard?
> On trial we shall find
> It makes us give up nothing more
> Than Anguish of the mind[5]

there is no situation in Life from the Throne to the footstool which exempts us from its troubles in this respect all things come alike to all Men— My Daughter Smith & Grandaughter left Me the beginning of Jan'ry for their residence in chenango. the col as soon as his House was finishd with the first snow came for them— I had determined that they should spend the winter with me, but when the col came I could do no otherways than consent that my daughter should do, as I would have done in her place follow the fortunes of My Husband, however less eligible his situation was than that I had before experienced. I have had pleasing letters from her, having found the country much better Setled than she expected, and as she writes me every necessary for living comfortably—that having a home, she is determined to be content; and to possess her mind in patience, altho Secluded from the luxeries and many of those things which are estimated convenionce'es in Life— that I can hear often from her is a consolation to me, having but one only daughter, and that daughter qualified to adorn any station in Life, I could have wisht that her lines had fallen to her in a pleasenter place[6] and that She might have enjoyd a goodlier Heritage but I must not forget the truths I have quoted, and therefore submit with patience to the Allotments of Providence. William S smith remaind with us through the winter, and that he might not be Idle, became an assistant in teaching Arithmatic for three Months in our School. it finishd last week, and he is now gone to visit his Parents, with a desire to get a commission in the Army. he is a young Man of modest deportment amiable Manners, regular habits & virtuous disposition. he has enough of his Father to make him a Brave officer and of his Mother to be a good Man— Mrs Adams thank you for your kind Remembrance of her. she is very well and has added an other daughter to my Family Since you left us— Both the President and Myself have enjoyed good Health through a winter much milder than the last and but for the anxiety we feel for the embarressments our country labours under, and the dangers which encompass ~~us~~ it, we should be as tranquil as a consienceness of having done the utmost in our power to Serve and Save it, can render us— nor are we of that fault finding uncandid ~~Number~~ party who will not give to ceasar the things due to Ceasar,[7] ~~nor~~ when the measures of the Government are just and wise as they appear to be towards Great Britain—condemn them because they are adminiterd by a Government, the individuals of which were not of our choice. Present Me to the Judge affectionatly tell him both the President and your Friend hope to see him return to his native state invigorated by his excursion. with your mourning Friends I shed the Sympathizing tear and to you my Friend ~~all the Love~~ and affection increased and matured by a long experience of the ~~Many~~ unbounded benevolence of your heart, and the virtues which have ~~so highly distinguishd~~ Shed a Lustre round you through Life. May you reap that reward in a better World which this can never bestow, or be exprest in Words—sufficiently strong by your faithfull & affec

Abigail Adams[8]

Dft (Adams Papers); notation by CFA: "Copy. Mrs Cushing / 1808." Filmed at March 1808.

[1] The dating of this letter is based on William Steuben Smith's 24 March departure from Quincy (AA to AA2, 18 March, note 8, above).
[2] Cushing to AA, 17 March, above.
[3] William Cushing's presence at the commencement of the U.S. Supreme Court session on 2 Feb. was reported in the Boston *Columbian Centinel*, 13 Feb., and the Boston *Repertory*, 16 February.
[4] John, 11:35.
[5] "Resignation, or Good Out of Evil," Hymn 202, lines 5–12, in Jeremy Belknap, *Sacred Poetry, Consisting of Psalms and Hymns, Adapted to Christian Devotion*, Boston, 1795, p. 216. The quoted lines are based on Edward Young, "Resignation," Part I, lines 77–80, 441–444.
[6] Psalms, 16:6.
[7] Matthew, 22:21.
[8] Hannah Cushing responded on 11 May with a brief note informing AA that she and her husband had returned to Scituate and thanking her for her condolences. She also expressed a hope that she might stop at Peacefield as she passed through Quincy on an upcoming trip to Portsmouth, N.H. (Adams Papers).

Abigail Adams to Louisa Catherine Adams

my dear Daughter   Quincy April 4th 1808

It is a long time since I wrote You, or rather since I Sent a Letter, for an unfinished one has lain by so long that like an old Almanack it is out of date. the writing spirit is not always present, and it is shy and coy. if you do not frequently solisit it, neglect is sure to be followed by indifference, and indifference by disgust; I need not any other prompter at present than the desire I have to write of Your children from whom you have not heard for some time. by a Letter from Atkinson I hear that George is very well, and a very good Boy.[1] Abbe shaw has been very sick; Even to an allarming degree, seizd with a puking which could not be checked for several Days untill she was reduced almost to the grave. I have my fears that it will terminate in a decline which will be to my poor sister a heart rending stroke, and will break it I fear.— She has never recoverd the loss of Betsy, altho like a good Christian, she has bowd with Submission, and devoted her time, and all the powers of her mind to the improvement of those Young persons committed to her care; by which, as she has some times said she has alleviated her affliction.[2] John is very well now, but he was Sadly troubled with fits of the cholick for Some time; so as to wake from his sleep and cry. some medicine which he took gave proof of the cause and he has been relieved by the dischare of several living creatures and I am now pretty well convinced that the gasping for Breath which at times has been So allarming; arose from some knot of those vile reptiles— we are all in pretty good Health, I cannot add Spirits. the aspect of public affairs throughs a gloom over the approaching Spring. the Husbandman can neither till or sow with a prospect of gain; as his handmaid commerce has both her hands lop'd of and her feet tied.[3] she is laid prostrate, and her Lovers go about the streets mourning. we may truly add we are beset on every side— who is wise enough to say what ought to be done?

I have thought the administration more blamed by the Federal party than they merited, during these critical times. they have too closely imitated their opponents during the former administration— I cannot defend very many of the Measures of the Government; I think they have brought us to the present crisis of our affairs, Yet those who See but, in part, & know but in part are not the most competent Judges.

~~I cannot see~~ how can congress ~~can be~~ be permitted to rise.[4] the Country is So Critically and So dangerously situated, that every Man should be at his post.— every wind May waft as tidings of vast importance—

Mrs [allcut?] mentiond to me when she was here, that she thought the Rooms of your House ought to be opend and aird and the furniture lookd too, if you did not return early in the Spring[5] would you have her do it, if she should be at leisure? you will write me what you would have done;

William smith left us last week, and is gone to his Father. his attention and punctuality to his school gave great Satisfaction, and after it closed he could not bear to remain Idle, and there were not any prospects for him here. his inclination leads him to the Army, and he is desirious of obtaining a commission there. his Grand Father told him he would write for him, both to the President and mr Madison & the Secretary of war— I should like to know his uncle's opinion, and if consistant with his judgement, whether he would mention him to mr Madison as a young Man of regular habits, modest, discreet & I believe brave. I should hope that his engagement with Miranda would be no bar to his employment in the Army. he was under age, and was placed with him by those in whom he naturally confided, and knew not Mirandas views—

I should have written to mr Adams Myself upon the subject, but shall wait to hear further from William and I only mention it now, merely to know if any Scruple lies in his own mind against recommending him.

Mrs Adams is well and her little ones; with me desires to be rememberd to Your sister Buchanna

Louissa has been in Boston this month—or she would request a Remembrance also—to you and your Friends a Kiss for My Boy Charles.

I suppose when I know him, he will claim an equal share of the Love and affection of his Grandmother with his Brothers— he must be very good to get as large a portion as John— I shall write next to my son
Your affectionate Mother   Abigail Adams

RC (Adams Papers); addressed: "Mrs Louissa Adams / Washington"; endorsed by JQA: "My Mother 4. April 1808. / 12. April rec$^{d:}$"; notation by CFA: "To the Same—"

[1] The most recent extant letter from Elizabeth Smith Shaw Peabody to AA was that of 15 Jan., above. Peabody also provided updates on GWA's education in her letters to JQA of 10 Jan. and LCA of 24 March, both above.

[2] For Elizabeth Quincy Shaw's 1798 death, see vol. 12:367.

[3] A possible reference to Thomas Jefferson's 4 March 1801 inaugural address in which he spoke of the "encouragement of agriculture, and of commerce as its handmaid" (Jefferson, *Papers*, 33:151).

[4] The 1st session of the 10th Congress adjourned on 25 April 1808 (*Annals of Congress*, 10th Cong., 1st sess., p. 2284).

[5] That is, Mrs. Alker, the nurse who helped deliver CFA (JQA, *Diary*, 18 Aug. 1807).

William Smith Shaw to John Quincy Adams

My dear Sir   Boston 9 April 1808

I had the honour to receive your letter to Mr Otis on Thursday evening last, and have attended to its publication, with as much expedition as possible— The printers have published an edition of a thousand copies the sale of them commenced this morning and the whole are now disposed of. Oliver & Munroe are now printing a second edition of a thousand more on their own account and have contracted with several of the democrats, with Eben Larkin bookseller at their head, to print three thousand more for general circulation in the Country.[1] In consequence of the great haste with which they were printed—some few errors have escaped us, which I shall see corrected in the second edition I sent you several copies last evening and now send you several more by this mail— I have also agreeably to your direction sent a copy to Govenour Sullivan & to Mr. Otis.

What shall I do with your tenant Guerney.[2] I have never been able to collect a cent from him since your absence. Your order for $350 on the branch bank I have received and deposited to your account. I have paid your father eleven hundred seventy two dollars and forty nine cents agreeably to your direction[3]

With most respectful attachment and ardent gratitude / I am very sincerely / your hum Sert   W$^{m\cdot}$ S. Shaw[4]

RC (Adams Papers); internal address: "John Quincy Adams Esquire."

[1] On 31 March JQA penned an open letter to Harrison Gray Otis, the president of the Massachusetts senate (FC, Adams Papers), in which he defended his support of the em-

bargo in response to Timothy Pickering's circular letter to Gov. James Sullivan of 16 Feb., for which see TBA to JQA, 24 March, and note 3, above. The British Orders in Council of 1807, the *Chesapeake-Leopard* Affair, and continued impressment of U.S. sailors all served as justification for the embargo, JQA wrote, arguing also that Pickering's contention that it would draw the United States into war was overblown.

JQA enclosed a Dupl of the letter (MBAt) in one to Shaw of 31 March 1808 (MWA:Adams Family Letters), instructing that it be published by Edward Oliver and Isaac Munroe of Boston. JQA's intent in drafting the letter, he informed Shaw, was "not meant for electioneering, but for self-defence; and to give the public my views of public affairs." The Otis letter was advertised for sale in the Boston *Independent Chronicle*, 11 April, then printed in full in the same newspaper on the 14th. JQA asked Shaw to send published copies to Otis, Sullivan, and JA (*Biog. Dir. Cong.*; Pickering, *Letter from the Hon. Timothy Pickering... Exhibiting to His Constituents a View of the Imminent Danger of an Unnecessary and Ruinous War*, Boston, 1808; Clarence S. Brigham, "Bibliography of American Newspapers, 1690–1820," Amer. Antiq. Soc., *Procs.*, 25:288 [April 1915]; JQA, *A Letter from the Hon. John Quincy Adams... to the Hon. Harrison Gray Otis*, Boston, 1808, Shaw-Shoemaker, No. 14270; JQA, *Diary*, 31 March). For the public response to JQA's letter, see JQA to Shaw, 23 April, and note 2, below.

[2] William Gurney, a stonemason, became JQA's tenant on 25 May 1807 (JQA, *Diary*, 23 May; *Boston Directory*, 1807, p. 80, Shaw-Shoemaker, No. 12180).

[3] See JA to JQA, 19 Feb. 1808, and note 1, above.

[4] JQA had previously written to Shaw on 8 Jan., reporting capital news and giving instructions on the management of his business affairs (MWA:Adams Family Letters).

Abigail Adams to John Quincy Adams

my dear son   Quincy [10] April   1808[1]

Altho I have not So frequently written to you It has not been oweing to Your having been less frequently in my Thoughts, than formerly; I found it so difficult to determine from a partial view, what were the wisest and best measures for the government to pursue, in a day so dark, and in times So perilous, that Silence was best for me, after having once given my opinion upon a subject where we had differd in judgement, altho from a more clear view of the subject, and the circumstances attending it; I have been led to think of it, in a different light.

we expect tomorrow to have your full view of our national affairs, altho you must expect that it will raise a Hornets next arround You. the Consciousness of having uprightly discharged Your duty to your country, will serve to shield you from their stings. Your Father has various times exprest a wish that you would come out, explicitly, and avow your sentiments, and opinions, and since the publication of a Brother senetors celebrated Letter he has thought it a duty which you owed to yourself and your constituents— as the Election in this state is now decided, it cannot be said to have been written with a desire to influence that. both Your Father and Brother attended the meeting here, but neither of them voted for Govenour.[2] from personal Friend-

April 1808

ship they would both have been willing to have given m^r Gore their vote, if other reasons and motives had not opperated more powerfully, in their minds, Some which led them to think a Change at this critical moment might not prove favorable to the true Interest of the state— Many things may be said, which it is improper to commit to paper. to us at a Distance, we cannot but look with astonishment, that no effective measures are adopted for defence even the Gun Boats are thought useless by striping them of their Men and at this eventfull crisis congress are about to rise—! as tho it was a time of profound peace— I own I cannot see through the wisdom & policy which directs the counsels of the Nation—

I will quit the Subject and say something respecting our domestic affairs. when William Smith, left us he exprest a desire to obtain a commission in the Army. I knew not whether you would think it consistant with your Ideas, after what had past respecting his Father, to Mention him Yourself—to mr Madison, or the secretary of war and I should not wish, or desire You to do any thing which would look like asking a favour from any of them. I had much rather write myself to mr Jefferson as I shall not have any scruple in doing ~~from our~~ when I hear from William.

Your son John is very well, grows fast. he dinned with us to day. George was well last week

I inclose my flower account which I will thank You to settle for me, as you come through Philadelphia[3]

My Love to mrs Adams— I wrote to her about a week ago.[4] we are all well, and shall be very glad to See you return, if you can do so, consistant with the public good

Your affectionate / Mother   Abigail Adams

RC (Adams Papers). Filmed at [*April 1808*].

[1] The dating of this letter is based on the publication and sale of JQA's open letter to Harrison Gray Otis, for which see William Smith Shaw to JQA, 9 April, and note 1, above.

[2] In Quincy, Democratic-Republican incumbent governor James Sullivan earned 59 votes while Federalist challenger Christopher Gore received 87 votes (Salem *Essex Register*, 6 April).

[3] The enclosure, which has not been found, was a bill from Philadelphia merchant Thomas Allibone (JQA to AA, 20 April, below).

[4] AA to LCA, 4 April, above.

Thomas Boylston Adams to John Quincy Adams

Dear Brother   Quincy 10th: April 1808.

I received your favor of the 30th: ult: on the 7th: current and also the pamphlet containing the documents respecting the Chesapeake.

I have read the whole with attention, and am particularly impressed with the concluding letter of M^r: Madison, which is universally admitted to be a very luminous and correct State paper. That it could not be answered or refuted, is very apparent from the replication given to it, by the Envoy Extraordinary; and I feel confident, that it will diffuse a proper and just sentiment on the subject of our disputes with England, among the people; *this* was a thing much to be desired, in this quarter; for, I verily believe, that the federal newspapers have created great doubts in the minds of many, as to the justice and propriety of our pretentions upon the great questions, which have been agitated between our Government & Great Britain.[1] The appearance of an undue influence on the part of France & Spain has been such as to create distrust and jealousy, and as the sources of correct information, on this point, were hidden from the view of the world, it is not surprising to me, that suspicions should grow out of a state of things, which prudence might have enjoined upon Government, as the best policy. There seemed to me in M^r: Quincy's speech upon his motion for more information upon the subject of our relations with France, sufficient grounds for such a call, and I was not at all displeased at any thing which he urged on that occasion.[2] There has been too little apparent sensibility in the Executive to French Tyranny; too anxious a solicitude to wink at insults and to smoother complaint against injuries of a very aggravated description to which our National interests have been subject for two years past, on the part of France. To what reasons of State this policy must be ascribed, is not for me to say. I can only find one apology or palliation for it—viz the *Naval* impotence of France and the Naval preponderance of Great Britain. The idea of a deeply rooted hostility to Commerce, existing in the dispositions of the South, obtains fresh credit in the North, from the first imposition & long duration of the Embargo; though many other indications have been given, which tend to a confirmation of such an opinion here, this measure is viewed as the first practical illustration of a very broad theory, and I think the feelings of our people have, in many instances, been successfully assailed by the outcry which has been made on this subject. Its effects are not visible so much in those places, where we should naturally look for them, (the sea port and fishing towns) but as among the farmers; there may therefore be some falacy in the inference that the Embargo, has been an unpopular measure, even in this quarter of the Union. It is too plain that without such a precaution on the part of Government, a vast proportion of our Navigation

April 1808

would have encountered other perils than those of the Sea, to the utter ruin of all the Insurers on the Continent.

So much has been said among your constituents of your agency in the passage of the Embargo Act, from which your Colleague dissented and has taken so much pains to condemn, that I feel much rejoiced at the prospect of a publick appeal on your part, which I understand is now in the press and will appear tomorrow. Whether you adopted this idea from your own sense of its propriety and expediency, or whether the step first taken by your Colleague forced it upon you; it is a general opinion among your friends that it had become absolutely necessary. To a certain class of your Constituents it will afford no pleasure, but to those who are well intentioned towards you, it will be very grateful. It appeared to me very clearly that the disposition to appretiate the conduct of your Colleague was greatly quickened by an opposite disposition towards you, and the freedom of remark in which some Gentlemen have indulged upon the course you have pursued during the present Session, of which I, of course, have heard only a small proportion, has not been calculated to inspire your friends with any very conciliatory sentiments towards them. Their language has been full of reproach and very much in the style formerly used towards your father upon his continuing to treat with the French Government in 1799.[3] I need not add that it has proceeded from the same sources and from a similar policy.

For electioneering watch-words the Junto adopted the *very significant* phrases "Gore & no Embargo"—"Gore & free trade"—"Sullivan and starvation." If M^{r:} Giles has not got the right scent for *cabalistick* words, in his late speech, I think he might perceive the odour very strong here.[4] The whole pack opened with this *view holla*, and have been in full cry ever since. I was *thrown out* in the first start and have never been able to come up with the hunters or even get a view of the game. I am but a poor Country 'Squire and ill-mounted for this kind of chase.

To me it was and yet is quite incomprehensible, how the election of M^{r:} Gore could effect the raising of the Embargo, and as to freetrade, so long as the foreign pressure existed upon our maratime rights, I could discern no other method of extricating the Nation from these difficulties, but by unconditional submission to the law of the strongest. For this step I did not feel prepared, and being rather dubious whether the non-election of the Junto favourite, would necessarily be followed by starvation, I concluded to take my chance for one year longer, under the present Governor, if he should be re-elected, leaving that event however to any body's agency but my own.

The votes given in are more numerous than I expected and the increase for Sullivan less. In many places there is a visible change, but as frequently in favor of one Candidate as the other. According to returns already published, M$^{r:}$ Gore has a majority of two thousand and upwards, but from a paragraph in yesterday's Sentinel I infer, that Major Russell thinks M$^{r:}$ Sullivan will prevail in the end.[5] I regret, that the principles on which M$^{r:}$ Gore's election was advocated were of a nature to cause the with holding from him my vote. Personal considerations had no agency in it; for surely I have no cause of dislike or enmity to the man; on the contrary I have a great respect and esteem for his character and an opinion of his talents which he would not think derogatory, himself being judge; but the party abused and vilified *you* for holding opinions such as M$^{r:}$ Gore was said to disclaim, and as I had not passed sentence of condemnation against you for those opinions I could not sanction by my vote, those who had. Another thing, M$^{r:}$ Gore was not in my judgment the man to whom the federal party were preeminently indebted, nor for whom this mark of their favor ought at this time to have been reserved. If any other motives deterred me from voting they were such as would receive no quarter from federalism, of course I have no pride in recording them.

Since the fever of Electioneering is over, for the present, and the publick pulse is reduced to its usual beat, you will not expect a very rapid circulation of your communication upon the State of the Nation. No Six-thousand copies of editions will find a sale in a few hours, though it is possible some of the Newspapers of one side or the other may reprint it. With a view to the May Elections it will find its way gradually through the State, most probably by the help of the Democrats, who will father it as a refutation of the Epistle of Timothy, if for no other reason; but so many have already believed in Timothy that the gospel of John will labour hard with them.[6] To convince the unconverted, (as our Braintree Minister who preached for us to day, *would be likely to say*), is as hard a task as to convert the unconvinced.[7]

I have made provision for discharging your Note to R Dexter, having received of Wm Shaw $130 towards it.[8] The amount of principal and interest is $337:90; and I expected ere now to have had sufficient funds collected from your tenants here, to discharge the debt; but only one has yet paid me and that a small sum; before your return I shall settle with them all; whether for cash or *approved notes* is somewhat dubious. Money is said to be scarce—this I presume you have heard of before now, but I begin to think there is some truth in the story as I find it impossible to collect any for myself.

Your children are well. John dined here to day and sends his love and duty to his parents— We heard from George a few days since, who was then in good health. My wife and children are also well and send much love to you and yours. / Farewell.

RC (Adams Papers); internal address: "J.Q Adams Esqr."; endorsed: "Adams— T. B. 10. April 1808. / 18. April rec^{d:}."

[1] In his letter of 30 March to TBA (MHi:Adams Papers, All Generations), JQA discussed U.S. negotiations with France and Great Britain and enclosed a pamphlet printed by order of Congress on 22 March, *Message from the President of the United States . . . on the Subject of the Attack on the Chesapeake*, Washington, D.C., 1808. The pamphlet included correspondence between James Madison and British envoy George Henry Rose about the negotiations over the *Chesapeake-Leopard* Affair. Madison concluded his part of the exchange with a 5 March letter that lamented "the exorbitant shape of hostility and of insult seen in the attack." Noting that Britain still held sailors impressed from the *Chesapeake*, Madison characterized the breach in Anglo-American relations as ongoing. This provided an opportunity to reach an accord on impressment, he wrote, thereby "converting a particular incident, into an occasion for removing another and more extensive source of danger to the harmony of the two countries." Rose in his response of 17 March reiterated that Britain disavowed the actions of the *Leopard* commander and was ready to negotiate reparations. He said, however, that his government forbade him to negotiate other issues and viewed the embargo as unwarranted retaliation (p. 64, 68, 72, 75, 76, 79).

[2] On 14 March Josiah Quincy III introduced in the House of Representatives a resolution calling on the Jefferson administration to turn over to Congress all dispatches received from France during the previous thirteen months. The House defeated the resolution by a vote of 66 to 44 (*New-England Palladium*, 22, 29 March).

[3] JA faced significant opposition from members of his cabinet and the press for sending a second diplomatic mission to France in late 1799, for which see vols. 13:416, 14:35–36.

[4] TBA was referring to an 11 Feb. 1808 Senate speech by William Branch Giles in support of a bill to codify the definition of treason, for which see JQA to AA, 24 Feb., and note 1, above. He was also quoting electioneering phrases used by the Essex Junto in the Massachusetts gubernatorial election to pin the economic hardships of the embargo on incumbent James Sullivan (Paul A. Gilje, *Free Trade and Sailors' Rights in the War of 1812*, N.Y., 2013, p. 161; *Annals of Congress.*, 10th Cong., 1st sess., p. 108–127; Washington, D.C., *National Intelligencer*, 19 Feb.; Northhampton, Mass., *Republican Spy*, 9 March; *New-England Palladium*, 25 March; Boston *Democrat*, 2 April; Salem *Essex Register*, 16 April).

[5] The Boston *Columbian Centinel*, 9 April, printed partial election results and predicted, "Those who love Governor *Sullivan*, and the *Embargo*, may congratulate themselves on the reelection of the former; and on the continuation of the latter for six months to come." Sullivan won reelection by almost 2,500 votes (A New Nation Votes).

[6] The Boston *Independent Chronicle*, 31 March, referred to Timothy Pickering's 16 Feb. letter to Sullivan as a "disorganizing Epistle" and reported that JQA was expected to issue a response.

[7] Rev. Sylvester Sage (1765–1841), Yale 1787, was the minister of Braintree's First Congregational Church, serving with Rev. Ezra Weld, whose health had begun to decline (Dexter, *Yale Graduates*, 2:631–632, 4:569–570).

[8] In his letter to TBA of 30 March, for which see note 1, above, JQA mentioned that Richard Dexter held a note from him and asked his brother to settle the debt.

John Adams to John Quincy Adams

My dear Son   Quincy April 12. 1808

In your favour of March 25th, you express a hope that nothing like a distribution of Money, among the Principal Leaders of our Parties, has occurred or will occur, among Us.[1] I agree with you in this hope and I will add that I Still entertain this belief. At least there is no one, on whom I can fasten even a Suspicion. But that foreign Money has been received by Sebastian, has been adjudged: that it has been offered, is proved by *Judge* Innis's deposition. These were not leaders You will Say. true. but where did Burr obtain the Sums, adequate to his vast Expences? What Shall We Say of the affair of Blount? Burr and Blount have been leaders.[2] We know that certain Powers of Europe have no Scruples to employ Money with Such as will receive it, when they think they can carry any Point by it: and is not Money as well beloved and as much wanted by Some among Us, as by any in Europe,?

Our Elections run very near the Wind. I have been neutral though neither Nations nor Parties will allow of Neutrality,. I expect to be captured by one, or burnt or Sunk by the other. For myself I care not which. For You and your Children I am anxious. Your Letter to Mr Otis is expected to day. The Effervescence is past. The Men of twelve per Cent a Month, will not be able to afford Money to pay for printing and diffusing twenty Editions of ten thousand Copies each.[3] What Should you Say if it should fall dead from the Press, as David Hume Says his Essay on Human Nature and his first History of England did?[4] I believe that very little will be Said about it. Our Brutus's have not forgotten, that Cicero would not Send fifty Horse, to compel their Creditors in Cilicia to pay Eight and forty per Cent Interest. You remember how he quarrelled with the orator. Yet Brutus you know was a pure virtuous and disinterested Republican, though a rich haughty and covetous Aristcrat. Our Speculators have not forgotten your opposition to their Bank in the Senate of this Commonwealth.[5]

Your Son John dined with Us yesterday in very good health and Spirits. George is very well and a good Boy as Mrs Peabody writes in a very late Letter.[6]

The Embargo tingles in every Vein. The Clamour against it will grow louder and louder and every Man who voted for it more and more unpopular with the Party who oppose it. We cannot give the Law to France nor England by this measure, and nothing is done to lay the

April 1808

foundation of a Navy, the only Arm that can protect Us. I See no System in the Conduct of Administration or of Congress.

From the government of John Bunyans Honourable Mr Penny wise, Pound foolish, good Lord deliver Us.[7]

A Repeal of the Embargo Laws, would instantly expose, many rash Adventurers to burn their Sails. Arming their Vessells would be of little or no Use, without Frigates to convoy and protect them. The present Congress will never declare War against England or France. Neither of those Powers will declare War against Us, ~~any~~ more explicitly than they have done already. Are We then to remain for Years in this Situation? We may be more disposed to War among ourselves, for what I know, than We are to fight with any foreign Power. The present humiliation of the northern States cannot long endure, without producing Passions which will be very difficult to restrain. I am weary of Conjectures.

My Love to your Family and all your Friends.

RC (Adams Papers). Tr (Adams Papers).

[1] In his letter to JA of 25 March (MWA:Adams Family Letters), JQA expressed hope that the United States would not be plagued by the political factions that had troubled ancient Rome, the Netherlands, and Sweden and lamented that money "envenomed" competing factions. He also provided an update on U.S. negotiations with Great Britain and France. JA had begun the exchange in his letter to JQA of 5 March, citing Cato on the sectional tensions that led to the downfall of Rome (Adams Papers).

[2] For the deposition of federal judge Henry Innes regarding Benjamin Sebastian's alleged bribe from Spain, see LCA to JQA, 15 Feb. 1807, and note 3, above. JA also alluded to the 1797 impeachment of Tennessee senator William Blount, for which see vol. 12:x–xi.

[3] Here and below JA referenced Cicero, *Epistles to Atticus*, Book V, epistle XVIII, par. 11, which notes that 12 percent was the legal rate of interest in Rome in the first century B.C.

[4] In his autobiography, David Hume commented that his *Treatise of Human Nature* "fell *dead-born from the press*, without reaching such distinction, as even to excite a murmur among the zealots" (Hume, *The Life of David Hume*, London, 1777, p. 7–8).

[5] A group of twenty Massachusetts merchants sought to establish a new bank in Boston in Feb. 1803. JQA, a state senator at the time, opposed the project because some of the bank's shares would be reserved for members of the legislature, which he viewed as "a species of influence so dishonourable to the legislature itself." JQA sought to add a provision requiring a public subscription list, but this suggestion was rejected. The Boston Bank was successfully chartered and opened on 16 May (JQA, *Diary*, 4, 7, 27, 28 Feb., 1, 3 March; *New-England Palladium*, 20 May).

[6] Not found.

[7] John Bunyan, *The Holy War*, London, 1790, p. 292.

John Adams to William Steuben Smith

My dear William   Quincy April 15. 1808.

I thank you for your agreeable letter of 31st March from Albany.[1]

Grumbles at the Embargo appear to me to be mere electioneering artifices. The orders and Proclamations of the king of England, and the Decrees of the Emperor of France at Berlin and Milan, ought to be and would be an embargo, if our Government had not interfered. Perhaps some Merchants would have adventured; but it would have been only to augment the Spoliations of one power or another. It is said that Merchants are the best judges of their own Commerce and the risks they may run. As far as respects their own private individual interest this may be true of some not all of them. But none of them are the best judges of the effects of their Commerce upon the great interests of the Nation. There are higher interests in Society than Commercial interests, great and important as they are. The interests of National defence involves the lives, liberties and property of the people, and these are surely of more consequence than trade. The Agricultural interest too, is of an higher order than the Commercial, though both are naturally useful to each other at all times, and necessary at some. To shew you the genius of Mercantile adventure, there is a Dutch anecdote well attested in history, which may convince you what sort of Judges some Merchants are of their own projects and of National duties, as well as interest. Prince William Henry of Orange laid siege to Antwerp, invested the City on all sides and blocked up the Port. Nevertheless, notwithstanding all his vigilance and activity, he found the inhabitants were from time to time supplied with provisions, ammunition, arms and even Cannon. With much anxiety and probably at great expense of spies & informers he at length discovered that Antwerp was supplied by a company of Merchants of Amsterdam. The Prince sent for those Merchants and reproached them severely with their ingratitude and treachery to their Country, asking them how they could be so base as to sacrifice their Country to its enemies for a paltry profit. The principal man of the Company answered that "trade ought to be free; and if it was necessary to go to Hell in the course of his Commerce he would run the risk of burning his sails."[2]

I wait for a letter from you at Smith's Valley. My love to your father and Mother and sister; compliments to your Uncles and Aunt. We are all well and join in regards to you all. I have had two kind letters from your brother, who writes in good spirits and seems to have a mind awake with a laudable curiosity for knowledge and ardor for study.[3]

I am with warm affection your Grandfather

LbC in TBA's hand (Adams Papers); internal address: "Mr William S Smith"; APM Reel 118.

[1] Not found.
[2] M. D. A. Azuni, *The Maritime Law of Europe*, 2 vols., N.Y., 1806, 2:79.
[3] John Adams Smith's letters to JA have not

been found. On 15 April, JA responded to a question posed by his grandson about the right of a belligerent nation's armed ships to search those of a neutral nation (LbC, APM Reel 118).

John Quincy Adams to Abigail Adams

My dear Mother. Washington 20. April 1808.

My wife received a few days since a letter from you, and I had the happiness of receiving one also from you, yesterday or the day before— In the former there seems to be an intimation that on our part, we had not been so punctual in our correspondence with you, as our duty and affection justly requires— My wife had written you not long before—[1] As for myself I have not indeed written you so often as my inclination would have dictated— But I hope you will impute it to any cause rather than to a failure in the dearest of my duties— Among the severest of the trials which have befallen me during the present Session of Congress (and they have been severe beyond any that I ever was before called to meet) that of having incurred in some particulars the disapprobation of both my Parents has been to me the most afflictive— Totally disconnected with all the intrigues of the various parties which have been in such a violent electioneering fermentation, I have been obliged to act upon principles exclusively my own, and without having any aid from the party in power have made myself the very mark of the most envenomed shafts from their opponents— Although I attended at M^{r:} Bradley's Caucus or Convention, yet it has been very explicitly understood by the principal friends of the Candidates that I had no intention to become the partizan of either— This neutrality with regard to persons, has of course neutralized the men of both sides in return, and having taken an active and decided part upon much of the public business, it has on one side been convenient to load me with the burthen of managing as much of it as I would assume, and on the other to leave me to defend myself as well as I could from the assailants of another Quarter— Hence there has been scarcely a measure of great public importance, but I have been obliged to attend to in Committee as well in the Senate; and in addition to all the rest a question of expulsion of a member has been imposed upon me, of great difficulty respecting the forms of proceeding, and the merits of the particular case, which I have been compelled to carry through almost alone— The question was taken about ten days since and the vote for expulsion was nineteen to ten— The Constitution requiring two thirds to carry the vote, it failed by a single vote— I could tell you though it may not be proper to say upon paper, by what a curious concurrence of parties the ten votes of acquittal was compounded—[2]

The Letter of M[r:] Pickering, is another document of which I could account for the origin from circumstances perhaps not known to you— I was not named in that letter, but it was hardly possible for me to avoid noticing it.[3] My Letter to M[r:] Otis was written in great haste, and of course in point of composition is incorrect— It touches only upon the leading inaccuracies of his statement, because both my own want of time, and a regard to the public patience, made it necessary for me to be as short as possible— Yet it engrossed every leisure moment I could command for a fortnight— I mention these things by way of excuse for not having written more frequently to you—

I have had no intention or desire of influencing Elections by what I have written— If an impartial person will consider the situation in which I was placed by M[r:] Pickering's letter, I think he will perceive that something from me was indispensible— The effects of my letter, will I hope, be what was intended— To promote Union at home, and urge to vigour against foreign hostile powers— If federalism consists in looking to the British Navy, as the only Palladium of our Liberties, I must be a political heretic— If federalism will please to consist of a determination to defend our Country, I still subscribe to its doctrines.

My father and brother write me that my letter to M[r:] Otis will not have much circulation—[4] I know very well that argument for Embargo, will not be so catching as invective against it, and if my countrymen are not inclined to hear me, I must bear their indifference, with as much fortitude and philosophy as I can command— I should hope at least that in future, the Legislature will not be taken by *surprize*, and driven to imprudent measures, by having a fire-brand thrown into their windows, in the midst of their Session—

We adjourn next Monday— In a fortnight from that time, I hope to have the pleasure of seeing you, and at least at Quincy I shall be sure of meeting no altered faces— I will take care of Allibone's Bill, which you enclosed— My wife and child are well.

Your's dutifully

John Quincy Adams.

RC (Adams Papers); addressed: "M[rs:] Abigail Adams. / Quincy."; docketed by JA: "April 1808."

[1] AA to LCA, 4 April, and to JQA, [10] April, both above. LCA last wrote to AA on 24 Jan., above.

[2] For the Senate expulsion trial of John Smith of Ohio, see TBA to JQA, 24 Jan., and note 1, above.

[3] For Timothy Pickering's 16 Feb. letter to Gov. James Sullivan, see TBA to JQA, 24 March, and note 3, above.

[4] TBA to JQA, 10 April, and JA to JQA, 12 April, both above.

April 1808

John Quincy Adams to William Smith Shaw

My dear Sir.   Washington 23. April 1808.

I have received your two letters of last Week, with a dozen copies of my letter to Mr Otis—And Mr Gardiner's fast Sermon— But the copies which you mention as forwarding with your's of the 15th inst^t have not come to hand.¹ I thank you most cordially for the promptitude with which you executed the charge of publication— I find the federal newspapers in Boston, which began with a system of silence about my letter, have at last found their tongues—² Of the use which their opponents make of this paper, I cannot be surprized— But if there be such a person as a candid and impartial federalist (and I trust the great majority of them are such) I ask him to say *who* is justly chargeable with my publication, and all its effects, whatever they may be— I had no party purposes—No electioneering views— But an attack so violent, and at such a time—and in such a manner, was a strong call upon me for notice— Yet I have most truly said that this alone, I would have overlooked— My Motives were altogether of a public Nature—

I expect to reach home about the 10th of next Month— I would thank you to see that the family in my house, have it opened and aired a day or two before that time— Mrs Alker mentioned to my mother that she would attend to it; and I will be obliged to you to speak to her for that purpose.

Your's faithfully   John Quincy Adams.

RC (MWA:Adams Family Letters); internal address: "W. S. Shaw Esqr"; endorsed: "Washington / 23 Ap 1808 / John Q Ada[ms]"; docketed: "1808 / Apr^l / 28." Some loss of text due to a tight binding.

¹ Shaw's letters to JQA were dated 9 April, above, and 15 April (Adams Papers), with which was shipped a copy of Rev. John Sylvester John Gardiner's *A Sermon, Preached at Trinity Church, in Boston, on Fast Day, April 7, 1808*, Boston, 1808, Shaw-Shoemaker, No. 15087.

² In the week after the 11 April publication of JQA's letter to Harrison Gray Otis, Federalist newspapers in Boston included advertisements for its publication. The Democratic-Republican Boston *Independent Chronicle*, 14 April, however, printed the letter in full and accused Federalists of favoring Great Britain and the Essex Junto by publishing Timothy Pickering's letter and suppressing JQA's letter. The Boston *Columbian Centinel*, 16 April, answered by pointing out that JQA's letter was written "to a federalist; and published by a federalist" (Boston *Repertory*, 12 April; *New-England Palladium*, 12 April; Boston *Columbian Centinel*, 13 April).

Abigail Adams to Abigail Adams Smith

My Dear Daughter   Quincy May 8th 1808—

I took My pen to write to you this morning in a placid temper of mind; the news papers of yesterday lay by me, which I had not lookd into comeing late last Evening from Boston; papers bearing the title of Federal. I found in them such a bitter spirit of Party, Such uncandid constructions, Such false conclusions and, Such mean crouching to one power; and such bigg Blustering against an other, that I own I felt My indignation strongly excited against the writers tho unknown to me. in every paper and upon every occasion they attack your Brother with a Venom and spight, which shows fully how much they dread his tallents, and how keenly they feel the force of his replie to col Pickerings Letter. so totally devoted to the essex junto are all the Federal Printers in Boston, that they have refused to publish a single line in answer to the false and scandelous publications with which there papers have teemed ever since the Report in the case of John smith appeard—[1] This is the fate of every public Man who wishes to do his duty with fidelity to his country, to impartially administer equal justice to all— the spirit of Party has become so Rancorous that a civil war will break out, unless some Method can be devised to subdue the base passions of envy, & jealousy, and Moderate the contending factions— candour, liberality and that Charity which the Gospel So highly recommends—which suffereth long and is kind, which envieth not which vaunteth not itself, is not puffed up, doth not behave itself unseemly seeketh not her own, is not easily provoked, thinketh no evil rejoiceth not in iniquity, but rejoiceth in the truth.[2] this truly Christian Spirit seems banished from the Hearts and pens of Men, and in lieu of it, calumny and evil speaking, falshood and deceit ~~prevail~~ take the lead, can the cause of truth and justice prevail, when thus borne down? this is no new thing under the Sun.[3] the History of the world is full of Such base ingratitude, and for this the judgements of heaven are abroad in the Earth, and for these sins we shall like other Nations be scourged. in proportion as our Family have been engaged in public Life have they shared from one and the other Party, their full proportion of obliqui and ill treatment, but I challenge either party; in their hours of calmness to produce a single instance, or one action where the honour independence and safety of the Country has not been the ultimate object of every member of the family where personal safety has not been hazarded, personal Property sacrificed and the whole

May 1808

long Life of its Most ancient Member Solely devoted to the public interest. having given vent to My feelings excited by news paper revileings I quit the subject, and its Authors, and ask forgiveness for them as I am instructed in holy writ—and notice your kind Letters of March 6th and April 24th which I received both together and thank You for them—⁴ to hear often from you is a great pleasure to me, one of the few left me in the decline of Life, when the days approach in which we are told there is no pleasure. there is an innocent pleasure to be derived from the renovating season of the spring which Charms us even in age. I feel its influence in the vivid Green which cloaths the Earth, in the beautious Blosom which adorn the trees, and in "the Charm of Earliest Birds"⁵ these are all before me. the Grass waves in the wind. I never saw it more forward at this season. on the 24 of April we cut our first Assparagrass, on the 25 our daffies Bloomd, our peach & pear & plomb trees are in full Bloom, peas ready to stick— I did not expect to hear from you, that your peas were up; I should like to have You state the progress of your Vegetation that we may compare notes— Our Barley is also up— I am glad to find that you have been so successfull in making maple Sugar—every manafactor which will render us less dependent, is a valuable acquisition.— My Immagination frequently visits you, and always find you occupied. to be Idel would be novel altogether to you. we cannot be sufficiently thankfull to our early ~~employers~~ instructors for teaching us habits of industery, training us up in the way we should go, that in age we may not depart from it—⁶ it is a true Saying, that the devil will find work for those who have not any employment. the mind is naturally active and the body requires it also—

> "Born to no end, we worse than useless grow
> as waters stagnate when they cease to flow.["]⁷

Mrs T B A desires me to ask You if you have not received a Letter which she wrote you in Feb'ry⁸ our little Abbe grows a little charmer. how she would delight to ramble with Caroline, and feed the chickins— she is a daily visitor to the puppy children as she calls them and runs as fast as a quail when she gets out. the little one is a very beautifull Baby, quiet as a Lamb, fine dark Eyes, and black Hair. She bids fair to out shine her sister in personal Beauty— Mrs Adams's Sister Foster has a son about a week old— Mrs B Adams has a daughter—⁹ So we increase and Multiply and replenish the earth¹⁰

Charlot Welch has been with us this fortnight— susan rambles with her. she wants Caroline too— Susan Scolds because caroline does not write. Your Father received Williams Letter and was satisfied with his reasons—[11] william must continue to write. tell him it is a habit the pleasure of which increases with the practise, but becomes urksome by neglect— Your Father Sends his Love to you all. Louissa Susan and all the domesticks desire me to make mention of their high consideration— I believe I wrote you that Mrs Dexter and family were removed to their own House— we expect your Brother and family to arrive this week— inclosed is a Letter for Caroline—[12]

affectionatly Your Mother   Abigail Adams[13]

RC (MHi:De Windt Family Papers); addressed: "Mrs Abigail Smith / Smith Valley / State Newyork."

[1] The most recent issues of Boston's Federalist newspapers offered growing criticism of JQA. The *Boston Commercial Gazette*, 5 May, argued that his support of the embargo coupled with his contention that enhanced defenses were needed lacked "common sense" because the embargo would reduce federal revenue to spend on protecting seaports: "From *such statesmen, in such times*, good Lord deliver us!" The Boston *Repertory*, 6 May, stated that "with regret" it could no longer extend JQA the benefit of the doubt offered on 15 Jan. when it published the report of his Senate committee recommending the expulsion of John Smith: "Mr. Adams's dereliction of his friends is no longer equivocal. His adoption into the phalanx of our political foes has been proclaimed and celebrated throughout the union." The Boston *Columbian Centinel*, 7 May, published a report from New York disparaging "QUINCY ADAMS'—famous letter" and aligning him with "friends of the Embargo" who had been "completely foiled" in recent local elections. The animosity between JQA and the Federalists culminated in June, for which see AA to AA2, 19 June, and note 3, below.

[2] 1 Corinthians, 13:4–6.
[3] Ecclesiastes, 1:9.
[4] Not found.
[5] Milton, *Paradise Lost*, Book IV, line 642.
[6] Proverbs, 22:6.
[7] William Whitehead, "An Essay on Ridicule," lines 59–60.
[8] Not found.
[9] On 2 May AHA's sister Frances Harrod Foster gave birth to John Harrod. On 15 April Elizabeth Crosby Adams, wife of Boylston Adams, gave birth to a daughter named Susanna Boylston (Pierce, *Foster Genealogy*, 1:270–271; Sprague, *Braintree Families*).
[10] Genesis, 1:28.
[11] Not found.
[12] Not found.
[13] In a prior letter to AA2 of 17 April, AA mentioned her concern for William Steuben Smith. She also commented on the publication of JQA's letter to Harrison Gray Otis, which she believed was "disclosing facts which the Nation ought to know at this critical juncture. it is however so bitter a pill, that the Anglo Americans cannot swallow it so they resort to revileing, and abuse, calumny and slander to injure the writer, and to draw down vengence upon him." Her next letter to AA2 was dated 20 May. AA wrote about her health, updates on family members and neighbors, her thoughts on JQA's reasons for writing the Otis letter, and her opinions on the embargo and its effect on party politics (both MHi:De Windt Family Papers).

Abigail Adams to Caroline Amelia Smith

My Dear Caroline: Quincy, May 28th, 1808.

Your letter of May the 8th, your grandpapa brought home with him from church, on Sunday the 20th;[1] owing to sickness I was not able to go, and am yet confined to my chamber. My fever and cough are

May 1808

both leaving me, and I hope a few days more will give me health sufficient to enjoy the fine season.

I have been reading a novel called the Wild Irish Girl. Why the term wild is given, I know not, unless as a ridicule upon those who imbibe national prejudices, merely from vague report. She is represented as living in an ancient barony with her father, who in the wars had been despoiled of his property, and had retired with his daughter, her old nurse, and Father John, a learned, polite, and liberal minded priest, from whom she received her education. Here she lived, a recluse from the world, but with a lively imagination, a sportive fancy, a devotion to music, which she practised upon her harp, the favourite instrument of her country. She studied, and was perfectly versed in the historic knowledge of her native land; as a resource, she became a botanist, and on a thousand occasions, displayed such a love of nature and its productions, which she describes so artlessly, with such a vivid display of superior powers, that she charms and enchants the reader. She had gathered the first rosebud of the spring, which she had watched with much care, and presented to a young stranger, whom chance had led to the barony, and who had for some months been an inmate there, and who at the request of her father had been her preceptor in drawing. In return she repeated to him a little ode from the French. "Oh beautiful! beautiful!" exclaimed Glorvina, "I thank you for this beautiful ode; the rose was always my idol flower in all its different stages of existence; it speaks a language my heart understands, from its young bud's first crimson glow, to the last sickly blush of its faded bloom; it is the flower of sentiment in all its sweet transitions; it breathes a moral, and seems to preserve an undecaying soul in that fragrant essence which still survives the bloom and symmetry of the fragile form which every beam too ardent, every gale too chill, injures and destroys."[2]

Your little darling A. has been sick, and looks like the flower or the bud in its faded form,[3] which I have just been describing; more interesting in decay than bloom—one exciting all the pleasing sensations, the other a softer and tenderer sentiment.

Our friends here are all well. To-morrow will be our general election day; the embargo should not be complained of by the federalists, for it has increased their number ten fold, and will be like to give them such a weight in the councils of the nation, as no other measure of a peaceable kind could have effected.

With the love and affection of the whole family, jointly and severally, I close my letter to my dear Caroline, and am her truly affectionate grandmother, A. A.

MS not found. Printed from AA2, *Jour. and Corr.*, 1:211–213.
[1] Not found.
[2] Sydney Owenson, *Wild Irish Girl*, 3 vols., London, 1806, 1:251–252.
[3] That is, TBA and AHA's daughter Abigail Smith Adams.

Elizabeth Smith Shaw Peabody to Abigail Adams

Atkinson June 18th. 1808

Mr Lion & his intended *I suppose so*, as the modern phrase is, called here last Wednesday— I was very glad to see any one from your house, that could give me any information of my Dear Sisters health & welfare— I told Mary, she I fancied, was going to add one more pair to the Nuptial Circle of your Dometicks—[1] She with down cast smiling simpers, blushed the Affirmative—

She talked as if she could not return to Quincy, but said You did not know of her tarry at home— I then urged her to return for this Summer, as I presumed it would be a disappointment to you, & leave an unfavourable impression upon your mind,—respecting the fairness of her conduct, as she acknowledged you, & the family had treated her with the greatest kindness—

I was very glad to have my Son come, though his Visit here was short, as Abbey was very desirous of seeing her Brother, & would often wonder why he could not come— He sees her so little, that he cannot love her half so much as he ought— Dear Girl, if pain, & sickness long & peculiarly destressing, give her any claim to his esteem, & attention, she stands high on the list— Her patience under suffering, I hope, arises from a better Source, than a mere happy temper—

I have not heard one word how our dear George does, since his return to his Parents— He certainly was as extraordinary a Child as I ever knew— I regretted Abbys sickness upon his account, for she delighted to assist him in English Grammer—& he seldom forgot what she told him— He was apt to be peevish sometimes, but we could always talk, & reason him into good humour—

Mr Peabody & I have been called to attend his Sister Mary, to the house appointed for all the living—[2] She died sudden at last, though she was very unwell for several weeks—[3] I hope her exchange of worlds, has been happy—she was a kind, inoffensive, worthy woman— In early life met with a sad dissappointment—& been like a lone solatary Dove ever since— Out of eight Children Mr Peabodys Brothers & Sisters, only three remain—& *we* are *all* aged, & are swiftly "marching downward, to the Tomb"—⁴ That we may stand, with loins girded up, ready to obey our heavenly Summons, is devoutly to be wished—

My Dear Abby remains very feeble, has a fever every day, & is unable to set up all day, She rides out, & always feels better—but seems too sick yet to go as far as Quincy—⁵

It requires not a little self-Government, to see in the papers, & to hear the unjust Censure, & the reproaches cast upon a Man, who I believe has been actuated by no sinister motives, nor a disposition to *change*, but from reflection, & agreeably to the dictates of his conscience, & best Information *he* could obtain, from the best Authority— I cannot believe that he wished any one to yield *implicit obedience* to the mandate of a Despot or even to the *best President*— If any thing droped of the kind, it must have been qualified—I think—

I find people differ in their Opinion respecting the policy, & wisdom of Mr Adams, resigning his seat in Congress—⁶

In great haste I must subscri[be . . . .] with proper regards to the President, & all Your family, your affectionate   Eliza. Peabody—

RC (Adams Papers); addressed: "M^rs. Abigail Adams / Quincy." Some loss of text where the seal was removed.

¹ That is, Mary Harrod, AHA's sister (AA to AA2, 19 June, below).
² Job, 30:23.
³ Mary Peabody (b. 1739), the sister of Rev. Stephen Peabody, died on 10 June. His remaining siblings were Sarah Peabody Stevens Peters (b. 1723), who died later in 1808, and Capt. John (Selim Hobart Peabody, comp., and Charles Henry Pope, ed., *Peabody Genealogy*, Boston, 1909, p. 25, 37; Salem *Essex Register*, 5 Oct.).
⁴ Isaac Watts, "A Funeral Thought," line 11.
⁵ On 9 May, Elizabeth Peabody also wrote to AA about Abigail Adams Shaw's health and reported on boarders in the household (Adams Papers).
⁶ JQA's resignation from the Senate, for which see AA to AA2, 19 June, and note 3, below, was reported in the *Newburyport Herald*, 14 June.

Abigail Adams to Abigail Adams Smith

My dear Daughter   Quincy June 19th 1808

Here we are Sitting by a good fire in the parlour, & wearing, our winter coats to meeting, whilst our windows are coverd with a profusion of roses, our Walls decorated with flowers expanding their Beauties to the cold Northern blast, which rudely lacerates their delicate texture, unmindfull of their Beauty; and headless of their fragrance

I rose the other morning delighted with the visit I had made You; and the pleasing interview I had with you, and the Coll. William your Brother Mrs st Hillair, all but my dear Caroline not least beloved, whom I did not see. Your Father accompanied me, and we came rather unexpectedly upon You, but were not the less joyfully received.— I was quite delighted with your Situation, and found you so cheerfull and happy, that it augmented the pleasure of my visit which was only interrupted by the strikeing of the clock at the morning hour when I usually rise. altho only a dream it left upon my mind so pleasing an impression, that I could not refrain communicating it at the Breakfast table, and calling upon the family to participate the pleasure.

It is some time Since I received a Letter from you. susan received one from Caroline of May 25th a few days since,[1] full of her lovely lively spirits which delighted us all. I have been much confined at home from indisposition, for three weeks to my chamber with a bad cough and some fever; it has now left me, altho a change of weather produces a hoarsness. I have not been in Boston Since Your Brothers return there. he comes to Quincy almost every Saturday, and passes sunday with us—but yesterday the rain and storm prevented him. Miss Kitty Johnson has been with us the week past. altho she has not so many personal Charms as Eliza, her manners are more correct, and pleasing to me. I think she resembles her Mother in person and manners, more than any of her other of her Daughters. our little Abbe is gone with her Aunt Mary to Haverhill. You may easily immagine how much we miss her. Mrs James Foster has an other Son—[2] thus far domestick occurrences—

You have no Doubt Seen that our state Legislature and Senate have a federal majority, and that they have Elected Mr Loyed a Senator to congress in the room of Your Brother.[3] Mr Loyed is the only son of dr Loyed, a Merchant, a Gentleman of tallents & Education, of a fair and honorable Character, whom I presume will not discredit the state.[4] how much of an Essex Man he is, time will disclose. during the present session of the House, a number of Resolutions were brought forward, and adopted, with instruction to the Representitives and senators, to use their influence in congress to carry them into effect. those of them which recommend a Navy for the defence of our harbours and commerce, and fortifications for our security,[5] not only your Brother, but every Man who is sensible of our exposed Situation, and the allarming state of our country with respect to Foreign powers, would most readily assent to, but these resolutions were connected with others which calld for a decided opposition to the National Government, and in the view of your Brother, relinquished our Neutral Rights, and deserted our Seamen Subjects which he had ardently mantaind, and strenuously asserted against British orders, and French Edicts, and which he considerd as essential to our independence. consistant therefore with

June 1808

his principles, he could not any longer hold his Seat in the Senate. he resignd it, by a Letter to the two Houses, like an honest Man and true American

The Federal Party have acted towards him a most ungenerous part— one which no honest man can justify they have vilified, abused and calumniated him because he could not adopt their principles, and become a party Man, because he would have an opinion of his own— every federal printer in Boston, refused to publish any thing which was written by way of justification, or explanation of his conduct. let us pull him down, by any means, and any falshood, was the language of their conduct; the Republicans Saw this, and eagerly caught the occasion to place him upon their side, and support him by their votes. this exasperated the federalist—and they rejected a Man whose conduct and principles will reflect honour upon his country in spight of all their mean jealousy, and narrow views. the Republicans have acted towards him, with more candour and liberality than they usually practise. they have not resorted to flattery but represent him as he really is, a man of a candid liberal mind, free from party views, of a pure heart, and unblemished Character, of distinguished tallents and integrity—

I cannot say that he has not felt, being wounded in the House of his Friends;[6] yet his elevation of mind will enable him to bear with mildness and patience the jealousy of his equals, which upon this occasion has been very conspicuous, the ill treatment of his fellow citizens, and the calumnies of his Enemies, being fully sensible that true greatness of Soul consists in Suffering these trials without complaining, or abateing any thing of zeal for the public good. Plutarch observes that the ill usage of our Country, like that of our Parents, should be borne with Submission—[7]

I must close this Letter with my best Love and regards to the coll, who has shared largely in these *Bounties* of his Country and who knows how to estimate good report, and evil report.

Verily there is a Reward for the Righteous.[8] let us act consciencously and leave the event—

with Love to every Branch of your Family from every twig of ours, I am my dear Daughter / most affectionately / Your Mother

Abigail Adams—

RC (MHi:De Windt Family Papers).

[1] Not found.

[2] Elizabeth Smith Foster gave birth to William Emerson (d. 1842) on 31 May (Richard D. Pierce, ed., "Records of the First Church in Boston, 1636–1868," Col. Soc. Mass., *Pubns.*, 40:440 [1961]; Thomas Francis Harrington,

The Harvard Medical School, 3 vols., N.Y., 1905, 3:1464).

³ The Mass. General Court convened in May with Federalists intent on replacing JQA as one of the state's federal senators, holding an election within days of the start of the session. On 2 June, nine months before the end of his term, members in the Massachusetts house of representatives cast 248 votes for James Lloyd Jr. and 213 for JQA. The following day, the senate confirmed the election with 21 votes for Lloyd and 17 votes for JQA. While the election was not to take effect until the end of JQA's term, he resigned his Senate seat on 8 June, writing to the Mass. General Court (LbC, APM Reel 135) that he was giving the people of Massachusetts the opportunity to send someone "who may devise and enforce the means of relieving our fellow-citizens from their present sufferings, without sacrificing the peace of the nation, the personal liberties of our seamen, or the neutral rights of our commerce." JQA reflected in his Diary: "I have the testimony of a good Conscience; and a firm belief that I have rendered essential service to my Country." After his resignation, the legislature held a special election on 9 June and voted to appoint Lloyd to serve out JQA's term (vol. 15:310; *New-England Palladium*, 3 June; Bemis, *JQA*, 1:149; JQA, *Diary*, 3, 8, 9 June, 11 July; *Newburyport Herald*, 14 June; A New Nation Votes).

⁴ Lloyd (1769–1831), Harvard 1787, a Boston merchant, was the only son of Dr. James Lloyd Sr. and was JQA's college classmate. During their years in Cambridge, JQA described Lloyd as "a good scholar, and a hard student" but "too much indulged in every childish caprice." Lloyd served in the U.S. Senate until 1813 and again from 1822 to 1826 (*Biog. Dir. Cong.*; JQA, *Diary*, 11 May 1787).

⁵ On 27 May 1808, Laban Wheaton of Norton introduced seven resolutions in the Massachusetts house that acknowledged a duty of the state's congressional delegation to support measures ensuring a strong national defense but questioned the constitutionality of an open-ended embargo. The house passed the resolutions on 2 June followed by the senate on 7 June. The passage of these "anti-embargo Resolutions" was a key factor in JQA's resignation from the U.S. Senate (*New-England Palladium*, 31 May; Boston *Columbian Centinel*, 8 June; JQA, *Diary*, 2, 8 June).

⁶ Zechariah, 13:6.

⁷ Charles Rollin, *The Method of Teaching and Studying the Belles Lettres*, 6th edn., 3 vols., London, 1769, 3:38, a copy of which is in JA's library at MB.

⁸ Psalms, 58:11.

Louisa Catherine Adams to Abigail Adams

My Dear Mother [ca. 2 July 1808]¹

I grieve to be under the necessity of informing you that I am again to be disappointed of passing next Monday with you at Quincy as the expence of a Carriage is double on account of the celebration of *Independance* I shall certainly keep this Anniversary in the full conviction that we are too much the creatures of circumstances to enjoy much of the boasted blessing or I should not at this moment have to repeat my regret In the hope however that it is only defer'd a short time I am dear Madam your affectionate daughter   L C Adams

P.S. Mrs Welsh will not have it in her power to go out & President will I hope pass the Night with us

RC (Adams Papers). Filmed at [1 July 1803].

¹ The dating of this letter is based on JA's attendance at Fourth of July celebrations in Boston, which allowed LCA to borrow his carriage to visit Quincy. JA and JQA visited the Massachusetts senate, attended services at the Brattle Street Church, walked in a procession, and dined at the governor's residence. On 5 July LCA returned to Boston with her

children, including an ill JA2, and JA returned to Quincy that evening (LCA, D&A, 1:275; JQA, Diary, 4, 5 July; Boston Repertory, 5 July; Boston Independent Chronicle, 7 July).

John Adams to William Smith Shaw

Mr. Shaw   Quincy July 10. 1808

I request the favour of you to insert the foregoing Letter in the next Anthology. It is a material Document in the Life of Washington, as well as in mine and my Sons. As I was bitterly reproached for promoting my Son, though I never did promote him, but only removed him with the Same Rank and Appointment from Lisbon to Berlin,[1] Washingtons Letter ought to have been considered as a Justification of it, or at least an Apology for it, if I had really promoted him. I have never before made any Use of this Testimony, and probably it would have remained forever unknown had not my son as well as myself been So cruelly used. But as Things are now circumstanced, I am determined it shall be published: and if you will not insert it I will Send it to Ben Russell, and if he will not, to the Chronicle. The original Letter all in Washingtons own hand, may be seen when you please.[2] affectionately yours   J. Adams.

RC (Adams Papers).

[1] For JA's nomination of JQA as U.S. minister to Prussia, see vol. 12:135–136.

[2] JA prefaced this letter with "A Letter from President Washington to his Successor," under which he transcribed George Washington's 20 Feb. 1797 letter to him (Adams Papers), where Washington declared that when JA became president he should not withhold diplomatic promotions from JQA, because he was "the most valuable public Character we have abroad." The letter was not published in the Monthly Anthology, the Boston Columbian Centinel, or the Boston Independent Chronicle. It was printed in the Boston Patriot, 29 April 1809, soon after JA began making regular contributions to that newspaper, for which see AA to AA2, 13 May, and note 1, below. See also vol. 12:5.

Abigail Adams to Abigail Adams Smith

                                                                            Quincy July 31 1808

do you know my dear Daughter that the date of your last Letter was the 3 of June, since which I have not received a line from you;[1] perhaps you may have been occupied as I have been by a large family— Providence has been So bountifull to us this season in the rich and ample Supply of Grass, that we can neither procure Sufficient hands to cut it; or Barns apple large enough to contain it. we have already cut 80 ton of English Hay, and shall nearly make an hundred— Such a Grass Season was never known—before; the misfortune is that labour is higher than I ever knew it, it being now in such demand, and Hay

So low as to be sold at 7 dollars pr ton— We have employd 12 Men for three weeks past, and for them were obliged to send more than 20 miles— I hope we shall finish in a week more—but the season has been So wet, that the Farmers have had bad luck in making their Hay. fruit will be very Scarce, partly oweing to the rain and partly to ~~an early~~ late Frost which occasiond it to drop from the trees— corn looks well, Barley not So good— whilst Heaven is pouring down upon us plenty, and abundence, blessing us with a season also of Health, we are murmuring and contending at our Rulers, at their Laws and restrictions— that We have had a weak, timid cowardly Administration is most certainly true—and that these measures have brought us into the present difficulties under which we are now suffering from the unjust decrees of one power, and the Hostile orders of counsel of an other power, I have no doubt— these led to the oppressive Embargo, which has cut up our commerce, dispersed our seamen, and brought distress upon the whole country, ~~which~~ and will terminate I fear in disobeidence to the Laws, in insurrection and civil war, if a Foreign war does not prevent it— the Embargo must be repealed—and the Vessels permitted to arm. the people of the Northern states will not Suffer it to continue much longer.

We are, says a late Writer the inhabitants of a wicked and avaricious world. to grant one privilege and to submit to one insult, is proved by a thousand instances only to be the invitation to others. to proclaim aloud that we will not defend ourselves or our property; that we will even destroy our implements of defence is the plainest language for the assassin and the Thief.[2]

Does all History present us with an other such picture as Spain—a Monarck resigning his crown, and commanding all his subjects to submit without a struggle to a foreign power?

August 8th

My Letter has lain for a week because I could not find time to fill up my paper— the weather has been intencly hot, and we have had company almost every day; there is not any solitude or retirement in our House now— Abigail is as wild as a Bird—and flies in all directions, and I have little John here too. he came sick from Boston a Month ago, fallen away so that you would not have known him pale as a corps and so languid I thought he was going into a decline but he has finely recruited, and is driving round now with Abbe enough to craize one— here sits susan too, for I have fled to your chamber as the quiet spot

July–August 1808

in the house, writing a Letter to her Mother,³ interupting me every few moments with some question (hold your peace Hussy) whom I expect here soon with Abbe— I suppose you are not unacquainted with her dissapointment— the Gentleman has lost all his Property—if he ever had any; I own I have my Doubts— there are So many imposters in the world that I think the greatest caution necessary inquiry ought to be made; every Man can tell his own story—but who knows more about him than what he relates of himself? his employment in this country must be known here— His story is that his Brother has ruind him, and that he has lost 80 thousand dollors— he returnd according to his engagement, and I presume offerd to Marry, from what she writes, but I believe Sally declind at present.⁴ I do not know sufficiently respecting the Gentleman to make up an accurate judgement— she is comeing to make me a visit. I shall then learn more about him— our Friends are all well Your Brother J Q A has become a private Man again to my intire satisfaction. I never saw him in better health or spirits. the responsibility he felt, the weight of buisness which devolved upon him the last session of congress, being upon every committe but three during the whole session kept him always anxious, and thinking differently upon public questions from his constituents. they sacrifised him to party views with a Malicious jealousy which will disgrace them in the Eyes of all those who are not devoted to Mammon. a more upright or honest man they never will find—but in times like the present, the post of honour is a private station—

we know not one day what an other will bring forth the whole world is in a turmoil. since I began this Letter accounts have reachd us, of the resistance of Spain to the usurpations of Beauonaparte.⁵ I most cordially wish them success—

we shall feel the effects of the revolution and find new arguments for removeing the Embargo.— the office of President has ever been [Strewd?] Stuck with thorns— It daily becomes a more difficult one to weild— a wise Man would find it a Hurculean task— who will Guide the helm upon the tempestous ocean I know not— there will be a struggle I presume— give my love to william and tell him to write to us— I have a Letter from Caroline— I shall write next to her

I inclose a Letter for her which came from Newark—⁶

Write to me my dear daughter, if it be only to tell me of your various occupations. Love to the col to William & Caroline—

From Your truly affectionate / Mother   Abigail Adams

RC (MCR-S); addressed: "Mrs Abigail Smith / Smith Valley / Chenango."

¹ Not found.
² AA quoted from a letter by Valius reprinted in the *Boston Commercial Gazette*, 28 July, which criticized the Jefferson administration and the embargo. The letter was the third of four originally published in the Baltimore *North American and Mercantile Daily Advertiser*, 9, 11, 12, and 13 July.
³ Not found.
⁴ SSA was being courted, probably by Boston merchant Edward Minchin. AA reported to AA2 on 20 May (MHi:De Windt Family Papers) that he recently returned from abroad and passed through New York on his way to Philadelphia to make good on an offer of marriage to SSA. Minchin (1765–1856), who returned from Scotland to New York in late March, was a former British naval officer and a widower with three children. He offered British imports from a shop on Broad Street until moving to Ireland in 1815 (Boston *Columbian Centinel*, 23 March 1808; John Wentworth, *The Wentworth Genealogy*, 2 vols., Boston, 1870, 2:391–392; *Massachusetts Mercury*, 2 Nov. 1798; Boston *Repertory*, 1 April 1808; *New-England Palladium*, 5 Dec. 1815).
⁵ Napoleon turned his sights on Spain to facilitate the movement of troops into North Africa and expand the French empire. The deteriorating relationships among the Spanish Bourbon family favored his imperial ambitions as King Carlos IV and his son Fernando, Prince of Asturias, fought each other for the Spanish crown. When French troops advanced into Spain on 16 Feb. 1808, Spaniards opposed to the king stopped him from fleeing and forced his abdication on 19 March. Napoleon mediated an agreement in Bayonne, France, between the factions, convincing Carlos IV to temporarily give him the crown and then on 6 May persuading Fernando to allow his father to continue to rule. When Napoleon abrogated the settlement and installed his brother Joseph as king, insurgents assassinated several French military governors and appealed to Great Britain for military aid. Reports of the events appeared in the Boston *Repertory*, 5 Aug. (Schom, *Napoleon Bonaparte*, p. 462–467).
⁶ Not found.

Abigail Adams to Abigail Adams Smith

my dear Daughter   Quincy August 29 1808

Do you know how long a time has elapsed Since you wrote a single line to Your Mother? You did not use to be thus neglectfull of your pen; I am myself frequently tardy, but I believe unless the post has failed: that I have written twice; since I recived a Letter from You. Caroline has written once to me; and once to susan So that my mind has been releived from the apprehension that you were Sick.¹ I have had an ill turn, and been confined to my chamber for a week past, with complaints similar to those which at this Season usually afflict me, an irregular intermitting fever, and Rhumatic complaints united—my head much affected, which has prevented my writing before. it is so common for me to be indisposed that it Seem's a Matter of course; but your Aunt Cranch has been much more sick than I have; being confined to her Bed with a Virtigo in her Head, so that she cannot bear a Ray of light, or walk or stand a moment. she has taken an Emitic & been Blisterd, but is not yet relieved. You will easily conceive how much her sickness has added to my anxiety and distress—that she to whom I am so much indebted for the tenderest care, and assiduity, when I have been brought low. Should herself want that aid, I am unable to afford

July–August 1808

her; it has so happend; that this is the ~~Annual~~ Season when mrs Greenleaf and family make their visit; she is there fortunately, alltho encumberd with 5 children, and near being confined with her sixth—[2] Yet why should I say encumberd; doth not the Scripture say, that children are an Heritage of the Lord?[3] and is not every married person desirious of building up a family. is it not their Duty to do so. He who says, or lives as if he thought that "it is good for man to be alone gives the lie to his Maker; sins against the constitution of his nature, dishonours his Parents; defrauds another of one of the justest rights of ~~his~~ humanity and exposes himself to commit offences against Society," says good Dr Hunter in his sacred Biography or history of the Patriarchs, a course of Lectures which I have lately been reading, and with which I have been highly pleased.[4] I wish I could convey them to you. they are instructive, and entertaining, excellent family Books— I should be delighted to have my Caroline read them. You must read uncle justise this admonition— altho seperated from You as appears to me, a much greater distance than when You resided in the city of Nyork, My imagination follows you; and I think of you hourly, regret the Seperation, and mourn that my only Daughter cannot more frequently visit her Parents. yet I cheeck myself, and say am I not ungratefull? has she not been with me through many of My most Dangerous, and painfull Sicknesses, a solace and comfort and consolation to me— might she not be placed in circumstances much more distressing for me to reflect upon—?

How is my dear William, laid asside his pen for the implements of Husbandery. can the wilderness make him forget the Social fire side of Quincy—the slate and pencil of his Grandfather over which he last winter Spent So many—shall I say *pleasent*, or usefull Evenings? From John we hear pretty often, he and his Grandfather are still correspondents— he writes for information, and instruction, which his Grandfather readily communicates—

I expect Susan's Mamma & sister every day to spend Some time with me. she seems to be unfortunate in her expected connexion, and sausy susan says, sighs and groans, as much as if she was a *young Girl*—for the slut got her Letters to me and read them— you know she is too knowing in some things for her years.

Caroline says to Susan—write me any thing but politicks— If you say So too, I shall hardly know how to comply—yet they are very vexatious topicks. But who can feel indifferent when the prevalence of party spirit, distorts every effort for the public good into a conspiracy to overturn the constitution; and native Americans unite with foreigners to degrade the Land which gave them Birth and Humiliate themselves to become tributary Vassels— the Vile spirit of Party, has sacrificed at their shrine, honour integrity and talents that corresponding opinions prevail in other states. I will coppy from the Newspaper an extract of a Letter from a Gentleman in South carolina to his Friend in this State—"The shamefull neglect of talents of integrity and Manly candour and firmness, which has occured with you in leaving out John Q Adams as Senator, excites here universal Sympathy in his favour, and a corresponding disgust at the conduct of his opposers. I hear him Spoken of with enthusiastic admiration, and I make no doubt but that the ill usage he has received, will in the long run, prove highly advantageous to him"—[5]

with respect to the Letter so much the subject of federal censure and abuse, there is every thing in it, which constitutes an upright honest candid Man—who loves his country better than Gold: and who dared to strip the mask from the face of deformity—and hold up to public view the true and real picture— I consider it as a family trophy— as a coat of Arms and pride myself more in being the Mother of Such a Son, than in all the honours and titles which Monarch could bestow

I am disgusted when I see low artifice Substituted, for candor, falshood, for truth, and the same arts resorted to support a good cause, which were used to accomplish a bad one. it has been publicly asserted that Your Father has said that he fully approved of the present Administration.[6] nothing could be more false he must first condemn all the great leading principles of his own which were neither weak, or timid, rash or voilent, cruel or vindictive— they were the Halcion Days of America. What is to be our future Lot—Heaven only knows. May the Righteous few save our Land.—

our Friends here are well, save those I have mentiond.— Remember me affectionatly to the col, to william and Caroline— I hope Mrs st Hilliar has recoverd from her fall for a sprain when first done, a Tea kettle of cold water poured upon it in a stream; is the best thing, I ever saw used, tho painfull it is salutary.

our little Abbe is a delightfull sensible forward child—but Eliza is the Beauty—fine large chesnut Eye, black hair, and fair skin, short Limbs round face—and a quiet child

I must bid you good night or I shall get a sleepless night—and then it will all be attributed to writing—

Your ever affectionate / Mother   Abigail Adams

RC (MHi:De Windt Family Papers).

¹ AA's letters to AA2 were of 19 June and 31 July, both above. In that of 31 July AA acknowledged receiving a letter from AA2 dated 3 June, which along with Caroline Amelia Smith's letters to AA and Susanna Boylston Adams have not been found.

² John and Lucy Cranch Greenleaf's five children were Lucy, John Jr., William Cranch (1801–1868), Daniel (1803–1827), and Mary Elizabeth (1806–1886). Lucy gave birth to their sixth child, Richard Cranch (d. 1887), on 9 Nov. (vols. 12:160, 13:530; Greenleaf, *Greenleaf Family*, p. 223–224; Sprague, *Braintree Families*).

³ Psalms, 127:3.

⁴ Henry Hunter, *Sacred Biography; or, The History of the Patriarchs*, 2d edn., 4 vols., N.Y., 1805–1807, 1:28.

⁵ AA copied almost verbatim from a letter published in the Pittsfield, Mass., *Sun*, 6 Aug., which declared that Federalists in Massachusetts should emulate those in South Carolina and endorsed JQA for vice president as an alternative to George Clinton.

⁶ AA's frustration with the press likely rose from a report in the Pittsfield *Sun*, 30 July, which stated that JA wholeheartedly supported the embargo. The newspaper claimed that the former president's "support of a great national measure, which his rival and successor had recommended, and which his own party were making a subject of party opposition" made him "much more honorable ... than many leading *Federalists*."

Abigail Adams to Susanna Boylston Adams

my dear susan   Quincy Sep^{br} 12th 1808

It is a week Since you left me, and you have not written me a line to tell me how you do, nor what you do, whether you feel content and pleased as I hope you do—¹ we miss Your capers not a little, and your chamber looks quite Solatary.

my Health is much better—Since my ride to Scituate where I went last week with your cousins Louissa and Abbe—and a very agreable visit we had. Mrs cushing is such a charming woman, so kind—so attentive to her company that we could not but be gratified and pleased. true kindness which is true politeness attends to the little wishes and wants of those we entertain, and we often remember slight attentions, after we have forgotten great benefits. thus a cup of cold water with a pleasent cheerfull countanance is more gra[tef]ull to your Guests, than a feast of fat things, or a profusion of farfetched Luxery, if good humour and affability are wanting. a desire to please seldom fails of Success. sweetness of temper, easiness of behaviour, and kindness of disposition are peculiarly engageing. all of which are blended in the character of this amiable Lady, who altho she has not personal Charms to recommend her, is beloved and esteemed by all her acquaintance, as one of the [. . . . of her Sex]²

It is probable my dear susan that you may make a visit to Haverhill, and that you may See some persons who knew your Father, as he resided in that place several years and received part of his School Education there— from his engageing deportment, and obligeing disposition he was much beloved there and Some persons may be disposed to notice you, for the regard they bore to your Father— do honour to his Memory as his daughter by a modest respectfull and engageing behaviour—

receive every admonition from your Aunt with gratitude—and be assured they are meant for your benefit.— Be a comfort to me in my advanced Age—and you will reap a sweet reward—the consciousness of having fullfilld Your duty—

since you left me I have not heard a word from your Mother. from your Aunt Smith I had a Letter Yesterday 23 August[3] She and caroline were well. our last Letters had not reachd them.

If you want any thing write me word Abbe talks of you every day.

I am Dear Susan / your affectionate / Grand Mother

Abigail Adams

I have written in the Ev[eni]ng and see but badly—

RC (private owner, 1957); addressed: "Miss Susan B Adams / Atkinson"; docketed: "No 1 / My Grand-Mothers Letters / Received September 20th / 1808—" Some loss of text due to a torn manuscript.

[1] In September and October Susanna Adams visited Elizabeth Smith Shaw Peabody in Atkinson, N.H. (AA to AA2, 3 Oct., MHi:De Windt Family Papers).
[2] Five words missing.
[3] Not found.

Abigail Adams to William Smith Shaw

Dear sir   Quincy october 1st 1808

shall we ever have the pleasure of a visit from you at Quincy. I can scarcly credit that you Should be so intirely weaned from a place, and Friends whom you once loved and esteemed. I know your avocations are numerous, your time fully occupied, but you may have leisure to visit the Atheneum, when your Friends here are to be no more Seen. Your uncle and Aunt Cranch have both been very sick. Your Aunt more so than I ever knew her; save once She is still very low. your good Sister is with her, administring to her comfort, a dear amiable Girl she is. you do not know her worth

I expect your mother next week—

I inclose You a Letter which came under cover to your uncle—[1] I think it is time to remind our Tennant that he must pay up his Rent in October. he will cry out the Embargo—but milk has not borne a less price than formerly, and he was very neglegent before the Embargo commenced— it is no favour to a Man to let him run behind hand. I am not for being hard with him, and we have waited upon him patiently— it would be well for you to inquire into his circumstances, and whether he was a punctual Man where he formerly lived— if he cannot pay his [Re]nt, he had better quit the Farm at the expiration of his year.² can you procure for me corrinna in Itally?³ affectionatly Your Aunt   Abigail Adams

RC (DLC:Shaw Family Papers); addressed: "William S Shaw esqr. / Boston"; endorsed: "Quincy 1 Oct 1808 / My Aunt Adams." Some loss of text due to an ink blot.

¹ Not found.
² Probably Joseph Arnold, who in 1808 leased the John Adams Birthplace and a large portion of the Penn's Hill farm (TBA to JQA, 27 Dec. 1807, and note 9, above).
³ Anne Louise Germaine Necker, Baronne Staël von Holstein (Madame de Staël), *Corrinna; or, Italy*, 3 vols., London, 1807.

Abigail Adams to Abigail Adams Smith

my dear Daughter   Quincy Nov^{br} 3^d 1808

Your Letter of sep'^{br} 25 together with Carolines came safe to hand, but I have been in a kind of Turmoil ever Since, and never felt retired, or quiet enough to sit down to my pen.¹ it is a great misfortune to me that I cannot see to write in an Evening, without injury to my Eyes. Your Aunt Cranch's Sickness has lain heavey at my heart. She is I hope recovering, but she has been much broken down. I have never been more distresst about her.— Mrs S Adams has been sick too, almost ever Since She came. the dr calls her compl[ai]nt, the Water Brush;² the pain in her stomack has been intence, and the water would flow from her mouth in great abundance, whilst her hands and feet would be an Ague cold. Little Abbe has had a slow fever, and been as fractious as a wasp— my daily cares You know: they are not lessned: but the Scripture tells us, that no Man liveth for himself—³ the Sordidness of that Idea, is Sufficient to stimulate the indolent, and prompt us all to do good and communicate, that the Sphere of your usefullness may be enlarged. I hope with You that You may return to the Society of your Friends and connections. to me the distance is unpleasent, yet I trust that there are pleasures, and comforts to be found there to a mind disposed to view objects in their best light, and to receive with gratitude the bounties of providence— Johnson in his Rassalass shows us that the happy valley must be in the mind.⁴

I have just procured Corrinna and am reading it— I will give you my opinion when I have finishd it.

If william should think of passing the winter at Philadelphia, I Should recommend him to an acquaintance with dr Rush's family. Richard Rush is a very fine young Man—and he will find a kind of home in the domestick circle of the dr— I will write to the dr in his behalf. his uncle Thomas will give him Letters to some of his Friends. M^rs S Adams thinks he may be of *essential* Service to his Aunt in the care of her affairs, particularly So, if she removes to her Farm as she proposes to do. a single woman whether maiden, or widow, wants some Friend of the other Sex to protect her, and her property or she becomes the prey of every sharper. William has Seen enough of the world—to be—even a Guide to a thoughtless giddy woman—and he may do it in a way, that may convince her, that her honour and reputation are his peculiar care. he is quick sighted, and will easily discern what is proper. at the same time, he will be upon his guard against the contagion of improper example. I have reasons for these hints. he will soon see whether they are well founded. I thought it probable that he might go to Philadelphia—and that he ought not to be improperly associated—

whether Commerce is ever again to shake of her shackles, as respects America, is doubtfull, not I fear untill she can do it, by the power of her own Navy, and the Thunder of her own Cannon— Brittain is jealous of our prosperity and fears us, as a rival. she is determined to check us in every way which she can France wishes to Embroil us with England; and to crush us in that way, least we should unite our power with hers, against France— thus are we hemed in on every Side— America is desirious of Dealing justly by Both—and extending her commerce as a Nutral Nation, to every part of the Globe. General Moreau compares America to the trunk and limbs of a Giant, with the Muscles of an Infant—[5] under the present Administration she has certainly totterd and limped, as if affraid to go alone. last week, the report was Current, that Napolean had declared war against the united states—[6] this was not believed by Your Father—who could not See any cause, or motive of policy in the measure. his decrees are more provoking than War; we shall soon have the Bugget opend— Mr Madison I think will be our next President— Pinckney is not the Man calculated to ride in the storm, and stem the torrent. if mr Madison can, he will perform wonders the people are so divided that it is like a House which cannot stand.[7]

we have had one Snow storm— I thought you must have had it deep with you. it is all gone, and this day is mild as May. Your Brother and sister are both well. they kept Sabbeth with us. John went home last week, having been with me four Months.— sister T B A asks if you received the Letter She wrote you Some months since.—[8] I was in Boston last week. our Friends all well— poor Aunt Edwards fell in her

Chamber & broke her Arm—regreets it much, as she was to have made her annual visit at Quincy on the same week.—[9]

I shall write to Caroline next. my Love to her. Caroline was so womanly so correct, and So pleasing in her manners, that those who come after her, when weighd in the balance are found wanting— susan is in a voilent hurry to take the Letter to her uncles. wait I say untill I send my Regards to all the family uncles Aunts and cousins and to my dear Daughter— / the affection of her Mother   Abigail Adams[10]

P S I had a Letter from John and have written to him his Grandfather had one this week[11]

RC (MHi:De Windt Family Papers); addressed: "Mrs Abigail Smith / Smith valley / Lebanon state / Newyork." Some loss of text due to an ink blot.

[1] Neither AA2's letter nor Caroline Amelia Smith's letter has been found; the latter was dated 28 Sept. (AA to Caroline Smith, 17 Nov., below).
[2] Pyrosis (*OED*).
[3] Romans, 14:7.
[4] Samuel Johnson, *The Prince of Abissinia: A Tale*, 2 vols., London, 1759, describes the protagonist's search for fulfillment in an edenic "happy valley."
[5] AA repeated views attributed to French expatriate Gen. Jean Victor Moreau in a letter from Benjamin Rush to JA of 13 June (Adams Papers).
[6] In late October, Boston newspapers reported an unfounded rumor that Napoleon had declared war on the United States (*Boston Mirror*, 29 Oct.; Boston *Democrat*, 29 Oct.; JQA, *Diary*, 25 Oct.).
[7] Mark, 3:25.
[8] Not found.
[9] That is, AA's aunt Hepsibah Small Edwards (vol. 10:325).
[10] AA previously wrote to AA2 on 3 Oct., providing updates on family and neighbors and expressing relief that AA2 was well. She also added a "seasoning of politicks," including comments on Spanish protests of Napoleon's rule and her desire that the United States stay out of war (MHi:De Windt Family Papers).
[11] Not found.

Abigail Adams to Caroline Amelia Smith

my dear Caroline   Quincy Nov'br 17th 1808

I can scarcly belive that I have not written to my dear Girl for so long a time as two Months, Yet upon opening her Letter in replie to mine, I find it bears date 28 sep'br [1]

This Letter I hope will receive a double welcome, for it incloses one from Your Friend which of them I know not, but it came under cover to your Grandpappa this week.[2] Your Aunt C Adams has been sick almost ever since she came, which has been a great trouble to me as well as to herself— I hope she is recovering. she is gone with Louissa to Boston to Day, the first time since she came. Susan and Abbe are gone out with Ann Hall to invite company to a party which Ann, is going to have this Evening.[3] I will tell You how the Girls were dissapointed. Ann had invited them for twesday, but it was a dire storm. she then appointed the next fair day. Wednesday mor'g being dubious, Ann did not Send, but they took it for granted as the afternoon was fair, she would certainly see them. accordingly, there was a brushing and polishing and Brightning up, and misses got all in prim order, susan every now & then taking a dancing step, and miss Abbe a stride after her. I sat in my easy chair trying to get a Nap. the chaise was orderd and pray misses, rousing up said Grandmamma, had you not better just send down and inquire first if Miss Ann expects You— the Message went, and the return was, the weather had been so uncertain that the party were not invited. what fools we were sister not to inquire before we drest? blank—whose the dupe? well says Miss Susan, I have just been reading the triumphs of Temper. I think I will try to imitate Serena, and quietly bear the dissapointment—[4] Abbe who is the mere child of imitation, followd the example—and undresst—then took her work, and Submitted with a good grace. to day their hopes are all renewed— the pleasure is yet to come— it would be greatly enhanced could you my dear Caroline add to the number, for when a model of ease and Elegance, is required, it bears the Name of Caroline Smith—not by the partial Eye, and fond attachment of Grandmamma alone, but through the whole Village—united to So modest a Demeanor there is not any danger of exciting an improper pride in the Bosom of innocence. pride you know was not Made for Man, nor Woman neither.[5] There are persons, there are countanances, there is a deportment, which strike at first sight, and create an interest which it is impossible to account for. it is the great hand of nature which engraves upon the external appearance; the internal Spirit and Character. Lavator the great Physiongnomist has given a Number of Rules for judging, of the Character by the countanance—[6] they are more fancifull than just I believe—and much depends upon Education— It is Tom Jones I think who says a good face is a Letter of recommendation—

You do well my dear to try to amuse your Mamma and Aunt in their solitude. they have many cares and anxieties to which you are yet a stranger; and the innocent playfullness of youth is a sweet solace— the comfort of humane Life, is a combination of little minute attentions, which, taken Seperately, are nothing, but connected with the circumstances of time place and manner, as comeing from the heart, as tokens of good will possess a value, and inspire a pleasure beyond the possession of gold and Rubies and it will ever be a satisfaction to you, to reflect upon your having contributed to the amusement and comfort of your parents, and the more so now, when they are seperated from most of their Friend and relatives. may you never want eitheir pleasure or amusement. we were made for active Life and idleness and happiness are incompatible

Your Aunt T B Adams and her little Girls are very well, and grow finely— our Friends in Boston are well, Your Aunt Cranch I hope is recovering— I do not write to your Mamma now—Writing to you is the Same thing. she will hear from us all— With Love and regards to the whole family I am your truly affection / Grandmother   A A[7]

RC (Adams Papers); docketed by AA2: "Caroline Smith."

[1] AA previously wrote to Smith on 30 Aug. about the importance of cultivating the virtue of hospitality. Smith's 28 Sept. reply has not been found (AA2, *Jour. and Corr.*, 1:213–214).

[2] Enclosure not found.

[3] That is, Ann Hall, niece of Moses Black (vol. 12:324).

[4] Serena is a character in William Hayley's *The Triumphs of Temper*, London, 1781.

[5] Ecclesiasticus, 10:18.

[6] Johann Caspar Lavater, *Essays on Physiognomy*, 3 vols., London, 1789.

[7] AA next wrote to Smith on 2 Feb. 1809, addressing topics of health and the weather. AA also admonished her granddaughter on politics, "You say you hate politics; but when your native country is so seriously threatened, you cannot be a descendant from the spirit of '76, to be totally indifferent to what is passing" (AA2, *Jour. and Corr.*, 1:214–217).

Abigail Adams to Abigail Adams Smith

my dear Daughter   Quincy december 8th 1808

I am indebted to you for two Letters one of   the last bearing date Nov^{br} 20th & 24th [1] I am always rejoiced to see Your handwriting, altho the contents of your Letters Some times give me pain, and none more so than those which contain an Idea that Your Relatives, and Friends have not exerted themselves for You as they might have done. With respect to William, Your Father himself went to Town; and advised with some of his commercial acquaintance, who oweing to the total supression of commerce did not like to take any Young Gentleman into their stores— most of those who had any Number were obliged to dissmiss them. dr welchs Youngest Son John returnd home, and he sent him to an accademy to keep him out of Idleness. mr Greenleafs son Price is returnd home. capt Beals two son, are here intirely out of Buisness.[2] the shop keepers have buisness for a time, but that is like to come soon to a close by the nonintercourse Bill which has recently past in congress—So that the youth of our country have not any other resourse, but to till the land for Bread to Eat.[3] this state of things cannot last long— We are wrought up to a crissis which must break forth in Vengence some where or other. Heaven preserve our country underserving as it is of the favour and protection of Providence. Parson Eackly told his congregation, that we were suffering the judgments of Heaven for having chosen an infidel President to rule over us.[4] we as a people have crying sins enough beside to draw down the punishments we feel. let each individual look into his own breast, and root out every evil and corrupt propencity, then may we expect to be a people saved of the Lord—

I am much grieved at the misfortune of Your Brother. a more generous benevolent Heart exists not in Man. the season of the year is in his favour, and I hope he will be spaired to his family and Friends. in the midst of Life we are in Death. we have had a recent instance of this in the late Death of Mrs Price, the Mother of Mrs Greenleaf— invited to a tea party, well and Vigorus as age can be, She declined only on account of the late hours of Return, rose from her chair was seizd with an oppression upon her lungs, went to her Bed, and expired the next day, to the inexpressible Greif of her distresst and afflicted Daughter—[5] by painfull experience I know how afflictive the death of Parents is, at a period when their Lives are usefull instructive and pleasent, the Source of our own Life seems dried up, our best Friends and counselors removed Yet this is the order of Nature, and we who are yet living must soon expect to follow our Aged Friend— our old Friend Gen'll Warren is also numberd with the Great congregation he was very infirm, and Aged—84 I think. I felt as tho former Friendhip demanded from me a Sympathizing Letter, and regreted that the bitterness of party Spirit had severd us, but after the injustice she had done Your Fathers Character in her History and the opportunity he had given her of Making some acknowledgm[ent] for it, which she wholy omitted to do, I thought a Letter of the kind would appear insincere—and altho I feel for her berevement, and know how keenly she must feel it, I have declined writing to her—[6]

We are all in pretty good Health at present. Mrs S Adams is much better. my dear sister Cranch is recoverd in some measure, but I can see that her whole frame is shaken, and that she is failing— Your Brothers family in Boston are well except John who I think in a very critical state of Health. he has many hetick symptoms—[7] they all kept thanksgiving with us, your uncle and Aunt Cranch & sister smith—all of whom desired to be affectionatly rememberd to you.[8] we calld you all to mind, and found our party incompleat. last year You were with us— Susan desires me to present her Duty to you—and to say to you, that she was at Atkinson when her Mother arrived here; and did not know it for a week, when be sure she was anxious enough to return, but was obliged to wait an other week for her Aunt Peabody— T B A and his Rib desire to be kindly rememberd to you— all our Domesticks remember you and yours with Love and affection— I was yesterday at Weymouth— our Friends there were well— We tallk of you— I expect Aunt Edwards tomorrow to make her Annual visit— she fell and broke her Arm in October, when she intended to come— I expected she would give up the Idea of her visit, but she sent me word her Arm was well, and she must come and kiss the President—

yours affec'ly   A Adams

RC (MHi:De Windt Family Papers); addressed: "Mrs Abigail Smith / Lebanon / state N york." Some loss of text due to a torn manuscript.

[1] Not found.

[2] That is, John Adams Welsh (b. 1792), son of Thomas and Abigail Kent Welsh; Ezekiel Price Greenleaf (1790–1886), son of Thomas and Mary Deming Price Greenleaf; and George Washington Beale (1782–1851) and Thomas Smythe Beale (1787–1815), sons of Capt. Benjamin Beale Jr. and Ann Copeland Beale (vol. 6:299; Greenleaf, *Greenleaf Family*, p. 210; Sprague, *Braintree Families*).

[3] From the start of the congressional session, senators and representatives focused on the repeal and replacement of the Embargo Act of 1807, including the interdiction of trade with Great Britain and France (*Annals of Congress*, 10th Cong., 2d sess., p. 16–17, 20, 123–124, 345, 422). For the resulting Non-Intercourse Act of 1809, see JQA to LCA, 8 Feb. 1809, and note 5, below.

[4] That is, Rev. Joseph Eckley of Boston's Old South Church (vol. 13:279).

[5] Ruth Avery Price (b. 1737), the mother of Mary Greenleaf, died on 25 Nov. 1808 (Boston *Repertory*, 29 Nov.; Greenleaf, *Greenleaf Family*, p. 210).

[6] Gen. James Warren, husband of Mercy Otis Warren, died on 28 November. At the time of his death, the Warrens and Adamses' friendship had broken down over Mercy Warren's portrayal of JA in her *History of the Rise, Progress, and Termination of the American Revolution*, 3 vols., Boston, 1805, for which see Warren to AA, 11 July 1807, note 4, above. It was more than a year before she wrote to Warren, in Dec. 1809, finally offering her condolences on James' death and attributing the delay not to the content of the *History* but rather to Mercy's refusal to retract her characterizations (Lee D. van Antwerp, comp., *Vital Records of Plymouth, Massachusetts, to the Year 1850*, Camden, Maine, 1993, p. 199; AA to Warren, 31 Dec., Dft, Adams Papers).

[7] All three of JQA and LCA's children were sick. GWA and CFA had the chicken pox, and JA2 had a fever. Hectic symptoms included fever and dry skin and were often associated with consumption (JQA, *Diary*, 1–9 Dec. 1808; LCA, *D&A*, 1:278; *OED*).

[8] Massachusetts residents marked a day of thanksgiving on 1 Dec. in accordance with a 9 Nov. proclamation of Gov. James Sullivan (*Boston Commercial Gazette*, 10 Nov.; JQA, *Diary*, 1 Dec.).

John Adams to John Adams Smith

Dear John   Quincy Dec.r 14. 1808

It is a long time Since I had a Letter from you. In the last I think you prophesied "Wonders in November."[1] I understood you to mean a wonderful Revolution in the Sentiments of the People, and a restoration of the Federalists to the Government of the Nation. But the month of November is past, and there appears, notwithstanding all the terrors and horrors of the Embargo, a wonderful Adherence of the People to that measure and its Projectors and Abettors. Pray tell me what Wonders you meant, and whether they have appeared or not.

There is one Wonder much lamented as I hear, and much celebrated far and wide in the Nation, and that is that your Grandfather has changed his Politicks; has come quite round; has altered his System; has become a Democrat; a Jacobin; a Disorganiser; a Republican; a Turncoat; an Apostate, &c &c. &c.[2]

This is an imaginary Wonder indeed.— Chimerical as it is, the very report is a wonderful Wonder of Wonders as ever this wondering World wondered at.

When the Sun remains fixed in the Center of the System, or at least revolving round it, in its own appropriate Circle, it appears, to the Savages of Africa and America and to the ignorant Vulgar of all civilized Nations, to revolve daily round the Earth, when in truth, these Stupid Starers themselves revolve daily round the Center of the Earth, or to descend, in the true Spirit of the Bathos from the Heavens to the Earth, when I Sailed up the Garonne on the first of April 1778 before a gale of Wind and a rapid tide, the Trees and Houses on each Side the River, appeared to run from me down the Stream as fast as a horse could gallop or a Bird fly.[3] But in reality it was myself who ran from them, up the River, and the Trees and Houses were Stationary.

It is your Grandfather who has been Steady to his System, and the Pretended Federalists, who have fled from it.

My System for four and thirty Years has been Neutrality, among the Nations of Europe, as long as possible. But when no longer possible, to war with the Aggressor. When two Aggressors at once render Peace untenable, to War with both, or at least with the worst. My Principle has been to Support a National Government National honor, National Union and National Independence. The Hyperfederalists are for hazarding all. It is my opinion, and has been So, ever Since our Independence and will be So for a long time to come, that the English are our natural Enemies. To be Sure, Alliances are Sometimes made from Necessity, Sometimes through Folly and Sometimes by the Intrigues and private Views of Princes or other Individuals or Parties, between natural Enemies. But I will certainly never consent to an Alliance with England, but in the last Extremity of Necessity. Some of the leading Federalists are driving at an allians with England, and at other Points, in which course I will not follow them, it least untill they get the Legal

Government. They broke away from me, when upon these Principles, I made a Peace with France in 1800.[4] They have been flying from me, ever Since that time, as fast as I Sailed from the Trees in my Voyage to Bourdeaux. And now the Jackanapes charge me with flying from them.—

How are the Proceedings of Congress received at New York?

J. Adams

LbC (Adams Papers); internal address: "John Adams Smith."; APM Reel 118. Tr (Adams Papers).

[1] John Adams Smith's most recent letter has not been found. JA previously wrote to Smith on 10 Oct. describing the characteristics necessary for the practice of law, his grandson's chosen profession. He explained, "Your natural aversion to politics will soon, too soon wear away. A lawyer must be a politician." He recommended several works and areas of law that Smith should study (Adams Papers).

[2] JA's politics, especially his attributed support for the embargo, were reported and reprinted in several newspapers; see, for example, the Newburyport *Statesman*, 7 Nov., 5 Dec.; the Washington, D.C., *Monitor*, 17 Nov.; and the Charleston, S.C., *Carolina Gazette*, 9 December. For earlier comments by AA, see her letter to AA2 of 29 Aug., and note 6, above.

[3] JA sailed the Garonne River at Bordeaux, France, on 30 and 31 March 1778 and employed similar imagery in his autobiography: "The Lands on each Side of Us and the Vessels in the River seemed to fly away from Us" (JA, *D&A*, 4:32–33).

[4] For the Convention of 1800 ending the Quasi-War with France, see vol. 14:437.

Elizabeth Smith Shaw Peabody to Abigail Adams

My Dear Sister, Atkinson Dec. 24th. 1808

I had anticipated a visit from Mrs Adams, & both her Children, for a few days at least, when she came to Haverhill, & we regretted very much that it was not in our power to send for them, or to visit her while there— Abby, & I, both went down a monday, and had the mortification to find she went to Boston the Saturday before— Mr Peabody was absent the whole of your Thansgiving week, & I could not go from home— The Trustees of Atkinson Academy requested Mr Peabody, to go to Concord, & proffer a Pettition in new-Hampshire Court, soliciting Lands, to be appropriated as a Fund for this Seminary—[1] I think it is doubtful, whether he succeeds with such an antifederal Court, who have implicitly adopted the Oeconomical, pusulanimous System of their *Master*; though it has many claims upon Equity, Generosity, & justice; yet where wisdom, & Candour does not preside, & party spirit rages, Institutions of Learning, can have but little prospect of relief, or liberal Benefactions

I could not but regret that my Time in Boston was so limited, that I could not call at your Sons House, & upon many other Friends, whom I wished to see— It really grieved me that I could not see our dear little George, I was in hopes his Parents would have told him to come, & seen me, though I could not visit them—

Yes, my dear Sister, I do indeed, rejoice with you, that you have a Son, of whom you have reason to be *gratefully proud*— His high sense of moral Obligations, his Virtue, his Talents, all give him a superior rank, in the estimation of the candid, the wise, & the good—& the parental breast cannot but glow with peculiar pleasure, when is rehearsed, the "wisdom, the Virtue, & prosperity, of a beloved Child"— That I can claim some share of this pure, & perfect Bliss, I count among my greatest Blessings—

> "O! speak the Joy, Ye, whom the sudden tear
> suprizes Oft."—[2]

I presume the time will come, when truth shall prevail—& things shall not be viewed through the false medium, which now obscures their sight— And though the tongue of slander, may reproach Mr J.Q. Adams, supposing him to have been actuated by sinister motives, yet, those who know him best, cannot believe, but, that, his conduct was the result of his best informed Judgment, & a high sense of the duties he owed his Country, though we may regret, that it is "human to Err," & that the best, are not exempt—[3]

When Virtue, & political Knowledge are Talents so much wanted to prop the falling States, we lament that his, should retire from publick life, & move in a lesser Sphere. If Wisdom, & Virtue, are the stability of a Nation, into what a Situation are we now plunged, for how little do we see in the present Administration— Heaven grant, the next Congress, may exhibit more wisdom—

It was so lately that we visited your Neighbour Mrs Price, in Quincy, & saw her happy in her Children, smiling in health, & surrounded with the elegancies & comforts of Life, that to hear of her sudden departure, was to me very surprizing. Yet what avails riches, honours, or any sublinary Enjoyment at the hour of Death— they must be less than nothing, at that all-important period— Happy, if we have learned, e'en now, "to relish, what alone subsists hereafter"—[4]

I know Mrs Nancy Adams will rejoice to hear that Haverhill has at last united in the Settlement of Mr Joshua Dodge—a worthy Man—& I hope, will prove a lasting Blessing—[5] Mr Harrod, I suppose has informed his Daughter, of the particulars relative to the Ordination— Entertainments &ccc—

Abby's *regrets* many indeed, I dare say were, that she had left her worthy, kind friends at Quincy, & could no longer enjoy the Instructive circle, she always found in her Venerable Uncles hospitable mansions— "What dear Mamma, said she, did you write to my Aunts? now—what will they think— I am sure it was nothing—the cloudy weather"—[6] Peace Child—what need you be concerned— I only related a simple circumstance, & I trust such, will never dishonour you—

I am rejoiced to find our dear Sister Cranch is better, & that she has been able to use her Eyes for the benefit of her absent Friends— I was delighted to receive a letter from her—

I am pleased to hear that Mrs Charles Adams has recovered her health— Please to present my kind regards to her, & her Daughters— I hope they will rapidly improve under her correct, & maternal Guidance—

With sincerest wishes for your health, & the happiness / of all your family, I am ever, your affectionate Sister   Elizabeth Peabody

PS Mr Peabody, & Abby desire their best regards may be accepted by the President—

RC (Adams Papers); endorsed: "Mrs Peabody dec^{br} / 28 1808."

[1] In May, the trustees of Atkinson Academy authorized Rev. Stephen Peabody to petition the N.H. General Court for a land grant for the school, which was approved in June 1809 (Harriet Webster Marr, *Atkinson Academy: The Early Years*, Springfield, Mass., 1940, p. 84–85).
[2] James Thomson, *The Seasons*, "Spring," lines 1154–1155.
[3] Alexander Pope, *An Essay on Criticism*, Part II, line 525.
[4] Edward Young, *The Complaint; or, Night Thoughts*, Night V, line 647.
[5] On 21 Dec. 1808, after more than five years without a settled minister, Rev. Joshua Dodge (1779–1861) was ordained pastor of the First Church in Haverhill, which he led until 1827 (Haverhill *Merrimack Intelligencer*, 24 Dec. 1808; Chase, *History of Haverhill*, p. 558–559).
[6] On 18 Nov. Elizabeth wrote a joint letter to AA and Mary Smith Cranch describing her return trip to Atkinson with Abigail Adams Shaw. Peabody wrote of Shaw's "terrible dull" feelings after visiting friends and how the "innocent ebulitions" of her daughter's "heart, made [me] smile" (Adams Papers).

Abigail Adams to Abigail Adams Smith

my dear Daughter   Quincy December 28 1808

what is the reason I do not get a Letter from my Mother I think I hear you say? why I will tell you Child. I have Sat down more than once, got through one page, been interrupted, laid it by—untill it seemd of no value. I love to be by Myself when I write and that is a difficult thing in the winter season— the parlour Your Father occupies all the forenoon in reading or writeing. it is proper he Should have it to himself. my own chamber is compleatly full this Winter, and I know not how to write in the Evening, So that I can only Snatch, a few moments at a time, and then with various interruptions. Since I began these few lines I have been twice calld away. Susan and Abbe are gone to Boston to day, in order to go to the play in the Evening.¹ Louissa has been there this week. little Abbe is sick, and Eliza is confined to the chamber, so that I am more still than usual. I improved the forenoon in writing a Letter to John and this afternoon I was detemined to write to you. Mrs C Adams has been writing in my chamber to Norfolk—from whence she had a Letter yesterday—² a correspondence is kept up, but whether more than Mere Friendship is Meant, or rather whether any connection will ever take place is very uncertain; I wish she was well setled in Life, but without good prospects, She is better as she is— Susan and Abbe are two overgrown Girls, both of them require a carefull attention & vigilenc Susan with all her foibles bids fair to make a valuable Woman if ~~directed and~~ duly imprest with a ~~proper~~ Sense of her Duty, She becomes properly attentive to them— I hope they will both make good women— as yet, they have not attaind to many of the graces particuliarly Abbe, who I really think an uncooth child in her behaviour. She is milder in her temper, and less usurping than susan but not half the intelect. I begin to think Grandparents not so well qualified to Educate Grandchildren as Parents. they are apt to relax in their Spirit of Government, and to be too indulgent. Yet that was not the case with my Grandmother whose memory I cherish with holy veneration, whose maxims I have treasured up, whose virtues live in My Memory— happy if I could Say, they have been transplanted into my Life—

How has the winter been with you. we have not had scarcly any snow, and but little cold weather. we have been sadly cut off with our cider— we made only 4 Barrels this year and scarcly a Bushel of winter apples—

Our Friends here are all well— your Aunt Cranch is better, but by no Means the Woman She has been I am affraid she has received a shock which she will never recover

My pen does not incline to run a race. tell Caroline I will write soon to her, and to william give my Love— his Grandfather has written to him lately and I sent on a Letter from Harriot Welch to you—³ I intended to have coverd it to you, but your Father Saw it, and frankd it— tell Caroline not to prevent her Friends Sending her Letters here if she is willing to wait a little longer for them— your Brother Johns children have all been Sick, but are getting better. he is going to washington to the supreeme court, in a cause of considerable importance—⁴ he expects to leave here in about three weeks—and to be absent about six weeks—

I shall not touch upon politicks now, but reserve them for the subject of an other Letter from / your affectionate Mother

A Adams

RC (MHi:De Windt Family Papers); addressed: "Mrs Abigail Smith / Lebanon state / NYork"; notation by AA2: "Cousin Louisa say some / thing about."

[1] James Kenney's *The World* was performed at Boston's Federal Street Theatre from 12 to 28 Dec. (*Boston Mirror*, 10 Dec.; *Boston Columbian Centinel*, 28 Dec.).

[2] AA's letter to John Adams Smith, [28 Dec.], is below. The letters to and from SSA have not been found.

[3] Neither JA's letter to William Steuben Smith nor Harriet Welsh's to AA2 have been found.

[4] For JQA's appearance before the U.S. Supreme Court, see JQA to LCA, 5 March 1809, and note 1, below.

Abigail Adams to John Adams Smith

Dear John [28 December 1808][1]

I always feel most disposed to write when I have just received a Letter, yet that is not the case now, but what is very Similar to it. I have just read one from you to Your Grandfather in which You mention judge Benson's having commenced a course of Law Lectures and express a wonder at what could be his object as he does not receive any pecuniary reward.[2] from the knowledge I have of Judge Benson and his Character, I should not hesitate to say that his object is the benefit and instruction of those Youths, who are more eager to obtain knowledge, than to pursue pleasure. of that number I believe my dear Grandson to be. Rollin tell us that it was a custom observed among the Romans to make the houses of old Lawyers the School of the Youth designed for the Bar.[3] What can be more Worthy a Great orator than to conclude the glorious course of his pleading by so honorable a function, like an old experienced pilot—to point out to the young students the course they are to steer and the Rocks they must shun. Such I presume are the Motives and views of Judge Benson— as a few days since I was reading upon this subject, it may not be unacceptable to you to receive a few of the Hints for the rule of your conduct. the first and principle thing, is to form a Grand Idea of Your profession. it is a profession which qualifies a Man best for the chief employments of the state. what esteem does it not gain those who distinguish themselves in it, either in pleading or giving counsel. Is there any finer sight, than to see a numerous auditory, attentive, immoveable, and as it were hanging upon the Lips of a pleader, who manages speech common to all with so much art that he charmes and ravishes the minds of his hearers, and Makes himself absolute master over them. But beside this Glory which would be Trifling enough were there no other motive, what solid ~~glory~~ joy is it for a virtuous man to think he has received a talent from God, which makes him the sanctuary of the unfortunate, the protector of Justice; and enables him to defend the lives, fortunes and honours of his Brethren? I am convinced that a Genius is the first and most necessary quality for a pleader but I am also certain that study is of the utmost importance Tis like a second nature, and if it does not impart a Genius to him who had none before, it rectifies, polishes, improves and invigorates it— these are the observations of Rollin— I have heard Your Uncle J Q Adams observe, that most of our public speakers both in our National Legislature, and at the Bar, are very deficient in point of Literature. it is polite Literature which embellishes and enriches the understanding, which diffuses a delicacy and beauty over discourse, and imparts a "charm beyond the reach of art"[4] To imbibe Rhetoric from the very fountain, to consult able Masters, to read carefully the ancient and moderns, to be constantly employd in composing and translating and to make the Greek language a particular study;—these were the exercises which Cicero thought necessary to form the great orator. it is reported of Demosthenes that he coppied Thucydides's history Eight times with his own hand, in order to make his stile more familiar to him.[5] What ever you undertake my dear son strive to excell in; I am glad to see Your mind so much engaged in the pursuit of knowledge. it is a young Mans best security against temptation, and dissipation—

I had a Letter last week from your sister Caroline she is well—and assures us that your uncle is upon the recovery—[6] we are all in good health at present it is probable you will see your uncle J Q Adams in about three weeks he is going to washington to the supreeme court ~~up~~ in a cause of consideral concequence— I shall leave politicks at present to the statesmen, recommending however to you to read all the debates and speeches you can procure upon both sides of the Great subjects, which now agitate and embarrass our country.

RC (Adams Papers); docketed by AA2: "John A Smith." Filmed at [1808].

[1] The dating of this letter is based on AA's letter to AA2 of 28 Dec., above, in which she mentioned that she wrote to John Adams Smith on the same day.

[2] Smith's letter to JA about Judge Egbert Benson, formerly chief judge of the second circuit of the U.S. Circuit Court, has not been found (vol. 9:339; *ANB*).

[3] Charles Rollin, *The Method of Teaching and Studying the Belles Lettres*, 6th edn., 3

vols., London, 1769, 2:118.
⁴ Alexander Pope, *An Essay on Criticism*, Part I, line 153.
⁵ In AA's comments on rhetoric, she referenced Cicero, *De Oratore*, Book I, ch. 34, and Rollin, *The Ancient History of the Egyptians,* *Carthaginians, Assyrians, Babylonians, Medes and Persians, Macedonians, and Grecians*, 5th edn., 7 vols., London, 1768, 4:239, a copy of which is in JA's library at MB.
⁶ Not found.

Abigail Adams to John Quincy Adams

my dear son   Quincy Jan^ry 16th 1809

I find from Dr Tufts that I have seventeen Hundred dollors of Eight prct Stock which is paid, and deposited in the Bank. seven hundred of them I should like to vest in the Market shares. the other thousand dollors I should wish to place so as to yeald me an interest of six pr ct. I know not how to let it lye useless as it is a large proportion of all I have, and the interest is necessary to Me for the supply of those who are immediatly dependent upon me— the payment of it; I consider as a real misfortune at this time. you mentiond to me that you should be obliged to sell some property, to make your own payment of shares—¹ You shall take the thousand dollors if you chuse, instead of parting with Your property only should a new loan be opened, I should then like to vest it in public securities— I will procure an order from dr Tufts for you to receive it, if agreable to you

I am my dear son / your affectionate / Mother

Abigail Adams

RC (Adams Papers); addressed: "Honble John Quincy Adams. / Boston"; endorsed: "Adams— A— My Mother 16. Jan^y: 1809."

¹ On 17 Jan. AA directed Cotton Tufts to withdraw these funds so that JQA could invest them (DNDAR). Mother and son finalized the transaction on 18 Jan., and AA received an initial interest payment of $53.12 on 27 July. TBA made at least three more interest payments on JQA's behalf during the following year (AA to JQA, [27 *July*]; to TBA, [9 *Feb. 1810*], [7 *May*], [7 *Aug.*], all Adams Papers).

Louisa Catherine Adams to John Quincy Adams

Boston Jan^ry 28. [1809]

Assured that a few lines from me will be acceptable to my best beloved friend on his arrival I seize the earliest opportunity of enquiring after his health and giving the pleasing information of the return to health of our darling Children Poor Kitty suffers severely for her imprudence she has a large Blister on her side and though not absolutely confined to her Bed it almost amounts to it she finds it intolerably irksome as she has an invitation to two Balls next Week, one to Mrs Derby's.¹ I am under the necessity of postponing the visit of your Brother & family for a few days—

Your Father & Mother have been here this Morning and were anxious to know if I had heard from you I told them I did not expect it untill you arrived at New York they laughed and said they supposed a few Franks might be of use and I have prepared a large packet—

Give my love to all at Hellen's and Boyds your family are all well and I forgive you though you did part with me very *cavalierly* and subscribe myself with pleasure your very affectionate Wife   L. C. Adams

P. S. Kitty sends your Watch paper with her love Caroline is in a Family way

RC (Adams Papers); addressed: "John Quincy Adams Esq[r.] / Washington City"; endorsed: "Adams— L. C. my wife. 28. Jan[y:] 1809. / 5. Feb[y:] rec[d.] / 6. Ans[d:]"; notation: "free" and by JA: "J. Adams."

¹ That is, Martha Coffin Derby (vol. 15:386).

John Quincy Adams to Louisa Catherine Adams

My dear Wife.   Baltimore 1. Feb[y:] 1809.

On leaving Boston I had formed the Resolution of travelling only in the day-time, but at the close of the second day, arriving at Hartford, I found I should be four days more in getting to New-York, unless I proceeded that same Evening, about forty miles to New-Haven— The roads were excellent for sleighing; I was alone in the Stage, and there was a moon bright almost as the morning— I therefore prevailed on the proprietors of the Stage to send me on that Night instead of the next day, and reached New-Haven about two in the morning.— After going to bed for about four hours I took the Stage again and arrived at New-York, Sunday Noon— I had found myself by experience so well able to travel in the Night, and had seen the chances of being delayed beyond the time I had allotted for my journey, that I concluded to try another Night's expedition— As I wrote you, at the Stage-Office in New-York, we arrived in Philadelphia, Monday Morning before daylight—¹ It had begun to Snow about an hour before, and continued to Snow almost through the whole day— I had taken lodgings at the mansion house, and pass'd the day by parcels, there, at M[r:] Hopkinson's, M[r:] Ewing's, and M[r:] C. J. Ingersoll's—² The next Morning, that is yesterday, I again took the Mail Stage, and after riding all last Night arrived here this day between 9 and 10. too late to go on to Washington by this day's Stage— I have taken my passage for to-morrow.

The roads from Philadelphia to this place are very bad, and my ride from yesterday morning was so fatiguing, and the severity of the weather chill'd me to such a degree, that I have not been able to avail myself as I should have wished, of this day to go out and see M{r:} and M{rs:} Buchanan.—[3] I have confined myself most of this day to my chamber at Gadsby's (the House formerly kept by Evans) and shall take an early bed, in order to be ready to start to-morrow morning at 6.[4]

My Journey has been remarkably dull and barren of incident, nearly one half of it having been performed alone.— My cough has been the only companion that hung by me faithfully the whole way, and increases in its attachment by habit and indulgence— When I get to Washington I hope it will grow tired of me.

I was in hopes I should have been unknown and unnoticed in my progress— But from the time when I met M{r:} Story, I have been known all the way— I have had little or nothing said to me, but have perceived much curiosity and speculation where and for what I am going—[5] You will readily conceive my feelings on the occasion.

Politics—the rage of politics, boiling every where with a fierceness I never knew before. In Massachusetts and Connecticut all was questioning—Had the General Court declared the Division of the States?— Had they recalled all their Members from Congress?—Were there forty sail of ships in Boston harbour, loaded, and waiting only the permission of the Legislature to sail?— All this, and I know not how much more such stuff had been reported, and seriously believed—[6] In New-York, Philadelphia and here, the current with equal violence sets the opposite way.

It is impossible I should have heard from you since I left you, and yet I am very anxious to hear from you— My thoughts are continually running on you and my dear children, whom I long again to embrace by my own fire side.

There have been some very warm personal altercations in Congress lately; and some which have given me great pain and concern— But I need not detail them, as you will see them told in the newspapers.[7]

We met the Vice-President yesterday, in his Carriage, on his way returning home— The report is revived that he intends to decline serving for the next Election.

M{r:} Calhoun called this afternoon to see me, and made particular enq[uiry for] you—[8]

Farewell my best beloved— Kiss Kitty and the children for me. / faithfully yours John Quincy Adams.

RC (Adams Papers); addressed: "M^rs: L. C. Adams. / Boston."; internal address: "M^rs: L. C. Adams."; endorsed: "J Q. Adams / Rec^d Feby 14 / Ans^d." Tr (Adams Papers). Some loss of text where the seal was removed.

[1] JQA's letter to LCA from New York City was dated 29 Jan. and reported on his journey, noting that he planned to depart for Philadelphia later that day (Adams Papers).

[2] William Renshaw opened the Mansion House Hotel in Philadelphia in 1807 in the former home of the Bingham family at 122 Third Street between Walnut and Spruce Streets. While in the city, JQA visited playwright Charles Jared Ingersoll (vol. 15:42; CFA, *Diary*, 1:18).

[3] Caroline Johnson and Andrew Buchanan lived four miles outside of Baltimore (LCA, *D&A*, 1:260).

[4] John Gadsby, who also owned Gadsby's Hotel in Washington, D.C., took over the Indian Queen Hotel after the 1807 death of previous owner William Evans. The inn was located at 187 Market Street in Baltimore (vol. 14:565; J. Thomas Scharf, *History of Baltimore City and County*, Phila., 1881, p. 514).

[5] JQA saw Joseph Story in Brookfield, Mass., on 26 Jan. 1809, and thereafter wrote of being recognized by fellow travelers. Newspapers also noted that he passed through Philadelphia on his way to the federal capital (*Biog. Dir. Cong.*; JQA, *Diary*, 28 Jan.; *Philadelphia Gazette*, 31 Jan.; Charleston, S.C., *City Gazette*, 15 Feb.).

[6] After the passage of the Enforcement Act, which was signed into law on 9 Jan. and authorized state militias and federal troops to enforce the embargo, several Massachusetts towns passed resolutions attacking the law as an abrogation of states' rights. Boston newspapers suggested it was grounds for disunion. The Mass. General Court met in a session beginning on 25 Jan. to discuss a response to acting governor Levi Lincoln's use of the law to order the militia to enforce the embargo. The legislature formally objected to Lincoln's actions and several Federalist members called for a meeting of New England states to discuss leaving the union and forming a confederation (Stephen W. Stathis, *Landmark Legislation 1774–2012: Major U.S. Acts and Treaties*, 2d edn., Los Angeles, 2014, p. 36; Dinah Mayo-Bobee, *New England Federalists: Widening the Sectional Divide in Jeffersonian America*, Madison, N.J., 2017, p. 135–137; Philadelphia *Democratic Press*, 30 Jan.; Boston *Repertory*, 31 Jan.; Boston *Columbian Centinel*, 18 Jan.; *The Patriotick Proceedings of the Legislature of Massachusetts*, Boston, 1809, p. 9–40).

[7] JQA was likely referring to recent threats of duels targeting Josiah Quincy III. During debate of the Enforcement Act in the House of Representatives, Quincy declared that even Democratic-Republicans would not renew the embargo if it had an expiration date. In response to his claims, Quincy was challenged to duels by "embargo patriots" in Congress, including John Wayles Eppes of Virginia. During debate in January over whether a special session of Congress was needed to further discuss the embargo, attempts to goad Quincy into a duel were again unsuccessful. Several newspapers reported the challenges, including the Boston *Repertory*, 6 Jan.; Washington, D.C., *Monitor*, 21 Jan.; New York *Commercial Advertiser*, 25 Jan.; and Boston *Columbian Centinel*, 1 Feb. (Boston *Repertory*, 3 Feb.; Boston *Commercial Gazette*, 2 Feb.; Mayo-Bobee, *New England Federalists*, p. 134).

[8] James Calhoun Jr. was a Baltimore merchant with whom JQA and LCA socialized in Europe in the 1790s (vol. 12:384, 385).

John Quincy Adams to Louisa Catherine Adams

My dear wife. Washington 8. February 1809.

I thank you for your letter, and Kitty for her watch-paper— I had like to have had no watch-case to put it in— For at Baltimore I lost my

February 1809

watch for several hours, I need not tell you how—for thereby hangs a tail.— Suffice it to say that having occasion for my seal, on closing my letter to you from that place, I found my watch was missing—[1] I immediately recollected where I had last left it; but it was no longer there— I wrote an advertisement for it to be put into the papers of the ensuing day; and Gadsby set enquiries on foot all round the neighbourhood— Late in the Evening, my watch was brought back to me, by a boy who had had the luck to find it, and the honesty to bring it back— So I was quit for a five dollar bill, and have got my watch-case again for Kitty's paper.

I am much concerned to hear that she continued so unwell, and had been obliged to have resort to a blister— The loss of the Balls too was a heavy misfortune, in these hard times, when pleasure is all that can be got.— I hope she has quite recovered by this time— You speak so shortly about the returning health of the children, without saying any thing in particular of Charles, that I was afraid his health had *not much* returned— But I hoped he was no worse; and must hope so still.

The abruptness of my departure was occasioned partly by the Stage-Driver's having come and contrary to the engagement made with me at the Stage-Office, called upon me to go there, and threatened not to call for me— But partly I had attributed it to yourself, for which I do not know whether I have yet *forgiven you*— I am sure I have not yet got over it—[2]

The first days after my arrival here, I paid and returned a few visits;[3] but since the Court has been in Session; that is since Monday I have principally confined my attendance to that.

The votes for President and Vice-President, were this day opened and counted by the two Houses, of Congress, assembled in the Representatives Chamber— M$^{r:}$ Madison was declared to be President elect and M$^{r:}$ Clinton Vice-President—[4] This latter Gentleman, probably not being very anxious to be present at this ceremony, went home some ten days since— I met him on the road between Philadelphia and Baltimore; but as his Carriage and our Stage merely pass'd by each other, I had not an opportunity to speak to him.

We are well here in this family, excepting M$^{rs:}$ Hellen, who is apprehensive of having a bad breast— They are also well at M$^{r:}$ Boyd's, where I have been several times and dined once—

Public Affairs continue to be much perplexed, and the prospect is still very gloomy— The House of Representatives have voted by a large majority that the Embargo shall come off, the 4$^{th:}$ of March. But having heretofore resolved against submission, they are now to provide something instead of the Embargo, and what that shall be they cannot agree upon.

They talked of issuing letters of Marque and Reprisal; but they have now decided against that— They talk of authorizing the merchants to arm their vessels—But neither will that succeed— They now talk of non-intercourse with France and England—of excluding armed vessels of all Nations from our Ports—Of raising 15000 Men—Of borrowing ten Millions of Dollars—[5] It would be passing strange if they should finish by doing nothing at-all.

The Ladies of our family are going this Evening to a party at M[r:] Brent's—[6] There are very few parties any where— This is the first since I came, and there has been but one Ball this Winter.

9. Feb[y:]

I have just received from my friend Gardner a letter giving me information of the decease of his wife—[7] Although this Event could not have been unexpected to him, he appears to be in great distress under it, and I very sincerely participate in his affliction— This circumstance has depress'd my Spirits, and if I should continue this Letter any longer, I should be apt to conclude it in a style too much contrasted with that of its first page— But, in Spirits high or low, in sorrow or in mirth believe me to be ever alike affectionately yours.

John Quincy Adams.

I will thank you to send the enclosed letter to M[r:] Gardner.[8]

RC (Adams Papers); addressed: "M[rs:] L. C. Adams. / Boston."; internal address: "M[rs:] L. C. Adams."; endorsed: "J Q Adams / Rec[d] Feb 21 / Ans[d] do 21."

[1] LCA to JQA, 28 Jan., and JQA to LCA, 1 Feb., both above.

[2] JQA was responding to the closing line of LCA's letter to him of 28 Jan., above.

[3] In Washington, D.C., JQA visited with George Boyd and Boston attorney William Stackpole. He also saw several members of Congress, including representatives Ezekiel Bacon and Orchard Cook of Massachusetts and Clement Storer of New Hampshire and senators Joseph Inslee Anderson of Tennessee, William Branch Giles of Virginia, and Buckner Thruston of Kentucky. He also met with Thomas Jefferson, cabinet members Robert Smith and James Madison, and diplomats Louis Marie Turreau de Garambouville of France and David Montagu Erskine of Great Britain (JQA, *Diary*, 2–6 Feb.; *Biog. Dir. Cong.*).

[4] On 8 Feb., Congress convened in joint session to count the electoral votes for president and vice president. Madison earned the majority for president with 122 votes while Charles Cotesworth Pinckney garnered 47 votes. For vice president, George Clinton received a majority with 113 votes and Rufus King was second with 47. For Madison's inauguration, see JQA to LCA, 5 March, and note 2, below (*Annals of Congress*, 10th Cong., 2d sess., p. 344–345).

[5] A firestorm of criticism against the Embargo Act of 1807 moved the House of Representatives to consider repeal and the possible alternatives outlined by JQA. The House debated the measure from 10 Nov. 1808 and on 3 Feb. 1809 approved a resolution calling for a

repeal. The resolution passed by a vote of 93 to 26 with 70 representatives supporting a 4 March deadline in a subsequent vote. Work then began on a replacement measure. On 6 Feb. the House rejected proposals to allow letters of marque and reprisal to be issued to U.S. privateers or to sanction the arming of merchant ships. Ultimately, the House on 27 Feb. concurred with a Senate bill to replace the embargo with a ban on U.S. trade with Great Britain and France while trade with other nations resumed. The president signed the Non-Intercourse Act of 1809 into law on 1 March. It went into effect on 15 March, but with no effective enforcement mechanism, it did little but further fuel tensions with Britain (*Annals of Congress*, 10th Cong., 2d sess., p. 345, 414–436, 451–452, 474, 1332, 1334, 1541; *U.S. Statutes at Large*, 2:528–533; Wood, *Empire of Liberty*, p. 655–658; Kevin R. C. Gutzman, *James Madison and the Making of America*, N.Y., 2012, p. 300; Burton Spivak, *Jefferson's English Crisis: Commerce, Embargo, and the Republican Revolution*, Charlottesville, Va., 1979, p. 188, 190, 191, 192–193, 195, 196; *Documentary Source Book of American History*, ed. William MacDonald, rev. edn., N.Y., 1918, p. 284–288).

[6] Robert Brent Sr. (1764–1819) served as the first mayor of Washington, D.C., from 1802 to 1812 (Columbia Hist. Soc., *Records*, 2:236, 239, 247 [1899]).

[7] Sarah Jackson Gardner (b. 1779) died on 29 Jan. 1809. In his letter to JQA of 2 Feb. (Adams Papers), John Gardner asked for a letter from JQA to distract him from his loss (Elizabeth Cabot Putnam and James Jackson Putnam, eds., *The Hon. Jonathan Jackson and Hannah (Tracy) Jackson: Their Ancestors and Descendants*, [Boston?], 1907, p. 30).

[8] JQA's letter to Gardner, not found, was dated 9 Feb. (LCA to JQA, 26 Feb., and note 3, below).

Louisa Catherine Adams to John Quincy Adams

My best beloved friend   Boston Feb$^{ry.}$ 12th 1808 [1809]

Your very kind letter was sent to me yesterday Morning from Quincy and as added to the anxiety of my mind from a conviction that the rappidity with which you travel'd has contributed very much towards encreasing your cold of which I hope you will now take every possible care for my sake if not for your own—[1]

Our family are still invalids and Kitty does not recover as fast as I could wish your Dear Mother has been very dangerously ill but thank God she is restored to her family once more to whom her loss would be irreparable—

Mon Ami you know not what it cost's me to distress you thus but alas we must endeavor patiently to submit to evils which are unavoidable and I am too well acquainted with the fortitude which you possess to doubt a proper exertion of it on the present occasion— I write this from my Sopha to which I was removed yesterday Morning after a confinement to my bed of four or five days my illness was caused by an unfortunate kick from poor little Charles who was very sick I am however getting very well over it and shall be quite strong before you return—[2]

Your Brother and sister left us this Morning after a visit of ten days She was confined the whole time with Abigail who has had a bad fever ever since she came to town she is however much better—

Adieu my best Friend the Children are much better Kitty desires to be remember'd to you and joins with me in love to all the family— Yours most affectionately   L C A.

excuse this scrawl I am too weak to do better—

RC (Adams Papers); addressed: "John Quincy Adams Esq[r.]"; endorsed: "Adams— L. C. 12. Feb[y:] 1809. / 17. Feb[y:] rec[d:] / 21. Ans[d:]."

[1] JQA to LCA, 29 Jan., for which see JQA to LCA, 1 Feb., and note 1, above.

[2] LCA was then pregnant. She later wrote that it was a fall, not the kick from CFA, that may have caused her miscarriage (LCA to JQA, 16 Feb., below; LCA, *D&A*, 1:279).

John Quincy Adams to Louisa Catherine Adams

My dear wife.   Washington 13. February 1809.

I have received but one letter from you since I left Boston, and that was written only two days after my departure—[1] So long an interval during which I have not heard a word from you, and neither your mother, nor any other of the families here have received a line, begins to make me uneasy; and the state of our Charles when I came away, and of Kitty's health when you wrote tends to increase that uneasiness—

I wrote you from New-York, from Baltimore, and twice since my arrival here.[2] I intended to have written you again yesterday; but as it was your birth-day, a day which in my heart is always associated with sentiments of affection and delight, I could not prevail on myself to sit down, and darken it by the communication of alarms and of distress— For the intelligence I must have given from here was such as I knew would be distressing to you— M[rs:] Hellen's youngest child has been for three days at such extremity that they have scarcely hoped its life from hour to hour—[3] Its disorder was first something of the croup, and afterwards inflammation of the bowels, which it is apprehended will terminate in a mortification— It has been twice bled, and had three blisters applied— During great part of the day yesterday, the night before last and Saturday, there was not a hope in the family, or the physicians that the child would recover— Last Evening and this morning there are some favourable symptoms; but such as yet leave it extremely doubtful what the event will be—

I have attended the Sessions of the Supreme Court very steadily the whole of the last week, and shall continue to attend them, untill they get through the part of the business in which I am concerned— I am very much afraid that I shall lose them all; upon questions entirely new, and unthought of by those who employed me. One of these ques-

February 1809

tions is whether a *Company*, or incorporated body can sue or be sued in the Courts of the United States— This question has never been made before, and they have decided hundreds of cases in which Corporations are parties— But now it is made a *point*, and there is great probability the Court will decide against their own right to sustain such suits.⁴

I have been into no Company, and have confined myself to a very few visits— I scarcely know what is going forward in Congress, being absorbed in the necessary attention to my own business.

The appointment of General Dearborn as Collector at Boston, has at length been confirmed by the Senate, and he will immediately proceed to take possession of his Office— After his nomination there were strong objections made against him on the ground of his having paid money without lawful authority to General Wilkinson— The fact I understand was clearly proved; but M$^{r:}$ Dearborn in his justification produced the President's orders—the opinion of the Attorney General, and promises from Gen$^{l:}$ Wilkinson to refund *advances*.— M$^{r:}$ Randolph has brought the subject forward in the house, and I suppose it will be talked of in public, unless objects of higher importance should continue to engross the attention of the Nation.⁵

Your mother yesterday received a recent letter from your brother, at New-Orleans, who is well— He writes on political affairs, and reasons on the present state of things in a manner very conformable to my own opinions—

The embargo is to come off on the 3$^{d:}$ of March—But in its stead [there is] to be a non-intercourse with France and England— Exclusion of all foreign armed vessels from our Ports and Harbours, and perhaps (but I doubt) a loan of money, and more men to be raised.

Adieu, my dearest Louisa; may Heaven grant you many, many *happy* returns of the yesterday's anniversary; and bless you more and more in your children present and to come—   John Quincy Adams.⁶

RC (Adams Papers); addressed: "M$^{rs:}$ L. C. Adams. / Boston."; internal address: "M$^{rs:}$ L. C. Adams."; endorsed: "J Q Adam / Rec^d Feby 22." Some loss of text where the seal was removed. Tr (Adams Papers).

¹ LCA to JQA, 28 Jan., above.
² JQA's letters to LCA were dated 29 Jan. and 1, 5, and 8 February. For that of 29 Jan., see the 1 Feb. letter, and note 1, above; for the 5 Feb. letter, see LCA's of 16 Feb., and note 1, below; the letter of 8 Feb. is above.
³ That is, MCHA.
⁴ Starting on 7 Feb., JQA attended the U.S. Supreme Court almost every day until he left Washington, D.C., in March. While he was primarily there to argue the case of Fletcher *v.* Peck regarding Yazoo land claims, for which see JQA to LCA, 5 March, and note 1, below, he also represented William Henderson Boardman in the case Hope Insurance Company of Providence *v.* Boardman and contributed to Bank of the United States *v.* Deveaux. Arguments in both cases centered on the question

of whether corporations have standing in U.S. courts. The Supreme Court handed down decisions in both cases on 15 March, ruling only on the constitutional question in reversing the decisions of lower courts. The decisions, especially in Bank of the United States v. Deveaux, proved to be foundational in extending some of the protections of citizen stockholders to corporate entities (JQA, *Diary*, 7 Feb.–15 March; Cranch, *Reports of Cases in the Supreme Court*, 5:57–92; Anne Ashmore, "Dates of Supreme Court Decisions and Arguments," p. 8, U.S. Supreme Court, www.supremecourt.gov; Adam Winkler, "*Bank of the United States v. Deveaux* and the Birth of Constitutional Rights for Corporations," *Journal of Supreme Court History*, 43:237–238 [2018]).

[5] Thomas Jefferson on 25 Jan. nominated Henry Dearborn to serve as collector of the port of Boston. Dearborn faced opposition owing to his decision while secretary of war to transfer funds without congressional approval to Gen. James Wilkinson, who was involved in Spanish border disputes. A Senate committee investigated the allegations from 26 Jan. to 8 Feb., and the full Senate confirmed Dearborn's appointment on 11 February. The issue was then again raised in the Senate by James Hillhouse and in the House of Representatives by John Randolph, and while the later debate drew extensive coverage in the press, Dearborn retained the post and served until 1812 (U.S. Senate, *Exec. Jour.*, 10th Cong., 2d sess., p. 97, 106, 108–109; *Alexandria Gazette*, 7 Feb. 1809; *New-York Gazette*, 20 Feb.; *Annals of Congress*, 10th Cong., 2d sess., p. 347–352; *New-England Palladium*, 7 Feb.; U.S. House, *Jour.*, 10th Cong., 2d sess., p. 537, 590–591; *Biog. Dir. Cong.*).

[6] JQA wrote again to LCA on 21 and 26 Feb., expressing concern about the health of his family and stating that he was busy with Supreme Court matters. He mentioned visiting Jefferson and noted that Congress planned to adjourn in a few days and that he expected to arrive home about 25 March (Adams Papers).

Louisa Catherine Adams to John Quincy Adams

My best Friend Boston Feb[ry.] 16 1808 [1809]

I hasten to answer the few lines I recieved from you this Morning to assure you that we are *all* rapidly recovering from the different indispositions which I mention'd in my last and I am regaining my strength[1] I mention'd that my illness was owing to a kick but I find it is the opinion of the D[r.] & Nurse that the injury which was very evident in the Child must have been done by a fall which I had in returning from M[r] Foster's—

The Town is full of your appointment as Secretary of War and your father and Brother ask'd me if I thought your would accept it[2] I told them I did not know but I rather thought you would not—

Since that M[r.] Sumner is come and your now said to be going to England to settle all the disputes as there is no other man in this Country can do it[3] I write you all the Nonsense I hear having nothing better to say but I fear you will never get through this *long letter* therefore I will only request you to remember us affectionately to all and believe ever / tenderly yours L C Adams

RC (Adams Papers).

[1] In a letter of 5 Feb. (Adams Papers), JQA wrote about his journey from Baltimore to Washington, D.C., noting that he fell ill before beginning that leg of the trip. On arrival in the capital, he reported that he was busy with social engagements. LCA's previous let-

ter to JQA was of 12 Feb., above.

² The Boston *Columbian Centinel*, 8 Feb., and other newspapers reported an unfounded rumor that JQA was nominated as secretary of war (*Philadelphia Gazette*, 3 Feb.; New York *Republican Watch-Tower*, 7 Feb.).

³ This was probably William Hyslop Sumner (1780–1861), Boston attorney and son of former Massachusetts governor Increase Sumner. The *New-York Gazette*, 31 Jan., falsely reported that JQA would sail to England on a diplomatic mission within a few days (vol. 14:469).

Louisa Catherine Adams to John Quincy Adams

Boston Feb^ry. 26 1808 [1809]

Percieving from your last letter my beloved friend that you suffer great anxiety concerning Charles; I can with pleasure assure you, that he is very fat, very handsome, and apparently very well; though he still has the Cough which is some times very troublesome.¹ Your Mother is recovering slowly and all the rest of our family are in good health—

Your father was in Town yesterday and brought George in to see us with whom he is quite delighted M^r. Whitney gives him a very high Character and has put him into Latin which he acquires unusually fast quick he is in perfect health and grows very fast he took up your letter and was much delighted to find he could read it I made him a trifling present by way of encouragement with which he was much pleased—

Dr Welsh called to see me to day he told me that there were letters in town from M^r. Q— saying that the Embargo would not be removed *at all*. that it is *here* thought that there has been too much *moderation* that therefore something more violent must immediately be attempted which it is supposed will effectually intimidate the Government and gain the desired end—²

I am not in the way of gaining much intelligence I write you what little I hear although I suppose you have correspondents who are able and willing to write you every occurrence worth notice—

I see The papers mention the death of John Gardners youngest Child I sent your letter to Mr Jackson who promised to deliver it—³

Most heartily do I rejoice in the recovery of Nancy's Child offer her my sincere congratulations and tell her I suffer'd much anxiety on her account—

Adieu my best beloved friend rest assured that every possible care and attention shall be paid to our dear Children and as far as the tender solicitude of an anxious Mother can prevent nothing shall be wanting for their Welfare and health Poor Mrs W. Payne is at the point of death in the last stage of a consumption the Physicians have pronounced it impossible for her to recover⁴ Remember me to all and believe me with the sincerest wishes for your welfare and the truest and tenderest affection yours.   L. C. Adams

P. S. Kitty desires her love to you and is highly flatter'd by the account you have given of her to the family

RC (Adams Papers); addressed: "John Quincy Adams Esqr"; endorsed: "Adams— L. C. 26. Feb^y: 1809. / 5. March rec^d:."

[1] In a letter to LCA of 15 Feb., JQA expressed continued anxiety over CFA's health and noted that the U.S. Supreme Court was expected to hear his case the following day (Adams Papers).

[2] Josiah Quincy III wrote at least four times in February from Washington, D.C., to his wife Eliza Susan Morton Quincy in Boston, for whom see Descriptive List of Illustrations, No. 7, above. He updated his wife on congressional debate of the repeal of the embargo and its replacement with the Non-Intercourse Act of 1809. Local sentiment was reflected in a report in the Boston *Democrat*, 25 Feb., which opined, "It is evident then that war, or submission is . . . inevitable" and stated further that if there was to be a military response, "*it should be immediate*." A writer in the *New-England Palladium*, 21 Feb., took the opposite position, arguing that diplomacy was a better option: "Here is the field for the exercise of the wisdom, the firmness, policy, and sound discretion of the real statesman, and the real patriot" (Edmund Quincy, *Josiah Quincy*, p. 184–186).

[3] The *New-England Palladium*, 24 Feb., reported the death of John Gardner's six-month-old daughter, Mary Tracy. Gardner wrote to JQA about the death in a letter of 25 Feb. (Adams Papers) and mentioned JQA's letter of 9 Feb., which has not been found. JQA's letter was carried by Patrick Tracy Jackson, Gardner's brother-in-law (Elizabeth Cabot Putnam and James Jackson Putnam, eds., *The Hon. Jonathan Jackson and Hannah (Tracy) Jackson: Their Ancestors and Descendants*, [Boston?], 1907, p. 30–31).

[4] Lucy Gray Dobell Payne died on 13 March (Whitmore, *Families of Payne and Gore*, p. 23).

Thomas Boylston Adams to John Quincy Adams

Dear Brother.   Quincy 28th: February 1809.

I intended to have written to you when at your own house or Office in Boston,[1] but was prevented by the intense *severity of the weather*, added to the general ill health of both your & my family, during the whole time we sojourned under your Roof, which, by the assiduity of your wife & Catharine and the faithful attendance of their domesticks was made, in every respect, *our own house*. My Daughter Abigail was taken sick the day after my wife went to Boston, and so continued nearly the three weeks they remained there, and the severe indisposition of your wife, from which she has happily recovered, while it added to our regret for the loss of her Society, made us feel anxious least we should unavoidably increase her illness by our poximity to her apartment. I never knew a colder spell of weather than that we passed in Boston, and its severity affected, in various ways, the health of almost every living creature. From the time of your departure, till now,

7. ELIZA SUSAN MORTON QUINCY, BY CHARLES BALTHAZAR JULIEN FÉVRET DE SAINT-MÉMIN, 1797
See page xii

there has been constant sleighing, but a warm wind & sun for three days past has nearly put an end to it.

I can tell you nothing *new* of the proceedings in our Genl Court; Their bile is pretty well worked off by this time, and they pretend to be on the eve of adjournment. I think the object of their coming together, this winter, has been misconceived, for, in stead of legislation they have done nothing, but pass Resolution's, Remonstrances & *Replications*. They have rivetted M^{r:} Gray to the Republican interest by actual violence— I have heard him speak several times, and my conclusion is, that he is a more decidedly honest *Republican* than Sam. Dana or William King—[2] I give him credit for acting from *conviction*. The Remonstrance of the two branches of the legislature is nothing more than Mr Gore's speech, in the House, upon Crowningshield's Resolutions, reduced to writing and revised by the Author—[3] Two of the tenets of the Junto are very explicitly announced in it—Viz That THE alliance with France was found to be more pernicious than *any war*, and that France, in the present rivalship of doing the most harm to the U S. has, in every instance, been first & foremost. Here is the whole secret; all the rest is but *inducement* (as the Lawyers say) I think that passage in the memorial relative to the late alliance with France, peculiarly striking, and comprehensive. If the language had been, that "we view with abhorrence the separation of these Colonies from Great Britain," it might have been more intelligible to some, but the sentiment would have been less striking. I do not, for my own part, concur with M^{r:} Morton in applauding the conduct of Washington, because he did not fulfill the Treaty with France, as to the Guarantee of their West India Isles, merely on the score of its being too hard a bargain on our part; nor would any real friend of Washington represent his conduct in that light; but, as we got into a difficulty on that ground, we had no right to claim exemption from the execution of that article, but by setting it off, against unwarranted infractions of the compact, on the part of France. This was the way in which that affair was balanced, as I understand it. I was a good deal entertained by listening to the arguments of the great party Champions in the two branches of our Legislature during the discussion of Crowningshield's Resolutions, but the crowd of auditors was so great that I lost the hearing of several speakers on both sides. Gore was the British Champion— Bangs the French.[4] But neither of them reached the cause of our embarrassments, as I *humbly conceive*, nor did either prescribe an efficient remedy for the disease that afflicts our Country. We are our own worst enemies. Our power is undervallued by all parties, with

February 1809

the same views; viz, the fear of expence; because expence begets taxation & taxation begets unpopularity. I am no Solomon, but this is my opinion.

I am requested by my wife's brother M{r:} Charles Harrod to ask the favor of your recommendation of him to the proper authority for a Commission in the Army, now raised, raising or to be raised.[5] He has been for a few months in the dry-good line, but finding that business too *dry* for him and little or no chance of rapid promotion in it, he has come to the resolution of relying upon his arms for future subsistence. He has been a private in a volunteer Militia Company; is of a good figure & stature; only a little more than 21 years of age and of a good character. If upon these hints you can speak a word or two for him, as a Captain, in case of a vacancy, or a first Lieut{t:} in lieu thereof, it may further the application which has already been made in his behalf at my instance, by Col. Boyd.

Friend Ewing of Philadelphia writes me that he was gratified by a visit from you and the promise of another on your return— He promises to send me some books if you can bring them. M{r:} Ingersoll also promised a copy of his work, but as I have purchased one since he informed me where they might be had, you need not incumber yourself with the portage, if at all inconvenient.[6]

Your family were pretty well a few days ago. George goes to M{r:} Whitney and is quite applauded for his aptness to learn latin.

My Mother has been extremely ill, since you went away, but I am happy to say is now in a great degree restored to health. M{rs:} C A. & Louisa Smith are both quite sick with colds. My wife & children are at present tolerably well. Your Father & all the family send love &{ca:} / Your brother. T. B. Adams—

RC (Adams Papers); addressed: "John Q Adams Esq{r:} / To the care of Walter Hellen Esqr should M{r:} / Adams have left the / City of Washington"; internal address: "J Q Adams Esq{r:}"; endorsed: "Adams— T. B. 28. Feb{y:} 1809. / 8. March rec{d:} / 9. Ans{d}."

[1] JQA's office was on Court Street (*Boston Directory*, 1809, p. 14, Shaw-Shoemaker, No. 17067).

[2] TBA compared Federalist state senator William Gray (1750–1825), a merchant of Salem, to Democratic-Republican state senators Samuel Dana, representing Middlesex County, and William King of Maine. Gray supported the embargo, and exchanges between him and Essex Junto Federalists led to talk of duels in the press; see, for example, the Salem *Essex Register*, 7 Jan. (LCA, *D&A*, 1:282; Mass., *Acts and Laws*, 1808–1809, *Resolves*, p. [i]–[vii]; Boston *Columbian Detector*, 6 Jan.; Edward Gray, *William Gray of Salem, Merchant*, Boston, 1914, p. 47; William Bentley, *The Diary of William Bentley*, 4 vols., Salem, 1911, 3:411; *Essex Register*, 9 Jan.).

[3] Federalist majorities in the Massachusetts senate and house of representatives on 17 and 18 Feb., respectively, approved a memorial to Congress declaring that the embargo violated their rights and predicting that a nonintercourse law would lead to war because it would not deter the British from impressing U.S. sailors. James Lloyd Jr. presented the memo-

rial to the Senate on 27 Feb., and it was read and printed. An earlier, related conflict in the legislature pitted Salem representative Benjamin Crowninshield Jr. against Christopher Gore of Suffolk County. On 16 Nov. 1808, Crowninshield proposed two resolutions pledging support for the federal government and the embargo. The proposal was assigned to a committee led by Gore, which issued a 28 Jan. 1809 report opposing the resolutions and instead arguing that U.S. trade would flourish by repealing the embargo and banning trade with France (Boston Commercial Gazette, 27 Feb.; Annals of Congress, 10th Cong., 2d sess., p. 444–450; Dinah Mayo-Bobee, New England Federalists: Widening the Sectional Divide in Jeffersonian America, Madison, N.J., 2017, p. 124, 137, 149; Boston Repertory, 3 Feb.).

⁴ In Mass. General Court debate on 23 Feb., Dorchester representative Perez Morton lauded George Washington's stance on neutrality, echoing language in the legislature's memorial to Congress that alluded to the "dignified, fair, and impartial negotiation" of "the immortal Washington" that led to the 1794 Jay Treaty. TBA took issue with Washington's 22 April 1793 Neutrality Proclamation, which critics saw as an abrogation of the United States' obligation to defend the French West Indies in accordance with the Franco-American treaties of 1778. Democratic-Republican Edward Bangs was a representative from Worcester (vol. 10:72–73; Boston Repertory, 24 Feb. 1809; Annals of Congress, 10th Cong., 2d sess., p. 446; Reginald Horsman, The New Republic: The United States of America 1789–1815, N.Y., 2000, p. 39–40; Boston Columbian Centinel, 25 Feb.; Mass., Acts and Laws, 1808–1809, Resolves, p. [i]–[vii]).

⁵ Charles Harrod (1787–1870) was AHA's younger brother. JQA mentioned Harrod's request for a commission during a 14 March visit to the War Department (Treat, Treat Family, p. 332–333; JQA, Diary).

⁶ Neither Samuel Ewing's nor Charles Jared Ingersoll's letter to TBA has been found. Ingersoll's new book was A View of the Rights and Wrongs, Power and Policy, of the United States of America, Phila., 1808, Shaw-Shoemaker, No. 15302.

Abigail Adams to John Quincy Adams

my dear son   Quincy Feb'ry 1809

The Saturday after you left Boston, I went to Town, and brought up George. he went the next week to his uncle Cranch's, and goes daily to school to mr Whitney. he appears well pleased, and learns to the Satisfaction of mr Whitney as I hear, who has put him into Lattin, which George says is not so hard as French. in his French Bible his Aunt hears him daily. he is a Good Boy, save now and then, a little mischief which all Boys are by nature prone to; I have every week had the pleasure of seeing your hand writing upon a cover of a Letter to Your Father inclosing one to mrs Adams, which have been regularly forwarded—and altho I have been very anxious for her, under her late misfortune, from which she is now happily restored. I have been So very ill that I have not been able either to see her, or render her that assistance which I wished, by taking John home as I Should have done— the day after I returnd from Boston, I was taken Sick, and have not Since been out of my chamber— I have not been so sick for these five years. I hope I am now mending tho it is by slow degrees.— My fever has left me, and I experience great Weakness, and debility. If I had not been sick, so sick, that I could not write a line, You would not have

February 1809

been so long absent without hearing from me. Your journey has been productive of many conjectures, Some of which have found their way into the News papers, as I presume You have seen, whilst the real buisness upon which You were known to be engaged in, has not been mentiond.¹ I have been so ill, that I have not read all the Roman Eloquence of our Senate and House of Rep's but I have read enough to see, that as wise men have lived before them—

I read the debates in congress when I am able, and think with shakspear, when he says, that ["]it is easier to teach twenty what were good to be done, than to be one of the twenty to follow the teaching"² upon the most mature reflection, as it respects Your honour Your interest and reputation, I do not wish to see You under existing circumstances any other than the private citizen You now are. the period is not yet arrived, when Your country demands you—at present your Family have prior claims— My trembling hand can only add, my best wishes for Your health and prosperity, and a Safe return to Your Family— Your Father is well and said he would write to You— I heard by dr Welch yesterday that Mrs Adams had rode out— I rejoice in her Speedy restoration She was very ill—

most affectionatly Your / Mother   Abigail Adams

P S— when you see mrs cushing give my Love to her—

poor Lovel is removed for Morten and the L Govenour has nominated Dr Eustise for high Sheriff.³

RC (Adams Papers).

¹ In addition to newspaper reports that JQA was nominated as secretary of war, for which see LCA to JQA, 16 Feb., and note 2, above, the Boston *Repertory*, 21 Feb., falsely claimed that he was nominated to be secretary of state.

² Shakespeare, *Merchant of Venice*, Act I, scene ii, lines 17–19.

³ James Lovell retained his post as U.S. naval officer at Boston, serving until his death in 1814, despite the resignations of two officers on his staff in early 1809 in response to his enforcement of the embargo and a communication in the Boston *Democrat*, 21 Jan., declaring him a traitor. On 20 Jan. Lovell placed a newspaper advertisement pledging that he would continue in his post despite the controversy, and the *Democrat*, 11 Feb., reported that senior naval officials had ruled Lovell's actions lawful and appropriate. In describing who would become Suffolk County sheriff after the 12 Feb. death of Jeremiah Allen, AA likely confused William Eustis with William Jarvis. Eustis was appointed as secretary of war in the Madison administration while Jarvis on 24 Feb. was nominated by acting governor Levi Lincoln as sheriff of Suffolk County. Jarvis did not assume the post, which remained vacant until Gov. Christopher Gore nominated Lt. Col. Samuel Bradford on 15 June and Bradford was sworn in the following day (*Biog. Dir. Cong.*; Boston *Columbian Detector*, 20 Jan.; *New-England Palladium*, 20 Jan.; Boston *Independent Chronicle*, 13 Feb.; *Newburyport Herald*, 28 Feb.; Boston *Columbian Centinel*, 15 March, 17 June; Dedham *Norfolk Repository*, 15 June).

Louisa Catherine Adams to John Quincy Adams

Boston ~~Febry~~ March 1st. 1808 [1809]

Mr Gurney having called on me yesterday, to give notice that he should quit your house next quarter day, and that he wished to settle with you as soon as possible, I have thought it best to write you my beloved friend, he having expressed a desire to leave it immediately, which I did not think you would approved; he mention'd not having it in his power to pay you at present, but will give you ~~an~~ the best security in his power which he hoped would prove satisfactory—

I have nothing to tell you whatever the Town still rings with your appointment some say to ~~the~~ be Secretary of State others to Europe it is so much credited here that your young men have talked of looking out for other Gentlemen to study with I ventured to tell Mr Loud that I thought they should take no steps in the business untill they heard from you having no doubt you wou'd give them sufficient notice if there was any truth in the report which I myself very much doubted and saw no reason whatever to believe.[1] I am so teazed with questions which I find it impossible to satisfactorily answer that I feel very much puzzled

General Dearborn arrived here yesterday— William Gray has bought the Governor's house and is coming to live in Boston[2] they have a story here of his being Raving mad and obliged to wear a straight Waistcoat I imagine because he would not unite with the popular party as he was in perfect health three days ago—

We have had several visitors here the last week Mr S Wells, Mr John Grey, Mr Shaw, Mrs Otis and Mrs W. Foster, who is a pretty lively french Woman not at all fitted for Boston—[3]

I presume we shall see you soon Mr Shaw told me he thought you would only be there long enough to recieve this letter I shall however venture to write one more—

Adieu, my beloved, and best friend, remember me affectionately to all, the Children are at length perfectly well and Kitty is well, and as much adm[ired a]s usual once more farewell Heaven grant you [. . . .]rtly return to your home and affectionate   L. C. Adams

RC (Adams Papers); addressed: "John Quincy Adams Esqr."; endorsed: "Adams— Louisa C. 1. March 1809. / 8. March recd: / 9. Ansd:." Some loss of text due to placement and removal of the seal.

[1] JQA's law students included Samuel P. Loud (1783–1875) of Weymouth, Alexander H. Everett, John Gallison, and William White (JQA, Diary, 22 Aug. 1845; William T. Davis,

Bench and Bar of the Commonwealth of Massachusetts, 2 vols., Boston, 1895, 2:197).

[2] Federalist state senator William Gray of Salem purchased the late Gov. James Sullivan's house at the corner of Summer and Hawley Streets in Boston (vol. 12:226; Edward Gray, *William Gray of Salem, Merchant*, Boston, 1914, p. 48).

[3] LCA received visits from Samuel Adams Wells (1787–1840), a Boston merchant and Samuel Adams' grandson; John Chipman Gray (1793–1881), a Harvard student; William Smith Shaw; and Sally Foster Otis and her sister-in-law, Marie Hortense Perron Foster, wife of William Foster Jr. (vol. 15:140, 141; Jefferson, *Papers, Retirement Series*, 14:227–228; CFA, *Diary*, 2:267; Betty G. Farrell, *Elite Families: Class and Power in Nineteenth-Century Boston*, Albany, N.Y., 1993, p. 124; Pierce, *Foster Genealogy*, 2:940–941; LCA, *D&A*, 1:280, 281).

John Quincy Adams to Louisa Catherine Adams

My dear wife.   Washington 5. March 1809.

We have at length got through the argument on the Cause for which I came here. It was finished yesterday after having taken up nearly four days—[1] The opinion of the Court will probably be given in the course of the week, and my intention is to leave this place, to-morrow week, which will be the 13th:— I depend therefore upon the pleasure of seeing you again at latest in three weeks from this day.

The Oath of office was yesterday administered to the new President in the chamber of the Representatives— He delivered a short speech, which you will without doubt see in the newspapers before you can receive this letter; it is in very general terms, and was spoken in a tone of voice so low, that scarcely any part of it was heard by three fourths of the Audience.[2]

The body of the house was excessively crowded, and the galleries were equally thronged; which gave it altogether a very magnificent appearance— The City was very much crowded with Strangers, and I believe I may say without exaggeration that in the course of the day yesterday I saw more people, than in the whole time I have ever been here.

Immediately after the ceremony was performed the President and his Lady, received company at their own house; I paid my visit with your Mamma and Mr: and Mrs: Hellen— It was not at the President's house, which Mr: Jefferson has not yet left.— He was with the company who visited his successor.

In the Evening there was a Ball at *Long's*, on the Capitol-Hill; the house which last Winter was kept by Stelle— The crowd there too was excessive—The rooms suffocating, and the entertainment bad— Your Sister Hellen literally took me with her, for I should not have gone, but at her special invitation that I would attend her— The President and his family were also there—and also Mr: Jefferson—[3] I had some conversation with him in the course of the Evening, in the course of which he asked me whether I continued as fond of POETRY, as I was in my youth— I told him yes—that I did not perceive I had lost any of my relish for good poetry; though my taste for the minor poets, and particularly for *amatory verses* was not so keen as it had been when I was young— He said he was still fond of reading Homer, but did not take much delight in Virgil.

Congress you know have broken up, after repealing partially the Embargo, after the 15th: of this Month, and totally at the end of the next Session of Congress—substituting a non-intercourse with France and England to commence on the 20th: of May. I believe that nothing better upon the whole could have been done; though in Congress it did not suit the views of either party— My time, my reason and my feelings have been so much engross'd by the business which brought me here, that I have neither examined, nor felt much in relation to the public—

The Senate are to continue in Session two or three days— Principally for the purpose of receiving nominations of the Heads of Departments— Report announces very confidently who they are to be, and adds that there has been some perplexity in fixing upon them— It had been determined that Mr: Gallatin should be Secretary of State— Mr: R. Smith Secretary of the Treasury—Mr: *Hamilton* of S. Carolina, Secretary at War, and Dr: Eustis Secretary of the Navy— But it is understood that the nomination of Mr: Gallatin to the Department of State would have met with such strong opposition in the Senate, that it was doubtful whether the appointment would be confirmed— The arrangement therefore now is changed, and Mr: R. Smith is to be the Secretary of State—Mr: Gallatin remaining at the head of the Treasury.— Dr: Eustis is certainly to be Secretary of the Navy.[4]

Mr: Blake has not yet arrived here; at least I have not seen him— If he should obtain some employment *abroad*, the occasion of uneasiness which you express, will cease—

I saw in the newspaper the paragraph to which I suppose you allude, admonishing the aspiring young federal members not to presume as Representatives of the People to have any opinions of their own— But I should not have suspected whence it came, nor whither it was directed, without the intimation in your letter.[5]

As I was going up to the Capitol yesterday morning, I met Mr: Quincy, going in a Hack to Georgetown, to get a passage homewards— He had been disappointed in the expectation of going early in the morning— I suppose he will reach home about the time that you will get this letter.

March 1809

I have been to Church again with the girls this morning; and heard M^r: Addison—⁶ M^r: and M^{rs}: Harper have been here since I began my letter, with the eldest Miss Caton—⁷ I think this young lady very beautiful; and wonder I never thought so before—

The roads as usual at this Season are breaking up; and the Stages as they come and go between here and Baltimore are breaking down— I hope the roads will be better before I leave this place— From Baltimore and New-York, I shall take the water passage— Your answer to this letter, could not get here before I shall be gone, but I shall long to hear from you so much that I would wish you to write me under cover to John A. Smith at New-York—requesting him to keep the letter untill I get there— I shall probably stop one day at Philadelphia.

In the hope of soon embracing you all once more in health and Spirits, I remain ever affectionately your's. A.

RC (Adams Papers). Tr (Adams Papers).

¹ JQA appeared before the U.S. Supreme Court from 1 to 4 March, arguing on behalf of Boston merchant John Peck in the case of Fletcher v. Peck. Peck and his New England Mississippi Land Company sold part of its Yazoo land claims to Amherst, N.H., speculator Robert Fletcher, who then lost his investment when Georgia nullified the sales. In 1803, with the tacit agreement of both parties, who hoped to force Congress to settle claims, the suit was brought before Judge William Cushing in U.S. Circuit Court but lay dormant by mutual consent as Congress debated the issue, for which see JQA to William Smith Shaw, 3 Feb. 1805, and note 3, above.

The case was revived in 1807 after Congress failed to reach a resolution. Cushing ruled for Peck, prompting an appeal by Fletcher that sent the case to the Supreme Court. On 14 Dec. 1808 Peck hired JQA to represent him. JQA's cocounsel was Robert Goodloe Harper. The two argued that Georgia was contractually obligated to honor a land sale it had improperly nullified. The court handed down its decision on 11 March 1809, ruling against Peck owing to flawed pleadings and not the merit of the case. The case was reargued the following term without JQA, who was by then serving as U.S. minister to Russia. The court reversed its earlier decision on 16 March 1810, deciding in Peck's favor and invalidating Georgia's rescission of Yazoo land sales and vesting buyers with title. Congress passed funding legislation in 1814, providing compensation for investors' costs during the years of unsettled title. The case would later be cited as precedent supporting decisons to strike down state laws as unconstitutional and authorize Native American land clearances by characterizing the dwellers as "occupiers" rather than owners of land (Marshall, *Papers*, 7:225-230; Charles F. Hobson, *The Great Yazoo Lands Sale: The Case of Fletcher v. Peck*, Topeka, Kans., 2016, p. 1-9, 57, 58-59, 88-89, 134-140, 206-207; JQA, *Diary*; Stuart Banner, *How the Indians Lost Their Land: Law and Power on the Frontier*, Cambridge, 2005, p. 170-174).

² James Madison's 4 March 1809 inauguration as the fourth president of the United States included the "liveliest demonstrations of joy" from assembled spectators, according to the Washington, D.C., *National Intelligencer*, 6 March. Madison, escorted by troops to the Capitol, wore a "full suit of cloth of American manufacture." In his address, the incoming chief executive spoke about domestic and international challenges facing the United States after a period of unprecedented growth, declaring that his administration would uphold the nation's neutrality to maintain prosperity without sacrificing its honor. Chief Justice John Marshall administered the oath of office at a ceremony attended by Thomas Jefferson and four other Supreme Court justices. In the week following, Madison's inaugural address appeared in Boston newspapers (JQA, *Diary*, 4 March; Madison, *Papers, Presidential Series*, 1:15-18; *New-England Palladium*, 14 March; Boston *Repertory*, 14 March).

³ An evening ball to mark the inauguration was attended by more than 400 revelers. The event was held at a hotel on 1st Street recently taken over by Robert Long after being operated by Pontius Stelle since 1804 (Washington, D.C., *National Intelligencer*, 6 March 1809; Bryan, *Hist. of the National Capital*, p. 519; JQA, *Diary*, 4 March).

⁴ Madison sent a list of cabinet nominations to the Senate on 6 March, proposing Robert Smith as secretary of state and William Eustis as secretary of war, both of whom were confirmed in a special session of the Senate. Madison had intended to nominate Albert Gallatin as secretary of state but dropped the plan after Senator William Branch Giles and Representative Wilson Cary Nicholas opposed the appointment of the Swiss-born immigrant. Madison offered to nominate Smith as secretary of the treasury in exchange for support of his favored choice, but Gallatin rejected the plan. He proposed remaining secretary of the treasury, and Madison agreed to continue him in the post. On 7 March, the president nominated and the Senate confirmed Paul Hamilton as secretary of the navy (U.S. Senate, *Exec. Jour.*, 11th Cong., special sess., p. 118–121; Raymond Walters Jr., *Albert Gallatin: Jeffersonian Financier and Diplomat*, Pittsburgh, Penn., 1957, p. 210–211; *Biog. Dir. Cong.*; Madison, *Papers, Presidential Series*, 1:10–11).

⁵ In her letter to JQA of 21 Feb. (Adams Papers), LCA noted that U.S. district attorney for Massachusetts George Blake was on his way to Washington, D.C. Blake drew comment from LCA for his frequent visits to their Boston house, a pattern she said was drawing "too much conversation." LCA also referred to a state representative with the initials W. S. who was in conflict with "Mr O," probably meaning freshman legislator William Hyslop Sumner and senate president Harrison Gray Otis, who was leading Federalist opposition to the embargo (A New Nation Votes; Mark Peterson, *The City-State of Boston: The Rise and Fall of an Atluntic Power*, 1630–1865, Princeton, N.J., 2019, p. 421–422).

⁶ JQA and Eliza and Adelaide Johnson attended a service led by Rev. Walter Dulany Addison (1769–1848) at St. John's Church in Georgetown, D.C. JQA previously heard Addison at the church on 26 Feb. 1809 (JQA, *Diary*; Sprague, *Annals Amer. Pulpit*, 5:403–410).

⁷ Marianne Caton (1788–1853) was the daughter of Mary Carroll and Richard Caton and the niece of Catharine Carroll and Harper (AA to AHA, 20 Sept. 1806, note 1, above; Jehanne Wake, *Sisters of Fortune: America's Caton Sisters at Home and Abroad*, N.Y., 2010, p. xviii).

John Quincy Adams to Louisa Catherine Adams

My dear Louisa.   Washington 9. March 1809.

I wrote you on Sunday,¹ and the same Evening I received yours of 26. Feb$^{y:}$— Yesterday yours of the 1$^{st:}$ inst$^{t:}$ came to hand— I rejoice to learn that the children are at length perfectly well; and Kitty continues to be admired.

I shall be very well satisfied to part with M$^{r:}$ Gurney as a Tenant, and if he can give me any *good* security for the payment of his rent, I shall very willingly take it.

I have now finished as much of my business here, as I suppose can be done, during the present Session of the Court— They have however not yet decided upon any of the questions in the Causes for which I was engaged— I shall not wait for their decisions, certainly longer than next Wednesday the 15$^{th:}$—

On Monday Morning M$^{r:}$ Madison sent his nominations to the Senate— The heads of departments, are as I wrote you they would be— He nominated me, to go to Russia— But the Senate took no vote on

March 1809

this nomination— They pass'd a Resolution that it was inexpedient, or unnecessary in their opinion that a Minister should be sent to Russia— M:^r Short had some time since been nominated by M:^r Jefferson, and the nomination rejected, as was said because the man was disliked.[2]

I believe you will not be much disappointed, at the failure of a proposition to go to Russia— In respect to ourselves and to our Children it would have been attended with more troubles than advantage— I had as little desire as expectation of that or any other appointment, and although I feel myself obliged to the President for his nomination, I shall be better pleased to stay at home, than I should have been to go to Russia—

The Senate finished their Session on Tuesday— The members of both houses are almost all gone, and the city has again the appearance of solitude— With the exception of the attendants upon the Supreme Court— It forms a contrast to the bustle and crowd of the inauguration day, when it is said there were ten thousand strangers here— This however I believe is exaggerated.

M:^rs Hellen had an Evening party here on Tuesday— She had invited a very large Company; but there was also a ball somewhere else, and not much of the Company came. M:^r & M:^rs Harper were here, and the two Miss Caton's.[3]

The Embargo, you know is to *come off*, in part, the 15:^th of this month, notwithstanding M:^r Quincy's predictions— It is to be entirely repealed from the end of the next Session of Congress— All the federal members but two however voted *against* this bill for repealing the Embargo.[4]

Neither D:^r Eustis nor M:^r Blake are yet here— Though we have heard of both of them at New-York.— M:^r Blake, we are told remains there, to be *married*—which I hope is true.[5]

I shall write you again before I leave this place— Last Evening I spent at M:^r Boyd's— M:^r Sheldon was there, and I had half a mind to deliver Kitty's message to it him in her own words—[6] Upon the whole I thought it would be carrying the joke too far— M:^rs Boyd is very unwell— M:^rs Buchanan is said to be at Bladensburg and expected here in two or three days.

your's ever affectionately John Quincy Adams[7]

RC (Adams Papers); addressed: "M:^rs Louisa C. Adams. / Boston."; internal address: "M:^rs L. C. Adams." Tr (Adams Papers).

[1] JQA to LCA, 5 March, above.
[2] On 6 March James Madison nominated JQA to be minister plenipotentiary to Russia and informed JQA of his nomination. On the 7th the Senate voted 17 to 15 that it was not necessary to send a minister to St. Petersburg.

On 25 Feb. the Senate had rejected a recess appointment of William Short made by Thomas Jefferson the previous summer (Madison, *Papers, Presidential Series*, 1:21; JQA, *Diary*, 6 March; U.S. Senate, *Exec. Jour.*, 12th Cong., 2d sess., 112; U.S. Senate, *Exec. Jour.*, 11th Cong., special sess., p. 118–120). For JQA's subsequent appointment to Russia, see William Steuben Smith to JQA, 1 July, and note 1, below.

³ Ann Johnson Hellen's gathering was attended by Marianne Caton and her younger sister Elizabeth (1790–1862). Henry Whetcroft, who was a notary public in Washington, D.C., hosted the ball (Anna Thornton Diary; Jehanne Wake, *Sisters of Fortune: America's Caton Sisters at Home and Abroad*, N.Y., 2010, p. xviii).

⁴ Philip Barton Key of Maryland and Joseph Lewis Jr. of Virginia were the two Federalist representatives who voted to repeal the embargo (*Annals of Congress*, 10th Cong., 2d sess., p. 1541; *Biog. Dir. Cong.*).

⁵ George Blake married his second wife, Sarah Olcott Murdock, in New Hampshire in 1810 (St. Albans, Vt., *Franklin County Advertiser*, 26 July).

⁶ Daniel Sheldon Jr. was a clerk at the U.S. Treasury Department (vol. 15:367–368).

⁷ JQA also wrote to AA, on 8 March 1809, expressing relief that her health had improved and providing an account of his work before the U.S. Supreme Court. He also reported his nomination as U.S. minister to Russia (Adams Papers).

John Quincy Adams to Louisa Catherine Adams

My dear Louisa.   Washington 12. March 1809.

Last night I received your kind favour of the 4th: instt: with the information the most delightful to my feelings, that my mother is recovering still; that the children are well, and that I may hope to find you so, upon my return.—¹ May God Almighty grant that this hope may be realized.

This is the last Letter which I purpose to write you from this place— Yesterday the Supreme Court delivered their opinion upon the principal Cause for which I came—or rather they declined giving an opinion upon the question itself, and decided it against us on a *defect in the pleadings*— This is one of the *mysteries* of the Law, which I could not explain to you so as to make it intelligible— It has nothing to do with the real questions in the case— The Court thought it most prudent not to decide these.

There are two other cases in which I was engaged here, which will go off upon points equally immaterial to the questions of right and wrong between the parties— There have been five or six learned arguments upon them, in two of which I have taken my part—² The Court are prodigiously perplexed about making up their opinions upon these points also; and I shall not wait for them any longer—

Wednesday morning the 15th: I intend taking my seat in the Stage for Baltimore. And I shall continue my journey by the water-Stage to Philadelphia; and then from New-York to Providence by the passage of the Sound.³

I think I wrote you on Thursday that Mrs: Buchanan was at Blad-

March 1809

ensburg, and soon expected here—[4] She arrived here with her husband that same Evening.— She is quite unwell, with a severe cough; which yesterday and this day has confined her to her chamber, and for which she has been bled by D[r:] Patterson—[5] M[rs:] Boyd has also been very unwell for several days; but is I believe now recovering— M[rs:] Hellen I think looks better than I have ever known since she was married— I should suspect she will grow fat— In which case I shall have somebody to keep me in countenance; for I continue to grow fat in spite of all my tribulations— Since the first week after I arrived here, when I was over-fatigued and unwell, I have more than recovered all the flesh I had lost. But my eyes have suffered by the intensity of my night-watches over my business; and I am more purblind than ever.

I have been to Church with M[r:] Hellen, M[r:] Buchanan, and the two girls, and heard M[r:] Addison preach a sermon upon meekness— Blessed are the meek, for they shall inherit the Earth— There was talk after the last day of the Congressional Session, of two or three probable duels between the ci-devant members— Among others, one was said to be necessary between M[r:] Eppes and M[r:] Key, but they did not fight—[6] Whether they ever had any thought of fighting, or whether they concluded on second thoughts to abate their manly rage, and wait for opportunities of new conflicts with the tongue I am not informed, but M[r:] Addison said much on the duty and obligation of forgiving injuries which I thought very just, and very wise.

The Union has arrived, after having been long expected— M[r:] Gibbon brings dispatches from England, and M[r:] Purviance from France— But still the news from Spain remains as contradictory as it had been for three weeks before— There has been an alteration in the English orders of Council, which will produce as I believe a material effect on the measures of Congress at their Session in May. I do not learn whether the reports that Buonaparte had repealed one of his most obnoxious decrees is also true.[7]

I am going with M[r:] Buchanan to dine at M[r:] Boyd's— Also with your mother and the girls. There is something between this family and that, which I much lo[. . .] to perceive existing, but I know not what it is, and of which I have taken [. . . .] because it has not been mentioned to me on either side— If it had been I should have been glad if it were in my power, to have reconciled parties, between whom I can conceive no reasonable ground of variance— Not knowing the cause, I have thought it would be considered that interference on my part would be officious

I dined yesterday with M[r:] Cranch— If you should have the opportunity, let his friends at Quincy know, that he and his family were then well.

For a few days more, my dearest friend, farewell

John Quincy Adams.

RC (Adams Papers); addressed: "M⁽ʳˢ⁾ L. C. Adams. / Boston."; internal address: "M⁽ʳˢ⁾ L. C. Adams." Tr (Adams Papers). Some loss of text where the seal was removed.

[1] In a short note to JQA of 4 March, LCA wrote of AA's and CFA's improved health (Adams Papers).

[2] For JQA's roles in the Supreme Court cases Hope Insurance Company of Providence v. Boardman and Bank of the United States v. Deveaux, see JQA to LCA, 13 Feb., and note 4, above. For the court's decision in Fletcher v. Peck, see JQA to LCA, 5 March, and note 1, above.

[3] JQA departed Washington, D.C., on 15 March, stopped in Baltimore, and arrived in Boston on the 26th (JQA, Diary).

[4] JQA to LCA, 9 March, above.

[5] This was probably Thomas Patterson, who operated a pharmacy on F Street in Washington, D.C. (Washington, D.C., National Intelligencer, 8 April 1805).

[6] The purported duelists were John Wayles Eppes and Philip Barton Key (Biog. Dir. Cong.). See also JQA to LCA, 1 Feb. 1809, and note 7, above.

[7] After weeks of anticipation, the Union arrived from Europe on 9 March with two messengers, a Lt. Gibbon, and John H. Purviance (ca. 1772–1820), who previously served as James Monroe's secretary in London. Gibbon brought dispatches from Great Britain, while Purviance brought news from France. The "dispatches ... do not otherwise change the subsisting relations between the U. States and Great Britain," reported the Washington, D.C., National Intelligencer, 13 March. On 21 Dec. 1808 the British government amended the Orders in Council of 1807 that required neutral ships to pay duties in Britain if trading with Europe, for which see JQA to LCA, 19 Feb. 1807, and note 3, above, excluding from it countries "in amity" with Britain. The exclusion would apply to the United States only if the Non-Importation Act was rescinded. Napoleon's Milan Decree, for which see TBA to JQA, 27 Dec., and note 2, above, had not been altered, leaving Franco-American relations unchanged. The *Union* also carried European newspapers with contradictory reports about the French Army's progress in Madrid that were similar to accounts in U.S. newspapers before the *Union* arrived (Jefferson, *Papers*, 35:445; Washington, D.C., *National Intelligencer*, 17 Feb. 1809, 10 March; Philadelphia *American Daily Advertiser*, 10 March; *Amer. State Papers, Foreign Relations*, 3:237–240; U.S. Senate, *Jour.*, 11th Cong., 1st sess., p. 374–376; Donald R. Hickey, *The War of 1812: A Forgotten Conflict*, Chicago, 1989, p. 17–18; *Alexandria Gazette*, 21, 23 Feb.; Baltimore *Federal Republican*, 10 March; *New-York Commercial Advertiser*, 14 March).

Abigail Adams to Abigail Adams Smith

My Dear Daughter:　　　　　　　　　　Quincy, April 10th, 1809.

Your two last letters of March 10th and 23d, came safe to hand.[1] They gave me great pleasure, not only from learning by them that you enjoyed good health, but your spirits were more animated from your little excursions from home, and from your prospects with respect to your family. I most sincerely rejoice in any event which looks like prosperity. Your trials have been many and various. You have hitherto been supported through them with dignity and firmness, with Christian patience I trust, and due submission to the allotments of Providence.

March–April 1809

It will greatly tend to improve our wisdom, to promote our piety, and increase our pleasure, to take frequent and particular views of our lives, and to observe the changes which have taken place in our circumstances, from time to time, in connection with the means and instruments which have been employed, and through which we have succeeded or failed in our enterprises, that by experience we may learn wisdom; and put our trust and confidence in that Being who holds the lives and fortunes of individuals in his hands, as well as the fate of kingdoms and nations. Let us say with Pope,—

> "What blessings thy free bounty gives,
> Let us not cast away."[2]

If we have not all we may wish, we have all that is best for us. When I look back upon my past days, I can see many faults, many errors, both of omission and commission, for which I have need of pardon and forgiveness. Many are the blessings which I have received, and am still in the enjoyment of. One of the first I consider the life and health of your father; who, thank God, is still vigorous, and in the full possession of his mental faculties, although the tremour upon his nerves I think increases. His books and his pen are his constant amusement. The effusions of his pen, though only a private letter, written in reply to two gentlemen, strangers to him, have drawn down upon him the abuse of the federal party. These gentlemen wrote him, by direction of a number who had met together for the purpose of consulting upon public affairs, a very respectful and handsome letter, addressing him as their venerable father, to whom they applied for counsel and advice; whose age, experience, long and faithful services, and sacrifices in the cause and service of his country, entitled him to its confidence and its gratitude. To this letter, which was a very long one, he returned the enclosed reply without any idea of its being published. I recollect our visit to the Baron de Stael; but think we did not dine with him; that, however, is not a matter of consequence. I enclose to you the letter. You see they made the most of it for electioneering purposes.[3] I have lived to see the day, when those who were the most clamorous against your father and his administration, now speak what I believe was then their true sentiments, though the spirit of party led many to deny the truth; and the desire of power and influence stimulated them to pull down an administration under which they saw little hope of obtaining it. For it is very true, that the federal party were as hungry and rapacious after office, as ever their opponents have been, and of a spirit quite as selfish and intolerant. I once said, or rather wrote to

Mr. Jefferson, "if you are a freeman, and can act yourself, you can do more than either of your predecessors could."⁴ Such was the bitterness of the federal party, or rather the leaders of it, and * * was one of them, that they would not hear a word of any nomination to office, of even the cool and moderate republicans. There will never be any harmony between parties, until public offices can be shared; and this your father used to tell them. The leaders in our State have gone great lengths, assumed powers which belong only to the national government; and are meditating schemes which they dare not openly avow; and which your father and mother think destructive to the Union, and independence of the country, and which will subjugate us to the power and domination of Great Britain. It was for lifting this veil, and declaring his private opinion and judgment, that writers in the federal papers have come out with as barefaced falsehoods, and as scurrilous language, as was ever used by the jocobins.

The times are perilous, and the country must not be forsaken by its friends, although men revile and persecute for righteousness' sake.⁵ May the blessing pronounced upon such, descend upon those who have hazarded life, health, fame, and fortune, to save their country.

Adieu, my dear daughter. Remember me kindly to the Colonel, Mrs. S. &c., and be assured of the tenderest love of / Your affectionate mother, Abigail Adams.

MS not found. Printed from AA2, *Jour. and Corr.*, 2:188–191; internal address: "To Mrs. Smith."

¹ Not found.

² Alexander Pope, "The Universal Prayer," lines 17–18.

³ Attorneys Daniel Wright and Erastus Lyman of Northampton, Mass., wrote a 3 March letter to JA, not found, in which they extolled the former president as "the great and wise and patriotic father of New-England" and sought advice on U.S. relations with Great Britain and France. JA responded on 13 March (LbC, APM Reel 118), stating, "I always consider the whole Nation as my Children." He wrote that the union should be preserved at all costs and the United States should maintain its neutrality unless forced into a conflict with Britain or France. JA also recalled a 1784 conversation on republican government with Jean, Comte de Diodati-Tronchin, then the Saxon minister to France, at a Paris dinner hosted by Erik Magnus, Baron Staël von Holstein. Wright and Lyman's letter was published in the *Boston Patriot*, 22 April 1809, after an extract of JA's response was printed in the same newspaper on 24 March. The Boston *Columbian Centinel*, 25 March, also reprinted the extract and condemned the exchange as "More Electioneering Trickery," attacking Democratic-Republicans for goading the former president into the correspondence and describing JA's response as electioneering fodder and "a degradation of conduct unworthy a Statesman." The copy of JA's letter that was enclosed by AA to AA2 has not been found (*Repertorium*, 3:244; Franklin, *Papers*, 41:342).

⁴ AA to Thomas Jefferson, 1 July 1804 (vol. 15:399–402).

⁵ Matthew, 5:10.

Thomas Boylston Adams to William Sullivan

Dear Sir. Boston 6th May 1809.

M^{r:} Thomas Greenleaf, who read law in my Office, for the space of Two years and nine months, and who is now under your professional guidance and direction, pursued, while with me, as near as I recollect, the following course of study.[1] Viz: Robertson's History of Ch: 5^{th:} 1 Vol: Blackstone's Commentaries Cook Litt: Wood's Institute—Woodeson's lectures—Espinasse N P. Fearne on Remainders & Devises; Park on Insurance; Chitty on Bills of Ex. Statutes of the Commth & Massachusetts Term Reports. The Title Please & pleading in Bacon's Abridg^t, and some other titles which Mr G. will remember better than I can. He has dipp'd occasionally into the Reporters, and has revised a second & third time some of the books above enumerated.[2] Of his improvement and acquisitions in the profession, you will soon form a judgment; I can venture to recommend him as a Gentleman & a Schollar, and subscribe with great / esteem & respect, / Your friend & serv^t

Thomas B Adams

RC and enclosure (MBBA); internal address: "W^{m:} Sullivan Esqr"; endorsed: "Thomas B. Adams / concerning— / Mr Greenleaf / 1809"; docketed by William Sullivan: "Thos Greenleaf— / 1809—"; notation by William Sullivan: "mr Savage."

[1] TBA enclosed with this letter an affirmation that Thomas Greenleaf Jr. studied with him between 29 July 1806 and 1 May 1809. TBA also described Greenleaf as a student who pursued his studies "with assiduity & diligence" (William T. Davis, *Bench and Bar of the Commonwealth of Massachusetts*, 2 vols., Boston, 1895, 2:197).

[2] In addition to classic texts by William Blackstone and Edward Coke, Greenleaf studied the following works: William Robertson, *History of the Reign of the Emperor Charles V*, 3 vols., London, 1769; Thomas Wood, *A New Institute of the Imperial or Civil Law*, London, 1704; Richard Wooddeson, *Elements of Jurisprudence Treated of in the Preliminary Part of a Course of Lectures on the Laws of England*, Dublin, 1792; Isaac Espinasse, *A Digest of the Law of Actions at Nisi Prius*, 2 vols., London, 1789; Charles Fearne, *An Essay on the Learning of Contingent Remainders and Executory Devises*, London, 1772; James Allan Park, *A System of the Law of Marine Insurances*, London, 1787; Joseph Chitty, *A Treatise on the Law of Bills of Exchange*, London, 1799; Matthew Bacon, *A New Abridgement of the Law*, 5 vols., London, 1736–1766; and Henry Cowper, *Reports of Cases Adjudged in the Court of King's Bench: from Hilary Term, the 14th of George III, 1774, to . . . 1778*, London, 1783.

Abigail Adams to Abigail Adams Smith

My Dear Daughter: Quincy, May 13th, 1809.

I have not had a line from you for several weeks. Your father visits the post-office every post day; and, although he frequently returns with his pockets full of letters, I do not find among them the superscription which is dearer to me than all the rest. You must know, since he has publicly avowed himself the *father* of the *whole nation*, he has a most prodigious number of letters from his adopted offspring, some of which he replies to, and some lie unanswered. He has also become a writer in the public paper called the Patriot, one of which I sent you; and, I have reason to think, done much good to his country, by his publication in defence of our seamen.[1] Although maligned and abused by the Anglo-American party, his arguments have silenced, if not convinced them; though, I suppose, they will be like those whom Hudibras describes:—

> "He who is convinced against his will,
> Is of the same opinion still."[2]

He is also publishing a series of papers and documents respecting the mission which he sent to France in the year 1799, and which was so much censured by * * * and his party,[3] and used by them as a powerful weapon to assail and abuse the administration, although the mission terminated the honour, peace, and prosperity of the country. * * * who thirsted for a war with France, finding his views frustrated in his determination to change the Executive, like Samson in pulling down the pillar, overthrew himself and his federal friends.[4] "He has passed away," but the baneful influence of his ambitious views still remain; he left his mantle upon the essex junto, whose objects and views are anti-American.[5] I enclose to you another Patriot, which contains subjects which will amuse you, and in which you will feel a family interest.[6] The clouds which overspread our horizon and looked so dark and gloomy as to threaten us with a volley of electric fluid, appear to be dispersing. "Returning Justice lifts aloft her scales;" may we not be found wanting when weighed in the balance, but be as ready to do justice as to receive it.[7]

When I sit down to write, I feel as though I could not pen a paragraph worth penning. My fire is out, my wit decayed, my fancy sunk. I long to imbibe a draught of that enthusiasm which is the wine of life; which cheers and supports the mind. What noble or tender emotion of the mind is excited without producing a degree of it? It is, to use the expression of the Letters from the Mountains, "the fan in summer and the fur in winter;"—pray have you met with these Letters from the Mountains?[8] If you have not, I will certainly send them to you; they are written by a Mrs. Grant, who was once in America;[9] her father was a British officer who was stationed in some fort beyond Albany, upon the frontiers, for she speaks of her Mohawk friends; her father was susperseded, and removed with his family to Albany, where he rented a small farm of Madam Schuyler, relict of Col. Schuyler, who was the father of the late Gen. Schuyler. Of this lady she draws a most interesting and amiable character; as she lived near to her, she was frequently with her, and passed two whole winters with her when she was only eight years of age. She says that Madam Schuyler, seeing her one day reading Milton's Paradise Lost with delighted attention, appeared astonished to see a child take pleasure in such a book, and no less so, to observe that she loved to sit thoughtful by her and hear the conversation of elderly and grave people. She adds, whatever culture my mind has received I owe to her: beyond the knowledge of my first duties, I should scarce have proceeded, or rather I should have become almost savage in a retreat which precluded me from the advantages of society as well as those of education. It appears by her letters that she left America just before the Revolution, and accompanied her father to the Highlands of Scotland; and that he was stationed for some time at a fort called Augustus. From these mountains her letters are written; they contain a series of years, from 1773 to 1801. I have never met with any letters half so interesting; her style is easy and natural, it flows from the heart and reaches the heart. In the early part of her life, and before she met with severe trials and afflictions, her letters are full of vivacity, blended with sentiment and erudition.[10] Though secluded from the gay world, she appears well acquainted with life and manners. Her principles, her morals, her religion, are of the purest kind;

> "Her mind was moral as the preacher's tongue."[11]

These letters contain so much matter particularly adapted to your situation and retirement, that when you read them you will call her sister-spirit, and imbibe for her kindred sentiments. When I took them up I had not formed any very favourable impression respecting them; but the more I read, the more I was delighted, until that enthusiasm which she so well describes, took full possession of my soul, and made me for a time forget that the roses had fled from my cheeks, and the lustre departed from my eyes; or that I was

> "Like a meagre mope adust and thin
> In a loose nightgown of my own wan skin."[12]

Nor was willing to believe, with Ossian, that age is dark and unlovely. I went back to the "Tales of the times of old," and felt the sparks of fancy kindle at the touch of memory, whilst I retraced the age of seventeen, with all its hopes and expectations.[13] I long to communicate to you this rich mental feast, "this feast of reason, and this flow of soul."[14] Mrs. S—— will share it with you.[15]

May, 21.[16]

This letter has lain unfinished for several days as you will see by the date, during which the weather has been cold, foggy, and gloomy; the season ungenial until yesterday, when the warm influence of the sun unfolded the buds; and the garden blooms like Eden.[17] All this I have waited impatient to hear from you, and learn

> "How springs the tender plant, how blows the balmy grove;
> How nature paints her colours!"[18]

or whether stern Boreas still usurps the domain of Vertumnus and banishes Flora from her rightful abode. To descend to plain prose, how is the season with you?[19] Girls, be silent: you would wonder how I can write a line, surrounded and interrupted twenty times within this hour.

Here comes little John: "grandmamma, I have lost my fourpence in the grass, when I was at play; now I cannot buy me a sword; won't you give me another?" ["]Hush child; don't you see I am writing?" Then in runs Elizabeth holding up her little arms for me to take her. Away with you all, or I will lock the door.

I heard of our dear Caroline last week.[20] I know you must deprive yourself of much enjoyment in parting with her; yet I think you did right to make the sacrifice. A total seclusion from that society, which at her age is desirable, might in process of time injure her. She has so much life and such a flow of spirits that shade, solitude, and retirement, would not so soon affect her as one of a more languid temper. We are all, in a measure, children of habit, and are apt to contract the manners and habits of those we most frequently see and converse with. Where there is mind there is manners;[21] but even in a college, we see that although science may form and enlighten the understanding, it is only by mixing with polished society that the rust is rubbed off, and the manners embellished and refined.

My paper will not allow me more space than to repeat what you are not now to learn, that I am, / Ever your affectionate mother,

Abigail Adams.

MS not found. Printed from AA2, *Jour. and Corr*, 2:192–198. Dft (Adams Papers).

[1] JA wrote a series of essays in the *Boston Patriot* from April 1809 to May 1812 that were prompted by his recent exchange with Daniel Wright and Erastus Lyman, for which see AA

to AA2, 10 April 1809, and note 3, above. JA's early *Boston Patriot* essays included a defense of American seamen on 29 April and 3 May, in which he declared impressment to be an attempt by Great Britain to assert dominion over the United States and called on the British to "keep their arbitrary powers at home: not practise them upon us, our ships, or seamen." His later writings centered on his presidency and foreign policy. JA in letters to JQA of 19 and 29 April asked his son to deliver manuscripts to the *Boston Patriot* (both Adams Papers); AA in a separate letter of 29 April (MHi:Adams Papers, All Generations) asked their son to visit them (*Boston Patriot*, 16 May 1812).

[2] In the Dft, instead of the previous sentence and quotation from Samuel Butler, *Hudibras*, Part III, canto iii, lines 547–548, AA wrote, "He has defended the cause of our imprest Seamen against the power which great Britain assumes over them, and very many of our British Americans were disposed to yeald to them by So Strong and forceable Arguments as to Silence if not convince them."

[3] In the Dft, AA wrote the phrase, "which excited so much wrath in Hamilton, and the essex Junto."

[4] Judges, 16:25–30.

[5] Instead of the previous two sentences, AA wrote in the Dft, "as a formidable engine to finally remove him from the chair of Government."

[6] AA probably enclosed the *Boston Patriot*, 29 April 1809, which also printed George Washington's 20 Feb. 1797 letter to JA about JQA, for which see JA to William Smith Shaw, 10 July 1808, and note 2, above.

[7] Alexander Pope, "Messiah," line 18.

[8] AA paraphrased a passage from Anne MacVicar Grant, *Letters from the Mountains*, 2 vols., Boston, 1809, 1:105–106. Grant (1755–1838) was born in Glasgow, where her father, Duncan MacVicar, served as a British military officer. Shortly after her birth, they moved to North America where he served at posts in Charleston, S.C., and Albany and Fort Oswego, N.Y. Grant met Margarita Schuyler (1701–1782), widow of Philip Schuyler (1696–1758), while living near Albany. In 1768 she returned with her family to Scotland and in 1773 moved to Fort Augustus on Loch Ness in the Scottish Highlands (*Women's Travel Writings in Scotland*, ed. Kirsteen McCue and Pam Perkins, 4 vols., N.Y., 2017, 1:xiii–xiv; Cuyler Reynolds, *Hudson-Mohawk Genealogical and Family Memoirs*, 3 vols., N.Y., 1911, 1:31).

[9] In the Dft, AA included the following sentence, "She came with her Father who was an officer and a Scotchman to this country when we were a part of the Subjects of George the 3d before the Revolution which seperated us from G Britain."

[10] Instead of the following sentence, in the Dft, AA continued here, "Literature & knowledge of the humane heart as make them highly impressive and instructive."

[11] Edward Young, *The Complaint; or, Night Thoughts*, Night II, line 448.

[12] Grant, *Letters from the Mountains*, 2:64.

[13] Grant in *Letters from the Mountains*, 1:53, quoting James Macpherson, "Carthon," par. 1.

[14] Pope, "The First Satire of the Second Book of Horace," line 126.

[15] That is, Margaret de St. Hilaire.

[16] In the Dft, AA dated this section "May 20th."

[17] In the Dft, AA wrote and then canceled, "Vertumnus presides and Flora accompanies him in all her Glory."

[18] John Milton, *Paradise Lost*, Book V, lines 21–24.

[19] In the Dft, AA concluded this paragraph and the next with the following: "I sit writing in my chamber with all the Chit Chat of two Girls, and little John who is on a Visit to me—they Scatter my Ideas and dissipate my thoughts."

[20] In the Dft, AA completed this sentence, "that she was gone to NYork."

[21] In the Dft, AA instead completed this paragraph, "and where the natural temper is mild and generous, deep impressions of integrity and early habits of benevolence must communicate to the Manners the unconstrained air of open Rectitude, and that animated Softness which a disinterested wish to please always produces—"

Abigail Adams to Abigail Adams Smith

My Dear Daughter: Quincy, May 23, 1809

Yesterday your father brought me the much-desired packet.[1] You mention General Eaton's town-meeting speech, which I had seen. I presume he was in *spirits* when he made it; his virulence against Mr. —— is really personal—thereby hangs a tale. Mr. Lear, you know, made a treaty with Tripoli, which, through the misrepresentation of Eaton and his intrigues, had like to have been rejected by the Senate. Mr. —— thought Lear sustained and defended him and his treaty so ably, as to convince the Senate, and the treaty was ratified. Eaton also made, as he thought, very inadmissible demands of money, and that to a great amount, which Mr. —— opposed, though in this he was not successful. All this was enough to make Eaton his enemy. Eaton is a bold, daring adventurer, with considerable talents, but without judgment, prudence, or discretion; he is too well known to do any essential injury. His story of a mission to Constantinople, is all a vision of his own imagination, never heard of before by any one.[2]

I fear we are very ungrateful for the many favours Heaven is bestowing upon us. When we have been threatened with calamities, and the scenes have been most gloomy and distressing in our view, we have been saved from the horrors and calamities of war, by the returning justice of the offending powers. I am full of the mind that the election of Mr. Madison to the Presidency has had a powerful weight in the British Cabinet to bring them to terms of accommodation. According to Lord Grenville's speech in the House of Lords, and M. Whitbread's in the House of Commons, the embargo and non-intercourse act, had a much greater effect on England than even the best informed Americans believed. It affected their revenue as much as it did ours: it deprived them of raw materials for their factories, and would, if continued much longer, have starved thousands.[3]

I believe I read the whole of the documents and correspondence between our own government, and that of the belligerents, as they are called, and I most solemnly declare that I could not see any disposition to favour one nation more than another; but the strictest impartiality which justice required. I read them too, with a scrutenizing eye, because so much had been said both in Congress and out of doors respecting a partiality to France: so much has the malignant spirit of party blinded and misled the people.[4] There is no despotism like that practised by the rulers of opinion. Virgil, in one of his odysseys, de-

May 1809

scribes Æolus as confining the winds in a bag, and relates the terrible havoc they made when unskilfully let loose.⁵ We may compare the spirit of party to these winds, which blew the embers of discontent in flames, and threatened destruction to every obstacle which opposes their progress.

I dare not trust myself with describing to you how much I want to see you. On reflecting upon the barriers which age and infirmities, as well as many other obstacles placed between us, that I still possess the faculty of communicating with you by letter, is a source of enjoyment to me. How many blessings does the bountiful hand of Providence scatter in various proportions, to alleviate the sorrows and sufferings of a state only meant as the pathway to felicity.

I am writing by candle-light, whilst all around me are fast bound in sleep. My eyes suffer; but there is a tranquillity around me that the busy cares of the day interrupt and obstruct: even faithful Juno lies snoring beside me. Tell Mrs. S—— that her sister Sally wonders she does not write to her. We are all well. Adieu, my dear daughter. The clock strikes 12, and I must retire to rest, or suffer on the morrow.

Your affectionate mother, A. Adams.

MS not found. Printed from AA2, *Jour. and Corr.*, 2:198–201; internal address: "To Mrs. Smith."

¹ Not found.

² Gen. William Eaton, who had been nominated by JA to be U.S. consul at Tunis and served in that position from 1797 until 1803, was then the U.S. naval agent to the Barbary States. Eaton addressed a town meeting on 3 April 1809 in Brimfield, Mass., attacking JA, JQA, and Thomas Jefferson, probably the person whose name was redacted from this letter. Eaton had endorsed a plan to oust Yusuf Qaramanli, pasha of Tripoli, for which see JQA to TBA, 5 Feb. 1806, and note 6, above. Jefferson initially supported the strategy, but later halted it and sent Tobias Lear to negotiate a treaty. In his annual address to Congress on 3 Dec. 1805, Jefferson announced that he would send the Tripolitan-American Treaty of Peace and Amity to the Senate, to which it consented on 12 April 1806. Eaton in his speech lambasted JQA for his support of the treaty and related payments of tribute to Tripoli. He further claimed that JQA had been promised the post of minister to the Ottoman Empire in exchange for his support of the treaty and condemned him for having "converted by ambition and hope from a thorough-going federalist to a courtly democrat" (U.S. Senate, *Exec. Jour.*, 5th Cong., 1st sess., p. 249–250; Springfield, Mass., *Hampshire Federalist*, 13 April 1809; Jefferson, *Papers*, 42:392; JQA to AA, 3 Dec. 1805, and note 4, above).

³ On 17 Feb. 1809 in the House of Lords, William Wyndham Grenville, 1st Baron Grenville, called on the British government to revoke Orders in Council of 1807 on neutral trade, seeking instead "measures less calculated to alienate from us the good disposition of the American Government and people." Samuel Whitbread (1764–1815) made a similar and equally unsuccessful appeal in the House of Commons on 7 March, calling the orders and the retaliatory measures of the United States "manifestly injurious to the interest of both countries." The speeches were reported in the Boston *Repertory*, 14 April, and the *New-England Palladium*, 21 April (Bradford Perkins, *Prologue to War: England and the United States 1805–1812*, Berkeley, Calif., 1970, p. 18, 302; *DNB*).

⁴ AA likely read John Lowell Jr.'s pamphlet *Analysis of the Late Correspondence Between Our Administration and Great Britain & France*, Boston, 1809, Shaw-Shoemaker, No. 17933. The pamphlet combined correspond-

ence printed in the Boston *Columbian Centinel* with analysis on foreign relations.

[5] Homer rather than Virgil told the story of Aeolus' gift of a bag of winds to Odysseus (Homer, *The Odyssey*, Book X, lines 19–49).

Abigail Adams to Elizabeth Smith Shaw Peabody

Quincy June 5th 1809

I was unable to replie to my dear Sisters Letter of May 19th when I received it, being visited by st Anthony, who scourged me most cruelly.[1] I am sure I wished well to the Spanish Patriots in their late Struggle for Liberty, and I bore no ill will to those whose tutular saint thus unprovoked beset me. I wish he had been preaching to the fishes who according to tradition have been his hearers, for so ill did he use me, that I came very near loosing my Senses— I think he must be a very bigoted Saint, a favourer of the inquisition, and a tyrant. If such are the pennances of Saints, I hope to hold no further intercourse with them— For four days and Nights my face was so swelld and inflamed that I was almost blind. it seemd as tho My Blood boild.[2] untill the third day, when I sent for the doctor, I knew not what the matter was. it confined me for ten days. My face is yet Red but I have rode out to day, and feel much better. I think a little journey would be of Service to Me, but I find as Years and infirmities increase My courage and enterprize diminish— "Ossian says Age is dark and unlovely"[3] when I look in my Glass, I do not much wonder at the story related of a very celebrated Painter Zeuxis who it is said died of laughing at a comical picture he had made of an *old* woman.[4] if our glass flatters us in youth, it tells us Truths in Age. The cold hand of Death has frozen up Some of the streams of our early friendships; the congelation is gaining upon our Vital powers, and marking us for the Tomb. May we so number our days as to apply our hearts unto Wisdom,[5]

"The man is yet unborn, who duly weighs an hour"[6]

when my family were Young around me, I used to find more leisure, and think I could leave it with less anxiety than I can now. there is not any occasion for detailing the whys and the Wherefores. it is said, if Riches increase, those increase that Eat them, but what shall we say, when the eaters increase without the wealth?

you know my dear sister, if there be Bread enough and to spair, unless a prudent attention Manage that sufficiency; the fruits of diligence will be Scatterd by the hand of dissipation.[7] no Man ever prospered in the world; without the consent and co operation of his wife.

June 1809

it behoves us, who are parents, or Grandparents, to give our Daughters & Granddaughters, when their Education devolves upon us, such an Education as shall qualify them for the usefull and domestic Duties of Life, that they should learn the proper use, and improvement of Time, Since "Time was given for use, not waste."[8] The finer accomplishments Such as Musick, dancing and painting, serve to sit off and embellish the picture; but the ground work must be formed of more durable coulours.

I consider it as an indispensable requisite, that every American wife, should herself know, how to order, and regulate her family, how to Govern her domesticks, and train up her Children. for this purpose, the all wise creator made Woman an help meet for Man[9] and she who fails in these duties; does not answer the end of her creation.

> "Life's cares are comforts; Such by Heaven design'd
> they that have none, must make them, or be wretched
> cares are employments; and without employ,
> The soul is on a rack, The rack of rest;"[10]

I have frequently said to my friends when they have thought me overburdend with cares; I had rather have too much, than too little. Life stagnates without action— I could never bear to merely vegetate, "Waters Stagnate, when they cease to flow"[11]

has your Son sent You, or his Sister the Letters from the Mountains?[12] I think them the finest Selection of Letters, which I have ever read. You may with safety recommend them to all your Young female Friend's. I cannot find in them any principle, either of Morals Manners or Religion, to which I cannot most heartily subscribe. read them and give me Your opinion of them.

Mrs T B Adams desires me to say to you, that her regreet at not seeing you, was mutual. she had a hired Horse and was confined to a weeks stay. She has left behind her one of our dear Sprigs. we miss her much, altho another is comeing forward to supply her place; as lively and as lovely. how they twine around our hearts, and Steal our affections, of such said our great teacher, is the Kingdom of heaven.[13] Our dear valued Friend dr Tufts is raised up to bless us Yet a little longer, not yet having done all the good assignd him— may he yet be Spared to us.

I want to recommend to your perusal and mr Peabodys a News paper under the tittle of the Boston Patriot; I know my dear Friends are of no Party, but that of Truth and Justice.[14] upon the 19 of April a series of Letters and publications were commenced in that paper, and are continued to this day, which will serve to inform the unprejudiced mind: and to ~~remove~~ erase those false coulourings which all our Federal Papers have thrown over our public affairs for the last 12 Months— there is also a review of the late mr Ames Writings which have lately been exhibited to the World under the Tittle of the Dangers of American Liberty. I inclose one of the papers.[15] If there is not any Body who takes the paper with you, I will endeavour to send you a course of them as they have been publishd, by some privat conveyance to mr Harods's at Haverhill— Our Friends here are well, as usual and all desire to be rememberd to You. So does Your truly affectionate Sister[16]

Abigail Adams.

RC (DLC:Shaw Family Papers); addressed: "Mrs Elizabeth Peabody / Atkinson." Dft (Adams Papers).

[1] In her letter to AA of 19 May, Peabody recalled her recent illness and expressed disappointment that it caused her to miss AHA's visit to Haverhill. In a previous letter of 6 March (both Adams Papers), Peabody wrote about her concern for AA's health, provided family updates, and discussed Haverhill's new minister, Joshua Dodge (Chase, *History of Haverhill*, p. 558).

[2] Instead of the previous seven words, AA wrote in the Dft, "Except in the Ague and fever I do not recollect So high a fever."

[3] James MacPherson, "Carthon," par. 49.

[4] Zeuxis was a painter in Athens in the fourth century B.C. (Oxford Art Online).

[5] Psalms, 90:12.

[6] Edward Young, *The Complaint; or, Night Thoughts*, Night II, lines 97–98.

[7] In the Dft, AA began the next sentence, "I have always wished to impress upon the minds of my children, that."

[8] Young, *Night Thoughts*, Night II, line 153.

[9] In the Dft, AA ended this paragraph and instead of the next paragraph wrote, "Altho surrounded with all the abundance of Paridice, 'Eden was tasteless, till an Eve was there' altho every creature was intended for his aid and delight, the flower with its beauty and fragrance the tree, with its Nutricious fruit; the animal tribes, with all their powers of ministring Satisfaction to the Senses or to the mind. Adam beheld them with delight. the understanding was employed, but the Heart wanted its object, a tender Sympathetic ear to which he could in unison join & say: These are thy glorious works, Parent of Good / Almighty, thine this universal Frame. / Thus wondrous fair; but where have I rambled? into Eden be sure, but this is not my abideing place—"

[10] Young, *Night Thoughts*, Night II, lines 160–163.

[11] William Whitehead, "On Ridicule," line 46.

[12] In the Dft, AA started the next sentence, "He has patronized the publication."

[13] Instead of referencing Matthew, 19:14, in the Dft, AA added here, "The World is wide enough for them, and the old are quiting the stage to give place to them—as our Fathers have done for us—"

[14] In the Dft, instead of the previous clause, AA wrote instead, "You will find in it, those Truths which are hidden from the public in general, or so disguised and misrepresented by all the federal papers as to mislead those who wish well to their Country, and who are of no party but that of Truth and justice. there are a Number of Letters published in them by him whom You justly stile the Friend and Father of his Country—"

[15] Fisher Ames died on 4 July 1808. After his death, several of his friends compiled his writings and published them as *Works of Fisher Ames*, Boston, 1809. The collection included his essay "The Dangers of American Liberty," written in 1805. The *Boston Patriot*, 29 April 1809, 24, 27 May, and 3 June included a serialized review of the collection. While the enclosed newspaper has not been found, it was likely the issue of 27 May or 3 June (*New-England Palladium*, 5 July 1808).

[16] In the Dft, AA instead closed the letter, "My paper reminds me to close, so indeed do my eyes which are yet weak affectionatly your sister."

June 1809

Elizabeth Smith Shaw Peabody to Abigail Adams

My Dear Sister, Atkinson June 13th. 1809

By last Friday mail, I received your very excellent Letter, wherein you observe, it was thought a journey might be of service to your health,[1] I have not time now to make any remarks, only upon this part of your Letter, & warmly would second the motion, & would wish you to set off immediately, without stoping to adjust every *preliminary*— For if you do, you will see, I fear so many Lions, in the way, that you will think you cannot come— Abby had a beautiful fly-away visit to Boston, scarcely thought of it, ten minutes before *little Madam* was in the Chaise with her Brother Webster— All she regreted, when she returned, was, that it was not in her power, as she hoped it would be, to spread her wings for Quincy, & pay her respects a few hours to her good Uncles, & Aunts— She set out from Boston in the Moring, & got here to dinner about four in the afternoon, & brought Elizabeth Foster with her—[2] She is a fine Child, & as happy as possible—

I am sensible that those who have large families, have many—very many *different* Cares, from what any young Lady knows of, however domesticated, & good, she may be— She may think she knows *all* about it—but in a Parents house—she will, & must remain a Novice— *Happy* for her Husband & Servants, if ~~she~~, when she takes the guidance of a family, She possesses those oeconimick Virtues, that will carefully "gather up the fragments, that their Garners may be full, & nothing lost["]—Happy for the Children of Want, & happy, for Society—[3]

Mr Peabody, & I, thank you for the communications contained in the Paper, you were so obliging as to send—& if it would not be too much trouble, we should be very glad to have you send it— The mail comes from Boston mondays, & Fridays— We will talk it over when you come—And I will again repeat, what this letter was begun for, that is, to request your coming here as soon as possible it may be convenient, before the very hot weather—& before Abby goes to Haverhill Coos— Which I expect will be when the Court rises at Concord Her Sister Webster has got her Husband to come in a chaise, & will be sadly dissapointed if she does not go up with him—which I expect will be the week after next—[4]

I cannot bear to think of her going, so far, as I fear the air, will not suit her— For she is like the Camilion—changes in her feelings, if not in her Coulour, & seldom has any pain in her Limbs, Arms, &cc—when she inhales the Sea Breezes—

If you could send me word by Friday mail, when you would be here, I should be glad—for I, would not be absent, nor Mr Peabody neither— no not an hour—

All my dear Connections at Quincy, I hope will be so good as to accept of our most affectionate / Regards— Yours in Love—& great haste

E Peabody—

RC (Adams Papers); addressed: "Honble. John Adams Esq / Mrs Abigail Adams. / Quincy"; endorsed: "Mrs Peabody / June 13 1809."

[1] AA to Peabody, 5 June, above.
[2] That is, Elizabeth Anne Foster, the daughter of AA's niece Elizabeth Smith Foster (vol. 15:396).
[3] John, 6:12.
[4] The N.H. General Court held a session in Concord from 7 to 28 June. Stephen Peabody Webster served as a representative from Haverhill, the seat of Grafton County in the Coos region of central New Hampshire (vol. 11:51; William Whitcher, *History of the Town of Haverhill, New Hampshire*, 1919, p. 34; *Journal of the House of Representatives of the State of New-Hampshire*, Concord, N.H., 1809, p. 5, 131, 136).

Abigail Adams to Abigail Adams Smith

My Dear Daughter: Quincy, June 19th, 1809.

I yesterday received your letter of June 1st.[1] I think letters are longer upon their passage than they used to be, when you were at Quincy. Since I wrote to you in May,[2] I have been visited by St. Anthony, and most severely scourged by him: he first attacked one of my ears, but as I was wholly ignorant of the holy visiter, I paid little attention to him, except endeavouring to quiet him by bread and milk; but when he seized my face, eyes, and head, I was obliged to bow to him, and acknowledge his power—even send for a physician and exorcise him. I swelled to such a degree, that I could see my cheeks project beyond my nose; the fever was violent, and the pain in my head excruciating. It kept continually flashing up, and reminded me of poor Mr. Bishop, who called it the northern lights:[3] it lasted me ten days, before it entirely left me; but I have been comforted by Dr. Dexter, who sent me word, that an attack of it, like that which mine was described to be, was as good as a fit of the gout, to mend the constitution.[4] It is certain I have felt much better since than I did before.

You alarm me when you tell me that you have preserved my letters, and collected them together, in order to transmit them to Caroline.[5] Your affection and your partiality to your mother, stamp a value upon them which can never be felt by those less interested in them; they are letters written without regard to style; and scarcely ever copying a letter, they must be very incorrect productions, and quite unworthy

June 1809

preservation or perpetuity: do not let them out-live you; you may select a few, perhaps, worth transmitting, but in general, I fear, they are trash. Can you inform me who is the editor of the Albany Register? he is republishing your father's letters, with high encomiums upon them.[6] I presume he is a republican, because no praise comes now from any other quarter, except when you find a genuine American, of which there are a small number who can judge impartially. I mean by this, that the spirit of party so warps the judgment, and blinds the understanding, as to lead good and honest men blindfold. I enclose to you, your father's letter upon the King of England's proclamation, which was first published in the Boston Patriot, the demand of which became so great, as to induce the printer to publish them in a pamphlet. His text, as he calls it, is a quotation from Col. Pickering's letter, to which your brother replied, and which cost him his seat in the Senate; but which I consider one, amongst many others, of his disinterested actions and true love of his country, and which will thus be considered by an impartial historian.[7]

No one can accuse Mr. Madison for want of a frank and honourable spirit of accommodation with Great Britain. When she held out her hand with a spirit of conciliation, he received it with true magnanimity; and I rejoiced sincerely that our causes of animosity were to be removed. I own I am not satisfied with the subsequent conduct of the British Ministry: what powers the new minister may be clothed with, time must disclose[8] I feel at present safe in the hands of Mr. Madison. I presume he will not permit himself to be cajoled into any relinquishment of our national rights, or infringement of our independence. Whatever predilection Mr. Jefferson had in favour of France, or has against Great Britain, I believe, in his public transactions, he strove to act with impartial justice towards both. I read all the despatches with care and attention, expecting to find what had so often been declared, a blind partiality towards France, and hatred towards England; but justice requires me to say, that I could discover no such thing: and when party spirit yields to reason and sober sense, this will be the equitable decision. I wish I could justify all Mr. Jefferson's measures with the same candour; but to his own Master, he must stand or fall.

The federalists are courting Mr. Madison—let them do him no wrong, and I am one who at present believe that he will do no wrong to his country. With respect to Mrs. Madison's influence, it ought to be such as Solomon describes his virtuous woman to be—one who should do him good and not evil all the days of her life, so that the heart of her husband may safely trust in her.⁹ I believe I may say with safety, that her predecessors left her no evil example.

* * * * * *

Our friends are all well. That health is a blessing, which may be enjoyed by all of us, is the sincere wish of / Your affectionate mother,

A. Adams.

MS not found. Printed from AA2, *Jour. and Corr.*, 2:201–204; internal address: "To Mrs. Smith."

[1] Not found.

[2] AA to AA2, 23 May, above.

[3] Probably Medford miller John Bishop, late husband of Abigail Tufts (vol. 4:8).

[4] That is, Dr. Aaron Dexter (vol. 15:408).

[5] For Caroline Amelia Smith's later publication of her mother and grandmother's correspondence as AA2, *Jour. and Corr.*, see vol. 1:xxix–xxx.

[6] Solomon Southwick Jr. (1773–1839) was the editor of the *Albany Register*. The newspaper on 28 April and 19 May reprinted JA's letters from the *Boston Patriot*, 15 April and 6 May. The newspaper included commentary condemning the Essex Junto and crediting JA with exposing the "wicked machinations of the British faction" (James M. Caller and M. A. Ober, *Genealogy of the Descendants of Lawrence and Cassandra Southwick of Salem, Mass.*, Salem, 1881, p. 167; Douglas C. McMurtrie, *A History of Printing in the United States*, 2 vols., N.Y., 1936, 2:176).

[7] The enclosure, not found, was JA's letter to Joseph Bradley Varnum of 9 Jan. (LbC, APM Reel 118), which appeared in installments in the *Boston Patriot*, 19, 26, and 29 April and then as a pamphlet published by David Everett and Isaac Munroe. In the letter JA quoted Timothy Pickering's letter to Gov. James Sullivan of 16 Feb. 1808 in which Pickering wrote that the 16 Oct. 1807 proclamation by George III giving British captains official license to impress sailors from neutral merchant vessels "could not furnish the slightest ground for an Embargo." JA outlined why he agreed that the proclamation violated the rights of U.S. citizens, an opinion previewed in a letter to Varnum of 26 Dec. 1808 (LbC, APM Reel 118) that was printed in the *Patriot*, 12 April 1809. There JA described the proclamation as "the most *groundless pretension* of all" that had not been "distinctly enough reprobated" (JQA to TBA, 14 Dec. 1807, and note 6; TBA to JQA, 24 March 1808, and note 3, both above; JA, *The Inadmissible Principles, of the King of England's Proclamation, of October 16, 1807—Considered*, Boston, 1809, Shaw-Shoemaker, No. 16795; Pickering, *Letter from the Hon. Timothy Pickering . . . Exhibiting to His Constituents a View of the Imminent Danger of an Unnecessary and Ruinous War*, Boston, 1808, p. 4).

[8] In December, British minister to the United States David Montagu Erskine informed British foreign minister George Canning that the Madison administration sought improved relations. Erskine then notified the United States that British Orders in Council restricting Anglo-American trade would be rescinded as of 10 June 1809. James Madison responded with a 19 April proclamation announcing that the Non-Intercourse Act would also be repealed on 10 June and normal relations between the countries would resume. Canning, angered by Erskine's actions, recalled him. On 17 July the news reached Boston that the British government disavowed the agreement made by Erskine (Nicholas Dungan, *Gallatin: America's Swiss Founding Father*, N.Y., 2010, p. 83, 87; JQA, Diary, 17 July).

[9] Proverbs, 31:11–12.

Abigail Adams to John Quincy Adams

Dear son   Quincy June 28th. 1809

Coll. Bradford came out to day with a card of invitation from the Govenour, and an other from the Govr and Senate requesting your

June–July 1809

Father to celebrate the fourth of july with them; he has accepted the invitation. if you receive an invitation, both your Father and I advise You to accept it.[1] if you do not, I shall depend upon the pleasure of Seeing you at Quincy with mrs Adams Kitty & the children—

Your affectionate / Mother A Adams—

We wish you to dine with us on saturday

RC (Adams Papers); addressed: "John Quincy Adams Esqr / Boston"; endorsed: "My Mother 28. June 1809. / 29. rec$^{d:}$."

[1] On 4 July, JA joined JQA in Boston and walked in procession from the State House to the Old South Church. JQA then joined a procession to a dinner of the Bunker Hill Association. Both JA and JQA attended a gathering of young Democratic-Republicans at the Exchange Hotel where they gave toasts to Boston youth, which were recorded in the Boston *Independent Chronicle*, 6 July. JQA ended the night by watching fireworks on Boston Common (JQA, *Diary*).

William Steuben Smith to John Quincy Adams

My dear Sir, New York July 1$^{st.}$ 1809.

I have this day heard of your appointment, as minister to the Court of St. Petersburg, by an almost unanimous vote of the Senate;[1] I embrace the earliest opportunity of congratulating you upon this fresh instance of the high consideration in which our country holds you.—

My situation here induces me to state to you, that I have been greatly disappointed in my endevours to procure some employment for myself in the mercantile line, not being able to succeed, I take the liberty of requesting, that if there is any situation connected with this mission, in which I can be of service to you Sir, I beg you will consider me as perfectly at your service—

I hope to be favoured with your commands by the earliest opportunity

I am Sir, your obed$^{nt.}$ Serv$^{t.}$ / and nephew

W. Steuben Smith

RC (Adams Papers); internal address: "John Q. Adams Esq$^{r.}$"

[1] On 26 June, James Madison resubmitted to the Senate JQA's nomination as minister plenipotentiary to Russia along with documents showing that Russia wanted to improve trade with the United States after cutting off trade with Great Britain. The Senate confirmed JQA's nomination on 27 June by a vote of 19 to 7. JQA learned of the appointment from newspaper reports on 3 July and received his commission on 4 July (Madison, *Papers, Presidential Series*, 1:266–267; LCA, *D&A*, 1:283; U.S. Senate, *Exec. Jour.*, 11th Cong., 1st sess., p. 126, 127; JQA, *Diary*, 25 June).

John Quincy Adams to William Steuben Smith

My Dear Sir. Boston 5. July 1809.

I received your favour of the 1st: instt: and thank you for your obliging congratulations— I am unable to give you at present a positive answer, in relation to your proposal to go with me, for the offer of which I give you my thanks— I know not whether the Secretary is appointed or indicated by the Government; or whether the choice will be left to my discretion. I have written to make the enquiry, and if upon receiving the answer I should find it practicable, you may depend on my disposition to accommodate your wishes, as far as may be in my power.[1]

In the mean time I am with great attachment and esteem, My Dear Sir, your sincere friend and uncle.

LbC (Adams Papers); internal address: "William Steuben Smith— New-York."; APM Reel 135.

[1] On 5 July JQA wrote to Robert Smith asking if he could choose his own secretary. The secretary of state responded on 13 July (Adams Papers) that the choice was JQA's and that the government would provide a secretarial salary of $1,350. JQA in a letter to William Steuben Smith of 10 July (LbC, APM Reel 135) requested his nephew come to Boston within ten days to depart with him as his secretary in Russia (JQA, *Writings*, 3:328–330; JQA, *Diary*, 5-7, 10 July, 5 Aug.).

Abigail Adams to Elizabeth Smith Shaw Peabody

my dear sister Quincy July 18th 1809

It looks like a want of those gratefull feelings which I am sure are inmates of My Heart, that three Weeks have Elapsed since I left my dear sister, and her Hospitable Mansion, and I have not written her a line to tell her that I was highly gratified with my ride and Visit;[1] that my Health, and that of Louissas was much benifited by it, and that I have wanted to hear directly from my dear Neice, whom I left rather indisposed. tho I have not had any direct communication, I have heard twice from her, and you, since I left You, through Mrs Foster, and Sister Cranch. I have been so constantly occupied since my return, both head hands, and I may say Heart full, that I have only Written one Letter, and that to mrs smith—[2] in the first place I have had a Succession of company—which added to the numerous family I have during Hay time, and the addition of aiding my sons family in prepareing for their Voyage all these circumstances will account to you for my silence— this Embassy to Russia sits heavey at My Heart, altho I know it to be a very important one at this eventfull period, to our country.

July 1809

yet the season is so far advanced, and the Voyage So long together with so many other painfull circumstances which occur to me, that I find it very difficult to reconcile My Mind in any measure to it. at the advanced years both of his Father and Myself, we can have very little expectation of Meeting again upon this mortal theater— both his father and I, have looked to him as the prop and support of our advanced and declineing years. his judgment his prudence his integrity, his filial tenderness and affection, his social converse and information, have renderd his society peculiarly Dear to us, and as the world receeded from us, with its pleasures and amusements, these qualities became daily more and more, our solace and delight. like sterling coin, the alloy alass is in our being deprived of them. indeed my dear sister, a Man of his worth ought not to be permitted to leave the country,—a country which Wants Such supports.— I say this to you, the world would call it vain glory but how much has one Man frequently in the History of Nations been able to accomplish.? "Envy will merrit, as its shade pursue"[3]

such is humane Nature, in all ages and countries. it has been the ~~vile~~ intolerant spirit of party, which has induced him to accept this mission—and the hope of yet being Serviceable to his Country, altho traduced and vilified by the same intollerent faction

you must not suppose by what I have written "respecting" my son JQA, that I depreciate the good and amiable qualities of my other Son, who has ever been towards me a Dutifull and affectionate Child, but being so much younger, and not having been placed in such conspicious stations, cannot be supposed to have the knowledge and experience of his Brother— he will now have a double task to perform, to fullfill the Duties which belong to himself and supply those of his Brother— mr Adamss takes with him as private Secretary William S Smith his Nephew. this I know will be a great Gratification to his sister, as it is to me— he proposes to leave George & John under my care to be placed at their uncle Cranchs—[4] I think I could not consent to part with them all— of the few Children I have had, how they have been divided, brought together again & then Scatterd— God knows what is best, his will—be done

my dear sister your bountifull hand has supplied the President with Many a supper for which he tenders You his thanks. you could not have Sent him a more acceptable present. he is so much delighted with it, that he asks the favour of you to see if you could procure one of Mr Little, an old one he wants; if the stage could take it to Haverhill to mr Harrods we could get it on to Boston—and he wishes to speak for one Hundred & 50 wt of the same kind of cheese for the present year when it is sufficiently dry— we have a very cold storm & voilent wind—unusual at this season— mrs T B A still keeps up cousin B smith is upon a visit to sister Cranch— Eliza smith is going to be married to mr Cruffts—[5] Aunt Edwards with mr smiths family made me a visit last week and dinned with me Aunt is 95 years old. she depends much upon her semi Annual visits she is indeed a very extradanary woman—

Adieu my dear sister with Respects to mr Peabody and Love to Abbe, I am Your truly / affectionate sister   Abigail Adams[6]

RC (DLC:Shaw Family Papers); addressed by Louisa Catharine Smith: "Mrs. Elizabeth Peabody / Atkinson."

[1] AA visited Peabody in Atkinson, N.H., from 21 to 26 June (JQA, *Diary*).
[2] Not found.
[3] Alexander Pope, *An Essay on Criticism*, Part II, line 266.
[4] On 23 July JQA formalized plans for GWA and JA2 to live with the Cranches while he and LCA were in Russia. LCA learned of these plans from TBA while visiting Quincy with her sons on 26 July. She later recalled that "every preparation was made without the slightest consultation with me and even the disposal of my Children and my Sister was fixed without my knowledge until it was too late to Change"

(JQA, *Diary*; LCA, *D&A*, 1:283–284).
[5] Elizabeth Storer Smith, daughter of Hannah Carter and William Smith, married Boston merchant Edward Cruft (1776-1866) on 9 Aug. 1810 (CFA, *Diary*, 3:31; LCA, *D&A*, 2:589; *New-England Palladium*, 14 Aug.).
[6] Peabody replied to this letter on 26 July 1809, lamenting JQA's pending move but declaring that "upon a political account" his appointment as minister to Russia was a reason to "rejoice." She also provided updates on her family and informed AA that "Mrs. Little" did not have any more cheese (Adams Papers).

Abigail Adams to John Quincy Adams

[*31 July 1809*]

My consolation is, that You cannot go

["]where universal love, smiles not around
Sustaining all You orbs, and all their Suns
From Seeming evil still educing good"[1]

Your Mothers Legacy May a blessing accompany it—

RC (Adams Papers); addressed: "John Quincy Adams—"; endorsed: "My Mother 31. July 1809."

[1] James Thomson, "A Hymn," lines 112–114.

Appendix

Appendix

LIST OF OMITTED DOCUMENTS

The following list includes 155 documents that have been omitted from volume 16 of *Adams Family Correspondence* and 7 documents that have come to the editors' attention since the publication of the volume in which they would have appeared. Each entry consists of the date, correspondents, form in which the letter exists (Dft, FC-Pr, LbC, RC, Tr, etc.), location, and publication, if known. All copies that exist in some form in the Adams Papers are noted.

The letters between John Adams and John Quincy Adams in their public roles that have been omitted from the *Family Correspondence* will be considered for inclusion in forthcoming volumes of Series III, General Correspondence and Other Papers of the Adams Statesmen.

1796

11 Nov.	John Adams to Thomas Boylston Adams, RC (private owner, 2023).
28 Nov.	Abigail Adams to Elbridge Gerry, RC (private owner, 2023).

1800

June	Abigail Adams to Unknown, Dft (private owner, 2013).

1803

16 July	Richard Cranch to Thomas Boylston Adams, FC (NAlI:Cranch-Greenleaf Papers).
22 July	Thomas Boylston Adams to Richard Cranch, RC (NAlI:Cranch-Greenleaf Papers).
10 Aug.	Richard Cranch to Thomas Boylston Adams, FC (NAlI:Cranch-Greenleaf Papers).
9 Dec.	Elizabeth Smith Shaw Peabody to Abigail Adams, RC (Adams Papers), filmed at 9 Dec. 1805.

1804

9 Nov.	John Quincy Adams to William Smith Shaw, RC (MWA:Adams Family Letters).
16 Nov.	John Adams to John Quincy Adams, RC (Adams Papers).
17 Nov.	Thomas Boylston Adams to John Quincy Adams, RC (Adams Papers).
19 Nov.	John Quincy Adams to John Adams, RC (Adams Papers).
19 Nov.	John Quincy Adams to Thomas Boylston Adams, RC (Adams Papers).
26 Nov.	John Quincy Adams to William Smith Shaw, RC (MWA:Adams Family Letters).
[28 *Nov.*]	John Quincy Adams to John Adams, RC (Adams Papers); PRINTED: JQA, *Writings*, 3:79–82.
2 Dec.	John Adams to John Quincy Adams, RC (Adams Papers).
3 Dec.	John Quincy Adams to Abigail Adams, RC (Adams Papers).
6 Dec.	John Adams to John Quincy Adams, RC (Adams Papers); Tr (Adams Papers).
6 Dec.	Thomas Boylston Adams to John Quincy Adams, RC (Adams Papers).
11 Dec.	John Quincy Adams to John Adams, RC (Adams Papers); PRINTED: JQA, *Writings*, 3:82–86.
13 Dec.	John Quincy Adams to Thomas Boylston Adams, RC (Adams Papers).
14 Dec.	John Adams to John Quincy Adams, RC (Adams Papers).
17 Dec.	John Quincy Adams to William Smith Shaw, RC (MWA:Adams Family Letters).
19 Dec.	Louisa Catherine Adams to Abigail Adams, RC (Adams Papers).
22 Dec.	John Adams to John Quincy Adams, RC (Adams Papers).
24 Dec.	John Adams to John Quincy Adams, RC (Adams Papers).
24 Dec.	John Quincy Adams to John Adams, RC (Adams Papers); PRINTED: JQA, *Writings*, 3:100–103.

Appendix

1805

8 Jan.	John Adams to John Quincy Adams, RC (Adams Papers).
22 Jan.	Abigail Adams to Hannah Carter Smith, RC (MHi: Smith-Carter Family Papers).
23 Jan.	Elizabeth Smith to Abigail Adams, RC (Adams Papers).
24 Jan.	John Quincy Adams to John Adams, RC (Adams Papers); PRINTED (in part): JQA, *Writings*, 3:104–106.
[ca. 27 Jan.]	Abigail Adams to John Rutledge Jr., Dft (Adams Papers), filmed at [1802?].
7 Feb.	John Adams to John Quincy Adams, RC (Adams Papers); Tr (Adams Papers).
8 Feb.	John Quincy Adams to Thomas Boylston Adams, RC (Adams Papers).
8 March	John Quincy Adams to John Adams, RC (Adams Papers); Tr (Adams Papers); PRINTED (in part): JQA, *Writings*, 3:106–114.
14 March	John Quincy Adams to John Adams, RC (Adams Papers); Tr (Adams Papers); PRINTED (in part): JQA, *Writings*, 3:114–122.
18 March	Ann Quincy Packard to Abigail Adams, RC (Adams Papers).
11 April	John Quincy Adams to Walter Hellen, LbC (Adams Papers), APM Reel 135.
3 Sept.	William Stephens Smith to Abigail Adams Smith, RC (NHi:William Stephens Smith Coll.); PRINTED (in facsimile): Roof, *Smith and Lady*, p. 262–263.
4 Sept.	William Stephens Smith to Abigail Adams Smith, PRINTED: AA2, *Jour. and Corr.*, 2:185–187.
5 Sept.	Thomas Boylston Adams to William Smith Shaw, RC (MHi:Misc. Bound Coll.).
12 Nov.	John Quincy Adams to Abigail Adams, RC (Adams Papers).
12 Nov.	Louisa Catherine Adams to Abigail Adams, RC (Adams Papers).
6 Dec.	John Quincy Adams to John Adams, RC (Adams Papers); PRINTED: JQA, *Writings*, 3:129–131.
14 Dec.	William Smith Shaw to John Quincy Adams, RC (Adams Papers).

16 Dec.	John Quincy Adams to Abigail Adams, RC (Adams Papers).
18 Dec.	John Quincy Adams to Thomas Boylston Adams, RC (Adams Papers).
30 Dec.	John Quincy Adams to Abigail Adams, RC (Adams Papers).

1806

6 Jan.	Louisa Catherine Adams to Abigail Adams, RC (Adams Papers).
27 Jan.	John Quincy Adams to William Smith Shaw, RC (MWA:Adams Family Letters); PRINTED (in part): Felt, *Memorials of William Smith Shaw*, p. 210–211.
31 Jan.	Abigail Adams to Ann Harrod Adams, RC (private owner, 2019).
5 Feb.	John Adams to John Quincy Adams, RC (Adams Papers); LbC (Adams Papers), APM Reel 118; Tr (Adams Papers).
[ca. 11 Feb.]	Abigail Adams to Ann Harrod Adams, RC (Adams Papers), filmed at [*April 1797*].
11 Feb.	John Quincy Adams to John Adams, RC (Adams Papers); Tr (Adams Papers); PRINTED: JQA, *Writings*, 3:134–137.
19 Feb.	John Quincy Adams to William Smith Shaw, RC (MWA:Adams Family Letters).
[*Feb.*]	Abigail Adams to Ann Harrod Adams, RC (MBBS).
9 March	Abigail Adams to Lucy Cranch Greenleaf, RC (MHi: Adams Papers, All Generations).
19 March	John Quincy Adams to Thomas Boylston Adams, RC (Adams Papers).
24 March	Abigail Adams to John Quincy Adams, RC (Adams Papers).
28 March	John Quincy Adams to John Adams, RC (Adams Papers); PRINTED (in part): JQA, *Writings*, 3:138.
4 May	John Quincy Adams to Louisa Catherine Adams, RC (Adams Papers).
11 May	Louisa Catherine Adams to John Quincy Adams, RC (Adams Papers).
[*13 May*]	Abigail Adams to John Quincy Adams, RC (Adams Papers).

Appendix

18 May	Louisa Catherine Adams to John Quincy Adams, RC (Adams Papers).
1 June	John Quincy Adams to Louisa Catherine Adams, RC (Adams Papers); PRINTED (in part): JQA, *Writings*, 3:143–144.
9 June	Louisa Catherine Adams to John Quincy Adams, RC (Adams Papers).
10 June	John Quincy Adams to Louisa Catherine Adams, RC (Adams Papers).
18 June	John Quincy Adams to Louisa Catherine Adams, RC (Adams Papers).
27 June	Thomas Boylston Adams to William Meredith, RC (PHi:Samuel Washington Woodhouse Coll.).
29 June	John Quincy Adams to Louisa Catherine Adams, RC (Adams Papers); Tr (Adams Papers); PRINTED (in part): JQA, *Writings*, 3:150–151.
30 June	Louisa Catherine Adams to John Quincy Adams, RC (Adams Papers).
2 July	John Quincy Adams to Louisa Catherine Adams, RC (Adams Papers).
10 July	John Quincy Adams to William Smith Shaw, RC (MWA:Adams Family Letters).
13 July	John Quincy Adams to Louisa Catherine Adams, RC (Adams Papers); PRINTED (in part): JQA, *Writings*, 3:152–153.
20 July	John Quincy Adams to Louisa Catherine Adams, RC (Adams Papers).
20 July	Louisa Catherine Adams to John Quincy Adams, RC (Adams Papers).
28 July	John Quincy Adams to Louisa Catherine Adams, RC (Adams Papers).
30 July	Louisa Catherine Adams to John Quincy Adams, RC (Adams Papers).
6 Nov.	John Quincy Adams to William Smith Shaw, RC (MWA:Adams Family Letters).
25 Nov.	Louisa Catherine Adams to John Quincy Adams, RC (Adams Papers).
5 Dec.	John Quincy Adams to Louisa Catherine Adams, RC (Adams Papers).
6 Dec.	Thomas Boylston Adams to Thomas Cadwalader, RC (PHi:Cadwalader Family Papers).

12 Dec.	John Quincy Adams to Louisa Catherine Adams, RC (Adams Papers).
15 Dec.	John Quincy Adams to Louisa Catherine Adams, RC (Adams Papers).
17 Dec.	John Quincy Adams to Louisa Catherine Adams, RC (Adams Papers).
18 Dec.	John Quincy Adams to Louisa Catherine Adams, RC (Adams Papers).
19 Dec.	Louisa Catherine Adams to John Quincy Adams, RC (Adams Papers).
26 Dec.	John Quincy Adams to Louisa Catherine Adams, RC (Adams Papers).
28 Dec.	Thomas Boylston Adams to John Quincy Adams, RC (Adams Papers).

1807

2 Jan.	John Quincy Adams to Louisa Catherine Adams, RC (Adams Papers).
9 Jan.	John Quincy Adams to Louisa Catherine Adams, RC (Adams Papers); Tr (Adams Papers).
11 Jan.	Louisa Catherine Adams to John Quincy Adams, RC (Adams Papers).
13 Jan.	John Quincy Adams to Thomas Boylston Adams, RC (Adams Papers).
19 Jan.	John Quincy Adams to Louisa Catherine Adams, RC (Adams Papers).
26 Jan.	John Quincy Adams to Louisa Catherine Adams, RC (Adams Papers).
26 Jan.	Louisa Catherine Adams to John Quincy Adams, RC (Adams Papers).
27 Jan.	John Quincy Adams to John Adams, RC (Adams Papers); Tr (Adams Papers); PRINTED (in part): JQA, *Writings*, 3:158–160.
29 Jan.	Abigail Adams to John Quincy Adams, RC (Adams Papers).
29 Jan.	Louisa Catherine Adams to John Quincy Adams, RC (Adams Papers).
1 Feb.	Louisa Catherine Adams to John Quincy Adams, RC (Adams Papers).
4 Feb.	John Quincy Adams to Louisa Catherine Adams, RC (Adams Papers).

Appendix

6 Feb.	John Quincy Adams to Louisa Catherine Adams, RC (Adams Papers).
10 Feb.	John Quincy Adams to Thomas Boylston Adams, RC (Adams Papers).
11 Feb.	John Quincy Adams to Louisa Catherine Adams, RC (Adams Papers).
17 Feb.	Louisa Catherine Adams to John Quincy Adams, RC (Adams Papers).
27 Feb.	John Quincy Adams to Louisa Catherine Adams, RC (Adams Papers); Tr (Adams Papers).
8 March	John Quincy Adams to Louisa Catherine Adams, RC (Adams Papers).
24 March	William Stephens Smith to John Quincy Adams, RC (Adams Papers).
25 April	Hannah Phillips Cushing to Abigail Adams, RC (Adams Papers).
18 June	John Quincy Adams to John Adams, RC (Adams Papers).
20 June	John Adams to John Quincy Adams, RC (MHi:Winthrop Papers).
17 Oct.	John Quincy Adams to William Smith Shaw, RC (MWA:Adams Family Letters).
28 Oct.	John Quincy Adams to William Smith Shaw, RC (MWA:Adams Family Letters).
7 Nov.	John Quincy Adams to William Smith Shaw, RC (MWA:Adams Family Letters); PRINTED (in part): Felt, *Memorials of William Smith Shaw*, p. 248–249.
12 Nov.	John Adams to John Quincy Adams, RC (Adams Papers); Tr (Adams Papers).
30 Nov.	John Quincy Adams to John Adams, RC (Adams Papers); Tr (Adams Papers); PRINTED (in part): JQA, *Writings*, 3:163–164.
14 Dec.	John Adams to John Quincy Adams, RC (Adams Papers); Tr (Adams Papers).
18 Dec.	John Quincy Adams to William Smith Shaw, RC (MWA:Adams Family Letters).
27 Dec.	John Quincy Adams to John Adams, RC (Adams Papers); Tr (Adams Papers); PRINTED (in part): JQA, *Writings*, 3:166–173.

1808

7 Jan.	Thomas Boylston Adams to Richard Cranch, RC (NAlI:Cranch-Greenleaf Papers).
8 Jan.	John Adams to John Quincy Adams, RC (Adams Papers); LbC (Adams Papers), APM Reel 118; Tr (Adams Papers); PRINTED (in part): MHS, *Procs.*, 44:422–428.
8 Jan.	John Quincy Adams to William Smith Shaw, RC (MWA:Adams Family Letters).
17 Jan.	John Adams to John Quincy Adams, RC (Adams Papers); Tr (Adams Papers).
12 Feb.	John Adams to John Quincy Adams, RC (Adams Papers); Tr (Adams Papers).
18 Feb.	John Quincy Adams to William Smith Shaw, RC (MWA:Adams Family Letters).
5 March	John Adams to John Quincy Adams, RC (Adams Papers); LbC (Adams Papers), APM Reel 118; Tr (Adams Papers).
7 March	John Quincy Adams to William Smith Shaw, RC (MWA:Adams Family Letters).
15 March	Thomas Boylston Adams to John Quincy Adams, RC (Adams Papers).
18 March	John Adams to John Quincy Adams, RC (Adams Papers); Tr (Adams Papers).
25 March	John Quincy Adams to John Adams, RC (MWA:Adams Family Letters); PRINTED (in part): Felt, *Memorials of William Smith Shaw*, p. 252–253.
27 March	Abigail Adams to Abigail Adams Smith, RC (MHi: De Windt Family Papers); PRINTED: MHS, *Procs.*, 66:131–133.
30 March	John Quincy Adams to Thomas Boylston Adams, RC (MHi:Adams Papers, All Generations).
15 April	John Adams to John Adams Smith, LbC (Adams Papers), APM Reel 118.
17 April	Abigail Adams to Abigail Adams Smith, RC (MHi: De Windt Family Papers); PRINTED: MHS, *Procs.*, 66:133–134.
9 May	Elizabeth Smith Shaw Peabody to Abigail Adams, RC (Adams Papers).

Appendix

11 May	Hannah Phillips Cushing to Abigail Adams, RC (Adams Papers).
20 May	Abigail Adams to Abigail Adams Smith, RC (MHi: De Windt Family Papers); PRINTED: MHS, *Procs.*, 66:137–140.
30 Aug.	Abigail Adams to Caroline Amelia Smith, PRINTED (in part): AA2, *Jour. and Corr.*, 1:213–214.
3 Oct.	Abigail Adams to Abigail Adams Smith, RC (MHi: De Windt Family Papers); PRINTED: MHS, *Procs.*, 66:145–147.
10 Oct.	John Adams to John Adams Smith, LbC (Adams Papers), APM Reel 118; Tr (Adams Papers).
18 Nov.	Elizabeth Smith Shaw Peabody to Abigail Adams and Mary Smith Cranch, RC (Adams Papers).
[1808?]	Abigail Adams to John Quincy Adams, RC (Adams Papers).

1809

17 Jan.	Abigail Adams to Cotton Tufts, RC (DNDAR:Americana Coll.).
29 Jan.	John Quincy Adams to Louisa Catherine Adams, RC (Adams Papers).
2 Feb.	Abigail Adams to Caroline Amelia Smith, Tr (Adams Papers), APM Reel 327; PRINTED: AA2, *Jour. and Corr.*, 1:214–217.
5 Feb.	John Quincy Adams to Louisa Catherine Adams, RC (Adams Papers).
15 Feb.	John Quincy Adams to Louisa Catherine Adams, RC (Adams Papers).
21 Feb.	John Quincy Adams to Louisa Catherine Adams, RC (Adams Papers); Tr (Adams Papers).
21 Feb.	Louisa Catherine Adams to John Quincy Adams, RC (Adams Papers).
26 Feb.	John Quincy Adams to Louisa Catherine Adams, RC (Adams Papers); Tr (Adams Papers).
4 March	Louisa Catherine Adams to John Quincy Adams, RC (Adams Papers).
5 March	Abigail Adams to Abigail Adams Smith, PRINTED: AA2, *Jour. and Corr.*, 2:191–192.
6 March	Elizabeth Smith Shaw Peabody to Abigail Adams, RC (Adams Papers).

8 March	John Quincy Adams to Abigail Adams, RC (Adams Papers).
23 March	Richard Cranch to Abigail Adams, LbC (Adams Papers), APM Reel 95.
19 April	John Adams to John Quincy Adams, RC (Adams Papers).
27 April	Joseph Adams to John Adams, RC (Adams Papers).
29 April	Abigail Adams to John Quincy Adams, RC (MHi:Adams Papers, All Generations).
29 April	John Adams to John Quincy Adams, RC (Adams Papers).
19 May	Elizabeth Smith Shaw Peabody to Abigail Adams, RC (Adams Papers).
10 July	John Quincy Adams to William Steuben Smith, LbC (Adams Papers), APM Reel 135.
24 July	Louisa Catherine Adams to Dolley Payne Todd Madison (private owner, 1974); PRINTED (in part): *Dolley Madison Digital Edition*.
26 July	Elizabeth Smith Shaw Peabody to Abigail Adams, RC (Adams Papers).

Chronology

Chronology

THE ADAMS FAMILY, 1804–1809

1804

5 Nov.: The 2d session of the 8th Congress convenes with JQA serving in the Senate; the session adjourns 3 March 1805.

5 Nov.: TBA loses a bid to represent the Norfolk District in the U.S. House of Representatives.

2 Dec.: Napoleon crowns himself emperor of France.

12 Dec.: Spain declares war on Great Britain.

1805

3 Feb.: Elizabeth Eliot Cranch, daughter of William and Anna Greenleaf Cranch, is born in Washington, D.C.

4 Feb. – 1 March: The Senate holds the impeachment trial of U.S. Supreme Court justice Samuel Chase; JQA joins the majority in voting for acquittal.

13 Feb.: Electoral votes are read before a joint session of Congress. Thomas Jefferson and George Clinton are elected president and vice president, respectively.

4 March: Thomas Jefferson is inaugurated for a second term as president of the United States.

19 March: JQA, LCA, GWA, and JA2 leave Washington, D.C., for Quincy. They arrive on 5 April after spending a week in Philadelphia and visiting AA2 in New York City.

8 May: TBA is elected to represent Quincy in the Mass. General Court, serving until 14 March 1806.

16 May: TBA and AHA wed in Haverhill.

4 June: The United States and Tripoli sign the Tripolitan-American Treaty of Peace and Amity, ending the First Barbary War. The Senate gives its consent on 12 April 1806, and the United States ratifies the treaty on the 17th.

13 Aug. – 11 Nov.: AA2, Caroline Amelia Smith, and William Steuben Smith visit Quincy.

11 Nov.: JQA and LCA leave Quincy for Washington, D.C., accompanied by AA2 and her children as far as New York City, and arrive in the capital on the 29th.

2 Dec.: The 1st session of the 9th Congress convenes and sits until 21 April 1806.

1806

2 Jan.: Sidi Soliman Mellimelli, Tunisian minister to the United States, visits Congress. Negotiations with the Jefferson administration on trade and tribute end without resolution in April.

2 Feb. – 2 Aug.: Francisco de Miranda leads an unsuccessful expedition to liberate Venezuela from Spanish rule, accompanied by William Steuben Smith, who survives two armed engagements before returning to the United States by Sept. 1807.

10 Feb.: Mary Carter Smith, daughter of William and Hannah Carter Smith, dies in Boston.

13 Feb.: JQA introduces a bill in the Senate to limit diplomatic immunity of foreign ministers to the United States; the bill is defeated on 7 March.

24 Feb.: William Cranch is confirmed as chief justice of the U.S. Circuit Court of the District of Columbia.

17 March: Thomas Jefferson dismisses WSS as surveyor of the port of New York.

6 April: Louisa Catherine Smith Foster, daughter of James Hiller and Elizabeth Smith Foster, is born in Boston.

7 April: WSS is indicted in U.S. Circuit Court on a charge that he supported an unauthorized military action by assisting the Miranda expedition. He is acquitted on 22 July.

13 April: Mary Elizabeth Greenleaf, daughter of John and Lucy Cranch Greenleaf, is born in Cambridge.

18 April: The Non-Importation Act of 1806 becomes the first of three retaliatory measures aimed at Great Britain. The law, which takes effect on 15 Nov., bans certain British imports to the United States.

26 April: JQA departs Washington, D.C., for Quincy, where he arrives on 3 May after visiting AA2 in New York City.

6 May: JA and JQA attend the installation of Samuel Webber as president of Harvard College.

13 May: Lucy Ann Norton, daughter of Rev. Jacob and Elizabeth Cranch Norton, is born in Weymouth.

Chronology

12 June: JQA is installed as the first Boylston Professor of Rhetoric and Oratory at Harvard College. He delivers 36 lectures before resigning on 28 July 1809.

22 June: LCA gives birth to a stillborn son.

4 July: JA is guest of honor at a Fourth of July dinner held at Faneuil Hall in Boston.

26 July: LCA departs Washington, D.C., for Boston, arriving on 10 Aug. after visiting AA2 in New York City.

29 July: Abigail Smith Adams, first child of TBA and AHA, is born in Quincy.

6 Aug.: John Adams Smith graduates from Columbia College in New York City.

19 Nov.: JQA leaves Boston for Washington, D.C., arriving on the 27th.

1 Dec.: The 2d session of the 9th Congress convenes and remains in session until 3 March 1807.

1807

22 Jan.: Thomas Jefferson submits evidence to Congress alleging that Aaron Burr committed treason by planning an insurrection against the United States. Burr is arrested on 19 Feb. and tried in Richmond, Va., where he is acquitted on 1 September.

24 Feb.: The Seventh Circuit Act of 1807 expands the federal judiciary and adds a seventh justice to the U.S. Supreme Court.

5 March: JQA departs Washington, D.C. AA2, John Adams Smith, and Caroline Amelia Smith accompany him from New York City to Boston, where they arrive on 18 March.

11 July – 27 Aug.: JA initiates an exchange of sixteen letters with Mercy Otis Warren objecting to her depiction of him in *History of the Rise, Progress, and Termination of the American Revolution*.

18 Aug.: CFA, third child of JQA and LCA, is born in Boston.

6 Oct.: John Adams Smith departs Quincy for Albany, N.Y.

10 Oct.: JQA, LCA, and CFA depart Boston for Washington, D.C., arriving on the 24th.

26 Oct.: The 1st session of the 10th Congress convenes and remains in session until 25 April 1808.

22 Dec.: The Embargo Act of 1807 is enacted, laying a general trade embargo. It is the second of three retaliatory measures aimed at Great Britain.

1808

- 1 Jan.: The Act Prohibiting the Importation of Slaves, passed by Congress on 2 March 1807, goes into effect, formally ending the international slave trade to the United States.
- 11 Jan.: AA2 and Caroline Amelia Smith leave Quincy to join WSS at a homestead in central New York's Chenango Valley.
- 9 Feb.: ECA, second child of TBA and AHA, is born in Quincy.
- 24 March: William Steuben Smith returns to his parents in central New York after spending the winter teaching geometry in the Quincy town school.
- 8 April: JQA delivers a speech in the Senate advocating the expulsion of John Smith of Ohio for aiding Aaron Burr's expedition. The Senate votes against expulsion the next day.
- 9 April: JQA's 31 March open letter to Harrison Gray Otis defending his support of the embargo is published in Boston.
- 15 April: JA begins a series of essays in the *Boston Patriot* that will continue until May 1812.
- 27 April: JQA, LCA, and CFA depart Washington, D.C., for Boston, where they arrive on 8 May.
- 8 June: JQA resigns his Senate seat before the end of his term after the Mass. General Court elects James Lloyd Jr. as his replacement.
- 7 Nov.: The 2d session of the 10th Congress convenes and remains in session until 3 March 1809.

1809

- 26 Jan. – 26 March: JQA travels to Washington, D.C., to serve as counsel in three cases before the U.S. Supreme Court: Fletcher *v.* Peck, Hope Insurance Company of Providence *v.* Boardman, and Bank of the United States *v.* Deveaux.
- 8 Feb.: Electoral votes are read before a joint session of Congress. James Madison is elected president and George Clinton vice president.
- 1 March: The Non-Intercourse Act of 1809, the third of three retaliatory measures aimed at Great Britain, lifts the general embargo except for ships bound to British or French ports.
- 4 March: James Madison is inaugurated as the fourth president of the United States.

Chronology

6 March: JQA is nominated by James Madison to be minister plenipotentiary to Russia, but the Senate refuses the mission. Madison renominates JQA on 26 June, and he is confirmed the following day.

10 July: JQA names William Steuben Smith as his secretary for his mission to Russia.

Index

NOTE ON THE INDEX

The index for volume 16 of the *Adams Family Correspondence* is designed to supplement the annotation, when possible, by furnishing the correct spellings of names, supplying forenames when they are lacking in the text, and indicating dates, occupations, and places of residence when they will aid in identification. Markedly variant spellings of proper names have been cross-referenced to what are believed to be their most nearly standard forms, and the variant forms found in the manuscripts are parenthetically recorded following the standard spellings. Cross references under maiden names are used for women who were single when first mentioned in the text and were married subsequently but before the end of July 1809.

Branches, departments, and positions within the U.S. federal government are indexed individually under the name of the entity, with subdivisions as appropriate. For example, the Supreme Court is found as a subentry under "Judiciary, U.S." while "Presidency, U.S." stands as a main entry.

Subentries appear in alphabetical order by the primary word of the subentry. Abbreviations are alphabetized as if they were spelled out, thus "JQA" is alphabetized under "Adams, John Quincy."

The Chronology, "The Adams Family, 1804–1809," has not been included in the index.

The index was compiled in the Adams Papers office.

Index

AA. *See* ADAMS, ABIGAIL SMITH (1744–1818, wife of JA)
AA2. *See* ADAMS, ABIGAIL, 2D (1765–1813, wife of WSS)
Abdee, Phoebe (Adams servant), 121, 301, 339

ADAMS, ABIGAIL, 2D (Nabby, 1765–1813, daughter of AA and JA, wife of WSS, designated as AA2 in *The Adams Papers*)

CHARACTER, APPEARANCE, HABITS
as "aunt Miff," 338–39; books and reading, 16, 59; character of, 16, 202, 299, 346; frugality of, 235–36; health of, 430; letter writing of, 374, 383; Elizabeth Peabody on, 194; religious beliefs of, 126–27

DOMESTIC LIFE
AHA and, 52, 59, 363, 380; correspondence with William Smith, 127; correspondence with WSS, 60; domestic work of, 127, 274, 363; relationship with LCA, 147–48, 185, 190, 191, 193, 254, 279, 287, 307; relationship with WSS, xxi, 130, 144, 153, 162, 194, 244, 299, 302; relationship with M. Warren, 217, 269–70; social activities of, 59, 127, 144, 240

LETTERS
Letters: To AA (1804), 16; To TBA (1805), 59; To Francisco de Miranda (1806), 88, 102; To Hannah Carter Smith (1806), 126
Letters: From AA (1808), 299, 336, 362, 367, 371, 374, 379, 383, 389; (1809), 418, 421, 426, 432
Letters to, from, omitted: From AA listed (1808), 448 (2), 449 (2); (1809), 449; From WSS listed (1805), 443 (2)

MENTIONED
x, 289, 342, 358

OPINIONS AND BELIEFS
human nature, xx, 16; F. Miranda and expedition of, xxi, xxii, 102, 127

RELATIONSHIP WITH CHILDREN
concern for children, 269, 275, 288; correspondence with William Steuben Smith, 186, 202, 269; Caroline Smith and correspondence of, 434; John Adams Smith's education and, xv, 185; on William Steuben Smith, 102; William Steuben Smith's career and, xv, 338, 437

RELATIONSHIP WITH PARENTS
AA on, 272, 299, 304, 338, 379, 418–19; AA's concern for, 143, 235–36, 266, 272–73, 302, 303, 304, 346, 382–83; AA's correspondence and, 383, 392, 432–33; AA sends publications to, 421, 422, 425, 433; correspondence with parents, xvi, xvii, xx, xxiii, 266, 267, 339, 343, 346, 363, 364, 378, 381, 392, 420, 436; separation from parents, xxiii, 16, 299, 302, 303, 346, 363, 367–68, 375, 379, 383, 421, 427; visits AA and JA, xvi, xxii, 60, 119, 162, 249, 254, 268, 285, 287, 288, 302, 345, 372, 384

RELATIONSHIP WITH SIBLINGS
on JQA, 336; JQA assists, 162, 184; JQA's concern for, 146, 202, 244; JQA visits, 3, 52, 56, 133, 142, 145–46, 147, 152, 201, 272; TBA's marriage and, 59, 60; correspondence with JQA, 186

RESIDENCES
in Lebanon, N.Y., xv, xvii, xxii, 254, 299–300, 302, 346, 375; in New York City, 63, 375

TRAVELS
to Lebanon, N.Y. (1808), 299, 302, 345; to New York City (1805), 61–62, 63; to Quincy (1807), 267–68

ADAMS, ABIGAIL, 2D (*continued*)

WRITINGS

Journal and Correspondence, 16, 306, 366, 420, 424, 427, 434

Adams, Abigail Louisa Smith (1798–1836, daughter of CA and SSA): AA and, 118, 143, 304, 305, 373, 375, 382, 390; JQA visits, 146; Elizabeth Peabody on, 389; social activities of, 381–82, 390

ADAMS, ABIGAIL SMITH (1744–1818, wife of JA, designated as AA in *The Adams Papers*)

BOOKS AND READING

Joseph Addison, 269; Aesop, 119, 235; Fisher Ames, 430; Jeremy Belknap, 345; Bible, 36, 46, 52, 112, 126, 133, 270, 272, 289, 302, 318, 345, 362, 363, 369, 373, 375, 379, 380, 382, 385, 420, 422, 424, 428, 429, 433–34; Robert Burns, 44, 45, 47; Samuel Butler, 422, 425; Earl of Chatham, 10, 20, 21; Cicero, 392, 393; congressional journals, 289; William Cowper, 29, 45, 46, 74, 103; Anne MacVicar Grant, 422–24, 425, 429; Homer, 29, 426–27; Henry Hunter, 375; Samuel Johnson, 29, 50, 51, 379; Johann Caspar Lavater, 382; John Lowell Jr., 427; John Milton, 305, 363, 424; Mary Pierrepont Wortley Montagu, 302, 304; Edwin Moore, 93; newspapers, 48, 73, 317, 318, 344, 350, 362, 363, 369, 372, 374, 376, 377, 409, 420, 421–22, 430, 433; Sydney Owenson, 365; Plutarch, 369; Alexander Pope, 132, 216, 268, 270, 273, 392, 419, 422, 424, 437; *Port Folio*, 19, 20, 110, 132; Ann Radcliffe, 269; Charles Rollin, 318–19, 369, 391, 392, 393; Thomas Scott, 303; Shakespeare, 44, 45, 409; John Shebbeare, 78; Madame de Staël, 379; Anne Steele, 50, 110; Jonathan Swift, 270; James Thomson, 438; Mercy Otis Warren, 384, 385; William Whitehead, 363, 429; Edward Young, 50, 51, 52, 345, 423, 428, 429

CHARACTER, APPEARANCE, HABITS

health of, 5, 7, 8, 9–10, 11, 12, 13, 14, 16, 19, 21, 28, 52, 64, 68, 70, 72, 76, 103, 200, 216, 222, 266, 267, 268, 272, 273, 275, 346, 364–65, 368, 374, 375, 377, 379, 399, 403, 407, 409, 416, 418, 428, 432, 436, 437; interest of in politics, xxiii, 375, 392; letter writing of, xvi, 73, 74, 86, 87, 92, 93, 125, 200, 274, 289, 302, 336, 347, 364, 372, 374, 378, 379, 383, 389–90, 422, 424, 427, 432–33; portrait of, 17, 22, 29, 30; religious beliefs of, 51, 109, 110, 269, 345, 384, 418–19, 427, 429, 437

DOMESTIC LIFE

advises and assists family, xvii, 30, 35, 103, 118, 120, 122, 143–44, 301, 302, 304, 393; attends funeral, 103, 232; church attendance, 17, 32, 92, 103, 112, 185, 192, 280, 306, 364, 367, 380; family visits to and by, 15, 69, 103, 112, 124–25, 185, 274, 280, 284, 287, 297, 373, 375, 378, 379, 380–81, 385, 388–89, 431, 432, 435, 436, 438; Johnson family and, 76, 160, 240, 368; pets of, 29, 45, 111, 274; relationship with AHA, xviii–xix, 30, 44, 45, 54, 103, 104, 143–44, 274; relationship with LCA, 13, 30, 36, 37, 46, 92, 154–55, 160, 214, 239, 253, 260, 266, 348, 370–71, 380, 394, 399, 408; relationship with Mary Cranch, 112, 374–75, 379; relationship with Cushings, 133, 335, 346, 409; relationship with Shaw-Peabody family, 120–21, 143, 153, 271, 305, 430, 431, 437–38; relationship with WSS, xx–xxi; relationship with Warrens, xvii, 215–16, 268, 269–70, 275, 276, 278, 384, 385; Louisa Smith as secretary for, 52, 438

FIRST LADY

AA's attitude toward, 346, 434

HOUSEHOLD MANAGEMENT

accounts of, 143, 253, 301, 351, 360, 393; Bird, Savage, & Bird failure and, 118, 119; carriage for, 143; domestic work of, xvi, 144–45, 303, 371, 379; management of tenants and farmhands, 48, 371–72, 378–79, 436; Medford property of, 58, 118, 121, 122, 143; purchases household goods, 104, 143–44, 252, 253, 300, 351, 437–38; servants of, 29, 111, 206, 207, 222, 272, 336, 339, 364, 366, 385; William Smith Shaw as agent for, 29, 121–22, 143, 379; Cotton Tufts as agent for, 393

LETTERS

Letters: To AA2 (1808), 299, 336, 362, 367, 371, 374, 379, 383, 389; (1809), 418, 421, 426, 432; To AHA (1805), 44, 52; (1806), 103, 112, 143, 199; (1807), 274; To JQA (1804), 9, 16, 20, 28; (1805), 47, 64, 68, 73; (1806), 85, 107, 124, 184; (1807), 235, 266, 280; (1808), 317, 350; (1809), 393, 408, 434, 438; To LCA (1804), 18; (1805), 36, 46, 68, 75; (1806), 92, 110; (1807), 280, 288; (1808), 347; To SSA (1806), 118; (1808), 302; To Susanna Boylston Adams (1808), 377; To Hannah Phillips Cushing (1808), 344; To Ann Quincy Packard (1805), 49; To Elizabeth Smith Shaw Peabody (1807), 272; (1809), 428, 436; To Eliza Susan Morton Quincy (1806), 131; To William Smith Shaw (1806), 121, 143; (1808), 378; To Caroline Amelia Smith (1808), 305, 364, 381; To Hannah

Index

ADAMS, ABIGAIL SMITH (*continued*)
Carter Smith (1805), 35; (1806), 109; To John Adams Smith (1808), 391; To Mercy Otis Warren (1807), 268

Letters: From AA2 (1804), 16; From JQA (1804), 22; (1805), 61, 70; (1806), 96, 127, 187, 193; (1807), 243, 252, 281, 283; (1808), 324, 359; From LCA (1804), 13; (1805), 42, 51, 72; (1806), 154; (1807), 286; (1808), 306, 370; From Hannah Phillips Cushing (1805), 61; (1806), 144; (1808), 333; From Elizabeth Smith Shaw Peabody (1806), 119, 152, 194; (1807), 270; (1808), 300, 366, 387; (1809), 431; From Eliza Susan Morton Quincy (1806), 136; From WSS (1805), 60; From Hannah Quincy Lincoln Storer (1805), 32; From Mercy Otis Warren (1806), 215; (1807), 275

Letters to, from, omitted: To AA2 listed (1808), 448 (2), 449 (2); (1809), 449; To AHA listed (1806), 444 (3); To JQA listed (1806), 444 (2); (1807), 446; (1808), 449; (1809), 450; To Elbridge Gerry listed (1796), 441; To Lucy Cranch Greenleaf listed (1806), 444; To John Rutledge Jr. listed (1805), 443; To Caroline Amelia Smith listed (1808), 449; (1809), 449; To Hannah Carter Smith listed (1805), 443; To Cotton Tufts listed (1809), 449; To Unknown listed (1800), 441; From JQA listed (1804), 442; (1805), 443, 444 (2); (1809), 450; From LCA listed (1804), 442; (1805), 443; (1806), 444; From Richard Cranch listed (1809), 450; From Hannah Phillips Cushing listed (1807), 447; (1808), 449; From Ann Quincy Packard listed (1805), 443; From Elizabeth Smith Shaw Peabody listed (1803), 441; (1808), 448, 449; (1809), 449, 450 (2); From Elizabeth Smith listed (1805), 443

OPINIONS AND BELIEFS

Individuals: AHA, 54, 103; SSA, 380, 390; F. Ames, 73; C. Buchanan, 76; S. Chase Sr., 21, 46; Anna Cranch, 133; William Cranch, 132; H. Cushing, 345, 377; W. Eaton, 426; H. Edwards, 438; A. Hamilton, 132; C. M. Johnson, 368; E. Johnson, 92–93, 289, 368; J. Lloyd Jr., 368; D. Madison, 433–34; J. Madison, 132, 336; E. Minchin, 373; F. Miranda, 69; Napoleon, 74, 289; Elizabeth Norton, 273; Elizabeth Peabody, 272, 347; C. C. Pinckney, 380; A. M. Quincy, 49, 50; Elizabeth Norton Quincy, 390; J. Quincy III, 131; M. Quincy, xii, 69, 92, 131, 133; J. Randolph, 108, 131–32, 137; B. Rush, 304; R. Rush, 379; M. de St. Hilaire, 300; Abigail Shaw, 378; C. Shaw, 118; William Smith Shaw, 273–74; Hannah Smith, 36; Justus Smith, 306; Louisa Smith, 103, 304; William Smith, 35, 36; WSS, 300, 346, 369; G. Stuart, 29; W. Sullivan, 48; U. Tracy, 73; A. Walter, 235; M. Ware, 269, 270; M. Washington, 434; Marquis de Casa Yrujo, 108

United States: American Revolution, xxiii, 383; Congress, 46, 125–26, 131, 132, 289, 318, 348, 351, 409; Democratic-Republican Party, 131, 137, 369, 419–20; Embargo Act (1807), xv, 336, 347–48, 364, 372, 380; Federalist Party, 131, 337, 348, 365, 369, 419–20, 422, 425, 430; Jefferson administration, 73, 108, 125, 132–33, 235, 289, 345, 346, 347–48, 372, 380, 419–20, 433; Madison administration, 433; Massachusetts government and politics, 17–18, 48, 368, 420; military preparedness, xxvii, 351, 380; partisanship in, 125, 132, 362, 375–76, 380, 426, 427, 433; presidential election (1808), 318, 336–37, 380, 426; U.S. foreign relations, xxvi–xxvii, 86, 108, 338, 345, 346, 372, 380, 381, 420, 422, 426, 433; U.S. government and politics, 130, 304, 373, 318

Miscellaneous: aging and death, 20, 36, 110, 384, 423, 428, 430; children and childcare, 29, 64, 92, 288–89, 375, 382–83, 390, 430; debt, 378; education, 382, 424, 429; Europe, 339, 373; fashion, 19, 76, 130; friendship, 318; human nature, xxiii, 45, 363, 373, 377, 382, 424, 425; legal profession, 391–92; Miranda expedition, xxii, 125, 235, 269, 270; pets, 29, 45; public service, xxvi, 17, 118, 303, 319, 362–63; race, 92–93; women, 18, 130, 200, 304, 346, 377, 380, 425, 428–29, 430, 433–34

RELATIONSHIP WITH JA

on JA, 30, 78, 346, 419; JA and correspondence of, 69, 426; JA on, 14, 77; JA's correspondence and, 78, 266, 270, 381, 419, 420; on JA's presidency and public service, xxvi, 346, 348, 362–63, 376, 419, 420, 422; JA's writings and, 270, 422, 425, 429–30; advises JA, 48; correspondence with JA, xxviii

RELATIONSHIP WITH CHILDREN

AA2: on AA2, 272, 299, 304, 338, 379, 418–19; AA2 and correspondence of, 383, 392, 432–33; AA2's correspondence and, 266, 374; AA2 visits, xvi, xxii, 60, 119, 162, 249, 254, 268, 285, 287, 288, 302, 345, 372, 384; concern for AA2, 143, 235–36, 266, 272–73, 302, 303, 304, 346, 382–83; sends publications to AA2, 421, 422, 425, 433

CA: on CA, 377–78

JQA: on JQA, xviii, 18–19, 20, 289, 319, 338, 369, 373, 376, 437; JQA as agent for, 48, 252, 253, 351, 360; on JQA's caucus attendance, 317–18, 320, 324, 336, 350, 359; JQA's correspond-

ADAMS, ABIGAIL SMITH (*continued*)
ence and, 224, 337–38, 339, 343; on JQA's *Letter*, 350, 364, 433; on JQA's public service, xxiv, xxvi, 362, 368–69, 373, 409, 436–37; advises and assists JQA, xvi–xvii, xxiv, 10, 17, 20, 23, 29, 36, 37, 43, 46, 47, 48, 64, 71, 73, 85, 86, 87, 93, 108, 130, 187, 193, 325, 359, 361, 393, 435; concern and affection for JQA, xxvii, 76, 107, 111, 131, 184, 438; seeks JQA's advice and assistance, 236, 252–53, 266, 348; visits with JQA, 166, 368, 435

TBA: on TBA, xviii, 437; TBA and correspondence of, 44, 47, 49, 53, 54, 64, 65, 109, 266; TBA as agent for, 58, 122; on TBA's marriage, 53

Miscellaneous: separation from children, xxiii, 16, 19, 67, 92, 289, 299, 302, 303, 346, 363, 367–68, 375, 379, 383, 421, 425, 427, 437, 438

RELATIONSHIP WITH GRANDCHILDREN
on Abigail Louisa Adams, 304, 382, 390; on Abigail Smith Adams, 236, 273, 274, 338–39, 363, 372, 376, 425, 429; on CFA, xix, 288; on ECA, xix, 338, 363, 376, 429; on GWA, 18, 29, 75, 235, 408; on JA2, 16–17, 18, 29, 64, 69, 75, 85–86, 131, 288, 349; on Susanna Adams, 103, 273, 304, 305, 373, 375, 381–82, 390; advises grandchildren, xvii, xxiii, 377–78, 379–80, 382–83, 391–92; cares for grandchildren, xiii, xv, xvi, 60, 69, 85, 86, 92, 96, 103, 108, 110, 111, 119, 122, 124, 131, 155, 215, 222, 232, 235, 237, 239, 252, 260, 266, 273, 280, 283, 284, 288, 295, 345, 346, 351, 355, 356, 371, 372, 380, 408, 424, 425, 435, 437; concern and affection for grandchildren, 16, 199, 254, 269, 280, 300, 305, 348–49, 364, 367, 368; education of GWA and JA2 and, 239, 280; patronage for William Steuben Smith and, 338, 351; separation from grandchildren, 21, 37, 305, 377; on Caroline Smith, 273, 304, 381, 382, 424; Caroline Smith and correspondence of, 432, 434; Caroline Smith's correspondence and, 364, 381; on John Adams Smith, 274; on William Steuben Smith, 288, 303, 338, 346, 348, 380

SOCIAL LIFE
attends wedding, 240; in Europe, 419; in Philadelphia, 55; in Quincy, 15, 103, 112, 435; visits to and by, 5, 61, 124, 144, 200, 201, 216, 284, 335, 347, 363, 368, 377

WRITINGS
CFA notates correspondence of, 19, 37, 47, 76, 93, 111, 290, 347, 349; ECA notates correspondence of, 45, 201; edits correspondence before sending, 37, 50–51, 270, 304–305, 425, 430

Adams, Abigail Smith (1806–1845, daughter of TBA and AHA): AA on, 236, 273, 274, 338–39, 363, 372, 376, 425, 429; AHA and, 189 (illus.), 198; ECA and, 339; JQA on, xi, 226, 326; Susanna Adams and, 378; TBA on, x, 192; appearance of, x, 192, 253; birth of, x–xi, xviii, 183, 188, 189 (illus.), 190, 192, 194; health of, xi, 189 (illus.), 233, 239, 271, 295, 297, 365, 379, 390, 399, 404, 407; Caroline Smith and, 305; visits to and by, 199, 200, 368, 377, 387; mentioned, 348, 355, 366, 383
Adams, Alice Hayward (wife of Micajah), 193; identified, 194

ADAMS, ANN HARROD (1774–1845, wife of TBA, designated as AHA in *The Adams Papers*)

CHARACTER, APPEARANCE, HABITS
appearance of, 175; rumored death of, 168, 190; health of, 152, 157, 169, 175, 177, 179, 181, 183, 185, 253, 266, 267, 307, 309

DOMESTIC LIFE
church attendance, 338; correspondence with Mary Cranch, 200; correspondence with Louisa Smith, 44, 45; family record by, x–xi, 189 (illus.); parents and siblings of, 108, 119, 121, 367, 388, 407, 408; Elizabeth Peabody and, 153; residence of, 226, 254; social activities of, 171, 265; visits Haverhill, Mass., 69, 199, 200, 273, 274, 288, 387, 429, 430

MENTIONED
67, 76, 239, 289, 295, 304, 335, 348, 355, 366, 383, 385, 438

RELATIONSHIP WITH TBA
TBA's correspondence and, 197–98; correspondence with TBA, 53, 54; courtship and engagement, 30, 43, 44, 45, 53; marriage, x, xvi, xviii, 44, 54, 59

RELATIONSHIP WITH ADAMSES
AA2 and, 52, 59, 363, 380; JA2 and, 69, 103, 112, 125; JQA's scientific studies and, 85; Susanna Adams and, 103; correspondence with AA, xviii–xix, 45, 54, 110; correspondence with LCA, 115; purchases goods for Adamses, 44, 104, 140, 143–44, 149; relationship with AA, xviii–xix, 45, 54, 103, 274; visits AA, 30; visits LCA, 206, 394, 399, 404

RELATIONSHIP WITH CHILDREN
Abigail Smith Adams' vaccination and, 297; birth of Abigail Smith Adams, 188, 190, 192, 194; birth of ECA, 323–24, 338, 339, 346

Index

ADAMS, ANN HARROD (continued)

LETTERS
Letters: From AA (1805), 44, 52; (1806), 103, 112, 143, 199; (1807), 274
Letters to, from, omitted: From AA listed (1806), 444 (3)

Adams, Boylston (1771–1829, nephew of JA), 363, 364
Adams, Charles (1770–1800, son of AA and JA, designated as CA in *The Adams Papers*), 377–78
Adams, Charles (1795–1877, son of Micajah, Adams servant), 37, 187, 193; identified, 194
Adams, Charles Francis (1807–1886, son of JQA and LCA, designated as CFA in *The Adams Papers*): identified, 279; AA on, xix, 288; AA's concern and affection for, 280, 348–49; GWA and, 344; JQA on, 281; LCA on, 290; appearance of, 287, 403; birth of, xix, 279, 349; edits JA's correspondence, xxviii; education of, 201, 311; health of, 284, 290, 306, 312, 316, 385, 390, 393, 399, 400, 403, 404, 414, 416, 418; library of, 193; notates AA's correspondence, 19, 37, 47, 76, 93, 111, 290, 347, 349; parents' concern for, 397, 400, 403, 404; travels of, 281, 282, 288, 436–37; visits AA, 371, 435; mentioned, xiii, 326, 396, 410
Adams, Deacon Ebenezer (1737–1791, cousin of JA), 292
Adams, Elizabeth Anne Crosby (wife of Boylston), 363, 364
Adams, Elizabeth Coombs (1808–1903, daughter of TBA and AHA, designated as ECA in *The Adams Papers*): identified, 324; AA and, 424, 425; AA on, xix, 338, 363, 376, 429; Abigail Smith Adams and, 339; JQA on, xi, 326; appearance of, xix, 376; birth of, xi, xviii, 323–24, 326, 338, 341, 342, 346; health of, xi, 390; notates AA's correspondence, 45, 201; notates TBA's correspondence, 332; mentioned, 348, 355, 383, 387, 407

ADAMS, GEORGE WASHINGTON (1801–1829, son of JQA and LCA, designated as GWA in *The Adams Papers*)

CHARACTER, APPEARANCE, HABITS, DOMESTIC LIFE
CFA and, 344; JA2 and, 64, 86; TBA and, 94; TBA on, 285; appearance of, 151, 156, 164, 168; baptism of, 247; church attendance, 125, 205, 206, 209; Cranches care for, xiii, 64, 65, 70, 77, 92, 111, 125, 154, 159; education of, 13, 18, 22, 69, 85, 94, 96, 156, 163, 165, 203, 209, 210, 214, 218, 228–29, 231, 280, 298, 299, 301, 311, 344, 349, 366, 403, 407, 408; family visits to and by, 265, 271, 408; foreign language skills of, 205, 207, 209, 211, 212, 222, 231, 234, 239, 280, 283; health of, 22, 51, 52, 54, 59, 64, 69, 75, 85, 104, 111, 122, 125, 140, 209, 212, 214, 217, 224, 228–29, 231, 267, 286, 351, 355, 385, 390, 393, 400, 410, 414, 416; letter writing of, 344; Elizabeth Peabody cares for, 280, 283, 284–85, 286, 287, 288, 297, 298, 299, 343–44, 347, 356; Elizabeth Peabody on, 271, 298, 343, 366, 388; residences of, 1, 158, 246, 268; Abigail Shaw and, 366; travels of, 52, 281, 408

LETTERS
Letters: To LCA (1806), 156, 160

RELATIONSHIP WITH AA AND JA
AA cares for, 237, 239; AA on, 18, 29, 75, 235, 408; AA's affection for, 16, 21, 37, 349; JA on, 8, 77, 101; visits AA and JA, 69, 86, 103, 108, 110, 235, 252, 266, 371, 435

RELATIONSHIP WITH PARENTS
JQA on, 22–23, 156, 181, 344; JQA's career and, 437, 438; LCA on, 155, 174, 205, 209, 403; LCA's correspondence and, 223; correspondence with LCA, 165; parents' concern and affection for, 65, 67, 72, 84, 85, 87, 96, 104, 168, 185, 224, 242, 244, 251, 263, 396, 403; separation from parents, xiii, xix, 62, 72, 74, 75, 86, 92, 96, 107, 108, 148, 151–52, 154–55, 156, 158, 160, 164, 165, 173, 175, 176, 178, 179, 183, 186, 187, 193, 218, 222, 252, 259–60, 265, 286, 344, 366

ADAMS, JOHN (1735–1826, designated as JA in *The Adams Papers*)

BOOKS AND READING
Joseph Addison, 39; annotates books, 78; Domenico Alberto Azuni, 358; William Belsham, 122; Bible, 14; Samuel Blodget Jr., 229; John Bunyan, 357; Cato the Elder, 357; Cicero, 101, 102, 356, 357; Daniel Defoe, 38–39, 40; devotion to, 30, 389, 419; Dionysius, 229, 231; Edward Gibbon, 77; Robert Henry, 39; David Hume, 356; library at MB, 15, 40, 78, 102, 193, 370, 393; library of, 191, 192; Cassius Longinus, 101; Conyers Middleton, 77, 78; Richard Valentine Morris, 6; newspapers, 12, 38, 39, 99; Plato, 101; Pliny the Younger, 100, 102; publications sent to, 67, 182; Sallust, 77; Thomas Salmon, 34, 39, 40; Senate journals, 99; Shakespeare, 14, 33, 34, 39; Duc de Sully, 14; Jona-

ADAMS, JOHN (*continued*)
than Swift, 14, 15; Thomas Sydenham, 38; Tacitus, 77, 78, 88, 90, 100–101, 102; Velleius Paterculus, 100, 102; Mercy Otis Warren, xvii, 231, 276, 278, 384, 385

CHARACTER, APPEARANCE, HABITS, DOMESTIC LIFE

church attendance, 15, 32, 232, 364, 370; family visits to and by, 15, 185, 260, 280, 287, 297; foreign language skills of, 102; health of, 17, 21, 30, 171, 216, 346, 419, 437; letter writing of, xvii, 389, 409, 419; love of rural life, 76–77, 123, 124, 358; portrait of, 29, 30; relationship with LCA, xix–xx, 206, 214, 229–30, 253, 283, 370, 394, 402, 403; relationship with Cushings, 335; relationship with Shaw-Peabody family, 153, 271, 389, 431, 437–38; relationship with WSS, xx–xxi, 60; relationship with Warrens, 216, 217, 268, 269–70, 275, 276, 278

FINANCES AND PROPERTY

accounts of, 143, 320, 349; JQA as agent for, 67, 68, 320, 425; Bird, Savage, & Bird failure and, 118, 119, 321; investments of, 67, 68, 136; land and properties of, 48, 101, 118, 119, 194, 226; William Smith Shaw as agent for, 143

LETTERS

Letters: To JQA (1804), 6, 7, 14; (1805), 33, 37, 76; (1806), 99, 122; (1807), 229; (1808), 320, 356; To William Smith Shaw (1808), 371; To John Adams Smith (1806), 134; (1808), 385; To William Steuben Smith (1808), 357

Letters: From JQA (1804), 1; (1805), 30; (1806), 88, 181; (1808), 311

Letters to, from, omitted: To JQA listed (1804), 442 (6); (1805), 443 (2); (1806), 444; (1807), 447 (3); (1808), 448 (5); (1809), 450 (2); To TBA listed (1796), 441; To John Adams Smith listed (1808), 448, 449; From JQA listed (1804), 442 (4); (1805), 443 (4); (1806), 444 (2); (1807), 446, 447 (3); (1808), 448; From Joseph Adams listed (1809), 450

OPINIONS AND BELIEFS

Europe: British government and politics, 33–34, 312, 422, 425, 434; European character, 269; France, 34, 122, 123

Individuals: J. Bayard, 38; W. Blount, 356; A. Burr, 8, 356; B. Franklin, 100; W. Giles, 34; A. Hamilton, 8; John Jay, 320; Marquis de Lafayette, 135; J. Madison, 320; Napoleon, 268–69, 275; J. Quincy III, 8; B. Rush, 38; J. Sullivan, 7, 8; James Warren, 278; G. Washington, 77

United States: A. Burr conspiracy, 230; Congress, 4, 123, 254, 357; Constitution, 33, 326; defense of, 230, 356–57; diplomatic immunity, 123–24, 129; economy, 100, 320; Embargo Act (1807), 356–58, 385–86; Federalist Party, xxv, 31, 39, 320, 386–87; foreign influence on, 77, 122, 123, 356; Jefferson administration, 12, 31, 77, 320, 357; literary culture, 38; Louisiana Purchase, 101; Massachusetts government and politics, 7–8, 356; Native Americans, 386; neutrality of, 337, 386, 420; New England, 15, 34; patronage, 123, 420; presidential election (1804), 12; presidential election (1808), xxvi, 230, 320, 385–86; regional divisions in, 31, 34–35, 86, 356; U.S. judiciary, 123, 320, 326; U.S. foreign relations, 6, 77, 101, 107–108, 109, 122, 320, 357, 380, 386, 425

Miscellaneous: African peoples, 386; balance of powers, 40; education, 134–35, 196; law, 15, 387; Miranda expedition, xxii, 135, 230

PUBLIC LIFE

Continental Congress: service in, 176, 177

Diplomatic Career: joint commissioner, 100, 102, 135, 229; minister to Britain, xxi

Presidency, 1797–1801: JQA as minister to Prussia and, 5, 371; cabinet of, 355; Congress and, 131, 289; franking privileges of, 390, 394; A. Hamilton and, 422, 425; nominations by, 4, 427; presidential election (1800) and, 100, 425; public attitudes toward, 100, 135, 137, 255, 316, 348, 353, 355, 371, 376, 419; William Smith Shaw as secretary for, 301; U.S. Army uniform regulation and, 4; U.S. foreign relations and, 295, 353, 355, 387, 422, 427

Retirement, 1801–1826: attends Fourth of July celebrations, 186, 370, 434–35; attends installation of Harvard president, 149, 152; attends militia review, 286; Federalist Party and, 377, 386–87, 419, 422; Jefferson administration and, 135, 338, 348, 376; Massachusetts gubernatorial election (1808) and, 350–51; newspapers and, xvii, xxv, 38, 40, 371, 376, 377, 387; public attitudes toward, xvii, 60, 135, 186, 198, 229, 231, 276, 278, 316, 335, 341, 384, 385, 386, 419, 420, 422, 427, 430, 433, 434

Miscellaneous: JA's attitude toward, 12, 14–15, 135, 420, 421–22; American Academy of Arts and Sciences and, 193, 194

RELATIONSHIP WITH AA

on AA, 14, 77; AA and correspondence of, 78, 266, 270, 381, 419, 420; AA on, 30, 78, 346, 419, 420; AA on presidency and public service of, xxvi, 346, 348, 362–63, 376, 419, 420, 422; AA's correspondence and, 69, 426; correspondence with AA, xxviii

Index

ADAMS, JOHN (continued)

RELATIONSHIP WITH CHILDREN

AA2: AA2 visits, 268, 384
JQA: on JQA, 8–9, 14, 312; JQA and correspondence of, 187; JQA and legacy of, xxv, 316, 425; JQA on, 32, 325; JQA's concern and affection for, 12, 15; JQA's correspondence and, 82, 182, 183, 281, 282, 332, 378, 408; JQA's debt to, 312, 320, 321, 349; JQA sends publications to, 37, 67, 88, 98, 99, 105, 116, 224, 229, 246, 291, 293, 295; JQA's *Letter* and, 350, 356, 360; on JQA's public service, xix–xx, xxvi, 33, 40, 253, 254, 320–21, 371, 402; JQA visits, 368; advises and assists JQA, 34, 86, 196, 311, 312, 320, 435; relationship with JQA, xxiv, 123, 124, 325, 359, 407, 437
TBA: on TBA, 7, 8; TBA and correspondence of, 78, 266, 358; TBA's correspondence and, 117, 190; advises and assists TBA, 196, 249; sends publications to TBA, 38
Miscellaneous: separation from children, 7, 8, 368, 425

RELATIONSHIP WITH GRANDCHILDREN

Abigail Smith Adams and, 192; on GWA, 8, 77, 101; JA2 and, xiii, 8, 77, 101, 151, 229; education of grandchildren and, 301, 304, 375, 387; grandchildren visit, xv, xxii, 260, 284, 346, 351, 356; Caroline Smith and, 305, 381; William Steuben Smith and, 135, 269, 301, 338, 346, 348, 375, 383

RESIDENCES

in France, 100, 102

SOCIAL LIFE

in Europe, 420; in Maine, 124; in Quincy, 17, 18, 103, 185; visits to and by, 32, 216, 285, 286

TRAVELS

in Europe (1778), 386, 387; U.S. to Europe (1778), 9, 135, 231

WRITINGS

Published: *Diary and Autobiography*, xxvii
1776: *Thoughts on Government*, 176, 177
1809: *Inadmissible Principles, of the King of England's Proclamation, of October 16, 1807– Considered*, 433, 434
1809–1812: letters to *Boston Patriot*, xvii, 371, 419, 420, 421–22, 424–25, 429–30, 431, 433, 434
Unpublished: Autobiography, xvii, 9, 14, 15, 31, 32, 135, 229, 231, 387

1790: "Dialogues of the Dead," 276
1806: "Memorandum on the Legal Status of Half-Moon Island in Quincy Bay," 226
1807: "Comments on Napoleon," 268–69, 270

Papers of John Adams: supplements *Adams Family Correspondence*, xxvii, xxix

ADAMS, JOHN, 2D (1803–1834, son of JQA and LCA, designated as JA2 in *The Adams Papers*)

CHARACTER, APPEARANCE, HABITS, DOMESTIC LIFE

AHA and TBA and, 69, 103, 112, 125, 171, 284; GWA and, 64, 86; appearance of, 151, 156, 164, 253; baptism of, 247; church attendance, 185, 206, 280; clothing for, 69, 75; Mary Cranch cares for, 280, 282–83, 284, 288, 290; education of, 86, 203, 209, 218, 239, 280, 311; foreign language skills of, 205, 207, 209, 212, 215, 234, 237; health of, 22, 51, 52, 57, 59, 64, 69, 75, 104, 111, 122, 124, 140, 155, 200, 254, 267, 282–83, 347, 351, 371, 372, 384, 385, 390, 393, 400, 410, 414, 416; letter writing of, 74, 237, 238; marriage of, 211; Elizabeth Norton and, 288; residences of, 1, 158, 165, 246, 268; Louisa Smith and, 69; travels of, 52, 124–25, 281

RELATIONSHIP WITH AA AND JA

AA cares for, xiii, 37, 69, 85, 86, 92, 103, 111, 119, 122, 124, 131, 155, 222, 232, 235, 273, 280, 283, 372, 380, 408, 437; AA on, 16–17, 18, 29, 64, 69, 75, 85–86, 92, 131, 288, 349; JA and, xiii, 8, 77, 101, 151, 229; visits AA and JA, xvi, 215, 252, 266, 295, 355, 356, 371, 424, 425, 435

RELATIONSHIP WITH PARENTS

on JQA, 239; JQA on, 29, 156, 181; JQA's concern and affection for, 67, 85, 96, 104, 185, 218, 242, 244, 251, 263, 290, 396; LCA on, 29, 209, 253; LCA's concern and affection for, 72, 93, 168, 282–83, 287, 290, 307, 403; separation from parents, xiii, xix, 62, 64, 72, 74, 75, 92, 96, 107, 108, 125, 148, 151–52, 154–55, 160, 164, 165, 173, 175, 176, 178, 179, 183, 186, 187, 193, 239, 252, 259–60, 265, 280, 290, 437, 438

ADAMS, JOHN QUINCY (1767–1848, son of AA and JA, designated as JQA in *The Adams Papers*)

BOOKS AND READING

Joel Barlow, 234, 261; Bible, 259, 417; Alden Bradford, 41; Mathew Carey, 199; Earl of Ches-

ADAMS, JOHN QUINCY (*continued*)
terfield, 228; Cicero, 194; devotion to, 55–56; John Gardner, 312; Thomas Gray, 176; Homer, 182, 257; library at MQA, 193, 230–31; James Madison, 94; John Marshall Sr., 79, 80; John Mason, 199; Comte de Mirabeau, 225, 227; Mary Pierrepont Wortley Montagu, 23, 24; *Monthly Anthology*, 78–79, 115, 136, 261, 316, 317, 323, 331; newspapers, 176, 207, 214, 225–26, 246, 252, 256, 291, 292–93, 327, 328, 329, 332, 361, 412, 435; Blaise Pascal, 113; Giovanni Battista Piranesi, 62; poetry, 412; purchases books, 24, 199, 213, 219, 223; Joseph Sarfati, 226, 227; Shakespeare, 208, 225; James Stephen, 115; Tacitus, 78, 88, 90; John Wolcot, 291

CHARACTER, APPEARANCE, HABITS, DOMESTIC LIFE

appearance and clothing of, 19, 130, 193, 202, 284, 289, 396–97; church attendance, 62, 63, 137, 185, 242, 246, 247, 370, 380, 413, 414, 417; education of, 169, 187, 370; exchanges publications with William Smith Shaw, 1, 4, 5, 6, 41, 78, 80, 82, 104, 115, 136, 201, 246, 261, 349, 361; family visits to and by, 146, 284, 417; foreign language skills of, 182, 196, 234; godparent to C. Whitcomb, 159; health of, xiii, 13, 18–19, 20, 29–30, 36, 37, 43, 46, 72, 87, 99, 107, 108, 111, 127–28, 131, 136–37, 224, 244, 260, 262, 284, 287, 289, 290, 395, 399, 402, 417; Johnson family and, 58, 59, 149, 151, 155, 166, 215, 224, 227–28, 237, 240, 242, 251, 395, 404, 417; letter writing of, xx, 14, 22, 113, 163, 182, 206, 213, 223, 224, 242, 243, 311, 332, 339, 359; Elizabeth Peabody on, 298, 301, 344, 367, 388, 438; religious beliefs of, 171–72, 181, 292, 416; romantic relationships of, 237, 238; seal of, 397; servants of, 23, 27, 28, 37, 187, 193, 194, 241, 255, 267; John Adams Smith and, 139, 141, 142, 162–63, 166, 184, 185–86, 203, 254; WSS seeks assistance from, 130, 133, 139, 141, 142, 184; temperament of, 14, 15, 20, 228, 311, 313, 338, 344

FINANCES AND PROPERTY

accounts of, 58, 59, 149, 151, 205, 225, 226, 241, 242, 312, 320, 321, 349, 354, 355, 393; TBA as agent for, 225, 249, 291, 292, 294, 295, 342, 354, 393; Bird, Savage, & Bird failure and, 321; church pew purchases, 27, 206, 207, 211, 239, 241, 246, 247; investments of, 67, 68, 135–36, 321, 393; property and farmland arrangements of, 205, 210, 211, 225, 240–41, 297; property purchased by, 158, 161–62, 163, 167, 169, 321; property sold by, 161–62, 163, 168, 175, 291, 292, 294; rental properties of, 41, 79, 135, 136, 161, 211, 212, 232, 237, 238, 241, 249–50, 267, 268, 292, 295, 297, 349, 350, 354, 378–79, 410, 414; William Smith Shaw as agent for, 6, 41, 67, 79, 80, 82, 95, 106, 135–36, 150, 210, 211, 239, 241, 245, 246, 267, 282, 312, 320, 321, 342, 349, 350, 354, 361, 378–79

LETTERS

Letters: To AA (1804), 22; (1805), 61, 70; (1806), 96, 127, 187, 193; (1807), 243, 252, 281, 283; (1808), 324, 359; To JA (1804), 1; (1805), 30; (1806), 88, 181; (1808), 311; To LCA (1806), 145, 149, 156, 160, 166, 169, 175, 180, 184, 201, 204, 207, 210, 212, 217; (1807), 219, 227, 233, 240, 250, 255, 262; (1809), 394, 396, 400, 411, 414, 416; To TBA (1804), 10, 12; (1805), 54, 65; (1806), 81, 93, 104, 113; (1807), 223, 291; (1808), 312, 326; To Walter Hellen (1805), 58; To Catherine Nuth Johnson (1807), 279 (2); To William Smith Shaw (1805), 41, 78; (1806), 135, 199; (1807), 245, 261; (1808), 361; To WSS (1806), 133, 141; To William Steuben Smith (1809), 436

Letters: From AA (1804), 9, 16, 20, 28; (1805), 47, 64, 68, 73; (1806), 85, 107, 124, 184; (1807), 235, 266, 280; (1808), 317, 350; (1809), 393, 408, 434, 438; From JA (1804), 6, 7, 14; (1805), 33, 37, 76; (1806), 99, 122; (1807), 229; (1808), 320, 356; From LCA (1806), 147, 164, 165, 173, 177, 178, 182, 186, 190, 205, 208, 211, 213, 214; (1807), 222, 231, 236, 238, 253, 264, 267; (1809), 393, 399, 402, 403, 410; From TBA (1804), 25; (1806), 140; (1807), 248, 284, 294; (1808), 308, 321, 339, 351; (1809), 404; From Elizabeth Smith Shaw Peabody (1808), 297; From William Smith Shaw (1804), 4; (1808), 349; From WSS (1806), 130, 139; From William Steuben Smith (1809), 435

Letters to, from, omitted: To AA listed (1804), 442; (1805), 443, 444 (2); (1809), 450; To JA listed (1804), 442 (4); (1805), 443 (4); (1806), 444 (2); (1807), 446, 447 (3); (1808), 448; To LCA listed (1806), 444, 445 (9), 446 (5); (1807), 446 (5), 447 (4); (1809), 449 (5); To TBA listed (1804), 442 (2); (1805), 443, 444; (1806), 444; (1807), 446, 447; (1808), 448; To Walter Hellen listed (1805), 443; To William Smith Shaw listed (1804), 442 (3); (1806), 444 (2), 445 (2); (1807), 447 (4); (1808), 448 (3); To William Steuben Smith listed (1809), 450; From AA listed (1806), 444 (2); (1807), 446; (1808), 449; (1809), 450; From JA listed (1804), 442 (6); (1805), 443 (2); (1806), 444; (1807), 447 (3); (1808), 448 (5); (1809), 450 (2); From LCA listed (1806),

Index

ADAMS, JOHN QUINCY (*continued*)
444, 445 (6), 446; (1807), 446 (4), 447; (1809), 449 (2); From TBA listed (1804), 442 (2); (1806), 446; (1808), 448; From William Smith Shaw listed (1805), 443; From WSS listed (1807), 447

OPINIONS AND BELIEFS

Europe: British government and politics, 93–94, 337, 350; European war, 93–94, 122, 129, 225–26, 227, 256, 260, 337

Individuals: MCHA, 228; J. Bayard, 91; J. Bowdoin Jr., 28; J. Boyd, 229, 242; A. Burr, 31, 55, 57, 243, 253; Marianne Caton, 413; S. Cleverly, 241; Anna Cranch, 284; P. Derbigny, 23; J. Destréhan, 23; W. Emerson, 241, 246; W. Giles, 31–32, 91; P. Grant, 157; T. Jefferson, 261, 337; S. Keene, 241–42; Meriwether Lewis, 219, 234, 261; J. Lloyd Jr., 370; Queen Louise, 256; J. Madison, 337; S. Mitchill, 56; P. Morton, 28; J. Payplat, 56; O. Pollard, 56; E. Preble, 55; J. Randolph, 225, 291; P. Sauvé, 23; Earl of Selkirk, 150; John Adams Smith, 142; S. S. Smith, 63; William Smith, 41; WSS, 146, 202–203, 244; William Steuben Smith, xxi, 202; J. Story, 113; B. Thruston, 80; U. Tracy, 70; L. Turreau de Garambouville, 24, 32; G. Wythe, 176

United States: Congress, 41, 57, 72, 79, 81, 87, 90, 91, 106, 128, 218, 225, 252, 261, 281, 284, 311, 315, 398; Constitution, 324; Embargo Act (1807), 296, 337–38, 349–50, 360; Federalist Party, 313, 328–29, 360, 361; foreign influence on, 356, 357; Jefferson administration, 204–205, 243, 281, 314, 331, 337, 343; literary culture, 331; J. Madison inaugural address, 411; Massachusetts government and politics, 5, 12, 170; military preparedness, 98; Native Americans, 82, 87, 91, 219; New England, 96–97, 104; Non-Importation Act (1806), 292; Non-Intercourse Act (1809), 412; political caucuses and conventions, 324–25; political divisions in, 65–66, 357, 395; presidential election (1808), 128, 329, 330–31; Quincy, 224; Southern states, 96–97, 284; U.S. judiciary, 57, 326–27; U.S. Navy, 79, 81; U.S. relations with Britain, 81, 87, 90, 93–94, 97–98, 106, 113, 115, 292, 311, 316, 337, 338, 343, 350, 355, 357, 417; U.S. relations with France, 113, 311, 355, 357; U.S. relations with Spain, ix, 62, 81, 87, 97, 134

Miscellaneous: boardinghouses, 176–77; courtship and marriage, 163; gender, 23, 180; law of nations, 2–3; Miranda expedition, xxi, 128–29, 134, 142, 202; oratory, 171–72, 392; poetry, 412; post offices, 184; race, 82; social class, xxv, 65–66, 94–95, 96; women, 94–95, 96, 326

PUBLIC LIFE

Law Career: JQA's attitude toward, 167, 311; appears before U.S. Circuit Court, 169; appears before U.S. Supreme Court, 390–91, 392, 397, 400–402, 404, 409, 411, 413, 414, 416, 418; Boston law practice, 180, 181, 404, 407; students of, 162, 410; studies for, 212

Diplomacy, 1796, Minister Plenipotentiary to Portugal: reassignment to Prussia, 371

Diplomacy, 1797–1801, Minister Plenipotentiary to Prussia: Anglo-American relations and, 338, 339; appointment as, 5, 371

Massachusetts Senate, 1802–1803: Boston Bank and, 356, 357

U.S. Senate, 1803–1808: JQA's attitude toward, xii, xxvi, 30–31, 32, 78, 93, 111, 128, 167, 223–24, 245, 257, 258, 264, 308, 311, 313, 325, 359; aid sought from, 79, 80; anti-impressment bill and, 99; attends Democratic-Republican caucus, xxvi, 308, 314, 316, 317–18, 320, 322, 323, 324, 327–29, 332, 336, 337, 350, 359; attends House debates, 262, 332; *Chesapeake-Leopard* Affair and, xii, xxiv, 276, 278, 292, 293, 316, 327; committee work of, 88, 91, 104–105, 106, 107, 141, 245, 262, 296, 310, 315, 316–17, 326, 327, 359, 364, 373; Democratic-Republican Party and, xxiii–xxiv, xxv, 369, 427; diplomatic immunity and, 114, 116, 123–24, 129; drafts legislation, 105, 114, 115, 123, 129; Embargo Act (1807) and, xii, xv–xvi, xxiv–xxv, 296, 309, 310, 312, 313, 316–17, 337, 340–41, 342, 343, 349–50, 353, 361, 364; expulsion of John Smith and, 308–309, 310, 313, 316, 317, 324, 359–60, 362, 364; Federalist Party and, xii, xxiii, xxiv, xxv, xxvi, xxix, 307, 308, 328, 337, 354, 359, 360, 361, 369, 376, 427; franking privileges of, 41, 252, 261, 291, 296; habeas corpus bill and, 245, 253, 254; infrastructure and, 234, 240, 247; interdiction of foreign ships and, 313, 316; judicial reform and, 261, 262, 318, 319, 320, 325–26; Library of Congress and, 199, 213, 219, 223; military preparedness and, 99, 253, 254, 364; newspapers and, xxv, 291, 292, 293, 310, 312–13, 316, 317, 318, 323, 324, 325, 327, 328, 332, 361, 362, 364, 376; Non-Importation Act (1806) and, xxiv, 93, 95, 253, 254; Northwest Territory governance and, 106; petitions to Congress and, 84, 85, 105, 106, 291–92, 293; Pickering-Sullivan exchange and, 343, 350, 360, 433; public attitudes toward, 276, 292, 301, 302, 307, 308–309, 310, 312–14, 316, 318, 319, 320–21, 322, 323, 327, 331, 337, 338, 340, 341, 353, 359, 361, 367, 369, 371, 373, 376, 377, 388, 427; Senate publications and, 308–309, 310, 316, 323, 324, 331, 342, 362, 364; service in, xii, xv–xvi, xxv, 161, 181, 311,

ADAMS, JOHN QUINCY (*continued*)
367, 368–69, 370, 373, 388, 433; slavery and, 245, 262; territorial expansion and, ix, xxiv, 106, 317; U.S. relations with Barbary States and, 82, 85, 106, 107, 141, 317, 427; U.S. relations with Britain and, xxiii–xxiv, 91, 105, 106–107, 114, 115, 124; U.S. relations with France and, 124; U.S. relations with Haiti and, 113–14

Harvard Boylston Professor, 1806–1809: JQA's attitude toward, 181, 224–25, 311; appointment and installation of, xx, 65, 150, 152, 156, 164, 166, 168, 169, 170, 171–72, 182, 251; lectures by, xx, 78, 172, 182, 188, 190, 194; preparations for, 177, 182, 184, 185, 187, 223; public attitudes toward, 172, 188, 309, 313, 316, 331

Diplomacy, 1809–1814, Minister Plenipotentiary to Russia: JQA's attitude toward, 415; commission for, xx, xxvii, 435; nomination and appointment as, 413, 414–15, 416, 435; William Steuben Smith as secretary for, xxii, 435, 436, 437

Secretary of State, 1817–1825: negotiates Adams-Onís Treaty, ix

Miscellaneous: JQA's attitude toward, 234, 325; American Academy of Arts and Sciences and, 193, 194; rumored appointments for, 402, 403, 409, 410, 426, 427; T. Jefferson and, xi, 2–3, 81–82, 84, 218, 219, 255–56, 260, 397, 398, 402, 411–12; patronage appeals to, 130, 133, 310–11, 348, 351; 407, 408, 435, 436; public attitudes toward, 252, 395, 402, 410; scientific studies of, 79, 80, 81, 85, 94, 96, 98, 105–106, 149, 150–51, 170–71, 172, 175–76; as possible vice presidential candidate, 309, 310, 314–15, 316, 322, 377; G. Washington and, 371, 425

RELATIONSHIP WITH LCA
on LCA, 218; LCA advises and assists, 149, 162–63, 166, 168, 205, 206, 214–15, 227–28, 232, 233, 234, 236, 240, 241, 242, 253, 410; LCA and birthday of, 186; LCA and career of, 415, 437; LCA and correspondence of, 398, 403; LCA on, 164, 187, 206, 255, 307; LCA on public service of, xix–xx, xxiv, 13, 173–74, 253, 307, 308, 402, 410; LCA's birthday and, 255, 256–60, 261, 267, 400, 401; LCA's concern and affection for, 13, 72, 88, 148, 155, 182, 186, 214, 222, 264, 399; LCA's correspondence and, 19, 76, 227, 252; LCA's dower rights and, 161–62, 163, 167; on LCA's letter writing, 208, 213–14, 226; advises and assists LCA, 149, 172, 242; concern and affection for LCA, 24, 146–47, 152, 166, 169–70, 180, 203, 204, 217, 224, 228, 241, 260, 400; correspondence with LCA, xix, 150, 152, 157, 159, 163, 165–66, 168, 172, 177, 181, 182, 185, 187, 191, 193, 194, 206, 215, 218, 224, 226, 228, 229, 234, 237, 242, 246, 251, 252, 260, 397, 398, 401, 402–403, 404, 408, 412, 418; exchanges goods with LCA, 150, 157, 163, 165, 168, 171, 206, 207, 209, 219; marriage, 154, 237, 247; separation from LCA, xiii, xix, 140, 142, 147, 155, 164, 168, 173–74, 176, 178, 183, 186, 191, 205, 208, 209–10, 212–13, 214, 253–54, 256, 259–60, 265, 267, 395, 413

RELATIONSHIP WITH CHILDREN
on CFA, 281; CFA's resemblance to, 287; on GWA, 22–23, 156, 181, 344; on JA2, 29, 156, 181; JA2 on, 239; JA2's resemblance to, 164; birth of CFA, 279; birth of stillborn son, 180, 181; children and career of, 155, 437, 438; concern and affection for children, 67, 70, 84, 85, 87, 96, 104, 185, 218, 224, 234, 237, 242, 244, 251, 263, 290, 297, 298, 311, 396, 397, 400, 403, 404; correspondence with JA2, 237; education of children and, 165, 205, 207; separation from children, xii–xiii, 62, 64, 74, 86, 96, 107, 108, 125, 151–52, 160, 165, 168, 175, 176, 187, 193, 222, 239, 252, 259–60, 265, 280, 344, 366, 437, 438

RELATIONSHIP WITH PARENTS
AA advises and assists, xvi–xvii, 10, 20, 36, 37, 71, 85, 86, 87, 93, 108, 130, 187, 193, 361, 393, 435; AA and correspondence of, 224, 337–38, 339, 343; AA on, xviii, 18–19, 20, 289, 319, 338, 369, 373, 376, 437; AA on public service of, xxvi, 317–18, 324, 336, 350, 362, 364, 368–69, 373, 409, 436–37; AA's concern and affection for, xxvii, 76, 107, 111, 131, 184, 438; JA advises and assists, 34, 196, 311, 312, 320, 435; JA and correspondence of, 82, 182, 183, 281, 282, 332, 378, 408; JA on, 8–9, 14, 312; JA on public service of, xix–xx, xxvi, 33, 40, 253, 254, 312, 320–21, 350, 371, 402; JA's correspondence and, 187; JA's legacy and, xxv, 316, 425; as agent for parents, 22, 48, 67, 68, 252, 253, 351, 360, 425; concern and affection for parents, 12, 15, 67; correspondence with AA, xxvi, xxvii, 17, 18, 21, 24, 30, 31, 36, 37, 63, 65, 69, 72, 74, 84, 86, 87, 104, 108, 122, 128, 130, 185, 240, 267, 284, 312, 320, 321, 324, 336, 339, 416, 425; correspondence with JA, xxvi, xxvii, 3, 9, 10, 11, 12, 13, 15, 17, 18, 20, 21, 31, 32, 34, 40, 54, 57, 78, 91, 108, 109, 116, 124, 128, 136, 224, 226, 230, 236, 243, 245, 254, 281, 282, 287, 312, 326, 332, 357, 360, 408, 425, 441; encourages JA to write autobiography, 14, 15, 32; parents' influence on, xxiv, 325, 359; parents seek advice and assistance of, 123, 236, 252–53, 266, 348; purchases property from JA, 312, 320, 321, 349; sends publications to JA, 37, 67, 88, 98, 99, 105, 116, 224, 229, 246, 291, 293, 295; separation from parents, 7, 19, 67, 425, 438; visits with parents, 166, 368, 380, 435

Index

ADAMS, JOHN QUINCY (*continued*)

RELATIONSHIP WITH SIBLINGS

AA2: on AA2, 202; AA2 on, 336; assists AA2, 162, 184; concern for AA2, 146, 202, 244; correspondence with AA2, 186; visits with AA2, 3, 52, 56, 133, 142, 145–46, 147, 152, 201, 272

TBA: on TBA, 15, 94; TBA advises, xxvi, 340, 341; TBA and correspondence of, 213, 319; TBA and publication of writings of, 5, 341; TBA on, 25–26, 188, 309, 322, 353, 354, 402; advises and assists TBA, xviii, xxv, 25, 82, 86, 87, 104, 141, 407; birth of TBA's children and, xi, 226, 326; correspondence with TBA, xi, xxvi, 7, 27, 68, 69, 70, 71, 73, 74, 79, 81, 88, 91, 95, 96, 108, 115, 141, 229, 236, 240, 242, 243, 245, 246, 247, 249, 250, 253, 292, 316, 324, 341, 342, 355, 360; exchanges publications with TBA, 10, 25, 95, 96, 104, 113, 224, 248, 252, 253, 329, 351, 355

RESIDENCES

in Boston, xvi, 161, 165, 166, 167, 170, 175, 176–77, 241, 246, 272, 348, 361, 388, 404; in Cambridge, 64, 65, 71, 73, 82, 86, 95, 96, 108, 146, 150, 156, 158, 161, 166, 170, 174, 175, 176, 177, 180, 181, 182, 186, 187, 370; in Europe, 20; in Quincy, 23, 29, 30, 48, 58, 158, 165, 186, 190, 291; in Washington, D.C., 1, 3, 65, 74, 76, 111, 137, 140, 147, 161, 244, 266

SOCIAL LIFE

attends Fourth of July celebrations, 185, 370, 435; attends Harvard presidential installation, 149–50, 152; attends J. Madison inauguration, 411; aversion to, 24, 256; in Boston, 150, 152, 156, 157, 167, 240; in Europe, 28, 256, 260, 339, 396; in Newburyport, 212; in New York, 56, 57, 62, 63; in Philadelphia, 55, 56, 57, 66, 67, 203, 394, 396, 407; visits to and by, 1–2, 11, 62, 63, 137, 145, 156, 244, 245, 395, 396, 397, 398, 407, 413; in Washington, D.C., xi, 11, 23, 24, 63, 78, 81–82, 84, 210, 211, 212, 218, 219, 233, 241–42, 245, 255–56, 260, 335, 401, 402, 415

TRAVELS

to Boston (1806), 175, 199; to Boston (1807), 241, 244, 252, 253, 256, 264, 267–68; to Boston (1808), 342, 361, 364, 368; to Boston (1809), 401, 402, 410, 411, 413, 414, 415, 416, 418; to Quincy (1805), 51, 52, 54, 56; to Quincy (1806), 141, 142, 145–46, 147, 149, 152, 159; to Silesia (1800), 5; U.S. to Europe (1778), 9, 229, 231; U.S. to Russia (1809), 436–37; to Washington, D.C. (1803), 247; to Washington, D.C. (1804), 1, 3, 4, 19; to Washington, D.C. (1805), 61–62, 63, 64, 65, 67, 69, 70, 72, 73, 75; to Washington, D.C. (1806), 167, 201, 202, 203, 204, 206, 207, 244; to Washington, D.C. (1807), 272, 280, 281, 282, 283, 284; to Washington, D.C. (1809), 390–91, 392, 393, 394–95, 396, 397, 399, 400, 402, 404, 408, 409

WRITINGS

Diary: on books and reading, 24; on A. Burr, 7; digital publication of, xxviii; on Harvard lecture preparation, 172; on House debates, 332; on Native Americans, xi; on science and scientific studies, 57, 149, 150, 158, 159; on Senate service, xii, 308, 370; on stillborn son, 181; on travel companions, 207

Published: correspondence in newspapers, 341, 343, 350, 361

1804: *Letters on Silesia*, 5, 6; Publius Valerius in *Boston Repertory*, 4, 5

1806: *Inaugural Oration . . . as Boylston Professor of Rhetorick and Oratory*, 182

1807: *Monthly Anthology*, "On the Discoveries of Captain Lewis," 234, 261; "Lines, Addressed to a Mother" ("To Mrs: Hellen"), 233, 234, 238, 239

1808: *Letter . . . to the Hon. Harrison Gray Otis*, 349–50, 351, 353, 354, 356, 360, 361, 362, 364, 376, 433

1810: *Lectures on Rhetoric*, 172

Unpublished:

1806: "On the Instability of National Greatness," 184, 185–86; "The Misfortune," 95, 96

1807: "Lines, To Miss In Full Un-dress at a Ball," 252, 255; "A Winter's Day. To Louisa.," 255, 256–60, 261, 267

Papers of John Quincy Adams: supplements *Adams Family Correspondence*, xxvii

Adams, Joseph (b. 1730, cousin of JA, of Green, Maine): letter to JA listed (1809), 450

ADAMS, LOUISA CATHERINE JOHNSON (1775–1852, wife of JQA, designated as LCA in *The Adams Papers*)

BOOKS AND READING

Bible, 239; Lewis Goldsmith, 183, 184; newspapers, 403; *Port Folio*, 207; publications sent to, 232; Sappho, 267

CHARACTER, APPEARANCE, HABITS

appearance of, 265; grief of, 178, 182, 183, 186, 214; health of, 62, 65, 84, 177, 178, 180, 187, 209, 212, 215, 217, 222, 224, 228, 279, 289, 312, 316, 409, 416; interest of in politics, 237, 263; letter writing of, xix, 159–60, 169, 173, 180, 191, 208, 213–14, 215, 218, 222, 226, 235, 240,

471

ADAMS, LOUISA CATHERINE JOHNSON (*continued*)
255, 267, 279, 307, 359, 360, 400; pregnancy and loss of, xix, 128, 140, 141, 142, 155, 163, 164, 165–66, 169–70, 173, 174, 175, 181, 184, 186, 204, 214, 399, 400, 402, 404, 408; religious beliefs of, 211–12; temperament of, 154

DOMESTIC LIFE

AHA assists, 140, 143, 149, 279; ECA's birth and, 326; TBA and, 198, 265, 295, 324, 342, 402, 438; church attendance, 206, 232, 380; correspondence with AHA, 115; Mary Cranch and, 65, 154, 160, 282; domestic work of, 155; family visits to and by, 52, 190, 191, 193, 272, 394, 399, 404; godparent to C. Whitcomb, 159; horse for, 58, 59; house fire and, 211–12, 217–18; household management by, xx, 43, 143, 149, 241; pets of, 191; relationship with AA2, 147–48, 185, 190, 191, 193, 254, 279, 287, 307; relationship with parents and siblings, 42, 206, 214, 219, 227, 229, 232, 239, 240, 278, 287, 290, 410; servants of, 23, 36, 37, 43, 46, 183, 206, 207, 222, 241, 253, 255, 267, 404; William Smith Shaw as agent for, 191

LETTERS

Letters: To AA (1804), 13; (1805), 42, 51, 72; (1806), 154; (1807), 286; (1808), 306, 370; To JQA (1806), 147, 164, 165, 173, 177, 178, 182, 186, 190, 205, 208, 211, 213, 214; (1807), 222, 231, 236, 238, 253, 264, 267; (1809), 393, 399, 402, 403, 410; To Mary Smith Cranch (1806), 159; (1807), 282, 290

Letters: From AA (1804), 18; (1805), 36, 46, 68, 75; (1806), 92, 110; (1807), 280, 288; (1808), 347; From GWA (1806), 156, 160; From JQA (1806), 145, 149, 156, 160, 166, 169, 175, 180, 184, 201, 204, 207, 210, 212, 217; (1807), 219, 223, 227, 240, 250, 255, 262; (1809), 394, 396, 400, 411, 414, 416; From Thomas Jefferson (1807), 278; From Elizabeth Smith Shaw Peabody (1808), 343

Letters to, from, omitted: To AA listed (1804), 442; (1805), 443; (1806), 444; To JQA listed (1806), 444, 445 (6), 446; (1807), 446 (4), 447; (1809), 449 (2); To Dolley Payne Todd Madison listed (1809), 450; From JQA listed (1806), 444, 445 (9), 446 (5); (1807), 446 (5), 447 (4); (1809), 449 (5)

OPINIONS AND BELIEFS

Individuals: AA2, 190; Abigail Smith Adams, 253; G. Boyd, 52; Joseph Bradford, 267; S. Cleverly, 206, 222; William Cranch, 160; W. Duer, 190–91; M. Foster, 410; H. Innes, 254; L. Lincoln, 254; A. Pichon, 265; L. Pichon, 265; W. Pickman, 212; J. Quincy III, 264; Daniel Sargent, 237; WSS, 147; J. Sullivan, 254; W. Thornton, 243; S. White, 44

United States: Fourth of July celebrations, 370; presidential election (1808), 306–307; U.S. relations with Britain, 290, 306; Washington, D.C., 43, 286

Miscellaneous: gender, 174, 215

RELATIONSHIP WITH AA AND JA

on AA, 399; AA advises and assists, xix–xx, 13, 30, 36, 37, 46, 65, 92, 143, 144, 348; on JA, 253; advises AA and JA, 93, 402; correspondence with AA, xii, xiii, xxiv, 37, 65, 88, 93, 160, 289, 307, 351, 359, 360; relationship with AA, 10, 126, 154–55, 239, 253, 408; visits with AA and JA, 206, 214, 229–30, 249, 253, 260, 266, 370–71, 394, 403, 438

RELATIONSHIP WITH JQA

on JQA, 164, 187, 206, 255, 307; JQA advises and assists, 149, 172, 242; JQA and birthday of, 255, 256–60, 261, 267, 400, 401; JQA and correspondence of, 19, 76, 227, 252; JQA on, 218; JQA's birthday and, 186; JQA's career and, 415, 438; JQA's concern and affection for, 24, 146–47, 152, 166, 169–70, 180, 203, 204, 217, 224, 228, 241, 260, 400; JQA's correspondence and, 398, 403; on JQA's public service, xix–xx, xxiv, 13, 173–74, 253, 307, 308, 402, 410; advises and assists JQA, 149, 150–51, 158, 159, 162–63, 166, 168, 205, 206, 207, 214–15, 227–28, 232, 233, 234, 236, 239, 240, 241, 242, 246, 253, 410; concern and affection for JQA, 13, 72, 88, 148, 155, 182, 186, 214, 222, 264, 399; correspondence with JQA, xix, 150, 152, 157, 159, 163, 165–66, 168, 172, 177, 181, 182, 185, 187, 191, 193, 194, 206, 215, 218, 224, 226, 228, 229, 234, 237, 242, 246, 251, 252, 260, 397, 398, 401, 402–403, 404, 408, 412, 418; exchanges goods with JQA, 150, 157, 163, 165, 168, 171, 206, 207, 209, 219; marriage, 154, 237, 247; sale of JQA's property and, 161–62, 163, 167, 168, 169, 175; separation from JQA, xiii, xix, 140, 142, 147, 155, 164, 168, 173–74, 176, 178, 183, 186, 191, 205, 208, 209–10, 212–13, 214, 253–54, 256, 259–60, 265, 267, 395, 413

RELATIONSHIP WITH CHILDREN

on CFA, 290; on GWA, 155, 174, 205, 209, 403; GWA's and JA2's resemblance to, 156, 164; on JA2, 29, 209, 253; JA2 and correspondence of, 237, 238; birth of CFA, xix, 279; concern and affection for children, 65, 72, 93, 168, 282–83, 290, 403; education of children and, 203, 205, 209, 222, 239, 298; separation from chil-

Index

ADAMS, LOUISA CATHERINE JOHNSON (*continued*)
dren, xii–xiii, xix, 62, 64, 72, 75–76, 86, 92, 107, 108, 148, 151, 154–55, 158, 160, 173, 178, 179, 183, 186, 280, 286, 344, 366, 438

RESIDENCES

in Boston, xvi, 161, 167, 203, 209, 210, 211, 212, 230, 235, 239, 241, 242, 246, 249, 268, 348, 361, 404, 414; in Quincy, 30, 43, 47, 58, 165, 186, 190; in Washington, D.C., 1, 3, 65, 111, 128, 141, 142, 147, 160, 161

SOCIAL LIFE

in Europe, 256, 260, 339, 396; in Massachusetts, xx, 61, 208, 209, 211, 212, 236–37, 238, 265, 402, 410; in Philadelphia, 56, 57; visits to and by, 72, 179, 206, 208, 232, 284, 290, 402, 403, 410, 414; in Washington, D.C., 43, 72, 81–82, 84, 178, 251, 256, 335

TRAVELS

to Boston (1806), 177–78, 179, 180–81, 182–83, 185, 187, 190, 191, 193, 203, 204; to Quincy (1805), 51, 52, 54, 155; U.S. to Russia (1809), 436–37; to Washington, D.C. (1805), 61–62, 63, 64, 69, 70, 72, 73, 75; to Washington, D.C. (1807), 280, 282, 288

WRITINGS

Diary and Autobiographical Writings, xxix

Adams, Micajah (Adams cousin), 187, 193; identified, 194
Adams, Micajah Newell (son of Micajah, Adams servant), 37, 187; identified, 194
Adams, Phineas (Boston schoolteacher), 80
Adams, Samuel (1722–1803, 2d cousin of JA), 411
Adams, Sarah Smith (Sally, 1769–1828, wife of CA, designated as SSA in *The Adams Papers*): AA advises and assists, xvii, 118, 143, 302, 304; AA on, 380, 390; correspondence with AA, 375, 378; correspondence with Susanna Adams, 302, 372–73; health of, 379, 381, 384, 385, 407; romantic relationships of, xvii, 373, 374, 375, 390, 391; M. de St. Hilaire and, 427; visits with Adamses, 146, 373, 375, 379, 381, 384
Letters: From AA (1806), 118; (1808), 302
Adams, Susanna Boylston (1796–1884, daughter of CA and SSA): AA advises and assists, 119, 377–78; AA on, 103, 273, 304, 305, 373, 375, 381–82, 390; JA and education of, 304; books and reading, 382; correspondence with SSA, 302, 372–73; correspondence with Caroline Smith, 339, 363–64, 367, 374, 375, 377; domestic work of, 111, 271, 274; social activities of, 363, 378, 381–82, 384–85, 390; mentioned, 112, 200, 289, 389
Letter: From AA (1808), 377
Adams, Susanna Boylston (b. 1808, daughter of Boylston), 363, 364

ADAMS, THOMAS BOYLSTON (1772–1832, son of AA and JA, designated as TBA in *The Adams Papers*)

BOOKS AND READING

Bible, 294, 407; Nathaniel Chapman, 191–93; William Cobbett, 308; congressional publications, 352; William Cranch, 26; Richard Cumberland, 196; law library of, 421; *Monthly Anthology*, 323; Thomas Moore, 195, 196; newspapers, 113, 248, 249, 285–86, 295, 309, 322, 323, 341, 354; *Port Folio*, 26; publications sent to, 195, 407; purchases books, 407; Shakespeare, 25, 248, 249; John Wolcot, 295; John Wood, 248

CHARACTER, APPEARANCE, HABITS, DOMESTIC LIFE

LCA and, 198, 265, 295, 324, 342, 402, 438; appearance and clothing of, 112, 192; church attendance, 354; correspondence with S. Ewing, 2, 3; family visits to and by, 206, 284, 394, 399, 404, 438; finances and property of, 67, 68, 225, 226–27, 341; foreign language skills of, 196; health of, 17, 19, 30; letter writing of, xviii, 248, 308, 321; William Steuben Smith and, 285, 380

LETTERS

Letters: To JQA (1804), 25; (1806), 140; (1807), 248, 284, 294; (1808), 308, 321, 339, 351; (1809), 404; To Thomas Cadwalader (1806), 116; To William Meredith (1806), 188, 195; To William Smith Shaw (1805), 58; (1806), 191; To William Sullivan (1809), 421
Letters: From AA2 (1805), 59; From JQA (1804), 10, 12; (1805), 54, 65; (1806), 81, 93, 104, 113; (1807), 223, 291; (1808), 312, 326
Letters to, from, omitted: To JQA listed (1804), 442 (2); (1806), 446; (1808), 448; To Thomas Cadwalader listed (1806), 445; To Richard Cranch listed (1803), 441; (1808), 448; To William Meredith listed (1806), 445; To William Smith Shaw listed (1805), 443; From JA listed (1796), 441; From JQA listed (1804), 442 (2); (1805), 443, 444; (1806),

ADAMS, THOMAS BOYLSTON (*continued*) 444; (1807), 446, 447; (1808), 448; From Richard Cranch listed (1803), 441 (2)

OPINIONS AND BELIEFS

Individuals: GWA, 284–85; S. Dexter, 223; C. Gore, 340, 354; W. Gray, 406; T. Greenleaf Jr., 421; C. Harrod, 407; W. Jackson, 322; T. Jefferson, 26, 294; G. Meredith, 197; P. Morton, 26; William Smith Shaw, 342; William Steuben Smith, 295, 342; J. Sullivan, 340; G. Washington, 406

United States: A. Burr conspiracy, 248–49; Congress, 25–26, 294, 295, 308; Jefferson administration, xxvi, 352; Maine, 117; Massachusetts government and politics, 140–41, 285, 309, 340, 341, 353–54, 406; presidential election (1808), 323, 339–40; trade and commerce, 93, 352–53; U.S. judiciary, 26–27, 321–22, 326

Miscellaneous: education, 188, 196; taxes, 406–407

PUBLIC LIFE

Law Career: attends court, 48, 200, 201, 224, 294; cases of, xviii, 58, 122, 226, 285, 286; students of, 162, 421

Massachusetts General Court, 1805–1806: as candidate for senate, 85; election to house of representatives, xviii, 84–85; judicial reform and, 113, 115; service in, xv–xvi, 82, 84–85, 86, 87, 95, 103, 104, 116–17, 119, 141

Miscellaneous: addresses Phi Beta Kappa Society, 188, 190, 196–97, 198; as candidate for U.S. House of Representatives, xviii, 6, 7, 8, 12, 27; political activities of, 140–41, 322–23, 350–51, 353, 406; Quincy governance and, 108, 295

RELATIONSHIP WITH AHA

AHA and correspondence of, 197; correspondence with AHA, 53, 54; courtship and engagement, 30, 43, 44, 45, 47; marriage, x, xvi, xviii, 53, 54, 59, 60, 385

RELATIONSHIP WITH CHILDREN

on Abigail Smith Adams, x, 192, 197; birth of Abigail Smith Adams, 188, 190, 194; birth of ECA, 323–24, 326, 341

RELATIONSHIP WITH PARENTS

AA and correspondence of, 53; AA on, xviii, 437; as AA's agent, 58, 122; AA's correspondence and, 44, 47, 49, 53, 54, 64, 65, 109, 266; JA and correspondence of, 117, 190; JA on, 7, 8; JA's correspondence and, 38, 78, 266, 358; parents advise and assist, 196, 249

RELATIONSHIP WITH SIBLINGS

AA2 and, 59, 60; on JQA, 25–26, 188, 309, 322, 323, 339, 353, 354, 402; JQA advises and assists, xviii, xxv, 25, 82, 86, 87, 94, 104, 141, 407; JQA on, 15, 94; as JQA's agent, 225, 249, 291, 292, 294, 295, 342, 354, 393; JQA's correspondence and, 213, 319; JQA's patronage and, 342; JQA's scientific studies and, 81, 85, 94, 105–106, 151; advises JQA, xxvi, 340, 341; correspondence with JQA, xi, xxvi, 7, 27, 68, 69, 70, 71, 73, 74, 79, 81, 88, 91, 95, 96, 108, 115, 141, 229, 236, 240, 242, 243, 245, 246, 247, 249, 250, 253, 292, 316, 324, 341, 342, 355, 360; exchanges publications with JQA, 10, 25, 38, 95, 96, 104, 113, 224, 248, 252, 253, 329, 351, 355; publication of JQA's writings and, 5, 341, 360

RESIDENCES

in Philadelphia, 1, 3, 56, 57, 65, 66; in Quincy, xvi, xviii, 48, 226, 249–50, 291, 341–42

SOCIAL LIFE

at The Hague, 27, 28; in Philadelphia, 55, 65; in Quincy, 145, 239, 265; visits to and by, 8, 15, 32, 69, 108, 288

WRITINGS

ECA notates correspondence of, 332
Published:
1806: "Disquisition upon the Philosophy of the Ancients," 198

Adams Family Correspondence: editorial methods of, xxvii; letters omitted from, 441–50; publication of JQA's correspondence in, xxvii

Adams National Historical Park. *See* Old House

Adams Papers: digital catalog for, xxviii; mentioned, 37, 172, 343

Addison, Joseph: *Cato*, 39, 40, 270

Addison, Rev. Walter Dulany (of Georgetown, D.C.), 413, 417; identified, 414

Aesop: "The Boy Who Cried Wolf," 235; *Fables*, 119; "The Grasshopper and the Ant," 205, 206, 209

Africa, 205, 262, 374, 386

African Americans, 27, 28, 57, 177, 179. *See also* Slavery and enslaved persons

Agriculture: JA's love of, 76–77, 123, 124, 358; clearing and preparing land, 73, 76, 77, 90; dairying, 378; fruit trees, 121, 122, 144–45, 163, 363, 372, 390; grains and hay, 76, 295, 363, 371–72, 436; harvesting, 1, 436; livestock, 176, 200, 225, 236, 363; in Massachusetts, 339, 363, 378–79; in New York, 363; in

Index

U.S., 56, 100, 284, 349; use of manure in, 77; use of seaweed in, 224, 226
AHA. *See* ADAMS, ANN HARROD (1774–1845)
Akin, James (U.S. engraver): identified, ix; "The Prairie Dog Sickened at the Sting of the Hornet," ix, 83 (illus.)
Albany, N.Y., 207, 285, 302, 357, 422, 425
Albany Register, 433, 434
Alexander, James (New Orleans lawyer), 244; identified, 245
Alexander the Great, 320
Alexandria, Va.: merchants in, 171, 172; physicians in, 210; ships to and from, 19, 58, 106, 150, 152, 163, 168, 171, 204; mentioned, 203, 334
Alker, Mrs. (Boston nurse), 348, 349, 361
Allegheny Mountains, 245
Allen, Jeremiah (Boston sheriff), 167, 169, 409
Allen, Martha. *See* Strong, Martha Allen
Allen, Phineas (Pittsfield, Mass., printer), 39; identified, 40. See also *Sun*
Allibone, Thomas (Phila. merchant), 67, 68, 253, 351, 360
Amelia Peabody Charitable Fund, xxviii
American Academy of Arts and Sciences, 193, 194
American and Commercial Daily Advertiser (Baltimore), 183
American Citizen (N.Y.), 60
American Revolution: AA on, xxiii; JA and, 32, 276; battles of, 2, 91; French support for, 25, 90, 91, 135; histories of, xvii, 231, 276–77, 384, 385; legacies of, xxiii, 63, 216, 254, 383, 406, 435; service in, 176; WSS's role in, xxi; mentioned, 85, 291, 423, 425
Ames, Fisher (Mass. politician), 73, 74, 86–87, 95, 132; *Works*, 430
Amherst, N.H., 413
Amory, Thomas Coffin (Boston merchant), 150, 152, 157
Amsterdam, Netherlands, 358
Anacostia River, 98
Anderson, Joseph Inslee (Tenn. senator), 107, 398
Anishinaabe Nation, 80
Anne, Queen of England, 40
Antwerp, Belgium, 358
Apicius, M. Gavius (Roman gastronome), 55, 57
Apthorp, George Henry Ward (of Quincy), 73, 75
Arbuthnot, John, 14, 15
Aristotle, 198
Armstrong, John, Jr. (U.S. minister to France), 115–16, 262, 263, 294, 296, 331, 333

Army, U.S.: A. Burr conspiracy and, 240, 249; Congress and, 91, 332, 333, 342, 398, 401; expansion of, 230, 282; movements of, 244, 291; Native Americans and, xi; public attitudes toward, 368; service in, 3, 4, 332, 407, 408
Arnold, Elizabeth Briesler (wife of Joseph), 297
Arnold, Joseph (of Quincy), 297, 378–79
Art. *See* Paintings and prints; Sculpture
Artists: James Akin, ix, 83; Irwin John David Bevan, xii, 277 (illus.); Charles Balthazar Julien Févret de Saint-Mémin, xi, xii, xiii, 220 (illus.), 221 (illus.), 405; Gilbert Stuart, 17, 18, 22, 29, 30; Zeuxis, 428, 430. *See also* Paintings and prints; Sculpture
Aruba, 202
Asian languages, 74
Astronomy, 170–71, 172, 175–76, 386
Athens, Greece, 430
Atkinson, N.H.: Adamses visit, 265, 280, 286, 287, 378, 384–85, 438; Elizabeth Peabody's residence in, 143, 265, 347, 389
Atkinson Academy, 121, 280, 298, 299, 301, 387, 389
Atlantic Ocean, 164
Attorney General, U.S., 9, 10, 11, 207, 237, 238. *See also* Judiciary, U.S.
Auckland, William Eden, 1st Baron (Brit. statesman), 262–63
Augusta, Maine, 198
August Ferdinand, Prince of Prussia, 225; identified, 227
Augustus (U.S. ship), 296
Aurora General Advertiser (Phila.), 68
Austerlitz, Battle of, 124, 129–30, 227
Austin, Benjamin, Jr. (Honestus, Boston merchant), 32, 39, 223
Austin, Charles (son of Benjamin, Jr.), 223
Austria, 75, 227
Austrian Army, 74, 75, 129–30
Azuni, Domenico Alberto: *Maritime Law of Europe*, 358

Bache, Benjamin Franklin (Phila. printer), 39
Bacon, Ezekiel (Mass. representative), 398
Bacon, John (of Stockbridge, Mass.), 172
Bacon, Matthew: *New Abridgement of the Law*, 421
Baker, Ebenezer (Boston merchant), 144
Baltimore, Md.: Adamses travel through, 1, 54, 55, 70, 145, 147, 183, 201, 202, 267, 281, 282, 284, 395, 396, 397, 400, 402, 413, 416, 418; courts in, 148; Indian Queen Hotel, 395, 396; Market Street, 396; newspapers in, 397; residents of, 280, 396; ships to and

475

from, 149, 206, 207; stagecoach from, 67, 203, 413; taverns in, 335, 336; trade and commerce in, 100, 395, 396; visitors to, 51, 106, 164, 344
Bangs, Edward (of Worcester, Mass.), 406, 408
Banks, Sir Joseph (Brit. botanist), 56, 57
Barbados, x, 158
Barbary States, 106, 205, 427. *See also* Tripoli; Tunis
Barbary War, First, 33, 80, 107
Barker, Rev. Joseph (Mass. representative), 6
Barlow, Joel (poet), 86, 87, 234, 261
Barrett, Elizabeth (wife of John), 69
Barrett, Maj. John (of Quincy): identified, 69
Barrett, Nathanial Augustus (son of John): identified, 69
Barrett, Samuel (son of John): identified, 69
Barron, Capt. James (of the *Chesapeake*), xii
Barry, Capt. James (Washington, D.C., merchant): identified, 44
Barry, Joanna Gould (wife of James), 43; identified, 44
Barton, John (husband of Penelope), 285, 286
Barton, Penelope Verchild Markham (granddaughter of James Verchild), 285; identified, 286
Bates, John (Weymouth housewright), 73, 75
Bates, Rev. Joshua (of Dedham), xi
Bath, Maine, 117
Bavaria, 75
Baxter, Anthony Wibird (of Quincy), 73, 75
Baxter, Capt. Daniel (of Quincy), 285, 286
Baxter, William, Sr. (of Quincy), 48; identified, 49
Bay, Mr. (in Baltimore), 148
Bayard, James Asheton (Del. senator), 21, 38, 91, 98, 234, 247
Bayonne, France, 374
Beale, Ann. *See* Wales, Ann Beale
Beale, Ann Copeland (wife of Benjamin, Jr.), 385
Beale, Capt. Benjamin, Jr. (of Quincy), 85, 103, 112, 172, 383, 385
Beale, George Washington (son of Benjamin, Jr.), 383; identified, 385
Beale, Capt. Richard Copeland (son of Benjamin, Jr.), 84, 85
Beale, Thomas Smythe (son of Benjamin, Jr.), 383; identified, 385
Belknap, Rev. Jeremy: "Resignation, or Good Out of Evil," 345, 347; *Sacred Poetry*, 345, 347
Bellows Falls, Vt., 236
Belsham, William: *Memoirs of the Kings of Great Britain*, 122, 124
Benson, Egbert (N.Y. judge), 391, 392

Berkeley, Adm. George Cranfield (Brit.), 313, 314, 315; identified, 316
Berlin, 256, 260, 294, 296, 338, 339, 371
Bernstorff, Andreas Peter von, Count (Danish diplomat): identified, 90
Berquin, Arnaud: *L'ami des enfans*, 209, 210
Betsey (Hellen family servant), 94–95, 96
Bevan, Irwin John David (Brit. artist): identified, xii; "The *Chesapeake* and the *Leopard*," 277 (illus.)
Bible: Adam and Eve, 30, 289, 430; Agur, 112; Amos, 46, 47; Cain, 270; 1 Corinthians, 362, 364; Ecclesiastes, 52, 53, 318, 319, 362, 364; Ecclesiasticus, 382, 383; Gad, 153; Genesis, 63, 153, 154, 239, 363, 364, 385, 424, 430; Hebrews, 110; Herod, 185; Isaiah, 302, 304; Jesus, 345; Job, 366, 367; John, 345, 347, 431, 432; John the Baptist, 185; Judges, 422, 425; Lazarus, 345; Luke, 14, 15, 294, 296; Mammon, 373; Mark, 380, 381; Matthew, 126, 347, 417, 420, 429, 430; Nimrod, 289; Proverbs, 112, 133, 137, 139, 363, 364, 433–34; Psalms, 36, 37, 195, 289, 290, 300, 302, 346, 347, 369, 370, 375, 377, 428, 430; Romans, 272, 274, 379, 381; Samson, 422; Solomon, 133, 318, 407, 433; Zechariah, 369, 370
Bidwell, Barnabas (Mass. politician), 81, 84
Bigelow, Timothy (Medford lawyer), 172
Bingham family, 396
Bird, Savage, & Bird (London banking firm), 118, 119, 321
Births: Abigail Smith Adams (1806), x–xi, xviii, 188, 189 (illus.), 190, 192, 194; CFA (1807), xix, 279, 349; ECA (1808), xi, xviii, 323–24, 326, 338, 341, 346; Susanna Boylston Adams (1808), 363, 364; Harriet Johnson Boyd (1781), 279; John Quincy Adams Boyd (1806), 202, 204; Isaac Coffin (1759), 152; Elizabeth Eliot Cranch (1805), 43, 44, 47; John Cranch (1807), 244, 245; Charles Phineas Foster (1806), 201; John Harrod Foster (1808), 363, 364; Louisa Catherine Smith Foster (1806), 152, 154, 164; William Emerson Foster (1808), 368, 369; Anne MacVicar Grant (1755), 425; Mary Elizabeth Greenleaf (1806), 157, 159, 160; Richard Cranch Greenleaf (1808), 377; Eilbeck Mason (1806), 164, 165; Samuel Ogden Meredith (1806), 188, 190; John Cranch Minot (1806), 201; Lucy Ann Norton (1806), 157, 159; Christopher Gore Payne (1807), 158; Ellis Gray Payne (1807), 158; Tilly Churchill Whitcomb (1806), 159
Bishop, Abigail Tufts (wife of John), 434
Bishop, John (Medford miller), 432; identified, 434

Index

Black, Esther Duncan (wife of Moses), 254
Black, Moses (of Quincy), 383
Blackburn, Catherine (daughter of Col. Thomas), 336
Blackburn, Mary (daughter of Col. Thomas), 336
Blackburn, Richard (son of Col. Thomas), 336
Blackburn, Sarah (daughter of Col. Thomas), 336
Blackburn, Col. Thomas (father of Julia Washington), 334; identified, 336
Blackburn, Thomas (son of Col. Thomas), 336
Blackstone, William: *Commentaries*, 421
Bladensburg, Md., 336, 415, 416–17
Blake, George (U.S. attorney for Mass.), xx, 207, 285, 412, 414, 415, 416
Blake, Joseph, Sr. (Boston lawyer), 48, 49
Blake, Rachel Baty (wife of George), 206; identified, 207
Blodget, Samuel, Jr.: *Economica*, 229, 230–31
Bloomfield, Joseph (N.J. governor), 32
Blount, William (Tenn. senator), 356, 357
Boardman, William Henderson (Boston merchant), 401
Bolingbroke, Henry St. John, 1st Viscount (Brit. politician), 39, 40
Bollman (Bollmann), Justus Erich (German physician), 240, 242, 244, 245, 246, 252, 256, 261, 263
Bonaparte, Jerome (brother of Napoleon), 183
Bonaparte, Joseph (brother of Napoleon), 374
Bonaparte, Napoleon: AA on, 74, 289; JA on, 268–69, 275; European war and, xxiii, 75, 124, 129–30, 225, 227, 256, 260, 373, 374; navigation decrees and, 263, 294, 296, 311, 358, 380, 417, 418; New York Academy of Arts and, 62, 63; U.S. attitudes toward, ix, 75, 83 (illus.), 157, 216, 275–76, 294, 296, 341; U.S. relations with France and, ix, 380, 381; U.S. relations with Spain and, 83 (illus.); mentioned, 34, 76, 184
Books and pamphlets: JA's library, 15, 40, 78, 102, 191, 192, 193, 370, 393; JQA's library, 193, 230–31; TBA's library, 421; advertisements for, 192, 350; of art, 62; booksellers and printers, 3, 5, 6, 40, 65, 199, 232, 290, 349; gifts of, 63, 168, 195; Library of Congress, 199, 213, 219, 233; printing and binding of, 5, 182; publication of, 67, 80, 172, 195–96, 349, 350, 351, 353, 356, 361, 407; purchase of, 24, 199, 201, 407; reviews of, 316, 317, 331, 430; on science, 172; subscription libraries, 246, 247
Bordeaux, France, 135, 387
Boston, Mass.: AA2 visits, 272; AA and JA visit, 124–25, 166, 229–30, 232, 284, 380, 383, 394, 403, 408; Abigail Louisa Adams visits, 390; JA honored in, 434–35; JQA and LCA's residence in, xiii, xxii, 150, 160, 166, 170, 175, 203, 206, 209, 210, 211, 213, 230, 235, 249, 266, 268, 272, 348, 361, 368, 372, 384, 414; JQA and LCA travel to and from, 155, 156, 180, 183, 186, 191, 193, 194, 202, 203, 207, 253, 282, 283, 370–71, 394, 397, 400, 402, 404, 408, 418, 436; JQA's properties in, 41, 158, 161–62, 163, 167, 172, 212, 232, 237, 238, 240–41, 246, 267, 268, 349, 350, 410, 414; Susanna Adams visits, 390; TBA and AHA visit, 82, 103, 108, 116, 119, 285, 399, 404; arts in, 157, 159, 237, 390, 391; attitudes toward JQA in, 308–309, 323, 410; banks and banking in, 48, 136, 152, 243, 285, 321, 357, 393; boardinghouses in, 222, 223, 251; booksellers, printing, and publishing in, 5, 6, 65, 199, 232, 290, 349, 350, 361; *Chesapeake-Leopard* Affair and, xii, xxiv, 278, 292, 293, 327; civil unrest in, 222, 223, 262; courts in, 61, 169, 213, 214, 215, 222, 223, 286; fires in, 236, 237; food prices in, 58, 59; Fourth of July celebrations in, 185, 186, 370, 434–35; French consul at, 57, 251, 252; lawyers in, 6, 49, 80, 343, 398, 403; mails to and from, 251, 264, 404, 431; merchants and tradespeople in, xvi, 18, 29, 41, 71, 103, 104, 119, 143, 144, 152, 163, 172, 206, 212, 238, 262, 266, 294, 302, 350, 368, 370, 374, 383, 411, 413, 438; newspapers in, 5–6, 31, 214, 231, 246, 250, 292, 293, 302, 309, 310, 323, 342, 361, 362, 364, 369, 381, 396, 413, 434; Peabody-Shaw visits to, 120, 387–88, 431; petitions to Congress from, 108, 109, 291–92, 293, 337; physicians in, 210, 238, 283, 297; politics in, 5, 8, 309, 320, 340, 341; port collector for, 401, 402; restaurants and coffeehouses in, 57, 157; schools in, 209, 210; sheriff of, 169; Louisa Smith visits, 336, 348, 381, 390; scientific studies in, 94, 106, 170–71, 172, 175–76; societies and clubs in, 49, 157, 159, 171, 172, 175, 246, 247, 378, 435; transportation to and from, 19, 44, 67, 106, 145, 152, 171, 172, 252, 262; U.S. embargo in, 309, 310, 342–43, 403, 404; U.S. Navy and, 229, 231, 409; visitors to, 76, 121, 186, 201, 238; mentioned, 17, 64, 127, 261, 339, 437

Buildings, Landmarks, Streets, etc.: Ann Street, 104; Beacon Street, 158, 247; Boston Common, 435; Boston Harbor, 395; Bowdoin Street, 210; Boylston Street, 163; Brattle Street (Square) Church, 32, 80, 206, 207, 239, 241, 370; Broad Street, 374; Central Wharf, 158; Chambers Street, 119; Columbian Museum, 236, 237; Concert

Hall, 183; Congress Street, 247; Cornhill, 6; Court Street, 37, 41, 199, 232, 240, 407; Dorchester Neck, 262; Exchange Hotel, 435; Faneuil Hall, 185, 186; Federal Street Theatre, 391; First Church, 207, 239, 240, 241, 246, 247; Frog Lane, 163, 212, 268; Half-Court Square, 41, 162, 163; Hawley Street, 411; Haymarket Theatre, 161, 163; Joy's Buildings, 247; King's Chapel, 152, 237; Long Wharf, 28, 71; Mall, 161, 222; Marlborough Street, 144; Nassau Street, 163, 212, 268; Old South Church, 385, 435; Poplar Street, 210; Southac's Court, 223; State House, 29, 30, 327, 435; State Street, 144; Sudbury Street, 231; Summer Street, 172, 411; Tremont Street, 163, 237; Trinity Church, 18, 159; Union Street, 103, 104; West Boston Bridge, 71; West Church, 206, 207; West Street, 143

Boston (Continental frigate), 9, 231

Boston Athenæum, 80, 246, 247, 378

Boston Bank, 136, 321, 356, 357

Boston Commercial Gazette: JQA's treatment in, 172, 293, 364; A. Burr's activities reported in, 115, 231; congressional activities reported in, 42, 374; deaths reported in, 238; elections reported in, 141, 169, 343; food prices reported in, 58, 59; poetry in, 246, 247

Boston Courier, 254, 324

Boston Patriot: JA's writings in, xvii, 371, 420, 421–22, 424–25, 429–30, 431, 433, 434; book reviews in, 430

Boston Public Library: JA's library at, 15, 40, 78, 102, 193, 370, 393

Bourbon, House of, 374

Bourn, Samuel: *Christian-Family Prayer Book*, 194, 195

Bowdoin, James, Jr. (Mass. politician), 26, 28, 31

Bowers, Margaret Phillips (sister of Hannah Cushing): identified, 61

Bowes, Elizabeth. *See* Ware, Elizabeth Bowes (3d wife of Henry)

Bowes, Nicholas (of Boston), 240

Bowes, Rebecca Wendell (wife of Nicholas), 240

Bowles, William Lisle: *Works of Alexander Pope*, 226

Boyd, Archibald (son of Harriet), 185, 186, 187, 214

Boyd, George (husband of Harriet): JQA visits, 233, 242, 251, 397, 398, 415; LCA on, 52; family of, 186, 187, 204, 218, 219, 255; Hellen family and, 417; C. N. Johnson visits, 211; marriage of, 51, 52; seeks patronage for C. Harrod, 407; mentioned, 208, 394

Boyd, Harriet Johnson (sister of LCA): JQA and, 204, 237, 242; LCA and, 178, 232, 239, 394; family of, 185, 186, 187, 202, 204, 218, 229; health of, 233, 279, 415, 417; Hellen family and, 417; marriage of, 51, 52; mentioned, 19

Boyd, John Quincy Adams (son of Harriet): identified, 204; JQA and, 229, 237, 242; birth of, 202; health of, 218, 219, 229, 233, 239, 242, 251, 255

Boylston, Nicholas (1716–1771, cousin of JA's mother), 172

Boylston, Ward Nicholas (2d cousin of JA), 172, 180, 181

Brackett, Elizabeth Odiorne (wife of Capt. James), 70

Brackett, James (1736–1825, Quincy tavern keeper), 88

Brackett, Capt. James (1769–1855, son of James), 18, 19, 266

Brackett, Lemuel (son of James), 87, 88

Brackett, Mary (daughter of Capt. James), 69; identified, 70

Brackett, Mary Spear (wife of James), 88

Brackett, Sarah Whitney (wife of Lemuel), 87, 88

Brackett, Thomas Odiorne (son of Capt. James), 69; identified, 70

Bradford, Alden (of Maine): identified, 41; *Sermon Delivered at Plymouth*, 41

Bradford, Rev. John (of Roxbury), 185; identified, 186

Bradford, Joseph Nash (Boston merchant), 211, 241, 246, 267; identified, 212

Bradford, Lt. Col. Samuel (Boston sheriff), 409, 434

Bradley, Stephen Row (Vt. senator): Political activities of, 316, 317, 320, 324, 327–29, 340, 359; slavery bill and, 262

Bradley, Capt. William (of the *Cambrian*), 2, 3

Braintree, Mass.: TBA and, 7, 8, 225; First Congregational Church, 355; ministers in, 51; property in, 18, 286; mentioned, 266. *See also* Quincy, Mass.

Brayton, Capt. Israel (of the *Sally*), 207, 223

Breck, Samuel, Jr. (of Phila.), 56, 57

Breckinridge, James (U.S. attorney general), 11, 237, 238

Brent, Catherine Walker Johnson (Kitty, cousin of LCA), 43, 44

Brent, Robert, Sr. (mayor of Washington, D.C.), 398; identified, 399

Brent, William (husband of Catherine), 43, 44

Brest, France, 181, 292, 293

Bridgewater, Mass., 271

Bridgton, Maine, 195

Index

Briesler, Esther Field (wife of John, Sr.), 17, 23
Briesler, John, Sr. (Adams servant), 17, 23, 225, 226, 265, 266, 297
Brimfield, Mass., 427
British Army, 63, 422, 425
British Navy: attacks on foreign shipping by, 3, 146, 147, 183; *Chesapeake-Leopard* Affair, xii, xxiv, 276, 277 (illus.), 278, 282, 286–87, 290, 292, 293, 296, 306, 307, 315–16, 317, 327, 331, 335, 338, 343, 350, 351–52, 355; at Halifax, Nova Scotia, 150, 152, 157, 316; impressment by, xii, xv, xxiii, 2, 3, 95, 98, 99, 105, 106, 109, 263, 292, 293, 296, 311, 312, 350, 355, 368, 370, 407, 422, 425, 433, 434; service in, xii, 147, 292, 374
"British Spy in Boston" (pseudonym), 19, 20
Broadnax, Lydia (Va. servant), 177
Bronson, Enos (Phila. printer), 328, 332. See also *Gazette of the United States*
Brookfield, Mass., 396
Brotier, Gabriel (translator), 100, 102
Brown, Andrew, Jr. (Phila. printer), 39, 40, 78
Brown, Charles Brockden: *British Treaty*, 316, 317, 323
Brown, Michael (Va. servant), 177
Brown, Robert (Penn. representative), 84
Brutus, Marcus Junius (Roman politician), 356
Buchanan, Andrew (husband of Carolina): identified, 239; JQA and LCA and, 219, 223, 281, 284, 395, 417; marriage of, 238, 239–40; residence of, 396
Buchanan, Ann (stepdaughter of Carolina), 239
Buchanan, Anne McKean (1st wife of Andrew), 239
Buchanan, Carolina Virginia Marylanda Johnson (sister of LCA): AA and, 76, 266; JQA and LCA visit, 281, 284, 287, 395; as LCA's companion, 179, 193, 203, 219, 267; correspondence with mother and siblings, 213, 218, 227, 242, 251; health of, 111, 206, 287, 289, 307, 394, 417; marriage of, 238, 239–40; residence of, 396; travels of, 51, 415, 416–17; mentioned, 19, 205, 208, 229, 263, 348
Buchanan, Mary (stepdaughter of Carolina), 239
Buchanan, Susan (stepdaughter of Carolina), 239
Buckminster, Rev. Joseph (father of Joseph Stevens), 32
Buckminster, Rev. Joseph Stevens (of Boston), 80; identified, 32
Buckminster, Sarah Stevens (mother of Joseph Stevens), 32
Buenos Aires, Argentina, 230

Bunker Hill Association, 435
Bunyan, John: *Holy War*, 357
Burke, Edmund (M.P.), 191, 192; *Works*, 193
Burns, Robert: "The Country Lassie," 47; "O Poortith Cauld and Restless Love," 47; "To a Mouse," 138, 139; *Works*, 44, 45
Burr, Aaron (vice president): AA on, 269; JA on, 8, 356; JQA on, 31, 55, 57, 253; TBA on, 248–49; conspiracy and treason trial of, 207, 208, 213, 230, 231, 235, 242, 243–44, 245, 248–49, 250, 252–53, 263, 264, 276, 278, 310; rumored diplomatic mission of, 113, 115; duel with A. Hamilton, 7, 32, 34, 55; New York politics and, 34, 35, 126; presides over Senate, 7, 31, 55, 57, 91, 308; public attitudes toward, 31, 207, 230, 231, 235, 240, 243, 246, 249, 250, 264, 276, 313, 314, 318; WSS and, 244
Burrell, Peter (Adams family tenant), 73, 75
Burrows, Col. William Ward (U.S.), 3; identified, 4
Bussey, Benjamin (Boston merchant), 171, 175; identified, 172
Bute, Mary Wortley Montagu Stuart, Countess (daughter of Mary Montagu), 24
Butler, Samuel: *Hudibras*, 422, 425
Butler, Col. Thomas (U.S.), 3; identified, 4

CA. *See* Adams, Charles (1770–1800)
Cabot, George (Mass. senator), 342
Cádiz, Spain, 63
Cadwalader, Mary Biddle (wife of Thomas), 117, 118
Cadwalader, Thomas (Phila. lawyer), 116–17, 118, 146; letter from TBA listed (1806), 445
    Letter: From TBA (1806), 116
Caleb (Adams servant), 213
Calhoun, James, Jr. (Baltimore merchant), 395, 396
Callender, James Thomson (Phila. printer), 39, 40, 77
Cambrian (Brit. frigate), 2, 3, 146, 147
Cambridge, Mass.: AA visits, 64; JQA's residence in, 64, 71, 73, 82, 86, 95, 96, 108, 146, 147, 150, 156, 161, 172, 180, 182, 186, 187, 193, 370; merchants in, 88; ministers in, 290; restaurants in, 57; societies and clubs in, 188, 190, 193, 194, 196–97, 198; teachers in, 187; mentioned, 58, 171, 264

Buildings, Landmarks, Streets, etc.: Arrow Street, 85; Blue Anchor Tavern, 156, 158; Boylston Street (now John F. Kennedy Street), 158; Braintree Street, 65; Brattle Street, 88; Cambridge Common, 163, 169; Cambridgeport, 64, 71; Cambridgeport Meeting House, 239, 240; Cambridge

479

Street, 163; First Church, 197, 198; Harvard Square, 158; Massachusetts Avenue, 163; Mount Auburn Street, 158; Waterhouse Street, 169
Campbell, George Washington (Tenn. politician), 328; identified, 332
Canada, xi, 117, 287
Canary Islands, 124
Canning, George (Brit. statesman), 292, 434; identified, 293
Caracas, Venezuela, x, 89 (illus.), 158, 159
Carey, Mathew: *Carey's American Pocket Atlas*, 199
Caribbean Sea, 183, 186
Carlos IV, King of Spain, 372, 374
Carolina Gazette (Charleston, S.C.), 387
Carroll, Charles (of Carrollton), 52
Carroll, Mary Darnall (wife of Charles), 52
Carter, Catherine Crafts (Boston boardinghouse keeper), 222; identified, 223
Cary, Rev. Samuel (of Boston), 149–50; identified, 152
Carysfort, John Joshua Proby, 1st Earl of (Brit. diplomat), 339
Casamajor, Justinian (Brit. secy.), 338; identified, 339
Caton, Elizabeth (daughter of Mary), 201, 415; identified, 416
Caton, Marianne (daughter of Mary), 201, 413, 415, 416; identified, 414
Caton, Mary Carroll (sister of Catherine Harper), 201, 414
Caton, Richard (husband of Mary), 414
Cato the Elder (Roman historian), 357
Cayenne, French Guiana, 4
Cervantes Saavedra, Miguel de: *Don Quixote*, 269
CFA. *See* Adams, Charles Francis (1807–1886)
Chapman, Nathaniel (Phila. physician), 56; identified, 57; *Proposals by I. Watts, for Publishing . . . Select Speeches*, 192; *Select Speeches, Forensick and Parliamentary*, 191–93
Charleston, College of, 37
Charleston, S.C., 19, 25, 37, 425
Charlestown, Mass., 311, 435
Chase, Samuel, Sr. (U.S. Supreme Court justice): AA on, 21, 46; health of, 106, 107, 252; impeachment of, 21, 26, 31–32, 33, 34, 43, 46, 48, 57
Chatham, Earl of. *See* Pitt, William (the elder), Earl of Chatham
Chaumont, Jacques Donatien Le Ray de (French speculator), 100; identified, 102

Cheetham, James (N.Y. printer), 39, 60
Chenango Valley, xxii, 254, 255, 304, 345
Cherokee Nation, 80–81
Chesapeake (U.S. frigate), xii, xxiv, 276, 277 (illus.), 278, 282, 286–87, 292, 307, 335, 355
Chesapeake and Delaware Canal Company, 246–47
Chesapeake Bay, xii, 54, 191, 201, 247
Chesterfield, Philip Dormer Stanhope, 4th Earl of (Brit. statesman and author), 228, 236
China, 30
Chitty, Joseph: *Treatise on the Law of Bills of Exchange*, 421
Churches: Associated Reformed Presbyterian Church, Washington, D.C., 243; Brattle Street (Square) Church, Boston, 32, 80, 206, 207, 239, 241, 370; Cambridgeport Meeting House, Cambridge, 239, 240; Congregational Church, Wiscasset, Maine, 41; First Church, Boston, 207, 239, 240, 241, 246, 247; First Church, Cambridge, 197, 198; First Church, Dedham, xi; First Church, Haverhill, Mass., 388, 389; First Church, Hingham, 187; First Church, Quincy, 27, 28, 73, 75; First Church, Randolph, 266; First Congregational Church, Braintree, 355; First Presbyterian Church, New York City, 63; King's Chapel, Boston, 152, 237; Middle Dutch Church, New York City, 185; Old South Church, Boston, 385, 435; St. John Church, Georgetown, D.C., 413, 414; St. Paul's Episcopal Church, Washington, D.C., 211, 213; Second Church, Roxbury, 186; Trinity Church, Boston, 18, 159; West Church, Boston, 206, 207; West Parish Church, Bridgewater, Mass., 271
Church of England, 34, 40
Cicero, Marcus Tullius (Roman philosopher): JQA on, 194; *Epistles to Atticus*, 356, 357; *De Oratore*, 392, 393; *Pro Sexto Roscio Amerino*, 101, 102
Cilicia, Turkey, 356
Claiborne, William Charles Cole (gov. of Orleans Territory), 23–24, 278
Clap, Samuel (Boston bookseller): identified, 232
Clark, Harriett (of Providence, R.I.), 59
Clark, William (U.S. explorer), ix, xi, 205, 234, 261
Classical references: Adonis, 85; Aeolus, 427, 428; Arachne, 322; Argos, 29, 30; Ariadne, 235; Boreas, 424; Diana, 29; Flora, 424, 425; Graces, 274; Hebe, 85; Hercules, 77; Ilium, 257; Muses, 267; Neptune, 186; Odysseus, 29, 30; Vertumnus, 424, 425

Index

Cleverly, Sarah Jones (Sally, Adams servant), 206, 222, 223, 241; identified, 207
Clinton, Cornelia Tappen (wife of George), 260
Clinton, DeWitt (mayor of New York City), 34, 35, 60, 126, 308
Clinton, George (vice president): family of, 260; presidential election (1804) and, 8; presidential election (1808) and, 306, 308, 312, 314, 317, 323, 324, 329–30, 332, 340, 377, 395, 397, 398; presides over Senate, 70, 71, 82, 85, 256
Clothing: accessories, 26, 223, 394, 396–97; for Adamses, xviii, 13, 18, 75, 112, 157, 165, 193, 206, 211, 219, 251, 367; caps and hats, 69, 127, 160, 251; for children, 75, 165, 168, 171, 218; coats, 19, 75, 367; fabrics, 26, 27, 104, 120, 127, 140, 143–44, 150, 157, 168, 193, 218, 239, 274, 300; fashions, 241–42, 252; fire and, 211, 217, 218; handkerchiefs and cravats, 19, 168, 193, 271; for J. Madison, 413; manufacture of, 104, 150, 168, 413; sealskin, 56, 57; for servants, 222; for William Smith Shaw, 120, 274; shirts, 75, 120, 193; shoes, 206, 219; for William Steuben Smith, 300; solar eclipse glasses, 171; stockings and socks, 18, 103, 120, 193; straitjacket, 410; undergarments, 120; wigs, 19
Clubs. *See* Societies and clubs
Cobbett, William: *Porcupine's Works*, 308, 310
Codes and ciphers, 248, 250
Coffin, Sir Isaac, Adm. (Brit.), 150, 156; identified, 152
Coke, Sir Edward: *Institutes*, 421
Coleman, William (N.Y. printer), 316, 323; identified, 60. See also *Evening Post*; *Herald*
Columbia College: president of, 191; scientific studies at, 57; John Adams Smith attends, 139, 142, 162, 184, 185–86, 190, 193
Columbian Centinel (Boston): JA's writings in, 371, 420; Adamses' treatment in, 186, 198, 361, 364, 402; advertisements in, 172; A. Burr conspiracy reported in, 231; duels reported in, 396; elections reported in, 5, 6, 48, 49, 169, 354, 355; Embargo Act (1807) reported in, 296; European war reported in, 74, 75; T. Jefferson address printed in, 71; Miranda expedition reported in, 231; U.S. foreign relations reported in, 91, 255, 296, 316, 428; U.S. Supreme Court cases reported in, 347; vaccination debated in, 295
Columbia River, 230, 261
Commercial Advertiser (N.Y.), 126, 130, 185–86, 396

Concord, Mass., 58, 290
Concord, N.H., 387, 431, 432
Congress, U.S.: AA on, 46, 125–26, 131, 132, 289, 318, 348, 351, 409; JA on, 4, 123, 254, 357; JQA on, 41, 57, 72, 79, 81, 87, 90, 91, 106, 128, 218, 225, 252, 261, 281, 284, 311, 315, 398; TBA on, 25–26, 294, 295, 308; adjournment of, 47, 128, 136, 142, 219, 332, 349, 360, 402, 412; attitudes toward JQA in, 114, 313, 314, 332; attitudes toward T. Jefferson in, 124, 133, 154, 315–16; cemetery for members of, 319; *Chesapeake-Leopard* Affair and, 282, 286–87, 293, 316, 331, 351–52, 355; diplomatic immunity and, 114, 116, 123–24, 129; economic policies of, 15, 72, 106, 179, 204–205, 315, 317; electoral process and, 318, 319, 324; executive powers and, 31, 129, 293, 302, 332, 333; habeas corpus and, 244, 245, 248, 250, 253, 254; impeachment proceedings in, 21, 26, 31–32, 33, 34, 43, 46, 48, 57; T. Jefferson submits messages and documents to, ix, 4, 10, 11, 63, 69, 71, 72, 73, 78, 79, 81, 84, 97, 99, 105, 106, 109, 115–16, 130, 204–205, 209, 210, 243–44, 245, 248, 262, 263, 281, 282, 284, 290, 293, 296, 308, 310, 326, 331, 333, 351–52, 355, 427; library for, 199, 213; J. Madison inauguration and, 411; members and composition of, xi, xii, 6, 11, 31–32, 44, 70–71, 80, 84, 91, 98, 99, 124, 132, 147, 179, 202, 204, 260, 262, 281, 282, 310, 317, 319, 332, 357, 368, 370, 396, 398, 416; military preparedness and, 78, 79, 81, 84, 91, 98, 99, 124, 253, 254, 290, 295, 297, 310, 315, 332, 333, 342, 351, 364, 368, 398, 401, 406, 407–408; petitions to, 24, 84, 85, 91, 105, 106, 109, 115, 234, 291–92, 293, 302, 316, 317, 337, 408; presidential election (1808) and, 308, 311–12, 327, 329, 330, 397, 398; public attitudes toward, 26, 225, 253, 284, 286, 293, 340–41, 344, 387, 388; purchase of the Floridas considered by, ix, 81, 83 (illus.), 84, 86, 87, 90, 139, 154; quorums for, 11, 70, 204; regulation of trade by, 72, 114, 115, 116, 246–47, 296; secrecy in, ix, 84, 95, 97, 108, 125, 131, 137, 139, 154, 293, 294, 296; sessions of, 3, 11, 71, 106, 180, 204, 205, 234, 261, 264, 281, 282, 306, 349, 417; territorial governance and, 23–25, 33, 106; treason law reform and, 326, 355; U.S. judiciary and, 57, 123, 124, 261, 262, 318, 319, 320, 321–22, 325–26, 327; U.S. relations with Barbary States and, 33, 81, 82, 85, 107; U.S. relations with Britain and, 97, 98, 99, 106–107, 114, 115, 124, 294, 333, 337, 417; U.S. relations with France and, 114, 124, 333, 352,

481

355; U.S. relations with Haiti and, 4, 113–14, 115–16, 122; U.S. relations with Spain and, 11; violence in, 178, 179, 332, 395, 396, 417; Yazoo land claims and, 41–42, 44, 136, 315, 317, 329–30, 413

 House of Representatives: actions and business of, 81, 84, 255, 281, 282, 315, 317, 355; JQA and, 225, 262, 332; TBA as candidate for, xviii, 6, 7, 8, 12, 27; chamber of, 287, 332, 397, 411; clerk of, 281, 282; committees of, 24, 79, 81, 84, 85, 234, 317; journals of, 10, 25, 37, 84, 88, 104, 139; powers of, 43, 330; Speaker of, 70–71, 124, 281, 282

 Legislation: Articles of War (1806), 91; Enforcement Act (1809), 395, 396; Judiciary Act (1802), 132, 133; Non-Importation Act (1806), xxiv, 93, 95–96, 128, 129, 253, 254, 291–92, 293, 296, 418; Non-Intercourse Act (1809), xxiv, 383, 385, 398, 399, 401, 403, 404, 407, 412, 426, 434; Potomac River Bridge Act (1808), 233–34, 240, 261, 262; Seventh Circuit Act (1807), 247, 248; Slave Importation Act (1807), 245, 261, 262

 Senate: absences from, 91, 99, 256; actions and business of, 105, 106–107, 111, 316, 337; JQA and, xii, xxv, 91, 181, 223–24, 367, 368–69, 370, 373, 388, 414–15, 433; advises and consents to treaties, 80, 107, 317, 426, 427; A. Burr and, 7, 31, 32, 55, 57; chamber of, 252; committees of, 88, 91, 105, 106, 107, 114, 141, 245, 262, 278, 292, 293, 296, 308, 310, 315, 316–17, 326, 359, 364, 402; confirmation of nominations by, 11, 32, 126, 130, 133, 238, 248, 401, 402, 412, 414–15, 416, 435; expulsion of John Smith considered by, 308–309, 310, 313, 316, 317, 324, 359–60, 362, 364; journals of, 10, 25, 37, 88, 99, 104, 105, 289; powers of, 26, 57, 330; president pro tempore, 70, 71, 256; special session of, 412, 414, 415

 See also Embargo Act (1807)

Connecticut: agriculture in, 144; attitudes toward embargo in, 395; congressional delegation of, 71, 84, 202, 204, 319; migration from, 117; presidential election (1808) and, 340

Connecticut Courant (Hartford), 154

Constantinople, Turkey, 426

Constitution, U.S.: AA on, 132–33; JA on, 15, 33; JQA on, 324; possible amendments to, 9, 32, 57, 205, 318, 319, 320, 321, 322, 325–26; congressional powers under, 26, 31, 43, 57, 318, 319, 321, 322, 359; electoral process under, 318, 319, 324, 325, 330; executive powers under, 26, 31, 245; judicial powers under, 57, 318, 319, 321, 322; public attitudes toward, 132, 375; slavery and, 262; 12th Amendment, 9

Constitution (U.S. frigate), 84, 85

Continental Army, 25

Continental Congress, 176, 177

Continental Navy, 229, 231

Cook, Elizabeth Johnson (aunt of LCA), 186, 187

Cook, Nathan (of Cape Cod), 295, 297

Cook, Orchard (Mass. representative), 398

Cook, Thomas (of Cape Cod), 295, 297

Cooke, William (Md. lawyer), 148, 149

Cookendorfer, Leonard (Washington, D.C., hackneyman), 151; identified, 152

Coos, N.H., 431, 432

Cordero y Bustamante, Manuel Antonio (gov. of Texas), 208

Coro, Venezuela, x, xxi, 89 (illus.)

Cortés, Hernán (Spanish conquistador), 153

Courts. *See* Judiciary, U.S.

Covell, Capt. (of the *Katy*), 19

Cowper, Henry: *Reports of Cases*, 421

Cowper, William: "Beau's Reply," 29, 30; "The Dog and the Water-Lily," 29, 30; "Retirement," 103, 104; "The Rose," 45; "On a Spaniel, Called Beau," 29, 30; "Table Talk," 46, 47; "The Time-Piece," 74, 75; "The Winter Evening," 138, 139

Cranch, Anna Greenleaf (Nancy, 1772–1843, wife of William): Adamses and, 133, 138, 179, 284, 290; birth of children, 43, 44, 47, 244, 245; residence of, 139, 160, 244, 245; social activities of, 335

Cranch, Elizabeth Eliot (1805–1860, daughter of William), 43, 47; identified, 44

Cranch, John (1807–1891, son of William), 244; identified, 245

Cranch, Mary Smith (1741–1811, sister of AA): LCA and, 65, 154, 160, 282; birth of Elizabeth Cranch and, 47; cares for GWA and JA2, xiii, 64, 65, 70, 77, 92, 125, 154, 159, 280, 282–83, 284, 288, 290, 437, 438; correspondence with AHA, 200; correspondence with Elizabeth Peabody, 194, 389, 436; William Cranch and, 153; family visits to and by, 15, 69, 103, 112, 284, 374, 378, 384, 408, 431, 438; health of, 21, 112, 374, 378, 379, 383, 384, 389, 390; opposes dancing, 265; Quincy family and, xiii, 92, 107, 108–109, 131, 136, 138; relationship with AA, 112, 374–75, 379; residence of, 286; letter from Elizabeth Smith Shaw Peabody listed (1808), 449; mentioned, 37, 145, 271, 273, 304, 307

 Letters: From LCA (1806), 159; (1807), 282, 290

Cranch, Richard (1726–1811, husband of

Mary): AA and, 109, 145, 153; JQA and, 183; TBA and, 117, 190, 285, 286; cares for GWA and JA2, 77, 111, 408, 437, 438; family visits to and by, 15, 69, 384, 431; health of, 17, 21, 27, 30, 37, 378; opposes dancing, 265; poetry by, 27, 28; as Quincy postmaster, 296; residence of, 286; letter to AA listed (1809), 450; letters to TBA listed (1803), 441 (2); letters from TBA listed (1803), 441; (1808), 448; mentioned, 160, 201, 271, 273, 290

Cranch, William (1769–1855, nephew of AA): AA and, 37, 131, 138; JQA and LCA and, 11, 59, 160, 179, 244, 245, 284, 290; TBA sends poetry to, 27; J. Johnson estate and, 58, 59; *Reports of Cases in the Supreme Court*, 26, 28; residence of, 84, 95, 139, 160, 244, 245; social activities of, 335; as U.S. judge, 125, 126, 132, 160, 245, 249; mentioned, 79, 285, 298

Credit. *See* Debt; Money

Creek Nation, 80

Crime: arson, 179; bribery, 254, 255, 356; counterfeiting, 48, 49; fraud, 48, 177; libel and slander, 39, 40, 148; murder, 2, 7, 32, 55, 102, 146, 176, 177, 214, 222, 223; piracy, 99; sedition, 39, 40, 250; smuggling, 4; treason, 63, 208, 240, 244, 245, 246, 249, 250, 254, 264, 326, 355

  Punishments for: confiscation of assets, 4; death penalty, x, 326; exile, 63; fines, 262; imprisonment, x, 63, 179, 244, 246, 252, 262

Crowninshield, Benjamin, Jr. (of Salem), 406, 408

Crowninshield, Jacob (Mass. representative), 9

Cruft, Edward (Boston merchant): identified, 438

Cumberland, Richard: *The Observer*, 196, 198

Cumberland River, 244

Curtis, Noah (Quincy shoemaker): identified, 292

Cushing, Abigail (sister of William): identified, 61

Cushing, Hannah Phillips (wife of William): AA on, 345, 377; correspondence with AA, xvii, 248, 334, 345, 347; health of, 333; relationship with AA, 133, 335, 346, 409; religious beliefs of, 333, 334; travels of, 54, 138, 144, 244, 333, 347; visits with Adamses, 18, 61, 144, 216, 245, 377; letters to AA listed (1807), 447; (1808), 449

  Letters: To AA (1805), 61; (1806), 144; (1808), 333

  Letter: From AA (1808), 344

Cushing, William (U.S. Supreme Court justice): health of, 106, 107, 144, 247–48, 252, 333, 334, 344–45, 346; J. Madison inauguration and, 413; relationship with Adamses, 335; service of, 61, 144, 334, 347, 413; travels of, 54, 144, 244; visits with Adamses, 200, 216, 245; mentioned, 145

Cutler, Benjamin Clarke (Norfolk Co., Mass., sheriff), 285; identified, 286

Daily Advertiser (Alexandria, Va.), 91

Daily Advertiser (N.Y.), 115

Dana, Samuel (Mass. senator), 406; identified, 407

Dana, Samuel Whittlesey (Conn. representative), 94, 96, 145, 147, 187, 202, 204

Dancing: LCA and, 265; balls, 256, 260, 262, 394, 397, 398, 411, 414, 415, 416; Cranches oppose, 265; Native American, xi; Quincy assemblies for, xx, 239, 240, 265; rope dancing, 213; schools and instructors for, 157, 159, 265, 300, 429; in Washington, D.C., 212

Davenport, Rufus (Boston merchant), 207, 239, 240, 241; identified, 71

Davenport & Tucker (Boston mercantile firm), 28

Davis, Elizabeth Hanckley (wife of Thomas), 36; identified, 37

Davis, Isaac P. (Boston lawyer), 201, 238; identified, 240

Davis, Susan Jackson (wife of Isaac), 238; identified, 240

Davis, Thomas (Mass. treasurer), 36; identified, 37

Dawson, John (Beau, Va. representative), 43, 44, 70, 71

Dearborn, Henry (U.S. secretary of war): JQA meets with, 311; appointed Boston port collector, 401, 402, 410; A. Burr and, 253, 262, 263, 264; military preparedness and, 333; patronage for William Steuben Smith and, 338, 342, 348, 351; presidential election (1808) and, 309, 310, 314; visits naval frigate, 99. *See also* War Department, U.S.

Deaths: Jeremiah Allen (1809), 409; Fisher Ames (1808), 430; Queen Anne (1714), 40; Charles Austin (1806), 223; Col. Thomas Blackburn (1807), 334, 336; Archibald Boyd (1806), 186, 187, 214; John Bradford (1825), 186; James Breckinridge (1806), 237, 238; Michael Brown (1806), 177; Joseph Stevens Buckminster (1812), 32; Thomas Butler (1805), 4; William Coleman (1829), 60; Elizabeth Johnson Cook (1806), 186, 187; Elizabeth Hanckley Davis (1803), 36, 37; Thomas Davis (1805), 36, 37; William Evans (1807), 396; Thomas Fayerweather (1805), 88; Eliphalet Fitch (1810), 57;

Mary Tracy Gardner (1809), 403, 404; Sarah Jackson Gardner (1809), 398, 399; Cornelia Clinton Genet (1810), 260; Nicholas Gilman (1814), 147; Alexander Hamilton (1804), 422; Peter Hardwick (1806), 194, 195; Walter Hellen Jr. (1806), 210–11, 212–13, 214, 218, 224, 234, 283; Washington Hellen (1802), 234; James Jackson (1806), 99; Joshua Johnson (1802), 42, 149; Jabez Kimball (1805), 52, 53; James Lovell (Mass. politician) (1814), 409; Ludwig Ferdinand, Prince of Prussia (1806), 227; James Mitchel (1806), 194, 195; Samuel Parker (1804), 17, 18; Theophilus Parsons (1813), 169; Lucy Gray Dobell Payne (1809), 404; Mary Peabody (1808), 366; Sarah Peabody Stevens Peters (1808), 367; Thompson Phillips (1808), 333–34, 335, 345; John Pierce (1806), 146, 147; Ruth Avery Price (1808), 384, 385, 388; Ann Marsh Quincy (1805), 49, 50; Mary Pickering Leavitt Sargeant (1805), 51, 52; Arria Sargent (1805), 53; Friedrich Wilhelm, Count von Schmettau (1806), 225–26, 227; Elizabeth Quincy Shaw (1798), 347, 349; Oakes Shaw (1807), 270; John Clarke Smith (1806), 224, 226; Mary Carter Smith (1806), 109–10, 111, 120, 126; Ebenezer Storer (1807), 229, 231, 232, 235; stillbirths, 177, 178; suicides, 179, 264; Uriah Tracy (1807), 318, 319; Elisha Turner (1806), 104; Mary Miller Veasey (1806), 227; James Verchild (1769), 286; William Vernon Sr. (1806), 229, 231; Mary Vose (1806), 120, 121; Arthur Maynard Walter (1807), 212, 235, 245–46, 247; Mary Otis Lincoln Ware (1807), 240, 264, 265, 269, 270; James Warren (1808), 384, 385; Jane Mildred Washington (1807), 334; Samuel White (1809), 11; Joseph Willard (1804), 74; George Wythe (1806), 176, 177

Debt: AA on, 378; JA on, 326; of Adamses, 118, 143, 225, 226, 241, 242, 312, 320, 321, 349, 354, 355, 393; bankruptcy, 35, 36, 37; of A. Burr, 264; extinguishment of U.S. state, 315, 317; mortgages, 161; owed to JQA, 410, 414; payment of interest on, 225, 354, 393; sale of property to pay, 37, 158; of William Smith, 35, 36, 37; sureties for, 37, 58, 414; of U.S., 398, 401. *See also* Money

Decatur, Como. Stephen (U.S.), 44
Decatur, Susan Wheeler (wife of Stephen), 44; identified, 43
Declaration of Independence, 323
Decrès, Denis (French minister of marine), 262, 263
Dedham, Mass., xi, 48, 49, 86, 147, 201, 294, 296
Defoe, Daniel: "The Shortest Way with Dissenters," 38–39, 40
Delaware, 11, 44, 238, 317, 340
Delaware Bay, 247
Delaware Nation, 80
Delaware River, 54, 145, 146, 201
Delisle, Caton (Boston restaurateur), 41, 79, 135, 161
Democrat (Boston): JQA's treatment in, 316; JQA's writings in, 343; advertisements in, 409; A. Burr's conspiracy reported in, 231; congressional activities reported in, 129, 310, 404; elections reported in, 141; trial reported in, 6
Democratic-Republican Party: AA on, 131, 137, 369; JA and, 38, 100, 135, 386, 435; JA on, 12, 356; JQA and, xxiii–xxiv, xxv, xxvi, 308, 313, 314, 322, 323, 324, 327, 336, 349, 354, 359, 361, 369, 427, 435; JQA on, 65–66, 225; LCA on, 306–307; TBA on, 25–26, 406–407; caucuses of, xxvi, 140–41, 308, 312, 316, 317–18, 320, 322, 323, 324, 327–29, 332, 336–37, 340, 359; Congress and, xxiv–xxv, 32, 42, 124, 129, 132, 296, 310, 332, 360, 396, 412; divisions in, 137, 306–308, 323, 329, 330, 332, 340; Federalist Party and, 327, 396; T. Jefferson and, 100, 123; J. Madison and, xxvi; in Massachusetts, xviii, 5, 6, 7, 9, 12, 17, 49, 85, 115, 140–41, 158, 167, 169, 170, 172, 222, 223, 231, 254, 285, 309, 339–40, 342, 343, 351, 407; in New Hampshire, 387; newspapers and, 129, 324, 341, 361, 433; in New York, 34, 35, 126; in Pennsylvania, 68; presidential election (1804) and, 6, 9; presidential election (1808) and, 306–308, 309, 323, 324, 336–37; public attitudes toward, 40, 196, 198, 420; in Tennessee, 332; U.S. foreign relations and, xxiv, 100; in Washington, D.C., 137–38
Demosthenes (Greek statesman), 392
Denmark, 91
Dennie, Joseph, Jr. (Phila. editor): JQA and, 1–2, 55, 66; TBA and, 190; literary culture and, 133, 196, 198, 207; residence of, 3. See also *Port Folio*
Derbigny, Pierre Augustin Bourguignon (of La.), 23; identified, 24
Derby, Martha Coffin (of Boston), 394
Destréhan, Jean Noël (of La.), 23; identified, 24
Dexter, Dr. Aaron (Harvard professor), 428, 432, 434
Dexter, Andrew, Jr. (Boston lawyer), 41, 163

Index

Dexter, Caroline (daughter of Richard): identified, 339
Dexter, Edward (son of Richard): identified, 339
Dexter, Rebeckah Tirrell (Becky, wife of Richard), 36, 46, 336, 339, 364
Dexter, Richard (Adams servant), 111, 112, 339, 354, 355
Dexter, Samuel (Mass. politician), 132, 223
Diana (ship), 149
Dickson, William (Tenn. representative), 43; identified, 44
Diligence (stagecoach line), 65–66, 67–68, 145
Dinmore, Richard (Washington, D.C., printer), 286. See also *Washington Expositor*
Diodati-Tronchin, Jean, Comte de (Saxon minister to France), 420
Dionysius: *Dionysiou Halikarnasseōs*, 229, 231
District of Columbia, 317
Dobson, Thomas (Phila. bookseller), 67
Dodge, Rev. Joshua (of Haverhill, Mass.), 388, 430; identified, 389
Domestic work: baking, 157; childcare, xvi, 69, 92, 138, 156, 343, 347, 424, 425; laundry, 103, 112; Elizabeth Peabody on, 431; sewing, 18, 44, 111, 127, 155, 160, 271, 274, 300; snow shoveling, 111; sugaring, xvii, 363; taking in boarders, 118, 121, 367. See also Servants
Domitor (pseudonym), 60
Dorchester, Mass., 408
Dorsey, John (Penn. politician), 68
Driver (Brit. sloop), 147
Duane, William (Phila. printer), 11, 39, 78. See also *Aurora General Advertiser*
Duels: JQA and, 328; between A. Burr and A. Hamilton (1804), 7; between B. Gardenier and G. Campbell (1808), 328, 332; rumored between members of Congress, 43, 178, 179, 395, 396, 417; rumored between members of Mass. General Court, 406, 407; mentioned, xx, 33
Duer, William Alexander (N.Y. lawyer), 190–91, 232; identified, 191
Duvall, Gabriel (U.S. comptroller), 256, 260
Dwight, Theodore (Conn. representative), 202; identified, 204
Dyer, Joseph (of Weymouth), 273; identified, 274

E. (pseudonym): "Resignation," 110
Early, Peter (Ga. representative), 123; identified, 124
East Braintree, Mass., 75
East Indies, 263, 288

Eaton, Gen. William (U.S.), 207, 245, 426, 427; identified, 208
ECA. See Adams, Elizabeth Coombs (1808–1903)
Eckley, Rev. Joseph (of Boston), 384, 385
Eden, William. See Auckland, William Eden, 1st Baron
Edinburgh, Scotland, 56
Education: AA on, 382, 424, 429; JA on, 134–35, 196; JQA on, 207; of AA2 and WSS's sons, xv, 134, 139, 142, 162, 184, 185–86, 301; of CA, 377; of CFA, 201, 311; of GWA, 13, 18, 22, 69, 85, 96, 156, 203, 207, 209, 214, 218, 228–29, 231, 280, 298, 299, 301, 311, 344, 349, 366, 407, 408; of JA2, 86, 203, 207, 209, 218, 239, 280, 311; of JQA, 169, 187, 370; funding for, 117–18, 205, 387, 389; of J. Hellen, 258; for lawyers, 212, 391, 392, 410, 421; in New England, 296, 297, 387, 389; Elizabeth Peabody on, 297, 344, 387; religious studies, 65, 187; schoolteachers, 295, 296; in science, 57, 188; of servants, 253; of women, 157, 429. *See also names of individual schools, colleges, and universities*
Edwards, Abigail Fowle Smith (1679–1760, grandmother of AA), 28–29
Edwards, Hepsibah Small (1717–1817, aunt of AA), 380–81, 385, 438
Eel River Nation, 80
Egypt, 62
Elections: AA on, 318, 336–37, 380, 426; JA on, 77; JQA on, 324–25; Massachusetts congressional, 5, 6–7, 9, 11, 12, 28, 354, 364, 365; Mass. General Court, 84–85, 168, 368; Massachusetts gubernatorial, 31, 48, 49, 140–41, 158, 159, 167, 169, 170, 254–55, 285, 286, 340, 341, 342, 343, 350–51, 353–54, 355, 356; in New York, 34, 35, 146, 147; in Pennsylvania, 66, 67, 68; presidential (1792), 324; presidential (1796), 324; presidential (1800), 320, 324, 425; presidential (1804), 5, 6, 7, 8, 9, 12; U.S. Constitution and, 318, 319, 324; in Virginia, 312
   Presidential (1808): AA on, 336–37, 380, 426; JA on, xxvi, 230, 320, 385–86; JQA and, xxvi, 307, 308, 309, 310, 314–15, 316, 317–18, 320, 322, 323, 324, 327–29, 332, 336, 350, 359, 377; JQA on, 128, 329, 330–31; TBA on, 323, 339–40; caucuses for, xxvi, 308, 314, 316, 317–18, 322, 327–29, 332, 340, 359; G. Clinton as candidate in, 312, 314, 323, 324, 340, 395, 397, 398; Congress and, 311–12; electioneering in, 128, 129, 306–308, 315, 317, 320, 324, 329–31, 332, 350, 359; electoral process, 318, 324, 330, 340, 397, 398; T. Jef-

ferson declines to stand, 296, 307; J. Madison as candidate in, xxvi, 307, 309, 312, 323, 327, 329, 330–31, 332, 340, 380, 397, 398; J. Monroe as candidate in, 149, 308, 309, 312, 314, 322, 323, 329, 330, 332; C. C. Pinckney as candidate in, 308, 380, 398; vice presidential candidates in, 307, 308, 312, 314, 323, 329, 330, 332, 377, 395, 398

Ellis, John (of Medway, Mass.), 85

Ely, William (of Springfield, Mass.), 202; identified, 204

Embargo Act (1807): AA on, xv, 336, 347–48, 364, 372, 380; JA and, 356–58, 377, 385–86, 387; JQA and, xii, xv–xvi, xxiv–xxv, 296, 309, 310, 312, 313, 316–17, 337–38, 340–41, 342, 343, 349–50, 353, 360, 361, 364; TBA on, 352–53; Democratic-Republican Party and, xxiv–xxv, 296; economic impact of, xxiv, xxv, 336, 338, 348, 352, 355, 357, 378, 383, 426; Enforcement Act (1809) and, 396, 397; Federalist Party and, xxiv–xxv, 296, 341, 342, 343, 356, 365, 396, 415, 416; Jefferson administration and, xv, xxiv, 294, 296, 332, 333, 342, 374, 377; New England and, 296, 309, 310, 341, 342–43, 344, 352–53, 357, 368, 370, 372, 395, 396, 403, 404, 406, 407, 408, 409; passage and repeal of, 72, 96, 263, 293, 294, 296, 312, 313, 317, 332, 333, 383, 385, 397–99, 401, 403, 404, 407–408, 412, 415, 416; public attitudes toward, 300, 352, 353, 355, 357–58, 360, 364, 377, 396, 398, 426; U.S. relations with Britain and, xii, 296, 355

Emerald (Boston), 246, 247

Emerson, Rev. William (of Boston), 207, 239–40, 241, 246, 247

Emlyn, Sollom: *State Trials* and, 40

England. *See* Great Britain

English language and literature: education in, 231, 280, 298, 299, 366; orations in, 139, 149, 171, 184; translations to, 77, 78, 90, 100, 102; mentioned, 23, 292

Enquirer (Richmond, Va.), 126, 176

Episcopal Church, 18

Eppes, John Wayles (nephew of T. Jefferson), 159, 396, 417, 418

Erskine, David Montagu Erskine, 2d Baron (Brit. minister to U.S.): identified, 152; JQA and, 241, 242, 398; Madison administration and, 434; residence of, 203, 204; social activities of, 260, 265, 287

Erskine, Frances Cadwalader Erskine, Baroness (wife of David), 256, 262, 265, 287; identified, 260

Espinasse, Isaac: *Law of Actions at Nisi Prius*, 421

Essex (Amer. ship), 95

Essex County, Mass., 7, 9

Essex Junto: AA on, 422, 425; TBA on, 341, 353, 406; elections and electioneering and, 12, 353, 355, 368; newspapers and, 361, 362, 406, 434

Essex Register (Salem, Mass.), 396

Eugenius (pseudonym), 129

Europe: JA on, 269; French influence in, xxiii, 122; interest of in U.S. affairs, xxii, 230; U.S. interest in, 157, 158, 339, 418. *See also names of individual countries*

European war: JQA on, 93–94, 122, 129, 225–26, 227, 256, 260, 337; Fourth Coalition and, 159; France and, 74, 122–23, 124, 183, 373, 374, 418; peace negotiations during, 256, 260; reported in Britain, 129, 130; reported in U.S., 124, 130, 158, 159, 260, 418; Third Coalition and, 75; trade and commerce affected by, xxiii, 263, 296, U.S. and, xxiii, 75, 93–94, 311. *See also names of individual countries, armies, navies, and battles*

Eustis, Jacob (brother of William), 4; identified, 6

Eustis, Dr. William (U.S. secy. of war), 4, 6, 8, 43, 409, 412, 414, 415

Evans, William (Baltimore innkeeper), 395, 396

Evening Post (N.Y.), 60, 91, 154

Everett, Alexander Hill (U.S. diplomat), 410

Everett, David (Boston printer), 434. *See also Boston Patriot*

Ewell, Elizabeth Stoddert (wife of Thomas), 157, 159

Ewell, Thomas (U.S. naval surgeon), 159

Ewing, Samuel (Phila. lawyer): JQA visits, 56, 57, 203, 394, 407; TBA and, 43, 47, 195, 407; correspondence with TBA, 2, 3, 44, 66, 407, 408

Exercise: AA on, 20; health and, 18, 72, 120; horseback riding, 37; riding in a carriage, 9, 17, 367, 409, 428; walking, 87, 186, 290

Exeter, N.H., 147

Fabius Maximus Verrucosus, Quintus (Roman general), 318–19

Faial Island, Azores, 25

Faxon, James (Adams family tenant), 249

Fayerweather, Thomas (Cambridge merchant), 86, 95, 96; identified, 88

Fearne, Charles: *Essay on the Learning of Contingent Remainders*, 421

Federalist Party: AA on, 131, 132, 337, 348, 365, 369, 419–20, 422, 425, 430; JA and, xxv, 31, 38, 39, 100, 320, 377, 386–87, 419, 422; JQA

Index

and, xii, xxiii, xxiv, xxv, xxvi, xxix, 307, 308, 313–14, 316, 328–29, 337, 354, 359, 360, 361, 364, 370, 376, 427; TBA and, 323, 340, 406–407; caucuses of, 140–41, 308, 323; Congress and, 129, 132, 310, 360; Democratic-Republican Party and, 327, 396; divisions in, 422; Embargo Act (1807) and, xxiv–xxv, 296, 341, 342, 343, 356, 365, 396, 415, 416; Enforcement Act (1809) and, 396; A. Hamilton and, 39, 100, 132; T. Jefferson and, 84, 123, 126, 322; J. Madison and, 328, 433; in Massachusetts, 5, 6, 7, 9, 12, 17, 49, 85, 140–41, 169, 170, 172, 185, 186, 223, 255, 339, 340, 341, 342, 343, 351, 362, 365, 368, 370, 377, 396, 407, 410, 414; in New England, xxv, 316, 339; newspapers and, 129, 254, 321, 341, 352, 361, 362, 364, 369, 412, 420, 430; in New York, 146, 147, 332; Non-Intercourse Act (1809) and, 412; in Pennsylvania, 66–67, 68; presidential election (1808) and, 307–308, 309, 323, 324, 329, 336, 340, 385; public attitudes toward, 26, 40, 198, 377; WSS and, 142; in South Carolina, 377; U.S. foreign relations and, xxiv, 28, 100, 293, 316, 331, 361; G. Washington and, 339; in Washington, D.C., 137–38; Yazoo land claims and, 42, 329
Fernando, Prince of Asturias, 374
Finances. *See* Debt; Investments; Money; Prices and costs; Taxes
Firearms. *See* Munitions
Fires: Adamses and, 211–12, 217–18; in Boston, 236, 237; in Georgetown, D.C., 179; for heating, 210, 264, 321, 367; insurance for, 135, 136; in New York, 218
Fireworks, 435
First Barbary War. *See* Barbary War, First
First Book of the Dying State of Federalism, 9
Fitch, Eliphalet (2d cousin of JA), 56; identified, 57
Fletcher, Robert (of Amherst, N.H.), 413
Florida: boundaries of, ix, 63, 84, 99; A. Burr conspiracy and, 250; Spanish-American relations and, 62, 90, 139, 154; Spanish control of, ix; U.S. considers purchase of, ix, 81, 83 (illus.), 84, 86, 87; mentioned, 320
Food and drink: alcohol, xi, 17, 19, 66, 84, 108, 222, 239, 390; bread, 259, 432; chocolate, xviii, 143; coffee, 177; confections, xi, 13, 18, 84, 104, 157, 163, 168, 171; crackers, xvii, 18, 19, 108; dairy products, 13, 17, 18, 259, 300, 378, 432, 437–38; fruits, xviii, 108, 144–45, 168, 239, 258, 261, 280, 363, 390; grains and flour, 58, 59, 67, 104, 252, 253, 351, 363; meats and fish, 17, 23, 92, 93, 104, 200, 258; pasta, 106; salt, 179; shortages of, 9; sugar, xvii, 72, 363; tea, 211, 212, 335, 384; vegetables, 23, 43, 76, 168, 363
Ford, Worthington Chauncey (editor), xxviii–xxix
Foronda, Valentin de (Spanish chargé d'affaires in U.S.), 109
Fort Adams, Miss., 4
Fort Augustus, Scotland, 423, 425
Fort Oswego, N.Y., 425
Foster, Charles Phineas (son of Frances), 201
Foster, Elizabeth Anne (1802–1875, daughter of Elizabeth Smith), 431, 432
Foster, Elizabeth Smith (Betsy, 1771–1854, niece of AA): children of, 152, 154, 164, 368, 369, 432; Elizabeth Peabody and, 121, 436; Louisa Smith and, 119
Foster, Frances Harrod (sister of AHA), 112, 119, 200, 201, 363, 364; identified, 103
Foster, James Hiller (1773–1862, husband of Elizabeth Smith), 154, 368
Foster, John Harrod (son of Frances), 363, 364
Foster, Louisa Catherine Smith (daughter of Elizabeth Smith), 152; identified, 154
Foster, Marie Hortense Perron (wife of William, Jr.), 410; identified, 411
Foster, Phineas (husband of Frances), 402
Foster, William (Boston tobacconist), 161; identified, 163
Foster, William, Jr. (Boston merchant), 411
Foster, William Emerson (son of Elizabeth Smith), 368; identified, 369
Fox, Charles James (Brit. statesman), 152
Fox Nation, 80–81
France: JA and JQA travel to, 135, 231; JA on, 34, 122, 123; American Revolution and, 25, 90, 91, 135; arts and culture in, 62; client states of, 75, 374; consuls from, 57, 252; decrees on navigation, 263, 311, 358, 368, 372, 417, 418; diplomatic appointments of, 4, 24, 25, 100, 116, 129, 242, 252; diplomatic appointments to, 116, 262, 296, 420; European war and, xxiii, 40, 122–23, 124, 183, 227, 260, 294, 296, 374; French Revolution, 9, 25, 34, 122, 216; influence on U.S., 15, 122, 123, 280, 317, 320, 332, 337, 352, 356, 426, 433; political conditions in, 38, 63; relations with Britain, xx, 3, 33–34, 263, 380; relations with Prussia, 159, 256, 260; relations with Spain, ix, 83 (illus.), 372, 373, 374, 381, 417; relations with U.S., ix, xxv, 2, 4, 24, 39, 83 (illus.), 87, 99, 100, 113–14, 115–16, 124, 243, 252, 262, 263, 294, 296, 306, 311, 320, 333, 342, 345, 352, 353, 355, 357, 372, 380, 381, 385, 386, 387, 398, 401, 406, 408, 412, 417, 418, 420, 422, 433; symbols of, 320, 321;

U.S. attitudes toward, 75, 101, 157, 294, 316, 317, 341, 406; mentioned, 152, 300. *See also* French Army; French Navy
Francis II, Holy Roman Emperor, 225, 227
Francis, Thomas Willing (Phila. merchant), 56, 57
Frankfort, Ky., 250, 251
Franklin, Benjamin, 90, 91, 100, 102
Frazier, Harriet (sister of Mary Frazier Sargent), 237; identified, 238
Frederick II (the Great), King of Prussia, 226, 227
Frederick William III, King of Prussia, 225, 227, 260
Frederick, Md., 202
Freemasons, 76
French, Moses, Jr. (former Adams tenant), 79, 80
French Army: in Austria, 124, 129–30; in Bavaria, 74, 75; Napoleon and, 124, 129–30, 227, 256, 374; in Saxony, 226, 227, 260; service in, 25; in Spain, 374, 418
French language and literature: GWA's and JA2's skills in, 205, 207, 209, 210, 211, 212, 215, 222, 231, 234, 237, 239, 280, 283, 408; T. B. Johnson's skills in, 278; publications in, 15, 408; mentioned, 23, 365
French Navy, 183, 352
French Revolution. *See* France
Frenchtown, Md., 1, 54, 70, 145
Freneau, Philip (Phila. printer), 39
Frothingham, Nathaniel (Boston coachmaker), 143
Frothingham, Thomas (Boston coachmaker), 143
Funerals: Mary Carter Smith (1806), 111; Ebenezer Storer (1807), 229, 231, 232; Elisha Turner (1806), 103, 104
Furniture and furnishings: baskets, 211; beds and bedding, 30, 280, 305, 384; candles, 210, 211, 217, 218, 427; chairs, 212, 382, 384, 399; chests and dressers, 211, 217, 218; clocks, 368; coffeepot, 104; fireplaces and mantelpieces, 212, 264, 321; lantern, 175–76; mirrors, 428; seals, 397; tables, 217; trunks, 58, 150, 158, 163, 164, 168, 171, 172, 193, 199; writing slate, 375

Gadsby, John (Washington, D.C., innkeeper), 395, 396, 397
Gallatin, Albert (U.S. secy. of the treasury), 204, 278, 296, 412, 414. *See also* Treasury Department, U.S.
Gallison, John (Boston lawyer), 410
Gamble, John (of Phila.), 68
Games and pastimes: cards, 242; folk traditions, 258; horse racing, 10, 11, 282; sledding, 111; toys, 111, 168, 205, 207, 209, 424
Gardenier, Barent (N.Y. representative), 328; identified, 332
Gardens and gardening: at JQA Birthplace, 29; in Boston, 171, 172, 175; cuttings for, 144–45; flower, 363; fruit and vegetable, 43, 168, 363; at Peacefield, 168, 185, 363, 424; in Quincy, 43, 48
Gardiner, Rev. John Sylvester John: *Sermon, Preached . . . April 7, 1808*, 361
Gardner, Henry (Boston merchant), 267; identified, 238
Gardner, John (of Boston), 312, 398, 399, 403, 404; identified, 316
Gardner, Mary Tracy (daughter of John), 403, 404
Gardner, Sarah Jackson (wife of John), 398; identified, 399
Gardner, Sarah Turner (wife of Henry), 237; identified, 238
Garonne River, 386, 387
Gay, Henry Turner (of Quincy): identified, 69
Gazette of the United States (Phila.), 323
Gelston, David (N.Y. customs collector), 142
Gender, 23, 174, 180, 215, 216
Genet, Cornelia Clinton (wife of Edmond), 256, 260
Genet, Edmond Charles (former French minister to the U.S.), 129, 260
George I, King of England, 40, 122
George III, King of England, 157–58, 292, 293, 296, 358, 425, 433, 434
Georgetown, D.C.: merchants in, 241, 242; residents of, 165, 179, 241, 255; St. John Church, 413, 414; ships to, 106, 168, 234; slavery in, 179; mentioned, 412
Georgia, 41–42, 98, 99, 124, 136, 413
German states, 34, 39
Gerry, Elbridge (Mass. politician), 7, 9; letter from AA listed (1796), 441
Gibbon, Edward: *Decline and Fall of the Roman Empire*, 77, 78
Gibbon, Lt. (U.S.), 417, 418
Giles, William Branch (Va. senator): identified, 31; JA on, 34; JQA and, 31–32, 91, 398; health of, 98, 99, 108; presidential election (1808) and, 332; Senate activities of, 31–32, 233–34, 247, 310, 326, 353, 355, 414; mentioned, 132
Gilman, Nicholas (N.H. senator), 146, 202, 204; identified, 147
Giraud, Marc Antoine Alexis (French consul at Boston), 251, 264–65; identified, 252
Glasgow, Scotland, 425
Glover, Elias (Ohio lawyer), 308; identified, 310

Index

Godolphin, Sidney Godolphin, 1st Earl of (Brit. lord high treasurer), 39, 40
Goldsmith, Lewis: *Secret History of . . . St. Cloud*, 183, 184
Goldsmith, Oliver (Irish writer), 133
Goodwin, Gen. Nathaniel (of Sandwich, Mass.), 195
Goodwin, Ruth Shaw (wife of Nathaniel): identified, 195
Gore, Christopher (gov. of Mass.): TBA on, 340, 354; Adamses socialize with, 156, 434; Embargo Act (1807) and, 406, 407; law career of, 223; as Massachusetts governor, 340, 342, 351, 353, 354, 409; U.S. relations with Britain and, 10, 108, 109
Gore, Rebecca Payne (wife of Christopher), 156
Gorham, Stephen (Boston merchant), 36, 41; identified, 37
Grafton County, N.H., 432
Grant, Anna Powell Mason (wife of Patrick), 157, 159
Grant, Anne MacVicar (Scottish writer): identified, 425; *Letters from the Mountains*, 422–24, 425, 429
Grant, Patrick (London banker), 157, 159
Gray, John Chipman (son of William), 410; identified, 411
Gray, Thomas: "Elegy Written in a Country Churchyard," 176, 177
Gray, William (Salem merchant), 406, 410, 411; identified, 407
Great Britain: JA on, 33–34, 312, 422, 425, 434; arts and culture in, xii, 39, 207; colonial possessions of, 191, 192, 202, 425; economy of, 107, 152, 418; European war and, 40, 75, 159; histories of, 39, 40; influence on U.S., 122, 320, 323, 331, 332, 337, 356, 420, 422, 425, 433; judiciary in, 91, 93–94, 95, 101, 123; Magna Carta, 33; Parliament, 40, 122, 191, 192, 262, 426, 427; Privy Council, 350, 372, 417, 418, 427, 434; relations with France, xx, 33–34, 263, 294, 296, 320; relations with Prussia, 158; relations with Spain, x, 122, 320, 374; religion in, 33; slavery and, 262; symbols of, 320, 321; U.S. attitudes toward, xxiii, 75, 101, 115, 129, 147, 157, 276, 293, 294, 361, 406, 434; War of the Roses, 33, 34

Relations with United States: AA on, xxvi–xxvii, 108, 338, 345, 346, 372, 380, 420, 426, 433; JA on, 6, 101, 107–108, 109, 320, 357, 386, 425; JQA and, xxiii–xxiv, 81, 87, 90, 91, 93–94, 97–98, 105, 106–107, 113, 114, 115, 124, 292, 311, 316, 337, 338, 343, 350, 355, 357, 402, 403, 410, 417; LCA on, 290, 306; TBA on, 342; Anglo-American peace negotiations, 15; attacks on U.S. shipping and, xv, xxiii, xxiv, 2, 3, 147, 292, 312, 355, 433, 434; British attitudes toward, 296, 427; *Chesapeake-Leopard* Affair and, xii, xxiv, 276, 277 (illus.), 278, 282, 286–87, 292, 293, 296, 306, 307, 315–16, 317, 331, 335, 338, 351–52, 355; Congress and, 97, 98, 99, 106–107, 114, 115, 124, 294, 333, 337, 417; Embargo Act (1807) and, xii, 296, 355; exchange of ministers, 72, 148, 149, 152, 158, 163, 164, 204, 242, 260, 287, 307, 434; Jay Treaty, xxv, 10, 11, 408; Jefferson administration and, 3, 71, 99, 204, 205, 333, 433, 434; J. Madison and, 3, 296–97, 426, 433, 434; Monroe-Pinkney Treaty, 149, 243, 262–63, 316–17, 330, 332, 337; J. Monroe's mission to, 2, 3, 11, 296–98, 333; Native Americans and, 191, 192–93; Non-Importation Act (1806) and, 95–96, 128, 129, 253, 254, 291–92; Non-Intercourse Act (1809) and, 385, 398, 399, 401, 412; U.S. attitudes toward, 106, 108, 109, 113, 116, 292, 300, 307, 310, 321, 336, 340, 341; possible war with U.S., xxix, 93–94, 284, 287, 290, 294, 338, 340, 357

See also Ireland; Scotland
Greek language and literature, 182, 196, 224, 245, 257, 316, 392
Greene, Gardiner (Boston merchant), 150; identified, 152
Greenleaf, Daniel (1762–1853, of Quincy), 73, 75
Greenleaf, Daniel (1803–1827, son of Lucy Cranch), 375; identified, 377
Greenleaf, Ezekiel Price (son of Thomas and Mary Deming), 383; identified, 385
Greenleaf, James (Washington, D.C., merchant), 56, 218
Greenleaf, John (1763–1848, husband of Lucy Cranch), 159, 185, 377
Greenleaf, John, Jr. (1799–1826, son of Lucy Cranch), 103, 104, 156, 375, 377
Greenleaf, Lucy (1797–1877, daughter of Lucy Cranch), 375, 377
Greenleaf, Lucy Cranch (1767–1846, niece of AA): birth of children, 157, 159, 160, 377; correspondence with AA, 104; visits Cranches, 375; letter from AA listed (1806), 444; mentioned, 37
Greenleaf, Mary Deming Price (wife of Thomas of Quincy), 29, 183, 201, 384, 385; identified, 30
Greenleaf, Mary Elizabeth (1806–1886, daughter of Lucy Cranch), 157, 159, 160, 375; identified, 377
Greenleaf, Richard Cranch (1808–1887, son of Lucy Cranch), 375; identified, 377

489

Greenleaf, Thomas (1755–1798, N.Y. printer), 39
Greenleaf, Thomas, Sr. (1767–1854, Quincy J.P.), 30, 73, 75, 201, 383, 385
Greenleaf, Thomas, Jr. (1788–1817, son of Thomas and Mary Deming), 200, 421; identified, 201
Greenleaf, William Cranch (1801–1868, son of Lucy Cranch), 375; identified, 377
Gregg, Andrew (Penn. representative), 70–71, 95, 128, 129
Grenville, William Wyndham Grenville, 1st Baron (Brit. statesman), 426, 427
Groton, Mass., 206
Guiana, Venezuela, x, 89 (illus.)
Guild, Benjamin, Sr. (husband of Elizabeth): identified, 65
Guild, Elizabeth Quincy (2d cousin of AA's mother), 64; identified, 65
Gulliver, Benjamin (Boston merchant), 210, 211, 235, 239, 241, 242, 253
Gulliver, Mary Bancroft (wife of Benjamin), 206, 251, 252; identified, 207
Gurley, John Ward (New Orleans lawyer), 135
Gurney, William (Boston stonemason), 349, 350, 410, 414
GWA. *See* ADAMS, GEORGE WASHINGTON (1801–1829)

Hague, The, Netherlands, 27
Haiti, 2, 4, 12, 101, 113–14, 115–16, 122
Halifax, Nova Scotia, 150, 152, 157, 316
Hall, Ann (niece of Moses Black), 381–82, 383
Hall, Joseph, Sr. (1761–1848, Boston lawyer), 237, 238, 337–38, 339, 341, 343
Hallowell, John (of Phila.), 66, 68
Hallowell, Maine, 117–18
Hamilton, Alexander: AA on, 132; JA on, 8; duel with A. Burr, 7, 32, 422; Federalist Party and, 39, 100, 422, 425; mentioned, 34, 248
Hamilton, Paul (U.S. secy. of the navy), 412, 414
Hamilton, N.Y., 285
Hannibal, 319
Hanover, House of, 39, 40
Hardwick, Frederick (Quincy cordwainer), 249, 250
Hardwick, Peter (of Quincy), 194; identified, 195
Hare, Robert, Jr. (Phila. chemist), 59, 242
Harper, Catherine Carroll (wife of Robert), 51, 200, 201, 413, 414, 415; identified, 52
Harper, Robert Goodloe (Baltimore lawyer), 43, 52, 132, 201, 413, 414, 415
Harrod, Ann. *See* ADAMS, ANN HARROD (1774–1845, wife of TBA)

Harrod, Anna Treat (mother of AHA), 121, 199, 200
Harrod, Charles (brother of AHA), 407; identified, 408
Harrod, Elizabeth Marston. *See* Stebbins, Elizabeth Marston Harrod
Harrod, Joseph (father of AHA), 121, 199, 388, 430, 437
Harrod, Mary (sister of AHA), 52–53, 366, 367, 368; identified, 53
Hartford, Conn., 202, 394
Harvard College: CFA attends, 201; JQA attends, 169, 187, 370; JQA's professorship at, xx, 65, 78, 150, 152, 156, 164, 166–67, 168, 169, 170, 171–72, 181, 182, 187, 188, 190, 194, 223, 224–25; TBA on, 188; American Academy meeting at, 194; benefactors of, 85; Boylston Hall, 75; commencement at, 60, 166, 181, 187, 188, 195, 196, 198; Corporation of, 64, 74, 172, 182, 188; faculty of, 64, 65, 74, 152, 172, 187; Phi Beta Kappa Society at, 188, 190, 196–97, 198; president of, 73, 74, 86–87, 95, 149–50, 152; real estate of, 64; rules and regulations at, 172, 182; William Smith Shaw attends, 212, 301; students of, 85, 370, 411; treasurer for, 229, 231
Harvard University Press, xxviii
Hastings, Seth (Mass. representative), 202; identified, 204
Hatzfeldt, Franz Ludwig, Prince von (Prussian diplomat), 256, 260
Hatzfeldt, Friederike Karoline, Princess von (wife of Franz), 256; identified, 260
Haverhill, Mass.: Abigail Smith Adams visits, 368; CA's residence in, 377; TBA and AHA visit, 8, 15, 54, 69, 199, 273, 274, 285, 288, 387, 429, 430; First Church, 388, 389; mentioned, 53, 121, 271, 272, 290, 437
Haverhill, N.H., 431, 432
Hawk (sloop), 168, 171, 172
Hayley, William: *Triumphs of Temper*, 382, 383
Health and illnesses: ague, 3, 205, 379, 430; allergic reaction, 282–83; bilious disorders, 3, 122, 155, 347; bowel issues, 18, 21, 85, 400; broken bones, 98, 99, 381, 385; burns, 43, 120; cancer, 119, 237; chicken pox, xi, 52, 236, 385; childbirth, xix, 160, 177, 178, 188, 204, 251, 252, 267, 279, 323–24, 326, 338, 349, 377; colds and coughs, 17, 21, 29, 36, 43, 46, 56, 62, 64, 65, 69, 72, 76, 85, 92, 111, 144, 171, 209, 212, 217, 228, 229, 231, 235, 255, 262, 266, 280, 301, 312, 334, 364, 368, 395, 399, 403, 407, 417; colic, 347; consumption, 111, 118, 119, 260, 385, 403; croup, 226, 400; deafness, 119; dysentery, 119, 233, 239; edema (dropsy), 98, 119; epilepsy, 87; ery-

sipelas, 428, 432; eye problems, 32, 52, 215, 235, 379, 389, 417, 428, 430; fevers, 3, 9–10, 107, 111, 119, 144, 152, 155, 189 (illus.), 200, 202, 205, 210, 248, 273, 297, 301, 343, 364, 367, 368, 374, 379, 384, 385, 399, 408, 428, 430, 432; gout, 107, 432; gunshot wounds, 332; hand injuries, 173, 203, 204, 213; headaches, 200, 215, 222, 228, 432; influenza, 171, 266; laryngitis, 56; leg and foot injuries, 17, 21, 27, 112, 271; mental disorders, 131, 132, 264, 410, 419; nursing, 177, 178, 233, 253, 266, 289, 397; pleurisy, 66; pneumonia, 36, 120, 273; poisoning, 177; pregnancy and miscarriage, xix, 94–95, 96, 128, 140, 141, 142, 152, 155, 156, 157, 163, 164, 165, 169, 173, 175, 177, 178, 179, 180, 181, 184, 185, 187, 200, 214, 251, 289, 307, 309, 375, 394, 399, 400, 402, 404, 408; pyrosis, 379, 381; respiratory ailments, 17, 43, 271, 347; rheumatism, 17, 21, 29, 30, 36, 46–47, 64, 120, 262, 266, 268, 374; scarlet fever, xi; skin conditions, 21, 51, 125, 210, 224, 273, 282–83, 384, 385; smallpox, 51, 52, 57, 189 (illus.), 295, 297; sore throat, 202, 209, 212, 217; sprains, 376; stomach disorders, 103, 108, 122, 301; stroke, 17, 87, 235; teething, xi, 22, 189 (illus.), 290, 306, 312; toothache, 64; travel affects, 51, 107, 180, 428, 431; tremors, 419; vertigo, 251, 374; weakness, 195, 251, 408; weather and climate affect, 29, 36, 51, 64, 200, 368; weight and, 18, 72, 107, 417; whooping cough, xi, 52, 59, 64, 119, 231; worms, 72, 119, 347

Remedies: arm slings, 203; arrowroot, 239; baths, 44, 376; bleeding, 400, 417; blisters and compresses, 36, 239, 374, 393–94, 397, 400, 432; castor oil, 65; cough drops, 21; dewormer, 347; diet, 108; emetics, 283, 374; goose oil, 283; Lockyer Pills, 334; magnesium, 239; medicine, 65, 118–19, 122, 124, 125, 164–65, 235, 252; oil of terpentine, 72; onion juice, 283; recipes for, 30, 283; salt air, 120, 143, 195, 431; spirit of hartshorn, 264, 265; straightjacket, 410; vaccination, xi, 51, 52, 57, 189 (illus.), 295, 297

See also Exercise

Heard, John, Jr. (Boston lawyer), 210
Heard, Susan Oliver (wife of John), 209; identified, 210
Heath, Maj. Gen. William (of Roxbury), 141
Hebrew language and literature, 74, 226, 227
Hellen, Ann Johnson (Nancy, sister of LCA): JQA and, 215, 227–28, 233, 234, 238, 239, 417; Adamses reside with, 1, 3, 151, 244, 394; correspondence with LCA, 227, 229; domestic life of, 94–95, 96, 239, 257, 258; family of, 75–76, 164, 400, 403; grief of, 211, 213, 214, 224, 227–28, 283; social activities of, 411, 415, 416, 417; mentioned, 19, 59, 232, 279, 397
Hellen, Johnson (son of Ann), 258
Hellen, Mary Catherine (1806–1870, later wife of JA2, designated as MCHA in *The Adams Papers*), 229, 258, 400, 401, 403; identified, 211
Hellen, Walter (1766–1815, husband of Ann): JQA and, 59, 149, 151, 181, 407; LCA and, 206; Adamses reside with, 1, 3, 137, 208, 244, 251, 394; correspondence with LCA, 227, 229; domestic life of, 94–95, 96, 257, 258, 417; grief of, 210, 211, 213, 224; health of, 41, 43, 164–65; as merchant, 148, 165; WSS and, 174; social activities of, 411, 417; letter from JQA listed (1805), 443
  Letter: From JQA (1805), 58
Hellen, Walter, Jr. (1804–1806, son of Ann): JQA on, 224; death of, 210–11, 212–13, 214, 218, 224, 234, 283; health of, 164, 185, 202, 205, 208, 214
Hellen, Washington (son of Ann), 234
Hemings, Sally (of Monticello), 261
Henry (Peabody boarder), 121
Henry, Robert: *History of Great Britain*, 39, 40
Herald (N.Y.), xxv, 144, 145, 316, 323, 324
Hillhouse, James (Conn. senator), 402
Hingham, Mass., 187, 312, 321
Hodson, Daniel (brother-in-law of Oliver Goldsmith), 133
Holidays: Christmas, 74, 79, 206, 289, 294; Fourth of July, 182, 185, 186, 370, 434–35; New Year's Day, xi, 81–82, 84, 219, 222, 223; thanksgiving days, 15, 206, 285, 286, 288–89, 384, 385, 387
Holland, Henry Richard Vassall Fox, 3d Baron (Brit. nobleman), 262–63
Holmes, Rev. Abiel (of Cambridge), 163
Holy Roman Empire, 227
Homer, 224, 257, 412; *Iliad*, 182; *Odyssey*, 29, 30, 426–27, 428
Hope Insurance Company of Providence, 401
Hopkinson, Joseph (Phila. lawyer), 56, 57, 66, 203, 242, 394
Horses: for Adamses, 37, 58, 59, 429; care of, 112, 295; racing of, 10, 11, 282
Hotels: Blue Anchor Tavern (Cambridge), 156, 158; City Hotel (N.Y.), 146, 147; Exchange Hotel (Boston), 435; Gadsby's Hotel (Washington, D.C.), 396; Indian Queen Hotel (Baltimore), 395, 396; Long's Hotel (Washington, D.C.), 411, 414; Mansion House Hotel (Phila.), 394, 396; in Quincy, 265, 266; Ross' Tavern (Bladensburg, Md.), 335, 336; Stelle's Hotel (Washington, D.C.), 234, 411

Hough, David (N.H. representative), 202; identified, 204
House of Representatives, U.S. *See* Congress, U.S.
Houses: in Cambridge, 64, 73, 74–75, 95, 96; cellars for, 121; construction and renovation of, 64, 143, 232, 240–41, 250–51, 254, 255, 302, 345; fire protection in, 211–12, 217, 218; heating of, 209, 210, 367; moving of, 121, 122; rental of, 29, 41, 46, 48, 74, 79, 86, 136, 143, 161, 162, 167, 180, 187, 210, 211, 212, 232, 237, 238, 246, 295, 297, 349, 354, 410, 414, 422; in Washington, D.C., 218. *See also* John Adams Birthplace; John Quincy Adams Birthplace; Old House; President's House (Washington, D.C.); *names of individual estates*
Howard, John Clarke (Boston physician), 236, 238, 295, 297
Howe, John (Mass. politician), 85
Howe, Capt. (of the *Augustus*), 296
Hull, Capt. Isaac (U.S.), 190, 191
Hume, David: *History of England*, 356; *Life of David Hume*, 357; *Treatise of Human Nature*, 356, 357
Humphreys, Capt. Salusbury Pryce (of the *Leopard*), xii, 355
Hunter, Elizabeth Orby (wife of Robert), 163; identified, 164
Hunter, Henry: *Sacred Biography*, 375, 377
Hunter, Robert (former gov. of N.Y.): identified, 164

Immigration, 34, 117, 374, 375–76, 412, 414
Independent Chronicle (Boston): JA's treatment in, 186; JA's writings in, 371; JQA's treatment in, 324, 355; JQA's writings in, 341, 343, 350, 361; advertisements in, 144, 350; A. Burr conspiracy reported in, 250; elections reported in, 49; Embargo Act (1807) reported in, 310; Fourth of July celebration reported in, 435; Miranda expedition reported in, 159; Pickering-Sullivan exchange in, 355
Indian Chief (ship), 151
Industry (stagecoach line), 65–66, 67, 68
Ingersoll, Charles Jared (Phila. playwright), 394, 396; *View of the Rights and Wrongs*, 407, 408
Innes, Henry (Ky. judge), 254, 255, 356, 357
Insurance, 37, 135–36, 353
Investments: of Adamses, 67, 68, 135–36, 321, 393; foreign in U.S., 107; interest and dividends on, 118, 135–36, 321; land speculation, xxi, 41–42, 44, 71, 116–17, 161, 162, 300, 317, 401, 413; speculation, 71, 87, 356, 357; stocks and bonds, 67, 68, 135–36, 247, 321, 393. *See also* Money
Ireland, 34, 96, 133, 196, 198, 365, 374
Irujo, Carlos Fernando Martínez, Marquis de Casa. *See* Yrujo, Carlos Fernando Martínez, Marquis de Casa
Irving, Peter (N.Y. editor), 60
Italy, 62, 82, 85, 219

JA. *See* ADAMS, JOHN (1735–1826)
JA2. *See* ADAMS, JOHN, 2D (1803–1834)
JA Birthplace. *See* John Adams Birthplace
Jackson, Dr. David (of Phila.), 240
Jackson, Esther Phillips Parsons (sister of Hannah Cushing), 61
Jackson, James (Ga. senator), 98; identified, 99
Jackson, Patrick Tracy (Boston merchant), 403; identified, 404
Jackson, Susan. *See* Davis, Susan Jackson
Jackson, Susan Kemper (wife of David), 240
Jackson, William (Phila. printer), 319, 322, 327, 328, 329. See also *Political and Commercial Register*
Jamaica, 56, 57, 287, 291, 293
Jarvis, William (Boston merchant), 409
Jay, John (former gov. of N.Y.), 320, 323
Jefferson, Thomas: AA and, 124, 338, 351; books and reading, 412; correspondence with T. Randolph, 179; health of, 203, 204, 296; relationship with S. Hemings, 261; travels of, 148, 149, 174, 178; as Virginia governor, 40
    Presidency, 1801–1809: AA on, 73, 108, 125, 132–33, 235, 289, 345, 346, 347–48, 372, 380, 419–20, 433; JA and, 135, 338, 348, 376; JA on, 12, 31, 77, 320, 357; JQA and, xi, 2–3, 81–82, 84, 203, 218, 219, 255–56, 260, 397, 398, 402, 411–12; JQA on, 204–205, 243, 261, 281, 292, 314, 331, 337, 343; TBA on, xxvi, 26, 294, 352; A. Burr conspiracy and, 207, 208, 235, 243–44, 245, 248, 249, 250; cabinet of, 10, 11, 72, 248; *Chesapeake-Leopard* Affair and, xii, xxiv, 282, 286–87, 290, 292, 293, 307, 315–16, 351–52, 355; congressional attitudes toward, 124, 133, 154, 315–16; diplomatic etiquette and, 108, 109, 265; inaugural address, 347–48, 349; J. Madison inauguration and, 411, 413; military preparedness and, 71, 81, 98, 99, 124, 282, 333; Miranda expedition and, x, xxii, 126, 128–29, 130, 134, 142, 235; Monroe-Pinkney Treaty and, 263, 308, 317, 330, 337; nominations and appointments by, 10, 11, 32, 125, 126, 130, 133, 149, 238, 248, 401, 402, 415, 416; patronage appeals to,

311; Elizabeth Peabody on, 367, 387, 388; presidential election (1804) and, 12; presidential election (1808) and, 100, 230, 294, 296, 307, 330, 340; proclamations by, 249, 282, 307, 315, 316; public attitudes toward, ix, 38, 40, 60, 83 (illus.), 113, 126, 129, 137, 141, 186, 230, 231, 234, 249, 291, 316, 317, 330, 339–40, 341, 342, 374, 377, 384, 426, 427; J. Randolph and, 137, 139, 154, 287, 293; regulation of U.S. trade and, xv, 4, 95, 263, 294, 296, 332, 333, 342, 374, 377, 399; Sedition Act (1798) and, 39; Senate expulsion of John Smith and, 308, 310; slavery and, 205, 261, 262; WSS and, 142, 174, 194, 195, 250, 303; social responsibilities of, xi, 81–82, 84, 213, 219, 411; submits messages and documents to Congress, ix, 4, 10, 11, 63, 69, 71, 72, 73, 78, 79, 81, 84, 97, 99, 105, 106, 109, 115–16, 130, 204–205, 209, 210, 243–44, 245, 248, 262, 263, 281, 282, 284, 290, 293, 296, 308, 310, 326, 331, 333, 351–52, 355, 427; territorial expansion and governance and, ix, 11, 24, 83 (illus.), 139, 205, 278; U.S. relations with Barbary States and, 80, 107, 141, 205, 426, 427; U.S. relations with Britain and, xxv, 97, 106, 109, 146, 147, 148, 152, 204, 205, 262, 282, 290, 333, 346, 433; U.S. relations with France and, 25, 115–16, 262, 333, 352, 355, 433; U.S. relations with Native Americans and, xi, 11, 205, 213, 219; U.S. relations with Spain and, ix, 11, 63, 84, 97, 109, 134, 205; Yazoo land claims and, 42
Letter: To LCA (1807), 278
Jena, Battle of, 226, 227, 260
Jenings, Edmund (of Md.), 15
John (Peabody boarder), 121
John Adams (U.S. frigate), 98, 99
John Adams Birthplace, 226, 295, 297, 378–79
John Quincy Adams Birthplace: JA2 on, 158, 159, 165; JQA and LCA's residence in, 23, 48, 58, 158, 186, 187, 190, 193, 291; TBA and, 249–50; caretakers for, 17, 226; farms and gardens at, 17, 23, 249; tenants of, 29, 30, 292; woodlot of, 291, 292, 294
Johnson, Adelaide (sister of LCA): church attendance, 413, 414, 417; correspondence with LCA, 214; health of, 205; social activities of, 210, 219, 233, 262; mentioned, 19, 232, 289
Johnson, Carolina Virginia Marylanda. *See* Buchanan, Carolina Virginia Marylanda Johnson
Johnson, Catherine Maria Frances (sister of LCA): LCA and, 410, 438; Adamses and, 257, 368, 396, 397, 404, 435; correspondence with C. Buchanan, 213, 218; health of, 393–94, 397, 399, 400; social activities of, xx, 210, 219, 233, 262, 394, 397, 414, 415; mentioned, 19, 43, 232, 289
Johnson, Catherine Nuth (mother of LCA): AA on, 368; LCA and, xix, 227, 229, 232; family of, 211, 227, 251, 281, 401, 417; health of, 202, 213; J. Johnson estate and, 148, 149, 151; social activities of, 81–82, 84, 210, 219, 233, 262, 411; mentioned, 19, 72, 76, 93, 111, 147, 236, 289, 400
Letters: From JQA (1807), 279 (2)
Johnson, Catherine Walker. *See* Brent, Catherine Walker Johnson
Johnson, Eliza Jennet Dorcas (sister of LCA): AA on, 76, 92–93, 289, 368; LCA and, 290; Adamses and, 51, 52, 75, 156; family of, 111, 242, 417; health of, 43, 51, 62, 65, 72, 76, 208, 255; social activities of, 61, 63, 210, 219, 233, 262, 289, 290, 413, 414, 417; mentioned, 19, 232
Johnson, Harriet. *See* Boyd, Harriet Johnson
Johnson, Joshua (father of LCA), 42, 58, 59, 149, 151
Johnson, Samuel (Brit. author), 29, 30; *The Idler*, 50, 51; *Prince of Abissinia*, 379, 381
Johnson, Thomas Baker (brother of LCA), 36, 37, 111, 205, 278, 401
Johnson, William (U.S. Supreme Court justice), 107, 413
Jones, Walter, Jr. (U.S. attorney for D.C.), 245, 249
JQA. *See* ADAMS, JOHN QUINCY (1767–1848)
JQA Birthplace. *See* John Quincy Adams Birthplace
Judiciary, U.S.: AA on, 318; JA on, 123; JQA on, 57, 326–27; TBA on, 26–27, 321–22, 326; Congress considers reform of, 123, 124, 318, 319, 320, 321–22, 325–26, 327; corporations and, 400–402; grand juries and, 262; Judiciary Act (1802) and, 132, 133; Seventh Circuit Act (1807) and, 247, 248

District and Circuit Courts: JQA appears before, 169; TBA appears before, 285, 286; A. Burr conspiracy and, 244, 245, 249, 264; William Cranch's appointment to, 125, 126, 160; service on, 392; sessions of, 61; WSS's trial in, 141–42, 143, 144, 145, 195, 250; Yazoo land claims and, 413

Supreme Court: JQA appears before, 390–91, 392, 397, 400–402, 404, 411, 413, 414, 416, 418; JQA on, 261; Bank of the United States v. Deveaux, 401–402, 416, 418; William Cranch publishes cases of, 26, 28; Ex parte Bollman, 245, 252, 253, 256, 261, 263; Fletcher v. Peck, 42, 401–402, 411, 413, 414, 416, 418; Hodgson v. Dexter, 28; Hope Insurance Company of Providence v. Boardman, 401–402, 416, 418; impeachment of S. Chase Sr., 21, 26, 31–32, 33, 34, 43, 46, 48, 57; Marbury v. Madison, 28; powers of, 413; service on, 124, 247–48, 252, 260; sessions of, 106, 107, 144, 242, 243, 244, 247–48, 256, 334, 336, 344, 347, 415; Yazoo land claims and, 317, 401, 413

See also Attorney General, U.S.

Juno (Adams dog), 29, 45, 111, 274, 427
Jusseaume, René (French-Canadian interpreter), xi

Katy (brig), 19
Kean, Miss (of Phila.), 59
Keene, Sarah Lukens (niece of Tacy Lenox), 164, 241–42; identified, 242
Kenney, James: *The World*, 391
Kenrick, William: "Epistles to Lorenzo," 216, 217
Kentucky: congressional delegation of, 80, 398; judiciary in, 247, 248, 250, 255, 264; mails and, 251, 264–65; mentioned, 238
Key, Philip Barton (Md. representative), 416, 417, 418
Kilty, William (D.C. judge), 126
Kimball, David Tenney (of Ipswich, Mass.), 198
Kimball, Jabez (Haverhill, Mass., lawyer), 52; identified, 53
King, Rufus (U.S. minister to Britain), 56, 57, 62, 146, 308, 398
King, William (Maine politician), 406; identified, 407

Lafayette, Marie Joseph Paul Yves Roch Gilbert du Motier, Marquis de, 135
Lancaster, Penn., 202
Landais, Capt. Pierre (of N.Y.), 78, 90; identified, 91
Larkin, Ebenezer (Boston bookseller), 5, 349; identified, 6
Latin language and literature: GWA's skills in, 403, 407, 408; orations in, 149–50, 152, 198; translations from, 77, 78, 90, 100, 102
Latrobe, Benjamin Henry (Phila. engineer), 287
Laurie, Rev. James (of Washington, D.C.), 242; identified, 243
Lavater, Johann Caspar: *Essays on Physiognomy*, 382, 383
Law and lawyers: AA on, 391–92; JA on, 15, 387; JQA on, 2–3; JQA's practice, 162, 167, 169, 180, 181, 212, 311, 390–91, 392, 397, 400–402, 404, 407, 409, 410, 411, 413, 414, 416, 418; TBA's practice, xviii, 48, 58, 122, 162, 200, 201, 224, 226, 285, 286, 294, 421; corporate law, 400–402; diplomatic immunity, 116, 123–24, 129; education in, 162, 212, 391, 392, 410, 421; habeas corpus, 244, 245, 248, 250, 252, 253, 254, 256, 261; law of nations, 2–3, 96; maritime law, 15, 312; powers of attorney, 67; probate, 18; property law, 167, 224, 226; John Adams Smith's planned practice, 387; women and, 18, 161–62, 163, 167

LCA. *See* ADAMS, LOUISA CATHERINE JOHNSON (1775–1852, wife of JQA)
Leach, Abigail (daughter of Benjamin), 271; identified, 272
Leach, Abigail Harriman (wife of Benjamin), 272
Leach, Benjamin (of Haverhill, Mass.), 272
Leander (Brit. warship), xxiv, 2, 3, 146, 147, 148, 153
Leander (ship), x, 144
Lear, Tobias (U.S. diplomat), 77, 426, 427
Lebanon, N.Y., xv, xvii, xxii, 191, 254, 255, 299–300, 302, 339, 345, 358
Lee, Anne Lucinda (daughter of Charles), 241; identified, 242
Lee, Charles (former U.S. attorney general), 242
Lee, Mrs. (Washington, D.C., schoolteacher), 13, 209, 210
Lenox, Tacy Lukens (of Phila.), 241; identified, 242
Leopard (Brit. warship), xii, xxiv, 277 (illus.), 278, 282, 286–87, 292, 355
Létombe, Philippe André Joseph de (French consul general to U.S.), 57
Lewis, Capt. Joseph (of the *Sylvia*), 172
Lewis, Joseph, Jr. (Va. representative), 416
Lewis, Meriwether (U.S. explorer), ix, xi, 205, 219, 234, 261
Lewis, Morgan (gov. of N.Y.), 35, 126, 174, 207
Lexington, Ky., 252
Library of Congress, 199, 213, 219, 223
Lincoln, Benjamin, Jr. (d. 1788, of Hingham), 240
Lincoln, Benjamin, III (1784–1813, son of Benjamin, Jr.), 240, 264, 269
Lincoln, James Otis (son of Benjamin, Jr.), 240, 269
Lincoln, Levi (U.S. attorney general), 10, 11, 254–55, 396, 409
Lincoln, Mary Otis. *See* Ware, Mary Otis Lincoln
Lincoln, Maine, 117
Lincoln County, Maine, 41

Index

Lion, Mr., 366
Lisbon, Portugal, 371
Literary characters: Adriano de Armado, 208; Bardolph, 225; Costard, 25; Don Quixote, 269; Falstaff, 33, 225; Father John, 365; Fluellen, 33; Glorvina, 365; Hodge, 291; Nym, 33; Peto, 33; Pistol, 33; Serena, 382, 383; Tom Jones, 382; Tweedledum and Tweedledee, 270
Little, Mr. (Atkinson, N.H., farmer), 300, 301, 437
Little, Mrs. (of Atkinson, N.H.), 438
Livermore, Samuel (N.H. politician), 144, 145
Liverpool, England, 149
Livingston, Brockholst (U.S. Supreme Court justice), 34, 35, 256, 260, 413
Livingston, Edward (La. lawyer), 24, 63
Livingston, Robert R. (N.Y. chancellor), 56, 57, 63, 86, 87
Lloyd, Dr. James, Sr. (father of James, Jr.), 368, 370
Lloyd, James, Jr. (Mass. senator), 368, 407–408; identified, 370
Lloyd, Thomas (Phila. stenographer), 39
Loch Ness, 425
Lombard, Capt. Hezekiah (of the *Rambler*), 152, 157
London, England: JA's residence in, xxi; JQA's writings published in, 5, 6; banking in, 321; diplomats in, 3, 263, 293, 307, 320, 321, 418; merchants in, 321; newspapers and publishing in, 5, 15, 130; Smithfield, 78; societies and clubs in, 57
Long, Robert (Washington, D.C., innkeeper), 414
Longfellow House–Washington's Headquarters National Historic Site, 88
Longinus, Cassius (Athenian philosopher): identified, 102; *On the Sublime*, 101, 102
Long Island Sound, 191, 416
Loud, Samuel P. (of Weymouth): identified, 410
Louisa (Peabody boarder), 121
Louise Auguste Wilhelmine of Mecklenburg-Strelitz, Queen of Prussia (wife of Frederick William III), 260
Louisiana: JA on, 101; JQA and, xxiv; boundaries of, 62, 63, 84; civil unrest in, 2; exploration of, ix, xi, 205, 219, 234, 261; government for, 11, 23–25, 33, 278; Louisiana Purchase, ix, xxiv, xxv, 11, 15, 73, 86, 87, 101, 230; Orleans Territory, 24, 84; slavery in, 24; trade and manufacturing in, 4, 56; U.S. relations with Spain and, 90
Lovell, James (1737–1814, Mass. politician), 409

Lovell, James (1768–1820, Weymouth physician), 73; identified, 75
Lowell, Rev. Charles (of Boston), 206; identified, 207
Lowell, John, Jr. (Boston lawyer), 157, 158, 161, 162, 163, 167; *Analysis of the Late Correspondence*, 427
Lowell, Rebecca Amory (wife of John, Jr.), 157, 158
Ludwig (Louis) Ferdinand, Prince of Prussia, 225; identified, 227
Lyman, Erastus (Northampton, Mass. lawyer), 419, 420, 424
Lynn, Mass., 169
Lyon, Matthew (Ky. representative), 39, 40
Lytle, Mrs. (Washington, D.C., medical practitioner), 218, 233, 239
Lyttelton, Thomas Lyttelton, 2d Baron: *Speech of Lord Lyttelton, on . . . the Canada Bill*, 191, 192

McCall, Archibald (Phila. merchant), 56; identified, 57
MacCarthy-Reagh, Justin de, Comte (Irish book collector), 94–95; identified, 96
McCormick, Daniel (N.Y. merchant), 56, 57
McDonald, William (stagecoach operator), 203
McFarland, Mr. (printer), 39, 40
McHenry, James (former U.S. secy. of war), 145, 147
McKean, Thomas (gov. of Penn.), 67, 68
MacLay, Samuel (Penn. senator), 310
Macon, Nathaniel (Speaker of the House), 70, 123, 124, 281, 282; identified, 71
Macpherson, James: "Carthon," 423, 425, 428, 430
McQueen, Mr. (shopkeeper at The Hague), 27, 28
McRae, Alexander (lt. gov. of Va.), 329; identified, 332
MacVicar, Duncan (Brit. officer), 422; identified, 425
Madeleine, Îles de la, Quebec, 152
Madison, Dolley Payne Todd (wife of James), 178, 307, 335, 411, 433–34; letter from LCA listed (1809), 450
Madison, James: AA on, 132, 336, 433; JA on, 320; JQA on, 337; JQA visits, 233, 241, 242, 398; LCA and, 178; cabinet of, 409, 412, 414; *Examination of the British Doctrine*, 94, 96; Federalist Party and, 317, 328, 433; health of, 335; inauguration of, 398, 411, 413, 414, 415; D. Madison and, 307, 335, 433–34; Miranda expedition and, x, 125, 128, 134, 142; nominates JQA as U.S. minister

495

to Russia, 414–15, 435; patronage for William Steuben Smith and, 338, 348, 351; patronage sought from, 111–12, 278; presidential election (1808) and, xxvi, 128, 230, 306, 307, 308, 309, 312, 314, 320, 323, 327, 329, 330–31, 332, 336, 340, 380, 397, 398; as secretary of state, 11, 90, 91, 109; WSS and, 142; U.S. relations with Britain and, 3, 108, 109, 149, 296, 297–98, 307, 316, 317, 335, 352, 355, 433, 434; U.S. relations with France and, 116; U.S. relations with Haiti and, 4, 115–16; U.S. relations with Spain and, 109. *See also* State Department, U.S.

Madrid, Spain, 418

Magruder, Patrick (clerk of House), 281, 282

Mail Pilot (stagecoach line), 65, 66, 67, 68

Mails: franking privileges, 41, 252, 261, 291, 296, 390, 394; lost letters, 213; postal routes and schedules, 25, 99, 140, 181, 192, 195, 208, 211, 227, 264–65, 281, 349, 374, 431, 432; postmarks, 251, 252, 265; post offices, 166, 184, 299, 421; sent via stagecoach, 66–67, 68, 201, 271, 394; weather affects delivery of, 214

Maine, 117–18, 407

Maitland, John (Brit. merchant), 148, 149, 151

Mandan Nation, xi, 219, 220 (illus.), 221 (illus.), 234

Manufacturing, 124, 413, 426

Maps, x, 89 (illus.), 199

Marine Corps, U.S., 4, 260, 311

Markham, Penelope Verchild. *See* Barton, Penelope Verchild Markham

Markoe, Peter (Phila. playwright), 39, 40, 78

Marlborough, John Churchill, 1st Earl of (Brit. officer), 39, 40

Marlborough, Mass., 50

Marriages: JA2 and MCHA (1828), 211; JQA and LCA (1797), 247; JQA on, 163; TBA and AHA (1805), x, xvi, xviii, 53, 54, 59, 60; John Barton and Penelope Verchild Markham (1807), 286; Betsey (Hellen servant) (1806), 95; George Blake and Sarah Olcott Murdock (1810), 416; George Boyd and Harriet Johnson (1805), 51, 52; Lemuel Brackett and Sarah Whitney (1806), 87, 88; William Brent and Catherine Walker Johnson (1805), 43, 44; Andrew Buchanan and Carolina Virginia Marylanda Johnson (1807), 239–40; Edward Cruft and Elizabeth Storer Smith (1810), 438; Isaac P. Davis and Susan Jackson (1807), 238, 240; Stephen Decatur and Susan Wheeler (1806), 44; Richard Dexter and Rebeckah Tirrell (1804), 339; Thomas Ewell and Elizabeth Stoddert (1807), 159; Patrick Grant and Anna Powell Mason (1807), 159; Robert Hare Jr. and Harriet Clark (1811), 59; Robert Goodloe Harper and Catherine Carroll (1801), 52; Benjamin Page and Mehitabel Newcomb (1807), 159; Henry Sargent and Hannah Welles (1807), 237, 238; Stephen Sewall and Rebecca Wigglesworth (1763), 74; Chester Stebbins and Elizabeth Marston Harrod (1807), 290; Theodore Strong and Martha Allen (1806), 167, 169; Thomas Beale Wales and Ann Beale (1806), 171, 172; Henry Ware and Elizabeth Bowes (1807), 240; Henry Ware and Mary Otis Lincoln (1807), 239, 240, 264. *See also* Weddings

Marsh, Ann Fiske (grandmother of Ann Packard), 50, 51

Marsh, Rev. Joseph (of Braintree, husband of Ann), 51

Marsh, Wilson, Jr. (Quincy draper), 27; identified, 28

Marshall, John, Sr. (U.S. Supreme Court chief justice), 107, 264, 413; *Life of George Washington*, 79, 80

Martin, Luther (Baltimore lawyer), 43

Martinique, 158

Mary (brig), 181

Mary and Eliza (schooner), 199

Maryland: congressional delegation of, 11, 70, 71, 84, 91, 99, 107, 282, 292, 416; government of, 148, 149, 233, 234; judiciary of, 148, 151; Potomac River bridge and, 233, 234

Mason, Anna Maria Murray (wife of John, of Georgetown, D.C.), 164; identified, 165

Mason, Anna Powell. *See* Grant, Anna Powell Mason

Mason, Eilbeck (son of John, of Georgetown, D.C.), 164; identified, 165

Mason, John (1706–1763): *Essay on Elocution*, 199

Mason, John (1766–1849, Georgetown, D.C., banker), 179, 255, 260; identified, 165

Mason, John Thomson (Washington, D.C., lawyer), 149

Mason, Jonathan, Jr. (Mass. senator), 157, 159

Mason, Susannah Powell (wife of Jonathan, Jr.), 159

Mason, William: "Musaeus," 119, 121

Massachusetts: AA on, 17–18, 48, 368, 420; JQA on, 5, 12, 170; TBA on, 30, 140–41, 285, 309, 340, 341, 353–54, 406; agriculture in, 363; attitudes toward JA and JQA in, 341, 344, 376, 419; attitudes toward Embargo Act (1807) in, 310, 342–43, 370, 383, 395, 406; attitudes toward Virginia in, 6, 339; banking and insurance in, 49, 135–36, 243, 356, 357; climate of, 255; congressional delegation of, xii, xxiii, 32, 71, 84, 204, 282, 319, 368, 370, 395, 398; congressional election in, 5, 6–7, 9, 11, 12, 28, 354, 364, 365; fast and thanksgiving days in, 15, 69, 70, 140, 206, 285, 286, 288–89, 361, 384, 385, 387; government of, 36, 37, 49, 141, 158, 167, 169, 170, 172, 285, 409; gubernatorial elections in, 31, 48, 49, 140–41, 158, 159, 167, 169, 170, 254–55, 285, 286, 340, 341, 342, 343, 350–51, 353–54, 355, 356; militia of, 286, 396, 407; political parties in, 5, 6, 7, 9, 12, 48, 85, 115, 140–41, 218, 231, 285, 339, 342, 343, 365, 370, 377, 396, 406–407, 410, 414; presidential election (1804) and, 5, 6, 7, 8, 9, 12; property law in, 226; Supreme Judicial Court, 41, 49, 167, 169, 223; U.S. attorney for, 207, 414

General Court: JA and, 7–8, 356, 370, 434; JQA's service in, 356, 357; JQA's U.S. Senate election and, xv–xvi, xxv, 368, 370; TBA's service in, xviii, 82, 84–85, 86, 87, 95, 103, 104, 116–17, 119, 141; Boston Athenæum incorporation and, 247; election dispute and, 141, 158, 167, 169, 170, 285; Enforcement Act (1809) and, 395, 396; legislation considered by, 113, 115, 117–18, 261, 262; members and composition of, xviii, 115, 124, 141, 158, 168, 169, 170, 172, 231, 309, 310, 342, 349, 368, 407, 411; petitions to and from, 18, 46, 230, 231, 315, 317, 319, 325, 368, 370, 406, 407–408; ratification of 12th Amendment, 9; J. Sullivan addresses, 309, 310

Massachusetts Fire and Marine Insurance Company, 135–36
Massachusetts Historical Society: JQA sends publications to, 199; digital resources of, xxvii–xxviii
Massachusetts Spy (Worcester, Mass.), 152, 321
Mathematics, 295, 303, 304, 346
Maxwell, Hugh (Phila. printer), 3. See also *Port Folio*
May, Dr. Frederick (of Washington, D.C.), 108, 177, 179, 183, 334–35
May, Henry K. (Alexandria, Va., merchant), 171; identified, 172
MCHA. *See* Hellen, Mary Catherine (1806–1870)
Mead, Cowles (acting gov. of Mississippi Territory), 253, 262, 263, 264
Medeiros, Capt. Antonio Francisco de (of the *Union*), 25
Medford, Mass., 58, 118, 121, 122, 434
Mediterranean Sea, 6, 55, 178, 191
Mellimelli, Sidi Soliman (Tunisian diplomat), 80, 81, 82, 84, 85, 91, 186
Mendon, Mass., 207

Mercer, John Francis (Md. politician), 148; identified, 149
Meredith, Gertrude Gouverneur Ogden (wife of William), 188, 190, 197–98
Meredith, Samuel Ogden (son of William), 188; identified, 190
Meredith, William (Phila. lawyer), 56, 57, 190, 197–98, 203; letter from TBA listed (1806), 445
Letters: From TBA (1806), 188, 195
Meredith, William Morris (son of William), 188
Merry, Anthony (Brit. minister to U.S.), 3, 72, 150, 152, 203, 265
Merry, Elizabeth Death Leathes (wife of Anthony), 72, 163, 203, 210, 265
Mexico, 153, 208, 245, 250, 320
Miami Nation, 80
Michel (Adams tenant), 48
Middlesex Canal, 58
Middlesex County, Mass., 58, 85, 407
Middleton, Rev. Conyers: *Life of Marcus Tullius Cicero*, 77, 78
Middletown, Conn., 202, 335
Milan, Italy, 296
Militia (U.S.): A. Burr conspiracy and, 249, 250; Congress and, 71, 98, 99, 282, 291, 396; in Massachusetts, 286, 396, 407; in New York, 63; in Pennsylvania, 57; in Washington, D.C., 84, 413
Miller, Maj. Ebenezer (of Quincy), 73, 75
Milton, John: *Paradise Lost*, 137, 139, 305, 306, 363, 364, 423, 424, 425
Milton, Mass., 18
Minchin, Edward (Boston merchant), 373; identified, 374
Minot, John (of Dorchester, Mass.), 201
Minot, John Cranch (son of John), 201
Minot, Thomazine Elizabeth Fielder Bond (wife of John), 200; identified, 201
Mirabeau, Honoré Gabriel Riquetti, Comte de: *Histoire secrète de la cour de Berlin*, 225, 227
Miranda, Francisco de (Venezuelan revolutionary), xxi, 62, 63, 69, 128, 142
Letters: From AA2 (1806), 88, 102
Miranda Expedition (1806): AA2 on, xxii, 88, 102, 127; AA on, xxii, 125, 235, 269, 270; JA on, xxii, 135; JQA on, xxi, 128–29, 134, 202; British assistance to, x; Jefferson administration and, xxii, 126, 128–29, 130, 134, 142, 204, 235, 250; map of, 89 (illus.); news of in U.S., xxi, 154, 158, 159, 177, 231; organization and execution of, x, xxi, 144, 202; public attitudes toward, 125, 127, 130, 153, 230; WSS and, xxii, 62, 126, 128, 130, 134,

497

141–42, 143, 144, 194, 250; William Steuben Smith joins, x, xv, xxi–xxii, 88, 102, 125, 126, 127, 135, 146, 186, 194, 202, 208, 217, 270, 342, 348
Mississippi River, 208, 230, 231, 320
Mississippi Territory, 4, 253, 264
Missouri River, 230
"Mr. Stewarton" (pseudonym). *See* Goldsmith, Lewis
Mitchel, James (of Quincy), 194; identified, 195
Mitchell, Nahum (of East Bridgewater, Mass.), 5; identified, 6
Mitchill, Samuel Latham (N.Y. politician): identified, 57; JA and, 123, 124; JQA on, 56; Yazoo land claims and, 315, 317, 329
Moellendorff, Richard Joachim Heinrich, Count von (Prussian officer), 226; identified, 227
Moffat, John (Scottish engraver), 89 (illus.); identified, x
Mohawk Nation, 422
Money: JA on, 356; JQA on, 356, 357; bank book, 205; bequests, 172; bounties, 99; counterfeiting, 48, 49; invoices, 48, 351, 360; money orders, 41, 79, 393; promissory notes, 37, 225, 321, 354, 355; receipts for, 79, 215; regulation of, 49; rewards, 397; salaries and wages, 206, 436; scarcity of, 354–55; tributes to Barbary States, 80, 107, 426, 427. *See also* Debt; Investments; Prices and costs; Taxes; *names of individual banks*
Monitor (Washington, D.C.), 387, 396
Monroe, James: JQA and, 322; Chesapeake-Leopard Affair and, 287, 292, 293; diplomatic service of, 2, 3, 10, 11, 128, 148, 149, 294–95, 296–98, 320, 321, 333, 418; Monroe-Pinkney Treaty and, 262–63, 332; presidential election (1808) and, 149, 308, 309, 312, 314, 320, 322, 323, 329, 330, 332; *View of the Conduct of the Executive*, 330, 332; as Va. gubernatorial candidate, 312
Montagu, Mary Pierrepont Wortley (English writer), 302, 304; *Works*, 23, 24
Montesquieu, Charles Louis de Secondat, Baron de la Brède et de: *Persian Letters*, 344
Monthly Anthology and Boston Review: AA and, 304; JA's correspondence and, 371; JQA on, 78–79, 81, 136; JQA's scientific studies and, 81, 94, 96; JQA's writings in, 80, 129, 172, 234, 261; TBA's writings in, 198; book reviews in, 115, 116, 316, 317, 323, 331; organization of, 80, 261; poetry in, 198, 234, 246, 247, 261; William Smith Shaw and, 79

Monticello (Va. estate), 148, 174, 186
Moody, Rev. Samuel (of York, Maine), 123, 124
Moore, Edwin: "The Panther, the Horse, and other Beasts," 93
Moore, Thomas: *Epistles, Odes, and Other Poems*, 195–96, 198; *Fairies' Revels*, 198; *Odes of Anacreon*, 198; *Poetical Works of the Late Thomas Little*, 198
Moreau, Gen. Jean Victor (French), 62, 380, 381; identified, 63
Morning Chronicle (N.Y.), 60
Morris, Gouverneur: *Answer to War in Disguise*, 116
Morris, Como. Richard Valentine: *Defence of the Conduct of Commodore Morris*, 1, 3, 6
Morrisville, Penn., 63
Morton, Perez (of Braintree): JQA on, 28; TBA on, 26; political activities of, 172, 309, 310, 406, 408; mentioned, 409
Moses (Hellen servant), 257
Mount Vernon (Va. estate), 77, 334
Mumford, Gurdon Saltonstall (N.Y. representative), 81, 84
Munitions: civilian use of, 223; Dutch trade in, 358; Miranda expedition and, 142; U.S. military and, 99, 291; U.S. supplies Tripoli with, 107; U.S. trade in, 2, 4, 113–14, 115–16
Munroe, Isaac (Boston printer), 349, 350, 434
Munsee Nation, 80
Murdock, Sarah Olcott (of Hanover, N.H.), 416
Murphy, Arthur (translator), 77, 78, 90, 100, 102
Murray, Capt. Alexander (of the *John Adams*), 98; identified, 99
Murray, Catherine Elizabeth (of Washington, D.C.), 157; identified, 159
Murray, William Vans (U.S. minister to Netherlands), 132
Music: harp, 365; "I'm in Love with Twenty," 207; politics and, 38, 84; singing, 258; tambourine, 241; women and, 429; mentioned, 24, 45

Nantes, France, 24, 25
National Endowment for the Humanities, xxviii
National Historical Publications and Records Commission, xxviii
National Intelligencer (Washington, D.C.): Adamses and, 286, 291, 292–93; A. Burr conspiracy reported in, 208, 245, 250, 253; S. Chase Sr. impeachment reported in, 31; European war reported in, 227, 260; T. Jefferson's treatment in, 71, 129; Lewis and

Clark celebrated in, 234, 261; J. Madison inauguration reported in, 413; U.S. foreign relations reported in, 99, 418
Native Americans: AA on, 92–93; JA on, 386; JQA on, xi, 82, 87, 91, 219; British attitudes toward, 191, 193, 422; clothing of, 82; dancing of, xi, 213; medicines of, 118, 119; portraits of, xi, 220 (illus.), 221 (illus.); relations with U.S., 11, 71, 79, 80, 205, 413; U.S. attitudes toward, 82, 91; visit Washington, D.C., xi, 84, 87, 91, 98, 99, 219, 234. *See also names of individual nations*
Navy, U.S.: AA on, xxvii, 380; JA on, 230, 356–57; TBA on, 295; *Chesapeake-Leopard* Affair, xii, xxiv, 276, 277 (illus.), 278, 282, 286–87, 290, 292, 293, 296, 306, 307, 315–16, 317, 327, 331, 335, 338, 343, 350, 351–52, 355; flags of, 98; funding of, 71, 78, 79, 81, 98, 253, 254, 295, 297, 351; T. Jefferson and, 98, 99, 282; movements of, 55, 191, 291; naval agents, 278, 409, 427; navy yards, 99, 191, 311; public attitudes toward, 98, 368; secretary of, 412, 414; service in, 5, 84, 85, 159, 178, 191, 351
Neale, James G. W. (of Quincy), 310–11
Neponset River, 227, 254, 266, 286
Netherlands, 20, 34, 39, 74, 75, 357, 358
Newark, N.J., 146, 373
New Bedford, Mass., 159
New Brunswick, N.J., 146
Newburyport, Mass., ix, 5, 194, 212, 238
Newburyport Herald, 195, 302, 367
Newburyport Statesman, 387
New Castle, Del., 1, 54, 70, 281
Newcomb, Charles (Braintree shoemaker), 159
Newcomb, Elizabeth (daughter of Jerusha, Adams servant): identified, 37
Newcomb, Jerusha Adams (Adams cousin), 36–37, 46, 159; identified, 37
Newcomb, Mehitabel. *See* Page, Mehitabel Newcomb
Newcomb, Prudence (daughter of Jerusha, Adams servant), 36, 43, 46; identified, 37
New England: as AHA's birthplace, xviii–xix; JA on, 15, 34; JQA on, 96–97, 104; attitudes toward JA in, xvii, 420, 427; attitudes toward South in, 86, 96–97, 339, 352; climate of, 124, 255; Embargo Act (1807) and, 296, 309, 310, 341, 342–43, 344, 352–53, 357, 368, 370, 372, 395, 396, 403, 404, 406, 407, 408, 409; political parties in, xxv, 316, 339–40; presidential election (1808) and, 310, 339–40; Yankee as term for, 104; mentioned, 116, 117, 158. *See also names of individual states*
New England Insurance Company, 321

New England Mississippi Land Company, 413
New-England Palladium (Boston): JA's treatment in, 38, 40; JQA's treatment in, 172, 309, 310; advertisements in, 104, 144, 152, 240, 247; A. Burr conspiracy reported in, 250; congressional activities reported in, 133, 254, 404; deaths reported in, 110, 404; European war reported in, 124; Harvard president reported in, 74; U.S. foreign relations reported in, 293, 296, 427
New Hampshire: congressional delegation of, xi, 84, 147, 202, 204, 398; General Court, 387, 389, 431, 432; migration to, 117; thanksgiving days in, 270; mentioned, 416
New Haven, Conn., 201, 202, 394
New Jersey, 7, 32, 144, 317
New Market, Md., 187
New Orleans, La.: A. Burr conspiracy and, 240, 243–44, 250, 261; T. B. Johnson at, 278, 401; judiciary in, 57, 244, 245; land claims in, 106; public attitudes toward, 190–91; residents of, 56, 112, 333, 335
Newport, R.I., 61, 229, 231
Newspapers: AA on, 362, 420; JA on, 12, 39; JA's treatment in, 152, 186, 376, 386, 387, 419, 420, 433, 434; JA's writings in, xvii, 419, 420, 421–22, 424–25, 429–30, 431, 433, 434; JQA on, 332; JQA's treatment in, xxv, 152, 172, 292, 293, 301, 302, 309, 310, 312–14, 316, 317, 318, 323, 325, 327, 328, 329, 331, 332, 361, 362, 364, 376, 396, 402, 409, 435; JQA's writings in, 4, 5, 341, 343, 350, 354, 361; TBA and AHA's marriage reported in, 59; TBA on, 309, 341; Adamses exchange, 252, 253, 291, 293, 295, 329, 421, 422, 425, 433; advertisements in, 18, 104, 119, 144, 150, 152, 171, 172, 207, 240, 246, 247, 300, 350, 361, 397, 409; Boston Athenæum reported in, 246; A. Burr's activities reported in, 113, 115, 207, 208, 231, 250, 252; congressional activities reported in, 31, 128, 129, 286, 315, 396, 402; William Cranch's appointment reported in, 126; deaths reported in, 3, 52, 110, 120, 176, 237, 270, 403; duels reported in, 395, 396, 407; elections reported in, 5, 6, 48, 49, 170, 254, 329; establishment of, 285–86; European war reported in, 74, 129, 226, 256, 418; fires reported in, 179, 218; Harvard president reported in, 73, 74; health and illness reported in, 3, 297; T. Jefferson address printed in, 71; Meriwether Lewis honors reported in, 234; J. Madison inauguration reported in, 413; Miranda expedition reported in, xxi, 125, 134, 154; party politics and, 109, 129, 321, 324, 329, 341, 342, 361,

362, 364, 369, 412, 420, 430, 433; WSS's trial reported in, 141, 153, 154, 194; Supreme Court session reported in, 344; U.S. foreign relations reported in, 2, 3, 63, 80, 91, 147, 149, 153, 307, 315–16, 352, 381; Yazoo land claims reported in, 41, 317. *See also names of individual papers and printers*

New York (packet), 147

New York Academy of Art, 62, 63

New York City: AA2 and WSS's residence in, xxii, 61–62, 63, 144, 206, 244, 375; JQA and LCA travel through, 1, 3, 6, 52, 54, 56, 61, 63, 65, 66, 68, 142, 147, 149, 152, 181, 183, 185, 190, 191, 193, 201, 202, 203, 244, 267, 280, 281, 282, 394, 396, 400, 413, 416; JQA on, 146; attitudes toward JQA in, 323, 364; fires in, 218; government and politics in, 60, 142, 207, 308, 395; judiciary in, 141–42, 146, 174; merchants in, 2, 57, 91, 100, 105, 106, 119; militia in, 63; newspapers in, 3, 59, 60, 63, 125, 141, 323; ships to and from, x, xxi, 24, 204; Caroline Smith visits, 424, 425; societies and clubs in, 62, 63; stagecoach from, 65–66, 67, 394; surveyor and port inspector for, xxii, 60, 126, 130, 133, 142, 144, 194, 195; travelers through, 334, 374, 415; U.S. relations with Britain and, xxiv, 3, 146, 147; mentioned, 46, 55, 199, 391

Buildings, Landmarks, Streets, etc.: Broadway, 147; City Hotel, 146, 147; First Presbyterian Church, 62, 63; Greenwich, 67; Middle Dutch Church, 185; New York Harbor, xxii; Wall Street, 63

New York County, N.Y., 207

New-York Gazette, 130, 218, 402

New York State: JA on, 34; attitudes toward JQA in, 318, 331; as British colony, 164; A. Burr indicted for murder in, 7; congressional delegation of, 84, 260, 317, 323, 329, 332; Council of Appointment, 207; debt of, 317; elections in, 34, 35, 146, 147, 308, 323, 324; illness in, 1, 3; political parties in, 34, 35, 125, 126, 146, 147, 318, 332; property law in, 226; U.S. Circuit Court in, 249; U.S. marshal of, 142; Yazoo land claims and, 315, 317, 329; mentioned, 300, 363, 387

Niagara Falls, 197

Nicholas, Wilson Cary (Va. politician), 32, 281, 282, 414

Nicholson, Joseph Hopper (Md. representative), 84

Nicholson, Capt. Samuel (of the *Constitution*), 84, 85

Norfolk, Va., 43, 111, 296, 390

Norfolk County, Mass.: congressional district for, 6, 7, 8; courts in, 49, 201, 224, 226, 294, 296; Mass. General Court delegation of, 85; sheriff of, 285, 286

North American and Mercantile Daily Advertiser (Baltimore), 374

Northampton, Mass., 299, 305, 420

North Carolina, 71, 282

North Dakota, xi

Northwest Territory, 106

Norton, Edward (1795–1814, son of Elizabeth Cranch), 69

Norton, Elizabeth (1802–1869, daughter of Elizabeth Cranch), 69, 288; identified, 290

Norton, Elizabeth Cranch (Betsy, 1763–1811, niece of AA): AA on, 273; AA visits, 112; family of, 37, 87–88, 157, 159, 164, 290; Elizabeth Peabody on, 152–53

Norton, Rev. Jacob (1764–1858, husband of Elizabeth Cranch), 69, 88, 159, 265–66, 290

Norton, Lucy Ann (b. 1806, daughter of Elizabeth Cranch), 157, 159

Norton, Mary Cranch (1804–1841, daughter of Elizabeth Cranch), 69

Norton, Thomas Boylston Adams (1799–1831, son of Elizabeth Cranch), 69, 86, 87, 156

Norton, Mass., 370

Norway, 91

Ogden, Peter V. (New Orleans merchant), 244; identified, 245

Ogden, Samuel G. (N.Y. merchant), 142, 144, 145

Ohio, 247, 248, 264, 310, 319, 360

Ohio River, 248, 249, 250

Old House (Peacefield, now Adams National Historical Park): AA as manager of, xviii, 303; JQA's library at, 193, 230–231; TBA resides at, xvi, xviii, 226, 249, 341–42; farms at, 73, 76–77, 101, 336, 363, 371–72, 390, 436; fire at, 212; furnishings of, 368, 382; gardens at, 185, 363, 424; holidays at, 288–89, 384; outbuildings at, 371; visitors to, xv, 44, 69, 145, 185, 201, 272, 285, 347, 368, 372, 375, 385, 388–89, 436, 438; weddings at, 339. *See also* AA—Household Management; John Adams Birthplace; John Quincy Adams Birthplace

Oliver, Edward (Boston printer), 349, 350

Orby, Sir James, Baronet of Croyland Abbey: identified, 164

Osage Nation, xi, 80–81, 213

Osgood, Peter (Boston stonemason), 205, 206, 232, 240–41

Otis, Harrison Gray (Mass. politician): JQA's Letter to, 349–50, 351, 353, 354, 356, 360, 361, 362, 364, 376; as Mass. senate president, 172, 349, 414

500

Index

Otis, James, Jr. (Boston lawyer), 270
Otis, Sally Foster (wife of Harrison), 410, 411
Otis, Samuel Allyne, Sr. (secy. of the Senate), 62, 63
Ottawa Nation, 80
Ottoman Empire, 427
Ovid, 100
Owenson, Sydney: *Wild Irish Girl*, 365, 366
Oxford, Robert Harley, 1st Earl of (Brit. politician), 39, 40

Pacific Ocean, 230
Packard, Ann Quincy (wife of Asa), 50, 51; letter to AA listed (1805), 443
    Letter: From AA (1805), 49
Packard, Rev. Asa (of Marlborough, Mass.), 50
Packard Humanities Institute, xxviii
Page, Capt. Benjamin (of New Bedford, Mass.), 157, 159
Page, Mehitabel Newcomb (wife of Benjamin), 157, 159
Paine, Thomas (author of *Common Sense*), 78
Paintings and prints: by Susanna Adams, 304; art education, 304; cartoons, ix, 83 (illus.); charcoal and chalk, xi; of *Chesapeake* and *Leopard*, xii, 277 (illus.); commissions for, xi; engraving, x, xiii, 62, 63, 83 (illus.), 220 (illus.), 221 (illus.); gifts of, 63; museums and exhibitions for, 62, 63, 237; of pets, 30; "The Prairie Dog Sickened at the Sting of the Hornet," ix; publication of, ix, 62; watercolor, x, xii; women and, 428, 429
    Portraits: AA, 17, 18, 22, 29, 30; JA, 29, 30; T. Jefferson, ix; Napoleon, ix; E. S. M. Quincy, xii–xiii, 405; J. Quincy III, xiii; Sheheke, xi, 220 (illus.); Yellow Corn, xi, 221 (illus.)
    See also Artists; *names of individual artists*
Papers of John Adams, xvii, xxvii, xxix
Papers of John Quincy Adams, xxvii
Paris, France: JA's residence in, 100, 102, 420; French Revolution in, 9; Hôtel de Valentinois, 100; Louvre, 62; mentioned, 63, 159, 251
Park, James Allan: *Law of Marine Insurances*, 421
Park, Dr. John (Boston printer), 4; identified, 5–6. See also *Repertory*
Parker, Daniel (Watertown, Mass., merchant), 86, 87
Parker, Rev. Samuel (Boston bishop), 17; identified, 18
Parsons, Theophilus (Newburyport lawyer), 19, 20, 167, 169
Pascal, Blaise: *Lettres provinciales*, 113, 115

Paterson, William (U.S. Supreme Court justice), 107
Patronage: JA on, 123, 420; JQA and JA's, 371; JQA on, 329; TBA and JQA's, 342; appeals to JQA, 130, 133, 310–11, 342, 348, 351, 407, 408, 435, 436; T. Jefferson and, 123, 126, 278, 310–11, 348; for T. B. Johnson, 111–12, 278; for WSS, 207; for William Steuben Smith, 338, 341, 348, 351
Patterson, Thomas (Washington, D.C., pharmacist), 417; identified, 418
Paulus Hook (Jersey City), N.J., 54, 66, 67, 145, 146
Payne, Christopher Gore (son of William), 158
Payne, Edward William (son of William), 156, 158
Payne, Ellis Gray (son of William), 158
Payne, Lucy Gray Dobell (wife of William), 156, 158, 211, 403, 404
Payne, William (Boston merchant), 156, 158, 212
Payne, William Edward (son of William), 156, 158
Payplat, Jean Baptiste Gilbert (Julien, Boston chef), 56; identified, 57
Peabody, Elizabeth Smith Shaw (1750–1815, sister of AA): books and reading, 119, 120, 153, 194, 195, 270, 300, 301, 344, 366, 367, 388, 431; concern and affection for children, 120, 271, 301, 366, 389, 431; health of, 430; letter writing of, 195; properties of, 58, 122; religious beliefs of, 270–71, 298; servants for, 271; takes in boarders, 121, 347, 367; visits to and by, 120, 366, 387–88; mentioned, 45
    Correspondence: with AA, xviii, 121, 143, 271, 274, 298, 301, 347, 349, 356, 367, 389, 430, 438; with JQA, 299, 343, 344, 349; with LCA, 344, 349; with Mary Cranch, 194, 389, 436; with Elizabeth Smith Foster, 436
    Opinions and beliefs: death, 119; education, 297–98, 344; Elizabeth Anne Foster, 431; Miranda expedition, 153; nieces, 121, 152–53; J. Quincy III, 298, 301; WSS, 194; U.S. government and politics, 298, 300, 344, 387, 388; M. Vose, 120; women, 300, 431
    Relationship with Adamses: on AA2, 194; AA2 and, 272; on AA, 120; AA on, 272, 347; Abigail Smith Adams and, 194; AHA and, 153; GWA and, 271, 283, 284–85, 286, 287, 288, 297, 298, 299, 343–44, 347, 356, 366; on JQA, 298, 301, 344, 367, 388, 438; assistance to and from Adamses, 120, 299, 300, 301, 429, 430, 431, 437–38; concern and affection for Adamses, 121, 153, 271, 430; visits to and by Adamses, 194, 265, 271, 274, 280, 297, 378, 384–85, 388, 431, 432, 436, 438

501

Letters: To AA (1806), 119, 152, 194; (1807), 270; (1808), 300, 366, 387; (1809), 431; To JQA (1808), 297; To LCA (1808), 343
  Letters: From AA (1807), 272; (1809), 428, 436
  Letters to, from, omitted: To AA listed (1803), 441; (1808), 448, 449; (1809), 449, 450 (2); To Mary Smith Cranch listed (1808), 449
Peabody, Capt. John (brother of Stephen, Sr.), 194, 367; identified, 195
Peabody, Mary (sister of Stephen, Sr.), 366–67; identified, 367
Peabody, Rev. Stephen, Sr. (1741–1819, 2d husband of Elizabeth Smith Shaw): AA and JA and, 297, 429, 431, 432; Atkinson Academy and, 387, 389; education of AA2's sons and, 280, 287, 344; education of GWA and, 299; family of, 153, 195, 271, 366, 367; mentioned, 274, 438
Peabody, Stephen, Jr. (son of Stephen, Sr.), 153, 154
Peacefield. *See* Old House
Pearson, Eliphalet (Harvard professor), 74, 161, 163, 187
Peaslee, Judith Kimball (grandmother of Nathaniel Sargeant), 53
Peck, John (Boston merchant), 413
Pennsylvania: congressional delegation of, 84, 95, 310, 329; government of, 66–67, 68, 296; illness in, 1, 3; judiciary in, 67, 68, 319; land speculation in, 116–17; newspapers in, 68
Peter Pindar (pseudonym). *See* Wolcot, John
Peter Porcupine (pseudonym). *See* Cobbett, William
Peters, Sarah Peabody Stevens (sister of Stephen Peabody, Sr.): identified, 367
Pets, 29, 30, 45, 111, 191, 274, 427
Phi Beta Kappa Society, 188, 190, 196–97, 198
Philadelphia, Penn.: JQA and LCA travel through, 1, 48, 52, 54, 55–56, 59, 62, 63, 65, 68, 70, 145, 146, 147, 155, 183, 191, 193, 201, 202, 203, 209, 252, 253, 267, 281, 394, 395, 396, 397, 407, 413, 416; Adamses' residence in, 1, 65, 197, 304; arts and literature in, 3, 67, 195–96, 199, 396; as federal seat, 280, 315, 317; government of, 68; illness in, 1, 3; lawyers in, 3, 190; merchants in, 48, 57, 68, 100, 105, 106, 291, 292, 293, 351, 395; militia of, 57; physicians in, 56, 57, 117, 192; William Steuben Smith's possible residence in, 379–80; societies and clubs in, 196, 198; stagecoach from, 65–66, 67, 203; travelers to and from, 144, 203, 287, 333, 374; mentioned, 238, 240, 242

  Buildings, Landmarks, Streets, etc.: Fourth Street, 204; High Street, 68; Mansion House Hotel, 394, 396; North Second Street, 3, 57; South Fourth Street, 203, 204; Spruce Street, 396; Third Street, 396; Walnut Street, 3, 204, 396
Philadelphia County, Penn., 66, 68
Philadelphia Gazette, 99
Phillips, Abigail (daughter of Thompson), 334; identified, 335
Phillips, Abigail Cheeseborough Mumford (wife of Thompson), 334; identified, 335
Phillips, Anne Duryee (daughter of Thompson), 334; identified, 335
Phillips, Capt. Thompson (brother of Hannah Cushing), 333–34, 345; identified, 335
Philosophy, 198
Phinney, Joseph (of Braintree), 227
Pichon, Alexandrine Émilie Brongniart (wife of Louis), 251, 265
Pichon, Louis André (French diplomat), 2, 4, 251, 252, 264, 265
Pickering, John (N.H. judge), 57
Pickering, Timothy (former U.S. secy. of state): JA and, 433; JQA and, 23, 24, 360, 433; correspondence with J. Sullivan, 340, 341, 342–43, 350, 354, 355, 360, 361, 362, 433, 434; U.S. relations with Britain and, 316, 317, 350, 353
Pickman, Benjamin, Jr. (Salem, Mass., merchant), 212
Pickman, William (Boston merchant): identified, 212
Pierce, John (Amer. sailor), 146, 147
Pilkington, Mary: *Rosina: A Novel,* 275, 276
Pinckney, Charles (S.C. politician), 10, 11
Pinckney, Charles Cotesworth (of S.C.), 308, 380, 398
Pinkney, William (of Md.), 10, 11, 148, 149, 151, 262–63, 293, 330
Piranesi, Giovanni Battista: *Opere di Giovanni Battista Piranesi, Francesco Piranesi, e d'altri,* 62, 63
Pitkin, Timothy (Conn. representative), 202; identified, 204
Pitt, Thomas (nephew of Earl of Chatham), 10, 21
Pitt, William (the elder), Earl of Chatham, 191, 192–93; *Letters . . . to His Nephew,* 10, 20, 21
Pitt, William (the younger, Brit. prime minister), 100
"Plain Facts" (pseudonym), 129
Plato, 198; *Timaeus,* 101, 102
Pliny the Younger, 100; identified, 102
Plumer, William (N.H. senator), xi, 84

Plutarch, 369
Plymouth, Mass., 145, 216
Plymouth County, Mass., 6
Poetry: about Abigail Smith Adams, 198; about JA, 198; JA on, 38; by JQA, 95, 96, 233, 234, 238, 239, 255, 256–60, 261, 267; JQA on, 412; about LCA, 255, 256–60, 261, 267; by Richard Cranch, 27, 28; T. Jefferson on, 412; about Meriwether Lewis, 234, 261; about pets, 29, 30; publication of, 110, 246, 247, 261; "Resignation, or Good Out of Evil," 345; by J. Sarfati, 226, 227; about G. Washington, 198; about women, 242, 252, 255
Political and Commercial Register (Phila.), 316, 317, 319, 322, 327–28, 329, 332
Pollard, Othello (Boston chef), 56; identified, 57
Polock, Isaac (of Washington, D.C.), 218
Pope, Alexander: "Eloisa to Abelard," 216, 217; *Essay on Criticism*, 388, 389, 392, 393, 437, 438; *Essay on Man*, 132, 133, 268, 270, 273, 274, 344; "First Satire of the Second Book of Horace," 424, 425; "Messiah," 422, 425; translation of Homer, 224; "Universal Prayer," 419, 420; *Works*, 14, 15, 226
Porter, Israel (Cambridge tavernkeeper), 158
Port Folio (Phila.): JQA's Silesia letters in, 5; "British Spy in Boston" in, 19, 20; William Cranch's *Reports* reviewed in, 26, 28; women contributors to, 198; mentioned, 2, 3, 110, 133, 207
Portraits. *See* Paintings and prints
Portsmouth, N.H., 32, 347
Portugal, 371
Post. *See* Mails
Potawatomi Nation, 80
Potomac River, 179, 213, 233–34, 240, 255, 257, 261, 262
Preble, Como. Edward (U.S.), 55
Presbyterian Church, 243
Presidency, U.S.: AA on, 373; Congress and, 124, 129; electoral process for, 5, 6, 7, 9, 12; inauguration for, 349, 398, 411, 413, 414, 415; powers of, 25, 26, 31, 129, 133, 245, 278, 293, 302, 332, 333. *See also* AA—First Lady; JA—Public Life: Presidency; Elections: Presidential (1808); Jefferson, Thomas: Presidency; Madison, James
President's House (Washington, D.C.), xi, 81–82, 84, 219, 265, 411
Price, Ruth Avery (mother of Mary Deming Greenleaf), 384, 388; identified, 385
Prices and costs: of books, 5; of building repairs and removal, 17, 121, 179, 232, 240–41; of church pews, 73; of clothing and fabric, 165, 212; of food, 59, 144, 300; of hay, 372; of medicine, 119; of Potomac River bridge, 234; of property, 163, 225, 227; of rents and leases, 29, 48, 79, 162, 249; of transportation, 37, 67, 370; of wood, 292. *See also* Money
Princeton, N.J., 203, 204
Princeton College, 62, 63, 204
Privateers and privateering, xxiv, 2, 4, 95, 398, 399. *See also* Ships and shipping
Providence, R.I.: Adamses travel through, 56, 61, 63, 65, 145, 147, 150, 157, 191, 268, 282, 416; mentioned, 333
Providence Gazette, 115
Prussia, 158, 159, 226, 227, 256, 260, 339, 371
Pseudonyms: JQA as Publius Valerius, 4, 5; "British Spy in Boston," 19, 20; William Cobbett as Peter Porcupine, 308, 310; Domitor, 60; "E.," 110; Eugenius, 129; Lewis Goldsmith as "Mr. Stewarton," 184; "Plain Facts," 129; Valius, 372, 374; John Wolcot as Peter Pindar, 291, 295, 297
Publius Valerius (pseudonym). *See* JQA—Writings
Purviance, John H. (former secy. to J. Monroe), 417; identified, 418

Qaramanli, Hamet, Pasha of Tripoli, 107, 141
Qaramanli, Yusuf, Pasha of Tripoli, 107, 427
Quakers. *See* Society of Friends
Quebec, Canada, 152, 156
Quincy, Abigail Phillips (1803–1893, daughter of Josiah, III), 65
Quincy, Ann Marsh (1723?–1805, wife of Col. Josiah), 49, 50
Quincy, Dorothy Flynt (grandmother of Ann Packard), 50; identified, 51
Quincy, Elizabeth Norton (1696–1769, grandmother of AA), 50, 51, 390
Quincy, Eliza Susan (1798–1884, daughter of Josiah, III), 131, 133
Quincy, Eliza Susan Morton (1773–1850, wife of Josiah, III): books and reading, 137, 138; correspondence with AA, xiii, xvii, 125, 126; correspondence with J. Quincy III, 403, 404; Cranch family and, 107, 131, 136, 153, 245; family of, xii–xiii, 65, 70, 92, 240; on party politics, 137–38; portrait of, xii–xiii, 405; residences of, 74, 137, 139, 157, 239, 244; visits with Adamses, 72, 137, 200
   Letter: To AA (1806), 136
   Letter: From AA (1806), 131
Quincy, Col. John (1689–1767, grandfather of AA), 51
Quincy, Col. Josiah, I (1710–1784), 50
Quincy, Josiah, III (1772–1864, later "the President"): AA on, 131; JA on, 8; JQA visits

with, 137, 157, 412; LCA on, 264; congressional service of, xii, 5, 6, 8, 85, 138, 291, 293, 298, 301, 302, 352, 355, 396, 415; correspondence with E. S. M. Quincy, 403, 404; family of, xii–xiii, 65, 69, 70, 79, 95, 108, 236; health of, 251; Elizabeth Peabody on, 298, 301; portrait of, xiii; residences of, 137, 139, 153, 245

Quincy, Maria Sophia (1805–1886, daughter of Josiah, III): identified, 70; AA on, xii, 69, 92, 131, 133; Mary Cranch cares for, xiii, 74, 108, 131, 138; health of, 236

Quincy, Norton (1716–1801, uncle of AA), 321

Quincy, Mass.: AA2 and children visit, xxii, 60, 146, 162, 268, 302, 339, 347, 432; AHA visits, 44; JA's properties in, 321; JA2 visits, 215; JQA and LCA visit, 48, 157, 166, 175, 180, 182, 183, 185, 186, 193, 194, 260, 368, 370–71, 438; JQA on, 224; JQA's properties in, 249, 295, 297, 354, 378–79; JQA's scientific studies in, 79, 81, 94, 151; TBA and AHA's residence in, 108, 197, 225, 326; TBA represents in Mass. General Court, xviii, 84–85; Adamses travel to and from, 1, 3, 19, 51, 52, 54, 56, 63, 65, 141, 142, 145–46, 147, 149, 152, 154, 360; agriculture in, 339; baptisms and weddings in, xi, 172; Cranches' residence in, 418; dancing assemblies in, xx, 239, 240, 265; education in, 296, 297, 303, 338, 342, 346, 348; floods in, 254; government and politics in, 6–7, 8, 27, 140–41, 226, 229, 350, 351; hotels in, 265, 266; Peabody-Shaw family visits, 143, 388, 389; property rights in, 18, 224, 226; road conditions in, 46; societies and clubs in, 17, 18, 103, 112; stagecoach from, 171, 191; tradespeople and artisans in, 28, 118, 250, 292; visitors to, 61, 76, 87, 121, 133, 285, 286, 367, 378, 381; mentioned, 127, 138, 153, 210, 366, 399

Buildings, Landmarks, Streets, etc.: Elm Street, 266; First Church, 27, 28, 73, 75, 171; Franklin Street, 49; Half Moon Island, 224, 226; Hancock Street, 266; Mill Pond, 292; Mount Wollaston, 321; Penn's Hill, 297, 379; Plymouth Road (later Adams Street), 18; School Street, 49, 69

See also Braintree, Mass.

Quincy family, 286

Race: AA and, 92–93; JA and, 386; JQA and, 79, 82, 241; TBA and, 27; British attitudes toward, 191, 192–93; U.S. attitudes toward, 2, 63, 82, 177; mentioned, 219

Radcliffe, Ann: *Mysteries of Udolpho*, 269, 270

Rambler (ship), 150, 152, 157, 174

Randolph, John (Va. representative): AA on, 108, 131–32, 137; JQA on, 225, 291; congressional service of, 41, 42, 81, 84, 123, 124, 133, 139, 153, 154, 286–87, 293, 401, 402; possible duels of, 43, 44, 178, 179; T. Jefferson and, 137, 139, 154, 287, 293; presidential election (1808) and, 230, 307–308, 329, 332

Randolph, Martha Jefferson (daughter of Thomas Jefferson), 72

Randolph, Thomas Mann (Va. politician), 178, 179

Randolph, Mass., 266

Red River, 230

Reed, Joseph, Jr. (of Phila.), 67; identified, 68

Religion: AA on, 51, 109, 110, 269, 345, 384, 418–19, 427, 429, 437; JA2 on, 288; JQA on, 171–72, 181, 292, 416; LCA on, 211–12; afterlife, 49, 50, 229, 301, 333, 334, 345, 366; baptism, xi, 95, 159, 189 (illus.), 192, 247, 342; in Britain, 33, 40; clergy and politics, 40, 140, 384; fast and thanksgiving days, 15, 69, 70, 140, 206, 270, 285, 286, 288–89, 361; T. Jefferson and, 230; ordination of clergy, 32, 152, 388, 389; Elizabeth Peabody on, 270–71, 297–98; pew ownership, 73, 75, 206, 207, 239, 240, 241, 246, 247; Providence, 28, 110, 126, 127, 243, 346, 371, 379, 383–84, 418, 427; Sabbath observance, 61, 63, 92, 103, 112, 125, 137, 185, 205, 209, 242, 280, 306, 364, 367, 380, 413, 414, 417; as source of solace, 333, 334, 345, 347; study of, 65, 187; M. Warren on, 275. See also Sermons; *names of individual religions and denominations*

Renshaw, William (Phila. innkeeper), 396

Repertory (Boston): JQA's treatment in, 364, 409; JQA's writings in, 4, 5; A. Burr conspiracy reported in, 231; congressional activities reported in, 129, 310; duels reported in, 396; editor of, 4; European war reported in, 74, 75, 159, 374; Harvard president reported in, 74; T. Jefferson address reported in, 71, 99; Massachusetts politics reported in, 4, 6, 84, 231; New York politics reported in, 126; U.S. foreign relations reported in, 109, 129, 293, 427; U.S. Supreme Court cases reported in, 347

Republican Argus (Northumberland, Penn.), 68

Revenge (U.S. schooner), 292, 293

Rhode Island, 255

Richard (sloop), xxiv, 147

Richmond, Va., 172, 177, 264

Riggs, Elisha (Georgetown, D.C., merchant), 241; identified, 242

Ripley, Rev. Samuel (of Waltham, Mass.), 289; identified, 290

Rippon Lodge (Va. estate), 336

Index

Robbins, Edward Hutchinson (Milton lawyer), 141
Roberts, Martha (Phila. boardinghouse keeper), 54
Robertson, William: *History of . . . Charles V*, 421
Rodney, Caesar Augustus (U.S. attorney general), 238, 401
Rogers, Daniel Denison (Boston merchant), 201
Rollin, Charles: *Ancient History*, 392, 393; *Method of Teaching*, 369, 370, 391, 392–93; *Roman History*, 318–19
Roman Catholic Church, 34
Roman Empire, 391
Romani, 241
Rome, Italy, 316, 318–19, 320, 357
Roscius, Sextus (the Younger, Roman citizen), 102
Rose (Adams servant), 63
Rose, George Henry (Brit. diplomat): identified, 307; *Chesapeake-Leopard* Affair and, 306, 315–16, 317, 331, 335, 343, 352, 355; secretary for, 338, 339
Rose, Robert Hutchinson (Phila. physician), 116; identified, 117
Ross, William (Md. tavernkeeper), 335, 336
Roxbury, Mass., 185, 186
Royal Society (London), 57
Rush, Dr. Benjamin (of Phila.): AA and, 304, 379–80; JA and, 38, 67, 381; JQA visits, 1, 3, 56, 57, 67, 108, 203; *Essays, Literary, Moral and Philosophical*, 67, 68; medical students and practice of, 57, 72; residence of, 203, 204
Rush, Richard (son of Benjamin), 203, 379
Russell, Benjamin (Boston printer), 354, 371. See also *Columbian Centinel*
Russia: JQA as U.S. minister to, xx, xxvii, 413, 414–15, 416, 435, 436–37, 438; European war and, 75, 129–30, 260
Rutledge, John, Jr. (former S.C. representative), 36, 37; letter from AA listed (1805), 443
Rutter, Samuel (husband of Sarah), 1, 3, 56, 66
Rutter, Sarah Jones (of Phila.), 1, 3, 56, 66

Sacheverell, Henry (Brit. cleric), 39, 40
Sac Nation, 80–81
Sage, Rev. Sylvester (of Braintree), 354; identified, 355
St. Domingue. See Haiti
St. Hilaire, Felix Leblond de (husband of Margaret), 300
St. Hilaire, Margaret Smith de (sister of WSS): AA2 and, 302, 424; AA on, 300; SSA and, 427; health of, 303, 376; mentioned, 358, 367, 382, 420, 425
St. Kitts, 286
Saint-Mémin, Charles Balthazar Julien Févret de (engraver), xi, xii, xiii, 220 (illus.), 221 (illus.), 405
St. Petersburg, Russia, xxvii, 415, 435
Salem, Mass., 115, 212, 407, 408, 411
Salem Gazette, 177
Sallust: *War with Jurgurtha*, 78
Sally (schooner), 207, 223
Salmon, Thomas (ca. 1679–1767, English historian): identified, 40; *State Trials*, 34, 39, 40
Salmon, Thomas (father of William), 40
Salmon, William (grandfather of Louisa Smith), 40
Sappho, 267
Sarfati, Joseph: *Biblia Rabbinica*, 226, 227
Sargeant, Mary Pickering Leavitt (wife of Nathaniel), 51, 52, 53
Sargeant, Nathaniel Peaslee (of Haverhill, Mass.), 51, 53
Sargent, Arria (daughter of Epes, Jr.), 52; identified, 53
Sargent, Daniel (Boston merchant), 237; identified, 238
Sargent, Dorcas Babson (wife of Epes, Jr.), 53
Sargent, Epes, Jr. (of Gloucester, Mass.), 53
Sargent, Hannah Welles (wife of Henry), 237; identified, 238
Sargent, Henry (brother of Daniel), 237; identified, 238
Sargent, Mary Frazier (wife of Daniel), 237, 238
Sargent, Mary Turner (mother of Daniel), 236–37, 241; identified, 238
Sauvé, Pierre (of La.), 23; identified, 24
Saxony, 420
Sayward, Jonathan (York, Maine, merchant), 124
Schenck, Peter A. (N.Y. merchant), 130, 133
Schmettau, Friedrich Wilhelm, Count von (Prussian officer), 225–26; identified, 227
Schuyler, Margarita Schuyler (wife of Col. Philip), 422–23; identified, 425
Schuyler, Col. Philip (father of Maj. Gen. Philip), 422–23; identified, 425
Schuyler, Maj. Gen. Philip (of N.Y.), 423
Schuylkill Permanent Bridge Company, 67, 68
Schuylkill River, 68
Science, 56, 57, 59, 80, 188, 365. See also Astronomy
Scituate, Mass., 216, 347, 377
Scollay, Anna Wroe (daughter of William), 209; identified, 210

Scollay, Catherine (daughter of William), 209; identified, 210
Scollay, Catherine Whitwell (wife of William), 210
Scollay, Lucy Cushing (daughter of William), 209; identified, 210
Scollay, Mary (daughter of William), 209; identified, 210
Scollay, William (Boston apothecary), 210
Scotland, 34, 374. *See also* Great Britain
Scott, Thomas: "The Importance of Time," 303, 305
Sculpture, 62
Sears, David (Boston merchant), 157, 158
Seaver, Ebenezer (Mass. representative), 5, 6, 7
Sebastian, Benjamin (Ky. judge), 255, 356, 357
Selfridge, Thomas Oliver (Boston lawyer), 213, 214, 215, 222, 223, 261
Selkirk, Thomas Douglas, 5th Earl of (Brit. politician), 150, 158, 163, 164; identified, 152
Senate, U.S. *See* Congress, U.S.
Seneca, Lucius Annaeus, 100
Sermons, 15, 41, 62, 63, 306, 361, 417. *See also* Religion
Servants: AA on, 29; in JQA's poetry, 257; for Adamses, 23, 27, 28, 29, 36, 37, 43, 46, 63, 92, 111, 183, 187, 193, 194, 206, 207, 211, 213, 222, 241, 253, 255, 267, 272, 336, 339, 364, 366, 385, 404; African American, 177; coachmen, 213; cooks, 23, 187, 210, 241; education of, 253; for Hellens, 94, 95, 96, 257; for Peabodys, 271; stewards, 57; wages for, 206, 222; women as, 179, 187, 193, 206, 207, 241; mentioned, 103, 429, 431. *See also* Domestic work
Seven Years' War, 93–94, 95, 97
Sewall, Rebecca Wigglesworth (wife of Stephen), 74
Sewall, Stephen (Harvard professor), 73, 86, 88; identified, 74
Shakespeare, William: JA on, 33; *Hamlet*, 16, 44, 45; historical plays of, 39; *King Henry IV, Part II*, 225, 227; *King Henry V*, 34, 35; *King John*, 248, 250; *King Lear*, 14, 15; *Love's Labour's Lost*, 25, 28, 208; *Merchant of Venice*, 409; *Much Ado About Nothing*, 248; *Troilus and Cressida*, 138, 139; *Twelfth Night*, 225, 227
Shaw, Abigail Adams (1790–1859, niece of AA): AA on, 378; GWA and, 298, 301, 366; health of, 120–21, 122, 143, 152, 153, 195, 271, 347, 366, 367, 431, 436; Elizabeth Peabody on, 389; William Smith Shaw and, 153, 366, 429; travels of, 387, 431; visits AA and JA, 143, 171, 195, 274, 378, 388–89; mentioned, 438

Shaw, Benjamin (Boston merchant), 119
Shaw, Charity Smith (sister of WSS), 118–19
Shaw, Elizabeth Quincy (Betsy, 1780–1798, niece of AA), 347, 349
Shaw, Francis (son of William), 18
Shaw, Rev. John (1748–1794, 1st husband of Elizabeth Peabody), 195, 271
Shaw, Judith Proctor (wife of William), 17, 23, 29, 30, 43, 46, 47, 48; identified, 18
Shaw, Oakes (brother of John), 270; identified, 271
Shaw, Robert Gould (Boston merchant), 29, 47; identified, 30
Shaw, William (Boston merchant), 18, 30, 46
Shaw, William Smith (1778–1826, nephew of AA): books and reading, 430; Boston Athenæum and, 247, 378; church attendance, 205, 209; clothing for, 112, 274; education of, 212, 301; W. Meredith and, 190; Elizabeth Peabody and, 120, 195, 265. 271, 301, 366; relationship with A. Walter, 211, 212, 235, 245–46; Abigail Shaw and, 153, 366, 429
   Relationship with the Adamses: AA and, 103, 273–74, 379; GWA's education and, 205; as JA's secretary, 301; JA's writings and, 371; as JQA's agent, 6, 41, 67, 79, 82, 95, 106, 135–36, 150, 210, 211, 239, 241, 245, 246, 267, 282, 312, 320, 321, 349, 350, 354, 361, 378–79; JQA's correspondence and, 180, 213; JQA's scientific studies and, 81, 94, 106; JQA's writings and, 78–79, 80, 309, 316, 323, 331, 342, 349, 350, 361; LCA and, 183, 232, 410, 411; TBA and, 58, 191–92, 342; as agent for AA and JA, 29, 121–22, 143; correspondence with JQA, 6, 79, 80, 136, 281, 282, 296, 321, 350; correspondence with TBA, x; correspondence with Abigail Shaw, 153; exchanges publications with JQA, 1, 4, 5, 6, 41, 78, 80, 82, 104, 115, 136, 201, 246, 261, 361; sends publications to JA, 182; visits AA and JA, 69, 200, 201
   Letters: To JQA (1804), 4; (1808), 349
   Letters: From AA (1806), 121, 143; (1808), 378; From JA (1808), 371; From JQA (1805), 41, 78; (1806), 135, 199; (1807), 245, 261; (1808), 361; From TBA (1805), 58; (1806), 191
   Letters to, from, omitted: To JQA listed (1805), 443; From JQA listed (1804), 442 (3); (1806), 444 (2), 445 (2); (1807), 447 (4); (1808), 448 (3); From TBA listed (1805), 443
Shawnee Nation, 80
Shebbeare, John: *The Marriage Act*, 78
Sheheke (Mandan chief), 219, 220 (illus.); identified, xi

Index

Sheldon, Daniel, Jr. (U.S. treasury clerk), 415, 416

Ships and shipping: JA on, 425; arming of U.S. merchant, xxiv, 2, 4, 310, 372, 398, 399; attacks on neutral, 11, 106; bills of lading, 157, 163, 164, 186, 223; blockades of, 263, 293, 294, 296; British attacks on French, 3, 183; British attacks on U.S., xii, xxiv, 91, 97, 276, 277 (illus.), 282, 286–87, 290, 292, 293, 296, 306, 307, 315–16, 317, 327, 331, 335, 338, 343, 350, 351–52, 355; capture and condemnation of, 37, 91, 95, 122, 181; carry goods for Adamses, 18, 127, 150, 157, 158, 163, 164, 168, 171, 191, 206, 207; French attacks on British, 183; impressment and capture of seamen, xii, xv, xxiii, 2, 3, 95, 98, 99, 105, 106, 109, 263, 292, 293, 296, 311, 312, 350, 355, 368, 370, 407, 422, 425, 433, 434; insurance for, 135–36, 353; permits for, 142, 398; shipwrecks, 199, 213, 223; U.S. attacks on Barbary, 80; U.S. interdiction of foreign, 282, 293, 307, 313, 315, 316, 398, 401. *See also* British Navy; Navy, U.S.; Privateers and privateering; Trade and commerce; *names of individual ships and captains*

Short, William (U.S. diplomat), 415, 416

Sicily, 124

Silesia, 5, 6

Skene, Capt. Alexander (of the *Leander*), 2, 3

Skinner, Capt. (of the *Indian Chief*), 151

Skipwith, Fulwar (U.S. commercial agent to France), 62, 63

Slavery and enslaved persons, xx, 9, 24, 35, 179, 205, 245, 261, 262. *See also* African Americans

Sloan, James (N.J. representative), 315, 317

Smith, Abigail Adams. *See* ADAMS, ABIGAIL, 2D (1765–1813, wife of WSS)

Smith, Ann (Nancy, sister of WSS), 146

Smith, Ann Witherspoon (wife of Samuel Stanhope), 203; identified, 204

Smith, Caroline Amelia (1795–1852, daughter of AA2 and WSS): AA and correspondence of, 364, 381; AA's correspondence and, 432, 434; Abigail Smith Adams and, 305, 338–39; JA and correspondence of, 381; Susanna Adams and, 339, 363–64, 367, 374, 375, 377; correspondence with AA, xvii, xxiii, 373, 374, 377, 379, 381, 383, 392; domestic work of, 274, 363; interest of in politics, xxiii, 375, 383; relationship with AA, xvii, xxiii, 273, 300, 304, 367, 368, 381, 382–83, 424; relationship with parents and siblings, 130, 338, 434; residences of, xvii, 299–300, 302, 345; travels to New York, 61–62, 63, 424, 425; visits AA and JA, xxii, 60, 146, 162, 267, 272, 288, 305; letter from AA listed (1808), 449; mentioned, 289, 358, 376, 378, 390

  Letters: From AA (1808), 305, 364, 381

Smith, Catharine Louisa Salmon (1749–1824, sister-in-law of AA), 121, 384

Smith, Elizabeth (Betsy, 1770–1849, cousin of AA), 35, 438; letter to AA listed (1805), 443

Smith, Elizabeth Quincy (1721–1775, wife of Rev. William, mother of AA), 194

Smith, Elizabeth Storer (1789–1859, daughter of William and Hannah Carter), 127, 438

Smith, George W. (Phila. merchant), 54; identified, 57

Smith, Hannah Carter (1764–1836, wife of William, cousin of AA): AA2 and, xxii, 126–27; AA and, xvii, 35, 109–10, 438; AA on, 36; JQA and, 41; LCA and, 42; children of, 110, 111, 226; letter from AA listed (1805), 443

  Letters: From AA2 (1806), 126; From AA (1805), 35; (1806), 109

Smith, John (Ohio senator), 308–309, 313, 316, 317, 359–60, 362, 364; *Queries Addressed by the Committee . . . to Mr. Smith with His Answers*, 308, 310

Smith, John Adams (1788–1854, son of AA2 and WSS): AA and JA advise, 387, 391–92; AA on, 274; JQA and, 139, 141, 142, 162–63, 166, 184, 185–86, 203, 254; LCA and, 190, 413; assists JQA, 203; correspondence with AA, 381, 390, 392; correspondence with JA, xxv, 339, 358–59, 375, 381, 387, 391, 392; education of, xv, 134, 139, 141, 142, 162, 184, 185–86; interest of in politics, 385, 387; relationship with parents, 130, 288; travels of, 146, 285; visits AA and JA, xxii, 267, 272, 303; letters from JA listed (1808), 448, 449

  Letters: From AA (1808), 391; From JA (1806), 134; (1808), 385

Smith, John Clarke (son of William and Hannah Carter), 224; identified, 226

Smith, John Cotton (Conn. representative), 70–71, 84; identified, 71

Smith, Justus Bosch (brother of WSS): Adamses and, 146, 305–306, 358, 367; residence of, 191, 255; Caroline Smith and, 375; John Adams Smith and, 190; WSS and, 56, 130, 133

Smith, Louisa Catharine (1773–1857, niece of AA): AA on, 103, 304; AA's correspondence and, 52, 438; JA2 and, 69; LCA and, 76; correspondence with AHA, 44, 45; domestic work of, 300, 307; family of, 39, 40; health of, 36, 42, 46–47, 51, 153, 253, 407, 436; visits to and by, 32, 61, 119, 336, 348, 377, 381, 390; mentioned, 13, 19, 53, 145, 287, 289, 335, 364

Smith, Margaret Stephens (mother of WSS), 146
Smith, Mary Carter (1799–1806, daughter of William and Hannah Carter), 109–10, 111, 120, 126
Smith, Robert (U.S. secy. of state), 99, 297, 398, 412, 414, 436
Smith, Samuel (Md. politician), 70, 71, 99, 107, 292, 293
Smith, Samuel Stanhope (pres. of Princeton), 62, 203, 204; identified, 63
Smith, Rev. William (1707–1783, father of AA), 118, 122
Smith, William (1755–1816, cousin of AA, Boston merchant): Adamses and, 35, 36, 41, 127; children of, 110, 224, 226; finances of, 35, 36, 37, 41, 42; visits to and by, 120, 438
Smith, William Stephens (1755–1816, husband of AA2, designated as WSS in *The Adams Papers*): AA on, 300, 346, 369; as JA's secretary, xxi; JQA on, 146, 202–203, 244; JQA visits, 3, 56, 133, 142, 201; LCA and, 147, 190; correspondence with AA2, 60; correspondence with William Steuben Smith, 186, 202; finances of, xx–xxi, 162; Miranda expedition and, x, xxi, xxii, 62, 102, 126, 128, 130, 133, 134, 141–42, 143, 144, 145, 153, 154, 162, 174, 194, 195, 250; as N.Y. surveyor and port inspector, xxii, 60, 126, 130, 133, 142, 144, 194, 195; relationship with AA2, xxi, 130, 144, 153, 162, 194, 244, 299, 302; relationship with AA and JA, xx–xxi, 60; relationship with children, 130, 338, 342, 346, 348, 351; residences of, xxii, 62, 63, 206, 254, 255, 303, 345; seeks JQA's assistance, 130, 133, 139, 141, 142, 184; seeks employment, 207, 244, 303; letters to AA2 listed (1805), 443 (2); letter to JQA listed (1807), 447; mentioned, 88, 119, 358, 367, 373, 376, 420
Letters: To AA (1805), 60; To JQA (1806), 130, 139
Letters: From JQA (1806), 133, 141
Smith, William Steuben (1787–1850, son of AA2 and WSS): AA advises, 379–80; AA and JA's concern for, 269, 364; AA on, 288, 303, 338, 346, 348, 380; AA's correspondence and, 336, 339; JA assists, 301, 375, 383; JA on, 135; JQA on, xxi, 202; as JQA's secretary, xxii, 435, 436, 437; TBA on, 295, 342; clothing for, 300; correspondence with JA, 364, 390, 391; education of, 135, 301; Miranda expedition and, x, xv, xxi–xxii, 88, 102, 125, 126, 127, 135, 146, 186, 194, 202, 208, 217; relationship with parents, 102, 130, 269, 275, 336; seeks employment, 285, 288, 303, 338, 342, 346, 348, 351, 383; teaches school in Quincy, 295, 297, 303, 338, 342, 346, 348; travels of, 61–62, 63, 339, 342, 347, 348, 379–80; visits AA and JA, xxii, 60, 288, 346, 351; letter from JQA listed (1809), 450; mentioned, 367, 373, 376
Letter: To JQA (1809), 435
Letters: From JA (1808), 357; From JQA (1809), 436
Societies and clubs: in Boston, 49, 157, 159, 171, 172, 175, 246, 247, 378, 435; in Cambridge, 188, 190, 193, 194, 198; in London, 57; in New York City, 62, 63; in Philadelphia, 196, 198; in Quincy, 17, 18, 103, 112. *See also names of specific societies and clubs*
Society for the Study of Natural Philosophy (Boston), 171, 172, 175
Society of Friends (Quakers), 233
Socrates, 198
South, 34, 86, 96–97, 284, 352. *See also names of individual states*
South America, xv, xxix, 230
South Carolina, 37, 84, 329, 376, 377, 412
Southwick, Solomon, Jr. (Albany, N.Y., printer), 433; identified, 434
Spain: boundaries of, 62, 63; colonial possessions of, ix, x, xv, xxi–xxii, 83 (illus.), 88, 99, 142; diplomatic appointments of, 109; diplomatic appointments to, 11, 28, 31, 296; proverbs of, 323; relations with Britain, 40, 122, 374; relations with France, ix, 40, 63, 372, 373, 374, 381, 417, 418; relations with U.S., ix, 2, 10, 11, 28, 31, 62, 63, 71, 77, 81, 83 (illus.), 84, 87, 90, 91, 97, 99, 109, 134, 139, 142, 204, 205, 208, 243, 255, 320, 352, 356, 357, 402; mentioned, 124, 219, 278
Spectator (N.Y.), 59
Spring, Marshall (Watertown, Mass., physician), 242; identified, 243
Springer, Lydia (Peabody family servant), 271, 272, 273, 298
SSA. *See* Adams, Sarah Smith (1769–1828, wife of CA)
Stackpole, William (Boston lawyer), 398
Staël von Holstein, Anne Louise Germaine Necker, Baronne (Madame de Staël): *Corinna*, 379
Staël von Holstein, Erik Magnus, Baron (husband of Anne), 419, 420
Starbuck, Capt. Daniel (of the *Hawk*), 172
State Department, U.S.: JQA's rumored appointment as secretary of, 409, 410; clerks for, 174; consular service of, 427; diplomatic secretaries, 436; dispatches to and from, 292, 293, 294, 333, 352, 417, 418; patronage and, 111–12; secretary of, 412, 414. *See also* Madison, James; Smith, Robert

Index

Stebbins, Chester (husband of Elizabeth), 290
Stebbins, Elizabeth Marston Harrod (sister of AHA), 200, 201, 288, 290
Stedman, William (Mass. representative), 5, 6
Steele, Anne: "On the Death of a Child," 110; "To the Same on the Death of Her Child," 50, 51
Stelle, Pontius Delare (Washington, D.C., innkeeper), 414
Stephen, James: *War in Disguise*, 115, 116
Sterne, Laurence: *Sentimental Journey*, 275, 276
Stoddert, Benjamin (U.S. secy. of the navy), 159
Stoddert, Elizabeth. *See* Ewell, Elizabeth Stoddert
Stoddert, Rebecca Lowndes (wife of Benjamin), 159
Stony Brook, Mass., 201
Storer, Charles (son of Ebenezer), 235, 236
Storer, Clement (N.H. representative), 398
Storer, Deacon Ebenezer (1730–1807, of Boston), 32, 86, 229, 231, 232, 235
Storer, Hannah Quincy Lincoln (1736–1826, wife of Ebenezer)
    Letter: To AA (1805), 32
Story, Joseph (Boston lawyer), 113, 395, 396; identified, 115
Strong, Caleb (gov. of Mass.): as gubernatorial candidate, 49, 141, 158, 167, 169, 170, 255; thanksgiving day proclaimed by, 15, 70; mentioned, 198
Strong, Rev. Jonathan (of Randolph), 265–66; identified, 266
Strong, Martha Allen (wife of Theodore), 167, 169
Strong, Theodore (son of Caleb), 167; identified, 169
Stuart, Gilbert (artist), 17, 18, 22, 29, 30
Suffolk County, Mass., 6, 408, 409
Sullivan, James (1744–1808, gov. of Mass.): JA and JQA visit, 285, 286, 370; JA on, 7, 8; JQA's *Letter* and, 349, 350; LCA on, 254; TBA on, 340; addresses Mass. General Court, 309, 310; attends militia review, 286; correspondence with T. Pickering, 340, 341, 342–43, 350, 354, 355, 360, 361, 362, 434; as gubernatorial candidate, 48, 49, 141, 158, 167, 169, 254–55, 340, 342, 351, 354, 355; as Mass. attorney general, 223; as presidential elector, 7, 9; public attitudes toward, 49, 355; residence of, 410, 411; thanksgiving day proclaimed by, 286, 385; Yazoo land claims and, 317
Sullivan, William (Boston lawyer), 48, 201; identified, 49

Letter: From TBA (1809), 421
Sully, Maximilien de Béthune, Duc de: *Memoirs*, 14, 15
Sumner, Charles Pinckney (Boston lawyer), 4; identified, 6
Sumner, Increase (former gov. of Mass.), 403
Sumner, William Hyslop (Boston lawyer), 402, 414; identified, 403
Sun (Pittsfield, Mass.), 40, 377
Supplement to the Encyclopædia, 67, 68
Supreme Court, U.S. *See* Judiciary, U.S.
Susquehanna County, Penn., 117
Swan, James (Boston merchant), 86, 87
Swartwout, John (U.S. marshal of N.Y.), 142
Swartwout, Samuel (of N.Y.), 240, 242, 244, 246, 252, 256, 261, 263; identified, 245
Sweden, 357
Sweeney, George Wythe, Jr. (of Richmond, Va.), 177
Swift, Jonathan, 14, 15; *Tale of a Tub*, 270
Switzerland, 414
Sydenham, Thomas (English physician), 38; identified, 40; *Observationes medicae*, 40
Sylvia (schooner), 171, 172
Syria, 62

Tacitus: *Annals*, 100; *Dialogue concerning Oratory*, 77, 78, 90, 100–101, 102; *Histories*, 100; *Opera Supplementis*, 102; *Works*, 77, 78, 88, 90
Taggart, Samuel (Mass. representative), 202; identified, 204
Talleyrand-Périgord, Charles Maurice de (French foreign minister), 69, 100, 113–14, 115–16
Tallmadge, Matthias B. (N.Y. judge), 142, 174, 249, 250
Taxes: TBA on, 406–407; British, 418; collectors of, 142, 278, 401, 402; customs duties, 15, 179, 205, 263, 333, 418; on salt, 204–205. *See also* Money
Tayloe, Col. John, III (Va. politician), 256, 260
Taylor, Peter (Va. gardener), 308; identified, 310
Taylor & Stroud, 148
TBA. *See* ADAMS, THOMAS BOYLSTON (1772–1832)
Teel, Benjamin (of Medford), 121, 122
Telegraphe and Daily Advertiser (Baltimore), 130
Tempelhoff, Maj. Gen. Georg Friedrich Ludwig von (Prussian), 226; identified, 227
Tennessee, 44, 107, 247, 248, 332, 357, 398
Texas, 208
Thacher (Thatcher), Rev. Peter (of Boston), 239

Thacher, Peter Oxenbridge (Boston lawyer), 79; identified, 80
Thaxter, Celia (of Hingham), 320, 321
Thaxter, Elizabeth (of Hingham), 320, 321
Thayer, Gen. Ebenezer, III (of Braintree), 79
Thayer, Elizabeth Thayer (wife of Obadiah), 265; identified, 266
Thayer, Obadiah (Boston merchant), 265; identified, 266
Theater: in Boston, 161, 163, 237, 390, 391; playwrights, 40, 396; as political commentary, 38; in Washington, D.C., xi
Thetis (Theatis, Adams dog), 274
Thompson, James (U.S. Marine Corps paymaster), 256; identified, 260
Thompson, Thomas Weston (N.H. politician), 202; identified, 204
Thomson, James: "A Hymn," 438; *The Seasons*, 300, 302, 388, 389
Thomson, John: *New General Atlas*, x
Thornton, William (Washington, D.C., architect), 210, 211, 242, 243
Thorp, Samuel (of London), 148, 149
Thruston, Buckner (Ky. senator), 80, 85, 398
Thucydides, 392
Ticknor, Elisha (Boston grocer), 144
Tiffin, Edward (Ohio senator), 319
Tirrell, Job (Adams servant), 111
Titcomb, Capt. Jonathan (of the *Mary*), 181
Tobacco, 165
Todd, Thomas (U.S. Supreme Court justice), 248
Tomkins, Rev. Isaac (of Haverhill, Mass.), 54
Torrey, Abner (of Quincy), 69; identified, 70
Townshend, Charles (Brit. chancellor of the exchequer), 191, 192
Tracy, Uriah (Conn. senator): AA on, 73; JQA on, 70; death of, 318, 319; health of, 209, 213, 239; mentioned, 21, 107, 145, 147
Trade and commerce: JA on, 6, 100, 101, 320, 358, 359; JQA on, 93; TBA on, 93, 352–53; between Britain and the Netherlands, 358; British regulation of, xxiii, 93–94, 95, 96, 97, 105, 109, 116, 263, 293, 296, 311, 337, 339, 350, 358, 368, 372, 417, 418, 427, 434; contraband, 263; European war and, 75, 263, 296; French regulation of, 263, 294, 296, 311, 358, 368, 380, 417, 418; fur trade, xi; T. Jefferson on, 349; between Russia and Britain, 435; in sugar, 57; in textiles, 96; between U.S. and Britain, xxiii, 95–96, 97, 101, 106, 109, 114, 128, 129, 263, 296, 321, 358, 374, 385, 398, 399, 401, 412, 426, 434; between U.S. and China, 30; between U.S. and East Indies, 263; between U.S. and France, xxv, 263, 358, 385, 398, 399, 401, 408, 412; between U.S. and Haiti, 2, 4, 12, 101, 113–14, 115–16, 122; between U.S. and Russia, 435; between U.S. and West Indies, 4, 263; U.S. regulation of, xv, xxiv, 4, 11, 93–94, 95–96, 106, 114, 115, 128, 129, 245, 253, 254, 263, 291–92, 293, 296, 332, 333, 336, 338, 342, 343, 352–53, 355, 357–58, 372, 377, 378, 380, 383, 385, 386, 387, 395, 397–99, 400–402, 403, 404, 406, 407–408, 412, 418, 426, 434. *See also* Embargo Act (1807); Ships and shipping
Tradespeople and artisans: JQA on, xxv, 65–66; apothecaries, 210, 418; apprentices, 30; auctioneers, 199; boardinghouse keepers, 222, 223; booksellers, 5, 6, 65, 199, 232, 349; chefs, 56, 57; coachmakers, 143; dance instructors, 159; engravers, ix; fishermen, 226; fowlers, 226; housewrights, 75, 222, 223; innkeepers and tavernkeepers, 121, 157, 158, 159, 266, 336; midwives, 204; millers, 434; notaries public, 57; painters, 232; printers, 3, 40, 290, 349, 362, 369, 433; shoemakers (cordwainers), 159, 250, 292; stagecoach drivers, 64, 204, 397; stonemasons and carpenters, 159, 206, 232, 350; woolgatherers, 310
Translations, 77, 78, 90, 100, 224
Travel: accidents, 98, 99; AA on, 92, 288; by boat, 1, 24, 46, 52, 54, 56, 61, 63, 70, 92, 145, 147, 163, 179, 183, 201, 202, 203, 247, 249, 267, 281, 282, 288, 335, 413, 416, 437; by carriage, 52, 54, 63, 87, 99, 111, 112, 152, 195, 251, 370, 377, 395, 397, 412, 431; by ferry, 67, 145; health and, 51, 107, 180, 428, 431; road conditions, 1, 44, 46, 47, 144, 252, 333, 335, 342, 394, 395, 413; by sleigh, 38, 103, 111, 265, 305, 394, 404, 406; by stagecoach, 1, 52, 54, 62, 65–66, 67–68, 92, 145, 146, 147, 160, 171, 191, 201, 202, 203, 207, 268, 282, 303, 394–95, 397, 413, 416, 437; transatlantic, 24, 437; weather affects, 56, 103, 108, 251, 252, 281, 282, 299, 305
Treasury Department, U.S.: A. Burr conspiracy and, 208; church services in offices of, 242, 243; clerk and comptroller for, 243, 260, 416; customs collectors, 142; reports of, 106, 204; secretary of, 412, 414; mentioned, 71, 85. *See also* Gallatin, Albert
Treaties: Adams-Onís Treaty (1819), ix; Anglo-American Preliminary Peace Treaty (1782), 15; Compromise of 1800, 406; Convention of 1800 (Treaty of Mortefontaine), 263, 387; Franco-American treaties (1778), 406, 408; Franco-Prussian armistice (1806), 256, 260; Franco-Prussian Cooperation Treaty (1806), 159; Jay Treaty (1795), xxv, 408;

Louisiana Purchase Treaty (1803), 24; Monroe-Pinkney Treaty (1806, unratified), 149, 262–63, 308, 316, 317, 330, 332, 337; Treaty of Pressburg (1806), 227; Treaty of Tilsit (1807), 260; Treaty of Utrecht (1713), 39, 40; Tripolitan-American Treaty of Peace and Amity (1806), 107, 317, 426, 427; U.S. with Cherokee Nation (1805) and (1806), 80; U.S. with Creek Nation (1805), 80; U.S. with Delaware confederation (1805), 80; U.S. with Wyandot confederation (1806), 80

Trinidad, 269

Tripoli, 6, 71, 106, 107, 141, 317, 426, 427. *See also* Barbary States; Barbary War, First

Trumbull, Col. John (artist), 10, 146

Trusler, John: *English Accidence*, 298, 299

Tucker, Richard Dalton (Boston merchant), 27; identified, 28

Tufts, Dr. Cotton (1732–1815, uncle and cousin of AA), 393, 429; letter from AA listed (1809), 449

Tufts, Cotton, Jr. (1757–1833, cousin of AA), 73, 75

Tunis, 71, 79, 80, 81, 82, 85, 186, 427

Turkey. *See* Ottoman Empire

Turner, Elisha (husband of Mary), 103; identified, 104

Turner, John (husband of Lydia), 69

Turner, Lydia Gay (Quincy schoolteacher): identified, 69

Turner, Mary Adams (1769–1830, niece of JA), 104

Turner, William (Boston dance instructor), 159

Turreau de Garambouville, Louis Marie (French minister to U.S.): identified, 25; JQA on, 24, 32; JQA visits, 241, 242, 398; clothing of, 26; U.S. relations with Haiti and, 113–14, 115–16

Turreau de Garambouville, Marie Angélique Lequesne Ronsin (wife of Louis), 24; identified, 25

Ulm, Battle of, 74, 75

Union (Portuguese brig), 25

Union (ship), 417, 418

Union Bank (Boston), 243

United States: AA on, 302, 304, 319, 347, 375–76, 380; JA on, xxii, 33, 34–35, 77, 86, 100, 101, 230, 320, 326, 420, 421–22; JQA on, 325, 395; attitudes toward Britain in, xxiii, 75, 101, 115, 129, 147, 157, 276, 293, 294, 361, 406, 434; attitudes toward France in, 75, 101, 157, 294, 316, 341, 406; attitudes toward Haiti in, 4; European attitudes toward, 196, 198, 230, 380; foreign influence on, 15, 122, 123, 280, 317, 320, 323, 331, 332, 337, 352, 356, 357, 420, 422, 425, 426, 433

Domestic Affairs: admission of states to, 24–25; arts and culture in, 133, 258, 261, 331, 392; attitudes toward government in, 208, 222, 223, 243–44, 245, 250, 276, 284, 291, 293, 296, 306, 309, 342, 346, 368, 372, 374, 396, 403, 407, 408, 420, 422; boundaries of, ix, 62, 63, 84, 91, 99, 402; concern for union of, 34–35, 395, 420; economic situation of, 100, 107, 124, 152, 203, 204, 205, 230, 247, 296, 300, 315, 326, 333, 380, 398, 401; flag of, xii; immigration to, 34, 375–76, 412, 414; military preparedness of, 71, 98, 99, 124, 282, 290, 297, 315, 317, 332, 333, 351, 364, 368, 370; partisanship in, 346, 356, 357, 375, 376, 426, 427, 433; regional divisions in, xxv, 34–35, 86, 96–97, 100, 284, 339–40, 342, 352, 396; slavery and, 9, 24, 35, 179, 245, 261, 262; states' rights and, 42, 396, 413; territorial expansion, ix, xi, xxix, 71, 81, 83 (illus.), 87, 90, 205, 230, 234, 243, 261, 302, 320; Yazoo land claims, 42, 136, 315, 317, 401, 413

Foreign Affairs: diplomatic appointments of, 4, 11, 28, 31, 90, 100, 116, 129, 262, 287, 296; diplomatic appointments to, 4, 24, 25, 109, 116, 242, 252, 287, 306; diplomatic etiquette in, 72, 108; neutrality of, 4, 100, 106, 129, 263, 311, 337, 356, 368, 370, 380, 381, 386, 406, 408, 413, 420, 427; relations with Barbary States, 6, 71, 79, 80, 81, 82, 85, 106, 107, 141, 186, 205, 317, 426, 427; relations with France, ix, xxv, 2, 4, 24, 39, 83 (illus.), 87, 99, 100, 113–14, 115–16, 124, 243, 252, 262, 263, 294, 296, 306, 311, 320, 333, 342, 345, 352, 353, 355, 357, 372, 380, 381, 385, 386, 387, 398, 401, 406, 408, 412, 417, 418, 420, 422, 433; relations with Native Americans, 11, 71, 79, 80, 205, 413; relations with Portugal, 371; relations with Prussia, 371; relations with Russia, xx, xxvii, 413, 414–15, 416, 435, 436–37, 438; relations with Spain, ix, 2, 10, 11, 28, 31, 62, 63, 71, 77, 81, 83 (illus.), 84, 87, 90, 91, 97, 99, 109, 134, 139, 142, 204, 205, 208, 243, 255, 320, 352, 356, 357, 402

Relations with Great Britain: AA on, xxvi–xxvii, 108, 338, 345, 346, 372, 380, 420, 426, 433; JA on, 6, 101, 107–108, 109, 320, 357, 386, 425; JQA and, xxiii–xxiv, 81, 87, 90, 91, 93–94, 97–98, 105, 106–107, 113, 114, 115, 124, 292, 311, 316, 337, 338, 343, 350, 355, 357, 402, 403, 410, 417; LCA on, 290, 306; TBA on, 342; Anglo-American peace negotiations, 15; *Chesapeake-Leopard* Affair and, xii, xxiv, 276, 277 (illus.), 278, 282, 286–87, 292, 293, 296, 306, 307, 315–16, 317, 331, 335, 338, 351–52, 355; Congress and, 97, 98, 99, 106–107, 114, 115, 124, 294, 333, 337, 417; exchange of ministers, 72, 148, 149, 152, 158, 163, 164, 204, 242, 260, 287, 307, 434; impressment and, xii, xv, xxiii, 2, 3, 95, 98, 109, 263, 292, 293, 296, 311, 312, 350, 355, 368, 370, 407, 408, 422, 425, 433, 434; Jay Treaty and, xxv, 10, 11, 408; Jefferson administration and, 3, 71, 99, 204, 205, 333, 433, 434; *Leander-Richard* incident and, xxiv, 147; Monroe-Pinkney Treaty, 149, 243, 262–63, 316, 317, 330, 332, 337; J. Monroe's mission to, 2, 3, 11, 296–98, 333; Non-Importation Act (1806) and, 95–96, 128, 129, 253, 254, 291–92; Non-Intercourse Act (1809) and, 385, 398, 399, 401, 412; Privy Council and, 311, 350, 358, 368, 417, 418, 427, 434; U.S. attitudes toward, 106, 108, 109, 113, 116, 292, 300, 307, 310, 321, 336, 340, 341; possible war with Britain, xxix, 93–94, 284, 287, 290, 294, 338, 340, 357

  See also Embargo Act (1807); Ships and shipping; Trade and commerce

United States' Gazette (Phila.), 91, 109, 124

United States' Gazette for the Country (Phila.), 328, 332

U.S. government. *See names of individual branches and departments*

United States' Mail Stage (stagecoach line), 65–66, 67, 68

Universal Gazette (Washington, D.C.), 307, 332

Unknown: letter from AA listed (1800), 441

Valius (pseudonym), 372, 374

Van Cortlandt, Gen. Philip (N.Y. representative), 256; identified, 260

Varnum, Gen. Joseph Bradley (Mass. representative), 70, 71, 281, 282, 434

Veasey (Vesey), Ebenezer, Jr. (of Quincy), 225; identified, 226

Veasey (Vesey), Mary Miller (of Quincy), 226

Veasey (Vesey), Mottram (of Quincy), 225, 226

Veasey (Vesey), Mrs., 36

Velleius Paterculus (Roman historian), 100, 102

Venable, Abraham Bedford (Va. senator), 31

Venezuela, x, xv, xxi–xxii, 88, 89 (illus.), 142. *See also* Miranda Expedition (1806)

Verchild, James (of St. Kitts): identified, 286

Vermont, 117, 236, 262, 319

Vernon, William, Sr. (Newport, R.I., merchant), 229; identified, 231

Vernon, William, Jr. (son of William, Sr.), 229; identified, 231

Verplanck, Daniel Crommelin (N.Y. representative), 256; identified, 260

Vétéran (French ship), 183

Vice Presidency, U.S.: JQA as candidate for, 307, 308, 309, 310, 314, 316, 322, 327, 377; G. Clinton's reelection to, 397, 398; powers of, 7, 70, 71, 82, 85, 256. *See also* Burr, Aaron; Clinton, George

Vinal, Maj. William (of Quincy), 73; identified, 75

Virgil, 412, 426, 428

Virginia: African Americans in, 177; congressional delegation of, 31, 32, 41, 44, 71, 131, 179, 281, 282, 310, 329, 396, 398, 416; government and politics in, 100, 128, 176, 186, 307, 312, 329, 330, 332; illness in, 1; T. Jefferson as governor of, 40; public attitudes toward, 6, 137, 196, 339; mentioned, 56, 62, 82, 234, 336

Vose, Elizabeth Quincy (daughter of John), 120; identified, 121

Vose, John (Atkinson Academy preceptor), 120, 121, 280, 298

Vose, Lydia Webster (wife of John), 121, 280

Vose, Mary (daughter of John), 120; identified, 121

Wagner, Jacob (State Department clerk), 174

Wales, Ann Beale (wife of Thomas), 103, 171, 172

Wales, Thomas Beale (of Quincy), 171, 172

Wallace, Johnson & Muir (Brit. mercantile firm), 149

Walter, Arthur Maynard (of Boston), 80, 211, 212, 235, 245–46, 247

Ward, George (stagecoach operator), 203

Ward, Joshua (stagecoach operator), 203

War Department, U.S., 3, 402, 403, 408, 409, 412, 414. *See also* Army, U.S; Dearborn, Henry; Eustis, Dr. William

Ware, Elizabeth Bowes (3d wife of Henry), 239; identified, 240

Ware, Rev. Henry (of Hingham), 239, 240, 264; identified, 187

Ware, Mary Otis Lincoln (2d wife of Henry), 239, 240, 264, 265, 269, 270, 275

War of Spanish Succession, 40

Warren, James (1726–1808, Mass. politician), 217, 269–70, 276, 278, 384, 385

Warren, James, Jr. (1757–1821, son of James), 217, 270, 276

Warren, Dr. John (Harvard professor), 8

Warren, Mercy Otis (wife of James): books and reading, 216, 275; on A. Burr, 276; on

Index

death, 216–17; *History of the Rise, Progress, and Termination of the American Revolution*, xvii, 231, 276, 278, 384, 385; on Napoleon, 275–76; relationship with Adamses, xvii, 215–16, 217, 231, 268, 269–70, 275, 276, 278, 384, 385

    Letters: To AA (1806), 215; (1807), 275
    Letter: From AA (1807), 268

Washington, Bushrod (U.S. Supreme Court justice), 107, 334, 336, 413
Washington, Corbin (brother of Bushrod), 336
Washington, George: JA on, 77; JQA and, 371, 425; TBA on, 406; correspondence with JA, 371, 425; presidency of, 131, 289, 332, 337, 408; public attitudes toward, 137, 198, 339
Washington, Jane Mildred (daughter of Corbin), 334; identified, 336
Washington, Julia Ann Blackburn (wife of Bushrod), 334, 336
Washington, Martha Dandridge Custis (wife of George), 77, 434
Washington, D.C.: JQA on, 24, 211, 415; LCA on, 43, 286; Adamses' residence in, xii–xiii, xix, 1, 3, 65, 74, 76, 111, 128, 137, 140, 141, 142, 147, 160, 161, 244, 266; Adamses travel to and from, 1, 3, 4, 19, 52, 54, 61–62, 63, 64, 65, 67, 69, 70, 72, 73, 75, 145, 147, 159, 167, 175, 180–81, 191, 199, 201, 202, 203, 204, 206, 207, 244, 247, 264, 267, 272, 280, 281, 282, 283, 284, 288, 390–91, 392, 393, 394–95, 396, 397, 400, 401, 402, 404, 408, 409, 411, 413, 415, 418; courts in, 125, 126, 160, 240, 244, 245, 246, 252, 264, 344; diplomats at, 72, 80, 81, 82, 84, 85, 91, 203, 287, 307; as federal capital, 146, 315, 317; T. Jefferson travels to and from, 148, 149, 174, 178; J. Madison's inauguration in, 411, 414; mails to and from, 25, 171, 251, 404; mayor of, 399; merchants and tradespeople in, 44, 204, 290, 418; militia in, 84, 413; Monroe-Pinkney Treaty arrives in, 263; Native Americans visit, xi, 80, 81–82, 84, 87, 91; newspapers in, 74, 285–86, 307; political parties in, 137–38, 336; Potomac River bridge and, 233–34; public attitudes toward, 138, 317; religion in, 137; scientific studies in, 79, 81, 94, 151, 171, 175, 250–51; slavery in, 179; society in, xi, xx, 24, 26, 72, 81–82, 84, 212, 234, 241–42, 255–56, 260, 261, 264, 282, 398, 415, 416; stagecoach from, 67, 413; visitors to, x, 219, 238, 296

    Buildings, Landmarks, Streets, etc.: Analostan Island, 179; Associated Reformed Presbyterian Church, 243; Capitol Hill, 411; Congressional Cemetery, 319; First Street, 414; Foggy Bottom, 204; F Street, 418; Gadsby's Hotel, 396; Greenleaf's Point, 139; G Street SE, 139; K Street, 3, 204; Long's Hotel, 411, 414; Pennsylvania Avenue, 139, 218; Rock Creek Cemetery, 211, 213; St. Paul's Episcopal Church, 211, 213; Six Buildings, 218; Stelle's Hotel, 234, 414; 21st Street NW, 218; 22d Street NW, 218; U.S. Capitol, 74, 76, 137, 139, 210, 227, 250, 252, 257, 287, 324, 332, 334, 412, 413; Washington Navy Yard, 99

    See also President's House (Washington, D.C.)

Washington Dance Assembly, 256, 260
Washington Expositor, 285–86
Washington Federalist, 84, 128, 154, 307
Washington Jockey Club, 11, 282
Waterhouse, Dr. Benjamin (Harvard professor): JQA lodges with, 86, 166, 168–69, 170, 174, 175, 180, 181; vaccinates Adams children, 189 (illus.), 295, 297
Waterhouse, Elizabeth Oliver (wife of Benjamin), 169, 183
Watertown, Mass., 243
Watts, Isaac: "Few Happy Matches," 153, 154; "Funeral Thought," 367
Wea Nation, 80
Weather: JQA studies, 79, 80, 81, 85, 94, 96, 98, 105–106, 149, 150–51, 158, 159; cold, 27, 29, 38, 41, 93, 98, 111, 209, 213, 214, 219, 235, 237, 242, 250, 251, 254, 255, 264, 301, 367, 372, 395, 404, 424; farmwork affected by, 168, 372; fog, 199, 424; health affected by, 29, 36, 51, 200, 368; heat, 47, 168, 170, 200, 272, 372, 424; mail delivery affected by, 214; mild, 70, 73, 76, 79, 90, 235, 346, 390; rain, 29, 36, 38, 68, 73, 145, 168, 254, 299, 368, 372; snow, 36, 38, 46, 85, 92, 103, 111, 112, 208, 210, 212, 213, 289, 299, 302, 303, 305, 345, 380, 390, 394; storms, 54, 170, 183, 250–51, 252, 255, 301, 305, 382, 438; thaw, 237, 252, 255, 305, 406; travel affected by, 56, 103, 108, 251, 252, 281, 282, 299, 305; wind, 62, 73, 251, 367, 424, 438
Webber, Samuel (pres. of Harvard), 74, 149–50, 152, 182
Webster, Mary Peabody (wife of Stephen), 153, 154, 431
Webster, Noah, 258
Webster, Stephen Peabody (of Haverhill, N.H.), 154, 431, 432
Weddings, 43, 95, 172, 339
Wednesday Evening Club (Boston), 157, 159
Weems, Dr. John (of Georgetown, D.C.), 178, 179, 210, 233, 239
Weld, Rev. Ezra (of Braintree), 355
Welles, Hannah. *See* Sargent, Hannah Welles

Wells, Samuel Adams (Boston merchant), 410; identified, 411
Wells, William (Boston bookseller), 199
Welsh, Abigail Kent (wife of Dr. Thomas, cousin of AA), 5, 127, 370, 385
Welsh, Charlotte (daughter of Dr. Thomas), 127, 363
Welsh, Harriet (daughter of Dr. Thomas), 127, 390, 391
Welsh, John Adams (son of Dr. Thomas), 383; identified, 385
Welsh, Dr. Thomas (of Boston), 5, 231, 283, 383, 385, 403, 409
Western World (Frankfort, Ky.), 250
West Indies, x, 4, 202, 263, 285, 286, 406, 408. *See also names of individual islands*
Weymouth, Mass., 73, 75, 274, 385, 410
Wheaton, Laban (of Norton, Mass.), 370
Wheeler, Luke (Norfolk, Va., merchant), 43
Wheeler, Susan. *See* Decatur, Susan Wheeler
Whetcroft, Henry (Washington, D.C., notary public), 416
Whitbread, Samuel (M.P.), 426; identified, 427
Whitby, Capt. Henry (of the *Leander*), 146, 147
Whitcomb, Catherine Louisa (daughter of Tilly), 157; identified, 159
Whitcomb, Elizabeth Epps (wife of Tilly), 157, 175, 183
Whitcomb, Tilly (former Adams servant): JQA lodges with, 150, 152, 157, 159, 166, 167; JQA's correspondence and, 106, 251; leases property from JQA, 161
Whitcomb, Tilly Churchill (son of Tilly), 159
Whitcomb, Mr. (son of Tilly), 157, 159
White, Anna (sister of Daniel), 120; identified, 121
White, Daniel Appleton (Newburyport lawyer), 121
White, Ebenezer (Boston housewright), 222, 223
White, Capt. Elihu (of East Braintree), 73; identified, 75
White, James (Boston stationer): identified, 232
White, Luther (Boston housewright), 222, 223
White, Mary (sister of Daniel), 120; identified, 121
White, Samuel (Del. senator), 10, 43, 44, 234, 317; identified, 11
White, William (law student of JQA), 410
Whitehead, William: "Essay on Ridicule," 363, 364; "On Ridicule," 429, 430
White House. *See* President's House (Washington, D.C.)
White Painted House (son of Sheheke), xi
Whitewood, Elizabeth (Washington, D.C., midwife), 203; identified, 204
Whitney, Elizabeth (sister of Peter, Jr.), 87, 88
Whitney, John (brother of Peter, Jr.), 303, 403, 407, 408; identified, 297
Whitney, Rev. Peter, Jr. (of Quincy): Abigail Smith Adams baptized by, xi, 189 (illus.); as Adams tenant, 29, 30; family of, 87, 88, 297; sermons of, 15, 306
Whitney, Sarah. *See* Brackett, Sarah Whitney
Whitwell, Benjamin (of Augusta, Maine), 197; identified, 198; "Experience," 198
Whitwell, Samuel (Boston merchant), 103; identified, 104
Wigglesworth, Rev. Edward (Harvard professor), 64, 71, 74; identified, 65
Wilkinson, Gen. James (U.S.): JQA visits, 3; A. Burr conspiracy and, 208, 240, 244, 245, 248, 250; correspondence with JA, 3, 4; U.S. relations with Spain and, 208, 401, 402
Willard, Rev. Joseph (pres. of Harvard), 74
Willaumez, Rear Adm. Jean Baptiste Philibert (French), 183
William III, King of England, Prince of Orange, 358
William (Adams servant), 43
Williams, David Rogerson (S.C. representative), 84
Williams, Capt. (of the *New York*), 147
Wills and estates: of J. Johnson, 58, 148, 151; of William Shaw, 18, 30, 46; of G. Wythe, 177
Winn, Timothy (U.S. Navy purser), 177, 179; identified, 178
Winthrop, William (of Cambridge), 82; identified, 85
Wiscasset, Maine, 41
Woburn, Mass., 178
Wolcot, John: "Farewell Odes for the Year 1786," 291; "Sir John Banks and the Boiled Fleas," 295, 297
Women: AA on, 18, 130, 200, 304, 346, 377, 380, 425, 428–29, 430, 433-34; JQA on, 94–95, 96, 326; JQA's poetry about, 252, 255; LCA on, 174, 215; TBA on, 197; as authors, 198; as boardinghouse keepers, 222, 223; clothing and fashion for, 76, 241–42, 252, 255; education of, 197, 200, 304, 429; legal petitions of, 18; as medical practitioners, 52–53, 118–19, 200, 204, 218, 233, 349; as merchants, 9, 118–19; Native American, xi, 219, 221 (illus.); Elizabeth Peabody on, 300, 431; portraits of, xi, xii–xiii, 221 (illus.), 405 (illus.), 428; as servants, 23, 29, 94, 96, 179, 193, 206, 207; as wives, xiii, 346, 428, 429,

431. *See also* Domestic work; Gender
Wood, John (Frankfort, Ky., printer), 39, 248, 250
Wood, Thomas: *New Institute of the Imperial or Civil Law*, 421
Wood, 118, 210, 291, 292, 294
Wooddeson, Richard: *Elements of Jurisprudence*, 421
Worcester, Mass., 305, 408
Worcester County, Mass., 6
Workman, James (New Orleans judge), 244; identified, 245
Wright, Daniel (Northampton, Mass., lawyer), 419, 420, 424
Wright, Robert (Md. senator), 10, 91, 99, 108, 109, 148, 149; identified, 11

WSS. *See* Smith, William Stephens (1755–1816)
Wyandot Nation, 80
Wythe, George (of Va.), 176; identified, 177

Yellow Corn (wife of Sheheke), xi, 219, 221 (illus.)
York, Maine, 124
Young, Edward: *Night Thoughts*, 50, 51, 52, 53, 120, 121, 301, 302, 388, 389, 423, 425, 428, 429, 430; "Resignation," 345, 347
Yrujo, Carlos Fernando Martínez, Marquis de Casa (Spanish minister to U.S.), 108, 109

Zeuxis (Athenian artist), 428, 430

¶The *Adams Family Correspondence* was composed in the Adams Papers office using Microsoft Office Professional with style sheets and programs created by Technologies 'N Typography of Merrimac, Massachusetts. The text is set in eleven on twelve and one half point using the Linotype-Hell Postscript revival of *Fairfield Medium*, a design by Rudolph Ruzicka that includes swash characters especially designed for *The Adams Papers*. The printing and binding are by Sheridan Books of Ann Arbor, Michigan. The paper, made by Pixelle, is a grade named *Natures Book Recycled Natural Offset*. The books were originally designed by P. J. Conkwright and Burton L. Stratton.